A HISTORY OF THE

BIBLE

John Anderson
October 1977

BLAC[K]

Troy

Corinth

Athens

Ephesus

Boghaz-Keu[i]

MEDITERRANEAN SEA

Knossos (PALACE OF MINOS)

Megiddo (SOLOMON'S STABLE[S]
Betsan (TEMPLE OF DAGON[)]
Jericho?
Rosetta
Gilgal
Qumran
(SCROLL[S]

Oxyrhynchus
(LOST SAYINGS OF JESUS)

Tell-el-Amarna
(TABLETS)

E G Y P T
RE[D]

Thebes
(VALLEY OF THE KINGS)
Karnak
(TEMPLES[)]

Elephantine
(PAPYRI)

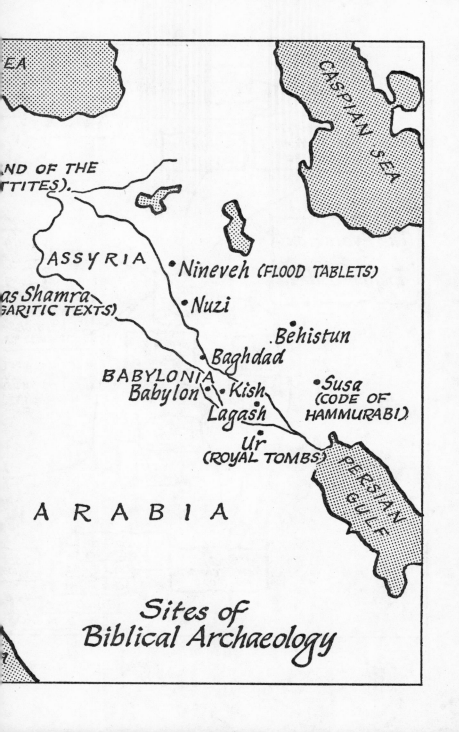

EA

CASPIAN SEA

ND OF THE
TTITES).

ASSYRIA

•Nineveh (FLOOD TABLETS)

as Shamra
GARITIC TEXTS)

•Nuzi

•Behistun

•Baghdad

BABYLONIA
Babylon•   •Kish

Lagash

•Susa
(CODE OF
HAMMURABI)

Ur
(ROYAL TOMBS)

PERSIAN GULF

ARABIA

*Sites of
Biblical Archaeology*

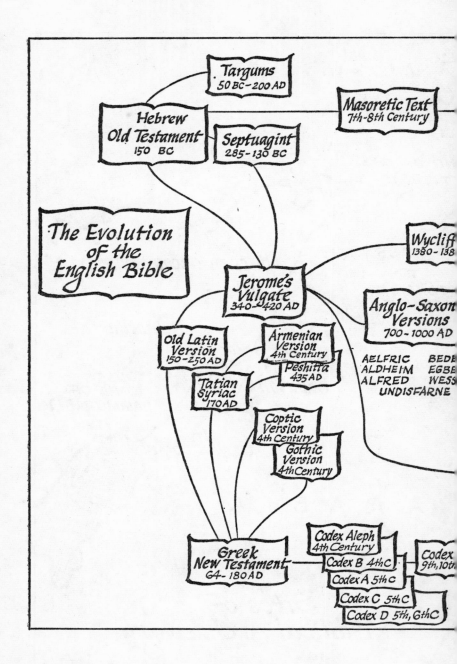

The Evolution of the English Bible

Targums
50 BC – 200 AD

Masoretic Text
7th-8th Century

Hebrew
Old Testament
150 BC

Septuagint
285 – 130 BC

Wycliff
1380 – 138

Jerome's
Vulgate
340 – 420 AD

Anglo-Saxon
Versions
700 – 1000 AD

Old Latin
Version
150 – 250 AD

Armenian
Version
4th Century

Peshitta
435 AD

AELFRIC   BEDE
ALDHEIM   EGBE
ALFRED   WESS
LINDISFARNE

Tatian
Syriac
170 AD

Coptic
Version
4th Century

Gothic
Version
4th Century

Greek
New Testament
64 – 180 AD

Codex Aleph
4th Century

Codex B 4th C

Codex
9th, 10th

Codex A 5th C

Codex C 5th C

Codex D 5th, 6th C

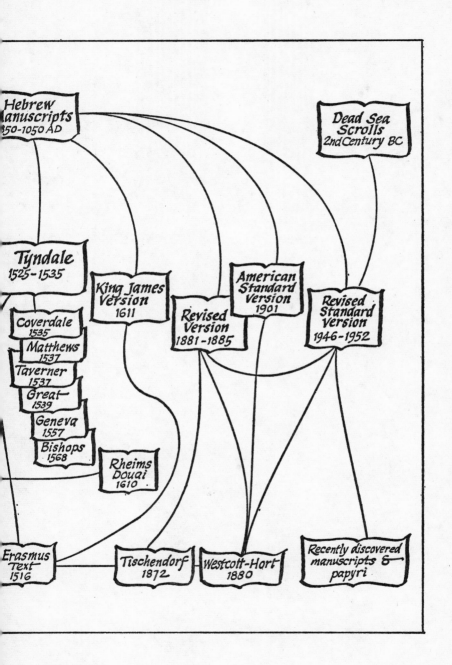

A HISTORY OF THE
BIBLE

An Introduction to the Historical Method

By FRED GLADSTONE BRATTON

Beacon Press   Boston

First published as a Beacon Paperback in 1967

Published simultaneously in Canada by Saunders of Toronto, Ltd.

Beacon Press books are published under the auspices
of the Unitarian Universalist Association

Printed in the United States of America

International Standard Book Number: 0–8070–1353–6

9 8 7 6 5 4

I wish to thank the following publishers for permission to quote
from the works cited below:

Ikhnaton's "Hymn to the Sun" reprinted with the permission of
Charles Scribner's Sons from *The Dawn of Conscience*, page 281,
by James Henry Breasted. Copyright 1933 James Henry Breasted;
renewal copyright © 1961 Charles Breasted, James Henry Breasted,
Jr., and Astrid Breasted Hormann.

Princeton University Press (excerpts from Akkadian and Egyptian
documents translated by E. A. Speiser, T. J. Meek, H. L. Ginsberg,
J. A. Wilson and reprinted from *Ancient Near Eastern Texts Relating to the Old Testament* edited by James B. Pritchard; copyright
1955).

University of Chicago Press (lines from "The Wisdom of Solomon"
and "Ecclesiasticus" reprinted from *The Apocrypha: An American
Translation* by Edgar J. Goodspeed; copyright 1938 by the University of Chicago).

Harper and Row (lines from "The Didache" and "The Shepherd
of Hermas" reprinted from *The Apostolic Fathers, an American
Translation* by Edgar J. Goodspeed; copyright 1950).

Contents

TO MY WIFE

Preface

In spite of the publication of the Revised Standard Version and other modern translations, the fact remains that the Bible is an ancient, oriental book. In order to understand it properly the reader must know something about its origin, history, and character. He must, in other words, have some guidance in his approach to the Scripture.

There are two ways of studying biblical literature: one deals solely with the content of the Scripture as a religious message; the other is concerned also with its composition, collection, canonization, and transmission. This book belongs to the latter class.

As a book *about* the Bible, this volume is designed to supplement, not to take the place of, the study of the Scripture itself. Reading the Bible, it goes without saying, is primary, but for a complete understanding of biblical literature it is necessary to know the facts about the Bible. "Who," "how," "when," "where," and "why" are just as important to the student of the Bible as "what."

There are also two schools of thought on how to read the classics. One school says that great books are universal in their content and therefore can and should be read *in toto* without being introduced, explained, or streamlined by professor or editor. Those who follow this school lament the present tendency to read *about* the Bible or Plato instead of reading the text itself. Text, they say, is sacrificed for context. The student is content with reading "the story of philosophy" and biographical sketches of the philosophers without familiarizing himself with what the philosophers actually wrote. To atone for this superficiality, some instructors have instituted courses in reading great books minus introductory notes and critical apparatus.

This point of view is thoroughly justified as a corrective of our quick-culture age; but it must be remembered that the classics (including the Bible) were written in another age, whose terms and concepts have changed with time. The twentieth-century reader is not qualified to read ancient literature until he has been oriented in the historical background and cultural context of any given book. Certain books are admittedly classic and therefore timeless but nevertheless are filled with terms, allusions, and concepts that are simply unintelligible to a modern reader who is not provided with the necessary explanatory notes. To put the Bible, for instance, into the hands of a young person without benefit of historical introduction and to expect him to understand it on the grounds that " great literature speaks for itself " is to invite confusion and frustration.

People are told to " read the Bible " as if it were a popular magazine! If all of the Bible were like the Twenty-Third Psalm, the layman could read it with a certain facility, but for most of the material in the Scripture the reader needs a suitable orientation in the authorship, dating, characteristics, purpose, and milieu. Such, at least, is the point of view of this book. It cannot replace a reading of the Bible itself, but it may perhaps make that reading more intelligible by supplying information in some of the areas not always adequately covered by textbooks in this field. Those areas have to do with the background and origin of biblical literature, the formation and canonization of the books, the story of the translation of the Bible, and the history of interpretation. It is hoped that this volume will serve not only as a text for courses in biblical literature but as a useful tool for the general reader.

It is not within the province of the present work to take up in detail the history of Israel, the teachings of the prophets, the life and teachings of Jesus, the career of Paul, and the beginnings of the Christian movement. The reader will find, however, a brief description of the contents of the important books of both the Old and New Testaments.

With the general reader and undergraduate student in mind, I have employed as far as possible a nontechnical vocabulary, keeping the documentation at a minimum and avoiding Hebrew and Greek quotations. Those who wish to pursue the various areas of study in greater detail are referred to the Bibliography. The expert will no doubt find more than one item that is not up to date or is entirely missing. Opinions in the field of Biblical Criticism change so rapidly that it is impossible to include the latest views. That is the function of the professional journals. It is really not of too much consequence for the student or general reader to learn that Professor X has just dated Hammurabi at 1790 B.C. instead of 1850 B.C. or that Professor Y has concluded that Ephesians was not written by Paul; for by the time the news is printed others have redated Hammurabi and have given Ephesians back to Paul. In a survey such as this we can only hope to review the main lines of biblical study and make the reader conscious of the chief critical problems.

Having explained the nature and purpose of the book, I hasten to point out that it contains nothing particularly new or original by way of research. My only aim is to offer a representative introduction to biblical study. Without proper guideposts, the student either will be confused by the forks and detours of critical study or will never get beyond the blind alley of pious literalism. For some, depending on background and previous training, the decision to take the route of historical and critical study is a painful experience, but, once the choice is made, there is an increasing satisfaction in the vistas encountered along the way.

In the preparation of the manuscript, as also in my thinking and teaching, I find myself indebted to many scholars — particularly Adolf Harnack and Adolf Deissmann, under whom I studied at the University of Berlin; E. F. Scott of Union Theological Seminary; S. J. Case of the University of Chicago; and my former teacher and later colleague, Robert H. Pfeiffer of Harvard University. More specifically I wish to thank Professor Morton S. Enslin of St. Lawrence University and Professor Ernest Cassara of Tufts University, both of whom read the manuscript and offered many valuable suggestions for its improvement. Finally, I wish to express my sincere thanks to Mr. Alan Levensohn of the Beacon Press for his generous help in the preparation of the manuscript.

Fred Gladstone Bratton

Springfield, Massachusetts
December, 1958

A HISTORY OF THE

BIBLE

Introduction

The Bible and the Twentieth-Century Mind

The general reader who is unfamiliar with biblical research may, upon picking up a book in this field, experience a certain amount of disillusionment over the conjectural nature of the discussion. The words "perhaps," "probably," "about," "presumably," "theory," "hypothesis," and "problem" are encountered on every page of his reading. It must be admitted that this cautious approach can be overdone. Some scholars are so afraid of oversimplification that they never seem to have the courage to end a sentence until they have qualified every observation.

On the other hand, there is a necessary and inevitable uncertainty about biblical studies owing to the very nature of the task. If the Bible had been written in English or if we had the original autographs of the Scripture, there would be no problem at all in regard to the text. But this is unfortunately not the case. Also, the paucity of information about the circumstances surrounding the writing of the Bible and the obscurity of events occurring in antiquity add to the conjectural nature of the treatment.

The absence of the original books of the Bible and the uncertainty attached to the history of the text make necessary a type of study called Criticism, of which there are two classes. The Lower or Textual Criticism is a study of the text of the

Bible with a view to determining the original wording as far as is possible from the comparative analysis of manuscript copies. Between the time of the original composition and the earliest manuscripts, as well as during the successive manuscript stages, numerous changes were made, both deliberate and accidental. So the textual critic is concerned primarily with the integrity of the text.

Higher or Historical Criticism deals with the more comprehensive problems of the authorship, dates, unity, sources, and general character of the books. The work of the higher critic has gone hand in hand with the advance of the modern scientific method and the development of archaeological and historical studies, and it has in turn produced a more intelligent study of the Bible.

The modern approach to the Bible, in fact, is a result of the development of several disciplines: archaeology, criticism, history, comparative religion, linguistics, and the biological and physical sciences. Archaeological discoveries have thrown much light on the cultural backgrounds of the Hebrew religion, unearthed Babylonian sources of Hebrew traditions, provided confirmation of biblical history, and enriched our knowledge of the Hebrew and Greek languages. The science of Textual Criticism has enabled us to arrive at a closer approximation of the original text, and the study of Higher Criticism has greatly enhanced our knowledge of the origin, order, authority, and authenticity of all the books of the Bible. Research in the history of religions and in comparative religion has shown that Judaism and early Christianity cannot be divorced from their environment and that there is a certain amount of religious syncretism in both. Our improved knowledge of the ancient languages has helped us to understand what the Bible intended to say and has compelled a continuous and thoroughgoing revision of the English text. Finally, nineteenth-century science has forced upon the Christian world a more vitalistic and evolutionary interpretation of the Scripture.

The Bible as a Library

From these branches of learning have emerged several important criteria or principles for the modern approach to the Scripture. The first is the recognition that the Bible is a collection of books consisting of various forms of literature. The idea that the Bible is *a book* is comparatively modern. It is not one book but a library of sixty-six books, written by almost as many authors during a period of one thousand years and on three continents. Ancient authorities were more cognizant of this fact than later writers, as seen in Jerome's Vulgate (*ca.* 400 A.D.), where the title " Bibliotheca Divina " (*divine library*) is used.

But in spite of this diversity there is a certain unity in the Scripture. The Bible is the continuous story of the religious growth of the Hebrew and early Christian people. Containing, as it does, the history and literature of these two religious movements, the Bible shows a steady continuity of theme. The integration of these sixty-six books is also seen in their religious message. The Bible is a revelation of moral and spiritual truth unsurpassed in all the writings of the ages in its ability to satisfy the religious needs of humanity. That message in essence and in its best expression states that at the heart of the universe there is goodness, that the stars in their courses are on the side of right, that God is our Father and all men are brothers. It teaches the sacred worth of the individual, the paramount importance of personal integrity, and the principle of service to others as the key to happiness.

Aside from any authoritative pronouncement of church or council, the Bible has held its place by virtue of its intrinsic appeal to conscience, insight, and reason. The books were accepted in the minds of the people as Scripture long before they were declared by councils to be canonical. Their inspiration was genuinely felt by their readers long before they were pronounced by the church to be infallibly inspired.

Inspiration Redefined

To speak of inspiration raises a problem for the twentieth-century reader. Are all the books of the Bible equally inspired? A careful scrutiny of the contents will readily convince one that there is a difference in the degree of inspiration. Lofty spiritual sentiment of the most inspiring character is found alongside of unworthy and decidedly uninspiring material. There is a vast difference, for instance, between the vengeful imprecations of Psalm 109 and the Parable of the Good Samaritan in Luke 10. Consider the disparity between the Song of Solomon and the Sermon on the Mount in moral and spiritual values. The conclusion of Ecclesiastes that " man has no pre-eminence above the beast " is certainly not on a plane with the Fourth Gospel, which says: " Beloved, now are we the sons of God."

Clearly the books of the Bible are not all on one level of inspiration. There are high peaks and low valleys. The traditional view regards every *verse* in the Bible as equally inspired, a presumption implied in the King James Version, in which the editors set up each sentence as an independent paragraph with a number. This arrangement gave to biblical usage a stilted and mechanical aspect from which it has never fully recovered. In this connection, the time-honored practice of preaching from a text might well be called into question as a form of bibliolatry not in accord with the intention of the original authors of the biblical books, which, as a matter of fact, had no verses. The Revised Version (1881–85), followed by the American Standard Version (1901) and the Revised Standard Version (1946–52), improved on the Authorized Version by arranging the material into paragraphs according to content. A preacher would do well, then, to prepare a sermon around a paragraph or a theme rather than around an isolated text.

But to pursue the problem still further: *What is meant by inspiration?* If by inspiration it is meant that the authors of the various books were passive instruments automatically and miraculously inspired by God to write and, therefore, were incapable of error, there are many who will question the inspiration of the Bible, because it clearly contains factual errors, anachronisms, unscientific ideas of the universe and unworthy ideas of God and man.

The historical or critical approach to the Bible has rendered the older view of inspiration untenable. The traditional interpretation assumed that since every sentence in the Bible had been dictated by God there could be no possibility of error. But contradictions, scientific errors, absurd statements, exaggerations, and immature views occur throughout the Bible and were detected by early church fathers, such as Origen, in the third century. In I Samuel 17:49, for instance, we are told that David slew Goliath. In II Samuel 21:19 another account of the same battle tells us that it was Elhanan who slew Goliath. Then a later redactor in Chronicles 20:5, noting the discrepancy, records that Elhanan slew the brother of Goliath! Whole volumes have been devoted to reporting inaccuracies, contradictions, and mistakes in the Bible, and it is not our purpose to labor that point here. The existence of these errors, however, does necessitate a new definition of inspiration.

On the other hand, the men who wrote these books were human and therefore capable of error; yet they were, for the most part, closely akin to the spirit of God and had unusual spiritual genius in their grasp of reality. They were able to express truths that stand the test of time and inspire mankind in any age or place. If this can be called inspiration, then it can be said that the Bible is really inspired. Whatever has the quality of insight that inspires one to a nobler conception of life is inspiring, whether it is regarded as " inspired " or not. Conversely, whatever degrades one's ideas of God, man, and human life is palpably not inspiring.

On this basis the Bible emerges as a truly inspiring book. Consider such mountain peaks of inspiration as the following: " So whatever you wish that men would do to you, do so to them; for this is the law and the prophets " (Matt. 7:12); " But seek first his kingdom and his righteousness, and all these things shall be yours as well " (Matt. 6:33); " Hear, O Israel, the Lord our God is one Lord, and you shall love the Lord your God with all your heart, and with all your soul, and with all your might " (Deut. 6:4); " So faith, hope, and love abide; these three, but the greatest of these is love " (I Cor. 13:13); " He shall judge between the nations, and shall decide for many peoples; and they shall beat their swords into plowshares and their spears into pruning hooks; nation shall not lift up sword against nation, neither shall they learn war any more " (Isa. 2:4); " But let justice roll down like waters and righteousness like an everflowing stream " (Amos 5:24); " I desire steadfast love and not sacrifice, the knowledge of God rather than burnt offerings " (Hos. 6:6); " He has showed you, O man, what is good; and what does the Lord require of you, but to do justice, and to love kindness, and to walk humbly with your God? " (Mic. 6:8); " The Lord is my shepherd, I shall not want " (Ps. 23:1). These teachings are *inspiring* whether they are " inspired " or not!

The Bible as a Progressive Discovery of Truth

Another criterion for an intelligent approach to the Bible is the recognition of the Bible as a progressive discovery of truth. Including, as it does, one thousand years of history, the Bible shows a steady growth or change in its ideas of God, man, and the moral life. Within that millennium one is prepared to find vast cultural differences and changes in life and thought. The Bible is not a preordained, supernatural deposit of truth but a record of the experience of man in his long search for that truth.

By reading chronologically, one can trace within the covers of the Bible a discernible progress in the conception of God. True, this is not an orderly or straight-line growth, proceeding from one level of thought to the next. The long-term progression includes retrogressions, and earlier phases of thought continue to exist in later periods.

In the earliest sources there are traces of polytheism, as seen in the use of plural names for deity. One of the authors of the Book of Genesis described God anthropomorphically, walking and talking as a human being. God is depicted as a jealous deity and an angry potentate, commanding the murder of women and children. Worship of this deity was by sacrifice of animals as an atonement for sin.

The God of Moses was a tribal deity, the protector of the Hebrew people. Entering the Promised Land, the Hebrews conquered the Canaanites, but the Canaanite religions conquered them, so to speak. The worship of Jehovah was confused with that of Baal, the Canaanite agricultural deity, and the Hebrew religion became syncretistic. Elijah later established the supremacy of Jehovah over Baal and recalled the people to the worship of their God.

The eighth-century B.C. prophet Amos declared that Jehovah was a God of justice and righteousness. He was followed by Hosea, who showed that Jehovah was also a God of mercy and compassion. Isaiah saw God as a spiritual being, a creature of awe and majesty. Jeremiah enhanced this growing conception of deity still further in his portrayal of God as a being with whom one could commune. Second Isaiah climaxes this process with his teaching of universalism ("Turn to me and be saved, all the ends of the earth," 45:22). Deuteronomy clarifies the monotheistic principle in the Shema (6:4): "Hear, O Israel, the Lord our God is one Lord. . . ." Still later, Jesus speaks of God as a loving, heavenly Father (Matt. 6:9). Finally, we encounter Paul telling the Athenians of that spiritual presence "in whom we live, move, and have our being" (Acts 17:22–28).

The progressive nature of the Bible is apparent also in the ideas of morality and human destiny as one proceeds from earlier to later writings.

The implication of this approach is that the materials must be seen as reflections of different stages of cultural growth and therefore as unequal in worth from the standpoint of religious maturity. To trace these changing ideas through the Bible in their development from elementary beginnings to their consummation is to recognize the importance of chronological order and historical sequence, an approach that earlier interpreters missed.

It must always be borne in mind that the present order of the books in the English Bible is not chronological but topical, and the first business of the scholar is to ascertain as accurately as he can the order of the books from the standpoint of their original composition.

Each Book in Its Own Setting

Another cardinal principle of biblical study is that of reading each book in the light of its own historical setting. The book must be interpreted with reference to its own time and place and must not be taken out of its context. One must hold the fact firmly in mind that these authors were not consciously writing " the Bible," nor were they writing for the twentieth century. Their message was primarily for their own time. If they had written for the distant future, their meaning would not have been intelligible to their immediate readers. Isaiah was concerned with the problems of his own people in the eighth century B.C. Paul's letters to the Corinthians were written to meet certain specific needs in Corinth in 55 A.D. In other words, we must first ascertain what the author intended to say to his original audience.

Having done that, we are qualified to inquire into the message of the book for us today, for in many instances there is a teaching of permanent as well as of transient value. Along with Isaiah's condemnation of the ceremonial system and idolatry of the Hebrews is a profound description of a peaceful world, the hope of humanity (Isa. 2:4). Along with Paul's discussion of the place of women and married life, totally irrelevant for our day, is found his lofty sermon on love (I Cor. 13).

This, then, is an indispensable method of the modern interpreter: first, to relate the book or chapter to its original setting with the idea of finding out what the author intended to say to his immediate audience; and then to extract from that passage whatever meaning there is for us today, always being frank to distinguish between the two approaches. We must be careful to disconnect our own inferences from the original truth of the passage. We must recognize that the abiding elements in the Bible are sometimes found in a transient and imperfect setting. Jesus, for instance, as a Jew of the first century, may have believed that the earth was flat and that the world was soon coming to an end, but the recognition of that fact need not detract from the abiding worth of the Sermon on the Mount.

This is the only intelligent way to " read the Bible "; it frees the interpreter from the necessity of accepting or teaching what he knows to be untrue. The author of the book of Joshua asserted that the sun stood still. He and his readers knew little or nothing of astronomy. Such a passage is merely the reflection of a pre-scientific age. But this acknowledgment need not minimize or detract from whatever religious teaching that book has for the twentieth century.

The Bible as a Book of Religion

Another principle of modern biblical study is the recognition of what the Bible is and what it is not. The Bible is a book of religion. It can be studied as literature, but its authors were not littérateurs and its purpose is not literary. To approach the Bible with the literary criterion in mind would be to miss the forest for the trees. True, the Bible contains passages which rank high as literary gems, but its *raison d'être* is not its rhetorical form.

For that matter, the beautiful style of the King James Bible has been acclaimed far out of proportion to its worth. In fact, there is nothing more difficult to read aloud than the King James Bible. The influence of the Authorized Version on English literature for two centuries or more was tremendous, and it is indeed fortunate that it was written during a period when the English language had reached a peak. But it would be a mistake to read the Authorized Version as a stylistic model for twentieth-century usage. To admire the King James Bible for its archaisms, however proverbial and felicitous, is to remove the Bible altogether from contemporary life.

Is the Bible to be admired as an object of antiquity, or should it be made to come alive for our day? The books of the Bible were originally written in a colloquial style. The Authorized Version also was written by and for the people of the seventeenth century. Those who devote themselves exclusively to the King James Version for the sake of church tradition and for aesthetic reasons seem not to be interested in making the Scripture relevant for our age.

By the same token, the Bible can also be studied as history with great profit, but it is not a book of history. It contains incidental history, but it is history with a didactic purpose. It is history undifferentiated from myth.

The chief value of the Bible lies in its moral principles and spiritual guidance. To regard it as authoritative in any other field is to fly in the face of modern knowledge. The Bible is not a textbook in science. Its world view is that of the childhood of the race, and this primitive cosmology is seen in all its references to the physical world. The earth is conceived as flat and stationary. The sky is a canopy or vault through whose windows the rain falls. The sun, moon, and stars are contained within this vault. Beneath the earth is Sheol, the realm of the dead. This world and the creatures in it, according to the Scripture, were made in six days. The world in which the Bible was written was one in which human destiny was determined by the stars, sickness was caused by demon possession, the dead were raised, angels stirred the waters of a pool for the healing of the sick, and the Red Sea was parted.

Many literalists, like Augustine, insist that "Scripture gives no false information" and that if it conflicts with science, so much the worse for science. But others, confronted with the vast discrepancy between the biblical world view and modern knowledge, can distinguish also between the passing and the permanent, between the abiding values of the Bible and their transient setting. They know that changes in civilization do not touch the vital and basic experiences of man. The outmoding of world views cannot belittle the permanence of the Scripture in its moral and spiritual values, its timeless aspirations and deathless convictions. The discoveries of Copernicus, Galileo, and Newton, of Pasteur, Darwin, and Einstein do not in any way impair the universal validity of faith, hope, and love.

Being Honest with the Bible

As a corollary of this approach to the Bible, there is a final principle of interpretation: the necessity of being honest with the Bible. We must take it for what it says and not for what we would like it to say. The translator has no right to inject into the text the slightest hint of his own point of view or that of any school of thought. (Fortunately, the translators of the King James Version, the American Standard Version, and the Revised Standard Version have been men of scholarly integrity and have been faithful to the original Hebrew and Greek wording as far as they could understand its meaning.)

The same cannot be said, however, of the reader who distorts the text in order to lend support to a particular theological or moral slant. Preachers often spiritualize or allegorize the Scripture, finding in it mystical and mysterious meanings that were obviously not intended by the author. Conversely, a literalist will read as factual history what was intended as a parable with a religious meaning. The Book of Jonah, for instance, is the most profound expression of universalism in the Old Testament with the exception of Second Isaiah. It is a parabolic tract against Jewish nationalism. Jonah, who had wanted to be a prophet with a mission, runs away from God's will and is swallowed by the whale. Given his second chance, he goes to Nineveh and preaches repentance. The Ninevites accept his message and repent, but he resents the idea that they should receive salvation, whereupon God rebukes Jonah for his narrowness. Israel, likewise, had a sense of world mission but did not carry it out. She was taken into captivity by the Babylonians. Given her second chance, she only withdrew into a more bigoted and exclusive nationalism. This prophetic message is completely lost on the literalist, who sees only the miracle of the whale swallowing Jonah.

But, to return to our caution against overspiritualization, there is the danger of reading into a parable allegorical details that are not implied at all. Nothing is more harmful to the study of the Bible than this extension of parabolic interpretation to include every detail of the story. Usually there is one central truth in a parable, and to go beyond that by spiritualizing all the minor details of the story is unwarranted.

If the reader will take the Bible for what it says, carefully distinguishing between his own views and the text itself, he will be saved much embarrassment. The ancient solution of the problem of miracle and prescientific material was to resort to allegory. Many people today hold to this method. More recent interpreters tried to harmonize all biblical passages with modern thought by the process of rationalism. They tried to save the text by logical explanation. It is possible, they would say, for the Red Sea to be parted by winds at certain times of the year. Recently a nationally known magazine ran a story by a writer who claimed that Joshua could have been correct in saying that the sun stood still and brought astronomical evidence to prove the point.

This type of intellectual interpretation is worse than uninformed literalism. It is a form of bibliolatry that attempts to square the Bible with science, and, for those who assume biblical infallibility, it offers an apparent reconciliation of the conflict between the scriptural world view and modern scientific knowledge.

Once the reader could pick up the Bible and not be bothered by the discrepancy between ancient mentality and modern knowledge. But today the informed reader has to take a stand on this issue. He recognizes the Bible for what it said at the time of its composition and is frank to label a passage as untrue, unworthy, and uninspired, if that is necessary. When he reads that God made woman out of man's rib, that there was a world flood that drowned all creatures but those who were in the ark, that the serpent literally spoke to Eve, that God wrote the Ten Commandments on stone, that God gave tremendous strength to Samson because he did not cut his hair or shave, and that Methuselah lived 969 years, he does not have to allegorize, harmonize, or take the Bible literally. He simply says: " That is what the passage says and that is what the author evidently believed, but as for me, I cannot go along in the world as if Copernicus, Newton, and Darwin never existed. I cannot live in a world of whimsicality and chance, cosmic lawlessness and divine caprice. If I must make the choice between miracle and law, I follow law."

The modern interpreter, however, does not stop there. He is quick to see the permanent in the midst of the transient, the timeless in the midst of the temporal. He knows that, when it comes to the fundamentals of human experience, the elemental needs of mankind, the moral and spiritual values, and the basic virtues of life, the Bible speaks with authority. He also knows that it is not enough to approach the Bible scientifically. A mere intellectual understanding of the Scripture is inadequate. One can have an encyclopedic knowledge of the Bible and still lack an appreciation of its rich religious message. Furthermore, a mere negative technique that succeeds only in ruling out former views can miss the very soul of the Bible by its intellectualism. Of this the modern scholar is profoundly aware.

These, then, are the criteria to be applied in the modern approach to biblical literature: recognizing the Bible as a collection of books, discovering within them degrees of inspiration, tracing progressive development of ideas, placing each book in its historical setting, distinguishing between the original message of the book and its possible relevance for our day, being honest with the content of each passage as far as its meaning can be learned, and seeing the Bible as primarily a book of religion and as authoritative in that field.

Part One

Archaeological Backgrounds of the Old Testament

Chapter One

Babylonian Parallels to Old Testament Traditions

1. Archaeology and the Bible

The historical approach to the study of religion has produced the criterion that no religion can be appraised, nor can its scriptures be interpreted, apart from an accurate knowledge of the cultural, historical, and religious background of that religion. The environmental study of Hebrew history has therefore emerged simultaneously with the growth of the science of archaeology. In supplying the data regarding the milieu of the early Hebrew religion and its sacred writings, archaeology has performed a most conspicuous service.

Our understanding of the early Hebrew writings would be woefully inadequate without a knowledge of Babylonian records. It is here that archaeology has made itself the greatest ally of biblical study. Discoveries of the tablets, monuments, and papyri in the Near East have made it possible for us to reconstruct the background of the Bible and to appreciate the world out of which it came.

The contribution of archaeological discoveries has worked two ways: we have been forced to give up some deeply embedded traditions related to biblical history; and, on the other hand, many biblical data that have been under suspicion by the critics have been accurately verified. The science of archaeology has therefore come as a fresh wind blowing through the pages of the Scripture, clearing away the mists and clarifying the air. Obscure references have been illumined, and missing links in the chain of religious history have been restored. Many a sweeping statement of a nine-teenth-century scholar has been completely discredited by the twentieth-century findings of archaeology.

It would be erroneous, however, to think that the Bible is to be wholly confirmed or wholly disproved by archaeology. There is such a thing as becoming too enthusiastic about any particular science. Archaeology is only one of several disci-plines in the historical and cultural approach to religion. Its function is corroborative, corrective, and illustrative. It has proved to be of inestimable value in the process of orienta-tion, enabling us to read the Bible with more historical per-spective.

Mysterious, semifabulous names, vaguely reminiscent of unknown or forgotten empires, have taken on new meaning, as the life, art, and spiritual aspirations of the dead past have been resurrected. As late as the mid-nineteenth century, only a few mounds of dirt remained to remind one of the Chaldees, and an uncertain reference in the Bible was all that was known of the Hittites; but soon thereafter great cities were to rise from the dust, and the dry bones of ancient monarchs were to take on flesh and blood. Thus science has not only re-duced distances but has foreshortened the dimensions of time. A magic carpet carries the ancient procession before our eyes — the magic carpet of archaeology.

2. Unlocking the Doors to the Ancient World

According to most anthropologists, civilization probably arose in the fertile valley of the Tigris and Euphrates rivers.

It is logical to suppose that human progress would occur first along the rivers of the warm countries. At any rate, the earliest deposits of civilized life are being found in Mesopotamia (modern Iraq). Take a map of the ancient world of the Near East. With Jerusalem as the center and with a radius of eight hundred miles, draw a circle. That circle constitutes the gold mine of archaeology, for it includes Egypt, Palestine, Mesopotamia, Asia Minor, and Greece. From the religious as well as the ethnic standpoint, Babylonia, Egypt, and Palestine are of the greatest interest to us, and it is these countries that have made excavation a romance and an adventure. But, before we tell the story of the modern discoveries and show their significance for biblical literature, we must explain how the archaeologists were able to read the inscriptions of these unknown peoples.

The secrets of Babylonia and Egypt were inscribed on two famous stones, and when these carvings were deciphered, the doors to antiquity were unlocked.

Champollion and the Rosetta Stone

One of the by-products of Napoleon's invasion of Egypt was the discovery in 1799 of the Rosetta Stone, which derives its name from the town where one of the French officers found it. This common block of black basalt, measuring forty-five by twenty-eight inches, was the master-key that opened the gates to one of the greatest civilizations of antiquity. Without it we should still be ignorant of the story of Egypt, and the monuments of Thebes, Karnak, and Luxor would still be as inscrutable as the Sphinx itself. But, because it was found and interpreted, our knowledge has received incalculable enrichment, and this small slab has become one of the most important objects in the British Museum.

The stone contains a trilingual inscription, with the lower register in Greek, the middle in Demotic script, and the upper in an unknown language. The Demotic was a development from the older cursive style of Egyptian writing and was in use after 900 B.C. The Greek section, of course, could be read, and it was found to be a priestly decree of thanksgiving addressed to the king, Ptolemy V, in 196 B.C. But what of the top register?

In 1801 the British came into possession of the Egyptian antiquities found by Napoleon's scholars, and the Rosetta Stone was placed in the British Museum. Thomas Young, the first authority to arrive at any conclusions regarding the text, deciphered the name of Ptolemy; but for the most part the stone remained a riddle for eighteen years. Then a French scholar, François Champollion, began to study it. The hieroglyph (for that was the writing of the top section) was at first completely baffling, but Champollion resolved to " fight it out on this line " until he either died or reached the solution. He worked on the assumption that the three sections represented different versions of the same message and that the upper register was the oldest. He brought to his task a knowledge of Coptic, a late Egyptian dialect, and, by a comparative analysis of the upper registers with their Coptic equivalents of the Greek characters, he succeeded in translating the hieroglyphics and soon thereafter gave to the world a new language. Champollion really sacrificed his life for this cause: he died shortly after of overwork. In this way, the door to the treasure-room of Egyptian antiquities was opened for all time; and discovery after discovery followed, down to the greatest of them all — the tomb of Tutankhamon — just a century later.

Rawlinson Finds the Key to Babylonia

The Babylonians, like the Egyptians, originally used picture writing, in which each picture represented an idea, but this system was later modified to make writing easier, and cuneiform (wedge-shaped) characters were used. The Persians simplified the cuneiform method by making an alphabet, and several Persian rulers wrote cuneiform inscriptions in three languages. For many years the scholars studied these inscriptions with little or no success. It remained for Henry C. Rawlinson to decipher first the Persian and later the Babylonian cuneiform. Rawlinson had learned Persian in India, and, when he was dispatched to Persia as a British army officer, he busied himself with the inscriptions that were carved on the rocks of Behistun.

In 516 B.C. Darius, king of Persia, determined to build himself a lasting monument. Instead of transporting stone to the place of his choice and building a pyramid, as the Egyptian Pharaohs did, he himself went to the stone and used the rocks in their original setting. He chose the rocks of Behistun, which tower seventeen hundred feet in the air, and, on the bare, smooth surface of this rock, his scribes chiseled the record of his victories. To make sure that the message would escape the ravages of time and the hand of man, he ordered it carved in a well-nigh unapproachable place several hundred feet above the ground. Then, in order that it might be intelligible to people of all the great nations, it was written in three languages; and, for the passers-by who could not read any language, the story was shown in life-sized picture form.

The relief, occupying the upper right-hand slab, shows Darius, accompanied by two of his attendants, giving thanks to the god Ahuramazda for his victories. His left foot is planted on the prostrate form of Gaumata, the usurper to the throne. In front of the king are nine rebel leaders, roped together, their hands tied behind their backs. Below the sculptured panel, which measures ten feet by eighteen, are the five columns of Persian text that tell the story of the king's vengeance. To the left of the Persian is a panel, just as large, bearing the Susian (Median) columns, and on the overhanging rock is the Babylonian version.

The story of Rawlinson's daring and courage in obtaining a copy of the Behistun carvings and of his scholarly ingenuity in interpreting the inscription is hardly surpassed by any contemporary tale of adventure. Carved on the face of a rock one hundred and fifty feet from the ground, it was a challenge to the twenty-five-year-old officer, and he made up his mind to get near enough to copy it. Scaling the cliff and suspending himself in front of the carving long enough to copy accurately a strange message in three languages was a feat that only an experienced Alpine climber can appreciate. In view of the modern difficulties encountered in climbing and copying the inscriptions, especially in the case of the Babylonian columns, which were inscribed on an overhanging boulder above the face of the Persian text, one is completely at a loss to conceive the dexterity and skill of those ancient workers who carved there so superbly for their king.

The story from this point resembles that of Champollion and the Rosetta Stone. In 1846 Rawlinson published his translation of the Persian column, which was a decree of King Darius. With his knowledge of the Persian cuneiform, he was able to find the corresponding characters in the Babylonian column. Eleven years after he had first climbed the great cliff, he mastered the entire inscription and forthwith published his translation of the Babylonian cuneiform together with a systematic treatment of the grammar of the language.

Rawlinson's deciphering showed that the ancient Babylonian language belonged to the Semitic family and was closely related to Hebrew, the language of the Israelites. Thus the second door was unlocked, through which Babylonia's palaces and tombs have yielded us the secrets of kings hitherto unknown.

3. *A Babylonian Odyssey*

No sooner had Rawlinson provided the key to Mesopotamia, than British, French, and German agents entered the beckoning land of the two rivers, and, from that time until the present, discoveries in Babylonia and Assyria have been revealing the great wonders of the past and illuminating the facts of biblical history.

In spite of the sensational and tremendously important discoveries of the present day, an archaeologist might well wish that he had lived in the mid-nineteenth century, before the long-buried civilization of Babylon had emerged from its grave and when the ruins of Nineveh, Ur, and a dozen ancient capitals lay waiting for the magic spade of the excavator. Botta, a French explorer, from 1843 to 1846 had excavated at Nineveh and had found many cuneiform tablets that he could not decipher. Layard was the other great name connected with early Assyrian archaeology. At the middle of the century he excavated palaces at Nineveh and Nimrud (the biblical Calah).[1]

[1] For the work of Botta, Layard, Rich, Place, Oppert, and Sarzec see George A. Barton, *Archaeology and the Bible* (Philadelphia, 1916–37); C. W. Ceram, *Gods, Graves and Scholars* (New York, 1951); Jack Finegan, *Light From the Ancient Past* (Princeton, 1946).

The discovery that precipitated the archaeological rush to Mesopotamia was the finding of the Babylonian account of the Deluge. In 1854 Hormuzd Rassam, continuing the excavation of Nineveh under Rawlinson's direction, uncovered a great palace. It was the royal residence of Ashurbanipal, who ruled Assyria from 668 to 626 B.C. Ashurbanipal is known today primarily for his great library, which embraced all forms of Babylonian literature, comprising religion, history, mathematics, laws, magic, and astronomy. (The volumes were clay tablets inscribed while in a soft condition with cuneiform or wedge-shaped characters and then baked until hard.[2]) Many of these works were copies of documents dating from many hundreds of years earlier. When Ashurbanipal died, his empire died with him, and all his treasures were buried in the destructive wake of Babylonian armies. British excavators have recovered over 20,000 tablets, which are now to be seen in the British Museum.

In 1872 George Smith, who had been deciphering some of these tablets, announced that one contained a Babylonian story of the Flood, closely resembling the biblical account (Gen. 7, 8). This particular tablet seems to have been the eleventh in a series of twelve composing the Nimrod Epic. The whole narrative dealing with the fortunes of a great hero named Gilgamesh is a kind of Babylonian Odyssey. The Flood tablet itself is from the seventh century B.C. and is of unusual interest to students of the Bible because of its resemblances to the Genesis account.

Ut-Napishtim tells Gilgamesh the story of the Flood — how the gods decided to destroy mankind with a deluge. Ea, the god of the earth, warned Ut-Napishtim to escape by con-

---

[2] For a well-illustrated volume on cuneiform tablets see Edward Chiera, *They Wrote on Clay* (Chicago, 1938).

structing a great ship. So he did and "pitched it within and without with pitch," supplied it with food and drink, and brought into it all kinds of living creatures and finally his family. Then came the storm, which raged for seven days. At the end of the seventh day the hero looked out and saw land. The ark grounded on Mount Nizir, and then after seven more days Ut-Napishtim sent forth a dove, a swallow, and a raven. The first two returned, but the raven found a resting place. Then the animals were disembarked and the hero offered a sacrifice on the mountain top.

The parallels with the Old Testament are evident in the following excerpts from the Gilgamesh Epic:

Shurippak — a city which thou knowest,
[And] which on Euphrates' [banks] is situate —
That city was ancient, [as were] the gods within it,
When their heart led the great gods to produce the flood. . . .

The warning
Man of Shurippak, son of Ubar-Tutu,
Tear down [this] house, build a ship!
Give up possessions, seek thou life.
Forswear [worldly] goods and keep the soul alive!
Aboard the ship take thou the seed of all living things.
The ship that thou shalt build,
Her dimensions shall be to measure.
Equal shall be her width and her length.
Like the Apsu thou shalt ceil her. . . .

He builds the ship
On the fifth day I laid her framework.
One [whole] acre was her floor space,
    Ten dozen cubits each edge of the square deck.
I laid out the contours [and] joined her together.
I provided her with six decks,
Dividing her [thus] into seven parts.

Her floor plan I divided into nine parts.
I hammered water-plugs into her.
I saw to the punting-poles and laid in supplies.
Six " sar " [measures] of bitumen I poured into the furnace,
Three sar of asphalt [I also] poured inside. . . .

The storm

With the first glow of dawn,
A black cloud rose up from the horizon.
Inside it Adad thunders. . . .
The gods were frightened by the deluge,
And, shrinking back, they ascended to the heaven of Anu.
The gods cowered like dogs
    Crouched against the outer wall.
Ishtar cried out like a woman in travail. . . .
Six days and [six] nights
Blows the flood wind, as the south-storm sweeps the land.
When the seventh day arrived,
    The flood[-carrying] south-storm subsided in the battle,
Which it had fought like an army.
The sea grew quiet, the tempest was still, the flood ceased.
I looked at the weather: stillness had set in,
And all of mankind had returned to clay.
The landscape was as level as a flat roof.
I opened a hatch, and light fell upon my face.
Bowing low, I sat and wept,
Tears running down on my face.
I looked about for coast lines in the expanse of the sea:
In each of fourteen [regions]
    There emerged a region[-mountain].
On Mount Nisir the ship came to a halt.
Mount Nisir held the ship fast,
    Allowing no motion.
One day, a second day, Mount Nisir held the ship fast,
    Allowing no motion.
A third day, a fourth day, Mount Nisir held the ship fast,
    Allowing no motion.

A fifth, and a sixth [day], Mount Nisir held the ship fast,
    Allowing no motion.

When the seventh day arrived,
I sent forth and set free a dove.
The dove went forth, but came back;
Since no resting-place for it was visible, she turned round.
Then I sent forth and set free a swallow.
The swallow went forth, but came back;
Since no resting-place for it was visible, she turned round.
Then I sent forth and set free a raven.
The raven went forth and, seeing that the waters had diminished,
He eats, circles, caws, and turns not round.
Then I let out [all] to the four winds
    And offered a sacrifice.
I poured out a libation on the top of the mountain.
Seven and seven cult-vessels I set up,
Upon their pot-stands I heaped cane, cedarwood, and myrtle.
The gods smelled the savor,
The gods smelled the sweet savor,
The gods crowded like flies about the sacrificer. . . .[3]

The similarities are so striking that most scholars agree
that either the Hebrew account is dependent on the Babylonian or that both are versions of an earlier original.. In both
versions the hero is informed by divine revelation that the
Deluge is to occur. Both are alike in the description of the
building of the ark, the embarkation, the cessation of the rain,
the resting of the ship on the mountain peak, the sending of
the three birds, the disembarkation, and the sacrifice. As in
other Hebrew-Babylonian comparisons, the Babylonian account reveals a more polytheistic and less ethical atmosphere
than the Hebrew, although it would be erroneous to claim

[3] James B. Pritchard (ed.), *Ancient Near Eastern Texts Relating to the Old Testament* (Princeton, 1955).

either an ethical point of view or monotheism in any Hebrew document before the sixth century B.C.

Several other Babylonian flood accounts were found, one of which, the Nippur tablet, dates from 2000 B.C. All of them reflect the same original tradition. Aside from the obviously greater antiquity of the Nippur tablets, the fact that those found in the library of Ashurbanipal were copies of Babylonian documents belonging to pre-Hebrew times would argue the priority of the Chaldean sources and the probable dependence of the Genesis material on them. The historical connections between the Hebrews and the Babylonians also render the dependence theory more likely.

Coming from the same period are two well-known Creation accounts. These tablets describe a great conflict between Tiamat, the representation of the original chaos, and Marduk, who became the champion of the gods and the supreme deity of Babylon. Marduk vanquished Tiamat, cut her body in two, and from it made the firmament and the heavens.

Primeval chaos

When on high the heaven had not been named,
Firm ground below had not been called by name,
Naught but primordial Apsu, their begetter,
[And] Mummu-Tiamat, she who bore them all,
Their waters commingling as a single body;
No reed hut had been matted, no marsh land had appeared,
When no gods whatever had been brought into being,
Uncalled by name, their destinies undetermined —
Then it was that the gods were formed within them. . . .

Marduk slays Tiamat

He cleft her like a shellfish into two parts:
Half of her he set up and ceiled it as sky,

Pulled down the bar and posted guards.
He bade them to allow not her waters to escape.
He crossed the heavens and surveyed the regions.
He squared Apsu's quarter, the abode of Nudimmud,
As the lord measured the dimensions of Apsu.
The Great Abode, its likeness, he fixed as Esharra,
The Great Abode, Esharra, which he made as the firmament.
Anu, Enlil, and Ea he made occupy their places. . . .

Making the heavenly bodies

He constructed stations for the great gods,
Fixing their astral likenesses as constellations.
He determined the year by designating the zones:
He set up three constellations for each of the twelve months.
After defining the days of the year [by means] of [heavenly]
    figures,
He founded the station of Nebiru to determine their [heavenly]
    bands,
That none might transgress or fall short.
Alongside it he set up the stations of Enlil and Ea.
Having opened up the gates on both sides,
He strengthened the locks to the left and the right.
In her belly he established the zenith.
The moon he caused to shine, the night [to him] entrusting.
He appointed him a creature of the night to signify the days:
Monthly, without cease, form designs with a crown. . . .[4]

It will be seen that there is less similarity here than in the
Flood story. The Genesis account may be dependent to some
extent on the older Babylonian forms, but the advanced religious genius of the Hebrews produced a loftier and vastly
more dignified description of what they, at least, thought was
the beginning of the world.

[4] *Ibid.*

4. The Origin of the " Eye for an Eye Morality "

One of the oldest sets of laws in the world is the Code of Hammurabi, inscribed by this king at least six hundred years before the time of Moses. Hammurabi (the Amraphel of Gen. 14:1) organized the first dynasty of Babylon and became the greatest administrator in the history of Babylonia.[5] He united the northern and southern sections of the country, unified the empire with Babylon as the capital, and extended his rule to the Mediterranean. He was a great patron of learning and assembled a vast collection of works including poetry, narratives, laws, astronomy, hymns, prayers, and rituals. He engaged in great building enterprises and encouraged art and religion.

The thing for which Hammurabi is now remembered, however, is his codification of the laws of Babylonia. The Code, consisting of 3,654 lines, was inscribed on a block of black diorite stone, eight feet in height, and was erected in the temple of Marduk in Babylon. At the top of the monument is a representation of King Hammurabi receiving the laws from the sun-god, Shamash. Under the picture are the various laws arranged in categories very much like our own statute books. During a siege in a later age, the Elamites took the pillar with them to Susa, where it was broken into three parts. In 1901 a French expedition under De Morgan, excavating at Susa, came upon this

[5] Excavations at Mari since 1936 have yielded over 20,000 clay tablets, some of which were written to Zimri-Lim, king of Mari, by other kings. These findings have necessitated the redating of Hammurabi to the eighteenth century B.C.

important treasure, pieced it together, and set it up in the Louvre.

Old as the Code is, it presupposes a highly advanced stage of civilization. As one reads the translation of these ordinances, one is profoundly impressed by their remarkably "modern" style and phraseology. A study of the Code gives us a fairly accurate knowledge of Babylonian life in the second millennium B.C. Here we find legislation affecting the clergy, lawyers, doctors, businessmen, tradesmen, farmers, carpenters, contractors, tailors, merchants, and slaves. Here are laws treating burglary, marriage, divorce, bankruptcy, partnership, debts, inheritance, adoption, assault and battery, wages, and slavery.

Since the Hebrews probably came from Mesopotamia originally and returned there in exile, it would not be surprising to find considerable dependence of the Old Testament laws on the Hammurabi Code. Such is the fact; indeed, in the case of some fifty articles in the so-called Mosaic laws the identity is practically verbatim.

Laws arise slowly out of long-felt social needs. When the Hebrews entered Canaan they found agricultural laws in operation, some of which were Babylonian in origin. In time, having become a part of an agricultural civilization, they found it necessary to utilize the same statutes. The Babylonian law of retaliation, for example, exhibits a close analogy to that of Exodus. This and other parallels will be of interest to students of comparative religion.

Hammurabi	*Exodus*
196,200 — If a seignior has destroyed the eye of a mem-	21:22 — If any mischief follow, then thou shalt give life

Hammurabi

ber of the aristocracy, they shall destroy his eye. If a seignior has knocked out a tooth of a seignior of his own rank, they shall knock out his tooth.

199,201 — If he has destroyed the eye of a seignior's slave or broken the bone of a seignior's slave, he shall pay one-half his value. If he has knocked out a commoner's tooth, he shall pay one-third mina of silver.

250,251 — If an ox, when it was walking along the street, gored a seignior to death, that case is not subject to claim. If a seignior's ox was a gorer and his city council made it known to him that it was a gorer, but he did not pad its horns [or] tie up his ox, and that ox gored to death a member of the aristocracy, he shall give one-half mina of silver.

252 — If it was a seignior's slave, he shall give one-third mina of silver.

125 — If a seignior deposited property of his for safe-keep-

Exodus

for life, eye for eye, tooth for tooth, hand for hand, foot for foot.

21:26 — If a man smite the eye or tooth of his servant or his maid and destroy it, then shall he let him go for his eye's sake [or tooth's sake].

21:28, 29 — If an ox gore a man or woman that they die, the owner of the ox shall be acquitted. But if the ox were wont to gore in time past, and it hath been testified to the owner, and he hath not kept him in, and he hath killed a man or woman, then shall the ox be stoned and the owner be put to death.

21:32 — If the ox gore a servant, he shall give unto their master thirty shekels of silver, and the ox shall be stoned.

22:7 — If a man shall deliver unto his neighbor money

Hammurabi	Exodus
ing and at the place where he made the deposit his property has disappeared along with the property of the owner of the house, either through breaking in or through scaling [the wall], the owner of the house, who was so careless that he let whatever was given to him for safekeeping get lost, shall make [it] good and make restitution to the owner of the goods, while the owner of the house shall make a thorough search for his lost property and take [it] from its thief.	or stuff to keep, and it be stolen out of the man's house, if the thief be found, he shall pay double.
14 — If a seignior has stolen the young son of a[nother] seignior, he shall be put to death.[6]	21:16 — And he that stealeth a man and selleth him, or if he be found in his hand, he shall surely be put to death.[7]

In 1952 Professor Noah Kramer of the University of Pennsylvania announced the discovery of a legal code prescribed by Ur-Nammu, a Sumerian king who lived before Hammurabi. Professor Kramer found a four-by-eight-inch tablet in a Turkish museum, where it had been stored along with some four thousand other tablets in 1890. This tablet contains enough of Ur-Nammu's laws to reveal that his brand of justice was less barbaric than that of Hammurabi. Undoubtedly, other legal codes will be found antedating Ur-Nammu.

[6] Pritchard, *op. cit.*
[7] American Standard Version.

5. Job's Forerunner in Babylon

Many documents that offer interesting parallels to Hebrew Wisdom literature [8] have been found and deciphered. Conspicuous among these is the Poem of the Righteous Sufferer, written about 2000 B.C. Tabu-utul-bel, a righteous man, suffers unjustly at the hands of the gods, and, like Job, questions the goodness of deity and defends himself against his critics. He rehearses his pious virtues and takes great pride in his observance of the acts of worship. Like the biblical hero, he is stricken with a terrible disease. In the light of the prevailing ancient conception that established a definite connection between sin and sickness or righteousness and prosperity, his suffering was incomprehensible. Surely, this was no fitting reward for such a noble life. The inscrutability of God's plans perplexed the Babylonian sufferer as well as the Hebrew Job. The cry of Tabu-utul-bel — " Who can understand the thoughts of the gods in heaven? Where may human beings learn the ways of God? " — has its counterpart in the lament of Job: " Behold I cry out, violence! but I am not heard; I cry for help but there is no justice."

Portions of the translation of the Babylonian poem follow:

I advanced in life, I attained to the allotted span;
Wherever I turned there was evil, evil —
Oppression is increased, uprightness I see not.
I cried unto god, but he showed not his face.
I prayed to my goddess, but she raised not her head. . . .
How deeds are reversed in the world!
I look behind, oppression encloses me
Like one who the sacrifice to god did not bring,

[8] See pp. 54–55.

And at meal-time did not invoke the goddess,
Did not bow down his face, his offering was not seen;
Like one in whose mouth prayers and supplications were locked,
For whom god's day had ceased, a feast day became rare. . . .
Who takes in vain the mighty name of his god; he says, I am like
   him.
But I myself thought of prayers and supplications;
Prayer was my wisdom, sacrifice, my dignity;
The day of honoring the gods was the joy of my heart. . . .
Who can understand the thoughts of the gods in heaven?
The counsel of god is full of destruction; who can understand?
Where may human beings learn the ways of god?
He who lives at evening is dead in the morning;
Quickly he is troubled; all at once he is oppressed;
At one moment he sings and plays;
In the twinkling of an eye he howls like a funeral-mourner. . . .
Into my prison my house is turned.
Into the bonds of my flesh are my hands thrown;
Into the fetters of myself my feet have stumbled.
With a whip he has beaten me; there is no protection;
With a staff he has transfixed me; the stench was terrible! . . .
Through torture my joints are torn asunder;
My limbs are destroyed, loathing covers me. . . .
My sickness baffled the conjurers,
And the seer left dark my omens. . . .

Then follows a section which tells of a messenger from the
god Marduk, who drives away the afflictions of Tabu-utul-
bel. The appearance of the god in the storm and the violent
demonstration accompanying the relief of the Babylonian sufferer find a counterpart in the book of Job, where Jehovah is
revealed in the powers of nature.

He sent a storm wind to the horizon;
To the breast of the earth it bore a blast,
Into the depth of his ocean the disembodied spirit vanished;

Unnumbered spirits he sent back to the underworld. . . . .
The roots of the disease he tore out like a plant.
The horrible slumber that settled on my rest
Like smoke filled the sky. . . .
The unrelieved headache which had overwhelmed the heavens
He took away and sent down on me the evening dew.
My eyelids, which he had veiled with the veil of night;
He blew upon with a rushing wind and made clear their sight. . . .[9]

While the Babylonian story is similar to that of Job in its development, the outcome differs considerably; for, whereas Job's suffering results in the end in his purified life, there is in the case of Tabu-utul-bel no moral improvement. Tabu-utul-bel simply gains relief from his physical distress through the spell of a sorcerer who drives away the evil spirits. The book of Job breathes a different atmosphere. Here the sufferer finds in his affliction the avenue to spiritual discernment. From the fires of adversity Job emerges to gain a new vision of God and his own soul.

6. Ur of the Chaldees

Until a few years ago Ur was associated only with the name of Abraham, but now we know that this Sumerian capital was over two thousand years old when the patriarch began his long trek to Canaan. For our increased knowledge of the antiquity of Ur and the Sumerian civilization we have to thank C. Leonard Woolley, the director of the joint expedition of the British Museum and the University of Pennsylvania, whose excavations at Ur date from 1927. For one thing, the work on this expedition points to the priority of

[9] Translation by George A. Barton: *Archaeology and the Bible.*

Mesopotamia as the oldest known culture in the world; the most recent discoveries in this region have shown a highly developed community life as early as 6000 B.C.[10]

The desolate plains of Ur would be sufficient to discourage the average digger — no vegetation, no water, no life. Most of the time a blinding sandstorm sweeps over the desert. The hot wind drives the fine sand with such force that it is almost impossible to breathe. It is the sand that buries cities and preserves them for archaeologists. Even Mr. Woolley was getting discouraged as he dug here and there in the mounds without striking anything. Finally, after making a new survey of the supposed site of Ur, he commenced operations on a mound that had impressed him as unusual in appearance. His workmen were not long in coming upon the sacred portion of the ancient city of Abraham. And then for the next two years the desert was rolled back; and there emerged the temple and tombs of a metropolis that thrived in the fourth millennium B.C.

Of primary importance to students of religion is the royal tomb of King Mes-kalam-dug and Queen Shub-ad, 3300 B.C., found by the Woolley expedition in 1927. Prior to this discovery, excavations in Mesopotamia had never revealed any evidence of human sacrifice. But here was a mammoth death pit containing the bodies of seventy-four victims, sacrificed in accordance with ancient Sumerian burial rites — proof enough of the early practice that became widespread in Canaan and against which the Hebrew prophets preached.

These victims were soldiers, grooms, and maidservants who had been put to death to accompany their king and queen into the next world. At one end of the tomb were nine

[10] See C. Leonard Woolley, *Ur of the Chaldees* (New York, 1938).

maidservants and four manservants. At the other end were nine court ladies with well-preserved headdresses and hair nets of gold. Near the entrance were six oxen harnessed to two four-wheeled wagons. In front of the oxen were two grooms; one driver was seated in the cart, while the other was on the floor nearby. The silver rings in the noses of the oxen and the collars prove they were trained to draw carts, the earliest instance, perhaps, of domesticated cattle. One of the court ladies wore an elaborate headdress of gold ribbons and gold poplar leaves strung with carnelian and lapis lazuli beads. Around her neck were a gold chain and carnelian beads. A gold pin had once fastened her cloak at the shoulder, and at her hand was a gold tumbler. All the women, in fact, were adorned in the most elaborate fashion.

In one corner were found four harps of gold, silver, copper, and mosaic. The best preserved lyre consisted of a silver and wooden top bar, uprights decorated with golden bands, and the golden head of a bearded bull, which was attached to the sound box. The sculptured bull's head is the finest of its kind found in the ancient world. It is of hammered gold with eyes of lapis lazuli and shell and with a beard of lapis lazuli. Evidently it was a representation of the moon-god, who was called " the young bull of heaven."

The objects found in another corner of the death pit proved to be of great interest and without parallel in the history of excavation. These were two rampant rams browsing on a thicket, to which they were linked by silver chains. The bodies are of wood overlaid with a fleece of shell; the manes, beards, and horns are of lapis lazuli; the heads and legs are of gold; and the bellies of silver. This representation, often seen by Mr. Woolley on shell plaques, recalls the biblical story of the ram found in the thicket by Abraham when he was about to sacrifice his son Isaac. The jewelry lavished on the sacrificial victims and the treasures deposited with the royal pair gave the floor of the tomb the appearance of a " carpet of gold," as one of the excavators described it. In another shaft was a wooden box containing two magnificent gold daggers and the gold helmet of the king. By the side of the queen were her crown, a silver boat, her wardrobe chest, and a wealth of objects, such as gaming boards, dice, bowls of gold and silver, and drinking goblets.

The presence of so many burial victims, most of whom were women, raises some questions for the religious historian. If this is a royal tomb, where is the king? Several conjectures might be made. The Babylonian tombs, like those in Egypt, were practically all plundered soon after the burial. The body of the king, therefore, may have been removed by the ancient robbers. On the other hand, the immediate successor to the king, fearing the tomb robbers, may have buried the king himself in an inconspicuous place in order to avoid disturbance. The early Sumerians believed that, if the body were disturbed, the soul also would be disturbed. It will be recalled that the tombs of the Egyptian kings were sealed with a curse on those who should disturb the remains.

The theory has been suggested that the human victims were offered to the deity as a substitute for the king. But if the figure of the ram had any such significance as in the Abraham story of the Bible, one wonders why human sacrifice was necessary at all. According to Sir James Frazer, the early animistic Sumerians sacrificed the ruler himself and with him his harem. Babylonian literature, rich as it is, contains no hint of burial sacrifice, but there is a reference from a later liturgy that refers to the lamb as a sacrificial substitute for a human being. This might well be a source for the Abrahamic incident. The predominance of women in the death pit presents still another problem. Their presence would seem to be connected with the idea of fertility and the continuance of the royal line in the next world. Suffice it to say, the Canaanite practice of human sacrifice was not without its Babylonian background, and there are, moreover, several instances of immolation in the Old Testament.

The Ziggurat and the Tower of Babel

We come now to one of the most spectacular features of the Ur discoveries — the ziggurat. The Sumerians came originally from the hills, and their gods were the gods of the hills. When they migrated to the plains of Mesopotamia and found there no hills on which to worship, they proceeded to *make* hills. The ziggurat uncovered by Mr. Woolley was built by Ur-Nammu, four hundred years before Abraham. It is a high mound two hundred feet in length and one hundred and fifty feet in breadth at the base. The center is of solid mud bricks, around which is a layer of burned bricks eight feet thick, each of which is inscribed with the name of Ur-Nammu. Modern archaeologists and native workmen can now use the three excellent flights of stairs that flank the northeast face of the ziggurat, just as priests and devotees five thousand years ago ascended to the Holy of Holies that surmounted the structure.

The biblical Tower of Babel is probably a Hebrew reference to this or some other ziggurat. Here again we can trace the influence of the Sumerian and Babylonian religious practices down through Canaanite and Hebrew history. When the Hebrews settled in Canaan, they found the people worshiping at " high places " where the deity was localized. In their assimilation of the Canaanite culture, the Hebrews took over many of these sacred hills and in some cases retained the Canaanite names. In fact, the Israelites for a long time identified the worship of Jehovah with the agricultural god, Baal. Reference to the " high places " as a center of worship occurs frequently in the Old Testament. Not until the Deuteronomic Reform of 621 B.C. was there an authorized effort to abolish the worship at the high places. The extent of the Canaanite influence is seen in I Kings 3:3, where even Solomon is said to have " sacrificed and burned incense in the high places." Recent excavations in Palestine have disclosed a number of these shrines.

7. *Visible Proof of a Flood*

The discovery of fish that are five thousand years old would appear to be a fish story indeed if it were not a demonstrated fact in the recent excavations in Babylonia. It was during the course of the 1929 campaign at Ur that the most astounding discovery was made. At the bottom of the death pit that had given up the bodies of a king and queen who ruled in the fourth millennium B.C., the excavators placed their picks in a clean water-laid stratum of clay, which extended through the whole area.

Mr. Woolley's men were digging in the cemetery at a depth of forty feet. They encountered layer after layer of rubbish. They came to the tombs of King Mes-kalam-dug and Queen Shub-ad and then more rubbish. The clay tablets, pottery, and implements were of the same character in each level, showing a continuous history. Suddenly the diggers found themselves in a totally different kind of soil. Seeing a layer of clean clay, they assumed that they had reached the original river or delta level (in prehistoric time the Persian Gulf covered what is now Babylonia), but at a depth of eight feet the clay stratum suddenly terminated, and then continued the regular soil with rubbish, implements, and various objects.

The significant phase of the whole event was that the articles under the water-laid stratum were of a different character from those above. The clay deposit (dated by Woolley at 3200 B.C.) had evidently produced a distinct break in historical continuity. A shaft was sent down some distance away from the death pit and revealed the same phenomena.

The importance of all this for students of biblical literature is at once clear. The bank of clay was made by a great inundation from the Euphrates, the magnitude of which must have been unprecedented, for it would require a tremendous amount of water to leave a layer of sediment eight feet thick. This flood, which wiped out a Mesopotamian civilization, assumed great importance in the minds of the Babylonians who came afterward, and without doubt it is the same deluge that is recorded in Genesis where it is described as a world flood.

The inundation was so complete and widespread that the civilization that it obliterated never reappeared. The objects found below the flood level consisted of painted pottery, metal, flints, and implements. Above the deluge deposit arose a people whose tools, art, and mode of living were manifestly different and whose early literature contained the story of the great flood. This tradition was handed down from one generation to another, and it is not surprising that the Hebrews, who had come originally from Babylonia, included the deluge account in their sacred books. While the flood was really local rather than universal, covering a territory approximately four hundred miles long and one hundred miles wide, it destroyed what to the Sumerians *was* the world — the Tigris-Euphrates valley.

Confirming the discovery at Ur came the startling news that Dr. Stephen Langdon at Kish had, at almost the same time, come upon a stratum one and one-half feet thick, consisting of fine river sand, shells, and small fish. Kish was another early capital of the Sumerians, founded as early as 5000 B.C., and, like Ur, it has yielded revolutionary discoveries. Langdon's excavations show the most complete and continuous stratification to be seen anywhere; the various levels from 100 B.C. back to 5000 B.C. are clearly distinguishable by their respective remains.

The alluvium stratum, containing fresh-water shells and small fish, clearly separates the debris above and below and runs along the entire site. Here we have another visible proof of the gigantic inundation that must have destroyed most of the Sumerian cities about 3200 B.C. Below the flood level, Langdon found the debris of a continuous civilization to a depth of fifteen feet. At the bottom of the shaft were found implements of the Neolithic age and painted ware dating from not later than 4000 B.C. Chief among the preflood pottery was a beautifully painted Sumerian head, which is the prize of the expedition.

The dependence of the Genesis flood story on an earlier Babylonian account has long been a recognized fact; but it was not until the Woolley and Langdon expeditions that the historical basis for the tradition was ascertained. Once again the soil serves as witness and joins legend with actuality.

8. The Hurrians of Nuzu

Before the excavations conducted by the American School of Oriental Research at Bagdad, the Iraq Museum, Harvard University, and the University of Pennsylvania in the twenties and thirties, little or nothing was known about the biblical Horites (Gen. 14:6). These were the Hurrians who lived in Nuzu (sometimes spelled Nuzi) near modern Kirkuk in Iraq. The Hurrians were of Armenoid stock and came into the northern part of Mesopotamia toward the end of the third millennium B.C. They settled in the Amorite country, where they became a dominant cultural group in the sixteenth and fifteenth centuries B.C.

The Nuzu tablets, written in the Babylonian cuneiform, throw light upon numerous obscure customs and events of the patriarchal period. In Genesis 15, for instance, mention is made of Eliezer, a servant, as the adopted son of Abraham and supposedly his heir. The birth of Isaac, however, prevented Eliezer from receiving the inheritance. The Nuzu tablets contain a detailed description of this custom, which provided that a man and wife without children could adopt a son, who would be expected to take care of them, in return for which he would inherit the estate, provided no son were born.

Sarah, one of Abraham's wives, was unable to have children, so she suggested that Abraham take her maid as a substitute (Gen. 16:1 ff.). The Nuzu literature shows this to be a recognized procedure of that period on the grounds that the function of marriage was exclusively for the production of children.

The discovery of Nuzu teraphim, or household idols, and also texts that contain inheritance laws has added greatly to our understanding of the Laban-Jacob incident (Gen. 29–31). Laban, having no male heir, adopted Jacob as his son and gave him his daughters, Leah and Rachel, as wives. The law provided that if Laban should later have a son, he should share the inheritance and take possession of the teraphim; otherwise, Jacob would inherit the teraphim. A further stipulation stated that if Jacob married any other woman, his inheritance would be forfeited. It turned out that Laban later had sons. Meanwhile, Jacob left for Canaan, and Rachel stole the teraphim. The household gods now rightly belonged to Laban's sons. Laban's search for the idols was unsuccessful, for Rachel had put them in her camel's saddle. The possession of the teraphim was the crucial point in this story. The Nuzu story of Nashwi and his adopted son, Wullu, parallels the Genesis account in practically every detail.

Other Nuzu similarities are seen in Esau's sale of his birthright (Gen. 25) and in the validity of deathbed wills or blessings (Gen. 27).

Chapter Two

Egyptian Discoveries

1. Indestructible Egypt

In spite of the greater antiquity of the Babylonian civilization, the land of the Nile will always have the greater charm because of the magnitude and the mystery of its pyramids, tombs, and temples. While they reveal to us the consummate egotism of the Pharaohs, these indestructible monuments are also symbols of immortality. The idea of the future life was an ancient belief in Egypt long before the Hebrews came into existence. The Egyptian faith in the future life produced a sense of permanence that constitutes the fascination that the Nile country has had for mankind.

Many fantastic ideas have been circulated with reference to the pyramids, but the simple fact is that they were the royal tombs. In addition to their intrinsic value and the presence within of mummies, the pyramids have provided by their inscriptions a wealth of information on the early religion of Egypt and particularly on the belief in immortality. A complete pyramid consisted of four parts: the introductory or entrance temple, situated at the edge of the Nile; the covered passage or incline; the pyramid temple where the priests performed their ceremony; and, finally, the pyramid proper, consisting of a tomb chamber containing the royal mummy and a tomb chapel where the offerings of food were made.

The great pyramid of Cheops (*ca.* 2700 B.C.) was 481

feet in height, and each of the four sides measured 755 feet 8 inches, with no side varying more than an inch. This pyramid contained 2,300,000 blocks of stone. The stones, measuring three feet in height and weighing about three tons apiece, were laid so as to form four staircases rising and narrowing to a central point. The whole edifice was made smooth with an outer casing, which in the course of time disintegrated and fell away. Quality, as well as quantity, is manifest in the joints between the stones, for they do not exceed one-fiftieth of an inch and in some cases are almost imperceptible. The stones were quarried from hills situated twelve miles away on the other side of the Nile. As to how the ancient Egyptians transported and piled these stones up to a point 481 feet high, the answer is: thousands of men, years of toil, rafts, ropes, pulleys, levers, and spiral incline.

The Egyptians built for eternity, and in their building they coupled the colossal with the microscopic. The pyramids testify to royal pride and power, but they also stand as awe-inspiring symbols of a sublime faith in the survival of life in the future realm. The Sphinx has seen far-flung empires rise and fall; more than a millennium of history had enacted itself at his feet before Moses led the Israelites out of Egypt. Egypt's " dwellings of eternity," in splendid ruin, even now defy the ravages of time and the hand of man.

2. *The Letters of Tell el-Amarna*

In 1888 an Egyptian peasant woman stumbled over some clay tablets in a field at Tell el-Amarna. They were of no importance to her, so she sold them for the equivalent of an American half-dollar. They proved to be of considerable importance, however, to authorities on Palestinian history.

El-Amarna was the new capital of Amenhotep IV, the heretic king who instituted a monotheistic worship. Ikhnaton, as he named himself, was a religious genius but a poor politician. While he was building a new religion, his tribute states were tearing down his imperial sway. The deterioration of the empire, resulting from the king's exclusive devotion to religious reform, is described in the Tell el-Amarna letters, which were written to Ikhnaton by his viceroys in Palestine, Phoenicia, and Mesopotamia. These tablets also give us important information about Palestine before the time of Joshua.

The most interesting of the letters are those written by Ebed-Hepa, vassal king of Jerusalem, appealing for help against invaders called the Habiru. Ebed-Hepa informs Ikhnaton that the Habiru " are taking the cities of the king " in Palestine and implores him to send mercenaries before it is too late. In one of his letters he adds an interesting personal note to Ikhnaton's cuneiform scribe, whom he apparently knew intimately: " To the scribe of my lord, the king, Ebed-Hepa the servant. Bring these words plainly before my lord, the king: ' The whole land of my lord, the king, is going to ruin.' "

The Habiru swept over Palestine, burning the towns and driving the people out of the land. As in the case of the northern provinces of the Egyptian Empire, the Palestinian vassals were in league with the invaders. Ebed-Hepa was the only loyal representative of Egypt in Palestine as Rib-Addi was in Phoenicia.[1]

The problem raised by this letter and five others from

[1] For translation and further discussion of these letters, see James B. Pritchard (ed.), *Ancient Near Eastern Texts Relating to the Old Testament* (Princeton, 1955), pp. 483–90; James H. Breasted, *History of Egypt* (New York, 1912), pp. 387–89.

Ebed-Hepa concerns the identification of the Habiru, who were besieging Palestine at the time of the correspondence. Scholarship differs in the answer. The word "Habiru" seems to stand for Hebrews. But how could the invaders be Hebrews when the letters were written in the Eighteenth Dynasty (reign of Amenhotep IV, 1360 B.C.), for it is usually thought that the Israelites did not leave Egypt until the Nineteenth Dynasty (Ramses II, 1225 B.C.). The solution that has most in its favor would be that the Habiru constituted another Hebrew tribe, which did not go into Egypt and which invaded Palestine earlier than Joshua. If this is the case, there must have been several phases in the conquest of Palestine by the Hebrews. It is pretty generally agreed that not all of the original Hebrew people went down into Egypt. At any rate, if Habiru stands for Hebrews, it seems necessary to hold that the Hebrew conquest took place in two parts.

The Tell el-Amarna letters also reveal much regarding Jerusalem three hundred years before the monarchy, the condition of Palestine during the breakup of Egyptian domination, and also the patriarchal period. Corresponding to the letters of Ebed-Hepa are those of Rib-Addi, a viceroy of Phoenicia, which contain a similar plea for help.

3. Reconstructing Jewish History in Egypt

When did the Jews begin their wanderings? It is generally thought that the Jewish Diaspora, or colonization outside of Palestine, did not take place to any great extent until the time of the Greek conquest, toward the end of the fourth century B.C. Yet some papyri found on the Egyptian island of Elephantine in 1895 indicate that a Jewish settlement existed there as early as the time of Ezra and Nehemiah, 444 B.C.

The surprising assertion is made in the Elephantine papyri that when Cambyses the Persian invaded Egypt in 525 B.C. he found a Jewish temple at Elephantine. How the Jews came to establish a colony and temple in Egypt at such an early date is somewhat mystifying, but the discovery of these important documents throws added light on the history of the Jews.

What excites our interest in the Temple Papyrus (written in 407 B.C.) is the statement that the temple had been destroyed by Waldrang, the Persian governor. The Jews, it appears, had previously written to the high priest at Jerusalem for help but had received no reply. In this letter they appealed to Bagoas, the governor of Judah, and also to the two sons of Sanballet, the governor of Samaria. Bagoas' reply, which we also have, favors the rebuilding of the temple and the restoration of the Jehovah-worship.

We know that the Deuteronomic Reform of 621 B.C. prohibited all temples other than the one in Jerusalem. How are we to account, therefore, for the existence of the one in Elephantine? According to one theory, the edict did not receive immediate and universal obedience, especially in distant places. The alternate view would be that the existence of the Jewish temple in Egypt calls into question the date of the Deuteronomic Reform. The former viewpoint seems to be the more reasonable one. At any rate, it is clear that the Jerusalem authorities did not favor the rebuilding of the temple, and it was not until appeal was made to the Samaritans that help came. This also seems natural, for the Samaritans, who had just revolted from Jerusalem, would not have been averse to aiding another competitor of the Jerusalem temple. The letter is therefore illuminating in regard to the Samaritan schism in its early stages.

Bagoas' reply was as follows:

Memorandum of what Bagoas and Delaiah said to me: Let this be
an instruction to you in Egypt to say before Arsames about the
house of offering of the God of Heaven which had been in existence in the fortress of Elephantine [5] since ancient times, before
Cambyses, and was destroyed by that wretch Vidaranag in the
year 14 of King Darius: to rebuild it on its site as it was before,
and the meal-offering and incense to be made on [10] that altar
as it used to be.[2]

Another Elephantine papyrus of great importance to
students of Hebrew history is the Passover letter from a certain Hannaniah in Jerusalem. The writer's purpose was to
instruct the members of the Jewish colony in the observance
of the Passover according to the ordinances as found in Exodus 12 and Leviticus 23. The problem here is: Why should
the Elephantine Jews as late as 419 B.C. need any instruction
regarding the Passover, if they possessed the Torah? One
scholarly opinion is that the Levitical code was not introduced until the reform of Nehemiah. That would harmonize
the chronology, if such were the case. Another authority
holds that the Levitical law was universally known, but it was
the custom for the authorities in Jerusalem to issue an annual
decree or proclamation containing detailed instruction regarding the Passover.

4. *Letters from an Egyptian Sage to his Son*

The hieroglyphic writings of Amen-em-ope, Egypt's
wise man, were found in 1888 by Sir Ernest Budge and were
subsequently taken to the British Museum, where they were
deciphered. Amen-em-ope lived about 1400 B.C., but this

---

[2] Translation from James B. Pritchard, *op. cit.*

papyrus comes from the reign of Darius I. The author held a position akin to that of Joseph: superintendent of cereals and regulator of wheat. "The Teaching of Amen-em-ope, son of Kanekht," as the work is entitled, was written in the form of confidential advice to his son, and constitutes a manual of moral instruction numbering thirty chapters.

In the introductory lines we are reminded of Proverbs 21 ff., and 3:1 ff.

> Give thy ears, hear what is said,
> Give thy heart to understand them.
> To put them in thy heart is worth while,
> [But] it is damaging to him who neglects them.
> Let them rest in the casket of thy belly,
> That they may be a *key* in thy heart.

Chapter two contains advice that finds parallels in Proverbs 14:13 and 28:27.

> Guard thyself against robbing the oppressed
> And against overbearing the disabled.
> Stretch not forth thy hand against the approach of an old man,
> Nor *steal away* the speech of the *aged*.

Resemblances to Proverbs will also be seen in the following four excerpts: [8]

> Do not carry off the landmark at the boundaries of the arable land,
> Nor disturb the position of the measuring-cord;
> Be not greedy after a cubit of land,
> Nor encroach upon the boundaries of a widow. . . .

> Better is bread, when the heart is happy,
> Than riches with sorrow.

[8] Cf. Prov. 23:10; 15:17; 11:1; 16:11; 6:9; 20:13.

Do not *lean on* the scales nor falsify the weights,
Nor damage the fractions of the measure.

Do not spend the night fearful of the morrow.
At daybreak what is the morrow like?
Man knows not what the morrow is like.
God is [always] in his success,
Whereas man is in his failure.[4]

These and other verses are so similar to Proverbs that authorities in this field see a real dependence of the Hebrew work on the Egyptian in ethical insight as well as in literary form. Both sets of writings exhibit the same motives and ideals: prudence, honesty, industry, obedience, and temperance.

5. *Two Kings: Tutankhamon and Ikhnaton*

Tutankhamon, a young Egyptian king, may have been somewhat famous, but he could not be called great. He was a reactionary, a pawn of the priests, and a caterer to popular demand. As a dead monarch he is a thousand times more famous than when alive, due to the fact that his was the only unplundered tomb ever found in Egypt, the contents of which constitute the richest and most bewildering array of funeral treasures seen in the history of excavation.

The entrance to the tomb of Tutankhamon is directly between, and only a few yards away from, the places where Theodore M. Davis had formerly dug; and thousands of unsuspecting tourists had walked above the now famous door. It was reserved for an Englishman, Howard Carter, to make,

[4] Pritchard, *op. cit.*

after six years' search, the most sensational find in the history of archaeology and to place the name of an obscure king of Egypt on the lips of countless people who up to that time hardly knew where Egypt was.

On November 4, 1922, Mr. Carter came upon a stone step just thirteen feet from the entrance to the tomb of Ramses VI. (When Ramses cut his tomb, he was unaware of the nearby Tutankhamon.) The excavators descended sixteen steps and found a door with its seals still intact. After entering, they descended thirty feet more to find a second door and, behind it, a profusion of wealth. It is fortunate that the discovery was reserved for our day, when archaeological technique could guarantee the safe removal of the numerous fragile objects and their preservation for the future.

For our knowledge of the Osirian ritual prescribed in the Book of the Dead, the mummy of Tutankhamon and the treasures of the sepulchral chamber provide a perfect commentary. The mummy wrappings revealed the ceremonial apron, a golden bird representing the spirit of the king, and hundreds of pieces of religious jewelry and precious stones. Venison, ducks, game, fruit, and all kinds of meat were embalmed or preserved and packed in small wooden boxes. This food was prepared for the " ka," or double, of the king in the future life.

Among other objects brought to light were some small statues of Tutankhamon, known as ushabti. Their purpose was to act for the king in the lower world and to perform for him any menial work that would be required, such as farming or irrigation. Besides showing the correct process of mummification, these statues were accompanied by model boats and various agricultural implements, which increase considerably our knowledge of Egyptian life.

Tempting as it would be to catalogue the remarkable treasures of this tomb, we must pass them by and accompany Tutankhamon's soul to the judgment hall of Osiris, where his place in the story of religion will be decided. Tutankhamon was one of history's " stand pats," who returned to the fold of Amon after his father-in-law, Ikhnaton, had broken with the priests and instituted the most significant reform in the history of Egypt. This explains why Tutankhamon was given such an elaborate burial by the grateful priests of Amon, whose power and wealth were restored, and why this king is completely overshadowed by his predecessor in the annals of the really great.

Ikhnaton, born Amenhotep IV, Tutankhamon's predecessor, made perhaps the first attempt in history to establish a monotheistic religion. He was the first great heretic. Impatient with the conventional forms of the priestly cults, he abandoned the old polytheism and chose the sun disc, Aton, as the one true god. When he sought to effect a religious reform on this basis, priestly opposition was so strong that he was forced to remove his capital to Tell el-Amarna 300 miles north of Thebes. Here he changed his name from Amenhotep (Amon is gracious) to Ikhnaton (spirit of the sun disc). For a brief period he carried on a purified religion; and with it came a more lofty literature, of which the hymn in praise of Aton is the most beautiful example.

> Thy dawning is beautiful in the horizon of the sky,
> O living Aton, Beginning of Life!
> When thou risest in the eastern horizon,
> Thou fillest every land with thy beauty.
>
> . . . .
>
> When thou settest in the western horizon of the sky,
> The earth is in darkness like the dead;

They sleep in their chambers
Their heads are wrapped up.

.   .   .   .

Bright is the earth when thou risest in the horizon.
When thou shinest as Aton by day
Thou drivest away the darkness.
When thou sendest forth thy rays,
The Two Lands [Egypt] are in daily festivity. . . .
All cattle rest upon their pasturage,
The trees and the plants flourish,
The birds flutter in their marshes,
Their wings uplifted in adoration to thee.
All the sheep dance upon their feet,
All winged things fly,
They live when thou hast shone upon them.

.   .   .   .

How manifold are thy works!
They are hidden from before us,
O sole God, whose powers no other possesseth,
Thou didst create the earth according to thy heart
While thou wast alone:
Men, all cattle, large and small,
All that are upon the earth. . . .
How excellent are thy designs, O Lord of eternity.[5]

This hymn, resembling as it does Psalm 104 and others, shows a deep, religious feeling, such as was never again attained in Egypt. The heretic king died while in his thirties and was succeeded by two sons-in-law in rapid order. The second, Tutankhaton, moved the court back to Thebes, reestablished the worship of the old gods, and incidentally restored the Amon suffix to his own name, which then became Tutankhamon.

[5] Translation by James H. Breasted, *The Dawn of Conscience* (New York, 1933).

Ikhnaton was a visionary, caring more for religious mysticism than for politics, and, while he caused imperial Egypt to lose its grip on foreign tribute states, he set free an ideal that was to be the making of a great people, whose leader was soon to be born among the slaves of Ramses!

Chapter Three

The Spade in Palestine

1. The Modern Conquest of Canaan

Every spadeful of Palestinian soil tells a story. It is the story of the rise and fall of successive civilizations from cave man to crusader. The technique of archaeology has woven together from broken fragments of pottery a fabric of history well coordinated and unified, confirming many of the data recorded in the Pentateuch.

The discoveries in Palestine, with the exception of the Moabite Stone and the Dead Sea Scrolls, have never been as spectacular as those in Egypt and Babylonia. No great and enduring civilization ever made its home in Palestine; that fact alone would preclude the possibility of discovering such monuments as those given up by the sands of Egypt or the palaces of the Euphrates. The Hebrew domination of Palestine was so short-lived and so precarious that no great works were even possible except during the regime of Solomon (and as a work of art or architecture his temple has perhaps been overrated).

Then when we reflect that from the twentieth century B.C. to the twentieth century A.D., Palestine has been a battle-ground, tramped upon by the armies of Egypt, Philistia, Assyria, Babylonia, Persia, Greece, Rome, Turkey, Arabia, and England, it is not to be expected that any ancient buildings or works of art could have survived the ravages of a hundred wars. And, even if the destructive hand of war had been stayed, the fact remains that the occupants of Palestine — Canaanites and Hebrews — were neither architects nor artists. Furthermore, as has frequently been pointed out, the climate and soil of the Holy Land are not conducive to the preservation of antiquities.

Being prepared, therefore, for a certain disappointment in Palestinian archaeology, we shall be able to appreciate more keenly the recent discoveries in that area.[1]

2. *The Hebrews Go Canaanite*

For thousands of years, from the most remote antiquity down to the Middle Ages, all roads led through (if not to) Beisan, the Biblical Beth Shan, which lies nine miles north of Jerusalem. Being the gateway to northern Palestine, Beisan was a perpetual battlefield, as the invading armies century after century attacked the fortress. The University of Pennsylvania Museum Expedition, under the direction of Alan Rowe, has laid bare the successive occupations of the " Mound of the Fortress," as Beisan was called, so that one may view a continuous stratification of temples from 1500 B.C. to medieval times. What a bird's-eye view of history the excavator has here, gazing upon the strata of Arabic, Byzantine, Hellenistic, Persian, Babylonian, Philistine, Egyptian, and Ca-

[1] For a complete and technical coverage of Palestinian archaeology see W. F. Albright, *The Archaeology of Palestine and The Bible* (New York, 1932); and *From the Stone Age to Christianity* (Baltimore, 1940); G. A. Barton, *Archaeology and the Bible* (7th ed.; New York, 1937); A. T. Olmstead, *The History of Palestine and Syria* (New York, 1931); J. Finegan, *Light from the Ancient Past* (Princeton, 1946); H. H. Rowley (ed.), *The Old Testament and Modern Study, A Generation of Discovery and Research* (Oxford, 1951).

naanite civilizations! On the Egyptian level are ruins of an
Egyptian fortress, statues of Ramses III, and an inscription of
Ramses II to the effect that he employed Semitic labor in
building his city in Egypt (Ex. 1:11).

Chief among the temple discoveries at Beisan are the two
mentioned in I Samuel 31:10 and I Chronicles 10:10: the
" Temple of Dagon " and the " House of Ashtoreth," respectively. It was upon the wall of Beisan that the Philistines
fastened the body of King Saul (I Sam. 31:10, 12). According to I Chronicles 10:10, " They put his armor in the house
of their gods, and fastened his head in the Temple of Dagon."
David, upon hearing of the death of Saul, took Beisan from
the Philistines and demolished it. The charred wood and reddened bricks found in the remains of the temple are sufficient
proof of the completeness of the job.

The temples of Dagon and Ashtoreth were rich in material relating to the Canaanite religion and the Philistines.
In the middle of a large hall, near the remains of a basalt column, was found part of an Egyptian stele, erected in honor
of the goddess Antit, or Ashtoreth. Above the portrait of the
female deity is the inscription, " Antit, queen of heaven, mistress of all the gods." This goddess, who became the Babylonian Ishtar and the Roman Venus, was the chief Canaanite
deity, the worship of whom wielded not a little influence
among the Hebrews in the direction of sex worship, as the
biblical records and archaeological discoveries clearly show.

The temple of Dagon (Resheph) contained a large hall
seventy-three feet long and twenty-six feet wide, with three
aisles. Just as in the great hall of the temple of Ashtoreth,
here also was found a sculpture dedicated to the temple deity.
The cylinder seal shows Ramses the Great with a war helmet,
shooting at two Canaanite captives; facing him is the war-god,

Dagon, holding in his hands the symbols of life and death. (Dagon is mentioned in I Sam. 5:2–7 and Judg. 16:23.)

Fortunately, we know the name of the builder of the temple of Dagon, for he was proud enough of his work to inscribe his name and portrait on the door jamb. Ramses Wesr-Khepesh, the builder, probably had been stationed by the Pharaoh over the fortress of Beisan. The titles following his name read " overseer of soldiers, commander of the bowmen of the Lord of the Two Lands, royal scribe, Great steward, Ramses Wesr-Khepesh, the son of the fanbearer at the right hand of the king, chief of the bowmen, overseer of foreign countries, Thotmes." The two temples yielded many objects used in connection with the worship of Ashtoreth, such as shrine houses, sacred boxes, lamps, bowls, vases, and kernoi, or sacred vessels consisting of rings with cups.

The fourth level was no less interesting, for it revealed a temple built by Seti I of Egypt about 1300 B.C. This temple had been partially " open air," and at the roofed end contained an altar room. Nearby were brick ovens, a great amount of flour, and jars of sesame seed, indicative of meal offerings to the deity.

Removing the Seti temple, Mr. Rowe and his force uncovered another one directly beneath, built during the reign of Amenhotep III, 1400 B.C. The cornerstone of this temple contained cylinder seals and a ring of Amenhotep III. Figures of Ashtoreth were plentiful here also. The contents of the fifth level were numerous and varied, showing Hittite, Cretan, and Syrian influences.

Not satisfied, the excavators struck deeper yet and found below the Amenhotep III level two Canaanite temples of 1500 B.C. These were not Egyptian, like the temples above, but were strictly Canaanite in origin.

The most important object in this temple was the mazzebah or sacred stone. It is a conical shaped form made of basalt and laid in a basalt foundation. In front of the stone is a libation cup into which the blood ran from the column. The mazzebah, emblematic of the deity, was a common feature of the Canaanite religion. Even today, Mr. Rowe tells us, the natives in Beisan regard with some respect a certain stone column upon which they sacrifice small animals to fulfill vows made in the tomb enclosure of a local saint, Sheikh Halabi. The Hebrews, after their invasion of Canaan, used many mazzebahs in their confused worship of Yahweh.

In the room of sacrifice was a large brick altar in which had been cut a channel for the outlet of blood. On the altar also was a hole for a peg to which the animal was fastened. The horns of the last bull to be sacrificed were lying beside the altar. The name of the deity to whom the temple was dedicated was found inscribed on an Egyptian stele in the mazzebah room — " Mekal, the god of Beisan." This discovery adds a new name to the procession of the gods. The other temple seems to have been dedicated to Ashtoreth, or to some early likeness of her.

Only by a thorough understanding of the Canaanite religion can we appreciate the preprophetic period of Israelitish history, when the Hebrews, in conquering Canaan, were in turn conquered by Canaan's gods. The idea that the religious practices of the Canaanites strongly influenced the Hebrews, producing for a time a syncretism or mixed type of worship, has ample proof in the writings of the prophets. The excavations at Beisan and other Palestinian sites have provided valuable data relating to the religious observances encountered by the Hebrews when they entered the Promised Land.

3. The Hittites Come into Their Own

In the fourteenth century B.C. King Shuppiluiumash (Suppiluliumas) ruled all Asia Minor, the land of the Hittites. His name was feared in Egypt, where the widow of Tutankhamon proposed to one of his sons. The widowed queen, realizing her precarious position upon the death of her husband, wrote to the Hittite king: " My husband is dead and I have no son. They say you have many sons. If you would give me one of them, he shall be my husband." The king was suspicious, however, and the marriage that would have united the royal houses of Hatti and Egypt did not materialize.

This leap-year proposal happened to be on one of several thousand clay tablets found in the royal library of Boghaz-Keui (Boghazköy) in Asia Minor (now Turkey). The finding of this library in 1906–07 by Professor Hugo Winckler was a major archaeological discovery. The Hittites were a powerful people in 1400 B.C. but by 1200 B.C. had vanished from the earth. Not many years ago, Professor A. H. Sayce, thinking that there must be a connection between Egypt and the early unknown inhabitants of Asia Minor, started the search for the lost empire. It was the discovery of the library of Boghaz-Keui that revealed for the first time the strategic importance of the Hittites in the ancient world.

The tablets are of clay, baked after inscription; they vary in size from small letters a few inches in length to formal inscriptions two feet high. The script used was the Babylonian cuneiform, but the texts were written for the most part in eight different Hittite dialects, totally unknown to the modern world. For twenty years scholars from Germany, England, France, and America have been translating these languages and piecing together the story of the Hittites. The documents included treaties with Egypt, Mitanni, and the Amorites, domestic treaties, royal decrees, detailed diplomatic correspondence with Egypt and Babylonia, wills, patents, inventories, military instructions, building plans, prayers, oracles, rituals, formulae, and catalogues of books, thoroughly indexed by authors' names.

From the Boghaz-Keui tablets we have been able to reconstruct some of the history of the Hittites. As far back as 2800 B.C. they revolted against Babylonian domination. At this early date the Hittites were not a united nation but independent states, chief among which were the two rival powers: Hatti, with its capital at Boghaz-Keui, and Kussara. The various states were later welded together into a great kingdom, whose domain extended from the Black and Aegean seas to Babylonia and Assyria. Under Hattusil I, Syria and Babylonia were conquered. Later, in 1469 B.C., Syria became the Alsace-Lorraine between Egypt and the Hittites, when Thotmes III attempted to expand the domain of Egypt.

The Tell el-Amarna letters are both confirmed and amplified by the Boghaz-Keui tablets, which show that the Egyptian vassals in Syria, while pleading for aid from Amenhotep IV, were at the same time making overtures to the Hittite king. The Syrian officials, probably anticipating Egypt's loss of imperial power due to Ikhnaton's all-absorbing interest in religious reform, attempted to effect an alliance with the Hittites. Although the Hittites did not enter Palestine, they did annex Mitanni, which was the northern portion of Mesopotamia.[2]

---

[2] For references to the Hittites in the Old Testament see Josh. 3:10; Num. 13:29; II Kings 7:6.

Further decipherment of the famous tablets enables us to follow step by step the campaigns of King Mursil III (1330 B.C.), under whom the Hittite Empire reached its zenith with the subjugation of Aleppo and the kingdom of the Amorites. At this point, Egypt, now ruled by the more ambitious Ramses II, again turned her attention to Syria. The Hittite king also prepared for action, and the clash of world powers occurred at Kadesh in 1296 B.C. The battle was disastrous for both combatants and was followed later by a treaty of peace.

Here the story of the tablets ceases, and we conclude that the Hittites disappeared before the onslaught of barbarians from the north about 1200 B.C. The very existence of the Hittite Empire, covering, as it did, all of Asia Minor, was completely forgotten, with the result that much later the name was applied only to the southernmost province. This accounts for the fact that in the Old Testament the people of Syria were called Hittites. Uriah the "Hittite" therefore was not a real Hittite.

As the Boghaz-Keui tablets show, the Hittites were familiar with the cuneiform writings of the Sumerians. Their own tablets were written in what is known as the boustrophedon system, in which the first line ran from left to right, the second from right to left, and so on.

Research in Hittite monuments has been concerned chiefly with deciphering and comparative philology. Some of the inscriptions are in Babylonian cuneiform, but the language itself is Hittite, an Indo-European tongue.[3] The most important name in Hittite translation is that of the Czech philologist Friedrich Hrozny (born in Poland in 1879).

---

[3] Compare present-day Yiddish — a German vocabulary written in Hebrew characters.

After several years of painstaking work on the Boghaz-Keui texts, he published his conclusion (1917) that the language of the Hittites belonged to the Indo-European family.

In 1947 an expedition, conducted by Professor Helmuth T. Bossert under the auspices of the University of Istanbul, discovered several Phoenician inscriptions at Karatepe in the southeast corner of Asia Minor. These texts begin on the body of a symbolic stone lion and continue through several group reliefs. Along with the Semitic texts were Hittite hieroglyphic signs. Thus Bossert had before him the one prerequisite for the deciphering of any unknown language — a bilingual inscription. On the basis of the Karatepe texts, he was able to decipher many important Hittite words.[4]

From a cultural standpoint there is a tendency today to exaggerate the importance of the Hittite Empire. True, it was one of the great military powers of antiquity, as seen in the battle of Kadesh. But, aside from military prowess, the Hittites did not make any cultural advance comparable with that of the Egyptians and the Babylonians. They had no unified language but used a borrowed script; they were indifferent to religion except in some local cults; they produced no great art or architecture; and they left the world no literature.

4. The Walls of Jericho

The walls of Jericho that Joshua faced were the two parallel inner walls, the foundations and lower parts of which

---

[4] Hittite bibliography has become very extensive, especially in French and German. For a popular and up-to-date summary of research in Hittite history, archaeology, decipherment, and also bibliography, see C. W. Ceram, *The Secret of the Hittites*, trans. Richard and Clara Winston (New York, 1956). See also O. R. Gurney, *The Hittites* (London, 1952).

are now uncovered. Signs of destruction by fire — reddened bricks, cracked stones, and ashes — are much in evidence. Remains of houses that had been burned to the ground were also found. When Jericho was taken, its attackers were able to ascend the citadel over the ruins of the walls, which had fallen outward and crumbled on the hillside. Having entered the city itself, the invaders set it on fire.

The determination of the occupational levels at Jericho has been from the first a complicated problem. The excavation was begun in 1907 under the auspices of the Deutsche Orient-Gesellschaft with Professor Ernst Sellin in charge. Remains of a prehistoric occupation were found, above which was the Canaanite city dating back to 2000 B.C. Sellin brought to light the defensive rampart of the early city on all sides except the east.

The citadel of the city was protected by a double wall of brick, the outer one being about six feet thick and the inner about twelve feet thick. It was thought that the outer rampart belonged to the later Israelite period and that the inner double wall was from an earlier period. Later, this conclusion was corrected, and the outer wall was assigned to 1800 B.C., but the belief persisted that the inner one belonged to a still earlier time. The German excavators believed that the wall around the crest of the hill had been destroyed about 1500 B.C. and had lain in ruin for six hundred years thereafter and that during the ninth century B.C. it was rebuilt by Hiel (I Kings 16:34).

The first authority to dispute this dating was P. H. Vincent. If the calculations were correct, he thought, the conquest of Jericho by Joshua (1200 B.C.) would have to be regarded as fiction, for there would then have been no walls of Jericho. Closer examination of the pottery showed that the inner wall dated from the late Bronze Age (1200 B.C.) rather than from the earlier period.

The Jericho excavation was continued by Professor John Garstang in 1930. The stratification was practically invisible because of the presence of former dumpings, the ancient destruction of the city, and the removal of remains for rebuilding purposes; but, after examining sixty thousand pieces of pottery and cutting an undisturbed stratification, Professor Garstang was able to confirm the opinion of the German authorities in dating the outer brick wall at about 1800 B.C. The double brick wall surrounding the citadel of the city proved to belong not to the earlier but to the later period — that of Joshua, as Père Vincent had surmised. The discrepancy was due to the fact that the inner brick wall had been built on an older fortification.

The conclusions finally reached were based primarily on the classification of pottery. Whatever certainty is achieved in the dating of the walls will be due largely to Père Vincent's expert knowledge of ceramics.

5. The High Places of Gezer

The completeness of the stratification at Gezer — where R. A. S. Macalister for many years conducted the work for the Palestine Exploration Fund — is probably due to its position somewhat removed from the beaten paths and the battlegrounds of empires. Its eight strata tell the story of the city from the cave man of 3000 B.C. to the Maccabean Wars of 165 B.C. (The archaeologist, unfortunately, has to start at the end of the story and read back to the beginning.)

The cave dwellers of Gezer left some extremely crude

pottery as the only record of their primitive life. It was molded by hand and was decorated with red and white lines. Of art and handicraft they apparently knew nothing, for the walls of the caves exhibit only meaningless scratchings. Evidence of primitive religious rites was found in the sacrificial rock, where pigs were probably slain by the tribal leader and the blood flowed into the room below.

The next stratum reveals a fortified town built by the early Semites who swept through the region and annihilated the cave dwellers about 2500 B.C. The wall of this hill town was twenty-five feet high and thirteen feet thick and supported parapets and towers. Entrance was made through a gigantic gate between two brick towers.

The outstanding discovery on the first Semitic level was the great tunnel cut through solid rock. The passage, which measures 12 feet across and 23 feet high, leads down 80 steps to a cave that is 94 feet below the courtyard level and 120 feet below the present surface. In the center of the cave is a spring. This feat of engineering was probably planned by Egyptian officials to insure water for the town in time of siege. Proof of the Egyptian domination during this period was at hand: a small Egyptian temple decorated with hieroglyphs and dedicated to one of the gods of the Nile country.

Even more noteworthy from the religious standpoint was the High Place of the native religious cult, where seven stone pillars stood as testimony to the bloody and barbaric worship of the early Semites. Here the god was appeased by the spilling of blood, which was sprinkled on the stones. There is little doubt as to the identity of the sacrificial victims. Dead bodies, being unclean, would not ordinarily be found in a sanctuary, but the whole area surrounding these monoliths is a cemetery filled with the skeletal remains of newborn infants. Sacrifice of the first-born was a common Semitic practice; a survival is seen in Genesis 22, where Abraham attempts to offer Isaac as a sacrifice to Jehovah. The law later provided for the sacrifice of a lamb (Ex. 34:20), but the custom seems to have reappeared in the time of Manasseh (II Kings 21:6; 23:10).

The stone pillars range from five to ten feet tall, and all but one were probably secured from the vicinity. One, however, had an indentation around it, indicating that it had been dragged to Gezer from Jerusalem or some other distant place. It is thought that this was the one sacred stone of the series and that the others were really not significant. This Canaanite High Place was probably used from 2000 B.C. down to the time of the Babylonian Exile.

The deity worshiped at the High Place of Gezer was Ashtoreth, the Canaanite goddess of fruitfulness, before whom devotees of the cult performed their ritual. The well-established sex-worship of the Canaanite shrines was the object of prophetic denunciation, and without doubt it was the reform preached by the eighth-century Hebrew prophets that led to the elimination of this corrupt type of worship from Hebrew life. The Ashtoreth plaques, found in great quantities on this and other sites, bear testimony to the prevalence of the Ashtoreth cult. It was inevitable that the Hebrews, in assimilating the culture of the Canaanites, should absorb also many of their religious practices.

The story of Gezer continues to unfold itself through the Philistine, Assyrian, Greek, and Maccabean levels, each occupation leaving its traces in bits of pottery and inscriptions. For the most part, the excavations at Gezer confirm the biblical data relative to the Hebrew conquest and later periods.

6. Solomon's Stables

The capital of the Great Plain district was Megiddo, a strongly fortified city containing the palace of the governor and the stables of Solomon. The references to Solomon's stables and chariot houses in I Kings 9:19 and II Chronicles 8:6 have been proved correct.

The stables, which are now cleared, could accommodate three hundred horses. The largest stable consisted of five sections, each with twenty-four stalls, twelve on each side of the central passage. Supporting the roof of the stables and separating the various stalls were stone pillars, through which holes were bored, showing that the horses were tied to them. Between each pair of pillars was a stone manger. The floor of the central passage had a lime-plaster pavement, and the stalls were paved with small, rough stones to keep the horses from slipping.

The excavation of Tell el-Mutesselim (the biblical Megiddo) was begun by the Deutscher-Palestina Verein in 1903 under the direction of Dr. Gottlieb Schumacher. The expedition found a stratification of seven occupational levels from the period of the Egyptian Twelfth Dynasty to the Hellenistic age.

In the lowest stratum, dating about 2000 B.C., was a tomb with skeletons, quantities of pottery, and many scarabs. In the fifth stratum from the bottom were the remains of a palace of the Hebrew period, in which was found a seal bearing the picture of a lion and the inscription " Belonging to Shema, the servant of Jeroboam," probably meaning Jeroboam II (784–744 B.C.).

The Oriental Institute of the University of Chicago, taking over the site in 1925, cleared and examined the four strata from the tenth to the fourth century B.C. The fourth stratum from the top was the Solomonic level, where the stables were found. The palace of the governor of the city stands close by the stables.

The Megiddo of Solomon's time was fortified by a new wall. The enemy would have had to climb the steep slope of the mound and would have encountered at the top a towered wall thirteen feet thick. Entrance by the gateway was just as difficult, for, if the outer gate were forced, the attacker would be caught in a trap between the outer and inner gate and would be under fire from the towers above.

Megiddo's " Main Street " led from the city gate straight to the palace. The governor's residence was approached by a lime-paved courtyard. An observation tower on the top of the palace commanded a fine view of the great plain below. The excavation of the palace and stables corroborates the traditional impression that Megiddo was rebuilt by Solomon and was one of the most strategic headquarters of the king's realm.

7. The House of Ahab

The excavation of Samaria was undertaken by Harvard University from 1908–10. References to the palace of Omri (886–875 B.C.) in I Kings 16:24 and to Ahab's (872–852 B.C.) " ivory house " in I Kings 22:39 took on new meaning with the discovery on successive levels of the remains of those royal residences and that of a third monarch. It is generally supposed that the third palace belonged to Jeroboam II.

Omri built his palace after the plans of those at Babylon, with open courts surrounded by small rooms. Workmen's marks appear here and there in the form of Hebrew letters or simple sketches of animals. Under the floors, which were of hard earth or slabs of stone, ran channels for sanitation. Adjoining Omri's palace and serving as a continuation of it was the "ivory house" of Ahab, who built a platform on a double wall that ran three hundred feet north and south, the outer wall being six feet thick. The foundation for the new palace was made by these walls and the debris, which was thrown inside them.

In the southwest corner of Ahab's court were found the royal archives and several hundred inscribed potsherds constituting some seventy ostraca or fragments of inscribed pottery. These ostraca were written in ink with a brush pen and represent the cursive form of the old Hebrew language. They contain lists of shipments of oil and wine to various localities and provide information regarding the tax system, the geography, and the administration of the Northern Kingdom. The ostraca are important also for the light they throw on the Hebrew language in the time of Elijah. These documents were written in the common script rather than in the formal biblical Hebrew that would be found in Jerusalem.

The excavation of Samaria was resumed in 1931 under the joint auspices of Harvard University, the Palestine Exploration Fund, and the Hebrew University of Jerusalem. The Hellenistic city was found to have been completely destroyed by Hyrcanus, but remains of the Roman and Herodian city were quite plentiful. These included a first-century temple, built by Herod; a palaestra or gymnasium, on the walls of which were names and sketches; and numerous houses — all of which give a fairly good idea of the Samaria of Jesus' day.

The last level to be investigated was the Byzantine. Valuable information is expected from the future excavation of

Samaria, especially with regard to the fortifications of the Israelite city and the Byzantine period.

8. The Dead Sea Scrolls

Whereas our best New Testament manuscripts come
from the fourth century A.D., the oldest Hebrew manuscripts
date from the ninth century A.D.[5] Such was the case, at least,
until 1947.

In the spring of that year a goat, seeking greener pastures,
climbed up on a high cliff overlooking the Dead Sea near
Jericho. The Arab goatherd followed and found the animal
near the mouth of a cave. Upon entering the cave he discovered some twenty ancient scrolls hidden in earthen jars.
These scrolls were later taken to the American School of
Oriental Research in Jerusalem for decipherment and were
found to be Hebrew manuscripts; the most important was
one of Isaiah from the second, or no later than the first, century B.C. This impressive manuscript, consisting of twenty-
four feet of sheepskin ten and one half inches wide, contains
the entire Hebrew text of Isaiah. (The Old Testament committee on the Revised Standard Revision of the Bible was able
to use the text in connection with the revision. Fourteen
changes were made on the basis of the Dead Sea manuscript,
but the changes are of no great significance and the newly
found manuscript only confirms the accuracy of the Masoretic text.[6])

The original discovery in the cave included several other
documents: a nonbiblical manual of discipline from an un-

[5] See pp. 225-226.
[6] The standard Hebrew text of the Old Testament is called the
Masoretic and is from the tenth century A.D.

known sect of the first century B.C.; a Hebrew commentary on Habakkuk on leather from the second century B.C.; an apocryphal book called Lamech, resembling the book of Enoch; some fragments of Daniel; a manuscript of Isaiah chapters 40–66, from the first century B.C.; and a volume of hymns or thanksgiving psalms. In a second search of the cave in 1949, some two hundred additional fragments were recovered, the most important of which were several scrolls containing portions of the Pentateuch, probably from the fourth or third century B.C. The American School of Oriental Research undertook to publish the Dead Sea Scrolls, but it will take several years to collate these documents and to appraise their value. It can safely be said that the discovery of the text of Isaiah is the greatest manuscript find of the twentieth century.[7]

Some of the scholars resident in Jerusalem at the time of these discoveries were reluctant to acknowledge the authenticity of the texts and in certain instances displayed not too much interest, at least in the initial stages of the investigations. The whole business was highly unorganized at first and the Scrolls were passed around from one official to another like " hot " jewelry. Their genuineness was recognized, however, by Professor W. F. Albright of Johns Hopkins, and subsequently the American School of Oriental Research in Jerusalem, the Hebrew University in Jerusalem, and the Jordanian Department of Antiquities took steps to organize the discovery, restoration, decipherment, and editing of the materials.

---

[7] The date of the Isaiah scroll was verified at the University of Chicago by radioactivity. This new technique, developed by radiochemist Willard F. Libby and known as the atomic calendar, measures the radioactivity of the carbon 14 present in any object. This process indicates when the carbon 14 was first created by the action of cosmic rays.

Altogether 267 caves in the Khirbet Qumran region have been explored. The presence of tens of thousands of scrolls in one area indicated that the caves contained a library of biblical, apocryphal, and other literature. Excavation revealed a stone building containing some thirty rooms and an adjacent cemetery with about a thousand graves. It is now thought that this building was a monastery of the Essene sect.[8] The Manual of Discipline, found in 1947, seems to have belonged to this monastic order and recalls the discovery of the Zadokite Fragments in Cairo in 1896. The Zadokite texts bear a strong resemblance to the Manual of Discipline in doctrine, language, and historical references. There is a connection also between the literature of the Essenes and some of the later apocryphal books. All of this gives added significance to the apocalyptic literature of the intertestamental period and its influence on early Christianity.

Two of the Dead Sea Scrolls are definitely apocalyptic in character — *The War of the Children of Light against the Children of Darkness* and a *Commentary on Habakkuk*. The latter, written probably in the middle of the first century B.C., refers to a Teacher of Righteousness, a prophet or priest who claims to have a revelation from God and who has a following among the poorer classes. The followers of the Teacher, who is called the Elect of God, are referred to as members of " the New Covenant." It is interesting to note that the Zadokite Fragments also mention a Teacher of Righteousness who is the leader of the New Covenant. The Book of Enoch (first century B.C.) speaks of " the Elect One " and " the Righteous

---

[8] The Essenes were a celibate monastic order of Jews existing in the two centuries preceding the Christian era. They observed strict rules regarding their daily life, fasting, ritualistic washings, sacraments, and work. Everything was held in common. In some of their tenets they resembled the Pharisees.

One." Obviously these titles are Messianic references and are similar to the allusions to Jesus in the gospels. The Dead Sea discoveries therefore establish more firmly than ever the continuity of Messianic ideas through the intertestamental period and into the New Testament itself.

Included in the intertestamental literature and also in the Qumran Manual of Discipline is a treatise on the dualistic doctrine of The Two Ways. The most prominent Christian expression of this theme is found in the Didaché or the Teaching of the Twelve Apostles, a manual of instruction in the early Christian church (*ca.* 125 A.D.).[9] The Manual of Discipline also contains a description of the sacred meal of the Jewish sect. This supper was presided over by the Teacher or Messiah, who blessed the bread and wine and distributed it to his followers.

The implications of the Dead Sea documents are not too clear at the present writing, but it is not an exaggeration to conclude that they do have a definite bearing on the questions of Jesus' uniqueness as a prophet, the originality of his teachings, the origin of Christian sacraments, and the influence of intertestamental Judaism on the beginnings of Christianity. The Teacher of Righteousness of the Scrolls would seem to be a prototype of Jesus, for both spoke of the New Covenant; they preached a similar gospel; each was regarded as a Saviour or Redeemer; and each was condemned and put to death by reactionary factions.

Previously it has been thought that in the sacraments of the Lord's Supper and baptism the early Christian church was influenced, if at all, more by the mystery religions of the Graeco-Roman world than by Judaism. But the Qumran findings seem to point to the supper of the Essenes as an ante-

[9] See pp. 203–206.

cedent of the Christian supper. Many of the teachings of the Essenes are reflected in early Christian literature. We do not know whether Jesus was an Essene, but some scholars feel that he was at least influenced by them.

In discussing the bearing of the Dead Sea Scrolls on the person of Jesus, much depends on one's theological and ecclesiastical position. Scholars like Millar Burrows, who are closely connected with the interpretation of the documents, are fairly objective; but some theologians have shown their apprehension by quickly assuring the public that orthodox Christology will in no way suffer by reason of the findings. To those who have always assumed a certain dependence of Christianity on earlier institutions and teachings, the implications of the Dead Sea Scrolls will not be too startling. Those who regard Jesus as uniquely the Son of God and Christianity as a divine and unchanging revelation will be somewhat disturbed, but all fair-minded scholars will be compelled to make some revision of their interpretation of the New Testament.[10]

[10] For a more complete coverage of the Dead Sea Scrolls see Millar Burrows, *The Dead Sea Scrolls* (New York, 1955), and *More Light on the Dead Sea Scrolls* (New York, 1958); H. H. Rowley, *The Zadokite Fragments and the Dead Sea Scrolls* (New York, 1953); E. L. Sukenik (ed.), *The Dead Sea Scrolls of the Hebrew University* (Jerusalem, 1955); A. Dupont-Sommer, *The Dead Sea Scrolls, A Preliminary Survey*, trans. E. Margaret Rowley (New York, 1952), *The Jewish Sect of Qumran and the Essenes*, trans. R. D. Barnett (London, 1954); Edmund Wilson, *The Scrolls from the Dead Sea* (New York, 1955); A. Powell Davies, *The Meaning of the Dead Sea Scrolls* (New York, 1956). See also the following articles: F. M. Cross, "The Newly Discovered Scrolls in the Hebrew University Museum in Jerusalem," *Biblical Archaeologist*, 1949, pp. 36–46; W. H. Brownlee, "The Jerusalem Habakkuk Scroll," *Bulletin of the American School of Oriental Research*, Dec., 1948, pp. 8–18, and "Excerpts from the Translation of the Dead Sea Manual of Discipline," *Bulletin of the American School of Oriental Research*, Feb., 1951, pp. 8–13; W. F. Albright, "The Chronology of the Dead Sea Scrolls," *Bulletin of the American School of Oriental Research*, 1951, pp. 57–60; J. C. Trevor, "The Discovery of the Scrolls," *Biblical Archaeologist*, 1948, pp. 46–57.

9. *The Oldest Alphabet in the World*

It had usually been supposed that the Phoenicians were the first people to use an alphabet, but the Ras Shamra excavations of Claude F. A. Schaeffer, begun in 1929, unearthed many clay tablets written in an earlier Semitic alphabetic script of twenty-nine characters. Several hundred such tablets were found in the scribal school or library, as well as dictionaries and Sumerian, Babylonian, and Hurrian texts. These Semitic inscriptions, coming from the fifteenth century B.C., represent the earliest alphabetic system known, antedating the Phoenicians by several centuries. The language has been described as proto-Phoenician or Canaanite.

Ras Shamra was a very ancient community — then called Ugarit — in the northwestern corner of Syria, opposite the eastern end of Cyprus. The excavations have established a fairly good historical sequence from the Neolithic age to the twelfth century B.C., when Ras Shamra disappeared. References to it have been found in Egyptian and Hittite documents and in the Tell el-Amarna letters.

The Ugaritic texts, found near the ruins of the temple of Baal, deal with certain Canaanitish myths, beliefs, and religious practices that influenced the Hebrews after their occupation of Canaan. The chief deity of Canaan, as described in these tablets, was El, whose wife was Asheran, the goddess of fertility, and whose chief offspring was Baal, the god of vegetation. Many stories about these three deities appear in the Ras Shamra literature, for which the Old Testament offers interesting parallels. El (plural Elohim) is the name of the god in one of the strands making up the Pentateuch.

Reminiscent of the tradition of the Babylonian god Shamash and Hammurabi — and also that of Yahweh and Moses

— is a Ras Shamra stele showing the king of Ugarit standing before the god El, who sits majestically on a throne. The Old Testament contains a number of references to the worship of Asherah, the mother-goddess (I Kings 16:33; 18:19; II Kings 21:7). The god Baal-zebul (II Kings 1:2 ff.) is probably a reference to the Baal of the Ugaritic texts, in which he is called Zabul. El and Baal, the two chief nature gods, were often linked together in the Canaanite religion. Both names are used in the Old Testament for the god of Israel; Saul and David named their children after Baal.

The Ugaritic texts of Ras Shamra have added materially to the existing evidence of the syncretistic nature of the Hebrew religion in the pre-prophetic period. It was not until the Deuteronomic Reform following the preaching of the eighth-century prophets that the Canaanitish influences of polytheism, sex-worship, fertility rites, and Baal ritual were abolished.[11]

[11] For pictures of Ras Shamra reliefs, statuettes, and tablets see G. Ernest Wright, *Biblical Archaeology* (Philadelphia, 1957), pp. 104-10; and James B. Pritchard, *The Ancient Near East in Pictures* (Princeton, 1954), pp. 81, 161, 165, 168. For translation of Ugaritic texts see James B. Pritchard, *Ancient Near Eastern Texts* (2nd ed.; Princeton, 1955), pp. 129-55.

Part Two

The Making of the Old Testament

Chapter Four

The Nature of the Old Testament Literature

1. Hebrew Prophecy

The books of the Old Testament, as far as content is concerned, can be grouped into seven categories, the first of which is prophecy.[1] The prophetic movement of Israel represents the Hebrew religion at its best and was the determining factor in all Hebrew history. There has been no more profound impact on Western civilization coming from antiquity, except perhaps the golden age of Greece. It is no exaggeration to say that the moral reform of the Hebrew prophets, with its continuation in the career of Jesus, is the most influential movement in religious history.

As a movement, Hebrew prophecy had its primitive origin, its early stages of growth, its maturity of expression, and its decline. The origin of prophecy can be traced to an element common to all primitive religions — the belief in a supernatural being who reveals his will to certain favored men. In the earliest times the will of the gods was ascertained through divination, the casting of lots, and soothsaying. Later, oracles and wise men claimed an intermediary relationship between God and man.

The first Hebrew form of prophecy was that of the ec-

---

[1] Some books contain a mixture of material. For instance, the so-called books of the Law (Gen., Exod., Lev., Num., and Deut.) contain much historical narrative, and the so-called prophetic books of Samuel and Kings are chiefly history.

statics or dervishes, a type of religious-political leadership in the eleventh century B.C. These ecstatics roamed about in groups like troubadours and worked themselves into a frenzy by means of music.[2] They were parasitic and had no real moral or religious message. In fact, they were regarded by the great eighth-century reformers as " false prophets."

Samuel is usually regarded as the first of the pre-literary prophets (*ca.* 1030 B.C.). It was Samuel who saw the need of a united front to protect the Hebrews from the warring tribes to the east and south of Canaan; he is credited with the institution of a united monarchy under Saul. The most important pre-literary prophet was Elijah (*ca.* 850 B.C.), who established the supremacy of Yahweh over Baal and other Canaanite gods and who initiated the typical prophetic message of doom. He was followed by Elisha, whose contribution as a prophet is difficult to perceive: by forcibly establishing Yahwehism as a formalized state religion, he helped to create the precise condition that provoked the moral reform of the eighth-century prophets.

The first literary prophet was Amos (750 B.C.), the Prophet of Righteousness. (Chronologically, Amos was the first actual book of the Old Testament.) By the middle of the eighth century B.C., the Hebrew religion consisted only of ritual and sacrifice; the poor were oppressed by the idle rich; bribery, injustice, and vice were rampant. To Amos such a condition would only spell doom unless the people repented of their sins. Standing in the streets of Bethel, a sanctuary of the northern kingdom of Israel, he proclaimed Yahweh as a god of righteousness who demands righteousness on the part of his people. He condemned the sacrifices of the priests and called the people to an ethical religion.

[2] See I Sam. 10:5-13.

I hate, I despise your feasts,
    and I take no delight in your solemn assemblies.
Even though you offer me your burnt offerings and cereal offer-
    ings,
    I will not accept them,
and the peace offerings of your fatted beasts
    I will not look upon.
Take away from me the noise of your songs;
    to the melody of your harps I will not listen.
But let justice roll down like waters,
    and righteousness like an ever flowing stream.[3]

Amos' condemnation of ritual was continued by Hosea, the Prophet of Love. "For I desire steadfast love and not sacrifice, the knowledge of God, rather than burnt offer-ings." [4] Yet, whereas Amos was a stern realist, Hosea was more sympathetic and spoke of the comprehensive and insist-ent love of God.

How can I give you up, O Ephraim!
    How can I hand you over, O Israel!
How can I make you like Admah!
    How can I treat you like Zeboiim!
My heart recoils within me,
    my compassion grows warm and tender.[5]

The prophetic portrayal of God was still further en-hanced by Isaiah (740–700 B.C.), the Prophet of Faith. He pictured God as a holy, transcendent being: "Holy, holy, holy is the Lord of hosts." [6] He condemned extreme ritual-ism as his predecessors had.

---

[3] Amos 5:21–24.
[4] Hos. 6:6.
[5] Hos. 11:8.
[6] Isa. 6:3.

Hear the word of the Lord, you rulers of Sodom!
Give ear to the teaching of our God, you people of Gomor'rah!
What to me is the multitude of your sacrifices?
  says the Lord;
I have had enough of burnt offerings of rams
  and the fat of fed beasts;
I do not delight in the blood of bulls,
  or of lambs, or of he-goats.

When you come to appear before me,
  who requires of you
  this trampling of my courts?
Bring no more vain offerings;
  incense is an abomination to me.
New moon and sabbath and the calling of assemblies —
  I cannot endure iniquity and solemn assembly.
Your new moons and your appointed feasts
  my soul hates;
they have become a burden to me,
  I am wearying of bearing them.
When you spread forth your hands,
  I will hide my eyes from you;
even though you make many prayers,
  I will not listen;
  your hands are full of blood.
Wash yourselves; make yourselves clean;
  remove the evil of your doings
  from before my eyes;
cease to do evil,
  learn to do good;
seek justice,
  correct oppression;
  defend the fatherless,
  plead for the widow.[7]

The doctrine of Messianism began with Isaiah. This teaching arose from the expectation of a divine intervention. Yahweh

[7] Isa. 1:10–17.

would deliver Israel, and, as later taught, a new era would be ushered in by a Messiah or king.[8]

One of the distinctive contributions of Isaiah to Hebrew history was his insistence on the subordination of political Israel to religious Israel. He challenged the people to have faith in God rather than in military alliances. This is the key to the survival of the Jewish community in spite of its political downfall. The religious destiny of Israel was made and was kept independent of its political welfare.

The prophet Micah (700 B.C.) served as the epitome of eighth-century prophecy in his succinct summary: " He hath showed you, O man, what is good; and what does the Lord require of you but to do justice, and to love kindness, and to walk humbly with your God? " [9]

Jeremiah, the Prophet of Personal Religion (626–586 B.C.), by the narration of his own experiences, portrayed religion as an inner personal feeling. God, for him, was a being with whom one can commune. Religion was the personal relation of the individual to God. In his confessions he reveals his bitterness, introspection, and weaknesses.[10] He complains to God of his persecution and condemns his enemies, but in the end he arrives at a more mature view of God and man.

. . . But this is the covenant which I will make with the house of Israel after those days, says the LORD: I will put my law within them, and I will be their God, and they shall be my people. And no longer shall each man teach his neighbor and each his brother, saying, " Know the LORD," for they shall all know me, from the least of them to the greatest, says the LORD; for I will forgive their iniquity, and I will remember their sin no more.[11]

[8] Isa. 2:4; 9:1–7; 11:1–9.
[9] Mic. 6:8.
[10] See Jer. 17:9–18; 18:18–23; 20:7–18.
[11] Jer. 31:33, 34.

The New Covenant of the heart will replace the covenant on paper. External laws and legal ordinances are not enough; the seat of man's religion is the heart. It is the inner man that must be changed.

The theme of individual responsibility is continued in the writings of Ezekiel, the Prophet of Individualism (592–570 B.C.). Here we encounter a surprisingly modern empirical doctrine, one that assuredly ran counter to the bulk of Old Testament writings. According to Ezekiel, every man is his own priest and is individually responsible to God. Every man will be judged by his own life. There is no such thing as inherited guilt or merit. Every man controls his own destiny.

The soul that sins shall die. The son shall not suffer for the iniquity of the father, nor the father suffer for the iniquity of the son; the righteousness of the righteous shall be upon himself, and the wickedness of the wicked shall be upon himself.[12]

This teaching, it must be cautioned, is quite fragmentary and undeveloped, for Ezekiel was more priest than prophet and his importance lies not in his moral reform so much as in his formulation of the priestly ideal (chaps. 40–48). He was not opposed to ritualism as were his predecessors. In the Babylonian Exile he held his people together through weekly meetings for religious instruction. These meetings were really the beginning of the synagogue as an idea, if not as an actual institution. He did much to establish the Sabbath as a sacred institution. He prepared the way for the return to Jerusalem, the rebuilding of the temple, and the restoration of the Jewish religious community.

With Ezekiel the priestly conception of holiness takes permanent form. Sin is ritualistic defilement, and holiness is

12 Ezek. 18:20.

separation from all forms of contamination. We see in Ezekiel, therefore, a reaction to prophetism and a swing back to ritualism, supplementing the work of the Deuteronomists.

Before that shift was made complete, there appeared one more great prophet, Deutero-Isaiah, the Prophet of Universalism (*ca.* 538 B.C.). The prophecies of this anonymous author came to be attached somehow to the Book of Isaiah (chaps. 40–66, or at least 40–55). Deutero-Isaiah celebrates the end of the Exile and refers to Cyrus as the Great Deliverer (44:28; 45:1; 48:14). He sees Israel as the "Suffering Servant" and looks to the new age of salvation when the Messiah will establish the world in peace and security. His contribution to the prophetic movement is his conception of universalism. "Turn to me and be saved, all the ends of the earth! For I am God and there is no other." [13] Deutero-Isaiah is the climax of prophecy, a point reached again only in the later Book of Jonah, with its universalistic implications.

Haggai, Zechariah, and Malachi represent the decline and disappearance of the prophetic movement and lead the way to post-Exilic legalism and exclusiveness. In that emphasis they are to be seen as priestly, rather than prophetic, influences.

The impact of the Hebrew prophetic movement on the history of religion in the Western world is profound. With the exception of Ezekiel, the prophets insisted on the religious inadequacy of ritual per se and defined religion in terms of morality or goodness. By doing this they made religion a potential agent for social progress and established its essential rationality.

An ethical religion cannot die because it is not dependent upon the cult. The prophets, declaring the moral independ-

---

[13] II Isa. 45:22.

ence of the individual and striving to free religion from nationalistic and parochial elements, gave to religion its permanent quality.

2. Legal Literature

It is easy to contrast legalism with prophetism in the Hebrew religion as a conflict between the conservative, ritualistic emphasis and the liberal, ethical emphasis. To a great extent this is true, but such a presentation does not do full justice to the place of the Law in the Hebrew consciousness. Prophecy was the soul and the Law was the body; one was content, the other, method. The Law, in short, became the Jews' ethics.

This way of thinking, of course, has its dangers, as may be seen in the Deuteronomic Reform. The Book of Deuteronomy (621 B.C.) was an attempt to achieve the ideal pattern for society through a system of legal precedents. Its priestly authors, mindful of the moral reform of the prophets, tried to establish a compromise between theory and practice by setting up specific rules of behavior. This resulted in a concrete formula for living the good life but at the same time produced a tendency toward legalism.

The purpose of the legal literature in general was to maintain the Mosaic tradition and the unity of the Hebrew people. The legislation of the Priestly Code (fifth century B.C.) aimed at the preservation of the sanctity of the Sabbath, circumcision, the priesthood, and the temple. The Levitical laws in this code dealt mostly with the sacrificial system, the various offerings, and the Day of Atonement.[14]

[14] For the P Code see pp. 111-112.

Some of the civil legislation in the Pentateuch, especially Exodus, shows an obvious dependence upon earlier Babylonian law.[15] This influence came by way of the Canaanites and was a product of the Hebrew-Canaanite amalgamation. The Hebrews took over not only the cultus of the Canaanites but much of their legal system, which in turn was Babylonian in origin.

Interest has always centered in the authorship of the Ten Commandments. Hebrew tradition, taking its cue from references in the Pentateuch itself, has always assigned the Decalogue to Moses.[16] But there are good reasons for thinking that Moses cannot be considered the author of the Ten Commandments in their present form (Exod. 20; Deut. 5).[17] Laws grow gradually out of civil, religious, and social situations and are not revealed prior to the history of a people. As conditions change and new situations arise in society, the laws are modified. The Decalogue, for instance, implies, on the whole, an agricultural setting that could only refer to the Hebrew settlement in Canaan rather than to the Mosaic period in the desert.

Another anachronism in the Decalogue, if viewed as Mosaic, is the advanced ethical tone of the legislation. The Deuteronomic Reform was based on the ethical teaching of the eighth-century prophets, and the Decalogue (Deut. 5) seems to reflect that influence. This reform was the first attempt to prohibit image-worship, another reflection of eighth-century prophecy. Prohibition of image-worship, in fact, was not heard of until the eighth century B.C. If the Second Com-

[15] See pp. 32–35.
[16] Note the discrepancy between I Sam. 30:21–25, where David makes a new law regarding booty, and Num. 31:25 ff., where Moses is given credit for the same law.
[17] Exod. 23 and 34 are two other recensions of the Decalogue.

mandment, directed against image-worship, had existed from the time of Moses, it seems to have been totally disregarded for several centuries! Furthermore, it must be noted that the eighth-century prophets made no appeal to the Decalogue.

While it is impossible to assign the Decalogue, as it appears in Exodus 20 and Deuteronomy 5, to Moses, it is reasonable to concede that some original impetus was provided by him. We must attribute to him some primitive statement of the worship of Yahweh and the necessity of loyalty to him. Upon this basic principle the later legislation was formulated.

3. Historical Narrative

The historical writings of the Old Testament take many forms: early war songs and ballads, stories about the patriarchs, legends of the Canaanite conquest, histories of the kings, temple records, royal annals, and post-Exilic redactions. The earlier stories, especially those about the patriarchs, are not primarily history but have a didactic quality and, at times, a great literary excellence. The story of Joseph, for instance, exhibits masterful character portrayal as well as dramatic prose style (Gen. 37–50). This type of narrative reaches its best expression in the biographical history of the united monarchy, with Saul, David, and Solomon as the heroes (I and II Sam.; I Kings). For charm and realism, the analysis of Saul's character, the narrative of David's exploits, and the description of Solomon's reign are unsurpassed in biblical literature.

A more reliable and systematic type of historical writing, although less dramatic, is found in the royal annals as preserved in I Kings. These annals were a record of the various reigns in the united commonwealth and the divided kingdom. Likewise, the temple records, kept by the priests, provided detailed information for later writers. The author of I Kings was also indebted to an unknown writer for the Elijah stories, which describe the triumph of Yahweh over Baal in Israel and Elijah's rebuke of Ahab.

For our knowledge of Hebrew history immediately after the Exile, we are indebted to Nehemiah and Ezra. With his capture of Babylon (538 B.C.), Cyrus freed all conquered peoples, including the Jews. Apparently he encouraged the return of the Jews to Judah and the rebuilding of their temple (Ezra 1:1–4). Confirmation of the Ezra passage is found in the Cyrus Cylinder: ". . . the gods, who dwelt in them, I brought them back to their places, and caused them to dwell in a habitation for all time. All their inhabitants I collected and restored them to their dwelling places." [18] This edict did not result in the immediate return of all the Jews in captivity. Many had intermarried and were content to remain in the fertile land of Babylonia. Those who did return rebuilt the temple (516 B.C.) under the inspiration of Haggai and Zechariah.

The rebuilding of Jerusalem remained for Nehemiah, the cupbearer of the Persian king Artaxerxes. In his book. Nehemiah relates that he received the permission of Artaxerxes to go to Jerusalem. In spite of considerable opposition, he rebuilt the walls, which had lain in ruins. This was in 445 B.C. Twelve years later, as occupational governor of Jerusalem he effected a great social, civic, and religious reform, organized and fortified the city, and introduced many measures that fostered exclusiveness and ritualistic conformity. One of

[18] R. W. Rogers, *Cuneiform Parallels to the Old Testament* (2nd ed.; New York, 1926), p. 383. Cf. II Chron. 36:23.

these laws was the prohibition of intermarriage, which caused the Samaritan schism, a revolt of certain Jews who had married foreigners. These events are recorded in the autobiography of Nehemiah, a lucid, straightforward, and highly trustworthy account.

The physical foundation of Judaism constructed by Nehemiah was supplemented by a religious foundation in the proclamation of the Book of the Law by Ezra, who came to Jerusalem during the regime of Nehemiah. Ezra's work in promulgating the Torah has been assigned to 458, 444, 432, 428, and 380 B.C. The Elephantine Papyri indicate that the Law had been introduced in Jerusalem before 419 B.C.[19] Regardless of the exact date (certainly by 400 B.C.), Ezra read the Law to the people, who formally adopted it, and something akin to canonization took place. The Book of Ezra also describes the return of the Jews to Jerusalem and the building of the second temple.

Hebrew history was rewritten in the late post-Exilic period by a Chronicler who, by a redaction of previous annals, cast everything in the priestly mold. The two books of Chronicles were written about 300 B.C. The author took his material about David and Solomon from the books of Samuel and Kings, but, whereas the former histories were secular or political in their treatment, the Chronicler sees David as purely a religious hero and modifies all earlier history in line with the ecclesiastical point of view. This necessitated a great amount of " white-washing " in the case of David and Solomon, with the omission of all instances of defection or questionable conduct. His history is concerned only with

[19] See C. C. Torrey, *Ezra Studies* (Chicago, 1907), pp. 196 ff., 333–35; R. H. Pfeiffer, *Introduction to the Old Testament* (New York, 1941), pp. 56–58. Cf. Ezra 7:8, 14; Neh. 8–10.

Judah, which, in his mind, was the seat of the Yahweh religion.

The ulterior motive that guided the pen of the Chronicler resulted, on the whole, in an unreliable document.[20] He falsely assumes that the Priestly Code and the priesthood existed from the beginning of Hebrew history. We must regard the Chronicler not as a historian, but as a doctrinaire who manipulated history in the interests of his sacerdotal point of view.

4. Literature of Revolt

The exclusiveness of the Nehemiah regime called forth two protests. The first was the Book of Ruth (about 400 B.C.), a short story opposing the prohibition of intermarriage. As literature this book is a gem and holds a high place in any anthology of the short story. The setting is the time of the judges. Because of a famine in Judah, Elimelech takes his wife Naomi and his two sons to Moab. Here the father dies and the two sons marry Moabite women, Orpah and Ruth. Later the two sons die. With improved conditions in Judah, Naomi decides to return, leaving the two daughters-in-law in Moab. Ruth insists on going back with Naomi. Arriving in Bethlehem, Ruth finds work in the barley fields of a Jew named Boaz. They are married and have a son, who is to become the grandfather of David.

The author is content to tell his story and draws no moral from it. Nevertheless, the feeling persists that his purpose was not merely to tell a story. The implication is that if the

[20] For contradictions and unhistorical statements of the Chronicler see J. A. Bewer, *The Literature of the Old Testament* (2nd ed.; New York, 1933), p. 286 ff.

great king David came from a mixed marriage there can be nothing wrong with foreign marriages. The Moabites particularly were discriminated against by the Jews of the post-Exilic community. Ruth is pictured as a modest person, loyal to the best Hebrew traditions.[21]

The universalism of Deutero-Isaiah was forgotten in the isolationist regime of Nehemiah, but its echo was heard in the brilliant satire of Jonah (400–300 B.C.). The Book of Jonah is parable at its best.[22] It is listed in the canon among the prophets. Chronologically it does not belong to the prophetic period, but from a didactic or moral standpoint this book is most prophetic. No more telling blow to religious exclusiveness and sectarianism was ever dealt. God's love, according to the author, does not stop with the Jews; even the Ninevites are God's children. In the light of the rabid desire of the Jews of that period to see Yahweh's extermination of surrounding nations (as proclaimed in Obadiah, Ezekiel, and Joel), this brilliant allegory stands as a voice in the wilderness proclaiming God's concern for all people.

5. The Wisdom Literature

As a result of the Dispersion, in which the Jews came into intimate contact with the Greeks, a new type of literature appeared in the books of Job, Proverbs, Ecclesiastes, Ecclesiasticus or the Wisdom of Jesus, son of Sirach, and the Wisdom of Solomon, the last two being in the Apocryphal list. These books date from 300 to 200 B.C. The authors of

---

[21] Some critics do not feel that this is a protest against Nehemiah's edict. Cf. R. H. Pfeiffer, *Introduction to the Old Testament* (New York, 1941), p. 719.
[22] See the Introduction, pp. 13–14.

the Wisdom books were true individualists and were concerned with human values and the philosophy of life. Wisdom in Hebrew usage had to do with common sense, prudence, morality, and the source of happiness.

The Book of Job might well be classified as literature of revolt in that it stands opposed to the prevailing theology of practically all of the rest of the Old Testament. The doctrine of retributive justice, as seen in the Psalms, Deuteronomy, Proverbs, and many other books of the Old Testament, says that if a man is pious he will be rewarded with filled barns and a long life; conversely, if he sins he will suffer both economic and physical adversity. Orthodoxy claimed that the righteous were favored by God with material rewards and sinners were punished with calamity. The Book of Job was written as a criticism of this theology, a protest that is unique in the Old Testament. While there is no systematic conclusion to the book, by implication it declares that there is no necessary connection between suffering and sin, that because a man is afflicted it does not follow that he has sinned. By the same token, it is not to be thought that goodness is requited in a material sense. God does not reward goodness with prosperity.

Job, a righteous man, is puzzled by his suffering and is told by his friends that he is receiving his just desert. This answer does not satisfy him, and he continues to question God about the suffering of the righteous while wicked people prosper and are happy. Job's solution comes not in an answer to the riddle of suffering but in a larger view of God, man, and the universe. The world is a complex process; God works in a mysterious way, but man can find internal peace in the faith that God is with him. The inner satisfaction of one's conscience and of God's approval is the reward for righteousness, rather than outward prosperity, health, or the approval of friends.

The Book of Proverbs is a collection of wise sayings from different periods brought together by an editor about 300 B.C. The theology of the sages who wrote these proverbial sayings is utilitarian and, for the most part, self-centered. It never reaches the profundity of Job or the selflessness of Jesus' teachings. It emphasizes shrewdness, personal happiness, goodness for the sake of gain, and the desirability of wisdom. Most of the proverbs take the form of a couplet in which the second line reinforces the first either by repetition or by contrast. Their main theme is the high worth of wisdom: " Wisdom is the principal thing; therefore get wisdom; and with all thy getting, get understanding " (4:7); " Keep thy heart with all diligence; for out of it are the issues of life " (4:23); " For wisdom is better than rubies; and all the things that may be desired are not to be compared with it " (8:11); " The fear of the Lord is the beginning of wisdom " (9:10a); " A soft answer turneth away wrath " (15:1a); " A good name is rather to be chosen than great riches " (22:1a); " As he thinketh in his heart, so is he " (23:7a); " Where there is no vision, the people perish " (19:18a).

Epicurean and Stoic influences are mixed in Ecclesiastes (ca. 200 B.C.), which inquires into the meaning of life and comes up with a pretty pessimistic answer. In fact, after pondering the matter for some time, the author concludes that life is a senseless rat race: " Vanity of vanity, all is vanity." There is nothing new under the sun. Life has no purpose, no meaning. Increased knowledge only means increased unhappiness. In the end there is death. Man and the beast go to the same place. There is no future life. There is a God but his ways are past finding out. Everything in the universe is predetermined and fixed, and there is nothing man can do about it. The author's advice is to accept life as it is, be temperate in all things, and be resigned to fate.[23]

6. Devotional Literature

The Psalms are the heart and soul of the Jewish people. They express the feelings of the ancient Jews at their highest point of spiritual aspiration and also at their lowest ebb of hatred and vengeance. As a revelation of man's innermost yearnings, fears, hopes, gratitude, love, hate, and longing for forgiveness, the Psalter is both timeless and universal in its appeal.

These prayers and praises of Israel became the chief source of all Christian hymnology. They express the universal moods of ecstatic joy and bitter sorrow, trust and despair, rejoicing and suffering. With such catholicity of sentiment, running the gamut of the religious life, the Psalms constitute the great common denominator for all Christian faiths today. The world's devotional literature contains no greater treasures than Psalms 1, 8, 19, 23, 34, 43, 84, 90, 91, 103, and 139.

7. Apocalypticism

The conquest of Judah by Antiochus Epiphanes reached its peak of violence in 168 B.C. The temple was plundered, the city walls were destroyed, Jewish rites were prohibited, and many Jews were killed. The climax of this outrage was

---

[23] For a discussion of Sirach and the Wisdom of Solomon, see chapter 6.

the sacrifice of swine on an altar to Zeus that had been erected in the temple. A revolt was led by Judas Maccabeus, and in 165 Jerusalem was once again in the hands of the Jews.

The Book of Daniel (168 B.C.) was written to encourage the Jews in their resistance to the Greeks and to assure the people of final victory. The author promised a kingdom ruled over by " the Son of Man," " an everlasting kingdom which shall not pass away " (7:13, 14). The book consists of a series of visions of things to come, including the defeat of the enemy, and the reward of the righteous in the hereafter. Daniel is the most pronounced expression of apocalyptic [24] in the Old Testament and is about the only canonical book that can be construed as referring to the future life. Joel (fourth century B.C.) is the only other eschatological book in the Old Testament.

[24] *Apocalyptic* — a type of literature devoted to revelations and visions; *Eschatology* — apocalyptic thought dealing with the end of the world or the last things.

Chapter Five

Canonization of the Old Testament

1. The Lost Library

In the light of the archaeological backgrounds (Part I) that reveal considerable source material for the Hebrew Bible, we are now prepared to proceed with the study of the formation of the Old Testament itself as a definite body of Scripture. As we do so, we must hold two distinct processes in mind: (1) the normal growth of a religious literature from oral tradition to written forms; (2) the selection and recognition of certain parts of that literature as sacred and authoritative canon.

The difference between these two stages hinges on the word " canon." The word originally meant a rod or ruler (cane). As an instrument of measurement, it then came to refer to the criteria by which something qualifies or measures up to the standard. The biblical canon can be defined as the authoritative or orthodox list of books that measured up to standard as sacred Scripture. Our purpose now is to trace the process by which certain books eventually won their way to this position of canonicity.

But before doing that, we must return to the subject of sources and compilation. In addition to the early non-Hebraic traditions that were drawn upon by Old Testament writers, there is evidence also of a lost library of early Hebrew folklore. The authors of the Old Testament seem to have been familiar with this literature and quote from it freely. In Numbers 21:14, for instance, reference is made to a book called "The Wars of Jehovah" as the source of the poem used by the author. "The Song of the Well," an early popular poem, is quoted in Numbers 21:17, 18; "The Song of Deborah" is quoted in Judges 5:1 ff.; and "The Fable of Jotham" is related in Judges 9:7 ff. Other fragments quoted are: "The Book of Jashar" (Josh. 10:13); "The Book of Nathan" (I Chron. 29:29); "The Book of Gad" (I Chron. 29:29); "The Book of Iddo" (II Chron. 9:29); "The Book of Shemaiah" (II Chron. 12:15); and "The Book of Jehu" (II Chron. 20:34).

These are some of the rivulets or small tributaries that found their way into the main stream of historical writing among the Hebrews. Except for these fragmentary quotations, this literature is completely lost. They were a part of the accumulation of ancient folklore — ballads, histories, legends, and songs about the early patriarchs and kings. Much of this tradition was orally transmitted from generation to generation, a fact that explains such confused and garbled accounts as, for example, Genesis 12 and 26, where the same story is told of Abraham and Isaac. Gradually these ballads and historical notes were gathered into written collections that became a part of the canonical books.

2. The Compilation of the Pentateuch

The first five books of the Old Testament are called the Pentateuch (from the Greek word "pentateuchos" meaning "the fivefold book"). The later books of the Old Testament, Jewish tradition in general, early Christian teaching, and the traditional or orthodox view of the present day all hold that Moses wrote these five books.

A careful reading, however, will reveal many post-Mosaic elements in the Pentateuch. For example:

So Moses, the servant of the Lord, died there in the land of Moab according to the word of the Lord, and he buried him in the valley in the land of Moab opposite Bethpeor; but no man knows the place of his burial to this day (Deut. 34:5, 6).

This statement was obviously written long after Moses' death.

Now the man Moses was very meek, more than all men that were upon the face of the earth (Num. 12:3).

It is hardly likely that Moses could have written that!

These are the kings who reigned in the land of Edom, before any king reigned over the Israelites (Gen. 36:31).

Whoever wrote this passage must have lived *after* the institution of the monarchy, which was some two centuries after the time of Moses.

And there has not arisen a prophet since in Israel like Moses, whom the Lord knew face to face (Deut. 34:10).

This likewise rules out Mosaic authorship.

Moses is referred to in the third person in Exodus 6:26, 27 and in Numbers 33:2. Many geographical terms used in the Pentateuch imply that the author in each case lived in Palestine and after the time of Moses (Num. 32; Deut. 1:5, 4:41, 34:1; Gen. 13:18, 14:14; Josh. 14:15). The father-in-law of Moses bears two different names (Exod. 2:18, 3:1). The statement that " the Canaanite was then in the land " (Gen. 12:6, 13:7) is unintelligible unless written after the conquest of Canaan by the Hebrews. Deuteronomy 2:12 also speaks in retrospect of the Canaanite period. The centralization of worship at Jerusalem is assumed in Exodus 15:13, 17. The agricultural setting of the Decalogue in Exodus 23 and 34 rules out the desert background of Moses.

Discrepancies are also evident in the legal portions of the Pentateuch. According to the Book of the Covenant, Yahweh may be worshiped in different places (Ex. 20:24, 25) but the Deuteronomic Code definitely prohibits the worship of Yahweh at local sanctuaries and restricts all worship to the temple at Jerusalem (Deut. 12:2–7).

These and many other passages preclude the possibility of Mosaic authorship of the Pentateuch. Those who defend Mosaic authorship do so in the face of obvious facts. Furthermore, modern scholarship questions the very existence in the nomadic period of some of the Hebrew words, as well as some of the advanced moral ideas, found in Deuteronomy.

The non-Mosaic authorship of the Pentateuch was hinted at in a fragmentary way by Rabbi ben Ezra (1092–1167), but it was not until after the Renaissance and the Reformation that individual critics began to direct their attention to the problem. Spinoza, in the seventeenth century, called attention to the internal evidence that automatically precluded the Mosaic authorship of the Pentateuch.

Simon, in his *Critical History of the Old Testament* (1678), detected different styles of writing in Genesis and recognized two independent and varying accounts of the Creation lying side by side, each of which had its own peculiar style and was complete in itself. In one story the making of man is the climax of God's creation, whereas in the second account the creation of man comes first. The first account has man and woman created at the same time, while the second has woman created from man's rib. The style of the first record is entirely different from that of the second (compare Gen. 1:1–2:4*a* with Gen. 2:4*b*–23). Simon also recognized two contradictory flood stories in Genesis 6–9. These two strands can be taken out and reconstructed separately. One gives the duration of the flood as 40 days, whereas the other speaks of 150 days. In one Noah took into the ark two of each kind of animal, but in the other account Noah took seven of each. These observations led Simon to assign the contradictory accounts to two different authors.

Jean Astruc, physician to Louis XV, was the first to note that in some sections of the Pentateuch the name employed for God is Yahweh and in other sections it is Elohim. For instance, the first account of the Creation uses the name Elohim exclusively, while the second account never mentions Elohim but uses only Yahweh. The same holds true throughout Genesis and other books of the Pentateuch. This led Astruc to conclude that "the memoir where God is called Elohim came from one hand, and the other, where God is called Yahweh, came from another."

Eichorn, in his *Introduction to the Old Testament* (1779), carried the point still further by listing words peculiar to the Elohim and Yahweh sections and also by describing the differences in style and atmosphere between the two records. At the beginning of the nineteenth century De Wette published his conclusion that the Book of Deuteronomy is a product of the seventh century B.C. and could not possibly be Mosaic. It is, he maintained, a reflection of the eighth-century prophetic reform, a "second law."

The investigations begun by these scholars were continued through the nineteenth century. Various theories were proposed to account for the facts observed: the Fragment theory, the Supplement theory, and the Documentary theory.[1] The last-named hypothesis underwent some modification and later appeared as the Graf-Wellhausen theory, which still is the most acceptable solution.

Graf and Wellhausen, two of the ablest scholars of the nineteenth century, formulated a developmental pattern to account for all the material. According to their hypothesis, sometimes called the Development or Documentary theory, the Pentateuch is a compilation of materials from different ages and from different authors and is made up of four distinct strata or strands indicated by the symbols J, E, D, and P.

Characteristics of the Four Documents

The oldest document, called J, was written about 850 B.C. Scholars called it J because it uses for God the name Jahweh (pronounced — and now commonly spelled — Yahweh). It is called the Bible of Judah, the Southern Kingdom. The author has naïve, primitive ideas and an anthropomorphic conception of God. Yahweh " walks in the garden in the cool of the day." He puts Adam in a garden where a serpent speaks. He calls to Adam and Eve. After they have sinned, he drives them out of the garden. He closes the door of Noah's ark. He leaves heaven and goes to earth to confuse men. He eats with Abraham, wrestles with Jacob, and almost kills Moses.

Whereas later writers resort to the supernatural to explain the action of deity, the Yahwistic writer sees God doing everything in a perfectly natural way. An east wind brought the locusts into Egypt, and a west wind drove them into the Red Sea. In the Garden of Eden story the author tries to account for the origin of sin in the world. The Tower of

[1] See *Abingdon Bible Commentary* (New York, 1929), p. 136.

Babel story tells how the different languages originated. He paints a graphic picture of Abraham about to offer Isaac as a sacrifice. He writes with dramatic emotional fervor, and his vocabulary throughout is picturesque.

The E document, from 750 B.C., is the Bible of Israel, the Northern Kingdom. The author uses only the name Elohim for the Divine Being, and speaks of God in a more refined and spiritualized manner. God is farther removed from man and reveals himself to man in dreams and visions or through the ministration of angels. Since God lives in heaven, he needs a medium through whom he can speak to man. The prophets spoke for God and were interpreters of God's will. Abraham and Moses were the mouthpieces of God. This spiritualized conception of God brought with it the supernatural element, so the Elohistic document speaks of miracles and signs and mighty works. Moses becomes a magician with a magic wand. The Elohistic writer also shows a greater moral sensitivity than was found in J, and many of the older traditions are corrected and refined.

The J and E documents differ in vocabulary and style. In the Bible of the North, "Sinai" becomes "Horeb," the "Canaanites" are called "Amorites," and "Israel" is referred to as "Jacob." [2]

J and E are found scattered throughout the Pentateuch, but our third document, known as D, is a separate book, complete in itself. The eighteenth year of King Josiah (621 B.C.) was a memorable one in the history of the Hebrew religion. In that year there was found a book that became the nucleus of the Old Testament canon and changed the course of Hebrew history. This was "The Book of the Law," which was

[2] Scholars agree that about 650 B.C. J and E were combined to form one complete book, which is designated JE.

discovered during the repairs of the temple. The scroll was taken to the king, who summoned the elders to Jerusalem and proclaimed it to be the divine book (II Kings 22). King and people pledged themselves to follow this new code as the law of the land.

This was the book of Deuteronomy, a new edition of Hebrew law. As the Law of the Lord and a divinely inspired book, Deuteronomy became the first hint of sacred Scripture. It virtually became the first official Bible of the Jews. The priestly authors of this book tried to effect a compromise between the older priestly religion and the later prophetic reform. Their aim was to embody in this document the ethical ideals of the eighth-century reformers. The logical way to do this, they felt, was to popularize the prophetic morality in the form of laws. The authors reasoned that the people needed specific regulations defining the good life. But, to a certain extent, it was a case of method killing spirit. They were sincere in their purpose to enforce a moral reform, but morals cannot be legislated. What went into the Book of Deuteronomy as prophetism came out as legalism, and, from 621 B.C. on, the Hebrew religion came to be more and more a religion of the book, a religion of laws in which the scribe took the place of the prophet. The sacrificial system henceforth prevailed. The Hebrew religion was recast in the mold of " commandments, statutes, and judgments."

But that is only one side of the picture. The second thing to note about this document is that it is the first clear expression of monotheism. The Shema (Deut. 6:4 ff.) becomes the focal point of all later Jewish worship:

Hear, O Israel, The Lord our God is one Lord; and you shall love the Lord your God with all your heart and with all your soul and with all your might. And these words which I command you this day shall be upon your heart, and you shall teach them diligently to your children, and shall talk of them when you sit in your house, and when you walk by the way, and when you lie down, and when you rise. And you shall bind them as a sign upon your hand, and they shall be as frontlets between your eyes. And you shall write them upon the doorposts of your house and on your gates.

The only valid place to worship God now is in the temple in Jerusalem. Deuteronomy effected a puritanical reform by abolishing the local sanctuaries and high places and by prohibiting sex-worship, image-worship, and all Canaanite practices. All representations of other gods were destroyed throughout the land.

In order to make this reform more binding, the promulgators of Deuteronomy created the impression that this law was from Moses, for only by ascribing their work to ancient authority could they hope to give it proper sanction. Now the Hebrews had a divinely inspired and authoritative book.

The fourth document of the Pentateuch is called P and is dated at approximately 500 B.C. It is the "Book of the Priests" and contains such narrative elements as the story of the Creation and the Deluge, stories about the patriarchs, the Exodus from Egypt, and the conquest of Canaan under Joshua. But its dominant theme is the rule of God and the laws of holiness. It embodies the priestly legislation formulated by Ezekiel in the Babylonian Exile and the Holiness Code (Lev. 17–26).

The Priestly Code completed the ritualistic transformation of religion begun by Deuteronomy. Now religion becomes identified with ceremonial purity. Sin is a matter of defilement. Here is the systematizing of all the laws concerning sacrifice, atonement, the annual festivals, the Sabbath, circumcision, the office of the priest, and the sanctity of the temple. Moreover, the author of P is exceedingly exclusive. His nationalistic ideal is a Hebrew theocracy, and his concept of religion is purely formal.

The Priestly Code thus formalized the Jewish religion and gave it a reactionary character. Professor Robert Pfeiffer calls it " the charter of the new Jewish church," a transformation in which " regulation took the place of spontaneity, discipline stifled freedom, solemnity displaced joyousness in the festivals, and holy sacraments were substituted for the religious exercises of the laity." [3]

3. The Canonization of the Torah

Thus far we have been concerned with the first of two processes: the growth of a body of religious literature. We are now ready to observe the second process: the recognition of this literature *as sacred and authoritative scripture*.

From the day of its promulgation in 621 B.C., the Book of Deuteronomy was invested with a certain sanctity and authority as " The Book of the Law." Sections of J, E, and P were also regarded as having semicanonical authority. J and E were brought together in the seventh century. Soon afterward Deuteronomy was added to JE, and finally P was interwoven with JE by a group of redactors.

It is this combined and redacted material which becomes by the end of the fifth century B.C. the first canon of the Jews. While the canonization of the Law is somewhat clouded in obscurity, it is generally agreed that the Torah,

[3] *Introduction to the Old Testament* (New York, 1941), pp. 256, 260.

consisting of J, E, D, and P, was formally proclaimed canon between 450 and 400 B.C. and that all references connect this proclamation with the name of Ezra the scribe. This promulgation of the Pentateuch as Scripture was coincidental with the reforms of Nehemiah, the governor of Jerusalem. According to Ezra 7:1–14, Ezra the scribe came from Babylonia to Jerusalem in the seventh year of Artaxerxes (458 B.C.), and in Nehemiah 8–10 we read that fourteen years later he read the law to the congregation in Jerusalem. Presumably this was about 444 B.C., but present-day authorities are inclined to doubt the trustworthiness of the chronicler at this point.

The best that can be done is to settle upon the latest possible date, which would be 400 B.C. It is fairly well established, however, that the Samaritans seceded from Judah in 432 B.C. and took with them the Pentateuch, which was considered by them and the Jews as the authoritative Bible. The Samaritans thereafter never added anything to the Torah. This, therefore, would place the first canon before 432 B.C.

The primacy and uniqueness of the Torah are attested in all post-Exilic writings of the Old Testament. The books of Chronicles, Ezra, and Nehemiah assume the canonicity of the Law and look upon it with great reverence. The prophet Malachi (4:4) appeals to the Law as final authority, as do Ecclesiasticus (22:23) and I Maccabees (1:57). The later Psalms define the religious life as obedience to the Law.

The editors of the Septuagint (the Greek Old Testament, 250–150 B.C.) exercised much greater care in their translation of the Pentateuch than in the rest of the Old Testament. The defective and often careless translation of the Prophets and the Writings shows that in their minds the Torah was the only authoritative Scripture.

The canonical status of the Torah is clearly implied in the Prologue of Ecclesiasticus (180 B.C.):

Since many great things have been communicated to us through the Law and the Prophets, and the others who followed after them, for which we must give Israel the praise due to instruction and wisdom; and since not only must those who read become expert themselves but those who love learning must also be able to be useful to the uninitiated, both in speaking and in writing, my grandfather, Jeshua, after devoting himself for a long time to the reading of the Law and the Prophets and the other books of our forefathers, and after attaining considerable proficiency in them, was led to write on his own account something in the line of instruction and wisdom, so that lovers of learning and persons who become interested in those things might make still greater progress in living accordance with the Law.

It is clear from this quotation that by this time (132 B.C.) the Prophets are also canonical.

Philo (an older contemporary of Jesus) regards the Law with extreme reverence as the divinely inspired book. The Torah was for a long time the only section of the Old Testament to be read in the services of the synagogue, while the Prophets and the Writings were never given much prominence. In fact, the word Torah seems to refer to the whole canon in some New Testament references (John 10:34; 12:34; 15:25; I Cor. 14:21).

By 400 B.C. the Torah was not only a distinct canon, but the interwoven documents had been rearranged and edited in the form of the present five books of the Pentateuch: Genesis, Exodus, Leviticus, Numbers, and Deuteronomy.

4. *The Canonization of the Prophets*

The date of the canonization of the Nebiim [4] is even less certain than that of the Torah. We can be certain, however, that by 200 B.C. the prophetic canon was a fact.

It was inevitable that the Law should be supplemented by the Prophets in the Jewish canon. While the Law never relinquished its primacy as the foundation of Israel's institutions, it was the moral and social teaching of the prophetic party that was to define Israel's greatest contribution to the world. Distrust of contemporary prophets and a growing veneration of the ancient spokesmen for God must have led to the popular desire to preserve the prophetic books in a formal way. Also, the possible reaction to extreme legalism under the influence of the Hellenistic culture (*ca.* 300 B.C.) hastened the recognition of the worth of the prophetic books. [5]

The leading reformers of the religion of Israel gave to the Western world its two important legacies: monotheism and morality. Samuel had been responsible for the institution of the monarchy. Elijah had established the supremacy of Yahweh over other gods. Amos had insisted on the religious inadequacy of ceremony in and of itself, declaring that " right " was more important than " rite." Hosea had said that mercy was more important than sacrifice and the knowledge of God than burnt offering. Isaiah had envisaged a day of universal peace when men would " beat their swords into plowshares and their spears into pruning hooks " and learn war no more. Micah had defined religion as doing justice,

---

[4] The Hebrew word "nabi" means "prophet"; plural, "nebiim."

[5] See H. E. Ryle, *The Canon of the Old Testament* (London, 1925), p. 118.

loving mercy, and walking humbly with God. Jeremiah had personalized religion, emphasizing the covenant of the heart. Ezekiel had individualized religion, placing freedom and responsibility in the person. Deutero-Isaiah (the Second Isaiah) had universalized religion, teaching that salvation was for all people.

The prophetic redefining of religion as ethical rather than ritualistic, as a social force rather than an ecclesiastical form, gave a rational, pragmatic, and permanent validity to prophetism as a historic movement. Like all radical reformers, these prophets were, for the most part, rejected by their contemporaries, but in time they loomed large in the minds of the people and took on a classic status. The recognition of the prophets as having scriptural authority could hardly have taken place in the period of the canonization of the Law, since that overshadowed everything else in Judaism. It is thought, therefore, that the period in which the prophets were canonized would have to be after 300 B.C. It is clear from literary evidence *after* 200 B.C. that prophetic canonicity had been established by that date.

Ecclesiasticus (the Wisdom of Jesus, Son of Sirach), composed in Hebrew about 180 B.C. and translated into Greek in 132 B.C., gives the Prophets equal standing with the Law as canon. The Prologue refers three times to the Prophets as a second authoritative group.[6] The Bible with Sirach consisted of the Law and the Prophets, as was also the case with New Testament writers. The original Ecclesiasticus reviews the Pentateuch and the work of all the Prophets except Daniel, which was not written until 168 B.C. The former Prophets are called " the famous men," and the minor Prophets are des-

---

[6] See p. 114. Notice the passing reference in Sirach to "the other books," which at that time were not accepted as canon.

ignated " the twelve." This shows that Sirach was in possession of the twofold Bible, confirms the fixation of the second canon at approximately 200 B.C., and establishes the fact that the canonicity of the Prophets was recognized *in toto* before any of the Kethubim (Writings).

Likewise, the Bible for New Testament writers uniformly consisted of the Law and the Prophets. Jesus uses that term as synonymous with the Scripture (Matt. 5:17; 7:12; 22:40; Luke 16:16, 29, 31; see also Acts 13:15; 28:33). Luke 24:44 is an interesting sidelight on the Psalms as the nucleus of the as-yet-uncanonized Kethubim.

The canonical order [7] of the Prophets is as follows:

Former Prophets: Joshua, Judges, I and II Samuel, I and II Kings.
Latter Prophets:
   Major: Isaiah, Jeremiah, Ezekiel.
   Minor: The Book of the Twelve — Hosea, Joel, Amos, Obadiah, Jonah, Micah, Nahum, Habakkuk, Zephaniah, Haggai, Zechariah, Malachi.

The reader may well inquire why Joshua, Judges, Samuel, and Kings are listed as Prophets, since they are mainly historical in character. One reason for their inclusion was the fact that they contained stories about the early prophets (or men who were supposed to be prophets) such as Samuel and Elijah. Also, in the later tradition these books were presumed to have been written by writers of the prophetic school.

---

[7] Bear in mind the difference between canonical and chronological order in the books of the Old Testament. The English Bible follows a topical order that is neither chronological nor canonical. It is to be observed also that the words " major " and " minor " in connection with the Prophets refer not to greater or lesser importance but to size. The books of the minor Prophets were so short that all twelve were included in one roll.

While on the whole their content is historical, there is a certain amount of didactic material, and that would stamp them as prophetic. The Book of Joshua was probably compiled during the Exile (586–538 B.C.) and originally was joined to the Pentateuch but was later separated. Judges and the books of Samuel, compiled from earlier sources, date from the same period. The Book of Kings shows definite Deuteronomic influence and was compiled at the close of the sixth century.

Interest in the prophetic books was not stimulated until after the Restoration chiefly because they prefigured a new order, a utopia, a Messianic era of peace. This prediction coincided with the nationalistic aspirations of the post-Exilic Jewish community, and the prophets were therefore given a more reverent and enthusiastic study. In fact, the later redactions of the prophetic books show interpolations emphasizing the overthrow of other nations and the ascendancy of the Jews, clear reflections of the post-Exilic feeling.

By 300 B.C. the Prophets were no more, and collections of the books were made preparatory to their canonization.

5. The Canonization of the Writings

The third canon was called "the Writings" (Hebrew: *Kethubim*) because it was made up of a number of unrelated books of diverse character. These books have little or nothing in common, and their ultimate canonization may be considered an appendix to the Law and the Prophets or an arbitrary grouping of miscellaneous but well-known writings left over after the first two canons were recognized. The Writings as finally canonized consisted of three groups:

The Poetical Books: Psalms, Proverbs, Job.

The Five Rolls: Canticles (Song of Solomon), Ruth, Lamentations, Ecclesiastes, Esther.

The Remainder: Daniel, Ezra, Nehemiah, I and II Chronicles.

Most of these books date from the fourth and third centuries B.C. and were in circulation at the time of the second canonization. The nucleus of the third canon was the Psalms. Undoubtedly the Psalter was the first book of the Kethubim to attain canonicity. As the hymnbook of the Hebrew people, it represents an accumulation of songs extending over a long period (750–150 B.C.).[8] Some of the Psalms were composed especially for the dedication of the second temple (*ca.* 520 B.C.). Originally in five books, the Psalms were brought together, edited, and arranged in their present form about 150 B.C.

The miscellaneous character of " The Writings " suggests a variety of reasons for their canonization. Although these reasons do not necessarily coincide with the modern criteria for evaluating their worth, it is appropriate at this point to indicate briefly the nature of some of the books.

The Psalms were automatically accepted by reason of their devotional and liturgical value. Proverbs gained recognition as a collection of wise sayings of an ethical type. These gems of wisdom were gathered from different sources and were finally edited in one volume. Like the Psalms, they came from different centuries, and, like the Psalms, they were attributed to one of the heroes of ancient Israel — in this case, Solomon.

[8] Authorities are divided on the question of Davidic authorship of the Psalms. According to some scholars, he may have written some of the Psalms but probably not more than a dozen.

Job was popular as a philosophical tract or perhaps as a mere narrative. As the latter, it has a certain literary value, to be sure, but, as the former, it is one of the most profound documents in all religious literature. Its theme is the oldest and most penetrating among all the questions of mankind: the problem of evil. Why do the righteous suffer? If God is good, why does adversity exist? The answer to that question is implicit rather than direct: more important than the reason for suffering is the attitude of the individual toward suffering when it comes. There is no necessary connection between suffering and sin; the rain falls on the just and the unjust, and nature is no respecter of persons. Adversity can be used to produce a greater strength of character and a supreme trust in the ultimate dependability of God. The Book of Job is a book of optimism and comes close to defining true religion as trust in the essential goodness of the universe.

The Book of Ruth (*ca.* 400 B.C.) is to be read against the backdrop of Nehemiah's prohibition of intermarriage. Here again is an outstanding piece of literature, but its value does not lie in its literary form, charming as that is. Back of the story is the aim of the author to oppose the edict of Nehemiah forbidding marriage with foreigners.

Canticles was the most questionable inclusion in the canon and precipitated no end of debate. Obviously this book is nothing more than a collection of oriental love poems, but it enjoyed a certain prestige as coming from Solomon. The embarrassment of admitting a book with such a secular theme was overcome by parabolic interpretation or allegorization. The writer's love for his spouse was interpreted to stand for Yahweh's love for Israel, and this symbolic interpretation helped to enhance the prestige of the book.

Popularity, of course, constituted a basic criterion for such books as Daniel, Esther, Ecclesiastes, Ruth, and Lamentations. Ecclesiastes obviously cannot compare with Ecclesiasticus (an extracanonical book) in ethical content, but it survived as a best seller, influenced, perhaps, by the current Hellenistic philosophy. Ezra, Nehemiah, and Chronicles, containing data of national importance, had an intrinsic historical value.

A final reason for admittance into the canon was anonymous authorship, which indicated antiquity, and that was paramount. As Pfeiffer points out, "Prophetic inspiration was thought to have come to an end immediately after the time of Ezra, and therefore no book later than Ezra could be regarded as inspired. No book could become canonical if positively *known* to have been written after Ezra." [9] The author of Ecclesiasticus (180 B.C.) was known to be Sirach, and the book was rejected; whereas Ecclesiastes was anonymous and therefore could be given proper prestige by assigning it to Solomon. The same procedure obtained in the case of Canticles and Proverbs, which would have been rejected if they had not been attributed to Solomon. Far from our modern preference for the new, the Hebrew mind regarded recent or contemporary known authorship as unfavorable. Attributing a contemporary or recently composed book to an ancient prophet or wise man (i.e., Moses, Solomon, Ezra) was common practice.

In the case of the Kethubim the process of canonization was gradual. The earliest information on this process is the Prologue to Ecclesiasticus (132 B.C.) already quoted. Three times in this one paragraph the author refers to "the Law, the Prophets, and the rest of the books." The last phrase indicates that he knew of a tripartite division of the Hebrew Scripture but does not give the third group canonical standing.

The process of canonization may have received its initial

[9] *Op. cit.*, p. 62.

impetus from the Maccabean period (from 168 B.C. to the end of the century). Without doubt the religious revival of that period and the new nationalistic feeling prompted the desire to expand the scope of sacred literature.

The Septuagint has little value as evidence for the third canon, for its chief interest is the Torah. The same holds true with Philo in the first part of the first century A.D. Coming to the New Testament, we find a number of allusions to "the Law and the Prophets" as constituting the complete canon but no real evidence for the third canon. The only valuable reference is Luke 24:44, where the canonicity of the Psalms is clearly recognized:

Then he said to them, "These are my words which I spoke to you, while I was still with you, that everything written about me in the Law of Moses and the Prophets and the Psalms must be fulfilled."

This passage clearly indicates that even as late as 80 A.D. the third canon does not exist as a complete and approved unit, but it does show that the Psalms had won their way to the status of Scripture. Ryle's theory that the New Testament evidence implies a fixed third canon is not warranted.[10]

While many of the books in the Kethubim had achieved canonicity before the first century of the Christian Era, it was the Council of Jamnia in 90 A.D. that confirmed the third canon and ratified once and for all the other two.[11] After the destruction of Jerusalem in 70 A.D. it was natural that the Jews

[10] "The references in the New Testament to the Old Testament Scriptures lead the unprejudiced reader to suppose that the Jewish Scriptures were regarded in the middle of that century as a complete and finished collection . . . (*op. cit.*, p. 163).

[11] Driver, however, says: "There is reason seriously to doubt the view that the canon was finally settled at Jamnia" (*Abingdon Bible Commentary*, p. 98).

should consolidate their position, reorganize, and give definitive form to their religion. It was also logical that they should close the canon of Scripture. This they did under the leadership of Rabbi Johanan ben Zakkai.

Another reason for holding the Council of Jamnia was the increasing popularity of the Septuagint among the Christians. It was imperative that a stand be taken with regard to the Greek version, which included fourteen books in excess of the Palestinian Bible. The Council of Jamnia upheld the Hebrew list of twenty-four books. Samuel, Kings, and Chronicles were listed each as one book, Ezra and Nehemiah were combined, and the twelve minor prophets were in one book. Breaking down these books we have a total of thirty-nine. After 90 A.D. no change was made in the Palestinian canon, which stands as follows:

The Law: Genesis, Exodus, Leviticus, Numbers, Deuteronomy.
The Prophets:
 The Former Prophets: Joshua, Judges, I and II Samuel, I and II Kings.
 The Latter Prophets:
  Major: Isaiah, Jeremiah, Ezekiel.
  Minor: The Book of the Twelve: Hosea, Joel, Amos, Obadiah, Jonah, Micah, Nahum, Habakkuk, Zephaniah, Haggai, Zechariah, Malachi.
The Writings:
 The Poetical Books: Psalms, Proverbs, Job.
 The Five Rolls: Canticle, Ruth, Lamentations, Ecclesiastes, Esther.
 The Remainder: Daniel, Ezra, Nehemiah, I and II Chronicles.

Contemporaneous with the late books of the New Testament as authority for the canon is Josephus, who wrote *Against Apion* (*ca.* 100 A.D.). Josephus used the Septuagint rather than the tripartite division of the Jewish canon and mentioned twenty-two books in the Old Testament as a well-defined, fixed collection. His list consisted of five books of Moses, thirteen books of prophecy, and four books of hymns and moral teaching. The Hebrew list comprised twenty-four books, but Josephus, writing for Greeks, used the Septuagint or Alexandrian canon of twenty-two books, combining Ruth with Judges and Lamentations with Jeremiah.

Thus the tripartite canon of the Old Testament was fixed by 100 A.D., although the canonical primacy of the Torah was never relinquished.

Early Greek manuscripts differ in the order and number of books in the Alexandrian or Septuagint canon. *Codex Vaticanus* contains forty-six books as against fifty in *Codex Alexandrinus*. In other words, the Apocryphal list in the Septuagint, i.e., books in excess of the Palestinian Hebrew canon, varied greatly.[12]

[12] For the Old Testament canonical lists of Melito of Sardis (*ca.* 170 A.D.), Origen (250 A.D.), Athanasius (365 A.D.), Jerome (400 A.D.), and the Eastern churches, see *The Interpreter's Bible* (New York, 1952), I, 40–42.

Chapter Six

Extracanonical Literature of the Old Testament

1. The Apocrypha

The Septuagint or Hellenistic Bible

Following the conquest of Alexander the Great (*ca.* 332 B.C.), there was a large emigration of Jews, both forced and voluntary, from Judah to all the countries of the Mediterranean world. This scattering is known as the Diaspora. There were, of course, earlier dispersions of the Jews as in the Babylonian Exile. In that connection it is a mistake to suppose that all the Jews returned to their homeland after the Persian victory over the Babylonians. Most of them remained in Mesopotamia, where they had intermarried, had settled down to trading and farming, and, on the whole, had become content with their new surroundings. The two centers of the Diaspora, or "Greater Israel," as it might be called, were Babylon and Alexandria. Our attention is now directed to the latter city, which in 300 B.C. contained more Jews than Jerusalem.

In the wake of Alexander's conquest followed the Greek language, which became the commercial and literary tongue of the Mediterranean world. That the Diaspora Jews normally wrote and spoke Greek is evident from contemporary synagogue inscriptions, which are in Greek. It is safe to say that most of the Jews in Alexandria were ignorant of their ancestral tongue and were therefore unable to read their own Bible. Thus in 250 B.C. during the reign of Ptolemy Philadelphus, arrangements were made for the translation of the Hebrew Bible into Greek for the benefit of these Greek-speaking Jews in Egypt.

This version is called the Septuagint. According to tradition, the translation was made by seventy men (Latin *septuaginta*, meaning seventy). The work was begun about 250 B.C. and was continued for at least seventy-five years. We have already referred to the extreme care exercised in the rendering of the Torah into Greek and the comparatively careless manner in which the other books of the Old Testament were handled. This laxity in regard to books other than the Torah is seen in the selection of books to be included in the Alexandrian canon.

Hellenistic Judaism, influenced by the tolerant, liberal outlook of the Greeks, became less exclusive and narrow than Palestinian Judaism. The Alexandrian Jews especially were liberal and comprehensive in their religious views, so it is easy to understand why the Alexandrian Septuagint contained several books not acceptable to Palestinian authorities. Specifically, in addition to the thirty-nine books of the Hebrew canon, the Septuagint contained the following fourteen books:

THE FIRST BOOK OF ESDRAS

THE SECOND BOOK OF ESDRAS

THE BOOK OF TOBIT

THE BOOK OF JUDITH

THE REMAINDER OF ESTHER

THE WISDOM OF SOLOMON

ECCLESIASTICUS OR THE WISDOM OF SIRACH

THE BOOK OF BARUCH

THE BOOK OF SUSANNA

THE SONG OF THE THREE CHILDREN

THE STORY OF BEL AND THE DRAGON

THE PRAYER OF MANASSEH

THE FIRST BOOK OF MACCABEES

THE SECOND BOOK OF MACCABEES

The order of the books in the Septuagint differs from the Hebrew list and no attention is given to the tripartite division of the canon. First and II Kings replace the two books of Samuel, III and IV Kings stand for I and II Kings, and II Ezra takes the place of Nehemiah.

History of the Apocrypha

Our chief interest is the inclusion in the Septuagint of the fourteen books that are outside the Hebrew Old Testament. These books are known as the *Apocrypha* (a Greek word meaning "hidden" and therefore "mysterious" or "spurious"). All of the Apocrypha except Sirach are anonymous, and all were written by Jewish authors, although some were written in Greek. The Apocryphal writings were known by the Palestinian rabbis at Jamnia, but they were emphatically rejected largely because they either were written in Greek or were recent in composition.

We have referred to the prevalence of Greek as the language of the Mediterranean world from 300 B.C. to 200 A.D. The earliest Christians were Jews who were loyal to the Law but who were also followers of Jesus. These Jewish followers of "The Way" most probably did not know Hebrew, so they had to use the Greek Old Testament. Christianity, while born a Jewish religion, after 50 A.D. became Gentile, and the early Christians outside of the Petrine circle in Jerusalem spoke and wrote Greek. It was natural, therefore, that the Scripture of the early Christian church should be the Greek Old Testament rather than the Hebrew. When Paul, for instance, quoted from the Old Testament, he used the Septuagint version and not the Hebrew.

Since the Septuagint contained the fourteen extra books, the Christians came to accept them as an integral part of the Bible and gave them at least a quasi-canonical status. As the Jewish element in Christianity receded, the leaders of Gentile Christianity ceased to distinguish between the Hebrew and the Alexandrian canons. Irenaeus, bishop of Lyons in Gaul (*ca.* 180 A.D.) quotes from three of the Apocryphal books as Scripture. Clement of Alexandria (*ca.* 200 A.D.), the city where the Septuagint originated, naturally assumed the canonicity of the Apocrypha, as did Tertullian (*ca.* 220 A.D.), bishop of Carthage.

The Old Latin version (*ca.* 175 A.D.) was translated from the Alexandrian Septuagint and therefore contained the Apocrypha. However, although the Septuagint became the normative Old Testament for early Christianity, as we come into the third and fourth centuries we notice a growing distrust of the Apocrypha on the part of the leaders of the church. Origen (*ca.* 250 A.D.), holding strictly to the Hebrew Old Testament, definitely excluded the Apocrypha from the canon. Eusebius, bishop of Caesarea (*ca.* 340 A.D.) and church historian, omits the Apocrypha in his official canonical lists but elsewhere refers to them as " disputed books." Cyril, bishop of Jerusalem (*ca.* 400 A.D.), admonishes his people to " read the twenty-two books of the Old Testament proper but have nothing to do with Apocryphal writings." Athanasius, bishop of Alexandria (*ca.* 365 A.D.), takes a position that anticipates the later Protestant view (and

Jerome as well) when he states: " All the books of the Old Testament are twenty-two in number; there are also other books not included in these nor admitted into the canon, which have been framed by the fathers for the benefit of those approaching Christianity " and follows with the Apocryphal list. Rufinus in Rome (*ca.* 410) concurs, citing the present Old Testament as canonical and referring to the Apocrypha as " ecclesiastical but not canonical."

A key figure in the history of the Apocrypha is Jerome (340–420), eminent scholar and churchman. He was commissioned by Pope Damasus in 383 to revise the Old Latin version. In 390 he undertook the translation of the complete Bible into Latin, a project that consumed some fourteen years. This was called the Vulgate, which became the Bible of Western Christendom for a thousand years and today is still the official Bible of the Roman Catholic Church.

Accepting the Septuagint as the Old Testament of the Christian church, Jerome included the Apocrypha in his translation; but he was influenced more by the Hebrew Old Testament, which he was translating, and therefore was inclined to relegate the extra books to a noncanonical position. After listing the twenty-two accepted books, he writes: " Whatever is beyond these must be reckoned as Apocrypha. Therefore these books are not in the canon. . . . The church reads them for the edification of the people." In spite of his own attitude toward the Apocrypha, Jerome felt it necessary to compromise to a certain degree and included the books in his translation. The Councils of Hippo (393) and Carthage (397) recognized the canonicity of the extra books, and the church at Rome in the fifth century, following the teaching of Augustine, included the books as Old Testament canon. Jerome's objections were forgotten, and throughout the millennium that followed no adverse comment was made except by Thomas Aquinas (thirteenth century), who was inclined to give the Apocrypha a secondary place.

In the early years of the Protestant Reformation Luther translated the Bible into German, going back to the Hebrew text for the Old Testament and to the Greek for the New Testament (1534). Not finding the extra fourteen books in the Hebrew canon, he took a definite stand against their inclusion as canonical works. He translated the Apocrypha and put them in an appendix to the Old Testament proper, commenting editorially that they were not on a par with Scripture but "were good and useful for reading," which is precisely what Jerome had said. Jerome, however, had scattered the Apocryphal books throughout the Vulgate, just as they were in the Septuagint. The Wycliffe Bible, translated into English from the Vulgate, has the same arrangement.

The English versions from Tyndale to the King James Bible printed the Apocrypha as an appendix to the Old Testament. Thus the Protestant position became firmly established (both Anglican and Lutheran) that the Apocryphal books were noncanonical but could be used for purposes of edification.

The Council of Trent (1546), acting more from an anti-Protestant feeling than from a desire to follow Jerome's views, fixed the Roman Catholic position as follows: "The Holy Ecumenical and General Council of Trent, following the example of the orthodox fathers, venerates *all* the books of the Old and New Testaments with an equal feeling of devotion." This statement is followed by a list of the biblical works, including the Apocrypha, and the announcement concludes with anathema on all who do not recognize all the books as equally inspired Scripture. But the decree was made over the objection of Cardinals Ximines and Cajetan, both of whom held to Jerome's views. The Vatican Council of 1870 ratified the canonicity of the Apocrypha as decreed by the Council of Trent.

The reader will now recognize the difference between the present Roman Catholic and Protestant Bibles and the history behind that difference. It is also apparent that the two conflicting points of view regarding the status of the Apocrypha go back to the earliest days of Christianity and are present throughout Christian history. In the present Vulgate and Douai versions of the Roman Catholic Church, the Apocrypha are an integral part of the Old Testament but are sometimes labeled "deutero-canonical," a term implying "secondary-canon." The Vulgate places some of the Apocrypha in an appendix after the New Testament (Prayer of Manasses, III and IV Esdras). The Greek church, inheriting the Septuagint, accepts the Apocrypha with variations in the order and placement of books.[1]

Character of the Apocryphal Books

Just as Deuteronomy was the nucleus and most important book of the Pentateuch and as the Psalms served in the same way for the third canon, so Ecclesiasticus may well be considered the most valuable book in the Apocrypha, at least from the standpoint of ethical and religious values. It was called "Ecclesiasticus," or "Church-book," because it was

[1] *The Apocrypha: An American Translation* by E. J. Goodspeed (Chicago, 1938), is an excellent English translation in an attractive format. It was issued in connection with the publication of *The Holy Bible: An American Translation*. See also R. H. Charles, *The Apocrypha and Pseudepigrapha in English* (Oxford, 1913); C. C. Torrey, *The Apocryphal Literature; a Brief Introduction* (New Haven, 1945); and R. H. Pfeiffer, *History of New Testament Times, with an Introduction to the Apocrypha* (New York, 1949).

used for a long time as a manual of instruction for young people entering the Christian church. It is the only book in the Apocrypha with known authorship. We gather from the text that Jesus, son of Sirach, was a sage in Jerusalem and conducted a scribal school. He published his essays in Hebrew (180 B.C.), and his grandson translated them into Greek (132 B.C.), adding a suitable preface.

Ecclesiasticus is the longest book of all the Wisdom literature of the Jews. The word "wisdom" in Hellenistic Judaism refers not to abstract philosophy but to practical ethics. The cultural and tolerant atmosphere of Ecclesiasticus reflects the Greek influence, which was felt even in the heart of Palestine in the second century B.C. As in the Book of Proverbs, the author here extols the virtues of prudence, kindness, obedience, discipline, humility, and learning, but the dominant theme is wisdom, not necessarily for its own sake but for a better understanding of the Law. The book is replete with shrewd, epigrammatic sayings about the good life and the pursuit of happiness: "He that toucheth pitch shall be defiled" (13:1); "Nothing can ever be taken in exchange for a true friend" (7:1); "Judge of thy neighbor by thyself" (31:15). The hymn entitled "Now Thank We All Our God" is based on 50:22–24: "Now bless the God of all. . . ."

Two of Sirach's poems are worthy of inclusion in any canon or anthology of verse. One is a tribute to the workingman and all forms of work:

It is so with every craftsman and builder,
Who keeps at work at night as well as by day.
Some cut carved seals,
And elaborate variety of design;
Another puts his mind on painting a likeness,

And is anxious to complete his work.
It is so with the smith sitting by his anvil,
And expert in working in iron;
The smoke of the fire reduces his flesh,
And he exerts himself in the heat of the furnace.
He bends his ear to the sound of the hammer,
And his eyes are on the pattern of the implement.
He puts his mind on completing his work,
And he is anxious to finish preparing it.
It is so with the potter, as he sits at his work,
And turns the wheel with his foot;
He is constantly careful about his work,
And all his manufacture is by measure;
He will shape the clay with his arm,
And bend its strength with his feet;
He puts his mind on finishing the glazing,
And he is anxious to make his furnace clean.
All these rely on their hands;
And each one is skilful in his own work;
Without them, no city can be inhabited,
And men will not live in one or go about in it.
But they are not sought for to advise the people,
And in the public assembly they do not excel.
They do not sit on the judge's seat,
And they do not think about the decision of lawsuits;
They do not utter instruction or judgment,
And they are not found using proverbs.
Yet they support the fabric of the world,
And their prayer is in the practice of their trade.[2]

The book closes with a review of the deeds of the great heroes of Israel: Abraham, Moses, Joshua, Samuel, David, Elijah, and Josiah. This résumé is introduced by a beautiful ode to great men, probably the most quoted lines in all the Apocrypha:

[2] 38:27-34.

Let us now praise distinguished men,
Our forefathers before us.
They are a great glory to the Lord who created them;
They show his majesty from of old.
Men who exercised authority in their reigns,
And were renowned for their might!
They gave their counsel with understanding,
And brought men tidings through their prophecy —
Leaders of the people in deliberation and understanding,
Men of learning for the people,
Wise in their words of instruction;
Composers of musical airs,
Authors of poems in writing;
Rich men, endowed with strength,
Who lived in peace upon their lands —
All these were honored in their generation,
And were a glory in their day.
There are some of them who have left a name,
So that men declare their praise;
And there are some who have no memorial,
And have perished as though they had not lived,
And have become as though they had not been,
With their children after them.
Yet these were merciful men,
And their uprightness has not been forgotten.
With their descendants it will remain,
A good inheritance for their posterity.
Their descendants stand by the agreements,
And their children also for their sakes;
Their posterity will endure forever,
And their glory will not be blotted out.
Their bodies are buried in peace,
But their name lives to all generations.
Peoples will recite their wisdom,
And the congregation declare their praise! [8]

[8] 44:1-15.

Next in importance are the Maccabean books, whose value is historical rather than ethical or literary. The first book of Maccabees (90–70 B.C.) is a fairly reliable source for information on the Maccabean Revolt (175–132 B.C.). Here are described the invasion of Jerusalem by Antiochus Epiphanes, king of Syria, the plunder of the temple and the city, the placing of the altar to Zeus in the temple, the burning of the books of the Law, and the martyrdom of the Jews. The author also describes the rebellion under the leadership of the Maccabean family, the death of Antiochus, and the liberation of the Jews under the Hasmoneans. The second book of Maccabees, dealing with the same period, tells of the desecration of the temple and the martyrdom of the Jews.

The Wisdom of Solomon (50 B.C.), called " the gem of the Apocrypha," is a philosophy of life written by an unknown author but attributed to Solomon. Again the Greek influence is seen, not only in the philosophical thought, but in the use of the classic Greek language and the stately style. At the same time, the author is attempting to establish the superiority of the Hebrew religion over the Greek culture. The intertestamental belief in immortality finds expression in a verse that has become a part of our church liturgy:

> But the souls of the upright are in the hand of God,
> And no torment can reach them.
> In the eyes of foolish people they seemed to die,
> And their decease was thought an affliction,
> And their departure from us their ruin,
> But they are at peace.
> For though in the sight of men they are punished,
> Their hope is full of immortality,[4]

[4] 3:1–4.

The climax of the book is the author's apotheosis of wisdom:

> Wisdom, the fashioner of all things, taught me.
> For there is in her a spirit that is intelligent, holy,
> Unique, manifold, subtle,
> Mobile, clear, undefiled,
> Distinct, beyond harm, loving the good, keen,
> Unhindered, beneficent, philanthropic,
> Firm, sure, free from care,
> All-powerful, all-seeing,
> And interpenetrating all spirits
> That are intelligent, pure, and most subtle.
>
> . . . .
>
> She is the breath of the power of God,
> And a pure emanation of his almighty glory;
> Therefore nothing defiled can enter into her,
> For she is a reflection of the everlasting light,
> And a spotless mirror of the activity of God . . .[5]

The Book of Tobit (*ca.* 175 B.C.), a piece of religious fiction, is a strange and charming story of the journey of Tobias, son of Tobit, from Nineveh to Ecbatana, accompanied by the angel Raphael.[6] In addition to being a faithful picture of Jewish piety and devotion to the Law, Tobit is especially important as showing the influence of Persian eschatology with its belief in angels and demons. New Testament apocalypticism is a continuation of Persian thought as developed in the intertestamental period.

Judith (*ca.* 150 B.C.) is another romance written to press home the paramount importance of obedience to the Law. The setting of the story is the siege of Bethulia by Holofernes, an Assyrian general. Judith, a beautiful Jewess, risked her

[5] 7:22–26.
[6] The famous Pollaioli painting "Raphael and Tobias" is based on this story.

life by entering the camp of the general and beheading him while he slept. She took his head back to the Jewish leaders, who promptly put to rout the army of Holofernes. This novelette has charmed many readers and was the inspiration for the great painting " Judith and Holofernes " by Tintoretto. The book may have been written, like Daniel, to encourage the revolt against the Greeks.

The Story of Susanna, the Song of the Three Children, and Bel and the Dragon are additions to the Book of Daniel in its Greek form and are therefore in the Septuagint and English Apocrypha but not in the Hebrew version. The Story of Susanna, written in the first century B.C., is undoubtedly of Pharisaic origin, having as its purpose the reform of Jewish laws regarding false witness. Two Jewish elders attempt to have relations with Susanna, the wife of a prominent Jew. She refuses and they accuse her of adultery. As she is being led to her execution, Daniel appears and demands that the accusers be examined separately. Upon examination, they contradict each other, and Susanna is acquitted. Jewish law required only two witnesses to establish the guilt of the accused. This book is a clever bit of propaganda against the practice of false witness.

The Song of the Three Children is a liturgical document depicting the delivery of Daniel's three friends from the fiery furnace. Bel and the Dragon also is associated with Daniel, who is shown preaching against the false gods of Babylon.

The two books of Esdras and the Prayer of Manasses belong to the Ezra-Chronicles literature. The first book of Esdras contains an account of the building of the second temple, while II Esdras is a series of apocalypses similar to Daniel. The Prayer of Manasses is a penitential song resembling the Psalms.

The Remainder of Esther is simply an addition to the canonical Book of Esther for the purpose of supplying the religious motif, which was clearly lacking in the former book.

The Book of Baruch, as the title implies, purports to be from the pen of Jeremiah's biographer. It was written about 100 A.D. and is liturgical in character.

2. The Pseudepigrapha

Pseudepigrapha ("false writings" or "writings under assumed names") is the title applied to a collection of eighteen Jewish books outside the Septuagint canon. They are largely apocalyptic and legendary in character and come from the late intertestamental period and the first two centuries of the Christian Era. Since they were not included in the Alexandrian Bible, Jerome rejected them. Today they are called Apocrypha by the Roman Catholic Church and Pseudepigrapha by the Protestant church.[7]

Although these books are known and quoted by New Testament writers, they are decidedly inferior to the canonical works of Scripture largely because of their predominantly apocalyptic nature. Apocalypticism is a type of Jewish literature that originated in the intertestamental period and continued throughout the early centuries of the Christian Era, the most prominent examples in the canonical Scripture being Daniel and Revelation.

This type of utterance might be regarded as an extension

[7] For an authoritative discussion of Apocrypha and Pseudepigrapha see R. H. Pfeiffer, *History of New Testament Times, with an Introduction to the Apocrypha* (New York, 1949), and the same author's two articles on the Apocrypha and the Pseudepigrapha in *The Interpreter's Bible* (New York, 1952), I, 391 ff.

of prophetic Messianism, a postponement, as it were, of the coming of the " Day of the Lord." With the failure of the Messianic era to materialize, the apocalyptic writers reasoned that there must be a future compensation or reward in a heavenly realm for all the persecution and martyrdom. Apocalypticism is a revelation of the last things, the prediction of a catastrophic ending of the world order and the ushering in of a new era, a " new heaven and a new earth." This is all in accordance with the predetermined plan of God.

Intertestamental apocalypticism shows the influence of Persian thought, particularly in the idea of the future life and the doctrine of heaven and hell. Another characteristic of this type of writing is its use of imagery and vision as a symbolic medium for its predictions.

The apocalyptists appeared comparatively late in the history of Jewish writing; so, in order to place their books within the framework of the period of inspired or revealed Scripture, they attributed their work to more ancient and well-known people such as Moses, Enoch, or Ezra.

The Book of Enoch (*ca.* 100 B.C.) is the most important of the Pseudepigrapha. Its influence is felt in several New Testament books, and it was actually considered as Scripture by Irenaeus, Tertullian, and Clement of Alexandria. The idea of Sheol as an intermediate realm of probation (see Roman Catholic doctrine of purgatory), or as the equivalent of hell, appears first in this book. Also used here for the first time is the Messianic title " Son of Man," a term found frequently in the New Testament. Other titles used here for the first time in a messianic sense are " the Righteous One," " the Elect One," and " Christ " or " the Anointed One." [8]

[8] Cf. *Commentary on Habakkuk* of the Dead Sea Scrolls for same Messianic titles. See pp. 78–79.

The Book of Enoch is preserved in two Ethiopic manuscripts and is therefore sometimes called Ethiopic Enoch.

The Secrets of Enoch or Slavonic Enoch (*ca.* 50 A.D.) also influenced the New Testament writers. The idea of the millennium, appearing for the first time in this book, became typical of Christian apocalyptic.

Since the Pseudepigrapha never appeared as a well-defined collection of sacred writings, there is no standard list of books under that title, but generally the following works are recognized:

THE BOOK OF JUBILEES

THE TESTAMENTS OF THE TWELVE PATRIARCHS

THE TESTAMENT OF JOB

THE LIFE OF ASENATH

THE PSALMS OF SOLOMON

THE BOOK OF ENOCH

THE SECRETS OF ENOCH (SLAVONIC ENOCH)

THE SIBYLLINE ORACLES

THE ASSUMPTION OF MOSES

THE APOCALYPSE OF BARUCH

III MACCABEES

IV MACCABEES

THE LETTER OF ARISTEAS

THE ASCENSION OF ISAIAH [9]

[9] For other pseudepigraphical lists, all of which are different, see R. H. Charles, *The Apocrypha and Pseudepigrapha* (Oxford, 1913); C. C. Torrey, *The Apocryphal Literature* (New Haven, 1945); R. H. Pfeiffer, in *The Interpreter's Bible* (New York, 1952), I, 421 ff.

Part Three

The Making of the New Testament

Chapter Seven

The Nature of the New Testament Literature

1. Correspondence

Letters of Paul

There are basically four classes of literature in the New Testament: gospel (the Four Gospels), history (Acts), correspondence (Pauline and other letters), and apocalypticism (Revelation). This grouping corresponds to the order of books in the English New Testament and might also be said to represent the order of their importance, but it is not the chronological order.

It would be natural to think of the gospels as the earliest of the Christian writings, but such is not the case. Why, then, were they placed first in the New Testament? The fact is that those who gathered the books into a collection had no interest in chronological order. Our modern scientific desire to arrange things in the sequence of their historical appearance held no appeal for them. Their sole interest was in content and from that standpoint the gospels were of paramount importance.

Our introduction to the literature of the New Testament will therefore follow a somewhat different pattern.

The earliest literature in the New Testament came out of a decidedly practical situation and was not thought of as literature at all, much less as Scripture. It consisted of letters written to various Christian communities in response to specific needs. Most of these letters were written by Paul between 52 and 64 A.D.

Paul had established the legitimacy of gentile Christianity at the Council of Jerusalem (*ca.* 48 A.D.) and subsequently had planted the gospel in the provinces of Galatia, Asia, Macedonia, and Achaia. Whether Jewish or gentile, these new converts were confused and had many questions to ask pertaining to both belief and practice. "How are we supposed to observe the Lord's Supper?" "What are we supposed to think about the return of Jesus?" "Whom are we to follow — you or Peter or Apollos?"

Paul's letters were written to answer these and many other questions that perplexed the minds of these young Christians. That this correspondence was to become either an integral part of a new Bible called the New Testament or a body of doctrine for the edification of posterity would have been news to Paul himself. Such an idea was far from his mind. He was writing personal letters to certain people, and, if he had been able to visit them in person, he would not have written. It is inaccurate, therefore, to call them "epistles," since an epistle is a literary form or a message for *general* reading. (The books of James and Hebrews may more properly be classified as epistles because of their formal character.)

Paul's letters were "occasional"; that is, they were written for certain, specific occasions. This distinction is important because the writer of a personal letter makes only casual comment on certain events and situations that are known to his immediate readers; later readers may find these comments unintelligible. The casual nature of the intimate letter also means that trivial but immediate problems are given as much emphasis as important matters, with the result that some of the most significant teachings are often out of focus. Here again we are confronted with the necessity of screening the transient from the permanent. First Corinthians 13 can be read with great profit by us today, but the same cannot be said for I Corinthians 7.

The importance of Paul's letters can be indicated in four ways, the first of which is their antiquity. They were written, received, read, passed about, and brought together as a distinct group before the earliest gospel was composed. In the second place, the fact that they are autobiographical — being the authentic correspondence of one of the greatest characters in Christian history after Jesus — increases their significance tremendously. They are historically valuable because they give us an insight into the life, customs, and problems of the early Christian communities. And, finally, they are permanently valuable to us because they are the record of one man's religious experience — an experience that he summed up in the phrase " in Christ."

These letters also reveal two Pauls: Paul the practical preacher of the gospel and Paul the theologian. The religion of the first is more important for us than the theology of the second, but, unfortunately, the church has often been unable to see the forest of the one for the trees of the other.

As to the dating of Paul's letters, the following chronological table represents a scholarly consensus:

I, II THESSALONIANS	50–52
GALATIANS	53
I, II CORINTHIANS	54–57
ROMANS	56–58
PHILIPPIANS	60–64
COLOSSIANS	60–64
PHILEMON	60–64
EPHESIANS (?)	60–64

These ten letters — with the exception of Ephesians — are usually accepted as Pauline, but the authenticity of the so-called Pastoral Epistles (I, II Timothy, Titus) is questioned by many authorities. Between those who accept the Pastorals as Pauline and those who emphatically reject them, there are some who recognize within these letters a nucleus of Pauline material. These fragmentary data, it is held, were later edited and amplified by a follower of Paul who was thoroughly familiar with his thought and style. Such a practice was not uncommon in ancient times.

The three letters to Timothy and Titus are called the Pastorals because they presumably carry instructions from Paul to his two pastors regarding the conduct of their parishes. But a close reading of these treatises will reveal, as Morton S. Enslin observes, that they are not letters at all, that they certainly are not from the hand of Paul, and that the author uses the names Timothy and Titus as a literary device or " stage setting." Certain Pauline expressions are used, especially at the beginning of each letter. Much of the instruction, purportedly given by Paul to Timothy, is information that Timothy must already have had by reason of his association with the apostle.

" The whole situation is impossible," writes Enslin, " not to say absurd and grotesque, if we assume the historic Paul writing personal letters to the historic Timothy and Titus in real situations. But if we admit that we have here the work of a later writer seeking to meet the circumstances of his own day and wishing to gain for his instruction the authority of the now long-dead Paul, the absurdity is removed." [1]

The authenticity of the Pastoral Epistles as Pauline hinges on the possibility of Paul's release from the Roman prison

[1] *Christian Beginnings* (New York, 1938), p. 300.

and a renewal of his missionary activity in new places. For this there is no evidence in the Book of Acts or in the accepted letters of Paul. In fact, the chief reason for rejecting the Pauline authorship of the Pastorals is that there is simply no place in the career of Paul where they can be placed.

But there are further reasons for rejecting these epistles as genuine. All three have a striking similarity of style, which is different from that of Paul's letters. The Pastorals refer to an ecclesiastical situation — an official hierarchy of bishops, elders, and other leaders with presumably understood functions — that did not exist in the time of Paul. Finally, the perfunctory character of the teaching stands in contrast to the typical thought of Paul.[2]

Paul's first letter (of those that are extant), and consequently the first book of our chronological New Testament, is I Thessalonians. The setting for this letter is Corinth between 50 and 52 A.D. On his second campaign Paul had crossed from Troas to Philippi, where he introduced Christianity to the Greeks of Macedonia, and then preached in Thessalonica, Berea, and Athens. At Athens he had been joined by Timothy, whom he had left in Berea with Silas. Timothy brought either a letter or an oral report from Thessalonica, and Paul's letter to the Thessalonians is an answer to this report. He praises them for their constancy but warns them against fair-weather loyalty, faintheartedness, and sexual immorality. He defends his mission against the Jewish opposition and closes with a word of encouragement for those who had lost loved ones and friends.

Apparently the letter to the Thessalonians did not suc-

---

[2] See E. F. Scott, *The Literature of the New Testament* (New York, 1936), p. 191 ff.

ceed in answering all their questions. There was some hysteria over the near approach of the Parousia.[3] Paul wrote a second letter, assuring the Thessalonians that the "Day of the Lord" was not yet at hand.

Galatians, the most spirited of all Paul's letters, was written to his followers at Iconium, Lystra, Derbe, and Antioch in Pisidia. Some Jewish Christians from Jerusalem had entered among these gentile converts, claiming that Paul's gospel was illegitimate and that he discouraged his converts from observing the Law. They claimed that a gentile had to become a Jew before he could become a Christian, that it was necessary, in other words, to be circumcised.

In defending himself against these "Judaizers," who were trying to undermine his work, Paul explained that his own apostleship was "from God and not man" and then (chap. 2) described the conference at Jerusalem, which he and Barnabas attended, accompanied by Titus, an uncircumcised gentile. In the debate with Peter and James, Paul used Titus as a test case, insisting that he was a bona fide Christian, although he was not circumcised and did not follow the Law. The apostle emphasizes his independence of the Jerusalem leaders and rejoices in his victory over them in establishing the validity of gentile Christianity.

Luke's account of the Council in Acts (chap. 15) has no mention of Titus and is calmly objective as compared with this letter, which shows Paul clearly on the defensive and in a passionate, if not a belligerent, mood. His career was at stake, as was the essence of Christianity itself: was it to be merely a part of Judaism, or was it to consist of faith in Christ alone? Paul eventually triumphed, and, mainly through his

[3] The time of the appearance or return of Christ as Messiah and the inauguration of a new era.

efforts, gentile Christianity won its independence from the domination of the Jewish Law.

When Paul reached Ephesus on his third campaign, word came to him of trouble in Corinth, due both to factions and to practical problems. Paul had evidently already written one letter (I Cor. 5:9–13), which we do not have.[4] Now he feels compelled to write another, rebuking the Corinthians for their divisions and giving them instructions in regard to marriage, the Lord's Supper, and the belief in the Resurrection.

This letter above all others reveals intimately the problems of the early church and Paul's technique in handling them. He rebukes the Corinthians for their divisions and calls them to the unity they all have in Christ. " I appeal to you, brethren, by the name of our Lord, Jesus Christ, that all of you agree and that there be no dissensions among you, but that you be united in the same mind and the same judgment. . . . For no other can anyone lay than that which is laid, which is Jesus Christ. . . . For by one spirit we were all baptized into one body — Jews or Greeks, slaves or free — and all were made to drink of one spirit. . . . For all things are yours, whether Paul or Apollos or Cephas. . . . All are yours and you are Christ's." [5]

Paul had sent Timothy to Corinth to help settle the disputes. Upon his return to Ephesus, Paul wrote the letter now designated as II Corinthians, in which he refers to an intermediate letter, which may be found in II Corinthians 10–13. There is also evidence that Paul left Ephesus, paid a short visit to Corinth, and returned to Ephesus (II Cor. 12:14; 13:1). This is not mentioned in Acts.

---

[4] II Cor. 6:14–7:1 may well be a part of this lost letter.
[5] I Cor. 1:10 ff.

Paul's letter to the church at Rome, which he had never visited, is more in the nature of a treatise or epistle than his other letters, differing from them in its objectivity and broad theological outlook. This fact probably accounts for its position at the head of the Pauline list in our English New Testament, a position given to the letter by reason of its importance or perhaps of the importance of the church at Rome.

As a general treatise addressed to strangers, this letter naturally contains no mention of anything local or specific as with his other letters, where he knows the problems and the history of each church. It is therefore surprising to find in the closing chapter a long list of personal greetings and also reference to certain individuals who were " causing divisions " and teaching doctrines contrary to the gospel they had received (presumably from Paul). The presence of this material has prompted many critics for the past century or more to question the authenticity of chapter 16 as part of the original letter. It is not to be expected that Paul would have so many intimate friends in a city he had never visited. Some authorities have concluded that what we have here is a later recension of Romans.

The letter, written during Paul's third visit to Corinth (*ca.* 56–58 A.D.), includes a vivid description of the life in the spirit:

The law of the spirit of life in Christ Jesus has set me free from the law of sin and death. . . . If Christ is in you, your spirits are alive because of righteousness. . . . All who are led by the spirit of God are sons of God. . . . We know that in everything God works for good with those who love him, who are called according to his purpose. . . . In all these things we are more than conquerors through him who loved us. For I am sure that neither death, nor life, nor angels, nor principalities, nor things present, nor things to come, nor powers, nor height, nor depth, nor anything else in all creation, will be able to separate us from the love of God in Christ Jesus, our Lord.[6]

Philippians, Colossians, Ephesians, and Philemon were written during Paul's imprisonment in Rome (60–64 A.D.). While Rome is not mentioned specifically, it is usually thought that " the letters of the captivity " were penned there rather than at Caesarea, where he was prisoner for two years, or Ephesus, which is vaguely connected with an earlier imprisonment of Paul. The first three of these letters contain some of the noblest religions and ethical teaching in the New Testament and define once and for all the nature of the Christian life.

Philippians is the most intimate and affectionate of all of Paul's letters. He tells his friends of his condition and of his hope of release. Then he describes his experience of oneness with Christ and admonishes them to preserve their unity in Christ.

For me to live is Christ. . . . I count everything as loss because of the surpassing worth of knowing Christ Jesus my Lord. . . . One thing I do: forgetting what lies behind and straining forward to what lies ahead, I press on toward the goal for the prize of the upward call of God in Christ Jesus. . . . So if there is any encouragement in Christ, any incentive of love, any participation in the spirit, any affection and sympathy, complete my joy by being of the same mind, having the same love, being in full accord and having one mind.[7]

Ephesians, Colossians, and Philemon are linked together by the mention of Onesimus and Archippus in Philemon and Colossians and Tychicus, the messenger, in Ephesians and

[6] Chapter 8.
[7] 1:21; 2:1; 3:7, 13, 14.

Colossians. Ephesus was the center of one of Paul's most successful and protracted campaigns. He had established a firm Christian community here and had made many friends. It is surprising, therefore, to encounter in the letter to the Ephesians a general religious and ethical tract rather than a warm personal greeting. The theme of Ephesians is the unity of the church in Christ:

That Christ may dwell in your hearts through faith; that you, being rooted and grounded in love, may have power to comprehend with all the saints what is the breadth and length and height and depth and to know the love of Christ which surpasses knowledge, that you may be filled with all the fullness of God. . . . There is one body and one spirit, just as you were called to the one hope that belongs to your call, one Lord, one faith, one baptism, one God and Father of us all, who above all and through all and in all . . . until we all attain to the unity of the faith and of the knowledge of the Son of God, to mature manhood, to the measure of the stature of the fullness of Christ [3:17-19; 4:4-6, 13].[8]

Colossians contains Paul's philosophy of religion, especially as opposed to Gnosticism and other contemporary forms of thought.[9] Here the apostle emphasizes his doctrine of reconciliation achieved by mystically dying and rising with Christ, a thought pattern that may reflect some of the teachings of the mystery cults. He concludes with the information that he is sending Tychicus to Colossae " and with him Onesimus, the faithful and beloved brother, who is one of yourselves."

Onesimus was a runaway slave whom Paul converted in

---

[8] The authenticity of Ephesians as Pauline has been questioned by some scholars, who regard it, like the Pastorals, as coming from a follower of Paul at a much later date. For arguments against Pauline authorship see Enslin, *op. cit.*, pp. 294 ff.

[9] Gnosticism was an oriental system of speculative belief emphasizing esoteric knowledge or mystical illumination.

Rome and was now sending back to Philemon, his master. The letter to Philemon is one of the most intriguing and intimate documents to come out of antiquity and reveals the downright humanity of the great campaigner.

Other Letters

The Epistle to the Hebrews (80–90 A.D.), like the Paulines, has both an occasional and an intellectual purpose. It was written during the reign of Domitian to encourage Jewish Christians, who were enduring bitter persecution and suffering. In the midst of such peril, ostracism, and risk of martyrdom, the loyalty of Christians was put to an almost intolerable test. The author of this epistle has but one purpose, and that is to warn these Christians against relapse and to plead with them to keep their faith. This leads to the thesis of the book: the finality of Jesus and the Christian religion.

This thesis is established on the background of Judaism, and the argument appears to be confined to Jewish thought; but that is true only in the terms used. The logic is thoroughly Greek, and the author, following the Platonic doctrine that earthly manifestations are imperfect copies of the absolute or heavenly reality, argues that Jesus' sacrifice for mankind takes precedence over all Jewish sacrifices and is the perfect medium for the redemption of mankind. The Jewish sanctuary, the Law, and the high priest were merely a preparation for the New Covenant. God has made his final provision for salvation in Jesus Christ, his son. In the author's idea of Jesus' cosmic significance as an emanation from God, he shows an affinity to the Fourth Gospel and Philo.

We do not know who wrote Hebrews or to whom it was addressed. Its doctrine and style rule out any possibility of Paul and point to some Alexandrian Jew as the author. No better conclusion has been found than that of Origen: "God only knows who wrote this book." Whoever did write it was a well-educated person; his Greek is, with Luke's, the most classical in the New Testament.

The other seven letters — James, I and II Peter, I, II and III John, and Jude — are called the Catholic Epistles, and in these instances the term seems rather appropriate, as they are more general in character than Paul's. With the exceptions of I Peter and I John, these letters were held to be noncanonical by Eusebius and other early authorities and never really attained equality with the rest of the New Testament.

James is a general religious tract rather than a letter and is traditionally thought to be from the brother of Jesus. Its strong ethical emphasis echoes the teaching of Jesus and the prophets: "Be ye doers of the word and not hearers only. . . . What does it profit, my brethren, if a man says he has faith but has not works? . . . Faith apart from works is barren. . . . You see that a man is justified by works and not by faith alone." [10] This does not contradict the doctrine of Paul and the Epistle to the Hebrews that "the just shall live by faith" rather than the works of the Law, since the "works" that Paul thought were inadequate were the ceremonial performances of religion. Salvation is not to be earned by sacramental works; it is a gift. "Works," to the author of James, means good deeds, moral and social proof of one's faith. With him, mystical faith must be accompanied by ethical action, a teaching that coincides with the best of Jesus and Paul.

The First Epistle of John resembles the Fourth Gospel so closely in style, thought, and vocabulary that common authorship is fairly certain. It probably comes from the same time

[10] 1:22; 2:14; 2:20b; 2:24.

as the Fourth Gospel. It is directed against a form of Gnosticism (Docetism) that denied the earthly existence of Jesus. The author emphasizes the reality of Jesus as the Christ and admonishes his readers to live in the "fellowship of love." He defines the religious life as obedience to the commandments of God, loyalty to Christ as the representative of God, and love of others.[11] His purpose is to assure his readers of the certainty of their faith in Christ. He emphasizes brotherly love and morality, which were minimized by the Gnostics. In defining religion as bearing witness to Christ, loving one's neighbor, and performing altruistic deeds, the author of this epistle has preserved the essence of the Christian message.

The other two Johannine Epistles have less theological and religious value, but they do add to our knowledge of the rapidly developing ecclesiastical organization at the end of the first century of the Christian Era. First Peter was written by a follower of Peter to some Christians in Asia Minor to encourage them under persecution. The style and viewpoint of II Peter reveal not only a different author but one who is superficial and somewhat lacking in sincerity. Second Peter was undoubtedly dependent upon Jude, which is a warning against those who would undermine the faith of the Christians. Jude is strongly apocalyptic, resembling the Book of Enoch.

2. Gospel

The Synoptic Problem

The first thing that impresses the attentive reader of the Four Gospels is the similarity of the first three and the unique-

[11] 2:3–5; 4:2, 3; 4:7–12.

ness of the fourth. Because Matthew, Mark, and Luke present a common view of the life and teachings of Jesus and tell substantially the same story, they are called the Synoptic Gospels. The term " synoptic " is Greek and means " to see together "; it is not too apt, but as applied to these three gospels it suggests their parallelism and common point of view.

The agreement among the three frequently extends to the smallest details. This striking similarity often continues for long sections, so that the three books can be arranged in parallel columns in the form of a synopsis or harmony. But

MARK	MATTHEW
12:36, 37: David himself, inspired by the Holy Spirit declared, " The Lord said to my Lord, Sit at my right hand, till I put thy enemies under thy feet." David himself calls him Lord; so how is he his son? And the great throng heard him gladly.	22:43–45: He said to them, " How is it then that David, inspired by the Spirit, calls him Lord, saying, ' Thy Lord said to my Lord, Sit at my right hand, till I put thy enemies under thy feet'? If David thus calls him Lord, how is he his son? "
6:41–43: And taking the five loaves and the two fish he looked up to heaven, and blessed, and broke the loaves, and gave them to the disciples to set before the people; and he divided the two fish among them all. And they all ate and were satisfied. And they took up twelve baskets full of broken pieces and of the fish.	14:19, 20: Then he ordered the crowds to sit down on the grass; and taking the five loaves and the two fish he looked up to heaven, and blessed, and broke and gave the loaves to the disciples, and the disciples gave them to the crowds. And they all ate and were satisfied. And they took up twelve baskets full of the broken pieces left over.

coexistent with this parallelism is a divergence no less striking. The combination of these two phenomena has given rise to the so-called Synoptic Problem, which aims to investigate the question of mutual relationship and to propose a theory that will account for both the similarities and the differences. This literary problem is one of the most complex in the history of Biblical Criticism, and its implications are highly important for the history of Christianity.

To break open the problem for the reader, let us note first some of the identities of language in the three books.

LUKE

20:42–44: For David himself says in the Book of Psalms, "The Lord said to my Lord, Sit at my right hand, till I make thy enemies a stool for thy feet." David thus calls him Lord; so how is he his son?

9:16, 17: And taking the five loaves and the two fish he looked up to heaven, and blessed and broke them, and gave them to the disciples to set before the crowd. And all ate and were satisfied. And they took up what was left over, twelve baskets of broken pieces.

MARK	MATTHEW
2:10, 11, 12: "But that you may know that the Son of man has authority on earth to forgive sins" — he said to the paralytic — "I say to you, rise, take up your pallet and go home." And he rose, and immediately took up the pallet and went out before them all; so that they were all amazed and glorified God, saying, "We never saw anything like this!"	9:6, 7: "But that you may know that the Son of man has authority on earth to forgive sins" — he then said to the paralytic — "Rise, take up your bed and go home." And he rose and went home.

Obviously, the individualities of these three writers have been overruled by some external norm. Their versions are clearly dependent upon some common original, for such detailed identities of language cannot be coincidental. In fact, practically all of Mark can be found in Matthew and Luke in outline and content.[12]

On closer inspection we notice that Matthew and Luke have accounts of the life of Jesus before his baptism and after his death. This material is not found in Mark, and in it Matthew and Luke are completely independent of each other, but, starting with the baptism of Jesus, they coincide with Mark.[13] In narrative material Matthew and Luke seem to be in agreement with Mark, but sometimes this agreement exists between Mark and Matthew; at other times, between Mark and Luke.

[12] For a demonstration of triple agreement, see R. L. Finney, *Huck's Synopsis of the First Three Gospels* (New York, 1907). (A. Huck, *Synopse der drei ersten Evangelien* [in Greek] was revised in 1931.)

[13] According to the best and most ancient manuscripts, Mark ends at 16:8. Verses 9 to the end represent a later addition.

LUKE

5:24, 25: "But that you may know that the Son of man has authority on earth to forgive sins" — he said to the man who was paralyzed — "I say to you, rise, take up your bed and go home." And immediately he rose before them, and took up that on which he lay, and went home, glorifying God.

We must note also that the chronological order of all three gospels is fundamentally the same. They present the same outline of the life of Christ: baptism, temptation, Galilean ministry, journey to Jerusalem, and passion. Further, there is a strange agreement in the selection of material. How does it happen that from the entire life of Jesus these three biographers give us the incidents from only forty or fifty days at the most and, furthermore, select for the most part the same incidents? That these three writers would choose such a relatively small portion of the life of Jesus for portrayal is astonishing, to say the least. (In Mark, only thirty-one days can be identified!) Would it not seem that this verbal correspondence and the agreement in outline, chronology, and selection of material all point to some common model?

Equally impressive, however, is the element of divergence. For example:

MARK

The Young Ruler:
10:17: And as he was setting out on his journey, a man ran up and knelt before him, and asked him, " Good Teacher, what must I do to inherit eternal life? "

The Great Confession:
8:29: And he asked them, " But who do you say that I am? " Peter answered him, " You are Christ."

The Blind Beggar Incident:
10:46: And they came to Jericho; and as he was leaving Jericho with his disciples and a great multitude, Bartimaeus, a blind beggar, the son of Timaeus, was sitting by the roadside.

The Temptation Story:

MATTHEW

19:16: And, behold, one came up to him, saying, " Teacher, what good deed must I do, to have eternal life? "

16:15, 16: He said to them, " But who do you say that I am? " Simon Peter replied " You are the Christ, the Son of the living God."

20:29: And as they went out of Jericho, a great crowd followed him.

4:1–11: Then Jesus was led up by the Spirit into the wilderness to be tempted by the devil. And he fasted forty days and forty nights, and afterward he was hungry. And the tempter came and said to him, " If you are the Son of God, command these stones to become loaves of bread." But he answered, " It is written, ' Man shall not live by bread alone, but by every

LUKE

18:18: And a ruler asked him, "Good Teacher, what shall I do to inherit eternal life?"

9:20: And he said to them, "But who do you say that I am?" And Peter answered, "The Christ of God."

18:35: As he drew near to Jericho, a blind man was sitting by the roadside begging.

4:1–12: And Jesus, full of the Holy Spirit, returned from the Jordan, and was led by the Spirit for forty days in the wilderness, tempted by the devil. And he ate nothing in those days; and when they were ended, he was hungry. The devil said to him, "If you are the Son of God, command this stone to become bread." And Jesus answered him, "It is written,

MARK

MATTHEW

word that proceeds from the mouth of God.'" Then the devil took him to the holy city, and set him on the pinnacle of the temple, and said to him, "If you are the Son of God, throw yourself down; for it is written, 'He will give his angels charge of you,' and 'On their hands they will bear you up, lest you strike your foot against a stone.'" Jesus said to him, "Again it is written, 'You shall not tempt the Lord your God.'" Again, the devil took him to a very high mountain, and showed him all the kingdoms of the world and the glory of them; and he said to him, "All these I will give you, if you will fall down and worship me." Then Jesus said to him, "Begone, Satan! for it is written, 'You shall worship the Lord your God and him only shall you serve.'" Then the devil left him, and behold, angels came and administered to him.

Mission of the Twelve:
6:8, 9: He charged them to take nothing for their journey except a staff; no bread, no bag, no money in their belts; but to wear sandals and not put on two tunics.

10:10: No bag for your journey, nor two tunics, nor sandals, nor a staff; for the laborer deserves his food.

LUKE

' Man shall not live by bread
alone.' " And the devil took
him up, and showed him all
the kingdoms of the world in
a moment of time, and said to
him, " To you I will give all
this authority and their glory;
for it has been delivered to
me, and I give it to whom I
will. If you, then, will worship me, it shall all be yours."
And Jesus answered him, " It
is written, ' You shall worship
the Lord your God, and him
only shall you serve.' " And
he took him to Jerusalem, and
set him on the pinnacle of the
temple, and said to him, " If
you are the Son of God,
throw yourself down from
here; for it is written, ' He
will give his angels charge of
you, to guard you,' and ' On
their hands they will bear you
up, lest you strike your foot
against a stone.' " And Jesus
answered him, " It is said,
' You shall not tempt the Lord
your God.' "

How are we to reconcile these and many other variations? Are we to suppose that Jesus was tempted twice, each time in a different order? Which of the three gospels reports correctly Peter's confession? Did Jesus command his disciples to take staves and sandals, or did he prohibit them? Did Jesus heal one blind man or two; and was it on the way to or from Jericho?

The discrepancies are easier to understand than the agreements. When one considers that nothing was written about Jesus for some thirty years after his death, it is not surprising to find changes in context and variations in report. Matthew and Luke invariably differ in the context of any given incident involving discourse. Difference between the two in content is illustrated in one of the Beatitudes. Matthew 5:3 says: "Blessed are the poor in spirit . . . ," while Luke 6:20 says: "Blessed are you poor. . . ." Additions and omissions on the part of Matthew and Luke can be attributed to their special sources or to differences in point of view. The textual problem must also be borne in mind. Repeated copying of the papyri and manuscripts in the period between the original autographs and the making of the fourth-century manuscripts would account for variations in phraseology and the reporting of incidents. Our Greek Testament is at best a resultant of many different manuscripts.

Such is the Synoptic Problem. But what is the solution? One of the earlier suggestions was that the form of the gospel record of all three books was fixed during the period of oral transmission. This oral theory held that a stereotyped tradition of teaching was passed about by word of mouth and was known and used by our three writers. Oral teaching was common practice with the Jews, who were reluctant to put their teachings into written form. This theory might explain certain variations, but it does not account for the material common only to Matthew and Luke and not found in Mark. Oral tradition, furthermore, would not produce such minute and parenthetical identities of language; nor can it account for the peculiar selection of common material and the high degree of fixity in the order and content of the tradition.

The solution must be found in a documentary, rather than an oral, theory. It has been suggested that for the triple tradition (material common to all three gospels) there must have been a common earlier source, a complete gospel. This idea breaks down in the face of the double tradition, in which Matthew and Luke are identical to the extent of some two hundred verses of discourse, which are totally absent from Mark. If Mark had such a source, it is inconceivable that he would have deliberately eliminated practically all the teaching material (Sermon on the Mount) and confined his report to narrative. The same argument rules out the priority of Matthew as a common source for Mark and Luke.

On closer scrutiny, it is to be noticed that Mark is the shortest book of the three, having only sixteen chapters, as compared with twenty-four for Luke and twenty-eight for Matthew. Mark bears a primitive appearance; it is blunt, unpolished, and unedited and lacks doctrinal interpolations. It gives the impression of originality and firsthand familiarity with detail. Its directness and realism indicate priority; and the vivid, fresh description of events gives the reader the feeling that the author either was an eyewitness to the original scene or had been with someone who was. The reader of Mark cannot escape the conviction that here he is on more historical ground than in the other three gospels.

The priority of Mark is not mere conjecture; we have as further evidence an interesting and valuable extra-biblical testimony. Papias, the bishop of Hierapolis in Phrygia, in the first half of the second century writes as follows: " And the

presbyter said this also: ' Mark, who had been Peter's interpreter, wrote down accurately, not in the proper order however, all that he remembered of what had been said or done
by Christ.' For he did not hear the Lord nor did he follow
him, but later, as I have said, accompanied Peter, who gave
his instructions according to the needs, but paid no attention
to the exact order of the Lord's discourses. So that Mark
made no mistake when he wrote down some things from
memory, for he had but one thing in mind: neither to overlook any of the things he had heard nor to falsify any of
them." [14]

Here, then, is our evidence: the fact that the bulk of
Mark is reproduced in Matthew and Luke; the primitive appearance of Mark; the statement of Papias that Mark was
Peter's interpreter and wrote down his reminiscences; the fact
that Matthew and Luke can be reconstructed on the basis of
Mark, while the reverse does not hold; and the fact that where
Matthew and Luke write independently at the beginning and
at the end of their gospels they are different, but when they
follow Mark they coincide with that work in narrative material. In view of this evidence, we conclude that Mark must
have served as a written source for Matthew and Luke.

This conclusion solves the first half of our problem:
namely, the triple tradition (passages common to all three gospels). We still have to deal with the double tradition, in
which we find some two hundred verses of discourse material
identical in Matthew and Luke, none of which is in Mark.
This material consists of sayings of Jesus — Sermon on the
Mount, parables, and other discourses — which take a similar
form, sometimes identical, in Matthew and Luke. Such a
parallel can only point to a second documentary source for

[14] Papias' own work is not extant. The quotation is found in
Eusebius *Ecclesiastical History* iii. 39, 15.

Matthew and Luke. Here again we have a statement from Papias to the effect that " Matthew composed the Logia in the Hebrew language and everyone interpreted them as he was able." [15]

This leads to the second conclusion: Matthew and Luke were dependent upon a second written source, now lost, called the Logia or Q (from German *Quelle* or source). The double tradition (material common to Matthew and Luke) can be reconstructed by extracting the duplicated sayings in the two gospels. This is evidently the substance of the Logia collected by Matthew. The later edited Gospel of Matthew was probably named after this disciple.

We have thus arrived at the Two-Source theory, which is the solution of the Synoptic Problem almost universally accepted today. This hypothesis states, in short, that Matthew and Luke are dependent upon two documentary sources: the Gospel of Mark and a Greek translation of the Aramaic Logia of Matthew, the follower of Jesus.

This theory has been held by most scholars for some fifty years. It has been supplemented more recently by the Four-Source theory, which, boiled down to its essentials, merely means that Matthew and Luke each had, in addition to Mark and Q, a special source. A more detailed investigation of these two gospels reveals a small amount of material unique to each. For this there must have been a local or special source in which each found some data not available to the other. The source for material unique to Matthew is called M, and material found only in Luke is attributed to a hypothetical source L.[16] Tradition in Matthew and Luke relating to the birth and passion of Jesus could well come from these two

[15] *Ibid.* iii. 39, 16.
[16] See B. H. Streeter, *The Four Gospels: A Study in Origins* (London, 1930).

sources, as it is different in each. Streeter has suggested that
the final edition of Luke is a composite of Mark and an earlier
form of his own gospel based on the Logia and L. This earlier
edition is called Proto-Luke.

Recent research in some quarters tends to oppose the existence of Q as a source for Matthew and Luke and as identical with the Logia mentioned by Papias. According to these
critics, the assumption that Matthew and Luke wrote independently is unwarranted, as is the theory that the double tradition points necessarily to a second written source — Q. The
double tradition is solved, rather, by the dependence of Luke
upon Matthew, who wrote earlier.[17] Such a theory is suggested in Luke's preface, where he speaks of previous writers
who had " taken in hand to draw up a narrative " of the life
of Jesus.

One or two questions remain. Did Mark know the Logia? Much has been written on this question, but it seems
like an unreasonable assumption, for it is highly improbable
that if Mark had access to the teaching of Jesus he would deliberately omit from his gospel such important material. Another question relates to the so-called Proto-Mark or earlier
Mark. To account for the discrepancy between the more
polished form of Matthew and Luke in the triple tradition,
which is based on the cruder, blunter style of Mark, and also
to account for some narrative material in Matthew and Luke
that is not in Mark, it has been proposed that Matthew and
Luke had before them an earlier edition of Mark. This theory is somewhat superfluous, since these few discrepancies
could be explained by independent sources or independent
editing of the same source, presumably Mark.

[17] See Enslin, *op. cit.*, pp. 426 ff.

Characteristics of the Synoptics

Mark. Each Gospel has its own peculiarities and telltale characteristics. Mark, as Papias testified, was Peter's interpreter and set down the reminiscences of the apostle. From Colossians 4:19 we gather that Mark was Barnabas' cousin, and in I Peter 5:13 he is referred to as Peter's " son." He may have been Peter's first convert. As a Diaspora Jew and a bilinguist, Mark was qualified to serve as an interpreter. It is possible that out of his experience with Peter he compiled his gospel.

Mark's style is noticeably terse, direct, and realistic. The word " straightway," or " immediately," occurs again and again throughout the book. There is something fresh and robust about this book. It speaks the language of the people with no attempt at elegance or polish. The author is economical in his choice of words, hastening on from one dramatic scene to the next. He avoids the abstractions of theology and caters to no school. This realism argues for priority. Here we are closest to the historic and human personality of Jesus.

The Gospel of Mark has neither introduction nor conclusion. It opens with a brief description of the baptism of Jesus and closes abruptly with his death. There is great doubt as to the authenticity of the last twelve verses, which speak of Jesus' resurrection. They are not found in our two most ancient and most reliable manuscripts, Aleph and B, the Sinaitic Syriac version, most of the manuscripts known to Eusebius, and the copies used by Jerome. Furthermore, they reveal a different style from the foregoing material. For these reasons, Mark 16:9–20, spaced separately in the American Standard Version and the Revised Standard Version, is commonly thought to be a later addition to the gospel, influenced by the endings of Matthew and Luke. Other manuscripts have a different and shorter ending consisting of one verse, which also is universally considered to be a later addition to the original gospel.

There is much discussion, as with all the books of the New Testament, about the date of Mark, but 70 A.D. has been the most acceptable. Mark wrote chiefly for gentile readers; his theme was the growing hostility toward Jesus, culminating in his death. Some Latinisms in his style and the fact that he was with Paul in Rome suggest that the book was written there, but the evidence is not too conclusive.

Matthew. Matthew was a man of motive and method. His chief interest was to demonstrate to Jewish readers that Jesus was the Messiah and the fulfillment of the Old Testament Messianic hope. That was his theme, and he really worked it for more than it was worth, especially in his use of the proof-text technique. In support of his Messianic doctrine he quotes the Old Testament at every turn and frequently uses a verse completely out of context to illustrate the fulfillment of Old Testament prophecy in the life of Jesus.

The absurdity of the proof-text method is seen in Matthew 2:14, 15: "And he arose and took the child and his mother by night, and departed to Egypt, and remained there until the death of Herod. This was to fulfil what the Lord had spoken by the prophet: 'Out of Egypt have I called my son.'" The quotation is from Hosea 11:1 where the prophet (in the eighth century B.C.) is reminding the Hebrews of God's care for them throughout their history: "When Israel was a child, then I loved him and called my son out of Egypt." What Hosea was saying in retrospect (referring to the Exodus under Moses in 1225 B.C.), Matthew twists into the prediction of the birth of Jesus, an event that occurred eight centuries later!

Due to Matthew's single-mindedness as a proof-text editor, Christians from that day to this have labored under the delusion that the Old Testament was merely a preparation for and a prediction of Jesus. " This was done in order to fulfil what the Lord had spoken through the prophet " became for Matthew the key to practically everything that Jesus did.

The redeeming feature of Matthew's gospel is its structure: the teachings of Jesus are arranged to present a well-coordinated theme. Because of this systematic arrangement, chapters 5, 6, and 7 are usually referred to as the Sermon on the Mount. According to Matthew, Jesus, following his baptism and temptation, delivered, at the outset of his public ministry and in one address, practically all of his teachings. This is psychologically inconceivable. Are we to suppose that Jesus, an Oriental, delivered a long series of disconnected epigrams, all on one occasion and without parabolic expansion or extended interpretation? Proof that this did not take place is seen in the Gospel of Luke, where the same teachings are found scattered throughout the career of Jesus, as certainly they must have occurred. The phrase " Sermon on the Mount " therefore represents not a historical fact but an editorial assembling of the sayings of Jesus into a compact unit.

The ethical teaching of Jesus as arranged by Matthew in the Sermon on the Mount may be outlined as follows:

5:1–12: The Beatitudes, containing the qualifications for membership in the Kingdom of God.

12–16: The social responsibility of the followers of Jesus.

17–48: *Spirit versus Letter:* Jesus defines religion as principle rather than law. For the laws on murder, divorce, adultery, oaths, revenge, and hate he substitutes the principles of fraternal love, the family inviolate, chastity of mind, personal integrity, unselfishness, and universal good will.

6:1–18: *Form versus Reality:* Worship as internal experience rather than an ostentatious display.

19–34: *Things versus Values:* Dedication of self to the ends for which we live rather than the means by which we live.

7:1–12: *Self versus Others:* The Golden Rule of sympathetic understanding.

13–23: *Creed versus Conduct:* The inseparable connection between religion and morality. "By their fruits ye shall know them."

24–27: *Conclusion:* Jesus' authority as a teacher and critic, an authority based on the appeal to conscience, reason, and insight.

In addition to the Sermon on the Mount proper, there are several extraneous passages that are important both for their intrinsic message and for the light they shed on the growing conflict with the Pharisees.

9:14–17: *Quantity versus Quality:* Religion with Jesus was not just a patch on the garment of life but a new cloth, not a spoke in the wheel but the hub itself, the central motivating force of life; not a specific formula of things to do or believe but a basic attitude toward life, not a quantitative form but a qualitative force.

12:1–13: *Institutions versus Values:* The well-being of man is more important than sacerdotalism with its rigid laws. Man is of more value than the Sabbath.

15:1–20: *External Form versus Internal Feeling:* Dietary pre-
scriptions and ceremonial washings miss the heart
of religion. Moral defilement is more serious than
ceremonial defilement.

The " Sermon on the Mount " is followed by a similar
block of material depicting in climactic sequence the miraculous deeds of Jesus (chapters 8, 9). Apparently Matthew
wished to demonstrate to his Jewish readers that Jesus was a
miracle-worker. He has a tendency to accentuate the miraculous element as compared with his Markan source.

In addition to his systematic arrangement of the teachings of Jesus, the compiler of the book of Matthew also offers
an opportunity for us to observe the self-consciousness of
Jesus in his life-struggle. The interpretation of the career of
Jesus has always been, and still is, a controversial task, but,
looking at it from the vocational standpoint and allowing for
Matthew's typical oriental imagery, we can reconstruct from
the gospel several important days of decision in Jesus' life.
These provide the key to both his personality and his mission.

The first is *The Baptism* (Matt. 3; Luke 3:21, 22; Mark
1:9–11). This experience was the dedication of Jesus to his
lifework. It was here that he came into the full consciousness that he was to become a leader, a prophet, and that God
had chosen him for this task. This was followed by a period
of meditation and decision called *The Temptation* (Matt.
4:1–11; Mark 1:12, 13; Luke 4:1–13). Jesus had to decide at
the outset what *kind* of Messiah he would be. The popular
expectation of a political leader of the Jews was widespread
and rabid. He had only to indicate his desire to be such and
he would be proclaimed the fulfillment of all Jewish hopes.

The Temptation experience can be interpreted as a dramatic description of a great mental and moral struggle that

continued throughout his career. It was not simply an event in the beginning of his ministry, after which all was clear sailing, but, rather, a problem that he faced every day of his life. Should he fall in with the popular demand and capitalize on his powers for his own advancement (turn stones into bread)? Should he try to impress the people by signs and wonders (cast himself from the pinnacle of the temple)? Should he compromise with the nationalists and give them what they wanted (fall down and worship Satan)? His decision was to become the humble teacher, the suffering servant, and not the political Messiah.

Jesus had set his sails, determined his direction. Now, as he set about his mission, the feverish demands to lead a political movement swept upon him from all sides and especially from his own disciples, who really did not understand him. From time to time he went into seclusion to rethink his initial decision. One of these occasions was *The Transfiguration* (Matt. 17:1–13; Mark 9:2–13; Luke 9:28–36). Occurring midway in the ministry of Jesus, this experience can be considered the watershed of his career. Here Jesus meditates on his mission. Should he go on? Is it God's will that he pursue the course he has thus far taken? At this time he gets high enough above things to see them in proper perspective. He looks backward and sees the continuity between himself and the prophets in their moral reform. He takes stock of his own spiritual resources and receives greater power from God. He also sees more clearly into the future and determines to see it through in spite of possible violence and death.

The time comes when Jesus decides to go to Jerusalem, for only in that city could he hope to accomplish his ends. His entrance into the city is called *The Triumphal Entry* (Matt. 21:1–11; Mark 11:1–10; Luke 19:29–38). How triumphal it was is a moot question. Was Jesus the kind of

Messiah whom the people welcomed at the edge of the city? It may be that theirs was a mistaken celebration. Jesus rode into the city as a prophet and an unarmed teacher, not as the king of the Jews. The demonstration had no results. On the contrary, upon entering the city Jesus drove the money-changers from the temple, an act that precipitated his arrest. Perhaps Jesus permitted rather than enjoyed the celebration, for he knew that the people who welcomed him that day could easily demand his death on the next.

Jesus' final decision day was at *Gethsemane* (Matt. 26:36–46; Mark 14:13–42; Luke 22:40–46). Here, forsaken by his closest followers, he fights out his last great decision. Perhaps it is not necessary to die a death of violence in order to accomplish his mission. Perhaps there is some other way. " Let this cup pass from me. . . . Nevertheless thy will be done." His struggle with destiny reaches its climax, and he emerges triumphant.

The key to Jesus' character and his career is found in the continuity of his moral struggle from The Wilderness to The Garden. If Jesus had no choice and all was predetermined, these decisions are meaningless; but if Jesus' battle was fought on the human plane, we are here face to face with something that can be called moral divinity.

There is in this gospel a strong Judaistic element, which might represent a subsidiary source. It certainly stamps the compiler as a Jew, well versed in the Old Testament and writing with a particularistic point of view. Matthew's gospel is to be dated about 80 A.D.

Luke. Luke is a gentile writer, and his Greek approaches the classical style, whereas all the other books of the New Testament, with the exception of Hebrews, are written in a more colloquial form. From the preface to the end of the book, the reader is conscious of the literary touch, the hand of the artist. In style and arrangement of material, the author shows himself to be a finished writer and a man of fine sensitivity and taste. Luke is the schooled man. Renan called the Gospel of Luke " the most beautiful book ever written."

There are three references to Luke in the New Testament: Philemon 5:24, II Timothy 4:11, and Colossians 4:14. In the last passage he is referred to as Paul's physician. There is a certain amount of medical terminology in the book, but this point has been given undue emphasis as an argument for Lukan authorship. As a doctor, Luke defined salvation as health of mind and body and saw in the person of Jesus the Great Physician. He takes pains to show the kindness and grace of Jesus. He is interested in Jesus' association with women and children and with the poor. There is a tender sympathy here that is not found in the other gospels.

Because of the emphasis on social reform, Luke's book has been called the Social Gospel or the Gospel of Humanity. Here are found two of the greatest parables — the Good Samaritan and the Prodigal Son. The broad humanitarianism of Luke is reflected in his interpretation of Jesus' teachings and deeds. He defends the Samaritans and is pro-gentile in his sympathies. Jesus' mission, according to Luke, was to " preach good news to the poor, . . . proclaim release to the captives, the recovering of sight to the blind, and to set at liberty those who are oppressed. . . ."

Luke's theme of the value of man in the sight of God is reflected in his parables, which present the truth of the gospel more eloquently than abstract teachings.

15:11–24: *The Prodigal Son.* The overtones of this pearl of all parables reveal Jesus' philosophy of life. The pursuant love of God is limited by the will of man. God's attitude of love is constant, but man must turn of his own will to God. God's forgiveness is unconditional. Man creates his own destiny.

18:9–14: *The Pharisee and the Publican.* You get as you bring. The Pharisee brought conceit and perceived nothing from the service of worship. The publican brought humility and a receptive spirit and went home blessed.

10:25–37: *The Good Samaritan.* This story shows the subtlety of Jesus in suggesting that a Samaritan could be good. Here is the teaching that true neighborliness is not reciprocal or calculating but is unbounded and goes beyond the line of duty.

The Fourth Gospel

Considerable water passed over the dam, theologically, between the writing of the Synoptics and the Fourth Gospel. As the reader proceeds from the first three to the Fourth Gospel, he finds himself in another world. He is immediately struck by the difference in language, concepts, and viewpoint. Whereas the Synoptics place the ministry of Jesus mostly in Galilee, the Fourth Gospel places it in Jerusalem. The Synoptics attempt to describe the events in the life of Jesus in the order of their occurrence; the Fourth Gospel has no interest in chronology. In the Synoptics, the cleansing of the temple takes place at the end of Jesus' public ministry; in the Fourth Gospel it occurs at the outset of his career. The first three gospels picture Jesus as a friend of all kinds of people; he is popular, intimate, lovable. The Jesus of the Fourth Gospel has only a limited circle of friends, is completely aloof, and is personally opposed to certain groups, such as the Pharisees.

The miracles of the Synoptics are exaggerated and heightened in John. The atmosphere of the Synoptics is on the whole irenic; that of the Fourth Gospel is controversial. The dominant interest of the Synoptics is biographical; that of the Fourth Gospel is doctrinal. The Jesus of the Synoptics grows in his self-consciousness as Messiah; the Jesus of John is the same divine creature throughout, the Eternal Word, the Son of God. The sayings of Jesus in the Synoptics are short, practical, and ethical; in John they are lengthy, abstruse, and metaphysical. In the Synoptics, Jesus calls the people to faith in God; in John, he insists that they believe in him. In the Synoptics, Jesus is the man of Galilee; in the Fourth Gospel, he is part of the Godhead.

It is not to be supposed that Matthew, Mark, and Luke are without a theological interest; they do have the miraculous element, and they speak of Jesus as Lord. But the general contrast is none the less real. In passing from one tradition to the other, the reader can only ask himself: "Is this the same Jesus?" The explanation can only be that the author of the Fourth Gospel is writing at a much later date (100–110 A.D.) and in a different place and is profoundly affected by Greek speculative thought. That his interpretation of Jesus as the Word shows the influence of Philo needs no argument.[18]

Early Christian tradition connected the Fourth Gospel with the apostle John, son of Zebedee, but in view of the contrast between the Synoptics and the Johannine tradition, it is inconceivable that this gospel could have come from the Galilean fisherman. Rather, it is more likely to be the reflections of an Alexandrian philosopher, who was familiar with

[18] Philo was a Hellenistic Jewish philosopher of Alexandria (late first century B.C. and early first century A.D.) who tried to harmonize Greek philosophy with orthodox Jewish thought.

Philonic thought. That he was Jewish is not too clear, but it is pretty certain that he was not a resident of Palestine.

This gospel stands as the christological bridge between the apostolic following of Jesus as the Messiah (however that term may be interpreted) and the Nicene period, when deification was practically complete and Jesus was regarded, at least by the orthodox world, as the Son of God with cosmic significance.

Historically the Fourth Gospel is of doubtful worth. Doctrinally it has wielded more influence on Christendom than the Synoptics. Perhaps both traditions are valuable: Jesus, the ethical teacher, and Christ, a symbol of the Eternal.

3. History

Acts

There are three reasons for thinking that the author of Acts was Luke. The first argument is that of the Prologue: " In the first book, O Theophilus, I have dealt with all that Jesus began to do and to teach. . . ." What was this " first " or " former " book? Obviously, it was the Gospel of Luke, which was also addressed to Theophilus: " Inasmuch as many have undertaken to compile a narrative of the things which have been accomplished among us, just as they were delivered to us by those who from the beginning were eyewitnesses and ministers of the word, it seemed good to me also, having followed all things closely for some time past, to write an orderly account for you, most excellent Theophilus, that you may know the truth concerning the things of which you have been informed." It follows that both books are by the same man.

The second argument for Lukan authorship is that of the so-called "we-sections" of Acts. There are four passages, taken from the travel diary of the author, in which he abruptly changes from the third person plural to the first person plural (Acts 16:10, 17; 20:5–15; 21:1–18; 27:1–28:16). The author of Acts must have been with Paul at Troas and Philippi on his second campaign (16:10–17), accompanied Paul from Caesarea to Rome (chap. 27) and been with the apostle in Rome (chap. 28). The men who were with Paul in Rome were Mark, Epaphras, Luke, Aristarchus, Demas, and Jesus Justus. They are specifically mentioned in Colossians 4:10–14 and Philemon 23, 24.

The author must be chosen from one of these six men. It is fairly clear from Acts 27:2 that only two people were with Paul on the voyage to Rome; one was Aristarchus, and the other, the unnamed author of the narrative: "And embarking in a ship of Adramyttium, which was about to sail to the ports along the coast of Asia, we put to sea, accompanied by Aristarchus, a Macedonian from Thessalonica." Since the author mentions Aristarchus in the third person, we can be sure he is not the writer. The name of Mark can be eliminated because in Acts 15:39 we are told that Paul refused to take him on the second campaign. Epaphras, a resident of Colossae, was probably unknown to Paul until his third campaign in Ephesus. Demas and Jesus Justus can hardly be considered likely candidates for the authorship since they are minor figures and are not mentioned elsewhere in the New Testament. This leaves Luke as the only person who satisfies all the requirements.

The third argument for Lukan authorship of Acts is based on style. There are some words that are not found in other books and may thus be regarded as peculiar to Luke and

Acts. It has also been maintained that both Luke and Acts contain a certain amount of medical terminology, which would point to common authorship. Earlier critics like Harnack held to this argument, but more recently there has been a tendency to abandon it.

Some doubt has also been expressed regarding the worth of the "we-sections" as proof of Lukan authorship on the ground that the author shows too little knowledge of Paul's career to be a travel companion.[19] It is thought that too many important events mentioned in Paul's letters are glossed over or are unknown to the author to justify our thinking that he was a travel companion of Paul.

There is little dissent, however, from the argument of the Prologue, which clearly points to Luke as our author. The dating of the book varies from 80 to 100 A.D. It seems clear that it was Luke's intention in these two books to trace first the origin of the gospel in Jesus and second the propagation of the gospel throughout the Roman world. The speeches of Paul as recorded in Acts are, of course, reproduced in Luke's style and are not verbatim reports.

The Book of Acts is important because it describes the most critical period in Christian history — a period about which there is little information. Acts can be divided into two sections: chapters 1–8 describe the growth of Christianity in Palestine among Jews under the leadership of Peter; and chapters 9–28 describe the spread of Christianity throughout the Mediterranean world under the impetus of Paul. Considered as a whole, Acts is the story of the birth and early growth of the church, first as "The Way" or Nazarene sect, and then as gentile Christianity, taking root in all the great centers of the empire. The author seems intent on showing

[19] See Enslin, *op. cit.*, pp. 416 ff.

that the propagation of the gospel was accomplished without hindrance from the Romans.

Approximate chronology of the contents of Acts:

Crucifixion of Jesus	29/30
Conversion of Paul	35
First Visit to Jerusalem	38
Second Visit to Jerusalem	44
First Missionary Campaign	45–47
Council at Jerusalem	48
Second Campaign	49–52
Third Campaign	52–56
Imprisonment in Caesarea	56–58
Arrival in Rome	59
Death of Paul	64

4. Apocalypticism

Revelation

The Book of Revelation is the New Testament counterpart of Daniel, written against the background of the Roman domination. It must be interpreted in the light of the historical situation rather than as allegory, mystery, or prediction. The symbolic imagery of the book has let loose a flood of attempts in all ages to identify " the beast " with historic figures — Mohammed, the Pope, Napoleon, Kaiser Wilhelm II, and Hitler. The book has always been used to predict wars and to date the end of the world. As a typical apocalyptist, the author looks for the near approach in his time of the end of the world and the judgment. Since this world has succumbed to the powers of evil, there must be another world where the

Christian martyrs will come into their own. Nero's persecution of the Christians, followed by the more widespread persecution of the cruel Domitian, could only mean that God himself would strike by sending Christ as the avenger and judge. There will be a judgment day when the faithful will be separated from the unfaithful, after which Christ will rule for a thousand years.

The book was written to encourage the Christians to stand firm against emperor-worship and to be faithful unto death. Domitian's persecution extended to Asia Minor, where emperor-worship was strong. It was to the seven churches in this province that Revelation was addressed.

Tradition assigns Revelation, along with the Fourth Gospel and the Johannine Epistles, to John, the son of Zebedee, but the book can hardly have been written before the end of the century, certainly too late to be from the hand of the disciple. Furthermore, the style of the Fourth Gospel is too much at variance to fit the author of Revelation. There is no evidence on authorship in the book itself. All we can conclude with any assurance is that the author was a Jew who had lived at Ephesus and who was later exiled to the island of Patmos, where he wrote the Apocalypse. Internal evidence pointing to church conditions later than Paul's time, to the presence of Nicolaitanism and other heresies, and to the extended persecution of Domitian, which did not stop until his death in 96 A.D., indicates that the book must be dated at the end of the century.

Chapter Eight

Canonization of the New Testament

1. Reasons for a Second Bible

The Bible of the Christians in the first century was the Septuagint Old Testament, which included the Apocrypha. This was their canon of Scripture, and they gave no thought to the creation of another Bible. But by the end of the fourth century the Christian church had a New Testament that was equal to the Old in authority and inspiration. Our task in this chapter will be to trace the process by which the Christian literature of the first century achieved the status of sacred and authoritative canon.[1]

The twentieth-century Christian takes the New Testament for granted. It is hard for him to realize that there was a period when Christians had no New Testament and a still longer period when they had one but they did not know what books were, or should be, in it! The books of the New Testament were not written as Scripture and for a long time were not read as Scripture. The "occasional" or local and, at times, self-centered character of Paul's letters is proof that neither Paul nor his readers thought there was anything sacred about them. We must, therefore, go back first of all to the period before the New Testament was a fact and ask: Why a *New* Testament?

[1] For the definition of "canon" see p. 103; see also C. R. Gregory, *Canon and Text of the New Testament* (Edinburgh, 1908), pp. 15–20.

During the quarter-century following the death of Jesus, nothing seems to have been written about his ministry or teachings. One reason for this inactivity was the common expectation of the Parousia or second appearance of Jesus, which the Christians derived from the older Jewish hope of a Messiah. If the world was soon to end and Jesus was to return shortly, why write books? Why prepare for the future? Furthermore, with eyewitnesses on hand — people who had heard and seen Jesus — there was no need to put the oral tradition into written form. For a generation, at least, an "interim" spirit dominated the early church. Even in the New Testament books themselves, an anticipatory or unsettled frame of mind is evident.

The sayings of Jesus were preserved through this period in oral form. "Daily in the temple and in every house they ceased not to teach and to preach Jesus Christ" (Acts 5:42). The stories of Jesus and his teachings were circulated by word of mouth and became more or less crystallized. Continued oral repetition would tend to produce a uniformity, a tradition. This was the "oral gospel" that Paul received (I Cor. 15:3, 4; II Thess. 2:15).

By the time Paul wrote his letters, "the word of the Lord" had taken on, if not scriptural authority, certainly an importance equal to that of the Law and the Prophets. First Corinthians 7:10–12 provides a graphic illustration of the differentiation Paul made between the authority of Jesus and his own opinion: "To the married I give charge, not I, but the Lord, that the wife should not separate from her husband. . . . To the rest, I say, not the Lord, that if any brother has a wife who is an unbeliever. . . ." In the first instance Paul is careful to point out that he is fortunate enough to have the teaching of Jesus (Cf. Matt. 19:5), but on the second matter he is frank to admit that he is giving only his own views. It is therefore clear that for Paul the sayings of Jesus were sacred and authoritative. That Paul may have received some sayings of Jesus now lost is indicated in Acts 20:35: "In all things I have shown you that by so toiling one must help the weak, remembering the words of the Lord Jesus, how he said: 'It is more blessed to give than to receive.'" The point is further illustrated in I Timothy 5:18, where the writer actually refers to a saying of Jesus as "Scripture" (Matt. 10:10).

With the failure of the Parousia to materialize and, also, with the spread of Christian missions, there arose a more obvious need for written records. The Logia underwent a transformation from oral to written form and then possibly from Aramaic to Greek. Mark's gospel appeared next, followed a decade later by Matthew and Luke, and still later by the Fourth Gospel. Meanwhile, Paul's letters and the other New Testament books were in existence, but, while they preceded the gospels in point of composition, their authoritative status came afterward.

In view of the fact that the Jewish Scripture was the only Bible for the Christians of the first century, it is logical to ask: What were the motives leading to the creation of a *New* Testament? The primary reason, which we have just described, was the growing importance of the words of Jesus. The phrase "The Scriptures and the Lord" is indicative of the emerging authority of the teachings of Jesus in the middle of the first century. There was also, from the earliest days, a theological interest in the death and resurrection of Jesus as related to the plan of salvation. The original tradition of the gospel was later supplemented by the apostolic tradition. The letters of Paul were lost sight of in the generation immediately following the period of his writing. Mark, Matthew, and Luke, in fact, show no acquaintance whatever with the Pauline letters. However, the author of Revelation seems to have known them and to have been strongly influenced by the collection.

There were two other reasons for making a *New* Testament. Both are later developments. One was the natural desire for a document that would distinguish the new religion from the Jewish religion and from the current heresies. (The Old Testament canon also emerged in a time of crisis. Indeed, it would be safe to say that all canons arise in periods of crisis, along with the consolidation of the cult along doctrinal and organizational lines.) In the second century the Christian church was thrown into confusion by the presence of various sects or heresies — Montanism, Docetism, Marcionism, and Gnosticism — and a clarification of the basic Christian religion was imperative. Hence, the appeal to the books of the New Testament as authority. A political factor also hastened the process of canonization: the recognition of Christianity as the official religion of the Roman Empire was possible only when there was unanimity in regard to the Scripture as the authoritative doctrine.

The other basic reason for canonization was the need to distinguish between the spurious and the genuine, to separate orthodox books from the heterogeneous mass of literature, more or less Christian, that was accumulating in the last decade of the first and early decades of the second century.[2]

An analysis of these motives lying behind the creation of a New Covenant points unmistakably to two nuclei or criteria around which the emerging New Testament revolved: the

---

[2] See Adolf Harnack, *Origin of the New Testament* (New York, 1925), pp. 16 ff.

Lord and the Apostles. All the books of the New Testament, including Revelation, can be, and were, classified under these two heads. The first criterion pertained to anything by or about Jesus. That was logical enough, but how account for the second criterion, which referred to anything by or about an apostle? It is explained by the fact that the apostolic writings acquired value as attestation and support of the original tradition. Ultimately " tradition " and " attestation " were regarded as equally inspired or sacred.

Two determining factors in the process of canonization must be mentioned: one is automatic, and the other, arbitrary. Certain books were being used in the services of worship along with the Old Testament. These books were read, not because they were Scripture, but for purposes of edification. This fact gradually and automatically placed these books (especially the gospels) on a scriptural plane. The more deliberate process of canonization was the selection or citation by bishops and presbyters of certain accepted works as canonical. But the second process was simply a result of the first. Certain books won their place automatically by their own merit and apostolic character.

2. Evidence for the Existence of Books

From this point on, two processes must be differentiated. The first is the proof of the existence of books by reason of citations on the part of certain authorities. The second and more important process is the listing of books as actually canonical.

Evidence for the existence of some of the Pauline letters and Acts is first seen in Clement's Epistle to the Corinthians

(95 A.D.). Ignatius, bishop of Antioch (110 A.D.), in his seven epistles shows a familiarity with the gospels and is the first one definitely to mention a collection of Paulines. The Epistle of Barnabas (130 A.D.) mentions Romans, Ephesians, Colossians, and Hebrews. The Didaché (110 A.D.) uses Matthew and Luke, and Hermas (100 A.D.) mentions Mark. Polycarp, bishop of Smyrna (*ca.* 110 A.D.), refers to some of the Paulines and assumes that his readers in Asia and Macedonia know of Paul's letters.

Marcion (140 A.D.) was the first to arrange the Pauline letters systematically. His order was as follows: Galatians, I Corinthians, II Corinthians, Romans, I Thessalonians, II Thessalonians, Laodiceans (Ephesians?), Colossians, Philippians, and Philemon. Marcion represents a second stage in the evolution of a canon. He flatly rejected the Old Testament with its immature ideas of God and nationalistic messianism, and, since Paul had been, in his mind, at least, anti-Jewish, he regarded his ten letters, the "apostolicon," as the new Scripture. He added to these the Book of Luke, with certain editorial changes of his own, but ignored the other New Testament writings.

Marcion's revolutionary attitude forced the Christian world into a more serious evaluation of its writings. Certainly the church was immediately aroused to a greater respect for the ten Paulines. His neglect of the gospels and Acts spurred Irenaeus and others to come to their defense, and his polemical writing drove all conservative leaders to a more forthright position regarding the canon.

Justin Martyr (*ca.* 150 A.D.), in his *Apology for Christianity*, says that the gospels were read at church services along with the Old Testament, but Justin's comments cannot be used as testimony for the canonicity of the gospels. Justin also knew the Apocalypse of John, Acts, I Peter, and the Paulines. Tatian (*ca.* 160 A.D.) in his *Diatessaron* or *Book of the Four* wove the Four Gospels together, omitting duplications. The composite gospel (at first in Greek and later translated, in 170 A.D., into Syriac) became the official Bible, along with the Old Testament, for the Syriac church and remained so until 435 A.D.

The Apostolic Fathers make no mention of Philemon, II Peter, II and III John, and Jude. These books seem to have had no status whatever throughout the first two centuries. On the other hand, several books, which were ultimately omitted from the canon, were not only popular in the first two centuries but were actually included as canon in the best manuscripts. These books were the Didaché (*ca.* 100 A.D.), Epistle of Barnabas (*ca.* 130 A.D.), the Apocalypse of Peter (*ca.* 125 A.D.), the Shepherd of Hermas (100 A.D.), and I Clement (95 A.D.).

3. *The Second Period*

The period of Irenaeus, Clement of Alexandria, and Tertullian, extending roughly from 170 to 220, offers clearer evidence for canonicity as compared with the fragmentary literature of the earlier period.

Irenaeus (135–200 A.D.), bishop of Lyons, writing about 180 A.D., is a strong witness for the canonicity of the Four Gospels. His emphasis on the gospels can be seen as a reaction to Marcion, who practically ignored all of them but Luke. The present order of the Four Gospels, i.e., Matthew, Mark, Luke, and John, can be traced to Irenaeus. This order differed from that of the Western text, which interchanged

Mark and John. He recognized also as Scripture the following books: Acts, 12 Paulines (omitting Philemon and accepting the Pastorals), Apocalypse of John, I and II John, I Peter, and Hermas. He omitted from his list Hebrews, II Peter, II and III John, James, and Jude.

Clement (150–215 A.D.), bishop of Alexandria and head of the catechetical school of Alexandria, was equally emphatic in giving the Four Gospels unquestioned authority. In his *Stromateis* he is careful to distinguish the four from the Gospel of the Egyptians: " We do not find this saying in the four Gospels that have been handed down to us, but in that according to the Egyptians." [3] Clement's New Testament consisted of the Four Gospels, Acts, 12 Paulines, Hebrews, I and II John, I Peter, Jude, Apocalypse of John, Epistle of Clement, Epistle of Barnabus, Apocalypse of Peter, and Shepherd of Hermas. The last two books were accepted by Clement without question. He rejected Philemon, II Peter, III John, and James.

Tertullian (155–222 A.D.), presbyter of Carthage and founder of Latin Christianity, accepted all the books of the present New Testament except Hebrews, II Peter, II and III John, and James. Tertullian knew the Latin version and spoke critically of it as a poor translation.

The opinions of Irenaeus, Clement, and Tertullian on canonicity coincided with the Muratorian Fragment, which is the earliest extant list of canonical books. This document was found in 1740 by Ludovico Antonio Muratori in the Ambrosian Library of Milan. It is usually dated about 195 A.D. and probably comes from the hand of Victor, bishop of Rome. It represents the official usage of the Roman church in the last quarter of the second century. The opening para-

[3] *Stromateis*, Bk. 3: Ch. 13.

graph is mutilated and lacks the names of Matthew and Mark, but the document must have begun with their citation as the first and second gospels, for the torn piece says that " the Gospel of St. Luke, the physician and companion of Paul, stands third." This is followed by mention of the Fourth Gospel. The Muratorian list is as follows: the Four Gospels, Acts, 13 Paulines, Jude, I and II John, Apocalypse of John, Apocalypse of Peter, and Wisdom of Solomon. It omitted Hebrews, James, I and II Peter, and III John. It qualifies the inclusion of Philemon and the Pastorals, and mentions Paul's letter to the Laodiceans and " several others which cannot be received in the Catholic Church." An additional note informs us that some church leaders were not willing to have the Apocalypse of John and the Apocalypse of Peter read in the church.

Thus far we have gathered authoritative statements from four important areas of the Christian world: Gaul, Egypt, Africa, and Italy. On the basis of this information we are now prepared to summarize the situation at the end of the second century. By 200 A.D. the following books were universally accepted as canonical: Matthew, Mark, Luke, John, Acts, 10 Epistles of Paul, Apocalypse of John, I John, and I Peter.[4] The following can be considered borderline books, with most authorities rejecting the first six and accepting the last four: James, II Peter, II and III John, Jude, Hebrews, Epistle of Clement, Barnabas, Hermas, and Apocalypse of Peter.[5]

[4] The Apocalypse of John was rejected by the Greek and Syriac churches until the fifth century.

[5] The Didaché (110 A.D.) was used by Clement of Alexandria and by Origen and was accepted in Egypt.

4. The Closing Period

The closing period of the canon (200–400 A.D.) sees the gradual acceptance of books that until this time were on the borderline — James, II Peter, II and III John, Jude, Hebrews, and Apocalypse of John — and the rejection, generally, of such works as Barnabas, Hermas, Didaché, the Apocalypse of Peter, and I and II Clement. It must be borne in mind, however, that Barnabas, Hermas, and possibly the Didaché were included in *Codex Sinaiticus* and I Clement in *Codex Alexandrinus*.

The first authority in this period is Origen, the great Christian teacher of Alexandria and later of Caesarea. Origen indicated three groupings: (1) undisputed books: the Four Gospels, Acts, Apocalypse of John, I John, I Peter, 13 Epistles of Paul, and Hebrews; (2) doubtful or disputed books: II Peter, II and III John, Jude, James, Barnabas, Hermas, Didaché, and the Gospel According to the Hebrews; (3) false books: Gospel According to the Egyptians, Gospel of Basilides, Gospel of the Twelve, Gospel of Thomas, etc. Tertullian regarded Hebrews as unscriptural and inferior to the rest of the New Testament, whereas Origen thought more highly of it.

It is surprising that Origen accepted the Apocalypse of John without qualification, for, although it was popular in Africa and the West, it was generally rejected in the East. Dionysius, his pupil and successor as head of the Alexandrian school, took a cautious view, following the general opinion rather than what seemed to be his own, more critical view. He writes: " But I should not dare to reject the book since many of the brethren hold it with zeal, and I accept as greater than my consideration of the book the general opinion about it."

Cyprian (200–258 A.D.), the influential bishop of Carthage, completely ignores James, II Peter, II and III John, Jude, and Hebrews but often quotes Revelation. Lucian (d. 312 A.D.), founder of the Antiochian school, devoted most of his career to the study of the text of the Old and New Testaments. His edition of the New Testament probably had much to do with determining the text of the best Greek manuscripts. His canonical list excluded Revelation, II Peter, II and III John, and Jude.

Eusebius of Caesarea (230–340 A.D.) was the intellectual child of Origen and, as such, followed his master in his threefold grouping, which, in view of his wide knowledge of the church in many areas, can be considered definitive for the first part of the fourth century. In his *Ecclesiastical History* he recognized the Four Gospels, Acts, 13 Epistles of Paul, I John, I Peter, and Apocalypse of John. The " disputed books " included James, Jude, II Peter, and II and III John. A second list of disputed but more " spurious books " included Acts of Paul, Hermas, Apocalypse of Peter, Barnabas, and the Didaché. He has a special note to the effect that the Apocalypse of John ought to be included in the spurious list " as some reject it, while others think it ought to be accepted." No mention is made of Hebrews. He adds a final list of " heretical books," including the gospels of Peter, Thomas, and Matthaias, and the Acts of Andrew, John, and others. The important thing about the list of Eusebius — and the same holds true with that of Origen — is that it represents not just his point of view but a consensus of the whole church, as far as he can ascertain the facts.

As far as the third and the first half of the fourth century are concerned, we have seen that there is little change in the position of the " doubtful books." Turning now to Athanasius (293–373 A.D.), bishop of Alexandria, we find a decided change. In his *Easter Letter*, written in 367 A.D., he issues an authoritative list of canonical books, which is the same as our present New Testament. Not until the time of Athanasius were James, II Peter, II and III John, Jude, Hebrews, and the Apocalypse of John unequivocally accepted as canon and Barnabas, Hermas, the Didaché, I Clement, and Apocalypse of Peter rejected. The latter books, plus some apocryphal gospels, were popular with the Egyptian Christians. It was the purpose of Athanasius to make a clear-cut distinction between the twenty-seven canonical books and the apocryphal ones. " In these alone," he writes, " is proclaimed the good news of the teaching of true religion. Let no one add to them nor remove anything from them." He does recommend the reading of the Didaché and Hermas by catechumens, but ultimately they, too, gave way to the exclusive use of the canonical works.

The Athanasian canon coincides with Jerome's New Testament as translated in the Vulgate, which became normative for the Western church. The councils of Laodicea (363 A.D.), Hippo (393 A.D.), and Carthage (397 A.D.), after considerable disagreement on some books, ratified the canon of twenty-seven books. The decree of the Council of Carthage (attended by Augustine) stated that " none except canonical writings are to be read in church under the title of divine Scripture." These councils, however, are not to be taken too seriously in the matter of the canon; they merely ratified a process that had already reached its consummation among the churches.

This virtually settled the question, at least for the West.

In the East there was less agreement. The canon of the Assyrian church, influenced by Tatian (172 A.D.), was for a long period confined to "the Gospel" (Tatian's *Diatessaron* — a synthesis of the Four Gospels or a weaving together of the four, omitting duplicating material), the Pauline Epistles, and Acts. This condition existed until Rabbula, bishop of Edessa, in 435 A.D. adopted the Antiochian canon of twenty-two books (II Peter, II and III John, and Jude were omitted). The Syriac church had from the earliest years excluded the Apocalypse and the Catholic Epistles. The Apocalypse, in fact, was not generally accepted in the Eastern church until after the fifth century. A Syriac New Testament of 508 includes it, and editions of the New Testament appearing in Asia Minor and Jerusalem likewise include it as canonical. The reluctance of the Greek church to accept the Apocalypse was balanced by the slowness of the African and Western churches to accept Hebrews.[6]

A thousand years elapsed before the discussion of the canon was resumed. With the coming of the Protestant Reformation in the first half of the sixteenth century, biblical research received a new impetus, the subjective or individual interpretation of Scripture became paramount, and Greek replaced Latin as the language of biblical scholarship. The result of all this was that the previously "disputed" books came in for fresh criticism. Luther questioned Hebrews, rejected the Apocalypse as unworthy of canonicity, called James an "epistle of straw," and rejected Jude. Erasmus questioned Hebrews and Revelation. Calvin and Zwingli regarded the Apocalypse as unbiblical.

As a necessary attempt to recover from the blow of the

---

[6] The Apocalypse of John is not used today in the liturgy or lessons of the Greek church.

Reformation, the Roman Catholic Church held the Council of Trent (1546), at which time, more as a countermove against Protestantism than as an objective definition of the canon, the Roman church ratified once and for all the twenty-seven books of the canonical New Testament and pronounced anathema upon anyone who " does not receive the entire books with all their parts as they are accustomed to be read in the Catholic Church."

And so the matter stands. For both Protestant and Catholic churches the canon as fixed in the fourth century has remained — and probably will remain — unchanged regardless of individual reservations or privately edited Bibles that omit certain sections.

Chapter Nine

Extracanonical Literature of the New Testament

1. The Apostolic Fathers

Most important by far among all the noncanonical Christian writings is a list of books called the Apostolic Fathers. Their importance is attested by the inclusion of at least some of them in several canonical lists of the third and fourth centuries. But they are also valuable because of their antiquity, their use in the public services of worship in the early Christian church, and their content.

While these books were known and used by early Christians, they were not grouped under the title of Apostolic Fathers until the seventeenth century. They were first published as a collection in 1672 by Cotelier, who included Barnabas, Hermas, Clement, Ignatius, and Polycarp. As manuscripts were discovered in the nineteenth century, the list was enlarged to include the Didaché, Papias, Quadratus, and Diognetus.[1]

The study of early Christian literature would be incomplete without at least an introduction to these writings which were so closely interwoven with the New Testament books

---

[1] Some of the modern editors of the Apostolic Fathers are Harnack, Zahn, Kunk, Lightfoot-Harmer, Lake (Loeb Classical Library), and Bonner. For an excellent translation, the reader is referred to E. J. Goodspeed, *The Apostolic Fathers: An American Translation* (Chicago, 1950).

themselves. Most of them represent the authentic correspondence of early Christian leaders in the age following the
apostles and are much more worthy than the apocryphal Gospels, Acts, Letters, and Apocalypses, which we shall discuss
later.

The Letters of Clement

First and Second Clement came to light, at least in the
Western world, when the Patriarch of Constantinople in
1628 presented the king of England with the famous fifth-
century manuscript, *Codex Alexandrinus*, which contained
these two early Christian documents. A complete Greek text
of I Clement in a manuscript dated 1056 was discovered by
Bryennius in 1873 in Constantinople and was subsequently
published by him. Since that time, Syriac, Latin, and Coptic
manuscripts have been found.

The First Letter of Clement to the Corinthians, from the
standpoint of date and inclusion in early canonical lists, comes
about as close to being an authentic New Testament book as
any other piece of literature not included in the accepted
twenty-seven books. Clement of Alexandria (*ca.* 200 A.D.)
includes I Clement as Scripture, and a twelfth-century Har-
clean Syriac version contains First and Second Clement as integral parts of the New Testament. It was written about
95 A.D. from the church at Rome to the church at Corinth as
a rebuke to the Corinthians for their lack of respect for
church officers, particularly the elders. While the author is
not named, it is usually considered to be from the hand of
Clement, bishop of Rome (88–97 A.D.). Eusebius in his *Ecclesiastical History* confirms Clement's authorship. Clement
shows familiarity with the then recently collected letters of
Paul and with Hebrews, but does not mention the gospels.

This letter, in fact, contains the first actual quotation of Paul's letters.

First Clement is reminiscent of I Peter and the Paulines in its instruction and counsel and is typical of that first form of Christian literature to come into existence — the letter. The author strongly condemns the rebellious spirit of the Corinthians toward their officers and reminds them of the humility of Christ. The authoritarian character of the letter may indicate the already growing importance of the Roman church. At least, it arrogated to itself the duty of instructing the church in Corinth. "Because of the sudden and repeated misfortunes and calamities that have befallen us," Clement writes, "we think we have been very slow in giving attention to the matters that are being discussed among you and to the foul and impious uprising, so alien and foreign to God's chosen people, which a few headstrong and wilful men have kindled to such a frenzy that your good name, respected and renowned and universally beloved, has come to be greatly reviled. . . ." [2]

In passages where the author admonishes his readers to have patience in suffering, he is noticeably influenced by I Peter: "It is right and proper then, brethren, for us to be obedient to God rather than to follow those who in arrogance and disorder are the instigators of detestable jealousy. It is right therefore that we should not be deserters from what God wills." In his reference to Christ as High Priest, Clement clearly reflects the Book of Hebrews: "This is the way, dear friends, by which we find our salvation, Jesus Christ, the High Priest of our offerings, the protector and helper of our weakness."

The letter designated as II Clement is more likely from

[2] 1:2 (Goodspeed's translation).

the pen of Soter, bishop of Rome (166–174 A.D.). This fact is confirmed by Eusebius in his *Ecclesiastical History*, where he quotes Dionysius, bishop of Corinth, in his reply to Soter. Since it was sent from Rome to Corinth, it was later attached to the letter of Clement. Unlike I Clement, this letter shows a familiarity with the Four Gospels and some apocryphal gospels. It urges the Corinthians to repent of their sins and " serve God with a pure heart."

The Letters of Ignatius

In the first quarter of the second century, Asia Minor, particularly the environs of Ephesus, was the scene of much literary activity. From this great Christian center came some of the Johannine literature, the collection of Pauline letters, and the first collection of the Four Gospels. This region was also the scene of the writing of the seven letters of Ignatius.

The circumstances can be reconstructed from the letters themselves. Ignatius, the bishop of Antioch, had been condemned to death, and now, in the charge of ten imperial guards, was being conducted to Rome to be thrown to the lions in the Colosseum. En route at Smyrna and Troas, Ignatius wrote these short but significant letters to the churches at Ephesus, Magnesia, Tralles, Rome, Philadelphia, and Smyrna, and to Polycarp, bishop of Smyrna. He either had passed through or had met delegations from these churches.

The fact that he apparently wrote nothing before or after — at least nothing that has survived — might indicate that this sudden outburst was the result of the urging of the two bishops, Polycarp of Smyrna and Onesimus of Ephesus, who were anxious that he help them combat heresy in Asia Minor. This is borne out by the fact that Polycarp later recommends the Ignatian Epistles in his letter to the Philippians and also by the rapidity with which all seven letters were publicized as a collection by the bishops.

The letters to Ephesus, Magnesia, Tralles, and Rome were written from Smyrna, where Ignatius had been joined by an Ephesian deacon named Burrhus who served him and accompanied him to Troas, where he wrote the other three letters.

The Ignatian letters are valuable as the first description in Christian literature of Docetism. This heresy maintained that since Christ was divine he could not have had a material body but only one that seemed real.[3] This view stemmed from a dualistic view that regarded the body — or any other material substance — as evil. The suffering of Jesus, therefore, was, in the mind of Docetists, not real but an appearance or semblance of suffering. In warning his readers against any schismatic tendency, Ignatius tells them to keep in line and obey their superiors. It is surprising to find such a strong ecclesiastical emphasis in a representative of the Eastern church — an emphasis that anticipates the hierarchical organization of a century later. "Flee from divisions and false teachings," he writes to the Philadelphians, "follow like sheep where the pastor is. . . . Obey the bishop, the elders, and the deacons. . . . Do nothing without the bishop."

A warm personal note also runs through these letters. The letter to the Ephesians is strangely reminiscent in style and content of Paul's letter to Philemon: "And Crocus too, who is worthy of God and of you, in whom I have received an example of your love, has refreshed me in every way. . . . May I have profit of you always. I do not order you as though I were somebody. For though I am in chains for the name, I am not yet perfect in Jesus Christ."[4]

---

[3] Greek, δοκεῖν, to seem.
[4] Goodspeed's translation, *op. cit.*, p. 207 ff.

The Didaché

In the middle of the second century of the Christian Era there appeared a manual of instruction called the Didaché or the Teaching of the Twelve Apostles. This little book became so well thought of that it was regarded by many later authorities as Scripture, or at least as one of " the disputed books." Its popularity probably accounts for its disappearance from view, as it became the nucleus for the more extensive works of the *Apostolic Church Ordinances* and *The Apostolic Constitutions,* which carry most of its content.

So the Didaché was lost sight of until 1875, when Bryennius discovered an eleventh-century manuscript containing the complete Greek text along with the Synopsis of the Scripture by Chrysostom, the Epistle of Barnabas, the two Epistles of Clement, and the Ignatian letters. Bryennius edited the Didaché in 1883. Since that time two Greek fragments and a Coptic fragment have been found.

The Didaché in turn is an expansion of an earlier form called the Doctrina. No Greek manuscript of this original source exists; hence, the title from the Latin recension of the Teaching. It contained about half of the Didaché and dates from about 100 A.D.

The Didaché is divided into two parts, the first of which is called " The Two Ways." The metaphor of " the two ways " is truly biblical and is found frequently in the Old Testament. Jeremiah 21:8, for instance, reads: " Thus sayeth the Lord: ' Behold I set before you the Way of Life and the Way of Death.' " The Psalms and the Proverbs speak of " The Way of the Wicked " and " The Way of Death." The New Testament abounds in references to " The More Excellent Way," " The Way of Wisdom," " The Way of

Peace," and " The Way of Righteousness." [5] The earliest followers of Jesus were called " those of the Way " (Acts 9:2). Christianity was a way of life. It was not until Paul had established Antioch as his headquarters that the Nazarenes or " followers of the Way " were called Christians (Acts 11:26). The material on " the two ways " shows further similarity to Hermas and Barnabas but is primarily dependent upon the earlier Doctrina.

The list of sins in the description of the Way of Death recalls Paul's letters, especially Romans:

Two ways there are: one of life and one of death, but there is a great difference between the two ways, The way of life, then, is this: First, thou shalt love God who made thee; second, thy neighbor as thyself, and all things whatsoever thou wouldst not have befall thee, do not to another. Now of these words, the teaching is this: Bless them that curse you, and pray for your enemies, for what thanks have ye if ye love them that love you? But love them that hate you and ye shall have no enemy. Abstain from fleshly and worldly lusts. If anyone give thee a blow on thy right cheek, turn to him the other also; if anyone compel thee to go one mile, go with him two. To everyone that asketh thee, give, and ask not back; for to all the Father desires to give of his own gracious gifts.

My child, flee from every evil thing, and from everything like it. Be not inclined to anger, for anger leadeth to murder; nor jealous or contentious, nor passionate. My child, become not a liar, nor avaricious, nor presumptuous, nor evil-minded, for of all these things blasphemies are begotten. Become long-suffering and gentle and good. Thou shalt not exalt thyself, but with the righteous and lowly thou shalt dwell.

Now the way of Death is this: first of all, it is evil and full of curse: murders, adulteries, lusts, thefts, idolatries, sorcery, false

[5] See also Deut. 30:15, 19; Matt. 7:13, 14. Cf. p. 79 on the Dead Sea Scrolls.

testimonies, hypocrisy, craft, arrogance, greed, hating truth and loving falsehood, loving vanity, pursuing revenge. May ye be delivered, children, from these.

These are the two ways: see that no one lead thee away from the teaching of the Lord.[6]

The author of the Didaché, probably a Jewish Christian, shows a strict reliance on the Gospel of Matthew, which he quotes verbatim in the Lord's Prayer (Didaché, chap. 8).

The second part of the Didaché (chaps. 7–16) consists of ecclesiastical regulations regarding baptism, the Eucharist, worship, and church organization. These regulations composed a manual for the instruction of catechumens preliminary to baptism and for Christian converts in general. The book is all the more interesting, coming from a period before any set rules were officially recognized by the church.

Some of these procedures are worth quoting:

Concerning baptism, thus baptize ye: having first declared all these things, baptize into the name of the Father, and of the Son, and of the Holy Spirit, in living water (running water). But if thou hast not living water, baptize in other water, and if thou canst not in cold, then in warm, but if thou hast neither, pour water three times upon the head. . . .

And concerning the Eucharist, thus give thanks. First, concerning the cup: " We thank thee, our Father, for the holy wine of David, thy servant, which thou didst make known to us through Jesus, thy servant. Glory be to thee for ever." And concerning the broken bread: " We thank thee, our Father, for the life and knowledge, which thou didst make known to us through Jesus, thy servant. Glory be to thee for ever. . . ."[7]

---

[6] Selections from chaps. 1–6. (Selections from the Didaché and other extracanonical writings are the author's translation.)

[7] Selections from chaps. 7 and 9. Note that the Eucharist follows the Lukan order: wine and bread.

Reference is also made to the appointment of bishops and deacons along with prophets and teachers. It can truly be said that no extracanonical work is more important than the Didaché, containing, as it does, the first reproduction of Jesus' teachings outside the New Testament, the first instructions on the Sacraments, and early church procedures.

The Shepherd of Hermas

In the Shepherd of Hermas (100–110 A.D.) we encounter a still different literary form — a revelation or vision. Hermas was undoubtedly familiar with the Apocalypse of John but shows little or no dependence upon the Johannine work. It has more in common with Hebrews in its concern with repentance.

The Book of Hermas, the longest of all the Apostolic writings, is a series of visions, in some of which the author converses with an angel disguised as a shepherd. In using the figure of a shepherd, Hermas could have been influenced by any number of sources, such as Hebrews, I Peter, or Ephesians, where Christ or some Christian leader was spoken of as a shepherd. This shepherd issues various commands that epitomize the good life of repentance:

First of all, believe that God is one, and he created all things, and organized them and out of what did not exist made all things to be, and contains all things, but alone is himself uncontained. . . . Be sincere and simple-minded, and you will be like little children, who do not know the wickedness that destroys the life of men. Speak evil of no one, and do not enjoy hearing anyone do so. . . . Love truth and let nothing but truth proceed from your mouth, so that the spirit which God made to dwell in this flesh may be found truthful in the sight of all men. . . . Be patient and understanding and you will prevail over all evil actions and do all upright.[8]

[8] From chap. 1, Commands. 1–5.

The Shepherd of Hermas received wide circulation and was included in the canonical lists of Clement of Alexandria and Origen and also in the *Codex Sinaiticus*. Numerous late Greek fragments have been found, but it has come down to us chiefly in its Latin form. There is also an Ethiopic version, indicating its popularity in Egypt and Abyssinia. A third-century papyrus of Hermas was found in 1922 and was later edited as the Michigan Papyrus.

The Epistle of Barnabas

The Epistle of Barnabas is important as an example of the early growth of the allegorical interpretation of Scripture. Barnabas was written about 125 A.D. in Alexandria, where the allegorical method had found earlier expression in Philo. As applied to the Old Testament, the allegorical system of Barnabas held that the Jewish Scripture was not to be taken literally but only figuratively and was not an end in itself but merely a prediction of the New Testament, Christianity, and Christ. This seems to have been a favorite method of Jewish-Christian writers who were appealing to a Jewish audience.

With chapter 18 the content and method of writing undergo an abrupt change. From allegory the author shifts to a series of commandments defining the Christian life. This section is clearly dependent upon an earlier form of the Doctrina or the Didaché, as it describes the Way of Life and the Way of Darkness. This indicates that the present Barnabas is made up of two previous forms. In fact, the two parts have been found in separate Latin recensions.

Both *Codex Sinaiticus* and the Bryennius manuscript found at Constantinople contained the complete Greek text of Barnabas. Clement of Alexandria included it in his New Testament, as did Origen, with some reservations.

Other Apostolic Writings

The remaining apostolic literature consists of a few short documents, one of which is the *Letter of Polycarp to the Philippians*. This is to be read in connection with the Ignatian letters. After Ignatius had left Philippi en route to Rome. the Philippians sent word to Polycarp, bishop of Smyrna, requesting that he send them the letters of Ignatius that he held. This he did and accompanied them by his own letter:

The letters of Ignatius that were sent us by him and the others that we had in our possession we send you as you instructed us to do; they are appended to this letter, and you will be able to derive great benefit from them. For they embrace faith, steadfastness, and all the edification that pertains to our Lord. And if you learn anything definite about Ignatius himself and those who are with him, let us know.

Polycarp's letter contains the usual ethical admonitions. His admiration for Paul is clearly evident in several passages:

I write you this, brethren, not taking it upon myself, but you first invited me to. For neither I nor anyone else can follow the wisdom of the blessed and glorious Paul, who when he was among you, face to face with the men of that time, carefully and steadfastly uttered his teachings about truth, and when he was absent wrote you letters, by poring over which you will be able to build yourselves up in the faith that has been given to you.

The Martyrdom of Polycarp is an ecclesiastical letter describing in detail the death of Polycarp in the arena at Smyrna about 156 A.D. Although it was written by representatives of the church at Smyrna and sent to the church at Philmelium, it was given a much wider circulation and became the prototype of a specific form of literature called martyrology. Polycarp had been in Rome conferring with the Roman

bishop Anicetus about the Easter controversy. Upon his return to Smyrna, he was arrested and put to death by stabbing
and burning. This document and the martyr literature that
followed served to encourage the early Christians under persecution. The letter is preserved in Eusebius' *Ecclesiastical
History*, and there are several Greek and Latin manuscripts.
Much of our information about Polycarp comes originally
from the writings of Irenaeus.

Another valuable series of fragments collected by Eusebius is that of Papias, bishop of Hierapolis. In his book, *Interpretations of the Lord's Sayings* (125–150 A.D.), Papias recorded his interviews with prominent people who served as
connecting links with the apostles.[9] (Papias is quoted by
many Christian writers before 1000 A.D.)

Other apostolic writings include the *Letter to Diognetus*,
a piece of apologetic literature from the third century, and
the *Apology of Quadratus*, a defense of Christianity by a
second-century Christian philosopher.

2. *The Apocryphal New Testament*

Further removed from the New Testament proper, both
in canonical status and in value as Christian literature, is the
vast collection known as the New Testament Apocrypha.

The New Testament books survived as canon by virtue
of their intrinsic worth. By the same token the apocryphal
books lost out and ultimately disappeared from view because
they had neither religious appeal nor historical value. On the
whole, they represent an accumulation of legendary tradition

---

[9] See pp. 165–167 for Papias' account of the writing of Mark and
the Logia.

in the form of gospels, acts, letters, and apocalypses and lack the ring of authenticity found in the Synoptic Gospels and Paul. Many of them are lost and can only be partially reconstructed from citations.[10] Mythology, of course, has its value in recording the ideas, the fears, the imaginations, the superstitions, and the theology of a people. That the age after the apostles produced an abundance of tradition unworthy of the name of Jesus or his disciples is well borne out by a perusal of some of this literature.

As with the Old Testament Apocrypha and also some of the later canonical works, many second- and third-century Christian writings were issued under older and more venerable names. This was done in order to gain more respect for those books and to give them the appearance of antiquity. Fortunately, through the work of Jerome and others the spurious character of these works was recognized. Their false or questionable nature is here pointed out in order to differentiate them from the writings of the Apostolic Fathers, which are certainly in another class.

Foremost among the New Testament Apocrypha are several gospels that have little to add to the content of the canonical gospels and that definitely are lacking in historical value. Of these the two most important are the *Gospel According to the Hebrews* and the *Gospel According to the Egyptians*. The *Gospel According to the Hebrews* was written about 125 A.D. and was popular among Jewish Christians in Egypt. Jerome had an Aramaic version of it, but its original form was probably Greek. No copy of it exists today; our only knowledge of it is from quotations by Origen, Clement of Alexandria, Eusebius, Jerome, and others. The author is

---

[10] The standard work in this field is M. R. James, *The Apocryphal New Testament* (Oxford, 1924).

obviously dependent upon the Gospel of Matthew, which he amplifies in places. In fact, the Aramaic recension of the *Gospel According to the Hebrews* has often been confused with the Aramaic original of Matthew.

It is highly probable that the *Oxyrhynchus Sayings of Jesus* are based on this gospel. Wherever there is additional or different material as compared with Matthew it borders on the grotesque, as is the case with all apocryphal literature. In the third century it is usually referred to as one of the questionable or false books, and by the fourth century it was virtually unknown.

The *Gospel According to the Egyptians* (*ca.* 130 A.D.) was used by gentile Christians in Egypt. Like its companion gospel, this was written in Greek and is preserved only through quotations by Clement of Alexandria and Origen, according to whom it was used by the Encratites, an ascetic sect in Egypt. Hippolytus and Epiphanius classified it as heresy.

The *Gospel of Peter* (*ca.* 130 A.D.) was written by an unknown author who hoped to gain more prestige for the book by the use of the apostle's name. It interprets the passion of Jesus from the standpoint of Docetism, a heresy that was attacked by the Fourth Gospel, the letters of John, and the Ignatian Epistles. A fragment of this gospel was discovered in Egypt in 1886, prior to which time our only knowledge of it came through patristic citation.

Gnosticism, another heresy of the second century, found expression in the *Gospel of Thomas*.[11] The author of this gospel retold the story of Jesus' childhood from the Gnostic point of view. Reading this gospel with its grotesque miracles that are attributed to the child Jesus, one can readily under-

[11] For Gnosticism, see p. 152.

stand why the word " apocrypha " came to be associated with the words " unworthy " and " spurious."

The apocryphal literature seems to be an amplification or extension of the chief literary forms of the canonical New Testament — the gospel, the letter, the acts, and the revelation. We have described briefly a few of the apocryphal gospels, all of which were imitations in the noncanonical literature of the second and third centuries.

In attempting to supply what purported to be information about individuals and movements mentioned in the canonical *Acts*, the later works took a fictional form and have provided not a little source material for twentieth-century novels. One of these apocryphal books is the *Acts of Paul* (*ca.* 160 A.D.), written, according to Tertullian, by a presbyter of Asia. Our chief evidence for the existence of this book is a mutilated Coptic manuscript of the sixth century and a recently discovered Greek papyrus from about 300 A.D. A section called " The Acts of Paul and Thecla " describes Paul's ministry at Iconium and his conversion of a Greek girl named Thecla, who becomes a strong Christian, is thrown to the lions, escapes, and subsequently becomes a teacher. Contrary to Paul's attitude in the New Testament, he here approves of women teaching and holding office. The story continues with incidents in Paul's later career at Myra, Perga, and Ephesus, where he is thrown to the lions, one of which was " let loose upon him, and it ran to him in the stadium, and lay down at his feet."

Following the *Acts of Paul*, another book appeared called the *Acts of John*, written by a Docetist about 160 A.D. The beginning of this book, dealing probably with the banishment of John to Patmos, is lost. The remainder, as found in a late Greek text (edited by Bonnet, 1898), tells of John's journey to Rome to appear before Domitian, who had heard of his preaching in Ephesus. The whole story is inelegant, crude, and, at times, offensive.

As might be expected, the Acts literature would not be complete without a similar book on Peter. The *Acts of Peter* (*ca.* 210 A.D.), modeled after the *Acts of John*, has been recovered in Coptic, Greek, and Latin manuscripts. This fictional biography of the apostle is typical of all apocryhal books in its trivial and grotesque quality and is the source of many later traditions such as the famous "Domine, quo vadis? " scene and the crucifixion of Peter head downward.[12] Other works of this type are the *Acts of Andrew*, the *Acts of Thomas*, the *Acts of Philip*, and the *Acts of Pilate*.

From II Peter, which has rarely been held as authentic, to the apocryphal epistles is not much of a jump. Forged or imitative letters did not become as numerous or as popular as apocalypses, owing to the difficulty of writing such documents and the possibility of detection. Among the few extant apocryphal letters, the most well-known are the fragments of the *Letters of Christ and Abgarus*, the *Correspondence of Paul and Seneca*, the *Epistle of the Apostles*, and the *Epistle to the Laodiceans*. Obviously the last-named work was written to supply the missing letter mentioned by Paul in Colossians 4:16.

It remains for us to consider briefly the apocalypse as a final form of apocryphal literature. The most important book in this category is the *Apocalypse of Peter*, which was included in several canonical lists and early manuscripts. This second-century work was quoted frequently by third- and fourth-century writers and is preserved, in part, in Greek

---

[12] Thomas B. Costain in his *The Silver Chalice* uses the story of the contest in Rome between Simon Magus and Peter and the attempted flight of Magus over the city.

and Ethiopic versions. It is devoted largely to a vivid description of the torments of hell and is a possible source for Dante's *Inferno*.

Less popular among ancient authorities was the *Apocalypse of Paul*, which appeared in the fourth century. The apocalypses of Thomas and Stephen complete the list of those bearing the names of New Testament personages.

In addition to the patristic and apocryphal literature, the noncanonical literature might also include the early apologies. On the other hand, the works of the apologists were not identified so closely with scripture as were the other two classes of writing. This form of literature arose out of the natural demand for a polemic or theological defense of struggling Christianity.[13] Ridiculed and condemned as treasonable and atheistic, the new religion had to find a quick defense or justification, the first of which was the *Preaching of Peter* (early second century), quoted by Clement of Alexandria and Origen. This was followed by the *Apology of Quadratus* (125 A.D.) and the *Apology of Aristides* (*ca.* 140 A.D.). Perhaps the best-known name among the apologists is that of Justin Martyr, who championed the cause of Christianity in Rome (150–165). His *First Apology* and *Dialogue with Trypho* defended the Christian religion against Jewish as well as Roman critics.

[13] "Apology," from the Greek 'απολογία — a treatise written in defense of Christianity.

Part Four

The Transmission of the Bible

Chapter Ten

Greek Manuscripts

1. The Problem of Transmission

Gutenberg's invention of the printing press had two important results: it increased the circulation of any given book a thousandfold, and it established the accuracy of the original text of that book for all subsequent printings. Before the fifteenth century no two copies of a book were the same. All books were in manuscript form and contained the inevitable errors or intentional changes of copyists. Once the autographs or original work were lost, no one could be sure of the original text.

The first fact to bear in mind as we take up the long story of the transmission of the Bible down to the present day, therefore, is that no original autograph of the Bible or any part of it exists today. The books of the Bible as first written — the Old Testament books on skins, the New Testament on papyrus — disappeared not long after their composition. But they were copied, and our only knowledge of their content comes from the study of manuscript copies or copies of copies. (This is also true of all Greek and Roman classics.)

The loss of the original books of the Bible has led to a science called Textual or Lower Criticism, which is a comparative study of manuscripts and versions with a view to approximating the probable content of the original documents. Owing to the errors of scribes in copying, to variant readings, and to corruptions in the texts of manuscripts, scholars can never be sure they have arrived at the original words of any part of the Bible, but the task continues to challenge them. We can appreciate the liability to error on the part of ancient copyists when we consider how difficult it is for us today to copy accurately a long — or even a short — document. In many instances the copyist was unable to read the handwriting of the previous scribe; in others, he misunderstood the abbreviations and peculiarities of writing. The task of the textual critic, therefore, is highly technical. He must be well trained in several ancient languages and familiar with all the peculiarities of manuscripts in their respective periods: size, number of columns, variety of contractions, and types of handwriting.

The original New Testament was probably written on papyrus with a reed pen and ink. Papyrus, found in great abundance in Egypt, was used for stationery as early as 3000 B.C. The inner bark was cut in strips, which were laid side by side. Other strips were placed on top of these at right angles, and the two layers were then pressed together, dried, and polished. Sheets were cut in various lengths from six to sixteen inches; where a single document required several pieces, they were glued together end to end in a scroll.

The writing originally followed the direction of the fiber strips; scrolls, therefore, were inscribed on the side on which the fibers were horizontal. The columns were narrow and there was no separation of words. The writer used no punctuation. In some instances the writer indicated a change in the content by a short horizontal line drawn in the margin — the origin of the English word " paragraph." [1]

The title of the book appeared at the end, and the whole

---

[1] παραγράφω, to write alongside of.

document was rolled up and put in a cylinder. The original Four Gospels and the Pauline letters were probably kept in such cylinders.

Papyrus gave way to vellum during the fourth and fifth centuries. This change was caused partly by the decrease in the amount of papyrus available but more especially by the greater practicability of vellum. Vellum, in the form of sheets, could be used on both sides; it was more durable and could be bound into books.

Down to the sixth century the scribes were a professional class, but from the sixth century on, manuscripts were produced and copied in monasteries by the monks. Most of the earlier manuscripts (from the fourth to the eighth century) were written in large, square, capital letters; these manuscripts are called *uncials*. Later manuscripts (generally after the eighth century) were written in a cursive or script style and are called *minuscules*. Some of the earliest manuscripts had four columns to the page, but as time went on the tendency was to reduce the number of columns, so that by the seventh or eighth century most of the manuscripts were done in one column. The words were still not separated, with the result that the modern scholar has the added task of dividing the letters correctly. In some cases this involves uncertainty, though usually it is not too difficult.

2. Uncial Manuscripts

Because the papyrus scrolls no longer exist, it is with the vellum manuscripts that we must begin our story of the transmission of the Bible. There are in existence some 2,500 manuscripts of the Bible, varying in length from the complete Bible

or New Testament down to a few verses, a chapter, or a portion of one book.

Some recently discovered fragments of the New Testament actually antedate the great manuscripts. These are the
Oxyrhynchus Papyri (third century), containing lost sayings
of Jesus as well as material from the canonical gospels and the
book of Hebrews. An earlier find was the Beatty Papyri,[2]
consisting of twelve fragments, some of which are from the
third century and contain parts of the gospels, Pauline letters,
and part of the Apocalypse of John. A noteworthy fact
about the Beatty Papyri is that they were in the form of three
codices or books rather than rolls. One of these codices, according to some scholars, dates from the middle of the second
century A.D. Originally the Beatty codices probably contained all the undisputed books of the New Testament (the
Four Gospels, Acts, the letters of Paul, and Revelation).
These documents, which have been edited and published, are
bound to have a bearing on the study of the early text of the
New Testament.

The main task of the textual critic is to reconstruct as far
as possible the correct text of the Bible. The Greek manuscripts are his first source for that task, the other two sources
being the ancient versions and patristic citations.

The two oldest and most valuable Greek manuscripts are
known as *Vaticanus* and *Sinaiticus*. *Codex Vaticanus* or *B* is
an uncial Greek manuscript of the early fourth century. It is
written on fine vellum and contains 759 leaves with three columns to the page. This manuscript has been in the Vatican
Library at least as early as 1481, when a catalogue of manuscripts was made. It probably contained all of the Old Testament at one time, with the exception of the books of Mac-

---

[2] Discovered by A. Chester Beatty in Egypt in 1931.

cabees. (In its present state it lacks Hebrews from 9:14 to the end, the Pastoral Epistles, Philemon, and the Apocalypse of John.) While its existence was long known, it was not until the nineteenth century that it was photographed and studied by textual critics. The paleographical evidence points to Egypt as the place of writing.

Second only to *B* in value and importance is *Codex Sinaiticus* or *Aleph,* which is written on vellum in uncial letters and contains 347 leaves with four columns to the page. It was discovered in 1859 by Count Tischendorf in the Monastery of St. Catherine on Mount Sinai. The manuscript was later purchased from the monastery by the Czar and kept in St. Petersburg until the accession of the Soviet rule, when it was purchased by the Parliament and people of Great Britain at a cost of half a million dollars. It is now in the British Museum.

Aleph contains the complete Bible including the Apocalypse of John, Epistle of Barnabas, and a part of the Shepherd of Hermas. According to some authorities, it may once have contained the Didaché. It is thought that *Aleph* and *B* were two of the fifty Bibles that Constantine ordered Eusebius, bishop of Caesarea, to have prepared for the Byzantine churches. Both are closely related textually and bear the earmarks of the same scribal school in Egypt. By the seventh century *Aleph* was in Caesarea and had undergone many corrections and editings.

Next in antiquity and importance is the uncial known as *A* or *Codex Alexandrinus.* It derives its name from the fact that it was in the library of Alexandria until 1621, at which time it was given to James I of England by the Patriarch of Alexandria. Its previous history places it in the Patriarchal Library of Cairo and before that at Mount Athos in Greece.

It is now in the British Museum. This codex is a fifth-century document and probably originated in Byzantium rather than Egypt. In addition to the books of the New Testament, it includes the letters of Clement, but it lacks parts of Matthew, the Fourth Gospel, and II Corinthians.

Codex Ephraemi Syri or *C* has an interesting history. It was written originally in the fifth century and contained the entire Bible in Greek. In the twelfth century, vellum having become somewhat scarce, some scribe partially rubbed out the original Greek and on top of it and between the lines transcribed in Syriac thirty-eight homilies of Ephraem, a Syrian Father of the fourth century. Such a manuscript is known as a palimpsest.[3] It is possible to read the fifth-century Greek fairly well in spite of the superimposition of the twelfth-century Syriac. Tischendorf edited the manuscript in 1843 and found that many leaves were missing. It is now in Paris.

Still another type of manuscript is the bilingual, the most celebrated example of which is *Codex D* or *Bezae*, which was written in Greek and Latin on the left and right sides, respectively. This manuscript has usually been assigned to the sixth century, but recent opinion places it in the fifth. It probably originated in France, where the people spoke Latin; hence, the need for a Latin " crib " of the Greek original. However, critical examination shows many discrepancies between the Latin and the Greek; it is obvious that the Latin side is not a direct translation of the Greek but has a separate origin. The Greek text is decidedly corrupt and shows signs of extensive editing by later scribes, who inserted marginal notes in the text itself and interpolated theological expansions. One theory holds that the Latin is a translation of a Greek manuscript from which the Greek of *D* was originally taken and that the

[3] πάλιν, again; ψῆν, to rub.

translator was familiar with current Latin versions. The Greek, in fact, has been corrected to conform to the Latin in many places.[4]

The manuscript was named for Theodore Beza, the Protestant reformer at Geneva, who obtained it from the Monastery of Saint Irenaeus at Lyons in 1562 and in 1581 gave it to the University of Cambridge. Its early history is associated with Lyons. *Codex Bezae* has only one column to the page. The gospels and Acts are not complete. The agreement, on the whole, between the earlier manuscripts *Aleph* and *B* as contrasted with *D* made possible a much more reliable text for the Revised Version of 1881–85 and further revisions that followed. It is generally agreed that the Western text, of which *D* is the representative, is less trustworthy than the Egyptian text of *Aleph* and *B*.

These five manuscripts are by far the most important and stand in a class by themselves. A few others, however, are taken into account in establishing the text:

D2 or *D Paul* or *Codex Claromontanus*, a Graeco-Latin uncial of the sixth century, is called *Claromontanus* because it was once at Clermont in Beauvais. This manuscript, now in Paris, is an important authority in the reconstruction of the text of the Pauline letters.

Codex E is a bilingual manuscript of the sixth century and contains only the Book of Acts. Its history starts with Sardinia and jumps to Northumbria, where it was used by Bede in the eighth century; it was later taken by Boniface to Würzburg, Bavaria, and finally in the seventeenth century fell into the possession of Archbishop Laud, who gave it to the Bodleian Library at Oxford.

---

[4] See F. C. Burkitt in the *Journal of Theological Studies*, 1901–02, III, 501–13.

H, once a complete sixth-century manuscript of the Paulines, now contains only a few leaves, which are divided among six European cities. They have value as a probable copy of an early recension of Pauline Epistles.

L, or *Codex Regius*, is an eighth-century Greek manuscript of the gospels, containing, incidentally, both endings of Mark.

The manuscripts designated *N*, *O*, Σ, and Φ are referred to as the Constantinople group because they have a common origin in that city, as the text and workmanship indicate. They are from the sixth century and contain only the gospels. The vellum in all four documents is stained purple, and the letters are in gold and silver.

In 1906 a manuscript was bought in Egypt by C. L. Freer of Detroit. This fifth-century uncial is called the *Washington Codex* or *W* and is noteworthy in that it gives the gospels in the so-called Western sequence — Matthew, John, Luke, and Mark — and also because of a peculiar interpolation within the longer ending of Mark, a textual oddity appearing in no other extant manuscript. This manuscript is now in the Freer Art Gallery in Washington, D.C.

3. Minuscules

Less important for textual study are the minuscules, which are valuable only as they support earlier uncial manuscripts. The minuscules, or cursive group, are indicated by numbers. They range from the ninth to the fifteenth century.

In the *B* and *Aleph* tradition is 33, a minuscule of the ninth or tenth century, containing the entire New Testament except Revelation. Most prominent among the minuscules is the " Ferrar Group," consisting of 13, 69, 124, 230, 346, 543, 788,

826, 828, 983, 1,689, and 1,709. Most of these manuscripts are from the eleventh century and are famous for their placement of the *pericope adulterai* — the passage about the woman taken in adultery — after Luke 21:38 instead of John 7:53.

The best example of the colored minuscule is 2,400, known as the Rockefeller-McCormick New Testament, a thirteenth-century Byzantine masterpiece. Edgar J. Goodspeed ran across this manuscript in an antiquarian shop in Paris in 1927. Even more noteworthy than the text, which is comparatively late (thirteenth century), are the 74 miniatures or colored illustrations that were found in this manuscript.

Another type of manuscript is that called the lectionary. The lectionaries are not continuous texts, but editions of the gospels or Acts made especially for reading in the public services of worship. They are so edited as to provide systematic readings through the church or calendar year. The lectionaries are difficult to place but probably do not antedate the eighth century.

4. *Hebrew Manuscripts*

Until the discovery in 1947 of the Dead Sea Scrolls, our oldest Hebrew manuscripts went back no earlier than the ninth century A.D. Not only did the Hebrew manuscripts, like the Greek uncials, have no word separation; they also had no vowels, which made reading still more difficult. The Hebrew text was standardized in the seventh century A.D. by the Masoretes. To preserve the text in its traditional form,[5] they simply copied it repeatedly for hundreds of years, introducing

[5] See James Hastings, *Dictionary of the Bible* (New York, 1919), IV, 729 ff.; W. R. Smith, *The Old Testament in the Jewish Church* (New York, 1912), pp. 69–83; and R. H. Pfeiffer, *Introduction to the Old Testament* (New York, 1941), pp. 71 ff.

no changes. Their text is the standard Hebrew Bible today.

The first extant manuscript of the Hebrew Old Testament [6] comes almost one thousand years after the Hebrew Scripture was canonized. In view of the length of the Old Testament as compared with the New Testament and also the longer time of transmission by hand, we might expect more variations and changes, but such is not the case. The reverence of the Hebrew scribes for the word of God made them meticulously careful in transcribing the text. Since the text was sacred, they copied even the obvious errors and inserted the correct words in the margin. Word division was introduced in the text about 500 A.D., and the consonantal and vocalic text reached its permanent form by the tenth century through the Masoretic school of Tiberias.

The oldest manuscript is the tenth-century *St. Petersburg Codex*, now in Leningrad. It contains the Prophets and consists of 225 folios, each arranged in two columns of 21 lines. The chief peculiarity of this manuscript is that the vowels are written above the text instead of below. The supralinear arrangement of vowel writing is known as the Babylonian system and is practically nonexistent outside of this codex.

The uniformity of the Hebrew text is explained by the fact that very early in the transmission (probably soon after the canonization in 90 A.D.) all Hebrew manuscripts were made to conform to one model, and variant texts were destroyed. This standardized form was called the *Sopherim* text, and it was faithfully copied as sacred. Further, when the vowel system was added in the seventh century, an even greater degree of stabilization was assured. In the period be-

---

[6] There are some 1,700 fragmentary Hebrew manuscripts but very few containing the entire Old Testament. For a discussion of Hebrew manuscripts, see C. D. Ginsburg, *Introduction to the Masoretico-Critical Edition of the Hebrew Bible* (London, 1897), pp. 469 ff.

tween the adoption of the standardized text and the time of the earliest known manuscripts (tenth century), the scribes made extensive marginal notes, dealing with peculiar words, spelling, pronunciation, mechanical notes, and errors. This marginal commentary is known as the Masorah.[7]

The first printed editions of the Hebrew Bible appeared at Soncino (1488), Naples (1491–93), Brescia (1494), and Pesaro (1511–17), but the most important was the Rabbinic Bible published by Bomberg at Venice in 1524–25 and edited by Jacob ben Chayyim. This edition, embracing the Masorah, became and remains the standard Hebrew Bible of the present day.

[7] For an extended description of the Masorah see the article by Arthur Jeffrey in *The Interpreter's Bible* (New York, 1952), I, 46–62.

Chapter Eleven

Early Versions

1. Latin Versions

As long as Christianity was confined to purely Greek-speaking localities, there was no need for the New Testament to be in any other tongue; but, with the increasing prominence of the Western or Latin church, centered in Rome, and with the rapid spread of the Christian religion in the far-flung provinces of the Graeco-Roman world, it became necessary to translate both the Old and New Testaments into Latin and other tongues. For a long time the educated class, even in Rome, used Greek, and the careless and crude form of the earliest Latin versions shows quite clearly that they were intended only for the uneducated. However, Latin was the official language of Carthaginian and African Christianity, so the Latin text of the Scripture was known there as early as 150 A.D.

In time, Greek became less of an international language, and, as Christianity penetrated into the hinterlands of Egypt, Ethiopia, Arabia, Syria, Gaul, Armenia, and North Africa, the necessity arose for versions in the languages of those places. Some of these versions were written before our best extant manuscripts; consequently, while they have the obvious defects of translation, their antiquity gives them great value in our attempt to approximate the original text. On the other hand, since many of them were secondary versions (translations of translations), their contribution to textual study is considerably diminished. If an Arabic version were made from an earlier Coptic, the Coptic in turn being a translation of the Greek, the Arabic is twice removed from the autograph copy and therefore is less trustworthy. This is why the Vulgate itself is less reliable, Jerome having based his translation in Latin upon several previous Latin manuscripts and the Septuagint.

The first version of importance for our study is the Old Latin, of which there were many African recensions. One might have expected Latin versions to appear first in Italy, but such was not the case. As late as the third and early fourth centuries, Greek was still the dominant language in Italy. The Christians in Rome wrote and spoke Greek, as did Roman officials and writers. But Latin was the official language of Carthage and northern Africa. Cyprian, writing in Carthage in the latter part of the second century, quotes extensively from a Latin Bible, which shows signs of being a translation of an earlier version; this points to a succession of Latin versions going back probably to 150 A.D. Bishop Nemesianus, for instance, when he attended the Council of Carthage in 256 A.D., used a Latin version that differed from Cyprian's Bible.

It is therefore safe to say that Tertullian (160–230 A.D.), the founder of Latin or African Christianity, was in possession of a Latin text. The gospel manuscripts known as *k* and *e*, from the fourth and fifth centuries respectively, came from Africa and contained the text used by Cyprian. The Fleury Palimpsest, *h*, is also an African text and contains the Book of Acts, fragments of the Catholic Epistles, and parts of Revelation.

Some manuscripts have been called the "European Latin" group to distinguish them from the "African Latin"; the relationship between the two has never been clarified.

The most valuable Latin manuscript of the European group is *Codex Vercellensis*, which is supposed to have been written by the bishop of Vercelli, Italy, about 365 A.D. It is written in narrow columns in silver on purple vellum and contains only the gospels. There are several fifth- and sixth-century European manuscripts that are more or less connected with the Western text.

It was Jerome (340–420 A.D.) who revised the earlier Latin recensions and brought out an official translation that would supersede all previous versions. With so many Latin versions in existence, all of which were different and contained mistakes of copyists, the need for revision became obvious. Jerome, whom Pope Damasus commissioned to do this important work, was well trained in Hebrew and Greek and can be considered one of the ablest scholars of his day. After serving as presbyter of Antioch, he was made secretary to Pope Damasus. He commenced his revision in 383 A.D. and continued the work in Bethlehem, where he lived for some twenty-five years. The result was the Vulgate (from the Latin, meaning " currently received " or " common "), which ultimately took its place as the accepted text and the authoritative Bible of the Roman church, although the Latin text of Jerome was actually not designated Vulgate until the Council of Trent (1546).

The Vulgate is not a translation from Greek originals but is chiefly a revision of an existing Latin text of the New Testament with occasional corrections based on Greek manuscripts. The particular Latin text used by Jerome is hard to determine, but ninety per cent of the Vulgate coincides with *Codex Brixianus* (*f*). Otherwise, his corrections of the Latin text, at least for the gospels, seem to be based on readings akin to those of the Egyptian school of manuscripts. He changed the order of the gospels from that of the Old Latin to that of the great uncials. The rest of the New Testament shows very little alteration, as Jerome was fearful of the opposition to any changes he might introduce. He seems to have used different texts for different sections of the New Testament.

Jerome worked fourteen years on the Old Testament, translating from Hebrew into Latin. He commenced his Old Testament work by revising the Old Latin Psalter, which was, like all the rest of the Old Latin versions, a translation from the Septuagint. But he soon saw that he could get better results by going back to the Hebrew text.

Jerome's revision was not universally accepted. On the contrary, while it had official sanction, it was opposed by many bishops and some later popes and by conservative people everywhere, just as all subsequent versions were opposed. During the reign of Pope Gregory in the sixth century, both the Old Latin and the Vulgate of Jerome were used in Rome. Augustine used the Vulgate for the gospels and the Old Latin for the rest of the New Testament. The Vulgate, in fact, did not attain supremacy until the ninth century and did not become the standard Bible of the Roman Catholic Church until it was so declared by the Council of Trent.

This indiscriminate use of the Old Latin versions and the Vulgate manuscripts caused no end of textual trouble, as the various texts were mixed in usage. The Vulgate text was purified somewhat by Alcuin, abbot of St. Martin of Tours, in 801, but a better job of correction was done at the University of Paris in the thirteenth century. The division of the Bible into chapters was made by Stephen Langton, archbishop of Canterbury, in 1228. The first complete book to come from the printing press of Gutenberg in 1455 was the Vulgate. In 1528 Stephanus published a critical edition, which was revised a decade later. The first official edition was based on the University of Paris text and was revised by Pope Sixtus V, who published it in 1590.[1]

2. Syriac Versions

Antioch in Syria was the earliest gentile-Christian center and the point from which Paul and his assistants worked in their missions. When Christianity penetrated the outlying districts of Syria (or Assyria), the need arose for Syriac translations of the New Testament. Syriac is closely related to the Aramaic that Jesus spoke. Added interest is therefore attached to the gospels in Syriac because the reader of these versions is dealing with practically the same vocabulary used by Jesus.

The first Syriac version, the Diatessaron of Tatian, made its appearance about 170 A.D. Confronting the fact that the Synoptics contained many doublets and triplets (material found two and three times in exactly the same wording), Tatian conceived the idea of combining the Four Gospels into one continuous narrative, eliminating duplications. His Diatessaron was based on a Greek text that was current in the middle of the second century. The resulting work was then translated into Syriac.

The Diatessaron remained the standard version of Edessa and the Assyrian Christians until the early part of the fifth century and was quoted by all Syriac Fathers up to that time. The text is a mixture of the Western and Neutral (or Egyptian), schools but is closer, perhaps, to the European Old

---

[1] The identification and collation of Vulgate manuscripts is a difficult task and is a field too technical to summarize here.

Latin and Bezae tradition than to the Egyptian. It is preserved in two Arabic manuscripts, which are in the Vatican.

The Assyrian church had a " Gospel of the Separated Ones " or separate gospels, of which we have two manuscripts, the Curetonian and the Sinaitic. This version, known as the Old Syriac, appeared about 200 A.D. The Sinaitic manuscript (fourth century) was discovered in the Monastery of St. Catherine on Mount Sinai in 1892. It is palimpsest and has been photographed repeatedly and treated with a reagent in order to make its text more readable. The Curetonian manuscript (fifth century) was discovered in 1842 in a monastery near Cairo. A comparative study of these two manuscripts of the Old Syriac helps greatly in the study of the Syriac text. The Sinaitic, for instance, follows the Neutral manuscripts, *Aleph* and *B*, in ending Mark at 9:8, whereas the Curetonian contains the longer ending.

The most important Syriac version is the Peshitta ("simple," "Vulgate"), which shows a great affinity to the Byzantine or ecclesiastical text. Its appearance was occasioned by the same set of circumstances that brought about Jerome's Vulgate: Bishop Rabbula of Edessa ordered a revision of the Old Syriac in line with the best current Greek manuscripts. It appeared in 435 A.D. and became standard for the Assyrian church.

The Peshitta was later expanded to include the rest of the New Testament with the exception of II and III John, II Peter, Jude, and the Apocalypse of John; these were included in a further revision by Polycarp of Heirapolis in 508. A further revision was made by Thomas of Harkel in 616; this is called the Harklean Version. These revisions made for a more literal rendering of the Syriac text to conform to the Greek manuscripts.

The Peshitta is now preserved in 243 manuscripts. An independent version called the Jerusalem or Palestinian version was made in the sixth century. The Peshitta Old Testament was made originally from the Hebrew, but the manuscripts differ in the number and order of books.

3. Egyptian Versions

In no province of the Roman Empire was the Greek language more firmly established than in Alexandria, home of the Septuagint, the Christian school of theology, and the best Greek manuscripts of the New Testament. But, in Egypt, as in other countries, when Christianity had moved into more remote districts and was found among the common people, versions in native dialects became necessary.

The Sahidic version of Upper Egypt, where Greek was not so prevalent, was probably the earliest to appear. This third-century version, otherwise known as the Thebaic, has been recovered from numerous fragments of papyri and parchment. Its text is closely akin to the Neutral school of *Aleph* and *B* in most readings, while in others it follows the Western text.

The Bohairic version, sometimes called the Coptic or Memphitic, arose in the Delta region and became the official text of the Coptic church. This version contains the entire New Testament and was probably written after the Sahidic. It has less Western influence than the Sahidic and is consistently Neutral in character.

The Latin, Syriac, and Egyptian versions are the primary ones, and we need not be concerned with secondary and later versions except to mention their names. They are the Gothic, which is a translation of both the Old and New Testaments by Bishop Ufilas (fourth century), the Armenian, the Ethiopic (Abyssinian), the Georgian, and the Arabic. These were formerly held to be of little value in Textual Criticism, but some contemporary scholars have more respect for them, particularly the Georgian and the Armenian versions.

4. Old Testament Versions

We have been considering versions related to both Old and New Testaments, but here we are concerned with Old Testament versions only. In the case of the Old Testament some of the manuscripts of versions are older than the extant Hebrew manuscripts, but it is difficult to get back to their original form because of emendations, corruptions, and changes occurring in the process of translation.

The Samaritan Pentateuch

The Samaritan revolt occurred shortly after the canonization of the Torah (444–432 B.C.). The Samaritans took with them to Shechem a copy of the Torah, which became known as the Samaritan Pentateuch. This remained their sole Bible. It is really an edition of the Hebrew text in the old Samaritan characters, and, although it was carefully preserved by the scribes, it contains many variants from both the Hebrew and Septuagint texts. Some of these changes were deliberate, others accidental. The Samaritan claims regarding their temple at Shechem gave rise to numerous changes in the text. "Gerezim," for instance, was substituted for "Ebal" in Deuteronomy 27:4. But, in spite of orthographic variants, dogmatic changes, interpolations, grammatical corrections of the Hebrew, and accidental scribal errors, the Samaritan Pentateuch in many respects represents a more reliable text than the Masoretic Old Testament, particularly when it agrees with the Septuagint in varying from the Hebrew.

The Targums

The Targums also are an aid in determining the Hebrew text. Toward the beginning of the Christian Era, Aramaic had become the popular language in Palestine. Since the Scripture continued to be read in Hebrew every Sabbath, the need arose for some translation or paraphrase for the congregation.[2] Originally these interpretations were made orally with the reading of the Hebrew Scripture, but eventually they were put into written forms and called Aramaic Targums. The seven extant Targums are from the fourth and fifth centuries A.D., but proof exists that the Targums were in written form before 200 A.D. They are textually valuable because they represent a paraphrasing of Hebrew text older than any we have in our best Hebrew manuscripts. The most important Targum is the Babylonian of Onkelos, a free translation of the Pentateuch.

The Septuagint

The Septuagint (285–130 B.C.) represents the first real translation of any part of the Bible.[3] The work of the translators varies considerably in quality, partly because many different men worked on it in the period of seventy-five or more years, and partly because the Pentateuch, being much more highly regarded, was therefore more carefully translated.

[2] Aramisms even appear in the Hebrew text of Ezra and Daniel.
[3] See pp. 125–127 ff. for the origin of the Septuagint.

One of the books of the Prophets, Daniel, was so carelessly translated that it was later supplanted by Theodotian's version in all copies of the Septuagint. The textual differences between the Hebrew Old Testament and the Septuagint are numerous, and the order of the books is different. No satisfactory reason for these differences is at hand except the partial explanation that the Septuagint translators were rather free in their handling of the Hebrew text, making additions and omissions in the text and even adding books to the Hebrew list.

A third-century papyrus fragment of the Septuagint was found at Oxyrhynchus, Egypt, in 1903. There are some thirty uncial manuscripts, the most important of which is *Codex Marchalianus*, a sixth-century uncial that contains only the Prophets. In addition to the uncials there are about three hundred cursives.

The popularity of the Septuagint throughout the Christian world in the first two centuries prejudiced the Jews against it, especially because of its inclusion of the Apocrypha. The Greek-speaking Jews wanted to keep their Old Testament intact and were aware of the many differences between the Hebrew and the Septuagint text. As a result there appeared several Greek Bibles for Jewish use, the first of which was that of Aquila. Aquila was a proselyte Jew from Pontus, Asia Minor, and, according to Jerome, a pupil of Rabbi Akiba. The chief characteristic of his version, which appeared about 170 A.D., is its literal quality. In order to achieve an accurate translation, Aquila tried to reproduce literally every word of the Hebrew text regardless of the form and idiom of the language he was using. This resulted in a stilted, wooden text, but it became the authoritative Greek version for Judaism.

The rapidly increasing Christian resentment to Aquila's

version was represented by Theodotion, an Ebionite Christian of Pontus (or Ephesus), whose version was produced about 190 A.D. Aquila's version had been a reaction to the Christian Septuagint; Theodotion's translation was a reaction to that of Aquila. Presumably a translation from the Hebrew Old Testament as a corrective of the Septuagint, it was in reality a revision of the Septuagint, which it improved noticeably. It exhibits a more facile, idiomatic Greek style than Aquila's version, so much so that parts of it were used to replace sections of the original Septuagint.

The third Greek version of the Old Greek Testament was that of Symmachus, another Ebionite Christian (*ca.* 200 A.D.). This translation is noted for its faithfulness to the Hebrew text and for its highly literary form. It was praised by Jerome for its clarity.

At this point we encounter the figure of Origen, the founder of Textual Criticism and the greatest biblical scholar of the first three centuries. Confronted with the Hebrew Old Testament, the Septuagint, and the three Greek versions, he decided to make a parallel study of all these in order to arrive at the most satisfactory Greek text of the Old Testament. This stupendous work is called the Hexapla, in which he arranged in parallel columns the Hebrew text of the Old Testament, the Hebrew text in Greek letters, the Greek translation of Aquila, the version of Symmachus, and Theodotion's translation. His own text of the Septuagint occupied the sixth column, which also contained his critical notes and emendations. Origen's Hexapla, which consumed twenty-eight years of his life, would, according to Nestle, fill 12,000 pages of manuscript, if complete, but it survives only in fragmentary quotations, copies, and palimpsests. The original manuscript, consulted by Jerome, was seen in the library at Caesarea in the seventh century.

Following Origen and largely influenced by his work, there were three Greek versions of the Old Testament, which aid greatly in determining the best readings of both the Septuagint and the Hebrew text. They were the work of Eusebius of Caesarea, Lucian of Samosata, and Hesychius in Egypt.

Syriac, Latin, Coptic, Armenian, Arabic, Ethiopic, and Georgian versions of the Old Testament made their appearance just as in the case of the New Testament.[4] All these versions except the Peshitta Syriac were translations of the Septuagint. Nothing else need be noted about these other than what has been said in connection with the New Testament.

5. Patristic Citations

Another important source of textual evidence is found in the quotations of the Scripture by early church fathers. The second century produced an astonishing amount of extra-canonical Christian literature, which, in view of the fact that it antedates our oldest manuscripts, is highly valuable in the reconstruction of the text of the Bible. A considerable portion of the New Testament could be restored, roughly at least, from these quotations, which were made from earlier manuscripts now lost.[5]

The chief Greek writers who quoted extensively from the Old and New Testaments were Marcion, Tatian, Justin Martyr, Irenaeus, Clement of Alexandria, Hippolytus, Origen, Pamphilius, Eusebius, Athanasius, Cyril of Alexandria, Basil of Caesarea, Gregory of Nazianus, Gregory of Nyssa, Epiphanius, and Chrysostom. The Latin writers were Tertul-

---

[4] See pp. 228–235.
[5] See pp. 188–192 ff. for patristic citations of the canon.

lian, Cyprian, Novatian, Hilary of Poitiers, Ambrose, Jerome, Augustine, Pelagius, and Cassiodorus. Syriac writings include *The Acts of Judas Thomas, Aphraates,* and *Ephraem.* In these quotations we find a mixture of the Western and Neutral texts. The chief value of these witnesses for the text is that in most instances they dated and located the manuscripts being used. The chief defect is that they were not too careful or precise in their quotation of the passages.[6]

6. The Problem of the Text

We have thus far surveyed the materials with which the search for the best text is conducted; namely, manuscripts, early versions, and patristic citations. The problem facing the textual critic is to get as close as possible to what may be considered the original text, which has been completely lost. This problem is complicated by the presence of countless variant readings (differences in the text of certain words or passages). Some of these variants were intentionally created by scribes in various ways: changing a manuscript to bring it in line with another, correcting what they regarded as errors of heresy, and carrying marginal explanatory notes of previous scribes over into the text itself.

There were also unconscious variants resulting from human fallibility. The copyist often omitted a line or a passage by mistake. If two lines began with the same word, the scribe might easily skip a line. If two lines ended with the same

[6] For further discussion on patristic writers see C. R. Gregory, *Canon and Text of the New Testament* (New York, 1927), pp. 419 ff.; A. Souter, *Text and Canon of the New Testament* (New York, 1910), pp. 76 ff.; and F. G. Kenyon, *Handbook to Textual Criticism of the New Testament* (New York, 1912).

word, he might easily repeat a line. Errors of spelling, hearing, and memory and errors due to misreading of Greek words by the copyist are numerous.

Changes were also made by editors of manuscripts for purposes of harmonization or smoothness. Finally, translators, from the earliest versions to modern English, have introduced many variations of text.[7]

In the face of these variant readings, the task of the editor from the second century on has been to standardize the text by collating and weighing the worth of the various manuscripts. To follow all the maneuvers that might be made in this battle for the text would take us far afield; let us look instead at the basic tactics most commonly followed today.

It became necessary to get back of the *Textus Receptus* — or Byzantine text, as it was called — to something closer to the first century. This was attempted by Griesbach in the mid-eighteenth century, by Lachmann in the mid-nineteenth century, and by Tischendorf, Nestle, and Westcott and Hort in the latter half of the nineteenth century. Coincidentally with the publication of the Revised Version in 1881–85, Westcott and Hort produced their critical edition of the Greek New Testament. This was the culmination not only of thirty years of research on their part but of centuries of scholarly labor.

In dealing with the corruptions of the text, these scholars evolved two tests for probability of textual purity: the intrinsic and the transcriptional. The intrinsic text tries to solve the problem of variants by deciding which reading

---

[7] For a more detailed discussion of the principles of Textual Criticism as applied to variants, see the article by Ernest C. Colwell in *The Interpreter's Bible* (New York, 1952), I, 72 ff.; also, his books, *The Study of the Bible* (Chicago, 1937), and *What Is the Best New Testament?* (Chicago, 1952).

makes more sense or best coincides with the context. In transcriptional probability, where two readings are involved, the decision is made in favor of that reading which seems to have produced the other.

These two methods obviously are not adequate for all situations, nor are they foolproof, as Westcott and Hort well recognized. They therefore went on to adopt the genealogical method, which places the emphasis on the comparative worth of manuscripts. Now, to choose a reading because it is supported by the greatest number of manuscripts is unreliable because a poor manuscript may have had many followers, while a superior manuscript may have been copied by very few. It is also dangerous to assume that the earliest manuscript is always the best, although usually antiquity is a good criterion.

According to Westcott and Hort, the main families of manuscripts are (1) the Byzantine (Syrian), (2) the Western (as in *D*), (3) the Neutral (*Aleph, A, B, 33,* and the Coptic versions), and (4) the Alexandrian (akin to the Neutral). Genealogical tables were made of all manuscripts as they were related to these four lines. These were later condensed into two main streams: the Neutral and Western (the Alexandrian is close to the Neutral and the Syrian is too late to have high value). Briefly, the theory is this: on the assumption that the Neutral school of manuscripts is more trustworthy, a reading supported by these manuscripts as against *D* is to be accepted. *B* is the manuscript to follow except where there are manifest scribal errors.[8]

[8] For canons of criticism see Kostantine von Tischendorf, *Critical Edition of The Greek New Testament* (8th ed., Leipzig, 1869–72); Henry Hammond, *Outlines of Textual Criticism Applied to the New Testament* (Oxford, 1902); Ira M. Price, *The Ancestry of the English Bible* (2nd rev. ed. by William A. Irwin and Allen P. Wik-

More recently the Westcott-Hort theory has been challenged. Von Soden introduced a new system of manuscript classification and nomenclature, but it proved to be decidedly unpopular. Then Rendel Harris sprang to the defense of the Western text but had little effect on followers of the Westcott-Hort theory. The discovery of the Koridethi gospels (Θ), the *Washington Codex* (*W*), and the Beatty Papyri [9] has already had some effect on recent Textual Criticism. Streeter fashioned a system of local texts, introducing a new family called the Caesarean, made up of 13, 1, Θ, and *W*, but this innovation in no way altered the validity of the Westcott-Hort theory.[10]

We can conclude that no serious change in Textual Criticism has occurred in the last fifty years; but one or two convictions can be set down. It has become evident that there is no strictly " Neutral " text in the sense of being the original uncontaminated Greek text. All manuscripts have different strains in them, and all manuscripts have been edited. Even *Codex Vaticanus* may well have been edited and corrected. The Neutral group of *Aleph* and *B* is still regarded as the most reliable source in the search for the best text.

gren, New York, 1949); B. F. Westcott and F J. A. Hort, *The New Testament in the Original Greek* (New York, 1882); E. C. Colwell, *op. cit.*
[9] See page 220.
[10] B. H. Streeter, *The Four Gospels* (London, 1924).

Chapter Twelve

English Translations

1. Anglo-Saxon Versions

Our story of the transmission of the Bible reaches its climax with the English translations, which originated for much the same reasons as the Latin or the Syriac versions, although the English was much later in putting in its appearance. The delay was due to the exclusive position of Latin as the official and sacred language of the Western church. It was inconceivable in the eyes of the Roman church that the Bible should be read in any other tongue. The people in England spoke Anglo-Saxon, but the Latin Vulgate was the only Bible permitted. The only vernacular translations from the fifth to the fifteenth century in the West were made by dissenting groups and were promptly prohibited by the church.

By the time Christianity had taken root in England, the Roman Catholic Church had established its tradition of apostolic succession, its doctrine of the primacy of the Roman See, and its claim to infallible authority and could therefore proscribe any such attempts to translate the Scripture into the language of the people. The availability of the Bible in the popular tongue was regarded as inimical to the unity and authority of the church in its dissemination of scriptural truth. The attempt was made, nevertheless, by reformers such as Peter Waldo. What Waldo did in the language of the Provence, John Wycliffe did in English — and met with the same result.

But the story of the English Bible actually starts before Wycliffe's time. The desire to render the Bible into the language of the common people found expression in several Anglo-Saxon versions. These were merely paraphrases of the Vulgate. The first was that of Caedmon, an illiterate farmer in Northumbria, who sang some biblical passages that were translated for him in the rough language of the seventh century. The only extant parts of his work are found in Bede's *Ecclesiastical History*.

The Psalter of Aldhelm, bishop of Sherborne (d. 709), was the first actual translation of any book of the Bible into English. The Psalms were conducive to metrical rendering and were the most popular part of the Bible in medieval England.

The first English version of the gospels was made by Bishop Egbert in the eighth century. The original copy is in the British Museum.

Bede, the most prominent scholar of eighth-century England, translated the Gospel of John into Anglo-Saxon. The story of his translation and his death comes down to us through Cuthbert, a student of Egypt. No trace of his translation exists today.

In the late ninth century, King Alfred translated the Ten Commandments, other sections of Exodus, and the Psalms.

Eadfrith, Bishop of Lindisfarne, edited Jerome's version of the gospels in the late seventh century. The Lindisfarne Gospels, as they were called, came into the possession of Sir Robert Cotton, who gave this excellent Latin manuscript to the British Museum. An interlinear Anglo-Saxon paraphrase of the Lindisfarne Gospels was made by Aldred, a priest, in

950 A.D. (Anglo-Saxon interlinear translations or paraphrases of the Latin Bible were made to assist preachers in teaching the Bible to the common people. The practice bears an analogy to the Aramaic Targums of the Old Testament.)

An independent Anglo-Saxon translation of the gospels (without the Latin) was made in Wessex in the tenth century. This is known as the Wessex Gospels and is preserved in six manuscripts, one of which is in the British Museum.

Finally, Aelfric, Archbishop of Canterbury (d. 1006), made a free translation of several Old Testament books. There are two extant manuscripts, one in the British Museum, the other in the Bodleian Library at Oxford.

2. *The Wycliffe Bible*

The first complete Bible in English was the work of John Wycliffe (1320–84), "flower of Oxford scholarship" and "morning star of the Reformation." Now for the first time in England the book that had been kept from the people became common knowledge. "The jewel of the clergy," as it was said, had become "the toy of the laity." Latin, the holy tongue, had given way to the harsh rough language of the peasant. (The complete absence of translations from Aelfric to Wycliffe, a period of some 350 years, is explained by the Norman influence throughout that period, which was naturally unfavorable to any attempt to convert the Scripture into English.)

Wycliffe's activity represents a pre-Reformation Protestantism. As a matter of fact, the revolt of Wycliffe and Huss was much more radical and thoroughgoing than that of Luther and Calvin. The same conditions existed: two extreme social classes, with the princes of church and state living in luxury, while the peasants starved in their filth; vice, materialism, and corruption; ignorance among the clergy; bribery at the courts; domination of the country by Rome; and, worst of all, prohibition of free speech and of reading the Scripture.

The Wycliffite dissent took the form of Lollardy. The "Lollards" were itinerant preachers [1] who wandered over the country proclaiming a gospel of simplicity, purity, and freedom. Under Wycliffe's leadership they opposed the temporal power of the church and actually persuaded Edward III to discontinue tribute to the Pope. Wycliffe preached against the worship of relics, pilgrimages to shrines, the mendicancy of friars, indulgences, monasticism, and sacramentarianism in all its forms. But his chief concern was the availability of the Scripture. How could the people follow the authority of the Bible if it was a sealed book written in Latin?

Fired with the idea of getting the Scripture to the people, Wycliffe undertook the translation of the Bible from the Vulgate into English. Half of the Old Testament was the work of Nicholas de Hereford, a Lollard leader. Also assisting in the translation was John Purvey, who worked on the New Testament and in 1388 made a complete revision of Wycliffe's Bible. Just how much of the translation can be credited to Wycliffe himself has not been determined, but it is clear that without his supervision the work would not have been done.

The Wycliffe Bible was the first complete Bible in English; it included the Apocrypha. The New Testament appeared in 1380 and the Old Testament in 1382. It must be borne in mind that this was merely a translation from the

---

[1] Compare the Beghards in Germany, the Vaudois in Switzerland, the Waldenses in France, the Patarenes in Italy, and the Bogomiles in Bulgaria.

Latin Vulgate. Wycliffe had no knowledge of Greek or Hebrew. This Bible became extremely popular and many handwritten copies were made; those which were done on illuminated vellum survive today. Some of the phraseology of the Wycliffe Bible worked its way permanently into the English language, and a few expressions survive in later translations. It is interesting to note that Wycliffe's New Testament, as revised by Purvey, contains Paul's letter to the Laodiceans, an apocryphal epistle.

Opposition was not long in coming. Within ten years Parliament banned the Wycliffe Bible, and in 1401 a law was passed confiscating and burning all copies of the English Bible. Many people were burned at the stake for reading it. The church had previously promulgated many laws prohibiting the publication and reading of any Bible in the vernacular; these pronouncements were strengthened by the Third Synod of Oxford in 1408 (Arundel's Constitutions), which forbade any person to translate any part of the Holy Scripture into English or to read the translation of Wycliffe or any other translation under penalty of " greater excommunication." In 1415 the Council of Constance had the bones of Wycliffe removed from their grave, and in 1428 they were dug up, burned, and thrown upon the River Swift. Purvey and Hereford were persecuted and thrown into prison.

Purvey's revision supplanted Wycliffe's edition as the popular Bible of the fifteenth century. In 1850 Forshall and Madden, after twenty-two years of intensive examination of the 170 manuscripts of the Wycliffe and Purvey Bibles, published both in parallel form. Prior to that time it was almost impossible to distinguish between them.

3. *William Tyndale*

The greatest name in the history of the English Bible is that of William Tyndale (1484–1536). His greatness lies in the fact that his is the first English translation to be made directly from the Greek New Testament and the Hebrew Old Testament. Back of the Tyndale Bible and accounting for its appearance in 1525 lay many potent forces, all of which can be summarized in one word — the Renaissance.

Between the times of Wycliffe and Tyndale, Europe had experienced an intellectual rebirth in one of the most creative periods in the history of civilization. The fall of Constantinople to the Turks in 1453 resulted in an influx of Greek scholars into Europe, where Greek had become almost extinct. In 1450 Gutenberg invented the printing press, and four years later movable type was being used. The Renaissance unleashed new forces of creativity. Otherworldliness gave way to realism. Individualism replaced medieval quiescence. Blind belief was supplanted by intellectual curiosity. Then came art, discovery, invention, and new scholarship. The Copernican theory produced a new universe; the discoveries of Columbus, Magellan, and da Gama revealed a new geography; and Galileo paved the way for modern science.

In the world of religion, the Renaissance took the form of a revolt against a corrupt and authoritarian church, as the suppressed desires and stifled rebellions broke loose upon Europe in the Protestant Reformation. Private judgment and individual freedom were the watchwords. Scholars everywhere began to search out and study Greek and Hebrew manuscripts. Greek grammars were published and Greek was placed in the curriculum of Oxford and the University of

Paris. Reuchlin issued a Hebrew grammar. The first printed Hebrew Bible appeared in 1488, and in 1516 Erasmus published the first Greek New Testament. The demand for the Bible again came to the fore, but this time that demand was for the Scripture in the original tongues. And now the printing press would guarantee a purer text, free from the multiplying errors of copyists.

All this lies back of Tyndale. Whereas Wycliffe had translated only from the Latin Vulgate, Tyndale could draw upon new and authoritative texts of the original tongues.

In spite of the new learning and religious revolt that had swept Europe, the Reformation had not as yet touched England. Henry was still "Defender of the Faith," and Sir Thomas More was strictly Catholic in his proposed reforms. The church was still opposed to the translation of the Bible into English and even more to Tyndale's Protestant ideas. It was therefore impossible for Tyndale to work under the patronage of the church. He appealed to Bishop Tunstall of London for approval but was spurned. In 1524, with the financial assistance of Humphrey Monmouth, a London merchant, he went to Hamburg, and within a year had finished the New Testament. The following year he appeared in Cologne with sheets for the printer.

The printing was suddenly stopped by church authorities who were told of the matter by an anti-Protestant informer named Cochlaeus. Tyndale fled to Worms, where the printing was completed. Some 6,000 copies were anonymously published and secretly shipped to England. The king and Cardinal Wolsey, however, had been warned by Cochlaeus of the possible shipment. Church authorities ordered the books burned at Paul's Cross in London. Only two copies of this edition survive today.

The much-publicized burning created a greater demand for the Bible and also greater financial support for Tyndale. This time help came from Augustine Packington, another London merchant. With this aid Tyndale revised his New Testament and printed another and larger edition. Now the tide could not be stemmed. Further revisions were made in 1534 and 1535.

Tyndale began work on the Old Testament in Marburg in 1527 and completed the Pentateuch by 1530. In May of that year it too was confiscated and burned in London. He completed his translation through Chronicles but was unable to complete the Old Testament before his death. After the split between Henry and the Pope, persecution became less severe, but agents of the opposition seized Tyndale in Antwerp and threw him into a dungeon in the Vilvorde prison. Here he languished for sixteen months and endured the mockery of a trial, in which Cromwell failed in his efforts to interfere on his behalf. Tyndale was put to death October 6, 1536, by being strangled and then burned at the stake. As he died, he said: "Lord, open the King of England's eyes."

In the work of translation Tyndale had before him the text of Erasmus' Greek New Testament, the Vulgate, and Luther's German translation. Compared with sources used later, these were inferior, but he did his work wonderfully well. The influence of Tyndale's translation is seen in the fact that eighty per cent of the Authorized Version retains his phraseology. He possessed not only a rare knowledge of Hebrew and Greek but also a prose style unparalleled in grace, felicity of expression, and vigor. It is not too much to say that Tyndale's translation was the making of the "King's English," the normative English usage, and, as incorporated in the King James Bible, remained such for three hundred years. What Luther accomplished through his German Bible, Tyndale did in his English translation. These two men gave to the German and English languages their permanent form, their grace, simplicity, and dignity.

4. The Coverdale Bible

Between Tyndale and the Authorized Version of 1611, several Bibles appeared, all of which were revisions of Tyndale's translation. The most important was that of Myles Coverdale, who was responsible for the publication of the first complete English Bible (1535).[2] Coverdale had Protestant leanings, and, encouraged, perhaps, by the changing attitude toward the English translations on the part of Thomas Cromwell[3] and Archbishop Latimer, he determined to supervise the publication of a complete Bible. Coverdale was more of an editor than a translator, but, as an editor, did much to improve the Tyndale Bible, adding many expressions that were more euphonius or rhythmical and also completing the Old Testament. For those books of the Old Testament not found in Tyndale's Bible, he used Luther's German Bible, the Vulgate, the Zurich Bible of Zwingli, and the Latin text of Pagninus. The Apocrypha were included, although not as canon.

The first edition, published in 1535, was dedicated to the king and therefore encountered little opposition. Whether

[2] Sometimes called the "Treacle Bible" from its rendering of Jeremiah 8:22: "Is there no treacle in Gilead?"

[3] Thomas Cromwell, not to be confused with Oliver Cromwell, was King Henry's chief adviser and acted successively as Privy-Councillor, Chancellor of the Exchequer, Secretary of State, Vicar-General, Lord Great Chamberlain, and supervisor of religious matters.

the 1535 edition was licensed by the king is uncertain, but his revision of 1537 had royal approval. Within one year of Tyndale's martyrdom, a Bible that was essentially his own was now published under the authority of the crown! Such is the irony of progress.

5. Matthew's Bible

The so-called Matthew's Bible was the work of John Rogers, who had been associated with Tyndale in Antwerp and who had acquired some of Tyndale's manuscripts. This Bible appeared in 1537 and was a slightly revised and completed edition of Tyndale's translation. Opposition to Tyndale was still strong, and publication under his name was out of the question. Perhaps for that reason, Rogers used the name Thomas Matthew as the editor. His Old Testament was Tyndale's from Genesis to Chronicles and Coverdale's for the remainder of the Old Testament and the Apocrypha. The New Testament was Tyndale's revised edition.

Rogers dedicated Matthew's Bible to King Henry and Queen Anne. The title page and dedication are signed by Thomas Matthew, whereas the introductory statement ends with the initials J. R., which presumably stand for John Rogers. The presence of both names poses a problem as to the identity of Thomas Matthew. Was he a benefactor who provided the money for the publication? Was he an earlier associate of Tyndale? Or was the name merely used by John Rogers as a pen name? The situation is further complicated by the initials W. T. at the end of the Old Testament; this is all the more perplexing since the latter half of the Old Testament was the work of Coverdale. The problem is partly clarified by the expression used in Roger's death sentence: " John Rogers alias Matthew."

Matthew's, like Coverdale's 1537 edition, was a licensed Bible. This is surprising since the prologue, notes, and most of the translation were known to be Tyndale's work. Royal sanction can probably be attributed to Cranmer's recommendation to Cromwell in which he said that " so far as I have read thereof I like it better than any other translation heretofore made." Despite this royal approval, its use in churches was prohibited.

This Bible, essentially the work of Tyndale, became the basis for all later translations. Its editor, John Rogers, shared Tyndale's fate. When Mary came to the throne, he was condemned as a heretic and burned at the stake.

6. The Great Bible

There were now two licensed English Bibles. Recognizing that both were in reality Tyndale's translation, Cromwell authorized Coverdale to prepare a revision of Matthew's Bible. In 1538 Coverdale, accompanied by Grafton, a London publisher, went to Paris, where the revision was begun, only to be confiscated and condemned. The publication was completed in London; upon its appearance in England it was supported by Cromwell and later received some episcopal support. It was called the Great Bible (1539) on account of its size.

The editors of the Great Bible made use of Münster's Latin Old Testament, the Vulgate, and the Complutensian Polyglot of Cardinal Ximines, but, in the final analysis, it was essentially a revision of Matthew's Bible, which meant that it was still Tyndale's translation. Because Archbishop Cranmer wrote a preface to the second edition, it has been called Cranmer's Bible. Ironically, the fourth edition was issued under the auspices of Bishop Tunstall, archenemy and persecutor of Tyndale!

The Great Bible enjoys the distinction of being the first — indeed, the only — officially " authorized " English translation.[4] Starting with the 1540 edition, the title page carried the injunction: " This is the Bible appointed to the use of the churches." Copies were placed in the churches by order of the bishops; but the church was evidently not ready for private reading and individual interpretation of the Scripture, for a proclamation was issued prohibiting all private discussion of the Bible, especially in " taverns and alehouses."

One improvement over previous Bibles was the elimination of marginal comments and sectarian introductions. Even Coverdale's attempts at marginal interpretations of " dark passages " were removed. On the title page appeared an elaborate woodcut showing King Henry VIII directing Cromwell and Cranmer to distribute copies of the Bible.

Henry's Protestantism was political rather than ideological. In the latter part of his reign he turned against the Protestant leaders and officially condemned every Bible except the Great Bible. Many Bibles were burned at this time and reading of the Scripture by the common people was prohibited. Cromwell was executed in 1540, and a general persecution of Protestants followed.

[4] The so-called Authorized Version of 1611 was produced under the sponsorship of King James, who actually appointed the committee of translators, but, as far as the records show, it was never officially authorized by him or any other authority.

7. *The Taverner Bible*

An independent revision of Matthew's Bible was published in 1539, the same year in which the Great Bible appeared. This was by Richard Taverner, a London lawyer and friend of Cromwell. Shortly after Cromwell's death, Taverner was imprisoned in the Tower of London. Although a layman, he had an excellent knowledge of Greek and was well known for his literary achievements. His New Testament, therefore, was checked against the original sources, but his work in the Old Testament was confined to arbitrary improvements in the English. Several of his words and phrases, such as " parable " for " similitude," were contained in subsequent translations. Regardless of its merits, Taverner's Bible was eclipsed by the Great Bible and played a relatively minor role in the drama of the transmission of the Scripture.

8. *The Geneva Bible*

Under Edward VI, England became more distinctly Protestant, and the Great Bible came into wider use. But Edward was succeeded by Mary Tudor, who rescinded all the pro-Protestant laws of her predecessor and turned England back officially to Catholicism. Reading of the English Bible was punishable by death. Under Bloody Mary, as the queen was dubbed, hundreds of Protestants suffered martyrdom. Among those put to death were Cranmer and Latimer. Coverdale, made bishop of Exeter under Edward VI, found himself in grave danger and fled to the Continent.

Many nonconformist Protestant leaders and prominent scholars went to Geneva, where they found a more favorable atmosphere. It was here that the Geneva Bible was translated and printed. The New Testament (1557) was largely the work of William Whittingham, a brother-in-law of Calvin and pastor of the English church in Geneva. The Old Testament was done by Anthony Gilby and others and appeared in 1560 along with a revision of Whittingham's New Testament.

The Geneva Bible, like previous and subsequent translations, was just another revision, which means that Tyndale was the chief source for the text. This was true more particularly of the New Testament. In the Old Testament, the Great Bible (a revision of Tyndale) was the immediate basis, with some reference to the Hebrew. The Geneva Bible was dedicated to Queen Elizabeth, who had meanwhile acceded to the throne and who was enjoined to " root out " popery and all forms of Catholicism. It was called the " Breeches Bible " from its rendering of Genesis 3:7 where Adam and Eve " sewed fig leaves together and made themselves breeches."

The most original work done in this Bible was in connection with those sections of the Old Testament not translated by Tyndale. Here the Hebrew text was consulted with great profit. In the New Testament, the commentary of Beza was used along with Latin texts.

The improvements in scholarship in the Geneva Bible were somewhat offset by the pro-Calvinist marginal notes, which ultimately weakened its influence. For a long time, however, it was popular because of this Protestant slanting. Later translators operated with greater professional integrity and were careful to avoid all sectarian bias and subjective interpretation. The work of the translator stops with the translation.

The Geneva Bible is famous for several innovations. It was the first to use Roman type. It was the first Bible to arrange the text in verses; that is, with each sentence printed as a separate unit. (This scheme was followed up to the Revised Version, which arranged the material in paragraphs according to subject matter.) It was the first English Bible to omit the Apocrypha. It was the first to use italics for all words not occurring in the original Hebrew or Greek text, but which needed to be added for sense or correct form. It was the first to omit the name of Paul in connection with the Book of Hebrews.

These features, along with the excellence of the translation itself and new mechanical features, helped to make it the family Bible of England and Scotland and the Bible of the early Puritans. It was the Bible used by Shakespeare and Bunyan. Its popularity is seen in the fact that at least eight editions appeared after the publication of the King James Version.

9. The Bishops' Bible

Elizabeth favored Protestantism for the same reasons that Constantine favored Christianity — political reasons. She reinstated the reading of the Scripture in the churches, and the Bible to be read was the Great Bible. However, the Geneva Bible was recognized as superior in scholarship and was certainly more popular, with the result that the Great Bible was unable to hold its own as the "official" Bible of England.

On the other hand, the Geneva Bible was partisan; it represented not the whole church but only the so-called liberal party.

Church authorities, therefore, decided to publish a Bible that would supplant both earlier versions and appointed Matthew Parker, archbishop of Canterbury, to undertake the task. His committee was composed mostly of bishops, a fact that led to the name, Bishops' Bible. Each translator was assigned a different section, and the whole was edited by Archbishop Parker. The translators were instructed to follow the Great Bible except where the Hebrew and Greek original required changes.

The Bishops' Bible was four years in the making and appeared in 1568. For a while it took the place of the Great Bible in an official way but actually did not displace the Geneva Bible as the Bible of the people. Since its official sanction was ecclesiastical rather than political, it lacked both royal approval and popular support. Its use among the clergy was endorsed by a convocation in 1571, but even this decree failed to make it popular.

10. Rheims-Douai Bible

The Rheims-Douai Bible is the Geneva Bible in reverse. Protestant scholars in exile under Mary produced the Geneva Bible. Now Roman Catholic scholars, fleeing from the persecution under Elizabeth, went to the Continent, where they published the Rheims-Douai Version in 1610. The publication of a Catholic Bible in English was not to be expected at any time in view of the official attitude of the church that held that Latin was the sacred language and that it was not wise for the common people to read the Scripture. The new version, therefore, was undertaken with great reluctance.

Why was it done at all? The answer can only be that it was a defensive move to offset the popularity of the Protestant English Bibles. The publication of an English version under Catholic auspices most certainly did not imply encouragement of lay reading of the Scripture. The preface, in fact, warns against use of the Bible by the people.[5] It was issued in self-protection or, perhaps, with the more aggressive motive of swinging political opinion back to Catholicism.

William Allen, an Oxford fellow, founded an English college at Douai in Flanders in 1568. The New Testament was commenced here under the leadership of Gregory Martin, also of Oxford. In 1578 the college was removed to Rheims, where the New Testament was published in 1609–10; hence, the name Rheims-Douai Version.

The translation, of course, was directly from the Vulgate, although reference was made to the Greek texts for the New Testament. The marginal interpretations were just as Catholic in their slant as the Geneva commentary had been Protestant. A typical example of the polemical exegesis is the marginal comment attached to Matthew 6:24 (" No one can serve two masters "), which reads: " Two religions, God and Baal, Christ and Calvin, Mass and Communion, The Catholic Church and Heretical Conventicles." As for the accuracy of the text as a translation of the Vulgate, nineteenth- and twen-

[5] The preface to the New Testament stated that the Scripture should not be read by " husbandmen, artificers, apprentices, boys, girls, mistresses, maids," and that it was not intended for " table talk, ale houses, boats, barges, and for every profane person and company." It further stated that " in those better times men were not so curious as to abuse the blessed book of Christ."

tieth-century translations based on fourth-century Greek manuscripts were to confirm certain Douai readings that were more accurate than other English versions of that period.[6] On the whole, the Rheims-Douai Version was couched in a stilted Latinized vocabulary. A revision was made by Bishop Challoner in 1750, and in 1941 it was again revised in accordance with Hebrew and Greek sources and completely modernized.

11. The King James Bible

In 1604 James I, who had succeeded Elizabeth in 1603, called a conference to consider the petition of the Puritans to change the Prayer Book and service of worship. The outcome of this conference was far different from all expectations. During the course of the hearings, and quite accidentally, the question of the Bible was broached. Dr. John Reynolds, president of Corpus Christi College, Oxford, and a Puritan himself, suggested that the king authorize the publication of a new Bible, inasmuch as those in use were " corrupt and not answerable to the truth of the original." The final result of that suggestion was the King James Bible or Authorized Version of 1611.[7]

Dr. Reynolds' motion was opposed by the bishop of London, who visualized a new translation every year if such a practice was continued; but the king, either for personal mo-

---

[6] The doxology at the end of the Lord's Prayer (Matt. 6:13), for instance, does not appear in the Vulgate or the Douai Version and is omitted in the American Standard Version and Revised Standard Version, since it is not found in the older Greek manuscripts. But it does appear in the Authorized Version.

[7] Many interesting sidelights on the English translations from Wycliffe to the Authorized Version are to be found in *The English Hexapla* (London: Samuel Bagster and Sons, 1841).

tives or because he resented the Puritan bias of the Geneva Bible, was heartily in favor of the project. Whatever the king's motive, his choice of translators was made with wisdom and catholicity; the committee of fifty-four men included Anglicans and Puritans, high churchmen and low, clergy and laymen. The work was begun in 1607 and forty-seven actually participated. The appointment of a large committee was an improvement, for previous revisions had been undertaken by one man, assisted by one or two friends. The committee was instructed to follow the Bishops' Bible mainly, but to consult the Greek text of Erasmus as revised by Stephanus and Beza, the Vulgate, and current Hebrew texts, including the Complutensian Polyglot. Free use was made of the Geneva and Rheims-Douai Bibles wherever it was thought advisable. Reference was also made to Luther's German and Olivetan's French Bibles, the Latin translations of Pagninus, Münster, and Castalio, and the Syriac New Testament. As a revision of the Bishops' Bible, the King James Version is virtually the Tyndale Bible (Tyndale→Matthew's→Great→Bishops'→King James).

The committee was divided into six sections, two to meet at Oxford, two at Cambridge, and two at Westminster. Each group was assigned a certain portion of the Scripture. The work of each group was reviewed by the other groups; in fact, every man passed judgment on the work of every other man, and six final revisions were made of the work in its entirety before publication.

The translators were instructed to use no marginal notes except necessary explanations of Hebrew and Greek words or alternate translations of original words. The preface of the 1611 edition indicates that the translators considered themselves revisers and no more; they were merely trying to "build on the foundation that went before." [8] The Authorized Version of 1611 included the Apocrypha, but later it was dropped as noncanonical. The chapter and verse division was the same as in the Bishops' Bible.

The first revised edition of the Authorized Version appeared in 1613 with some three hundred changes. This was followed by revisions in 1629, 1638, 1762, and 1769. The 1769 edition represented a more thoroughgoing modernization and is substantially the edition of the present day. Bishop Lloyd's edition, issued in 1701, was the first to use Archbishop Usher's chronology, which dated the creation of the world at 4004 B.C. (!). This chronological pattern has had an influence throughout the English-speaking world out of all proportion to its worth.

The sources for the Authorized Version naturally were inferior to those used by later translators. No consistency was observed in proper names and measurements, and the same object was given a variety of renderings. The translators' knowledge of Greek and Hebrew usage left much to be desired. Archaisms, solecisms, and erroneous translations, of which there were many, came under much closer scrutiny in the latter part of the nineteenth century when the Revised Version appeared.

In time, the Authorized Version replaced both the Geneva edition as the popular Bible and the Bishops' as the offi-

---

[8] For accurate information on the justification of revision, method of procedure, rules and objectives, the reader is referred to the prefaces of the Authorized Version, Revised Version, and American Standard Version. There is no substitute for these original statements of the translators. Unfortunately, in the case of the Authorized Version, modern editions carry only the obsequious, florid dedication to King James and omit the more important preface of the translators.

cial or ecclesiastical Bible. There was no thought of another Bible for two hundred and seventy years. The King James Bible became *the* Bible for the Protestant world. Its influence on the speech and literature of England is vast and well known.[9] From 1900 to 1950 some eleven hundred titles of books, mostly novels in English, were taken from the Bible (usually the Authorized Version). Biblical phrases in common usage today are numerous: " the apple of his eye," " cast thy bread upon the waters," " a still small voice," " the little foxes that spoil the vines," " precept upon precept, line upon line," " the signs of the times," " a thorn in the flesh," " labor of love," " the handwriting on the wall," " the widow's mite," " the highways and hedges," " a pearl of great price," " stand in awe," " the fat of the land," " the end is not yet," " to entertain angels unaware," " tell it not in Gath."

The paramount position of the Authorized Version in England and America became so firmly fixed that to this day it is not uncommon to hear a parishioner remark (after hearing the preacher read from the American Standard Version or Revised Standard Version or a modern translation): " That was interesting, but I prefer the Bible." For him and thousands like him, the King James is the only form in which the real Bible ever appeared. The problem of the Hebrew and Greek texts, manuscripts and versions, translations and revisions, is not in his world.

Like all the other Bibles, the Authorized Version contained many misprints and mistranslations, one of the most famous being Matthew 23:24: " Ye blind guides, which strain at a gnat, and swallow a camel." It should read: " strain

        9 See C. A. Dinsmore, *The English Bible as Literature* (Boston, 1931); J. H. Penniman, *A Book about the English Bible* (New York, 1919); M. B. Crook, *The Bible and Its Literary Associations* (New York, 1937).

out a gnat," but the mistake still appears in the present edition.[10]

12. The Revised Version

The Revised Version (1881–85) was part of a concatenation of events that caused an intellectual upheaval in the Western world almost as momentous as that which precipitated Tyndale's translation. The cultural rebirth of Europe and America in the nineteenth century was almost as far-reaching in its consequences as the Renaissance. Nothing less could have threatened the monopoly that the King James Bible enjoyed for two hundred and fifty years.

The Authorized Version was revised several times in the seventeenth century because of the increasing criticism of the translation. During the reign of the Stuarts, England became so unbelievably pagan that very little thought was given to the Bible. By the middle of the eighteenth century the King James Bible had taken on such an aura of sanctity that even the idea of revision was a sacrilege. But by the middle of the nineteenth century a combination of developments forced the issue. One was the discovery and availability of older and more authoritative manuscripts than those known in 1611; namely *Codex Alexandrinus*, a fifth-century manuscript, and the great fourth-century manuscripts, *Sinaiticus* and *Vaticanus*. These texts carried many important readings that differed from the *Textus Receptus*. Some of the New Testa-

---

10 Matthew's Bible was nicknamed the "Bug Bible" because it retained a misprint from Coverdale: "Thou shalt not nede to be afrayed for eny bugges by night" (Ps. 91:5). The Authorized Version as revised in 1631 came to be known as the Wicked Bible from an unfortunate omission in the rendering of Ex. 20:14, which read: "Thou shalt commit adultery."

ment of the *Textus Receptus* was from the Vulgate, and the Old Testament was taken from four inferior Hebrew recensions. Tischendorf's discovery of *Codex Aleph*, the editing of *B*, and the appearance of new critical Greek New Testaments by Tischendorf and by Westcott and Hort would have been reason enough for a new translation of the Bible.

Textual Criticism, which in the early part of the seventeenth century was unknown, had become a specialized science with a well-defined critical apparatus and trained biblical scholars. With two thousand manuscripts available for examination, collation, and editing — two of them from the fourth century — a closer approximation of the original was guaranteed. Further, knowledge of the Hebrew and Greek languages had increased tremendously, and scholars were much better qualified for the work of translation.

The pervasive influence of the theory of evolution, with its implication of the inevitability of change in all things, called into question the belief in static revelation, the idea of the absolute, the infallibility of Scripture, and the biblical account of creation. The theory of evolution supported the empirical method and the ideas of process, immanence, and emergence. The nineteenth century also gave birth to the science of Historical Criticism, which applied the genetic method to religion and biblical literature; on this background arose a new study of comparative religion, the history of religion, philology, and the social sciences. This resulted in the developmental view, which approached Scripture from the standpoint of hereditary factors and environmental influences.

The scientific outlook of the nineteenth century, in short, revolutionized man's thinking, and a new interest in biblical research was one of the results of this revolution. For scholars, therefore, if not for the people at large, a new translation was a necessity.

But one of the most cogent reasons for the Revised Version was the change in the English language in two hundred and seventy years. Hundreds of Elizabethan expressions were now obsolete and meaningless. How could the nineteenth-century reader of the King James Bible know that " knave " meant " boy," that " honest " meant " chaste," that " leasing " meant " falsehood," that " purtenance " meant " inward," that " carriages " meant " baggage," that " scrip " meant " wallet," and that " chapiter " meant " capital of a column "? According to the Authorized Version, the head of John the Baptist was brought in on a " charger " (Mark 6:28). To a modern reader this could only mean a galloping horse rather than a platter. Confronting Acts 28:13, the twentieth-century reader wonders why the travelers " fetched a compass " (this originally meant " circled around " or " made a circuit "). Such archaisms pointed clearly to the need for a new translation that would suit the vocabulary of modern times.

Many grammatical slips were also in need of correction. It is useless to teach a boy in school that the nominative, rather than the accusative, follows the expression " I am," when he reads in Mark 8:27: " Whom do men say that I am? " Likewise, any schoolboy knows that the pronoun " which " should not follow " Our Father " in the Lord's Prayer. Jesus was not tempted " of " but " by " the Devil. These and many other examples of poor usage called for a modernization of the Authorized Version.

On February 10, 1870, Bishop Samuel Wilberforce suggested that a revision of the Authorized Version be made with the idea of correcting errors, improving the vocabulary, and

embodying renderings more in accord with the older manuscripts. A committee [11] was formed and rules of procedure
were drawn up. The New Testament work was initiated in
Westminster Abbey on June 22, 1870, with Bishop J. C. Elli-
cott presiding. A subcommittee of American theologians under the chairmanship of Philip Schaff was appointed to collaborate with the British committee. The New Testament was
published in 1881, the Old Testament in 1885, and the Apocrypha in 1895.

Several mechanical changes were made, the most noticeable of which were the rearranging of the text in sense
paragraphs, the printing of poetical material in verse form, the
omission of all commentary and headings, and the incorpora-
tion of critical footnotes citing alternate or more literal readings. From the standpoint of Textual Criticism, the changes
surpassed all predictions. A sample of textual change is seen
in I John 5:8, which in the Authorized Version reads: " For
there are three that bear record, (in heaven — the Father, the
Word, and the Holy Ghost, and these three are one. And
there are three that bear witness in earth) the Spirit, and the
Water, and the Blood, and these agree in one." The section
in parentheses is not found in the older manuscripts and was
therefore omitted from the Revised Version as a theological
interpolation. The doxology found at the end of the Lord's
Prayer in the Authorized Version was omitted for the same
reason. Many other sentences found only in *Codex Bezae*
were omitted in the Revised Version. The longer ending of
Mark (16:9–20) was included, but a note was attached indicating that it was not found in the two older manuscripts.

[11] The committee consisted of such distinguished Hebrew and
Greek scholars as A. B. Davidson, S. R. Driver, A. H. Sayce, T. K.
Cheyne, H. Alford, J. Eadie, F. J. A. Hort, J. B. Lightfoot, W. F.
Moulton, R. C. Trench, and B. F. Westcott.

Many obsolete expressions were modernized: " cake " for " cracknel," " living " for " quick," " boil " for " botch," and " distress " for " straitness." " Holy Spirit " was substituted for " Holy Ghost " and " Sheol " for " Hell."

The Revised Version represented the fruits of two centuries of study. No previous scholars could have had the linguistic knowledge and the technical equipment possessed by this committee. The Greek text for the New Testament was that of Westcott and Hort, although other editions were consulted. The Masoretic text of the Hebrew had, by that time, been re-edited and improved. The result of their ten years' labor was a great gain for students of the Bible, if not for the layman. The Revised Version has been widely criticized as being too literal and altogether lacking in the lofty, spiritual tone that made the King James Bible so popular. But what it lost in beauty it gained in accuracy, and that was important. The Pauline Epistles, especially, appeared in a more intelligible form.

Opposition was not long in asserting itself, as has been the case with every revision. The Revised Version did not displace the Authorized Version in England largely because of the long familiarity with the literary form of the King James Bible and the emotional associations attached to it. But it did take its place in universities, church schools, and among the clergy and students.

13. The American Standard Version

The American subcommittee appointed to collaborate with the British revision committee had taken its work seriously and had submitted many suggestions, many of which were ignored. Numerous obsolete expressions and faulty translations of the original Hebrew and Greek appeared in the final draft of the Revised Version over the protest of the American committee. It was natural, therefore, that the members of the American committee would want to publish a revision of their own.

The American committee was pledged to give no sanction to the publication of the Revised Version in America in any form for a period of fourteen years. But the committee continued to function and at the expiration of that period published the American Standard Version (1901), which received immediate and widespread use for religious education, in schools and colleges, and among the clergy. In spite of its obvious superiority over all previous translations, however, the American Standard Version has never replaced the Authorized Version as the family and pulpit Bible of America. The general human inertia and apathy toward biblical scholarship is reflected in bookstores and libraries, where, in many instances, supposedly informed clerks do not know one version from another.

The American committee revised the appendix of the Revised Version, which had been written hastily, and added many significant changes in the text. "Jehovah," for instance, was substituted for "Lord" and "God" on the grounds that "a Jewish superstition, which regarded the Divine Name as too sacred to be uttered, ought no longer to dominate in the English or any other version of the Old Testament.[12] In the interest of grammatical accuracy the pronoun "who" was used in place of "which" when relating to persons. The orthography and idiom of 1611, which the Revised

[12] For complete details on the procedure and reasons for changes, see the preface of the American Standard Version.

Version had retained in many passages, were brought up to date.

The chief concern of the members of the American committee was to include readings that they had recommended on the basis of superior documentary evidence but that had been declined by the British reviewers. Also, many of the changes were made for the sake of consistency, where the Revised Version had translated the same word in different ways. The Babylonians and the ancient Hebrews regarded the liver, the kidneys, and the bowels as the seat of affection. Assigning mental and emotional attributes to physical organs has survived in the modern poetic use of " heart," but the Hebrews used what to our taste would be more offensive terms. These were removed in the American Standard Version, and more euphemistic expressions were substituted. The word " bowels," for instance, wherever used in the psychological sense, was changed to " compassion," " anguish," or " heart." " Reins," meaning " kidneys," was changed to " heart," " dung " to " refuse," and " stinketh " to " decayeth." Because of the change in the connotation of " charity," the word " love " was substituted in I Corinthians 13.

14. The Revised Standard Version

The American Standard Version was really only a correction or revision of the Revised Version, and, while it contained improvements, the changes were neither drastic nor thoroughgoing. Biblical research and archaeological discovery in the half-century that followed only confirmed the inadequacy of the 1901 edition. In the half-century following the publication of the Revised Version, archaeologists had learned much about the Koiné Greek of the New Testament from potsherds and papyri found in Egypt. They had also been at work reconstructing the Babylonian sources for the Old Testament traditions. During the first three decades of the twentieth century new manuscripts were discovered and edited, notably the Dead Sea Scrolls, the Washington and Koridethi gospels, and the Chester Beatty Papyri. These discoveries shed new light on the Hebrew and Greek texts.

Scholars soon realized that the modernization of the King James Bible was not fully accomplished by either the Revised Version or the American Standard Version. Modern private translations appearing in the first quarter of the twentieth century emphasized the need for a more thorough revision, but such translations do not have the official support of the church. It remained for the Revised Standard Version of 1946–52 to accomplish this goal.

The work was initiated in 1930 with the formulation of a committee under the chairmanship of Dean Luther A. Weigle of Yale.[18] Old and New Testament sections were organized, and meetings were held for the determination of policy. The aim of the committee, in its own words, was to produce " a revision of the present American Standard Edition of the Bible in the light of the results of modern scholarship, this revision to be designed for use in public and private worship, and to be in the direction of the simple, classic English style of the King James Version." The members of the committee were chosen with three things in mind: competence in biblical scholarship, appreciation of the best taste in English literature, and

---

[18] The committee consisted of the following: Luther A. Weigle, Julius A. Bewer, Henry J. Cadbury, Edgar J. Goodspeed, James Moffatt, William R. Taylor, Walter Russell Bowie, George Dahl, Frederick C. Grant, William A. Irwin, Willard L. Sperry, Leroy Waterman, Millar Burrows, Clarence T. Craig, Abdel R. Wentz, Kyle M. Yates, William F. Albright, J. Philip Hyatt, Herbert G. May, James Muilenburg, Harry M. Orlinsky, and Fleming James.

experience in the conduct of public worship and religious education.

We can assume that their directions to attain the " simple, classic English style of the King James Version " referred not so much to phraseology as to spirit, for obviously one of the chief reasons for the undertaking was to avoid the archaisms and inaccurate paraphrasing of the Authorized Version. More specifically, their task was to attempt to sail between the Scylla of the free translation of the King James Version and the Charybdis of the literal or prosaic renderings of the Revised Version and the American Standard Version; to combine, in other words, readability and accuracy — a difficult commission.

The cumulative critical opinion regarding the Revised Standard Version, as of the present writing, is that this two-fold aim of readability in public usage and accuracy of translation has been achieved in the most satisfying manner. To appreciate the smooth, natural flow of language of this version, one should read aloud such passages as Luke 10 and Acts 11:19–26. Elizabethan expressions that had been retained in the American Standard Version were now eliminated. " You " and " your " took the place of " thou " and " thine," " to " was substituted for " into," and " enter " for " enter into." Such antique expressions as " on this wise," " set at nought," and " privily " were modernized. The American Standard Version had kept such seventeenth-century usages as " provided " for " foreseen," " providence " for " provision," and " suffer " for " allow." These likewise were corrected. The unpardonable " much people " of the American Standard Version was changed to " many people " (Acts 11:24), and the spies who " feigned themselves to be righteous " now " pretended to be sincere " (Luke 20:20).

The improvement made by the Revised Standard

Version is appreciated in the following sample from Luke 9:17:

American Standard Version: "And they ate, and were all filled: and there was taken up that which remained over to them of broken pieces, twelve baskets."

Revised Standard Version: "And all ate and were satisfied. And they took up what was left over, twelve baskets of broken pieces."

The Revised Standard Version was published by Thomas Nelson and Sons and now appears under the copyright of the National Council of the Churches of Christ in the United States of America. Perhaps the best way to appreciate the fact that the Revised Standard Version is a church-sponsored Bible in the direct line of descent from Tyndale and the Authorized Version is to read the title page, which has retained the same wording as all previous versions. The committee will continue as self-perpetuating in order to make future changes in the text. The Revised Standard Version has been well received (except in obscurantist circles) and is rapidly taking the place of the American Standard Version in classrooms, church schools, pulpits, and among the laity as well as the clergy.[14]

15. Private Translations

It remains for us to call attention to some of the modern-speech or private translations of the Bible. These, in every

[14] For the description of the procedure of the committee and other interesting data on the Revised Standard Version, see the preface of the *Holy Bible; Revised Standard Version* (New York, 1952); H. S. May, *Our English Bible in the Making* (Philadelphia, 1952); I. M. Price, *The Ancestry of our English Bible* (2nd rev. ed.; New York, 1949).

instance, are the work of individuals and are not authorized by any church or council. They are published with two things in mind: to provide a more common or conversational type of translation than is permitted in the authorized Bibles, and to improve, wherever possible, on the renderings of the Hebrew and Greek texts. The impetus behind these private translations, at least in the case of the New Testament, was the growing realization, at the turn of the century, that the Koiné Greek of the New Testament was the language of the common people, differing completely from both the classical and the Septuagint Greek, and therefore should be translated, not in a literary style, but in a conversational or household English.

The first important private translation was the Weymouth New Testament which appeared in 1903. This was an independent free translation based on the Resultant Greek Testament of the translator, Richard F. Weymouth. *The New Testament in Modern Speech*, as it was called, was a British publication, but an American edition was published in 1943. It was issued with the idea of supplementing or correcting the Revised Version, and Weymouth did succeed in eliminating some antiquated expressions.

The *Twentieth Century New Testament*, another British publication, was originally issued " tentatively " in 1901, but appeared in its revised form in 1904. This anonymous translation represented the combined efforts of some twenty scholars who wanted to give the New Testament to the people in the language they used in their daily life. One radical change made was the arrangement of the books in the order of their composition; that is, Mark came first in the gospel section, and I Thessalonians in the Paulines. The names of the translators have never been known by the public.

In 1885 R. G. Moulton, of the University of Chicago, undertook the publication of the Revised Version in separate volumes. The complete twenty-one-volume edition appeared in 1907 under the title, *The Modern Reader's Bible*. This is not a modern-speech translation but is included here because of the typographical arrangements that provided greater readability. The text is actually the Revised Version with some modifications.

The Riverside New Testament (1923) was the work of William G. Ballantine, late professor of Biblical Literature at Springfield College. Dr. Ballantine used Nestle's Greek text and held to a more literal policy of translation.

In 1913 James Moffatt published *The New Testament: A New Translation*. This became a popular translation on both sides of the Atlantic.[15] Professor Moffatt taught formerly at Glasgow and later at Union Theological Seminary and was recognized as one of the leading authorities in the field. His New Testament was not only well translated but was couched in the idiom of the twentieth century. His Old Testament was published in 1924, and the complete Bible in 1926. In his translation of the Old Testament Moffatt revised the Masoretic text in many places.

The most distinctively American and one of the most satisfactory private translations is that of Edgar J. Goodspeed. Weymouth and Moffatt unconsciously retained British idioms, and Ballantine's translation was not entirely free of the influence of the King James Bible. Goodspeed's *New Testament: An American Translation* (1923), comes closer to the American language than any other and, having the appearance of a novel, is most attractive from the mechanical and typo-

---

[15] This was the outgrowth of his *Historical New Testament* (Edinburgh, 1901), a critical introduction to the New Testament.

graphical standpoint. Many of the improvements of the Revised Standard Version, such as the substitution of " you " for " thou " and " cents " for " shillings," were anticipated by Goodspeed, although as a member of the committee he made it clear that the Revised Standard Version was not to be another " Goodspeed Bible."

In 1927 the University of Chicago Press issued *The Old Testament: An American Translation.* This was edited by J. M. P. Smith of the University of Chicago. Smith's Old Testament and Goodspeed's New Testament were published as *The Bible: An American Translation,* sometimes called the Chicago Bible. In 1933 Goodspeed brought out *The Short Bible: An American Translation,* a volume chronologically arranged and containing only those books and passages which, in the mind of the editors, were historically or religiously valuable. In 1938 Goodspeed made a completely fresh translation of the *Apocrypha,* which was issued in connection with the Chicago Bible, and finally in 1950 he published *The Apostolic Fathers.*

The Centenary Translation of the New Testament (1924) was the work of Mrs. Helen Barrett Montgomery. It was published in connection with the celebration of the hundredth anniversary of the founding of the American Baptist Publication Society.

S. H. Hooke of the University of London supervised the publication of *The Basic Bible* (1950). *The New Testament in Basic English* had appeared in 1941. For the New Testament only 850 different words were employed, but the basic vocabulary was increased to 1,000 for the Old Testament. This was a novel experiment but imposes an undue restriction on the translators.

C. H. Rieu, editor of the Penguin Classics, published *The*

Four Gospels: A New Translation in 1953 and *The Acts of the Apostles: A New Translation* in 1957. One might question his assertion in the introduction that "the four gospels are spiritually supreme largely *because* they are great literature" and that the church chose them because of their literary and artistic superiority. Mr. Rieu has, however, rightly avoided the classical and literary style in his translation, which preserves the power and urgency of the original text and is, at the same time, unpretentious in style and totally free of word-for-word literalness.

J. B. Phillips' *The New Testament in Modern English* appeared in 1958. This translation conveys the spirit of the original Greek of the New Testament to the modern reader in a language that is at once comprehensible and faithful to the original tongue. It is a skillful rendering with no trace of subjective interpretation or slant, but with a precise knowledge of the vernacular of both first-century Greek and twentieth-century English.

Recent Roman Catholic Bibles can hardly be called private translations, but it is interesting to note in passing that several scholarly revisions have been made in the twentieth century, notably *The Westminster Version of the Sacred Scripture* (1935), *The New Testament of our Lord and Savior Jesus Christ*, edited by C. J. Callan and J. A. McHugh and translated by F. A. Spencer (1937), *The New Testament Translated from the Latin Vulgate; a Revision of the Challoner-Rheims Version* (1941), and, in England in 1944, a translation of the Vulgate by Ronald Knox.

The only recent English work by Jewish scholars has been *The Holy Scriptures According to the Masoretic Text, a New Translation*, published by the Jewish Publication Society in 1917.

From Wycliffe to Rieu is a long distance. Some of the changes in English usage may be noted in the forms in which the following sample verse (Acts 17:22) appears:

Wycliffe: Men of Atenes, bi alle thingis, I se zou as veyn worschipers.

Tyndale: Ye men of Attens, I perceave that in all things ye are to supersticious.

Geneva: Ye men of Athens, I perceave that in all things ye are to superstitious.

Rheims: Ye men of Athens, in all things I perceive you as it were superstitious.

Authorized Version: Ye men of Athens, I perceive that in all things ye are too superstitious.

Revised Version: Ye men of Athens, in all things I perceive that ye are somewhat superstitious.

American Standard Version: Ye men of Athens, in all things I perceive that ye are very religious.

Revised Standard Version: Men of Athens, I perceive that in every way you are very religious.

Weymouth: Men of Athens, I perceive that you are in every respect remarkably religious.

Centenary: Men of Athens, I perceive that in all respects you are remarkable religious.

Twentieth Century: Men of Athens, On every hand I see signs of your being very religious.

Moffatt: Men of Athens, I observe wherever I turn that you are a most religious people.

Ballantine: Men of Athens, I see that you are in every way unusually reverential to the Gods.

Basic English: O men of Athens, I see that you are overmuch given to fear of the Gods.

Goodspeed: Men of Athens, from every point of view I see that you are extremely religious.

Phillips: Gentlemen of Athens, my own eyes tell me that you are in all respects an extremely religious people.

Rieu: Men of Athens, I notice that you are in many ways very interested in religion.

Part Five

A Brief History of the Higher Criticism

Chapter Thirteen

Exegesis in the Early Church

The term " Criticism " must be understood as a purely technical term, which does not carry the adverse or destructive connotation usually associated with the everyday use of the word. It means, rather, an objective analysis of biblical literature and can be divided into two classes: Lower and Higher. The Lower Criticism aims to determine as far as possible the original form of the text. This is done by a comparative study of manuscripts and early versions.

The Higher Criticism has to do with the origin, purpose, meaning, authenticity, characteristics, and chronology of the books of the Bible. The higher critic studies the sources that were used by the author of the book, the milieu in which the book was written, its dependence upon previous or contemporary cultures, its unity or lack of it, and its teachings. An appropriate example of the work of Higher Criticism is the discovery of the composite authorship of the Pentateuch and the formulation of a documentary theory regarding it, or the Two-Source — and Four-Source — theory proposed to solve the problem of the interrelation of the Synoptic Gospels.

The science of Biblical Criticism has a long history, and scholars of all faiths, Jewish and Christian, have contributed to its growth. To these dedicated persons we owe all that we know about the Bible.

1. Jewish Interpretation

Having described the formation, canonization, and transmission of the Bible, we turn now to the history of interpretation. Our survey will be confined to those periods in which there were distinct changes in the methodology of interpretation; namely, the critical or early period of the church, the post-Reformation period, and the twentieth century.

The classical Jewish interpretation of the Old Testament was focused almost exclusively on the Law as the absolute revelation of God, supernaturally revealed to Moses, who wrote the entire Pentateuch. The rabbinical approach to the Scripture was not critical or historical. It was literal in regard to the requirements of the Law, but symbolic or mystical in its treatment of numbers and letters. Hillel (30 B.C. to 9 A.D.), however, while not scientific in his method, held that a verse must always be considered in the light of its context, a basic criterion of modern criticism.

The most important early Jewish interpreter was Philo of Alexandria (contemporary of Hillel). A Greek-speaking Alexandrian, he was thoroughly eclectic, being heir to both the Jewish Law and Greek philosophy. For him, Moses and Plato were coequal. His aim was to reconcile the Jewish religion with the Greek culture.

Philo represents the first clear divergence from the static, literal interpretation of Scripture. Recognizing that certain passages obviously could not be taken literally, he resorted to allegorization, a method used by Greek writers in harmonizing their philosophy with the older poets. In order to obviate contradictory or absurd passages, he read a hidden meaning into them. For example, in his commentary on Genesis 2:1

he says it is foolish to think that the world was created in six days: the number six is used purely in a symbolic sense. Likewise, he questions both the biblical account of the creation of woman and the statement that Cain built a city, when there were supposedly only three human beings in existence at that time.

Philo thus rules out the literal meaning just as emphatically as modern critics do, though he was seeing hidden meanings. His method was purely arbitrary: numbers and names had sacred and esoteric meanings — the meanings he wanted them to have. Scripture with him was miraculously and verbally inspired; the writer, Moses, was a passive instrument in the hands of God.

An appraisal of Jesus' interpretation of the Scripture would be of supreme interest, but the gospel record is, unfortunately, too scanty and too subjectively written to be trustworthy. It is too difficult to distinguish between what Jesus actually said and thought and what his biographers claimed he said and thought. But we can be reasonably certain that, as a biblical critic, Jesus had little in common with the current Jewish method. The essence of his interpretation was discrimination. He allied himself with the prophetic tradition and was radically opposed to Pharisaic legalism.

The key to his attitude toward the Scripture is found in the introduction to the Sermon on the Mount (Matt. 5:17–20), where he declares his intention to fulfill the Law in its spiritual, rather than its technical, meaning. For the old Law he substituted a new principle: the active cultivation of brotherly love rather than a passive abstention from murder; the maintenance of a wholesome mind rather than a mere avoidance of adultery; the life of integrity rather than casuistry; and sacrificial good will rather than reciprocal or calculated kindness. He placed human welfare above sacerdotalism and man above institutions. He was impatient with the current casuistical interpretation of Scripture and placed ethical purity above ceremonial purity.

His distinction between the definitely religious values in the Old Testament and the cultic regulations is seen in such passages as Matthew 12:1–8 (the well-being of man is more important than strict observance of the Sabbath); Matthew 15:1–20 (moral defilement is a more serious sin than ceremonial defilement); and Matthew 9:10–13 (righteousness is more important than ritual). His differentiation of the prophetic or ethical element in the Old Testament from the priestly or ceremonial is further demonstrated in Matthew 22:34–40 and Mark 12:28–34, where he quotes the Shema, adding to it the love of neighbor, and concludes: " There is no other commandment greater than these."

The closing verses of the Sermon on the Mount reveal the self-consciousness of Jesus as a critic and as an authority in his own right. He was convinced that his ethical principles constituted the *summum bonum* and that a man could build his life on them as bedrock. It was said that " he taught them as one who had authority and not as their scribes." The scribes quoted the Law, which they had memorized; the authority of Jesus was experiential and pragmatic, an appeal to conscience, insight, and conviction.

Jesus clearly transcended the current ceremonial interpretation of the Law; otherwise he was essentially Jewish in his attitude toward the Scripture. He regarded the Pentateuch as inspired writing and Moses as its author. He took the Old Testament literally and, if the evangelists are to be relied on, interpreted the Messianic passages as a prediction of his own life.

Paul's exegesis is rabbinic, but with a Christocentric application. He uses the Law as a forensic medium or bridge for his presentation of Jesus to his Jewish constituency. His preaching to the gentile world necessitated the use of Hellenistic ideas and practices, but, whatever the source of his teaching, it was only as a means to an end — the exaltation of Jesus. The typological use of the Old Testament as a prefigurement or preparation for Christ and the New Covenant is seen more specifically in the Book of Hebrews, a good example of the allegorical method.

2. Patristic Interpretation

The writings of the early church fathers and apologists must be viewed in the light of the New Testament, which had been written by the second century and, if not canonized, was at least regarded as having scriptural authority. Second-century interpretation differs little from that of New Testament authors, in that the Old Testament was regarded as a prediction of the New Testament and Christ as the fulfillment of Old Testament prophecy. Such is the exegesis of Clement of Rome (100 A.D.), who was completely lacking in historical sense. He read back into the Old Testament his own views and those of early Christianity. In fact, he treated the Old Testament as Christian literature.

The author of the Epistle of Barnabas (100–125 A.D.) shares with Clement of Rome the semi-Gnostic or esoteric view of Old Testament interpretation: the Old Testament was parabolic throughout, full of mysteries, unintelligible to the Jews, and understood only by Christian teachers who possessed the " gift " or ability to decipher it. Barnabas uses both the rabbinical method of assigning numerical values to letters and the typological exegesis that flouirshed among later writers. Everything in the Old Testament was a prototype of Christ. When Moses stretched out his arms in the battle with the Amalekites (Ex. 17:12), he was prefiguring the death of Jesus on the cross!

The second-century apologists — Justin Martyr, Theophilus, and Athenagoras — continued the earlier tendency to see the Old Testament as a prediction of Christ and the New Testament. Since the prophets were inspired as passive instruments in the hand of God, they naturally possessed foreknowledge and predicted future events specifically. Needless to say, this misinterpretation of the prophetic function has flourished to the present day.

Throughout the Old Testament, Justin identifies God the Father with the Logos or Christ. He also makes use of the allegorical method. Christ's death on the cross, for instance, was symbolized in the roasting of the paschal lamb (Ex. 12:8).

The mystery, then, of the lamb which God enjoined to be sacrificed as the passover, was a type of Christ . . . and that lamb, which was commanded to be wholly roasted, was a symbol of the suffering of the cross which Christ would undergo. For the lamb, which is roasted, is roasted and dressed up in the form of the cross. For one spit is transfixed right through from the lower parts up to the head and one across the back, to which are attached the legs of the lamb.[1]

With Justin, the allegorical method reached its most fantastic form.

The most important second-century interpretation was that of Irenaeus, bishop of Gaul, whose exegesis was most effective when he was refuting the Gnostics. In his treatise *Against Heresies*, he insists that biblical passages must never

[1] *Dialogue with Trypho,* chap. 40.

be taken out of context, a principle that alone is enough to give him a high place in the history of criticism. He recognized that to do so made it possible to prove anything by Scripture. In his accusation of the heretics, he writes:

Then, again, collecting a set of expressions and names scattered here and there in the Scripture, they twist them, as we have already said, from a natural to a non-natural sense. In so doing, they act like those who bring forward any kind of hypothesis they fancy, and then endeavor to support them out of the poems of Homer so that the ignorant imagine that Homer actually composed the verses with that particular hypothesis in mind. . . . In like manner, he who retains unchangeable in his heart the rule of truth . . . will doubtless recognize the names and expressions taken from the Scripture, but will by no means acknowledge the blasphemous use which these men make of them. But when he has restored every one of the expressions quoted to its proper position, and has fitted it to the body of the truth, he will prove the figment of these heretics to be without foundation.[2]

So much for the one permanently valuable element in the exegesis of Irenaeus. In all other respects, he was no better than his contemporaries. He judged the Scripture by the authority of apostolic theological tradition and, by identifying the two, rendered impossible an objective reading of the Bible. He regarded the Old Testament as one complete prediction of Christ in all the details of his life and teaching. He also used the typological method in both the Old and the New Testament.

3. *The Alexandrian School*

As we enter the third century and move to Alexandria, the Athens of early Christianity and a great cosmopolitan cen-

[2] *Against Heresies*, Book I, chap. 9, sec. 4.

ter of learning, we encounter a more philosophical and eclectic point of view. The two great teachers of Alexandria,
Clement and Origen, tried to accommodate the Christian religion to the Greek tradition and give it a more rational ground-
ing. Clement of Alexandria (150–220 A.D.), who succeeded
Pantaenus as head of the school of Alexandria, was primarily a
philosopher. As an exegete, Clement tried to reconcile the
Christian gospel with Greek thought, just as Philo had previously tried to bring together the Jewish Law and Greek philosophy. Philosophy, according to Clement, should be not
the enemy but the handmaid of the Christian religion. Faith,
in other words, does not rule out reason. Clement's system of
thought was a synthesis of biblical and philosophical learning,
an attempt to legitimize the Greek way of thinking within the
framework of the apostolic tradition. It was an eclecticism
calculated to broaden the appeal of Christianity in Hellenistic
circles.

The key to Clement's exegesis was allegory, but, with
him, it took a more elaborate and scholarly form than with
Philo, Justin, or Irenaeus. For Clement, both the Old and
New Testaments are symbolic. He interpreted Scripture as
having several meanings — historical, moral, or mystical — depending upon the particular verse. Whatever its character,
each verse was interpreted within a Christocentric frame of
reference or, at least, Christian truth.

With Origen (185–254) allegorization assumes a still
more systematic form. Many passages in the Scripture, he
says, are impossible if taken literally; they are to be interpreted
figuratively. All Scripture, in fact, has a symbolic or mystical
meaning, a revelation of some spiritual truth. Although in
some instances this truth may be unfathomable, it is our task
to pursue the ultimate mystery of the Scripture as far as pos-

sible. Sometimes this higher truth is concealed in a narrative or law that, though it may appeal to the ignorant, is not to be taken literally.

Origen's allegorical method proceeds from his dualistic world view: the terrestrial is the image of the celestial. Some texts have a bodily or physical sense, others a spiritual sense. He further sees a threefold meaning in Scripture: the bodily or literal, the moral, and the spiritual. His main concern was to grasp the inner or spiritual truth, which was for him in every case, a justification of the Christian faith and a refutation of heresy.

Apparently Origen resorted to the allegorical interpretation as a way out of the dilemma of literalism. He could see the impossibility of accepting certain passages in the Bible as factual or historical; yet he lacked the perspective of later scholars, who would be able to assign such passages to garbled report, myth, or lack of proper knowledge. It must be said, however, that Origen's manipulation of the text is more intelligent and less dominated by the doctrines of the church than that of any previous interpreter. The allegorical method in the hands of Origen was the best that could be expected at that time and might be said, moreover, to have saved the Christian religion from blind literalism and unreason.

Not only in the allegorical interpretation was Origen a child of his age but also in his view of inspiration as dependent upon the Christian tradition rather than upon the biblical content itself. He believed that Christ was the fulfillment of Old Testament prophecy. As a critic he lacked in historical sense, and some of his symbolic interpretations are fantastic and arbitrary. On the other hand, his rejection of the literal view was in itself a step in the direction of scientific criticism. For example:

For who that has understanding will suppose that the first, and second, and third day, and the evening and the morning, existed without a sun, and moon, and stars? and that the first day was, as it were, also without a sky? . . . And if God is said to walk in the paradise in the evening, and Adam to hide himself under a tree, I do not suppose that any one doubts that these things figuratively indicate certain mysteries, the history having taken place in appearance, and not literally. . . . And what need is there to say more, since those who are not altogether blind can collect countless instances of a similar kind recorded as having occurred, but which did not literally take place? Nay, the Gospels themselves are filled with the same kind of narratives; e.g. the devil leading Jesus up into a high mountain, in order to show Him from thence the kingdoms of the whole world, and the glory of them.[8]

In the same work he mentions passages that " are not literally true but absurd and impossible." [4]

Regarding some of the so-called laws of Moses, he comments: " And if we come to the legislation of Moses, many of the laws manifest the irrationality, and others the impossibility, of their literal observance." [5] He revolted against the anthropomorphisms of the Old Testament and said that those who insist that Moses saw God " fall into the absurdity of asserting that God is corporeal." [6] He regarded as barbarous the divine command in Genesis 17:14 to kill uncircumcised children.

Origen's critical treatment of the New Testament is remarkably advanced, for he calls attention to various discrepancies and contradictions in the gospels.[7] He was one of the first to escape from the Jewish and Zoroastrian eschatology; for him, as for Paul, immortality was a spiritual continuity

---

[8] *de Principiis*, IV, 1, 16.
[4] *Ibid.*, IV, 1, 18.
[5] *Ibid.*, IV, 1, 17.
[6] *Ibid.*, II, 4, 3.
[7] Commentary on John X, 2–3; *de Principiis*, IV, 1, 18.

rather than a resurrection of the physical body.[8] His eschatology was at variance with the current thought on judgment, heaven, and hell. With him, the death of Christ was not a substitutionary atonement. Finally, the modern relegation of miracle to a secondary and unimportant role was to a certain degree anticipated by this great third-century teacher in his assertion that the power of healing diseases is not evidence of anything especially divine.[9]

4. The Antiochian School

The critical spirit of Origen may well be regarded as the foundation of the Antiochian school. In fact, it would not be inappropriate to consider Origen as a representative of the Syrian tradition rather than the Alexandrian. After his expulsion from Alexandria, he lived in Caesarea, where, as a lecturer, he attracted pupils from far and near. A school was organized at Caesarea by Pamphilus (d. 309), who established also an exegetical library in which Origen's Hexapla was kept. The founding of the school at Antioch is credited to the famous scholar Lucian (240–312), who studied in Caesarea under Origen and became the teacher of Arius and Eusebius of Nicomedia.

The Antiochian school differed from the Alexandrian in its Jewish backgrounds and its more literal interpretation of Scripture. This twofold difference is seen in the teaching of the early Antiochian leaders: Paul of Samosata, Lucian, Dorotheus, and Theodore of Mopsuestia, a difference that results, on the one hand, in a more monotheistic and less trinitarian

[8] *Contra Celsum,* VI, 29.
[9] *Ibid.,* III, 25.

tendency and, on the other, in less emphasis on allegory. These two tendencies mark the Antiochian school as the prototype of a later liberal theology and of Historical Criticism.

The two most important representatives of the Antiochian school were Theodore of Mopsuestia (350–428) and John Chrysostom (347–407). These two exegetes paved the way for the scientific method in biblical interpretation, but they owed much to their teacher Diodore (fourth century), who wrote the first actual treatise on the principles of interpretation, a discussion of the historical method as contrasted to the allegorical.

Theodore was a presbyter of Antioch and later bishop of Mopsuestia. He was a Greek and had studied philosophy in the Sophist school of Libanius before becoming a pupil of the Christian Diodore. Theodore's commentary on the Epistles of Paul is strikingly modern and exceptional among ancient writers. In like manner, his other commentaries show an independent mind unhampered by the traditional view of inspiration. He questions the inspiration of Ecclesiastes; in fact, he assigns all the Wisdom literature to a noncanonical position as merely a form of Greek learning, edifying but not divinely inspired.

Since he lived during and after the closing period of the New Testament canon, his views on canonicity are all the more noteworthy. He rejected the Catholic Epistles and James as unworthy of canonization. He also anticipated modern criticism in assigning some of the Psalms to the Maccabean period. A final modern touch separating him from his contemporaries is his refusal to see the Old Testament as merely a prediction of the New. This view of prophecy was, for the time, nothing less than radical. He read the prophets as related to their times rather than as predictions of Christ and the church.

An Arian tendency is also seen in Theodore's Christological interpretation. He held that Christ was not recognized as divine by his apostles but only as Messiah.

Theodore's greatest achievement was his insistence on holding to the original or literal sense of the Scripture, as far as that could be ascertained, rather than reading into it ulterior meanings by way of allegory. His greatest weakness was the dogmatic bias with which he approached the Scripture. His theological preconceptions kept him from being truly scientific.

What has been said of Theodore, as an exegete, can to a certain extent be applied to John Chrysostom, who broke away from Alexandrian allegorization and took a more literal view of the Scripture, but who was influenced by ecclesiastical tradition even more than his contemporary. There is, in other words, more theological bias in Chrysostom and consequently less freedom in his interpretation. However, he shared Theodore's view of inspiration, which diverged strongly from the Alexandrians.

The critical approach of Origen and the Antiochians is continued, to a degree, in Jerome (340–420), who pioneered in Hebraic study, archaeological research, and translation. His work on the Vulgate shows an affinity with the scholars of Antioch in their interest in the Hebrew text. Like his predecessors, however, he made extensive use of allegory in his exegesis.

Augustine (354–430), whose theology became the norm for Catholic thought, held an uncritical and mystical view of Scripture in contrast to the more historical approach of the

Antiochians. For him scriptural numbers had spiritual meanings, Old Testament prophecy was a specific prediction of Christ as Messiah, and all Scripture was interpreted in the light of the authoritative tradition of the church.[10] His primary interest was in the hidden spiritual meaning of Scripture rather than in the critical problems of the text; in this he differs from Jerome. It might be said, therefore, that Jerome was influenced by the Antiochian tradition, while Augustine was allied more with the Alexandrian school, although theologically he represents the African or Latin tradition of Cyprian and Tertullian.

5. The Bible in the Middle Ages

The semihistorical method of the Alexandrian school was evidently premature. It disappeared as the more orthodox authoritarian teachers of Western Christianity molded the thought of the medieval church. According to Irenaeus, Tertullian, Cyprian, Augustine, and Leo the Great, the church has the key to all truth and through its apostolic succession is uniquely qualified to interpret Scripture.

This authoritarian doctrine, simple and therefore assuring to the faithful, gripped the Western world in a thousand years of quiescence, during which time little or no progress in biblical learning occurred within the church. The Bible was subordinated to the church itself as the custodian of truth, and interpretation was made only in the light of ecclesiastical theology. Gregory the Great (540–604), Alcuin (735–804), and Bede (673–735) depended entirely upon ecclesiastical tradition and the patristic writings. Although highly influential in

10 See Augustine, *Christian Doctrine.*

philosophy and theology, they were without originality and independence when it came to scriptural interpretation.

With the rise of the universities, the Bible was studied in connection with glosses, which were marginal or interlinear interpolations of a theological character. The interpretation of the text itself was usually allegorical. Following the Augustinian method, the medieval teacher interpreted each text of the Scripture in a two-, three-, or fourfold sense. By means of this method the exegete could show that all truth is to be found in the Scripture, hidden behind symbolic forms.

Thomas Aquinas (1225–74) inclined to the literal method, which gave firmer support to his conception of infallible revelation.[11] Since the Scripture is literally inspired and is the complete truth, it is necessary to know exactly what it says. Aquinas, however, made room also for the symbolic sense as something emerging from the primary sense, but his use of allegory was not as elaborate as that of previous exegetes, and he regarded it as purely secondary in value. The allegorical interpretation, he says, tends to confuse the truth of the text. It thus appears that Aquinas achieved a degree of objectivity in his approach to the Scripture and, by doing so, freed exegesis to a certain extent from theological bonds. This contribution, coupled with his rationalism, might be considered one of the important advances made within the church in the Middle Ages.

There were also a few nonconformists who, influenced by medieval Jewish scholars, held to a more or less rational view of the Scripture. One was Johannes Scotus Erigena (833–80), who made a critical study of the text and examined variant readings. His originality, however, is seen in his philosophical rationalism rather than in his Biblical Criticism. A

[11] See *Summa Theologiae*, I: 1, 8 and 9.

more important step toward the historical exegesis was the
work of Hugh and Andrew of St. Victor (twelfth century),
both of whom were strongly in debt to Rashi.[12] Andrew, the
more radical of the two, leaned toward the humanistic approach and was uninfluenced by traditional theology. He
went so far as to side with Jewish authorities in rendering the
Hebrew *almah* (Isa. 7:14) as "young woman" rather than
"virgin." Rashi's influence is seen even more emphatically in
the writings of Nicholas of Lyra (1270–1340), a Norman
Franciscan and professor at the Sorbonne. Nicholas, praised
by Luther as an excellent Hebraist, was interested in the textual
approach and endeavored to discover, beneath the fog of allegory and symbol, the meaning of the words in their original
Hebrew and Greek form.

[12] See p. 300.

Chapter Fourteen

The Rise of Higher Criticism

1. Jewish Precursors of the Historical School

The Higher Criticism, as it came to be known in the nine-teenth century, was no sudden development, but simply the steady flow of certain seventeenth- and eighteenth-century streams of thought, which, in turn, were fed by more remote tributaries of the pre-Renaissance period. Not the least im-portant among these tributaries was medieval Jewish learning. Even the Talmudists called attention to scores of discrepan-cies and contradictions in the Old Testament. It was observed by one that the flood was not a world catastrophe but local in character, by another that Moses and Elijah did not ascend to heaven, and by a third that the birds that fed Elijah were human.

Then, in the ninth century, there was the independent exegete and biblical critic, Al-Balkhi Hivi (Hiwi). His crit-ical study was probably a reflection of the Zoroastrian anti-biblical teaching to which he had been exposed. He gathered together biblical difficulties that had been rationalized by ear-lier Talmudists, such as the discrepancy between II Kings 8:26, where Ahaziah's reign is assigned to his twenty-second year, and II Chronicles 22:2, where it is assigned to his forty-second year. He anticipated the rationalistic exegesis in his suggestions that the crossing of the Red Sea was made at low tide and that the paleness of Moses' face (Ex. 34:29) was due to a long period of fasting on the mountain.

Hivi's arguments against the divine authorship of the Pentateuch were denounced as heresy by the Karaites, a Jewish sect founded in the eighth century B.C., which professed to follow the Bible to the exclusion of rabbinical traditions and laws. While antagonistic to Jewish sacramental and ecclesiastical laws, the Karaites were highly conservative regarding the so-called Mosaic laws; hence, their opposition to Hivi.

The revolt of Karaism from the Talmudic domination, as well as the Arabic learning of Saadya, which followed on its heels, helped prepare the way for a more systematic rationalism. Gaon ben Joseph Saadya (892–942), head of the Jewish Academy at Sura in Babylonia, translated the Old Testament into Arabic and thereby brought to his interpretation an improved philological apparatus. His rationalistic exegesis was continued in the following century by the Cordovan scholar, Ibn Janah, and by Rabbi Isaac of Toledo. The latter observed that Genesis 36:31 (" before there reigned any king over Israel ") could have been written only after the accession of Saul as king, thus implying the non-Mosaic authorship of the Pentateuch. Rashi (1040–1105), another prominent Jewish commentator, held to a strictly literal interpretation of the original Hebrew text.

By far the greatest impetus to the developing critical method coming from medieval Judaism was the work of the prolific Abraham ben Ezra (1092–1167). This fascinating figure — theologian, philosopher, poet, mathematician, and biblical scholar — was the inspiration of Browning's poem, Rabbi ben Ezra. In his commentary on the Pentateuch, Ben Ezra rejects allegorism along with the Midrashic interpretation in favor of his own historical and common-sense method. Of verbal inspiration he will have none, and the miraculous plays no significant role so far as he is concerned.

He could not believe that biblical writers anticipated history. Commenting on Genesis 12:6 ("and the Canaanite was then in the land"), he observed that such a passage was necessarily post-Mosaic in authorship. It was clear to him, in view of the retrospective language used in Genesis regarding the Canaanite period, that the Pentateuch, in its entirety, could not be attributed to Moses. The observation of variant recensions of the Decalogue and linguistic differences within the Pentateuch only confirmed his doubt of Mosaic authorship. Ben Ezra was one of the first to detect a second authorship in Isaiah, a hand that was undoubtedly post-Exilic, for the references to Cyrus as the deliverer of the Jews could hardly have been written by the eighth-century Isaiah. He also ventured the suggestion that the latter part of II Samuel was of different authorship from the first part.

In spite of the spread of Jewish learning in Spain, the age was not ready for a critical approach to the Scripture. Ben Ezra therefore discreetly veiled his statements in ambiguous and cryptic phraseology. His masterly knowledge of Hebrew enabled him to clarify many obscure passages and render the original text more accurately. He was greatly instrumental in spreading Arabic and Jewish learning when learning was really scarce and can be considered an important forerunner of modern Biblical Criticism.[1]

2. *Interpretation in the Reformation*

In the long run, the Reformation, by virtue of its important principle of individual freedom of interpretation, was an added impetus to the rise of Historical Criticism. The philos-

---

[1] Ben Ezra's rationalism was echoed in the writing of Maimonides (1135–1204), who called into question the historicity of various biblical narratives. See *Guide to the Perplexed* (2nd ed.; London, 1928), pp. 234 ff.

ophy of private judgment, inherent in both the Reformation and modern democracy, has obvious implications for the study of the Bible. This conscious release from ecclesiastical authority precipitated a new and popular interest in the Bible and bore fruit in the historical school of the nineteenth century, when Biblical Criticism was almost exclusively a Protestant movement.

But it would be a mistake to suppose that Luther and Calvin brought to their biblical study free and critical minds. Reformation interpretation was not without its interest in theology. Protestant scholars, in the period immediately following the schism, used the Scripture chiefly as a means of justifying the new faith. It is possible, therefore, to trace the progress of historical criticism as passing from the Jewish scholars of the late Middle Ages to the nineteenth century by way of the Renaissance and the Enlightenment rather than by way of the Reformation.

The chief innovation in Biblical Criticism made by the Reformation was its insistence on the independent validity of the Scripture as authority in itself. The Protestant movement effected a shift in the location of religious truth: authority now was vested in the Bible as the Word of God, not in the church. This shift had two results: it created a popular interest in the use of the Bible, but it also made the Bible an external, absolute, and binding authority over men's minds. The latter result has proved inimical to general intellectual progress from the sixteenth century to the twentieth.

Luther was influenced to some extent by Nicholas of Lyra in his literal interpretation, but he occasionally followed Augustine and the Fathers in using the allegorical method. He was well equipped, with his exceptional knowledge of Hebrew and Greek, for the grammatical and historical approach to the Scripture, but this shows only in connection with his translation of the Bible, where he considered the question of canonicity. He practically excluded from the canon, as far as his translation was concerned, such books as Revelation, Jude, Hebrews, and James. Ecclesiastes, he claimed, could not have come from the hand of Solomon. He recognized the work of redactors and later editors in some of the Old Testament books.

For Luther, historical interest is subordinated to "spiritual" interpretation, which is subjective. The Scripture, as the Word of God, holds the key to salvation, and its message is revealed to the reader by the Holy Spirit. In regarding both the Old and the New Testament as a revelation of Christ, Luther differed little from the early Fathers, and in the field of Biblical Criticism he had little to add to his predecessors. For him, the Psalms and Genesis witnessed Christ, and the prophets spoke in New Testament terms. His attention was given largely to the doctrinal Epistles of Paul, to the neglect of the Synoptic Gospels and the ethics of Jesus. All too often he ignored the historical situation of a passage in extracting from it a theological meaning.

Melanchthon followed Luther's exegetical method in reading the New Testament into the Old, and in using both as the source of Christian doctrine.

The primacy of Scripture reaches its zenith in the writings of John Calvin (1509–64). He rejected unequivocally all forms of allegory. The Bible, he said, contains "all things necessary for salvation," but it can be read only by those who have faith. Since the authors of the Bible were merely the "clerks" of the Holy Spirit and wrote under dictation, it follows that every word of Scripture is literally true as it stands. In throwing aside the allegorical method, Calvin went to the extreme of literalism, a tendency that characterized all later orthodox Protestantism.

Calvin failed to distinguish between fact and fiction, the poetry of imagination and the prose of history. The Bible was all on one infallible level of inspiration. He speaks of it as a progressive revelation of God's truth but is altogether lacking in historical sense when he interprets the Psalms or Genesis. He saw no difference in principle between the Law and the Prophets. His lack of critical judgment is seen in his statement that the writers of the gospels were in " perfect agreement." Finally, as a dogmatist, Calvin saw in the Scripture just what he wanted to see — his own particular brand of theology, which was clearly Augustinian. Like his predecessors, he used the Old Testament to prove the deity of Christ; to do so, he took each verse out of context and gave it unwarranted meanings.[2]

The Reformers, in short, whatever else they may have accomplished — and there was much — did not advance the cause of scientific Biblical Criticism to any appreciable degree. While they added to our knowledge of the text through their translations, they were not primarily interested in literary sources, problems of unity, date and authorship, and historical questions. Their concern was theological rather than critical and historical.

The Protestant principle of individual study of the Bible was intended to promote not objective scientific inquiry but religious and theological insight. In contrast to the claims of Catholicism that the church alone possessed the true interpretation of the Scripture and the divine right to mediate that truth to its followers, Luther and Calvin taught that the individual believer himself, with the assistance of the Holy Spirit,

[2] See *Institutes*, I: 13:9.

could grasp divine truth through reading the Scripture. The Bible, not the church, was the authority for doctrine and religious instruction. The individual did not need the mediation of the church in his apprehension of God's will or his assurance of salvation.

The Reformers, then, merely shifted the basis of authority. In place of ecclesiastical authority they substituted that of the Bible. This shift eventually worked against individual interpretation as the Bible became an external objective authority in doctrinal matters. Protestant theology became a rigid formula, and the Bible became merely an instrument for proving its soundness. Since the Scripture was the infallible Word of God and the source of doctrine, it made little difference who wrote what or why, for every book and every word was of equal weight. Such an atmosphere clearly was not conducive to scientific criticism.

3. *The Era of Rationalism*

Considering Erasmus (1466–1536) as a Humanist rather than a Reformer, we find in his writings a greater degree of independent criticism than was present in Luther and Calvin. Erasmus' genius lay in the textual field. To him belongs the distinction of preparing the first Greek New Testament. His collection of the best available manuscripts and his exegetical notes accompanying the text helped to set the stage for later textual and literary criticism. Under his critical eye the text of the New Testament was substantially improved. He detected many theological emendations and editorial insertions, such as I John 5:7 and the last twelve verses of Mark. He did not hesitate to place the ethical portions of the New Testament above the anthropomorphic fables of Genesis. He questioned the canonicity of Hebrews, James, Revelation, II and III John, and II Peter. His exegetical notes accompanying the New Testament were welcomed and were widely used by the leading scholars of Europe. Luther at first leaned rather heavily upon them but later, resenting their humanistic and rationalistic flavor, spurned them.

With Thomas Hobbes (1588–1679) and Isaac de la Peyrere (1594–1676) we come a little closer to the actual beginnings of literary criticism as applied to the Bible. Hobbes was both anti-Protestant and anti-Catholic in his view of the Scripture. As a free-lance philosopher, with no theological axe to grind, he introduced into the stream of critical history a fresh and independent element. He opposed both the Protestant idea of scriptural authority and the Roman Catholic tendency to read the Bible only as subservient to the church and its faith. According to Hobbes, the Bible is not the Word of God; it is the word of some men who knew God better than other men. In other words, he denied the authority of the Bible as conceived both by the Reformers and by the Roman Catholic Church. Among other things, he cited much internal evidence to throw doubt on the Mosaic authorship of the Pentateuch.[3]

La Peyrere was of Jewish extraction, but his family became Protestant. He published two unorthodox treatises, *Praeadmaitae* and *Systema Theologicum*. In the first book he argued that, according to the evidence in Genesis, human beings existed before Adam. In the second he continued Hobbes's proof of non-Mosaic authorship of the Pentateuch and introduced the rationalistic interpretation. He questioned the miracles of both the Old Testament and the New

[3] *Leviathan*, Part 3, chap. 33.

and assigned to natural causes many supposedly supernatural phenomena.

The rationalism of Hobbes and la Peyrere was continued on a more elaborate and systematic scale by Spinoza (1632–77) in his *Tractatus Theologico-Politicus*. Spinoza was also indebted to ben Ezra, Maimonides, and ben Gerson for his rationalistic views. He began by attacking the traditional use of the Bible as a means of supporting Christian theology. The theologians, he asserted, were interested only in propagating their particular doctrines, to which " they have made Holy Writ conform." He brushed aside the mysterious and the mystical and approached the Bible as he would any other book — first by a critical examination of the text; then by a historical study of date, composition, authorship, and setting; and finally by ascertaining what the text says, not what he would like it to say. This procedure, as outlined by Spinoza, defines the spirit of modern criticism.

Fearless, unprejudiced, possessing a mind at once mathematical and philosophical, Spinoza cleared away the old structures of both allegory and literalism, then proceeded to lay a new foundation — the *Tractatus Theologico-Politicus*, which might well be called the Magna Charta of Biblical Criticism. His contribution to biblical study lies in his anticipation of the two successive stages: Rationalism, or the harmonizing of the Scripture with natural law, and Historical Criticism, which assigns Scripture to its age and setting and does not try to " save " its contents. Today the rationalistic method appears as fallacious as allegory, but it was significant that Spinoza, in the seventeenth century, should make use of the first and at least point the way to the second.

The defect of the rationalistic method is that Scripture is assumed a priori to be truth, that the world of nature is also truth, and that the latter really determines the meaning of the former. Following this principle, certain interpreters even today reconcile the Red Sea story, or the story of the sun standing still for Joshua, with some unusual but "altogether possible" natural phenomenon. Spinoza, however, did not abuse the rationalistic method. He insisted on the right to refute Scripture where it was contrary to nature, just as he would the Talmud or the Koran.[4]

Spinoza's scientific attitude is most clearly seen in his literary criticism of the Pentateuch, where he acknowledges his debt to ben Ezra. Mosaic authorship is rejected on the basis of anachronisms, such as the iron bedstead mentioned in II Samuel 12:29, 30; of retrospective allusions to sources later than Moses, such as Numbers 21:14;[5] and of the presence of material that must be dated as late as the Exile. Spinoza points out that the Pentateuch must be seen, along with Joshua and Judges, as the work of editors, culminating with Ezra. He intimates that the Pentateuch was made up of distinct strands or documents that were later edited and observes the evidence of compilation and editorial correction.[6]

Spinoza places the Book of Nehemiah as late as the second century B.C. and the publication of the Book of Psalms in the time of the second temple. Regarding Chronicles, which is dated very late, he expresses surprise that such an unreliable book should be admitted to the canon and the Wisdom of Solomon be excluded. He assigns Proverbs to a post-Exilic date, denies unity to Jeremiah, regards Job as a translation of a gentile poem, and questions the genuineness of Daniel.

Spinoza hesitates to apply his criticism to the New Testa-

---

[4] *Cogitata Metaphysica*, 2:8.
[5] This evidence appeared before Spinoza in the *Systema Theologicum* of La Peyrere, 1655.
[6] See *Tractatus Theologico-Politicus*, in loco.

ment because of his lack of Greek, but insists, at any rate, that the apostles and evangelists had no miraculous powers and wrote simply as human beings. With respect to Jesus, he is surprisingly orthodox, even from a dogmatic Christian point of view, although he qualifies the traditional view of the Trinity as held by the Christian church. He shares with ben Ezra a belief in the spiritual rather than the literal or bodily resurrection of Christ and claims Paul as his authority. However, he thinks that the writers of the gospels thought that Christ rose bodily. In view of Spinoza's observation of the editorial or redactional nature of Hebrew literature and his differentiation between the thought of the New Testament writers and that of a later age, it can be truly said that he stands at the threshold of the critical period and did much to give it birth.

It thus appears that the foundation of scientific Biblical Criticism was laid, for the most part, by thinkers outside the church, chiefly Jews. Much of the superstructure also was the work of independent critics, philosophers, and poets.

4. The Birth of the Critical Spirit

The spirit of Literary and Historical Criticism was a product of the eighteenth century; its systematic method was developed in the nineteenth.

In the eighteenth century, men cut loose from tradition and authority. Bacon, Descartes, Locke, and Newton threw Aristotelianism and Scholasticism out the window. The eighteenth-century man did his own thinking; he cared nothing for the Fathers or ecclesiastical theology. Truth had to be tested by reason and experience. The Encyclopedists in France, the Deists in England, and the poets of the Aufklärung in Germany all created a new intellectual climate. The eighteenth century was a second Renaissance, especially in France, where the Enlightenment brought forth the ideas of representative government and popular sovereignty, freedom of contract, separation of church and state, freedom of conscience, civil liberty, belief in social progress, and natural rights.

In this eighteenth-century atmosphere, criticism was born — the application of scientific methods to the textual and literary problems of the Bible. The word " critical " now took on real meaning, as the traditional ideas of infallibility, revelation, and inspiration were cast aside to make room for the objective approach to the Scripture. But whom shall we call the founder of scientific Biblical Criticism — Simon, Astruc, Bentley, Eichhorn, Michaelis, Wettstein, Bengel, Semler? These were the great men associated with the birth of criticism, and they all played an important part.

Richard Simon (1638–1712) has been called the " Father of Biblical Criticism," but such a tribute exaggerates his contribution and works an injustice upon other eighteenth-century critics. As *one* of the founders of scientific criticism, Simon simply applied Spinoza's principles to the Old Testament. He ruled out Mosaic authorship for portions of the Pentateuch and asserted that most of the Old Testament in its present form was a product of the post-Exilic period. In other respects, however, he exhibited an uncritical spirit. He operated strictly within the confines of Catholic thought. Truth, he said, has been revealed to the church, and ecclesiastical tradition is supported by the Scripture, which is " infallible and of divine authority, since [it proceeds] immediately from God." [7] Alterations, additions, and later redactions of

[7] *A Critical History of the Old Testament* (London, 1682), p. 1.

the text, he adds, do not in any way detract from its authority. Tradition, in any case, is necessary, as Scripture in itself is neither clear nor self-sufficient.

Further impetus to critical study was given by Richard Bentley (1662–1742), who was the first to apply the principle of internal evidence to ancient writings. The importance of this principle to biblical studies is evident in those portions of the text which display a diversity of literary style, contradictory reports, and anachronisms. Bentley's theory of literary criticism led to the still more important formulations of Jean Astruc (1684–1766), a Roman Catholic physician, who noted in Genesis a variety of styles inconsistent with unity of authorship. He saw that there were two distinct names used for deity — Elohim and Yahweh — and that these two names belonged to two different accounts of the same events; namely, the Creation and Flood accounts. This observation pointed to two ancient sources used by the author of Genesis, who, in Astruc's mind, was Moses. In that discovery we can recognize the inspiration for the later documentary hypothesis of the Pentateuch.

The historical method made great headway in the work of Johann Semler (1725–91), the "Father of German Rationalism." In his *Treatise on the Free Investigation of the Canon* he broke the static and immutable view of the Scripture by showing that the formation of the canon was a purely human process, an historical growth in which all the churches differed for several centuries regarding the authoritative list of books. He then attacked the traditional theory of inspiration, which held that everything in the Bible was equally inspired and valuable. He pointed out differences in religious worth within the New Testament canon and insisted that the Scripture must be studied as any other product of the human mind. That meant that one should study the text in the light of its intrinsic meaning, unprejudiced by dogma. The reader must take into account the historical setting of a book, the cultural background of the writer, and the literary relationships of the book with other books.

In line with Semler in the historico-literary approach, but less original, were Johann Ernesti (1707–81), Johann Eichhorn (1752–1827), and Johann Michaelis (1717–91). The two greatest exegetical influences in the eighteenth century were the *Gnomon Novi Testamenti* of Johann Bengel (1687–1752) and the *Prolegomena ad Novi Testamenti* of Johann Wettstein (1693–1754).

The eighteenth century produced two other major critics, who were from the literary field. The first was Gotthold Lessing (1729–81), who startled the world with his questioning of the miracles of the New Testament. He also took a less bibliocentric view of religion, which was a long overdue criticism of Protestantism. Christianity as a religion, he writes, existed before the New Testament was written or even dreamed of. The Christian gospel does not depend on the New Testament writings for its validity; in fact, there is a vast difference between the religion of Jesus and that of the apostles. There is no basis in the teachings of Jesus for either the trinitarian formula or the sacraments of the church.[8]

Johann Herder (1744–1803) advanced the idea of Semler that the Bible is the work of men and should be read as such. His chief interest was in the Hebrew poetry as an interpretation of both nature and human nature. He regarded the early chapters of Genesis as poetry rather than history and took the same view of the Book of Jonah.

The rationalism of the seventeenth and eighteenth centuries, in brief, undermined the authority of dogma, weakened

[8] *Sämmtliche Werke*, ed. Karl K. F. Lachmann, pp. 99 ff.

the orthodox doctrine of inspiration, and introduced the historical and literary method in criticism — a process that reached its peak in the latter part of the nineteenth century.

5. *The Scientific Age*

The intellectual progress of the nineteenth century, one might say, was momentous. The study of archaeology, the study of comparative religion and the history of religion, the theory of evolution, the empirical emphasis in philosophy, and paleography — all occurring in the mid-nineteenth century — had, in every instance, a direct bearing on the development of scientific Biblical Criticism. Darwin's theory of organic evolution completely undermined the traditional world view and demanded a new formulation of theology, philosophy, ethics, anthropology, and psychology. Men now saw that the world is not fixed, that nature in all its forms changes constantly. Absolutism yielded to relativism, dogma to scientific verification. Belief in static revelation and the infallibility of Scripture, therefore, was no longer tenable.

The breakdown of scriptural authority, prefigured by eighteenth-century rationalism, which had substituted reason for revelation, was now completed by the Higher Criticism of the nineteenth century. The character of Jesus and moral values became the authoritative norm, rather than the Bible per se. The facts of history replaced the assumptions of dogma. Jesus' ethics became more important for the study of the New Testament than his miraculous activities. Nothing was too sacred for investigation. Instead of a transcendent God, above and apart from the world, theologians now thought in terms of divine immanence, the world as process, and God as an immanent force at work, an "infinite and eternal energy."

The scientific point of view made itself felt in the field of biblical literature through the idea of evolution, the use of the inductive and empirical method, and the genetic or developmental conception of religious history. Students of the Bible began, for the first time, to speak of the growth of the idea of God in the Bible, the evolution of early Christianity, progressive revelation as seen in the Scripture, and the growth of the canon.

With the discovery of pre-Hebrew documents, the dependence of Old Testament writers upon Babylonian traditions and laws was inferred from the parallels in the earlier literature of Assyria and Babylonia. Babylonian tablets from 2000 B.C. began to pour into the British Museum to be deciphered: they carried Creation stories, Flood accounts, and other myths, which duplicated passages in Genesis. Persian eschatology and Egyptian wisdom were seen as influencing the later books of the Old Testament. The mystery religions of the Graeco-Roman world were found to have influenced the thought-forms and practices of Pauline Christianity. Older and more trustworthy manuscripts of biblical documents were discovered, which revolutionized the study of the text.

Progressive scholars came to see that it was unsound to limit religious inspiration to the contents of the canonical books of the Bible, that historical inquiry must be concerned with an organic process, not a book. It was now clear that no religion can be properly understood without a knowledge of its sources and the influences affecting its early growth. The Hebrew-Christian religion must be studied in the light of archaeological backgrounds in the Near East and, beyond those backgrounds, in primitive religion. The Bible itself must be seen as a cultural growth in the course of history, not as an end in itself, complete and self-sufficient. It could not be studied in a vacuum; it required an historical context. The teachings of Jesus, for example, had to be studied against the background of Jewish law and history. Paul's letters could not be dissociated from the pagan religions of the first century. The Fourth Gospel could only be understood in connection with the writings of Philo.

This genetic point of view helped to usher in the scientific study of Scripture known as Historical or Higher Criticism, which, by 1870, attained a systematic form.

The Dominance of Germany

Professional criticism arose not in England, although the scientific temper was there most evident, or in France, but in Germany. Throughout the nineteenth century, the critics of importance were, for the most part, professors in German universities.

One reason for this dominance was that the German universities nourished the scientific spirit. In France, scientific criticism could make itself felt only in spite of the Roman Catholic Church, which defended the older dogmatic interpretation and which had an authoritative grip on scholarship. The exceptional scholars — Renan, Duschesne, Loisy — who had the courage to break through to an independent position, were either excommunicated or condemned. In England, the universities were held down by the conservative Anglican church, and the outstanding English scholars were the independent literary or ecclesiastical figures. In Germany, however, biblical research became a precise discipline under the auspices of the universities rather than the church. Biblical

Criticism was conducted along the same scientific lines as any other discipline, and was untouched by a conservative church.

The controlling principles of Historical Criticism were developed in connection with the analysis of two major problems — those of the Pentateuch and the Synoptic Gospels — although there were many other critical studies, involving such questions as the authorship and date of all the books in the Bible (especially Isaiah), the life and personality of Jesus, and the Pauline authorship of the Pastoral Epistles.

New Testament Criticism

The first major critic of the nineteenth century was Friedrich Schleiermacher (1768–1834), who represents a threefold transition: from the rationalistic to the purely historical position, from a preoccupation with the Old Testament to the field of New Testament study, and from a bibliocentric to a Christocentric emphasis. The normative authority for him was Christ, not the Bible. This transfer of interest marks the beginning of both liberal theology and modern Historical Criticism.[9] With Schleiermacher, biblical research turns to the New Testament and for a half-century remains there.

As the most influential German theologian in the first half of the nineteenth century, Schleiermacher can be considered the founder of the liberal school, represented later by such eminent theologians as Ritschl, Bleek, Neander, Tholuck, Dorner, Lotze, Harnack, Loofs, and Troeltsch. The Schleiermacher-Ritschlian school was known as the "mediating" school because it corrected and combined previous tendencies in a higher synthesis, defined the evangelical faith as resting on experience rather than dogma, and regarded religion pri-

9 See *Reden über die Religion* (Berlin, 1799).

marily as an inward feeling rather than a prescribed code of ethics or a superimposed body of doctrine. This combination of the critical spirit of interpretation with a personal experiential faith attracted American scholars, who, for a half-century, flocked to Berlin and other German centers of learning. In the fields of theology, church history, and criticism, therefore, Schleiermacher and his followers molded American thinking more than any other one force.

Schleiermacher tended to minimize the importance of doctrine and to relegate the miraculous element in the New Testament to a nonessential position. He rejected the virgin birth and the bodily resurrection of Jesus as having no significance and insisted that the crux of New Testament criticism, as of Christianity itself, is " the historical Christ." [10] Schleiermacher's importance lies in his integration of science and religion, which had been divorced in the eighteenth century. He showed that if religion is based, not on fourth-century dogmas, biblical cosmology, or ecclesiastical authority, but on a valid emotional experience and moral values, there can be no real conflict between science and religion.

The next great name in nineteenth-century criticism is that of Ferdinand Christian Baur (1792–1860), founder of the Tübingen school. The source of Baur's system of interpretation is the philosophy of Hegel, who fashioned an evolutionary or dialectical explanation of history. All history, he said, proceeds from thesis (the status quo or traditional pattern) to antithesis (the conflict produced by an opposing force) to synthesis (the higher resultant arising from the impact of the first two forces).

Baur used this Hegelian dialectic to explain the history of early Christianity and the New Testament writings. From

[10] *Leben Jesu* (1864) (posthumous).

the serious conflict of Petrine-Jewish Christianity (thesis) with Pauline-gentile Christianity (antithesis) — a conflict of which there can be no historical doubt — emerged early Catholic Christianity (synthesis). The New Testament books are not independent ends in themselves but part of a tendency or trend, representing certain stages through which Christianity was passing. The Pastoral Epistles, for example, are the emergent result of the Petrine-Pauline conflict. Baur's use of the Hegelian formula gave rise to the Tübingen school and was known as the *Tendenz* theory.[11] His investigations led to the rejection of the Pastoral Epistles as non-Pauline; he accepted only Romans, I and II Corinthians, and Galatians as coming from Paul.

Baur has received more than his share of criticism. It must be admitted that he applied the *Tendenz* theory to the New Testament canon in a sweeping manner and followed a deductive method in doing so, but he did shake men's minds loose from the pious and static conception of the Apostolic Age that all was peace and unity, and he gave a greater impulse to the historical method. The Rationalism of the eighteenth century, continued to some extent by Schleiermacher but more so by Paulus, was now at an end.

The third and perhaps the most powerful influence in New Testament scholarship was the *Life of Jesus* by David Friedrich Strauss (1808–74), a book that accomplished the spade work in Synoptic criticism and made all New Testament critics for the following century its debtor.[12] It had become apparent from the writings of de Wette that a biography of Jesus, in the true meaning of the term, was impos-

---

[11] See *Die Sogenannte Pastoral briefe* (1835); *Paulus der Apostel Jesu Christi* (Stuttgart, 1845); *Kritische Untersuchungen über die kanonischen Evangelien* (Tübingen, 1847).
[12] *Leben Jesu* (1835).

sible, owing to the paucity of information and absence of documentary material. Nevertheless, as a result of Strauss's work, the trend was established, and the century that followed produced thousands of lives of Jesus. As a pupil of Baur, Strauss appreciated the successive environmental influences that went into the making of the gospels. He was, in fact, the first to differentiate clearly between the Synoptics and the Fourth Gospel. He was one of the first to undertake a study of the interrelationship of the first three gospels — a study from which the Two-Source theory later emerged.[13]

Popular reaction to Strauss's *Life of Jesus* was decidedly unfavorable. The public (and also his colleagues) viewed with alarm his statement that Jesus was " a wise man " theologized by myth into a supernatural magician. Strauss's humanistic or liberal representation of Jesus caused a furore at that time, but many of his findings were soon taken for granted among critics.

Approaching the gospel records with no presuppositions, Strauss recognized the mythical or legendary character of most of the gospel, including all accounts of Jesus' life before his baptism and after his death. He came to this " mythical theory " by way of the Hegelian dialectic — the mythical theory being the synthesis developing from the supernaturalistic (thesis) and the naturalistic or rationalistic (antithesis). Hence the modern view, which rejects both miraculous revelation and the naturalistic explanation of supposedly miraculous events and recognizes that all ancient writings — including the Bible — contain legendary growths, which are heightened by the passage of time. The difference between

[13] For a discussion of the Synoptic Problem see pp. 155–164 ff. For the Two-Source theory, see especially pp. 164–168. The Two-Source theory was developed in its representative form by Heinrich Holtzmann and Bernhard Weiss.

the Synoptic tradition and the Johannine tradition is a case in point. Strauss rejected the Fourth Gospel as having no historical value. In his earlier work he interpreted the self-consciousness of Jesus in terms of Jewish eschatology: Jesus' role in his own mind was Messianic.[14] In his later *Life of Jesus* (1864), however, he modified his eschatological views.

The priority of Mark and the Two-Source theory were given a more systematic argument by Christian H. Weisse, who continued the investigations of Strauss, and Christian G. Wilke. The work of these two critics was in turn the point of departure for the extended research of Bruno Bauer (1809–82), whose skeptical treatment anticipated the later " Christ-Myth school " of Drews. Bauer's rejection of the gospel narratives as historically unreliable was shared by an earlier critic, H. S. Reimarus (1694–1768). Both regarded the figure of Christ as an idealization concocted by the evangelists. The skeptical or imaginative view of Jesus found a representative in France in Ernest Renan (1823–90), whose romantic *La Vie de Jésus* (1863) was, by comparison, somewhat superficial in scholarship, but exceedingly popular and charming.

German New Testament scholarship continued to occupy itself with the person of Jesus, the Synoptic Problem, and the formation of the New Testament. In the writings of Daniel Schenkel, Karl Weizsäcker, Heinrich Holtzmann, Karl T. Keim, Adolf Hilgenfeld, Otto Pfleiderer, Karl B. Hase, Willibald Beyschlag, Bernhard Weiss, and Adolf Jülicher — the creators of the so-called " liberal " school — there was an increasing tendency to reject the eschatological view of Jesus and to present him as a Messiah of a moral and spiritual reform, preaching the inward nature of the Kingdom. The

[14] See my article in *Journal of Biblical Literature*, 1929, XLVIII, 149–61.

use of the Synoptics rather than the Fourth Gospel in reconstructing the life of Jesus became axiomatic with Weizsäcker and Holtzmann. Heinrich Holtzmann (1832–1910) and Bernhard Weiss (1827–1918) gave the Markan hypothesis a more secure footing and did much to establish the Two-Source theory of the Synoptics.

In the last quarter of the nineteenth century and the opening years of the twentieth century, the eschatological question was revived. Otherwise, there was a general advance in the liberal interpretation of the New Testament as a whole. Johannes Weiss, in his *Preaching of Jesus concerning the Kingdom of God* (1892), maintained an exclusively Messianic and apocalyptic interpretation of Jesus, a view opposed by Wilhelm Bousset (1865–1920), who related Jesus' life and teachings to the present world of the spirit and not to the cataclysmic ending of the world. The Kingdom of God is the realization of God's will in the heart of the individual here and now: "The Kingdom of God is within you."

Theologically, Bousset belonged to the then rapidly rising *Religionsgeschichtliche* school, the left wing of the historical school, which stressed the importance of environmental influences in the growth of early Christianity. Another member of this group was William Wrede (1859–1906), who viewed the New Testament from the standpoint of the history of religion rather than theologically. With him there is no such thing as "biblical theology." Wrede's contribution was in his clarification of the differences between the Johannine and Synoptic traditions and in his analysis of the Jesus-Paul problem. Here he maintained that Paul effected a complete break with the original Christian community and founded a new gentile Christianity based on his own thinking. Wrede strenuously opposed the eschatological interpretation of Johannes Weiss and Albert Schweitzer. Wrede's position on eschatology was supported by Otto Pfleiderer (1839–1908), a follower of Baur. His chief investigations were in the Apostolic Age, where Karl von Weizsäcker (1822–99) excelled. Not the least important product of the German schools of criticism was the publication of the first great commentaries and numerous introductions.

The Historical Criticism of the nineteenth century was confined almost exclusively to Germany. German scholars, at any rate, can be credited with the development of the historical method in its definitive form. The influence of German scholarship began to be felt in England early in the century in the work of Coleridge (1772–1834), who rejected outright the traditional idea of revelation and mechanical inspiration. His criterion was that whatever calls up the best that is in you is inspiration. The test of inspiration is experience. This was a thoroughly modern idea.

Coleridge's view of the Scripture as strictly a product of human insight was shared by Thomas Arnold and Bishop John W. Colenso. Colenso inclined toward the radical wing of the German school and came into conflict with the church.[15] The historical method gained ground in England with the semitechnical writings of Matthew Arnold, who unequivocally rejected both the orthodox view of inspiration and the miraculous element in the Bible; with the investigations of Henry H. Milman in the history of early Christianity; and with the broad-church views of John F. D. Maurice, Frederick W. Robertson, Charles Kingsley, and Frederic W. Farrar.

[15] The heresy trial of Bishop Colenso in England was paralleled at the end of the century by the dismissal in the United States of Charles A. Briggs and Henry Preserved Smith by the Presbyterian church and Hinckley G. Mitchell by the Methodist church.

Old Testament Criticism

We now turn to the Old Testament field, where the problem of the Pentateuch dominated the scene. The Documentary theory had been suggested and partially developed by Astruc, Eichhorn, de Wette, and Ilgen. In 1853 Hüpfeld made a fresh attack on the problem and demonstrated the presence of three distinct authors in Genesis: two using the term "Elohim" for God, and the third, "Yahweh." He identified one of the Elohist documents as the Priestly Code and regarded it, erroneously, as the earliest of the documents. Karl Graf, following the earlier findings of Reuss, established the post-Exilic dating of P. (*ca.* 500 B.C.) and was supported in this by Kuenen, a Dutch scholar.

To this preliminary research was added the finishing touch of Julius Wellhausen (1844–1918), the most famous Old Testament scholar of the century.[16] He observed that three strands ran through Genesis, Exodus, Leviticus, and Numbers, and that Deuteronomy represented a fourth and independent authorship. He concluded that one author could not be responsible for the parallel, but contradictory, accounts of the Creation and the Flood or for the variety of literary styles. Laws and customs from different periods in history stood side by side, clearly indicative of several chronological strata. It became evident that Deuteronomy reflected a seventh-century situation and was written in the light of the eighth-century prophets. He held that the four documents, J (850 B.C.), E (750 B.C.), D (621 B.C.), and P (500 B.C.),

---

[16] See *Israelische und Jüdische Geschichte* (3rd ed.; Gutersloh, 1897) (Eng. trans., *Sketch of the History of Israel and Judah* [London, 1891]); also *Prolegomena zur Geschichte Israels* (3rd ed.; Berlin, 1886) (Eng. trans., *Prolegomena to the History of Israel* [Edinburgh, 1885]).

were combined in the post-Exilic period and later called the Torah.

Wellhausen's work produced a turning point in the history of Old Testament criticism. Applying the Hegelian idea to Hebrew history, he showed that the canonical order of Old Testament books is just the reverse of the actual facts of Hebrew history. The Law, in other words, was not the beginning but, in its present form at least, an end result. The editing of the Pentateuch was a post-Exilic movement, part of the restoration. After Wellhausen, the history of Israel was studied from an evolutionary or dialectic standpoint — polytheistic in the preprophetic period, henotheistic in the prophetic era, and monotheistic in the post-Exilic restoration. The Graf-Wellhausen theory, as it came to be known, has, with some minor modifications, held the field to the present day.

The historical method was then applied to other sections of the Old Testament. Critical work on the Prophets was done by George Adam Smith, W. Robertson Smith, and Bernhard Duhm. The earlier contention that the Book of Isaiah was composite in authorship was now given more systematic confirmation. In the introductions and commentaries of Marti, Duhm, Cornill, Ewald, Reuss, Fürst, Geiger, Wildboer, Kautzsch, and Delitzsch, the Psalms and Wisdom literature were assigned to the late post-Exilic period, new studies in Hebrew chronology and canon were made, and archaeological discoveries in Mesopotamia were used to throw light on the early Hebrew documents. Wilhelm Gesenius (1776–1842) was responsible for the great advance in the modern study of Hebrew grammar and textual analysis. Zecharias Frankel (1801–75), founder of the historical school of

modern Judaism, applied the critical method to biblical literature in his monumental work on the Septuagint and in his
study of the influence of Talmudic exegesis on the Alexandrian School. Abraham Geiger (1810–74), Jewish theologian and authority on Jewish history and institutions, is
known for his critical study of the Torah and the Talmud.

Our review of the nineteenth century comes to a climactic conclusion with Adolf Harnack (1851–1930), whose pro-
ductive career spans the last quarter of the nineteenth and the
first quarter of the twentieth century. Following in the tradition of Schleiermacher and Ritschl, Harnack became at
once the leading representative of the liberal school and without doubt the most influential theologian at the turn of the
century, exerting a profound influence on liberal Protestant
thought throughout the first half of the twentieth century.
The instrument that did most to mold the typical " modern-
ist " theology was *Das Wesen des Christentums*, a series of
extracurricular lectures at the University of Berlin in 1899–
1900.[17] These sixteen lectures, delivered to an audience of almost a thousand students, became the basis of liberal American thought in the first few decades of the twentieth century.

In these lectures Harnack distinguished clearly between
dogmatic Christianity and the gospel of Jesus, between the religion *of* Jesus and the religion *about* Jesus. The essence of
Christianity, he said, is the teaching of Jesus — not the dual-
ism of Paul, the Christology of the Fourth Gospel, the legalism of Latin Christianity, the asceticism of the Eastern church,
or ecclesiastical tradition in general. There is, in other words,
a difference between Jesus and the historic church. To define
Christianity, we must get back to the basic teachings of Jesus,

---

[17] Eng. trans., *What Is Christianity?* (New York, 1901).

which are, in essence, the fatherhood of God and the divine worth of the human personality as a child of God. The Kingdom of God is the rule of God in the individual soul. Salvation lies in the mental attitude of the individual, in an internal experience that effects a change or deliverance, not in any outward compulsion.

Harnack's chief field of concentration was the Apostolic Age and the ante-Nicene period. His theory was that the emergence of the Roman Catholic Church of the year 200 is not explained by the internal history of the early church alone. Nor can it be explained by the Tübingen theory, which saw Catholic Christianity emerging as a synthesis of the Petrine-Pauline conflict. The only adequate explanation must include non-Christian influences exerted upon the growing church.

The character of the early church, Harnack declared, was influenced specifically by Greek thought and practice. The Hellenization of Christianity started as early as Paul's campaigns and produced a permanent change, theologically and sacramentally. Christianity, in its early growth, was syncretistic and must be studied as developmental, not as a static deposit, immune to its milieu. Bruno Bauer and Edwin Hatch had previously suggested the possibility of Greek influences in early Christianity, but it was Harnack who worked out in detail the theory of Hellenization and religious syncretism.[18]

Some of Harnack's most significant work was done in the

[18] See *Die Mission und Ausbreitung des Christentums in den ersten drei Jahrhunderten.* (Leipzig: 1902): Eng. trans. by James Moffatt, *Mission and Expansion of Christianity in the First Three Centuries* [2nd ed.; New York, 1908]; *Dogmengeschichte* (Berlin, 1886) (Eng. trans. by N. Buchanan, *History of Dogma* [Boston, 1895]); *The Date of Acts and of the Synoptic Gospels* (New York, 1911); *The Acts of the Apostles* (New York, 1909).

history of the canon and the making of the New Testament.[19] While some of his theories were later criticized as extreme, Adolf Harnack still stands as the most towering theological figure of prewar German criticism and as the " prince of church historians."

[19] See *The Origin of the New Testament*, trans. J. R. Wilkinson (New York, 1925); also *Das neue Testament um das Jahr 200* (1889).

Chapter Fifteen

Twentieth-Century Interpretation

1. Christological Studies

Our task in this chapter will be to trace the principal paths taken by Old and New Testament criticism in the first half of the twentieth century and to point out trends in interpretation current at the beginning of the second half of the century. Biblical Criticism during the first two or three decades of this century was occupied with the consolidation of previous ground gained, the extension of the principles of the historical school along the lines established in the nineteenth century, and also the modification or correction of theories previously held.

One of the most controversial issues bridging the two centuries was the Christological problem, dealing with the historicity and identity of Jesus, his concept of himself, and the nature of his message. The liberal school of Bousset, Harnack, and Wernle had emphasized the Jesus of history. He was first and foremost a human being, a historical personage, whose divine character is appreciated only in the light of an intense moral struggle on the human plane. He preached a religion of fellowship with God the Father; his Kingdom was the achievement of God's will on this earth and in the lives of individuals.

In contrast to the view of the liberal school was the Christ-Myth theory of radical criticism, current in the first decade of the century. Mythical theories about Jesus and the origin of Christianity had appeared from time to time, but the position of the radical school was given its definitive form by Arthur Drews of Karlsruhe.[1] He maintained that Jesus never actually lived but was an imaginary Jewish Messianic figure, an incarnated God-man, whom Paul elevated to the plane of divinity as a redeemer-saviour and around whom Paul built a cult.

The Christ-Myth problem stirred up popular debates throughout Germany, and refutation was not long in coming from such representatives of the liberal school as Harnack, Jülicher, von Soden, Weinel, Johannes Weiss, and Clemen. These scholars pointed out that the historical life of Jesus is supported by the Pauline letters, the Synoptic Gospels, and the Apostolic Fathers. Reference to Jesus on the part of Roman historians was hardly to be expected in view of the obscurity and remoteness of Judea, but extra-biblical evidence for the historicity of Jesus was found in the writings of Tacitus, Suetonius, Pliny the Younger, and Lucian. Josephus and the Talmud also mentioned Jesus.

If the historicity of Jesus cannot be proved, neither can the nonhistoricity be proved.[2] In the final analysis the question is gratuitous, for, whether or not Jesus ever lived, we still have to account for the Sermon on the Mount and the parables. If Jesus did not exist, somebody else is responsible for these unparalleled teachings. Someone provided the impetus for the Christian movement; if not Jesus, then the equivalent of Jesus. We cannot ignore the personal equation in history.

Another focal point of scholarly debate at the turn of the

---

[1] *Die Christusmythe* (Jena, 1909).

[2] The outstanding American coverage of this problem is in S. J. Case, *The Historicity of Jesus* (Chicago, 1912). See also M. Goguel, *Jesus: Myth or History?*, trans. F. Stephens (New York, 1926).

century was the eschatological question. Johannes Weiss in 1892 had argued that Jesus, as an apocalyptist, preached the near end of the world and regarded himself as the Messiah who would reign in the new era to be established either in his lifetime or later. This purely eschatological point of view was opposed by Harnack, Bousset, and Wrede, who interpreted Jesus as an ethical reformer and the Kingdom as the rule of God in the lives of people here and now. The champion of thoroughgoing eschatology was Albert Schweitzer, who was strongly opposed to the liberal school: [3]

We modern theologians are too proud of our historical method, too proud of our historical Jesus, too confident in our belief in the spiritual gains which our historical theology can bring to the world. . . . We must be prepared to find that the historical knowledge of the personality and life of Jesus will not be a help, but perhaps even an offense to religion. . . . That which is eternal in the words of Jesus is due to the very fact that they are based on the eschatological world-view, and contain the expression of a mind for which the contemporary world with its historical and social circumstances no longer had any existence.[4]

For Schweitzer, Jesus was not the ethical teacher but the transcendent spiritual Messiah, a mystical Christ. The eschatological interest is central in the gospels, which are to be studied not objectively but as an inspiration to faith. Jesus was concerned with the imminent end of the world rather than with moral values and the social ethic; his teachings were only an " interim ethic," a " temporary way of living " for those who waited for the end of the world.

To this extreme view some liberal critics replied by disclaiming any eschatology in Jesus' self-consciousness and

---

[3] *Das Messianitäts und Leidensgeheimnis* (Tübingen, 1901); *Von Reimarus zu Wrede* (Tübingen, 1906) (Eng. trans., *The Quest of the Historical Jesus* [London, 1910]).

[4] *The Quest of the Historical Jesus*, pp. 398 ff.

teaching; others declared it was present but subsidiary to his ethical philosophy; still others thought it was a product of the later church tradition that became a part of the gospels. M. S. Enslin, an influential contemporary critic in the liberal school, has recently confessed to being — at least as far as early Christianity is concerned — an eschatologist. He criticizes as fallacious the tendency to modernize Jesus and the assertion by many critics that Jesus was not understood by his contemporaries. Enslin claims that Jesus was clearly understood and that his message was eschatological, although he did not necessarily see himself as the apocalyptic " Son of Man." [5]

The eschatological problem has been a basic factor in New Testament study throughout the first half of this century. Today practically all critics agree that the eschatological element is present in the gospels. The Enochian term " Son of Man " has an apocalyptic connotation. Schweitzer's thoroughgoing eschatology dovetailed nicely with the current neo-orthodox emphasis on crisis and despair. But neither as a world view nor as a standard of morality does it carry the weight of the religion of prophetism.

The natural reaction to the otherworldly view of Jesus and his message was the Social-Gospel school. The eschatologists said that Jesus had no interest in making the world better; he was interested only in its cataclysmic end. In that case, there is no permanent value in his teachings; they were only an interim stopgap. Strongly contrasted to this view was a school of thought, a product of liberal criticism, which emphasized the Social Gospel. The advocates of this view saw in the teachings of Jesus a practical program of social action. The Kingdom of God was the achievement of moral values in society.

[5] *Journal of Biblical Literature*, Vol. 75, Pt. 1, pp. 19-26.

For these critics, the teachings of the prophets and Jesus represented the really permanent element in the Bible. Social reform was the end of religion, not orthodox theology or passive mysticism. Such a view coincided with the pragmatism of William James and the pioneer spirit of the New World. After two world wars and an economic depression, the Social Gospel went out of fashion, as Neo-Orthodoxy, reflecting the pessimism and despair of Europe, reverted to the Calvinistic emphasis on sin, corruption, and divine grace. At mid-century, a reaction to Barthianism and Neo-Calvinism is noticeable.

These pendulum swings should warn us of the dangers of subjectivism in the interpretation of Jesus and his message. There is a Christ of faith as well as a Jesus of history; there is an eschatological element in the gospels as well as a social and ethical gospel; but whoever or whatever Jesus was, he must be kept, for purpose of interpretation, in his historical setting.[6]

2. History of the Gospel Tradition

Another prominent area of concentration in the early years of the century was that of the origin of the gospels and their interrelationships. The Two-Source theory retained its popularity with minor modifications. B. H. Streeter proposed the Four-Source theory, which says that in addition to Mark and Q (the Logia), Matthew and Luke had access to independent local sources, M and L respectively. Streeter and others have suggested that there was a Proto-Luke (a

[6] See H. J. Cadbury, *The Peril of Modernizing Jesus* (New York, 1937)

combination of L and Q), which was later to produce the present Luke.[7]

Greater attention, however, has been given to the question of oral tradition. At this point Form Criticism entered, presumably as a corrective of the purely literary method. Form Criticism was born in the period of the First World War and, like Neo-Orthodoxy, to which it seems to be indirectly related, is a reflection of the postwar *Zeitgeist*. It is also related to the socio-environmental approach of the same period. It is chiefly concerned with the growth of tradition in the life of the early church (30–70 A.D.), the cultic use of the gospel tradition, and the relation of the oral tradition to the life and thought of the early Christian community before the formation of the present gospels.

The initial work in the application of Form Criticism to the gospels was done by Martin Dibelius, Karl L. Schmidt, and Rudolf Bultmann.[8] These scholars, and those who followed, recognized the existence of legends, sayings, parables, texts, and independent stories about Jesus. These types of tradition — called "forms" — were preserved by the early Christians, used in their services of worship, and transmitted orally as independent units (*pericopae*) in the various communities. The early church used these oral sayings and stories for apologetic, homiletic, and didactic purposes. From the present gospels, which represent an artificial editing of these

---

[7] See B. H. Streeter, *The Four Gospels, A Study of Origins* (New York, 1925); B. S. Easton, *The Gospel According to St. Luke* (New York, 1926); G. D. Burton, *Some Principles of Literary Criticism and their Application to the Synoptic Problem* (Chicago, 1904).

[8] See Martin Dibelius, *Die Formgeschichte des Evangeliums* (Tübingen, 1919); K. L. Schmidt, *Die Rahmen der Geschichte Jesu* (Berlin, 1919); Rudolf Bultmann, *Die Erforschung der synoptischen Evangelien* (Göttingen, 1925).

earlier forms, the critic tries to reconstruct the original forms in their life-situation (*Sitz im Leben*).

Form Criticism was a reaction to the literary method, which was not sufficiently concerned with the life and thought of the early church. In emphasizing the life-situation, the Form critics swung to an extreme position. Their preoccupation with the theological process of the early Christian community caused them to neglect the historic person of Jesus. Also, their claims to objective classification of the stories existing in the tradition are now seen to be exaggerated. Schmidt's rejection of the established Markan theory and Bultmann's assertion that nothing can be known about the Jesus of history did not help the cause in England and America. Recent appraisal shows that the method was entirely too subjective and pretentious.[9]

In America the historico-literary method soon reasserted itself. E. F. Scott restored balance to Synoptic criticism by recovering Jesus as a historical figure and a teacher of ethics and by calling attention to the Jewish backgrounds and Hellenistic influences in early Christianity.[10] Shirley Jackson Case, the leading American representative of the socio-historical school, related the gospel tradition to its milieu and described early Christianity as a developmental movement rather than a *sui generis* deposit, a growing organism influenced by its religious and cultural environment rather than

---

[9] Form Criticism came to the attention of American scholars largely through the writings of Burton S. Easton and Frederick C. Grant. See B. S. Easton, *The Gospel Before the Gospels* (New York, 1928); F. C. Grant, *Form Criticism* (New York, 1934). For critical appraisals of this method see E. F. Scott, *The Validity of the Gospel Record* (New York, 1938); A. M. Hunter, *Interpreting the New Testament* (Philadelphia, 1951).

[10] *The Gospel and Its Tributaries* (Edinburgh, 1928); *The Ethical Teachings of Jesus* (New York, 1925); *The New Testament Today* (New York, 1921).

" a divine insert into history." The same genetic tendency is seen in his treatment of Jesus, where he traces the changing conception of Jesus' identity through the first century and then on through the entire history of Christianity.[11]

The Aramaic origin of the gospels was another question that engaged the minds of the critics in the first half of this century. Most scholars today agree that Jesus spoke Aramaic, a dialect of the ancient Hebrew, and that the Koiné Greek of the gospels is a Semitized Greek that contained the Aramaic idiom and that shows signs of translation from Aramaic originals. From this point on there is disagreement.

The most prominent name connected with the earlier research in the Aramaic problem is that of Gustaf Dalman. He made modern scholars conscious of the Aramaic background of the Synoptic Gospels and the Aramaic language that Jesus used. Further than that he did not go.[12]

The most extreme position was taken by C. C. Torrey of Yale, who maintained that all four gospels were originally written in Aramaic before 50 A.D. Such a view obviously rules out the oral-tradition theory and holds that the sayings of Jesus and the narrative material concerning his life took written form in Aramaic immediately after his death and that the present gospels are Greek translations of the original Aramaic complete gospels. All unintelligible or difficult passages in the Greek are seen as mistranslations of the Aramaic. Torrey, therefore, corrected the English translation to conform to what he supposed was the original Aramaic word. This could only be done with certainly if he had con-

[11] *The Evolution of Early Christianity* (Chicago, 1914); *Jesus Through the Centuries* (Chicago, 1932); *Jesus, a New Biography* (Chicago, 1927); *The Social Origins of Christianity* (Chicago, 1923); *Experience with the Supernatural in Early Christian Times* (New York, 1929).

[12] *The Words of Jesus* (New York, 1902).

temporary documentary evidence for the meaning of the Aramaic words in question. More often than not, that evidence was lacking.[13]

The middle ground was taken by Matthew Black, who concluded that all we can say is that there was an Aramaic source for the sayings of Jesus, written or oral.[14] Most present-day scholars are in agreement with this conclusion.

Recent research in the Synoptic Gospels has studied them not so much as historical documents but as religious testimony or cultic forms. This shift of emphasis from "the quest of the historical Jesus" to the appreciation of the gospels as witness to "the revelation of God" is pointed out by C. H. Dodd, who seems to think that we are through with the historical approach.[15]

Our brief survey of research in the gospels would be incomplete without mention of the significant contribution of Adolf Deissmann in his analysis of the Koiné Greek of the New Testament. The discovery of first-century papyri and ostraca containing words used by Jesus shed new light on their meaning. Deissmann demonstrated the popular (common) character of the Koiné Greek, and his papyri findings necessitated numerous changes in the English renderings.[16] Also of critical importance was the work of H. L. Strack and P. Billerbeck in establishing the rabbinic parallels to Jesus' teachings.[17] The Jewishness of Jesus' ideology and vocabu-

---

[13] The Four Gospels (London, 1933); Our Translated Gospels (New York, 1936); Documents of the Primitive Church (New York, 1941).

[14] An Aramaic Approach to the Gospels and Acts (Oxford, 1946).

[15] History and the Gospel (New York, 1938).

[16] See — Licht vom Osten (Tübingen, 1908) (Eng. trans. by L. R. M. Strachan, Light from the Ancient East [London, 1910]).

[17] Kommentar zum Neuen Testament aus Talmud und Midrasch (Munich, 1922–28).

lary had previously received attention in the writings of Claude Montefiore, Israel Abrahams, and Gerald Fried-lander.[18]

3. Pauline Letters

In the first quarter of the century much critical thought was given to Paul — his theology, his letters, and his permanent influence on Christianity.[19] The Hellenization theory, suggested by Harnack, became popular through the writings of Reitzenstein, Bousset, Lake, Heitmüller, Angus, and Dieterich.[20] By citing parallels in the mystery cults, by calling attention to Paul's emphasis on the rites of the sacramental meal and baptism, and by quoting Paul's use of terms found in the mystery cults, these critics made much of the paganizing of early Christianity under Paul. Some, in fact, regarded early Christianity as a soteriological mystery religion, similar to Mithraism, its chief competitor.

That Paul's mysticism and sacramentalism show an affinity to the cults, there can be no doubt, but analogies and parallels do not necessarily imply the transformation of a Jewish religion into a pagan rite. Later criticism tended to

[18] See C. Montefiore, *The Synoptic Gospels* (London, 1910); I. Abrahams, *Studies in Pharisaism and the Gospels* (Cambridge, 1917, 1924); G. Friedlander, *The Jewish Sources of the Sermon on the Mount* (London, 1911).

[19] For a critical appraisal of the relation of Paul to Jesus and the relative importance of Jewish and Hellenistic influences in Paulinism, see my article, "Continuity and Divergence in the Jesus-Paul Problem," *Journal of Biblical Literature*, 1929, Vol. 48, parts 3 and 4, pp. 149–61.

[20] See R. Reitzenstein, *Die hellenistischen Mysterie-religionen* (Leipzig, 1910); and S. Angus, *The Religious Quests of the Graeco-Roman World* (New York, 1929), and *The Mystery Religions and Christianity* (New York, 1921).

modify the Hellenization theory as the basic Jewishness of Paul was recognized. However, the opponents of Hellenization will have to concede that Paul used a Hellenistic idea in defining the Christian religion as a mystical union with Christ. This, even more than the doctrine of justification by faith, is the key to Paul's religious experience; it also defines mystical Christianity. The magical union of devotee and God in the pagan cult became for Paul the spiritual fellowship of the Christian with the living Christ (ἐν Χριστῷ).[21]

Another Pauline problem engaging the attention of scholars through the first half of this century was the authenticity of Ephesians and the Pastorals. Earlier critics had questioned all the letters of Paul except Romans, Galatians, and I and II Corinthians. More recently, however, the tendency has been to accept I and II Thessalonians, Colossians, Philippians, and Philemon as also genuine. Great doubt still exists with regard to Ephesians, which many authorities ascribe to a Paulinist.

Goodspeed has suggested that after the writing of Acts (*ca.* 85 A.D.), a close follower of Paul (possibly Onesimus) wrote Ephesians as a summary of Pauline thought and as a means of spreading Paul's influence more widely. The writer modeled his letter after Colossians, with which he was well acquainted, and published a collection of Pauline letters with his own Ephesians as the introduction. According to Goodspeed, the later collections — the Pastorals, the Johannine Epistles, and the Catholic Epistles — show the influence of this Pauline collection, which set the style of grouping books together. Goodspeed's theory has appealed to some as highly plausible (accounting for the similarity of Ephesians and

[21] See Adolf Deissmann, *The Mysticism of Paul the Apostle* (1931).

Colossians), but to others it leaves some questions unanswered.[22]

As to the Pauline authorship of the Pastoral Epistles, opinion has been greatly divided. Conservative scholars, of course, hold to their authenticity, but others, like E. F. Scott, assign them to a Paulinist who edited and enlarged upon some genuine notes of Paul that he had in his possession. The Pastorals are rejected because they cannot be reconciled to Luke's life of Paul in Acts; they reflect an ecclesiastical organization that could only prevail after Paul's time; and their style differs considerably from that of the apostle. Between the extreme positions of total rejection and total acceptance, Scott's theory of fragments seems to be reasonable; namely, that a later follower of Paul worked over some genuine fragments and published them under Paul's name. This theory explains the stylistic differences as well as the intimate notes, which certainly smack of authenticity.[23]

4. The Fourth Gospel

The Johannine Problem, as related to the Fourth Gospel, loomed large throughout the half-century. It has several facets: authorship, unity, Aramaic nucleus, relation to the Synoptics, and, finally, its reliability as a true representation of Jesus. With few exceptions, the weight of scholarly opinion in the earlier part of the century was against apostolic authorship.

[22] See Edgar J. Goodspeed, *New Solutions of New Testament Problems* (Chicago, 1927), and *The Meaning of Ephesians* (Chicago, 1933).

[23] Outstanding among Pauline studies in this period were: "The Acts of the Apostles," *The Beginnings of Christianity*, eds. F. J. Foakes-Jackson and Kirsopp Lake (New York, 1920–33); H. J. Cadbury, *The Meaning of Luke-Acts* (New York, 1927).

It was recognized by most German and American critics that the Fourth Gospel is not historically reliable but represents a speculative interpretation of Jesus to a Hellenistic constituency; it is a reflection of the Philonic doctrine of the Logos, is anti-Jewish, and could only come from the second century.[24]

More recent discussion, however, seems to have shifted in the direction of the conservative view in regard to authorship and date. Rudolf Bultmann, using the principle of Form Criticism, said the author had three sources: Aramaic sayings of Jesus, miracle stories, and passion narratives. On the basis of a fragment of the Fourth Gospel found in Egypt and dated not later than 125 A.D., Bultmann concluded that the gospel could not have been written later than 100 A.D.[25] Middle-of-the-road critics regard the author as John the Elder (mentioned by Papias) or a follower of the apostle John, while the more radical school assigns the gospel to an unknown writer who lived in the vicinity of Ephesus. Strangely enough, some scholars look to rabbinic Judaism rather than to Hellenism for the ideological background to the gospel!

Along with the current resurgence of theology in general, many critics since 1940 have tended to minimize the importance of the historical emphasis and to give more consideration to revelation in their interpretation of the Fourth Gospel.

5. Old Testament Studies

Among the significant developments in the Old Testament field during the first half of this century have been the

[24] See E. F. Scott, *The Fourth Gospel* (New York, 1906).
[25] *Das Johannes-Evangelium* (Göttingen, 1937–41).

archaeological discoveries; the publication of new introductions, commentaries, and histories of Israel; the rise of Form Criticism; and a new interest in Old Testament theology.

Literary criticism was supplemented by an increased knowledge of Hebrew life and religion, made possible by archaeological discoveries. It was now recognized that the Hebrews did not live in a religious vacuum but were influenced throughout their history by the surrounding cultures. The study of cognate languages and Near East religions became an integral part of Old Testament research. Archaeological excavations threw new light on Mesopotamian backgrounds of the Old Testament; on Egyptian parallels to the Wisdom literature; on the Hebrew-Canaanite amalgamation, the Hittite and Hurrian civilizations, and the various periods of Hebrew history; and on the text of Isaiah, the Psalms, and post-Exilic writings.[26]

Form Criticism, first applied to the Old Testament by Hermann Gunkel in his *Genesis,* has not been as influential, perhaps, as in the New Testament field. In recognizing older forms and traditions in the later-edited books, Form critics were not proposing anything especially new, but they have helped in the pursuit of sources and earlier stages of tradition. Form Criticism has modified the position of the literary school by assigning certain traditions, laws, and literary forms to an earlier period than formerly held.

Gunkel felt that the literary analysis of the written documents was inadequate as a means of determining the religious history of the Hebrews. He maintained that the literary forms present in the later documents came from an earlier age, and were, in turn, taken from pre-Hebrew sources. Hebrew literature developed along certain literary lines (*Gat-*

[26] See Part I.

tungen), which came out of " life situations." [27]   It is clear, however, that Form Criticism is really just an extension of the history-of-religion method in its citation of Egyptian, Babylonian, and Persian traditions as possible source materials for Hebrew literature.[28]

Another reaction to the liberal school was seen in the new interest in biblical theology, which rose concurrently with the revival of theology in general and the appearance of Neo-Orthodoxy.[29]   Attention was now given to the Bible as a whole, as a book about salvation and God, a unified revelation — not just a collection of literary documents with an antiquarian value.   How significant this shift is remains to be seen.   A study of the Old Testament purely on a topical or theological basis tends to ignore the historical development of ideas and proves less adequate than the older historical method.   Even in books on the religious values of the Old Testament, the authors, in order to make sense, had to resort to the evolution of these concepts within the Old Testament itself.[30]

As a matter of fact, how can there be such a thing as a unified biblical theology per se?   In a series of documents appearing over a period of a thousand years, there are *many* theologies.   One cannot escape the fact that the Old Testament represents an evolutionary process, without which there

[27] *Genesis, Übersetzt und Erklärt* (Göttingen, 1901), and *Einleitung in die Psalmen* (Göttingen, 1933).

[28] For an objective analysis of Form Criticism and the Old Testament see Herbert F. Hahn, *Old Testament in Modern Research* (Philadelphia, 1954).

[29] K. Barth, *The Word of God and the Word of Man* (Boston, 1928); *The Doctrine of the Word of God* (New York, 1936).

[30] See A. B. Davidson, *The Theology of the Old Testament* (New York, 1904); A. C. Knudson, *The Religious Teachings of the Old Testament* (New York, 1918); H. P. Smith, *The Religion of Israel* (New York, 1914).

is no life. Current orthodoxy, in decrying the emphasis of the older liberal school on the historical or evolutionary method, finds itself opposing the most valid and most valuable element in the Bible — growth, the progressive achievement of faith, the *élan vital* that is discernible in history. In attempting to discover the unity of the Old Testament as a revelation, scholars of the neo-conservative school have had the tendency to neglect the fruits of historical study. Such a procedure can lead only to a new obscurantism.

The observations of Albright and the methodology of Form Criticism have combined to throw some doubt on the adequacy of Wellhausen's developmental theory. While recognizing the lasting contribution of the Wellhausen school in the reconstruction of literary traditions, many leading scholars feel that the reconstruction of history cannot be solved by literary criticism alone. Many of the Hebrew documents are now regarded as having been written long after the events described, which in the interval had become a part of a growing cultic or ritualistic pattern. Here again there is the danger that exponents of new theories will go too far in their claims. The explanation of Hebrew history on the grounds of cultic usage cannot be maintained without taking into account other factors, such as the influence of environmental cultures, archaeological evidence, and literary criticism.

But the documentary hypothesis of the Pentateuch has not been discarded by all critics. With certain variations, the Wellhausen tradition was upheld by Robert H. Pfeiffer in his *Introduction to the Old Testament*, which, incidentally, was one of the most scholarly publications in America during the half-century.[31]

[31] *Introduction to the Old Testament* (New York, 1941). For a review of recent Pentateuchal criticism see H. R. Willoughby (ed.), *The Study of the Bible Today and Tomorrow* (Chicago, 1947).

Certain modifications have been proposed by Form critics who interpreted the Yahwist document strictly in theological terms. Recent criticism has tended to credit J and E with religious and ethical ideas previously thought to have appeared only in the genius of the eighth-century prophets. The tendency has been to establish a definite dependence of the prophets upon the earlier Yahwistic religion. Thus the theological unity of the Old Testament is achieved at the expense of the originality of the prophets.[32] Emphasis has shifted from the revolutionary character of the individual prophets to the theological import of the books *in toto*.

In the first half of the century special attention was given to the books of Ezekiel, Ezra, and Nehemiah. The instigator of all this post-Exilic controversy was C. C. Torrey, who maintained that the Book of Ezekiel, rather than being the chief instrument in the making of Judaism and a product of the Exile, was a purely Palestinian forgery from the third century B.C. This view was opposed by W. F. Albright, S. A. Cooke, and others. As for Ezra, Nehemiah, and Chronicles, Torrey sees little historical worth in their account of the Exile and the restoration. The Babylonian Captivity, he says, did not take many Jews from Palestine and the story of the restoration, occurring about 538 B.C., is fiction.[33]

Form Criticism has also made itself felt in recent research in the Psalms. The typical view of the historical school placed most of the Psalms in the post-Exilic period. The application of both Form Criticism and the method of compara-

[32] See H. H. Rowley (ed.), *Studies in Old Testament Prophecy*, Edinburgh, 1950.

[33] For recent post-Exilic criticism see C. C. Torrey, *Ezra Studies* (Chicago, 1910), and *Pseudo-Ezekiel, and the Original Prophecy* (New Haven, 1930); *The Second Isaiah, A New Interpretation* (New Haven, 1928); W. A. Irwin, *The Problem of Ezekiel* (Chicago, 1943); I. G. Matthews, *Ezekiel* (Philadelphia, 1939).

tive religion has resulted in establishing a relation between Hebrew usages and the cultus of Egypt, Babylonia, and Canaan. Some of the Psalms are recognized as liturgical chants and ritualistic hymns belonging to the period of the United Monarchy. Much is made of Babylonian and Egyptian parallels. The tendency, therefore, has been to assign many of the Psalms to a pre-Exilic date.[34]

6. At Mid-Century

As we pass the mid-century mark we can identify several contemporary trends in biblical research: the tendency to revert to a more conservative (earlier) dating of the books; a shift in emphasis from the text, which has become fairly well established, to its application to life, both at the time of its composition and today; a greater respect for archaeological findings, especially as they seem to confirm biblical materials; the use of Form Criticism and history of religion in identifying earlier sources for all books; and, finally, a new preoccupation with the theological character of both Old and New Testament books and the Bible as a whole.

By 1950 there appeared a noticeable attempt to establish a doctrinal homogeneity in the Old Testament and a systematic theology of the New Testament.[35] It was held that the

[34] See S. Mowinckel, *Psalmstudien* (Kristiania, 1921–24); W. O. E. Oesterly, *A Fresh Approach to the Psalms* (New York, 1937); O. R. Sellars, " The Status and Prospects of Research Concerning the Psalms," *The Study of the Bible Today and Tomorrow, op. cit.*

[35] See F. C. Grant, *An Introduction to New Testament Thought* (New York, 1950); R. Bultmann, *Theologie des Neuen Testaments* (Tübingen, 1948–51); K. Barth, *Kirchliche Dogmatik* (Munich, 1948); A. N. Wilder, " New Testament Theology in Transition," *The Study of the Bible Today and Tomorrow, op. cit.;*

time had arrived when we should recognize the uniqueness and unity of the New Testament message. Historicism had had its inning; it had recovered the Jesus of history. Now it was time to recover the Christ of faith. The Jesus of the historians must give way to the God-man of the theologian. The Bible must be seen as a unity and the church recognized as the keeper of the revelation of God and the means of salvation. The dependence of early Christian thought upon previous Jewish teachings and environmental influences was admitted, but syncretism and the developmental approach were made subsidiary to the all-important theological interest.

After dominating the field for a century, the religio-historical method of biblical research was called into question as failing to provide a profound insight into the religious message of the Bible. By mid-century it was felt in many quarters that Historical Criticism had reached the point of diminishing returns and that it was time now for an approach more synthetic than analytic, more sympathetic than objective. Historical and literary criticism, it was held, stopped with the scientific investigation of sources, dates, authorship, and characteristics of the Old and New Testament books. If the Scripture was analyzed like any other literature in history, everything was reduced to the human, the rational, and the secular.

This shift to biblical theology, however, was not a complete return to the traditional view of revelation. It was conceded that human and historical factors are involved in the

S. Minear, *Eyes of Faith* (Toronto, 1946); M. Burrows, *Outline of Biblical Theology* (Philadelphia, 1946); A. M. Hunter, *The Unity of the New Testament* (London, 1943); F. Filson, "The Study of the New Testament," *Protestant Thought in the Twentieth Century*, ed. A. S. Nash (New York, 1951).

making of the Scripture and that critical research is necessary, but it was also felt that the critical approach did not give proper emphasis to " God's place in history," " the eternal and final nature of biblical revelation," "the central place of Christ in history," and the over-all theological importance of the Bible. The influence of Barthianism is clearly seen in this revival of theology as a reaction to historicism. It has not gone unchallenged, however, for the liberal-historical school still has its defenders.[36]

Opponents of the new orthodoxy are still convinced that, while objective historical study can and should include the investigation of the religious life and teachings of the Old and New Testaments, there can really be no such thing as a coherent biblical theology. They also sense the grave danger of attempting to operate without proper use of the critical apparatus provided by historical study. Exclusive emphasis on sin, judgment, atonement, and salvation can only result in the appearance of a neo-Fundamentalism in biblical interpretation.

It is too early to predict what will evolve from the impact of current theories upon traditional ones, but we can be sure that the results of centuries of biblical scholarship will not be entirely discarded in favor of the present vogue. There must be a happy medium between the acceptance of traditional theories as final and the enthusiastic espousal of new methods as providing the answers to all problems. The tendency to adopt new hypotheses to the exclusion of all previous ones suggests that there are styles in biblical scholarship, just as in architecture and automobiles. To follow the most recent

[36] See R. E. Wolfe, " The Terminology of Biblical Thought," *The Journal of Bible and Religion,* 1947, pp. 143-47; E. W. Parsons, *The Religion of the New Testament* (New York, 1939); E. F. Scott, *Varieties of New Testament Religion* (New York, 1943).

fashion in the belief that the latest is the best is to lose all historical perspective.

The student of Biblical Criticism, trained in the liberal-historical school, is somewhat startled today when he encounters such terms as empathy, ritual patterns, eschatological symbol, myth and ritual school, *kerygma*, existential dimension, cultic background of eschatology, demythologizing the New Testament, and divine revelation. Such phrases reveal a new slant in interpretation, a type of criticism that has originated largely in European circles and is regarded by its extreme exponents as replacing the historical method.

An appraisal of the current trends is premature at this time, but it may be appropriate to point out certain dangers inherent in the methods of Neo-Orthodoxy, Form Criticism, the Cultic theory, and biblical theology. This conservative turn in American criticism stems from the confessional dogmatism of Europe, especially Germany, and it might be noted that the more ecumenical American theology becomes, the more conservative it has to be.

The chief limitation of the theological approach to Biblical Criticism is its *a priori* procedure. It insists on certain presuppositions or assumptions that must be maintained in spite of passages that would contradict such assumptions or new discoveries that would prove them invalid. One of these preconceptions is that God is manipulating history and that His chief concern is with Jewish and Christian history as revealed in the Scripture. The dogmatic propositions of Augustine and Calvin are read into the Bible as eternal and revealed truth. Finding in the Bible only those passages which serve the current interests of Neo-Orthodox theology is a kind of proof-texting once considered untenable. Those who follow this method have less interest in the Sermon on the Mount than in the Pauline letters because the latter serve their theology better. The teaching of Jesus about the potentiality of man as a child of God is passed over in favor of Paul's intimations of determinism.

Philosophically speaking, the confinement of God's purpose and activity to one book and to one people appears as an anachronism in our cosmic age. The Neo-Orthodox critics operate within the framework of the church and its dogmas, whereas the liberal school follows a more cultural approach that does not isolate Biblical Criticism from the world of history and science. A greater danger is that Neo-Orthodoxy may find itself unwittingly a part not only of the current antihistoricism but, by reason of its rejection of the rational method, also of the current anti-intellectualism.

As to the more recent Myth, Symbol and Ritual school, there is the danger of attributing to ancient writers a subtlety that they could not have possessed. Were the writers of these primitive accounts consciously using these stories as " symbols of reality," or did they believe in them as facts? Was the New Testament writer in describing the Transfiguration using a " mythological symbol," or was he relating in typical oriental fashion an event that he believed did take place? Is the eschatology of the New Testament, as it is suggested, merely symbolic or cultic in nature, or does it represent an actual hope of first-century Christians? It would seem that some contemporary critics are only reverting to the allegorical method of Alexandria in trying to make a system out of the symbolic theory.

The second half of the century should see a synthesis or compromise, combining the historical and theological methods.[37] The historical approach may have lacked spiritual depth, but, if biblical scholars in the future turn to theology as the dominant method, they will have cut loose from their foundations with the loss of all the great gains of the last two centuries. The direction taken by any individual critic, toward either historical objectivity or theological subjectivity, will be determined by his leanings toward naturalism, on the one hand, or supernaturalism, on the other. It should be possible to combine elements from the two positions.

The wise interpreter will see the Bible as historically conditioned, containing purely transient material along with permanent truths. He will see the Bible, not as a predetermined divine insertion in history, but as an integral part of the historical process. He will understand that the Bible is not an infallible revelation from God, but only a part of man's search for the truth of God. He will be adequately informed in the literary and philological problems of the text, but he will also appreciate the moral and spiritual values of the text for himself and for the modern world.

The wise reader will not forget that the gospels without the gospel are dead and that the intellectual study of the former can mean nothing for the world without the practical application of the latter. While he sees the importance of relating the Book of Amos to its original setting in ancient Bethel, he will also be concerned with the relevance of the prophet's message for his own times. He will always remember that experience precedes literature and that life is deeper than logic. Finally, he will understand that historical analysis must be joined to religious insight for a proper use of this book we call the Bible.

[37] Such is the position of Cunliffe-Jones, *The Authority of Biblical Revelation* (London, 1945), and R. M. Grant, *The Bible in the Church* (New York, 1948).

Chronology
Bibliography
Index

The Chronology of Biblical Literature

Note: The following dates are, in practically every instance, approximate and the list is limited to material found in or directly related to the Bible, including early literary fragments of the Old Testament and extra-canonical works of both the Old and the New Testaments.

Old Testament Literature

Song of the Well (Numbers 21:17 ff) . . .	1200 B.C.
Song of Deborah (Judges 5)	1100
Fable of Jotham (Judges 9:7–15)	1100
Song of Miriam (Exodus 15:21)	Before 1000
Fragment from "Book of Jashar" (Numbers 21:14 ff)	" "
Fragment from "Wars of Jahweh" (Joshua 10:12 ff)	" "
David's Lament (II Samuel 1:19–27)	1013–933
The Parable of Nathan (II Samuel 12:1–4) .	"
Code of the Covenant (Exodus 20:23–23:19)	"
"J" Decalogue (Exodus 34)	"
"J" Document	850
"E" Document	750
Amos	750
Hosea	740
Isaiah 1–39	740–700
Micah	725–700
"J" and "E" combined	650

Deuteronomy (promulgated 621) 650
Nahum 630
Zephaniah 630–627
Jeremiah 626–580
Proverbs (an early collection) 621–600
Habakkuk 605
Ezekiel 593–570
Obadiah 580
Lamentations 580
Holiness Code (Leviticus 17–26) 560
Second Isaiah (Chapters 40–55) 540
Zechariah 520
Haggai 520
Collection of Psalms 520
Judges (final form) 560–500
I, II Samuel (final form) 560–500
I, II Kings (final form) 560–500
"P" document (Priestly Code) 500
Joshua 450–400
Job 450–400
Third Isaiah (56–66) 450
Canonization of the Law (Torah) 444–400
Ruth 430–400
Malachi 420
Joel 400
Jonah 400–300
Song of Songs 300
Nehemiah (edited form) 300
Ezra (edited form) 300
I, II Chronicles (edited form) 300
Proverbs (final collection) 300–250
Septuagint begun 250
Ecclesiastes 250–200
Recognition of Prophets as Canon by . . . 250–200
Esther 200–150
Wisdom of Sirach (Apocrypha) . . . . .
(Greek Trans. 132) 180

Tobit (Apocrypha) 175
Song of the Three Children (Apocrypha) . . 170–150
Daniel 167
Psalms (final collection) 150
First Esdras (Apocrypha) 150
Judith (Apocrypha) 150
Remainder of Esther (Apocrypha) 150
Prayer of Manasseh (Apocrypha) 150–50
Story of Susanna (Apocrypha) 100
Bel and the Dragon (Apocrypha) 100
First Maccabees (Apocrypha) 90–70
Second Maccabees (Apocrypha) 50
Wisdom of Solomon (Apocrypha) . . . 50 B.C.–40 A.D.
Second Esdras (Apocrypha) . . . . . . 66 A.D.–250 A.D.
Baruch (Apocrypha) . . . . 70 A.D.
The Books of the Pseudepigrapha . . . . . 100 B.C.–200 A.D.

New Testament Literature

I, II Thessalonians . . . . 50–52 A.D.
Galatians 53
I, II Corinthians 54–57
Romans 56–58
Philippians 60–64
Colossians 60–64
Philemon 60–64
Ephesians . . (if non-Pauline: 75–90) . . 60–64
Gospel of Mark 70
Epistle of James 75–100
Gospel of Matthew 80–90
Gospel of Luke 80–85
Acts 80–100
Hebrews 90
I Peter 90
Revelation 90–100
I Clement (Apostolic Fathers) 95

Gospel of John 100–110
I, II, III John 110
I, II Timothy 125
Titus 100–125
Didache (Apostolic Fathers) 100–125
Jude 110–125
Shepherd of Hermas (Apostolic Fathers) . . 110–130
Epistles of Ignatius (Apostolic Fathers) . . 110–120
II Peter 130
Epistle of Barnabas (Apostolic Fathers) . . . 125–130
II Clement (Apostolic Fathers) 150–175
Letter of Polycarp (Apostolic Fathers) . . . 150
New Testament Apocryphal Writings . . . 125–200
Muratorian Fragment (Roman Canonical List) 195–200
Easter Letter of Athanasius (establishing canon) 367

New Testament Chronology

Jesus and Roman-Jewish History

Birth of Jesus . . . . 6 B.C.
Death of Herod I . . . . 4 B.C.
Philip Tetrarch (to 34 A.D.) . . . . 6 A.D.
Annas High Priest (to 15) 6
Caiaphas High Priest (to 35) 18
Pilate Procurator (to 36) 26
Baptism of Jesus 27
Ministry . . . . 2½ yrs.
Death of Jesus 29/30
Accession of Caligula (to 41) 37

Life of Paul

Birth of Paul . . . . 1 A.D
Death of Stephen 34
Conversion of Paul 35

Bibliography

NOTE. — In line with the general plan of this book I have limited the bibliography to English titles except in a few instances. The divisions in the following list correspond to the chapters of the book. I have therefore omitted the citation of references dealing with the history, content, and interpretation of the individual books of the Old and New Testaments and other phases of biblical study not included in the present book. No attempt has been made to repeat here all the titles mentioned in the text. Where a volume has pertinent value, however, the title is repeated.

INTRODUCTION
THE BIBLE AND THE TWENTIETH-CENTURY MIND

ANDERSON, BERNHARD W. *Rediscovering the Bible.* New York: Association Press, 1951.

BRUNNER, EMIL. *Revelation and Reason.* Translated by OLIVE WYON. Philadelphia: Westminster, 1946.

CLARKE, WILLIAM N. *Sixty Years with the Bible.* New York: Scribner, 1909.

COLWELL, ERNEST C. *The Study of the Bible.* Chicago: University of Chicago Press, 1937.

CUNLIFFE-JONES, HUBERT. *The Authority of the Biblical Revelation.* London: Clarke, 1945.

DODD, CHARLES H. *The Authority of the Bible.* New York: Harper, 1929.
———. *The Bible Today.* New York: Macmillan, 1947.

DUGMORE, CLIFFORD W. (ed.). *The Interpretation of the Bible.* London: Society for Promotion of Christian Knowledge, 1944.

FOSDICK, HARRY E. *The Modern Use of the Bible.* New York: Macmillan, 1924.

KENT, CHARLES F. *The Origin and Permanent Value of the Old Testament.* New York: Scribner, 1906.

MOFFATT, JAMES. *The Approach to the New Testament.* London: Hodder and Stoughton, 1921.

NEIL, WILLIAM. *The Rediscovery of the Bible.* New York: Harper, 1954.

PEAKE, ARTHUR S. *The Bible; Its Origin, Its Significance, and Its Abiding Worth.* (5th ed.) London: Hodder and Stoughton, 1924.

RICHARDSON, ALAN. *Preface to Bible Study.* Philadelphia: Westminster, 1944.

ROWLEY, HAROLD H. *The Relevance of the Bible.* New York: Macmillan, 1944.

CHAPTER ONE
BABYLONIAN PARALLELS TO OLD TESTAMENT TRADITIONS

BARTON, GEORGE A. *Archaeology and the Bible.* (7th ed.) Philadelphia: American Sunday School Union, 1937.

CERAM, C. W. *Gods, Graves, and Scholars.* Translated by E. B. GARSIDE. New York: Knopf, 1951.

CHIERA, EDWARD. *They Wrote on Clay.* Chicago: University of Chicago Press, 1938.

FINEGAN, JACK. *Light from the Ancient Past.* Princeton: Princeton University Press, 1946.

JASTROW, MORRIS, JR. *Hebrew and Babylonian Traditions.* New York: Scribner, 1914.

KENYON, FREDERICK. *The Bible and Archaeology.* New York: Harper, 1940.

KING, L. W. *Legends of Babylonia and Egypt in Relation to Hebrew Tradition.* Oxford: Oxford University Press, 1918.

MERCER, S. A. B. *Extra-Biblical Sources for Hebrew and Jewish History.* New York: Longmans, 1913.

PRITCHARD, JAMES B. (ed.). *Ancient Near Eastern Texts Relating to the Old Testament.* Princeton: Princeton University Press, 1950 (2nd ed., 1955).

——. *The Ancient Near East in Pictures, Relating to the Old Testament.* Princeton: Princeton University Press, 1954.

——. *Archaeology and the Old Testament.* Princeton: Princeton University Press, 1958.

ROGERS, ROBERT W. *Cuneiform Parallels to the Old Testament.* (2nd ed.) New York: Abingdon, 1926.

WRIGHT, G. ERNEST. *Biblical Archaeology.* Philadelphia: Westminster, 1954.

CHAPTER TWO
EGYPTIAN DISCOVERIES

BAIKIE, JAMES. *The Amarna Age.* New York: Macmillan, 1926.

BREASTED, JAMES A. *Ancient Records of Egypt.* Chicago: University of Chicago Press, 1906.

——. *A History of Egypt from the Earliest Times to the Persian Conquest.* (2nd ed.) New York: Scribner, 1912.

——. *The Dawn of Conscience.* New York: Scribner, 1933.

——. *The Development of Religion and Thought in Ancient Egypt.* New York: Scribner, 1912.

ERMAN, ADOLF. *The Literature of the Ancient Egyptians.* Translated by A. M. BLACKMAN. London: Methuen, 1927.

PETRIE, W. M. FLINDERS. *A History of Egypt from the Earliest Kings to the XVIth Dynasty.* (11th ed.) London: Methuen, 1924.

PRITCHARD, JAMES B. *The Ancient Near East in Pictures, Relating to the Old Testament.* Princeton: Princeton University Press, 1954.

WILSON, JOHN A. *The Burden of Egypt.* Chicago: University of Chicago Press, 1951.
WRIGHT, G. ERNEST. *Biblical Archaeology.* Philadelphia: Westminster, 1957.

CHAPTER THREE
THE SPADE IN PALESTINE

ALBRIGHT, WILLIAM F. *Archaeology and the Religion of Israel.* (2nd ed.) Baltimore: Johns Hopkins Press, 1946.
——. *Archaeology of Palestine.* Harmondsworth: Penguin, 1949.
——. *From the Stone Age to Christianity.* (2nd ed.) Baltimore: Johns Hopkins Press, 1946.
BURROWS, MILLAR. *The Dead Sea Scrolls.* New York: Viking, 1955.
——. *More Light on the Dead Sea Scrolls.* New York: Viking, 1958.
——. *What Mean These Stones?* New Haven: American Society for Oriental Research, 1941.
CERAM, C. W. *The Secret of the Hittites.* Translated by RICHARD and CLARA WINSTON. New York: Knopf, 1956.
DAVIES, A. POWELL. *The Meaning of the Dead Sea Scrolls.* New York: American Library of World Literature, 1956.
DUPONT-SOMMER, A. *The Jewish Sect of Qumran and the Essenes.* Translated by R. D. BARNETT. New York: Macmillan, 1955.
FINKELSTEIN, LOUIS (ed.). *The Jews: Their History, Culture, and Religion.* New York: Harper, 1949.
MACALISTER, R. A. S. *A Century of Excavation in Palestine.* New York: Revell, 1925.
McCOWN, C. C. *The Ladder of Progress in Palestine.* New York: Harper, 1943.
OLMSTEAD, A. T. *History of Palestine and Syria.* New York: Scribner, 1931.
PRITCHARD, JAMES B. *The Ancient Near East in Pictures, Relating to the Old Testament.* Princeton: Princeton University Press, 1954.
ROWLEY, HAROLD H. *The Zadokite Fragments and the Dead Sea Scrolls.* New York: Macmillan, 1955.
WILSON, EDMUND. *The Scrolls from the Dead Sea.* Oxford: Oxford University Press, 1955.
WRIGHT, G. ERNEST. *Biblical Archaeology.* Philadelphia: Westminster, 1954.

CHAPTER FOUR
THE NATURE OF THE OLD TESTAMENT LITERATURE

ANDERSON, BERNHARD W. *Understanding the Old Testament.* Englewood Cliffs: Prentice-Hall, 1957.
BARTON, GEORGE A. *The Religion of Israel.* Philadelphia: University of Pennsylvania Press, 1928.
BEWER, JULIUS A. *The Literature of the Old Testament.* New York: Columbia University Press, 1922.

DRIVER, S. R. *Introduction to the Literature of the Old Testament.* New York: Scribner, 1898.

GRAY, GEORGE B. *A Critical Introduction to the Literature of the Old Testament.* New York: Scribner, 1920.

KNOPF, CARL SUMNER. *The Old Testament Speaks.* New York: Thomas Nelson, 1933.

LESLIE, ELMER A. *Old Testament Religion.* New York: Abingdon, 1936.

MOORE, GEORGE F. *The Literature of the Old Testament.* New York: Holt, 1913.

MOULD, ELMER W. K. *Essentials of Bible History.* New York: Ronald Press, 1946.

OESTERLEY, W. O. E. and ROBINSON, T. H. *Introduction to the Books of the Old Testament.* New York: Macmillan, 1937.

PFEIFFER, ROBERT H. *Introduction to the Old Testament.* New York: Harper, 1941.

RANKIN, O. S. *Israel's Wisdom Literature.* Edinburgh: T. and T. Clark, 1936.

ROBINSON, THEODORE H. *Prophecy and the Prophets in Ancient Israel.* New York: Scribner, 1923.

SIMPSON, DAVID C. *Pentateuchal Criticism.* London: Hodder and Stoughton, 1944.

SKINNER, JOHN. *Prophecy and Religion.* Cambridge: Cambridge University Press, 1922.

SMITH, HENRY PRESERVED. *The Religion of Israel.* New York: Scribner, 1925.

SMITH, J. M. P. *The Prophets and their Times.* (2nd ed.) Revised by W. A. IRWIN. Chicago: University of Chicago Press, 1941.

WELLHAUSEN, JULIUS. *Die Composition des Hexateuchs und der historischen Bücher des Alten Testaments.* (2nd ed.) Berlin: Reimer, 1889.

CHAPTER FIVE
CANONIZATION OF THE OLD TESTAMENT

BEWER, JULIUS A. *The Literature of the Old Testament in Its Historical Development.* New York: Columbia University Press, 1933.

DRIVER, GEORGE ROLLIS. "The Formation of the Old Testament," *Abingdon Bible Commentary,* pp. 91 ff. New York: Abingdon, 1929.

LEWIS, FRANK GRANT. *How the Bible Grew.* Chicago: University of Chicago Press, 1926.

MARGOLIS, M. L. *The Hebrew Scriptures in the Making.* Philadelphia: Jewish Publishing Society of America, 1922.

ROBINSON, H. WHEELER. *The Old Testament: Its Making and Its Meaning.* Nashville: Cokesbury, 1937.

RYLE, HERBERT EDWARD. *The Canon of the Old Testament.* (2nd ed.) London: Macmillan, 1925.

SIMMS, P. MARION. *The Bible from the Beginning.* New York: Macmillan, 1929.

SIMPSON, DAVID CAPELL. *Pentateuchal Criticism.* London: Hodder and Stoughton, 1944.

STRACK, H. L. "Canon of Scripture," *The New Schaff-Herzog Encyclopedia*, II, pp. 388 ff. New York: Funk and Wagnalls, 1908.

TRATTNER, ERNEST R. *Unravelling the Book of Books.* New York: Scribner, 1929.

WOODS, F. H. "Old Testament Canon," HASTINGS, JAMES (ed.). *A Dictionary of the Bible*, III, 604 ff. New York: Scribner, 1900.

CHAPTER SIX
EXTRACANONICAL LITERATURE OF THE OLD TESTAMENT

CHARLES, R. H. *The Apocrypha and Pseudepigrapha of the Old Testament in English.* Oxford: Clarendon, 1913.

——. *Religious Development between the Old and New Testament.* New York: Holt, 1914.

FULLER, LESLIE. "The Literature of the Intertestamental Period," *Abingdon Bible Commentary*, pp. 187 ff. New York: Abingdon, 1929.

GOODSPEED, EDGAR J. *The Apocrypha: An American Translation.* Chicago: University of Chicago Press, 1938.

——. *The Story of the Apocrypha.* Chicago: University of Chicago Press, 1939.

OESTERLEY, W. O. E. *An Introduction to the Books of the Apocrypha.* New York: Macmillan, 1937.

PFEIFFER, ROBERT H. *History of New Testament Times, with an Introduction to the Apocrypha.* New York: Harper, 1949.

——. "The Literature and Religion of the Apocrypha," *The Interpreter's Bible*, I, 391 ff. New York: Abingdon, 1952.

——. "The Literature and Religion of the Pseudepigrapha," *The Interpreter's Bible*, I, 421 ff. New York: Abingdon, 1952.

TORREY, C. C. *The Apocryphal Literature: A Brief Introduction.* New Haven: Yale University Press, 1945.

CHAPTER SEVEN
THE NATURE OF THE NEW TESTAMENT LITERATURE

BACON, BENJAMIN W. *An Introduction to the New Testament.* New York: Macmillan, 1924.

BARNETT, A. E. *The New Testament: Its Making and Meaning.* New York: Abingdon-Cokesbury, 1946.

CADBURY, HENRY J. *The Making of Luke-Acts.* New York: Macmillan, 1927.

CRAIG, CLARENCE T. *The Beginning of Christianity.* Nashville: Abingdon-Cokesbury, 1943.

DIBELIUS, MARTIN. *A Fresh Approach to the New Testament and Early Christian Literature.* New York: Scribner, 1936.

EASTON, BURTON S. *The Gospel before the Gospels.* New York: Scribner, 1928.

ENSLIN, MORTON SCOTT. *Christian Beginnings.* New York: Harper, 1938.

FILSON, FLOYD V. *Origin of the Gospels.* New York: Abingdon, 1939.

FOAKES-JACKSON, F. J. and LAKE, KIRSOPP. *The Beginnings of Christianity.* London: Macmillan, 1920–33.

GOODSPEED, EDGAR J. *An Introduction to the New Testament.* Chicago: University of Chicago Press, 1937.

――――. *New Chapters in New Testament Study.* New York: Macmillan, 1937.

GRANT, FREDERICK C. *The Earliest Gospel.* New York: Abingdon, 1943.

――――. *The Growth of the Gospels.* New York: Abingdon, 1933.

HUCK, A. *Synopse der drei ersten Evangelien.* (In Greek.) Tübingen: Mohr, 1922.

JÜLICHER, ADOLF. *An Introduction to the New Testament.* Translated by JANET P. WARD. New York: Putnam, 1904.

KEE, HOWARD CLARK and YOUNG, FRANKLIN W. *Understanding the New Testament.* Englewood Cliffs: Prentice-Hall, 1957.

LAKE, KIRSOPP. *The Earlier Epistles of St. Paul.* London: Rivington's, 1914.

LYMAN, MARY E. *The Christian Epic: A Study of the New Testament Literature.* New York: Scribner, 1936.

MOFFATT, JAMES. *Introduction to the Literature of the New Testament.* New York: Scribner, 1923.

PEAKE, ARTHUR S. *A Critical Introduction to the New Testament.* New York: Scribner, 1920.

RIDDLE, DONALD W. *The Gospels: Their Origin and Growth.* Chicago: University of Chicago Press, 1939.

――――. *New Testament Life and Literature.* Chicago: University of Chicago Press, 1946.

SCOTT, ERNEST FINDLAY. *The Literature of the New Testament.* New York: Columbia University Press, 1932.

STREETER, B. H. *The Four Gospels.* (4th ed.) London: Macmillan, 1930.

TAYLOR, VINCENT. *The Formation of the Gospel Tradition.* London: Macmillan, 1933.

CHAPTER EIGHT

THE CANONIZATION OF THE NEW TESTAMENT

GOODSPEED, EDGAR J. "The Canon of the New Testament," *The Interpreter's Bible,* I, 63 ff. New York: Abingdon-Cokesbury, 1952.

――――. *The Formation of the New Testament.* Chicago: University of Chicago Press, 1926.

GREGORY, CASPAR RENÉ. *Canon and Text of the New Testament.* New York: Scribner, 1927.

HARNACK, ADOLF. *The Origin of the New Testament.* Translated by J. R. WILKINSON. New York: Macmillan, 1925.

KNOX, JOHN. *Marcion and The New Testament.* Chicago: University of Chicago Press, 1942.

LEIPOLDT, JOHANNES. *Geschichte des neutestamentlichen Kanons.* Leipzig: Hinrichs, 1907.

LEWIS, F. G. *How the Bible Grew.* Chicago: University of Chicago Press, 1924.

SMYTH, J. PATERSON. *The Bible in the Making in the Light of Modern Research.* New York: Pott, 1914.

SOUTER, ALEXANDER. *The Text and Canon of the New Testament.* New York: Scribner, 1910.

WESTCOTT, BROOKE FOSS. *A General Survey of the History of the Canon of the New Testament.* London: Macmillan, 1896.

CHAPTER NINE
EXTRACANONICAL LITERATURE OF THE NEW TESTAMENT

CADBURY, HENRY J. "The New Testament and Early Christian Literature," *The Interpreter's Bible*, VII, 32 ff. New York: Abingdon-Cokesbury, 1951.

CAMPBELL, J. M. *The Greek Fathers.* New York: Longmans, 1929.

DIBELIUS, MARTIN. *A Fresh Approach to the New Testament and Early Christian Literature.* New York: Scribner, 1936.

GOODSPEED, EDGAR J. (ed. and tr.). *The Apostolic Fathers: An American Translation.* New York: Harper, 1950.

——. *A History of Early Christian Literature.* Chicago: University of Chicago Press, 1942.

GRANT, ROBERT M. *Second-Century Christian Christianity: A Collection of Fragments.* London: Society for Promotion of Christian Knowledge, 1946.

HARNACK, ADOLF. *Geschichte der altchristichen Literatur.* 3 vols. Leipzig: Hinrichs, 1893–1904.

HARRIS, J. RENDEL. *The Teaching of the Twelve Apostles.* Baltimore: Johns Hopkins Press, 1887.

HENNECKE, EDGAR. *Handbuch zur den neutestamentliche apokryphen.* Tübingen: Mohr, 1914.

JAMES, MONTAGUE R. (ed. and tr.). *The Apocryphal New Testament.* Oxford: Clarendon Press, 1924.

KRÜGER, GUSTAV. *History of Early Christian Literature in the First Three Centuries.* Translated by CHARLES R. GILLETT. New York: Macmillan, 1897.

LAKE, KIRSOPP and OUTLON, J. E. L. *Eusebius: The Ecclesiastical History, with an English Translation.* (Loeb Classical Library.) 2 vols. London: Putnam, 1926.

—— (tr.). *The Apostolic Fathers.* (Loeb Classical Library.) London: Heinemann, 1912.

ROBERTS, A. and DONALDSON, J. (trs.). *The Ante-Nicene Fathers.* 24 vols. Edinburgh: Clark, 1867–72

VON SODEN, HERMANN. *The History of Early Christian Literature: The Writings of the New Testament.* Translated by J. R. WILKINSON. New York: Putnam, 1906.

CHAPTER TEN
GREEK MANUSCRIPTS

BUHL, FRANTZ. "Bible Text," *The New Schaff-Herzog Encyclopedia.* New York: Funk and Wagnalls, 1908.

CLARK, KENNETH W. *A Descriptive Catalogue of Greek New Testament Manuscripts in America.* Chicago: University of Chicago Press, 1937.

COLWELL, ERNEST C. *The Study of the Bible.* Chicago: University of Chicago Press, 1937.

———. *What Is the Best New Testament?* Chicago: University of Chicago Press, 1952.

GOODSPEED, EDGAR J. *The Making of the English New Testament.* Chicago: University of Chicago Press, 1925.

GORDIS, ROBERT. *The Biblical Text in the Making.* Philadelphia: Dropsie College, 1937.

GREGORY, CASPAR R. *The Canon and Text of the New Testament.* New York: Scribner, 1907.

KENYON, FREDERIC G. *The Text of the Greek Bible.* London: Duckworth, 1937.

KITTEL, R. *Biblia Hebraica.* (3rd ed.) Stuttgart: Priviligierte Würtem bergische Bibelanstalt, 1929.

LAKE, KIRSOPP. *The Text of the New Testament.* London: British Academy, 1916.

MACPHERSON, J. "Canon and Text of the Old Testament," *The New Schaff-Herzog Encyclopedia.* New York: Funk and Wagnalls, 1908.

NESTLE, EBERHARD. *Einführung in das griechische Neue Testament.* (4th ed.) Revised by E. VON DOBSCHÜTZ. Göttingen: Vandenhoeck and Ruprecht, 1923.

———. *Novum Testamentum Graece cum apparatu critico curavit.* (16th ed.) Revised by ERWIN NESTLE. Stuttgart: Priviligierte Württembergische Bibelanstalt, 1936.

PFEIFFER, ROBERT H. *Introduction to the Old Testament.* New York: Harper, 1941.

PRICE, IRA M. *The Ancestry of Our English Bible.* Edited and revised by W. A. IRWIN and ALLEN WIKGREN. New York: Harper, 1949.

ROBERTS, B. J. *The Old Testament Text and Versions.* Cardiff: University of Wales Press, 1951.

SOUTER, ALEXANDER. *The Text and Canon of the New Testament.* New York: Scribner, 1913.

STRACH, H. L. "Text of the Old Testament," HASTINGS, JAMES (ed.). *A Dictionary of the Bible.* New York: Scribner, 1904.

SWETE, H. B. *An Introduction to the Old Testament in Greek.* (2nd ed., rev.) New York: Macmillan, 1914.

WESTCOTT, B. F. and HORT, F. J. A. *The New Testament in the Original Greek.* (Vol. I, *The Text;* Vol. II, *Introduction and Appendix.*) New York: Harper, 1882.

CHAPTER ELEVEN

EARLY VERSIONS

COLWELL, ERNEST C. "Text and Ancient Versions of the New Testament," *The Interpreter's Bible,* Vol. I. New York: Abingdon, 1952.

———. *What Is the Best New Testament?* Chicago: University of Chicago Press, 1952.

GORDIS, ROBERT. *The Biblical Text in the Making.* Philadelphia: Dropsie College, 1937.

GREGORY, CASPAR RENÉ. *The Canon and Text of the New Testament.* New York: Scribner, 1907.

JEFFERY, ARTHUR. "Text and Ancient Versions of the Old Testament," *The Interpreter's Bible,* Vol. I. New York: Abingdon, 1952.

KENYON, FREDERIC G. *Handbook to the Textual Criticism of the New Testament.* (2nd ed.) New York: Macmillan, 1912.

———. *The Text of the Greek Bible.* London: Duckworth, 1937.

LAKE, KIRSOPP. *The Text of the New Testament.* Edited by SILVA NEW. London: Christophers, 1928.

NAVILLE, E. H. *The Text of the Old Testament.* London: British Academy, 1916.

NESTLE, EBERHARD. *Textual Criticism of the Greek New Testament.* Translated by WILLIAM EDIE and edited by ALLAN MENZIES. London: Williams and Norgate, 1901.

ROBERTS, B. J. *The Old Testament Text and Versions.* Cardiff: University of Wales Press, 1951.

SOUTER, ALEXANDER. *The Text and Canon of the New Testament.* New York: Scribner, 1913.

VAGANAY, LEO. *An Introduction to the Textual Criticism of the New Testament.* Translated by B. V. MILLER. St. Louis: B. Herder Book Co., 1937.

CHAPTER TWELVE

ENGLISH TRANSLATIONS

American Revision Committee. *An Introduction to the Revised Standard Version of the New Testament.* New York: International Council of Religious Education, 1946.

American Standard Version. New York: Thomas Nelson and Sons, 1901.

BAGSTER, SAMUEL (ed.). *The English Hexapla.* London: Samuel Bagster & Sons, 1841.

BALLANTINE, WILLIAM G. *The Riverside New Testament.* Boston: Houghton Mifflin, 1923.

BATES, ERNEST SUTHERLAND. *A Biography of the Bible.* New York: Simon and Schuster, 1937.

BUTTERWORTH, CHARLES C. *The Literary Lineage of the King James Bible.* Philadelphia: University of Pennsylvania Press, 1941.

CAMMACK, M. M. *John Wycliffe and the English Bible.* New York: American Tract, 1938.

CROOK, MARGARET B. (ed.). *The Bible and Its Literary Associations.* New York: Abingdon, 1937.

GARDINER, JOHN H. *The Bible as English Literature.* New York: Scribner, 1907.

GOODSPEED, EDGAR J. *The Making of the English New Testament.* Chicago: University of Chicago Press, 1925.

———. *Problems of New Testament Translation.* Chicago: University of Chicago Press, 1945.

GREENSLADE, S. L. *The Work of William Tyndale.* London: Blackie & Son, 1938.

KNOX, RONALD. *The New Testament Newly Translated from the Vulgate.* New York: Sheed and Ward, 1944.

MAY, HERBERT GORDON. *Our English Bible in the Making.* Philadelphia: Westminster, 1952.

MOFFATT, JAMES. *The Bible: A New Translation.* New York: Harper, 1926.

MOULTON, RICHARD G. *The Modern Reader's Bible.* New York: Macmillan, 1907.

MOZLEY, JAMES FREDERIC. *William Tyndale.* New York: Macmillan, 1937.

PENNIMAN, JOSIAH H. *A Book about the English Bible.* New York: Macmillan, 1919.

PHILLIPS, J. B. *The New Testament in Modern English.* New York: Macmillan, 1958

PRICE, IRA M. *The Ancestry of Our English Bible.* (2nd ed.) Revised by WILLIAM A. IRWIN and ALLEN P. WIKGREN. New York: Harper, 1949.

Revised Standard Version. New York: Thomas Nelson and Sons, 1952.

RIDDLE, M. B. *The Story of the Revised New Testament.* Philadelphia: Sunday School Times, 1908.

RIEU, E. V. *The Four Gospels: A New Translation.* Baltimore: Penguin, 1953.

———. *The Acts of the Apostles: A New Translation.* Baltimore: Penguin, 1957.

SIMMS, P. MARION. *The Bible in America.* New York: Wilson-Erickson, 1936.

SMITH, J. M. P. and GOODSPEED, EDGAR J. (eds.). *The Bible: An American Translation.* Chicago: University of Chicago Press, 1931.

SMYTH, J. PATERSON. *How We Got Our Bible.* New York: James Pott and Co., 1912.

The Twentieth Century New Testament: A Translation into Modern English. New York: Revell, 1904.

WEIGLE, LUTHER A. *The English New Testament from Tyndale to the Revised Standard Version.* New York: Abingdon, 1949.

WEYMOUTH, R. F. *The New Testament in Modern Speech.* Edited and revised by E. H. COOK. Boston: Pilgrim Press, 1943.

WIKGREN, ALLEN. "The English Bible," *The Interpreter's Bible,* Vol. I. New York: Abingdon, 1952.

WILD, LAURA H. *The Romance of the English Bible.* New York: Doubleday, Doran, 1929.

WILLOUGHBY, H. R. *The First Authorized English Bible and the Cranmer Preface.* Chicago: University of Chicago Press, 1942.

CHAPTER THIRTEEN

EXEGESIS IN THE EARLY CHURCH

BRIGGS, CHARLES A. *General Introduction to the Study of the Holy Scripture.* New York: Scribner, 1899.

CHASE, F. H. *Chrysostom.* Cambridge: Deighton, Bell and Co., 1887.

CONYBEARE, F. C. *History of New Testament Criticism.* New York: Putnam, 1910.

CROMBIE, FREDERICK (tr.). *The Writings of Origen.* Edinburgh: T. and T. Clark, 1878.

DUGMORE, CLIFFORD W. (ed.). *The Interpretation of the Bible.* London: Society for Promotion of Christian Knowledge, 1944.

FAIRWEATHER, WILLIAM. *Origen and Greek Patristic Theology.* New York: Scribner, 1901.

FARRAR, FREDERIC W. *History of Interpretation.* New York: Dutton, 1886.

GILBERT, GEORGE H. *Interpretation of the Bible.* New York: Macmillan, 1908.

GILDERSLEEVE, BASIL L. (ed.). *The Apologies of Justin Martyr.* New York: Harper, 1877.

GRANT, ROBERT M. "History of the Interpretation of the Bible: Ancient Period." *The Interpreter's Bible,* Vol. I. New York: Abingdon, 1952.

————. *The Bible in the Church.* New York: Macmillan, 1948.

KNOX, JOHN. *Marcion and the New Testament.* Chicago: University of Chicago Press, 1942.

ROBERTS, A. and DONALDSON, J. (eds.). *Ante-Nicene Christian Library. Translations of the Writings of the Fathers.* Edinburgh: Clark, 1879.

ROBERTS, ALEXANDER and RAMBAULT, W. H. (ed. and tr.). *The Writings of Irenaeus.* Edinburgh: Clark, 1880.

RYPINS, STANLEY. *The Book of Thirty Centuries.* New York: Macmillan, 1951.

SMITH, H. P. *Essays in Biblical Interpretation.* Boston: Marshall, Jones Co., 1921.

VINCENT, MARVIN R. *A History of the Textual Criticism of the New Testament.* New York: Macmillan, 1899.

WOOD, JAMES D. *The Interpretation of the Bible.* London: Duckworth, 1958.

CHAPTER FOURTEEN

THE RISE OF HIGHER CRITICISM

BAUR, FERDINAND C. *Kritische Untersuchungen über die kanonische Evangelien.* Tübingen: Fues, 1847.

BRIGGS, CHARLES A. *General Introduction to the Study of the Holy Scripture.* New York: Scribner, 1899.

EICHHORN, JOHANN. *Einleitung in das Alte Testament.* Leipzig: Weidmann, 1803.

ELWES, R. H. M. (tr.). *The Chief Works of Benedict de Spinoza.* London: Bell, 1883.

ERNESTI, J. A. *Principles of Biblical Interpretation.* Translated by C. H. TERROT. Edinburgh: Clark, 1832.

GILBERT, GEORGE H. *Interpretation of the Bible.* New York: Macmillan, 1908.

GRANT, ROBERT M. *The Bible in the Church.* New York: Macmillan, 1948.

HARNACK, ADOLF. *The Acts of the Apostles.* Translated by J. R. WILKINSON. New York: Putnam, 1909.

————. *Das Wesen des Christentums.* Leipzig: Hinrichsche Buchhandlung, 1920. (English translation by T. S. SAUNDERS. *What Is Christianity?* New York: Putnam, 1901.)

HARNACK, ADOLF. *Die Mission und Ausbreitung des Christentums.* (English translation by J. MOFFATT. *The Mission and Expansion of Christianity in the First Three Centuries.* [2nd ed.] New York: Putnam, 1908.)

———. *Dogmengeschichte.* Tübingen: Mohr, 1898. (English translation by N. BUCHANAN. *History of Dogma.* Boston: Roberts Bros., 1895.)

———. *The Sayings of Jesus.* Translated by J. R. WILKINSON. New York: Putnam, 1908.

HUPFELD, HERMANN. *Die Quellen der Genesis.* Berlin: Weigandt und Prieben, 1853.

JACOBS, C. M. (tr.). *Works of Martin Luther.* Philadelphia: Muhlenberg Press, 1932.

MCNEILL, JOHN T. "History of the Interpretation of the Bible, Medieval and Reformation Period," *The Interpreter's Bible,* Vol. I. New York: Abingdon, 1952.

NASH, HENRY S. *A History of the Higher Criticism of the New Testament.* New York: Macmillan, 1901.

NEWMAN, LOUIS I. *Jewish Influence on the Christian Reform Movement.* New York: Columbia University Press, 1925.

RENAN, ERNEST. *La Vie de Jésus.* Paris: Michel Levy Frères, 1863.

REU, J. M. *Luther and the Scriptures.* Columbus: Lutheran Book Concern, 1944.

RYPINS, STANLEY. *The Book of Thirty Centuries.* New York: Macmillan, 1951.

SCHWEITZER, ALBERT. *The Quest of the Historical Jesus.* (2nd ed.) Translated by W. MONTGOMERY. New York: Macmillan, 1922.

STRAUSS, DAVID. *Das Leben Jesu.* Tübingen: Osiander, 1835.

WELLHAUSEN, JULIUS. *Die Composition des Hexateuchs.* Berlin: Reimer, 1899.

———. *Prolegomena zur Geschichte Israels.* (3rd ed.) Berlin: Reimer, 1899. (English translation by J. S. BLACK and ALLAN MENZIES. *Prolegomena to the History of Israel.* Edinburgh: A. & C. Black, 1885.)

CHAPTER FIFTEEN

TWENTIETH-CENTURY INTERPRETATION

NOTE. — This list is limited to general surveys or definitive works on criticism in the twentieth century. See footnotes of chapter 15 for individual books and authors.

BARTH, KARL. *Der Römerbrief.* Munich: Kaiser, 1923.

———. *The Word of God and the Word of Man.* Boston: Pilgrim Press, 1928.

CUNLIFFE-JONES H. *The Authority of the Biblical Revelation.* London: James Clarke, 1945.

DIBELIUS, MARTIN. *Gospel Criticism and Christology.* London: Nicholson, 1935.

DODD, CHARLES HAROLD. *History and the Gospel.* New York: Scribner, 1938.

DUGMORE, CLIFFORD W. (ed.). *The Interpretation of the Bible.* London: Society for Promotion of Christian Knowledge, 1944.

FILSON, FLOYD V. *One Lord, One Faith.* Philadelphia: Presbyterian Board, 1943.

FULLERTON, K. *Prophecy and Authority; A Study in the History of the Doctrine and Interpretation of Scripture.* New York: Macmillan, 1919.

GRANT, FREDERICK C. *The Bible in the Church.* New York: Macmillan, 1948.

———. *Form Criticism. A New Method of New Testament Research.* Chicago: Willett, Clark, 1934.

———. *The Growth of the Gospels.* New York: Abingdon, 1933.

HAHN, HERBERT F. *Old Testament in Modern Research.* Philadelphia: Muhlenberg Press, 1954.

HOSKYNS, E. C. and DAVEY, F. N. *The Fourth Gospel.* London: Faber and Faber, 1948.

HUNTER, ARCHIBALD M. *Interpreting the New Testament, 1900–1950.* Philadelphia: Westminster, 1951.

KNOX, JOHN. *Criticism and Faith.* New York: Abingdon, 1946.

KRAELING, EMIL. *The Old Testament Since the Reformation.* New York: Harper, 1956.

McCOWN, CHESTER C. *The Search for the Real Jesus.* New York: Scribner, 1840.

NASH, ARNOLD S. (ed.). *Protestant Thought in the Twentieth Century.* New York: Macmillan, 1951.

PARSONS, ERNEST W. *The Religion of the New Testament.* New York: Harper, 1939.

ROBINSON, T. H. "The Methods of Higher Criticism," *The People and the Book.* Edited by A. S. PEAKE. Oxford: Clarendon, 1925.

ROWLEY, H. H. *The Old Testament and Modern Study.* Oxford: Clarendon, 1951.

SCHWEITZER, ALBERT. *The Quest of the Historical Jesus.* (2nd Eng. ed.) Translated by W. MONTGOMERY. New York: Macmillan, 1922.

SEISENBERGER, MICHAEL. *Practical Handbook for the Study of the Bible.* New York: Wagner, 1925.

STREETER, BURNETT H. *The Four Gospels: A Study of Origins.* New York: Macmillan, 1925.

TAYLOR, VINCENT. *The Formation of the Gospel Tradition.* London: Macmillan, 1933.

TERRIEN, SAMUEL. "History of the Interpretation of the Bible: Modern Period," *The Interpreter's Bible.* Vol. I. New York: Abingdon, 1952.

TILLICH, PAUL. *Biblical Religion and the Search for Ultimate Reality.* Chicago: University of Chicago Press, 1955.

TORREY, CHARLES C. *The Four Gospels.* London: Hodder, 1934.

WILDER, AMOS N. *Eschatology and Ethics in the Teaching of Jesus.* (Rev. ed.) New York: Harper, 1950.

WILLOUGHBY, HAROLD R. (ed.). *The Study of the Bible Today and Tomorrow.* Chicago: University of Chicago Press, 1947.

WREDE, WILLIAM. *Das Messiasgeheimnis in den Evangelien.* Göttingen: Vandenhoeck and Ruprecht, 1901.

Index

DOVER · THRIFT · EDITIONS

A Connecticut Yankee in King Arthur's Court

MARK TWAIN

DOVER PUBLICATIONS, INC.
Mineola, New York

DOVER THRIFT EDITIONS

GENERAL EDITOR: PAUL NEGRI
EDITOR OF THIS VOLUME: KATHY CASEY

Bibliographical Note

This Dover edition, first published in 2001, is an unabridged republication, from a standard edition, of the work originally published in 1889 by the author's Charles L. Webster Publishing Co., New York. The introductory Note was written for the Dover edition.

Library of Congress Cataloging-in-Publication Data

Twain, Mark, 1835–1910.
 A Connecticut Yankee in King Arthur's Court / Mark Twain.
   p. cm. — (Dover thrift editions)
ISBN 0-486-41591-0 (pbk.)
   1. Americans—Great Britain—Fiction. 2. Arthurian romances—Adaptations. 3. Knights and knighthood—Fiction. 4. Kings and rulers—Fiction. 5. Time travel—Fiction. 6. Britons—Fiction. I. Title. II. Series.

PS1308 .A1 2001
813'.4—dc21

00-065654

Manufactured in the United States of America
Dover Publications, Inc., 31 East 2nd Street, Mineola, N.Y. 11501

Note

WHEN MARK TWAIN wrote *A Connecticut Yankee in King Arthur's Court*, he had been increasingly famous, admired, and prosperous for 20 years, as the author of several successful books, including *The Innocents Abroad*, *The Adventures of Tom Sawyer*, *The Gilded Age* (with Charles Dudley Warner), *The Prince and the Pauper*, and *The Adventures of Huckleberry Finn*. The book marked a turning point in his life. Its creation was closely linked, both in time and by Twain's need to generate more income, with his mounting investment in the perfection of the Paige typesetting machine, which he hoped would revolutionize printing and make his family financially secure for life. *A Connecticut Yankee* was published by Twain's own publishing company, under the editorship of his nephew Clarence Steadman. They hoped that, when the manuscript was ready for publication, the machine would be operational—and a double triumph would ensue. In reality, the Paige machine was outdone in the market by another inventor's work, and the publishing company went bankrupt. With complete integrity and an indomitable will, though, the 60-year-old Twain set out in 1895 on an around-the-world lecture tour to earn money, and within three years paid all of his debts. *Following the Equator* (1897) was written on the basis of his experiences during this two-year trip.

Critics, as well as readers in general, have differed greatly in their interpretations of Twain's intentions in writing *A Connecticut Yankee*. This is not surprising, considering the mixed messages that seem to mingle in the tale. The conclusions drawn depend greatly on the extent to which the reader thinks that the Yankee's motives and opinions consistently represent those of Twain. Several things are unmistakable: the author used Hank as a spokesperson for his views on hereditary monarchy and to express his abhorrence of the effects on society of an established religion whose leaders work hand-in-glove with the governing forces.

Capitalism, with a free-market economy in which individuals may sell their labor and skills to the owners of land and capital goods, is assumed as the best economic system developed by the late 19th century, and not likely to be replaced by any form of socialism or communism. Likewise, democracy is presented as the only proper form of government for human beings. The question of whether women should be citizens on an equal basis with men is not dealt with explicitly, but despite continual references to "being a man," Twain several times in A *Connecticut Yankee* praises the courage and acknowledges the suffering of women in the society ruled by Arthur—and married couples are to be admitted to the Boss's "Man Factory." Slavery, by any name, and regardless of whether it involved people from the same gene pool, was unacceptable.

Some readers see the story as an affirmation of the social and political rightness of the attitudes of the self-confident, practical, individualistic Yankee. Others perceive the Boss as a Fascist figure. Basic questions regarding war and peace, and relating to the replacement of handcrafts with the use of advanced technology and mass production, also are raised by the novel.

Whatever "messages" one finds in the narrative, it is a rich, fast-paced story, somehow plausible despite its labored beginnings (the blow to Hank's head, the coincidence of the solar eclipse with his "arrival" near Camelot, and the fact that Hank happens to know and remember its exact date). Of course, one can think of it as a dream, and of the prelude as the encounters of the objective narrator with a man who never has emerged from his memories of the epoch-making dreamed experiences.

In preparing to write the book, Twain depended greatly on Malory's 15th-century *Morte d'Arthur*. He also referred in the novel to background material, artifacts, and even specific incidents from sources that had been written a millennium or more after Arthur's supposed reign in Wales. This accounts for some definite or probable anachronisms in details of armor, etc.

Contents

Preface

THE UNGENTLE laws and customs touched upon in this tale are historical, and the episodes which are used to illustrate them are also historical. It is not pretended that these laws and customs existed in England in the sixth century; no, it is only pretended that inasmuch as they existed in the English and other civilizations of far later times, it is safe to consider that it is no libel upon the sixth century to suppose them to have been in practice in that day also. One is quite justified in inferring that wherever one of these laws or customs was lacking in that remote time, its place was competently filled by a worse one.

The question as to whether there is such a thing as divine right of kings is not settled in this book. It was found too difficult. That the executive head of a nation should be a person of lofty character and extraordinary ability was manifest and indisputable; that none but the Deity could select that head unerringly was also manifest and indisputable; that the Deity ought to make that selection, then, was likewise manifest and indisputable; consequently, that He does make it, as claimed, was an unavoidable deduction. I mean, until the author of this book encountered the Pompadour and Lady Castlemaine and some other executive heads of that kind; these were found so difficult to work into the scheme that it was judged better to take the other tack in this book (which must be issued this fall) and then go into training and settle the question in another book. It is of course a thing which ought to be settled, and I am not going to have anything particular to do next winter anyway.

MARK TWAIN

Hartford, July 21, 1889

A WORD OF EXPLANATION

IT WAS IN Warwick Castle that I came across the curious stranger whom I am going to talk about. He attracted me by three things: his candid simplicity, his marvelous familiarity with ancient armor, and the restfulness of his company—for he did all the talking. We fell together, as modest people will, in the tail of the herd that was being shown through, and he at once began to say things which interested me. As he talked along, softly, pleasantly, flowingly, he seemed to drift away imperceptibly out of this world and time, and into some remote era and old forgotten country; and so he gradually wove such a spell about me that I seemed to move among the specters and shadows and dust and mold of a gray antiquity, holding speech with a relic of it! Exactly as I would speak of my nearest personal friends or enemies, or my most familiar neighbors, he spoke of Sir Bedivere, Sir Bors de Ganis, Sir Launcelot of the Lake, Sir Galahad, and all the other great names of the Table Round—and how old, old, unspeakably old and faded and dry and musty and ancient he came to look as he went on! Presently he turned to me and said, just as one might speak of the weather or any other common matter—

"You know about transmigration of souls; do you know about transposition of epochs—and bodies?"

I said I had not heard of it. He was so little interested—just as when people speak of the weather—that he did not notice whether I made him any answer or not. There was half a moment of silence, immediately interrupted by the droning voice of the salaried cicerone:

"Ancient hauberk, date of the sixth century, time of King Arthur and the Round Table; said to have belonged to the knight Sir Sagramore le Desirous; observe the round hole through the chain-mail in the left breast; can't be accounted for; supposed to have been done with a bullet since invention of firearms—perhaps maliciously by Cromwell's soldiers."

My acquaintance smiled—not a modern smile, but one that must

1

have gone out of general use many, many centuries ago—and muttered apparently to himself:

"Wit ye well, *I saw it done.*" Then, after a pause, added: "I did it myself."

By the time I had recovered from the electric surprise of this remark, he was gone.

All that evening I sat by my fire at the Warwick Arms, steeped in a dream of the olden time, while the rain beat upon the windows, and the wind roared about the eaves and corners. From time to time I dipped into old Sir Thomas Malory's enchanting book and fed at its rich feast of prodigies and adventures, breathed-in the fragrance of its obsolete names, and dreamed again. Midnight being come at length, I read another tale, for a nightcap—this which here follows, to wit:

How Sir Launcelot Slew Two Giants, and Made a Castle Free.

Anon withal came there upon him two great giants, well armed, all save the heads, with two horrible clubs in their hands. Sir Launcelot put his shield afore him, and put the stroke away of the one giant, and with his sword he clave his head asunder. When his fellow saw that, he ran away as he were wood,* for fear of the horrible strokes, and Sir Launcelot after him with all his might, and smote him on the shoulder, and clave him to the middle. Then Sir Launcelot went into the hall, and there came afore him three score ladies and damsels, and all kneeled unto him, and thanked God and him of their deliverance. For, sir, said they, the most part of us have been here this seven year their prisoners, and we have worked all manner of silk works for our meat, and we are all great gentlewomen born, and blessed be the time, knight, that ever thou wert born; for thou hast done the most worship that ever did knight in the world, that will we bear record, and we all pray you to tell us your name, that we may tell our friends who delivered us out of prison. Fair damsels, he said, my name is Sir Launcelot du Lake. And so he departed from them and betaught them unto God. And then he mounted upon his horse, and rode into many strange and wild countries, and through many waters and valleys, and evil was he lodged. And at the last by fortune he happened against a night to come to a fair courtelage, and therein he found an old gentlewoman that lodged him with a good will, and there he had good cheer for him and his horse. And when time was, his host brought him into a fair garret over the gate to his bed. There Sir Launcelot unarmed him, and set his harness by him, and went to bed, and anon he fell on sleep. So, soon after there came one on horseback, and knocked at the gate in great haste. And when Sir Launcelot heard this he arose up, and looked out at the window, and saw by the moonlight three knights come riding after that one man, and all three lashed on him at once with swords, and that one knight turned on them knightly again and defended him. Truly, said Sir Launcelot, yonder one knight shall I help, for it were

---

*Demented.

shame for me to see three knights on one, and if he be slain I am partner of his death. And therewith he took his harness and went out at a window by a sheet down to the four knights, and then Sir Launcelot said on high, Turn you knights unto me, and leave your fighting with that knight. And then they all three left Sir Kay, and turned unto Sir Launcelot, and there began great battle, for they alight all three, and strake many strokes at Sir Launcelot, and assailed him on every side. Then Sir Kay dressed him for to have holpen Sir Launcelot. Nay, sir, said he, I will none of your help, therefore as ye will have my help let me alone with them. Sir Kay for the pleasure of the knight suffered him for to do his will, and so stood aside. And then anon within six strokes Sir Launcelot had stricken them to the earth.

And then they all three cried, Sir knight, we yield us unto you as man of might matchless. As to that, said Sir Launcelot, I will not take your yielding unto me, but so that ye yield you unto Sir Kay the seneschal, on that covenant I will save your lives and else not. Fair knight, said they, that were we loth to do; for as for Sir Kay we chased him hither, and had overcome him had ye not been; therefore, to yield us unto him it were no reason. Well, as to that, said Sir Launcelot, advise you well, for ye may choose whether ye will die or live, for an ye be yielden, it shall be unto Sir Kay. Fair knight, then they said, in saving our lives we will do as thou commandest us. Then shall ye, said Sir Launcelot, on Whitsunday next coming go unto the court of King Arthur, and there shall ye yield you unto Queen Guenever, and put you all three in her grace and mercy, and say that Sir Kay sent you thither to be her prisoners. On the morn Sir Launcelot arose early, and left Sir Kay sleeping: and Sir Launcelot took Sir Kay's armour and his shield and armed him, and so he went to the stable and took his horse, and took his leave of his host, and so he departed. Then soon after arose Sir Kay and missed Sir Launcelot: and then he espied that he had his armour and his horse. Now by my faith I know well that he will grieve some of the court of King Arthur: for on him knights will be bold, and deem that it is I, and that will beguile them; and because of his armour and shield I am sure I shall ride in peace. And then soon after departed Sir Kay, and thanked his host.

As I laid the book down there was a knock at the door, and my stranger came in. I gave him a pipe and a chair and made him welcome. I also comforted him with a hot Scotch whiskey; gave him another one; then still another—hoping always for his story. After a fourth persuader, he drifted into it himself, in a quite simple and natural way:

The Stranger's History.

I am an American. I was born and reared in Hartford, in the State of Connecticut—anyway, just over the river, in the country. So I am a Yankee of the Yankees—and practical; yes, and nearly barren of sentiment, I suppose— or poetry, in other words. My father was a blacksmith, my uncle was a horse doctor, and I was both, along at first. Then I went over to the great arms factory and learned my real trade; learned all there was to it; learned to make everything; guns, revolvers, cannon, boilers, engines, all sorts of labor-saving machinery. Why, I could make anything a body wanted—anything in the world, it didn't make any difference what; and if there wasn't any quick new-fangled way to make a thing, I could invent one—and do it as easy as rolling off a log. I became head superintendent; had a couple of thousand men under me.

Well, a man like that is a man that is full of fight—that goes without saying. With a couple of thousand rough men under one, one has plenty of that sort of amusement. I had, anyway. At last I met my match, and I got my dose. It was during a misunderstanding conducted with crowbars with a fellow we used to call Hercules. He laid me out with a crusher alongside the head that made everything crack, and seemed to spring every joint in my skull and make it overlap its neighbor. Then the world went out in darkness, and I didn't feel anything more, and didn't know anything at all—at least for a while.

When I came to again, I was sitting under an oak tree, on the grass, with a whole beautiful and broad country landscape all to myself—nearly. Not entirely; for there was a fellow on a horse, looking down at me—a fellow fresh out of a picture book. He was in old-time iron armor from head to heel, with a helmet on his head the shape of a nail keg with slits in it; and he had a shield, and a sword, and a prodigious spear; and his horse had armor on, too, and a steel horn projecting from his forehead, and gorgeous red and green silk trappings that hung down all around him like a bed quilt, nearly to the ground.

"Fair sir, will ye just?" said this fellow.

"Will I which?"

"Will ye try a passage of arms for land or lady or for—"

"What are you giving me?" I said. "Get along back to your circus, or I'll report you."

Now what does this man do but fall back a couple of hundred yards and then come rushing at me as hard as he could tear, with his nail keg bent down nearly to his horse's neck and his long spear pointed straight ahead. I saw he meant business, so I was up the tree when he arrived.

He allowed that I was his property, the captive of his spear. There was argument on his side—and the bulk of the advantage—so I judged it best to humor him. We fixed up an agreement whereby I was to go with him and he was not to hurt me. I came down, and we started away, I walking by the side of his horse. We marched comfortably along, through glades and over brooks which I could not remember to have seen before—which puzzled me and made me wonder—and yet we did not come to any circus or sign of a circus. So I gave up the idea of a circus, and concluded he was from an asylum. But we never came to any asylum—so I was up a stump, as you may say. I asked him how far we were from Hartford. He said he had never heard of the place; which I took to be a lie, but allowed it to go at that. At the end of an hour we saw a faraway town sleeping in a valley by a winding river; and beyond it on a hill, a vast gray fortress, with towers and turrets, the first I had ever seen out of a picture.

"Bridgeport?" said I, pointing.

"Camelot," said he.

* * *

My stranger had been showing signs of sleepiness. He caught himself nodding, now, and smiled one of those pathetic, obsolete smiles of his, and said:

"I find I can't go on; but come with me, I've got it all written out, and you can read it if you like."

In his chamber, he said: "First, I kept a journal; then by and by, after years, I took the journal and turned it into a book. How long ago that was!"

He handed me his manuscript, and pointed out the place where I should begin:

"Begin here—I've already told you what goes before." He was steeped in drowsiness by this time. As I went out at his door I heard him murmur sleepily: "Give you good den, fair sir."

I sat down by my fire and examined my treasure. The first part of it—the great bulk of it—was parchment, and yellow with age. I scanned a leaf particularly and saw that it was a palimpsest. Under the old dim writing of the Yankee historian appeared traces of a penmanship which was older and dimmer still—Latin words and sentences: fragments from old monkish legends, evidently. I turned to the place indicated by my stranger and began to read—as follows.

I. CAMELOT

"CAMELOT—Camelot," said I to myself. "I don't seem to remember hearing of it before. Name of the asylum, likely."

It was a soft, reposeful summer landscape, as lovely as a dream, and as lonesome as Sunday. The air was full of the smell of flowers, and the buzzing of insects, and the twittering of birds, and there were no people, no wagons, there was no stir of life, nothing going on. The road was mainly a winding path with hoofprints in it, and now and then a faint trace of wheels on either side in the grass—wheels that apparently had a tire as broad as one's hand.

Presently a fair slip of a girl, about ten years old, with a cataract of golden hair streaming down over her shoulders, came along. Around her head she wore a hoop of flame-red poppies. It was as sweet an outfit as ever I saw, what there was of it. She walked indolently along, with a mind at rest, its peace reflected in her innocent face. The circus man paid no attention to her; didn't even seem to see her. And she—she was no more startled at his fantastic makeup than if she was used to his like every day of her life. She was going by as indifferently as she might have gone by a couple of cows; but when she happened to notice me, *then* there was a change! Up went her hands, and she was turned to stone; her mouth dropped open, her eyes stared wide and timorously, she was the picture of astonished curiosity touched with fear. And there she stood gazing, in a sort of stupefied fascination, till we turned a corner of the wood and were lost to her view. That she should be startled at me instead of at the other man, was too many for me; I couldn't make head or tail of it. And that she should seem to consider me a spectacle, and totally overlook her own merits in that respect, was another puzzling thing, and a display of magnanimity, too, that was surprising in one so young. There was food for thought here. I moved along as one in a dream.

As we approached the town, signs of life began to appear. At intervals we passed a wretched cabin, with a thatched roof, and about it small

fields and garden patches in an indifferent state of cultivation. There
were people, too; brawny men, with long, coarse, uncombed hair that
hung down over their faces and made them look like animals. They
and the women, as a rule, wore a coarse tow-linen robe that came well
below the knee, and a rude sort of sandals, and many wore an iron collar. The small boys and girls were always naked; but nobody seemed to
know it. All of these people stared at me, talked about me, ran into the
huts and fetched out their families to gape at me; but nobody ever
noticed that other fellow, except to make him humble salutation and
get no response for their pains.

In the town were some substantial windowless houses of stone scattered among a wilderness of thatched cabins; the streets were mere
crooked alleys, and unpaved; troops of dogs and nude children played
in the sun and made life and noise; hogs roamed and rooted content-
edly about, and one of them lay in a reeking wallow in the middle of
the main thoroughfare and suckled her family. Presently there was a
distant blare of military music; it came nearer, still nearer, and soon a
noble cavalcade wound into view, glorious with plumed helmets and
flashing mail and flaunting banners and rich doublets and horsecloths
and gilded spearheads; and through the muck and swine, and naked
brats, and joyous dogs, and shabby huts it took its gallant way, and in its
wake we followed. Followed through one winding alley and then
another—and climbing, always climbing—till at last we gained the
breezy height where the huge castle stood. There was an exchange of
bugle blasts; then a parley from the walls, where men-at-arms, in
hauberk and morion marched back and forth with halberd at shoulder,
under flapping banners with the rude figure of a dragon displayed upon
them; and then the great gates were flung open, the drawbridge was
lowered, and the head of the cavalcade swept forward under the frown-
ing arches; and we, following, soon found ourselves in a great paved
court, with towers and turrets stretching up into the blue air on all the
four sides; and all about us the dismount was going on, and much greeting and ceremony, and running to-and-fro, and a gay display of moving
and intermingling colors, and an altogether pleasant stir and noise and
confusion.

II. KING ARTHUR'S COURT

THE MOMENT I got a chance I slipped aside privately and touched an ancient common looking man on the shoulder and said, in an insinuating, confidential way—

"Friend, do me a kindness. Do you belong to the asylum, or are you just here on a visit or something like that?"

He looked me over stupidly, and said—

"Marry, fair sir, me seemeth—"

"That will do," I said; "I reckon you are a patient."

I moved away, cogitating, and at the same time keeping an eye out for any chance passerby in his right mind that might come along and give me some light. I judged I had found one, presently; so I drew him aside and said in his ear—

"If I could see the head keeper a minute—only just a minute—"

"Prithee do not let me."

"Let you *what*?"

"*Hinder* me, then, if the word please thee better." Then he went on to say he was an undercook and could not stop to gossip, though he would like it another time; for it would comfort his very liver to know where I got my clothes. As he started away he pointed and said yonder was one who was idle enough for my purpose, and was seeking me besides, no doubt. This was an airy slim boy in shrimp-colored tights that made him look like a forked carrot; the rest of his gear was blue silk and dainty laces and ruffles; and he had long yellow curls, and wore a plumed pink satin cap tilted complacently over his ear. By his look, he was good-natured; by his gait, he was satisfied with himself. He was pretty enough to frame. He arrived, looked me over with a smiling and impudent curiosity; said he had come for me, and informed me that he was a page.

"Go 'long," I said; "you ain't more than a paragraph."

It was pretty severe, but I was nettled. However, it never fazed him; he didn't appear to know he was hurt. He began to talk and laugh, in

9

happy, thoughtless, boyish fashion, as we walked along, and made himself old friends with me at once; asked me all sorts of questions about myself and about my clothes, but never waited for an answer—always chattered straight ahead, as if he didn't know he had asked a question and wasn't expecting any reply, until at last he happened to mention that he was born in the beginning of the year 513.

It made the cold chills creep over me! I stopped, and said, a little faintly:

"Maybe I didn't hear you just right. Say it again—and say it slow. What year was it?"

"Five thirteen."

"Five thirteen! You don't look it! Come, my boy, I am a stranger and friendless: be honest and honorable with me. Are you in your right mind?"

He said he was.

"Are these other people in their right minds?"

He said they were.

"And this isn't an asylum? I mean it isn't a place where they cure crazy people?"

He said it wasn't.

"Well, then," I said, "either I am a lunatic, or something just as awful has happened. Now tell me, honest and true, where am I?"

"In King Arthur's Court."

I waited a minute, to let that idea shudder its way home, and then said:

"And according to your notions, what year is it now?"

"Five twenty-eight—nineteenth of June."

I felt a mournful sinking at the heart, and muttered: "I shall never see my friends again—never, never again. They will not be born for more than thirteen hundred years yet."

I seemed to believe the boy, I didn't know why. *Something* in me seemed to believe him—my consciousness, as you may say; but my reason didn't. My reason straightway began to clamor; that was natural. I didn't know how to go about satisfying it, because I knew that the testimony of men wouldn't serve—my reason would say they were lunatics, and throw out their evidence. But all of a sudden I stumbled on the very thing, just by luck. I knew that the only total eclipse of the sun in the first half of the sixth century occurred on the twenty-first of June, A.D. 528 O.S.,[1] and began at three minutes after twelve noon. I also knew that no total eclipse of the sun was due in what to *me* was the present year—*i.e.*, 1879. So, if I could keep my anxiety and curiosity from

---

1. O.S. means Old Style—that is, according to the Julian calendar, not the Gregorian.

eating the heart out of me for forty-eight hours, I should then find out for certain whether this boy was telling me the truth or not.

Wherefore, being a practical Connecticut man, I now shoved this whole problem clear out of my mind till its appointed day and hour should come, in order that I might turn all my attention to the circumstances of the present moment, and be alert and ready to make the most out of them that could be made. One thing at a time, is my motto—and just play that thing for all it is worth, even if it's only two pair and a jack. I made up my mind to two things; if it was still the nineteenth century and I was among lunatics and couldn't get away, I would presently boss that asylum or know the reason why; and if on the other hand it was really the sixth century, all right, I didn't want any softer thing: I would boss the whole country inside of three months; for I judged I would have the start of the best-educated man in the kingdom by a matter of thirteen hundred years and upwards. I'm not a man to waste time after my mind's made up and there's work on hand; so I said to the page—

"Now, Clarence, my boy—if that might happen to be your name—I'll get you to post me up a little if you don't mind. What is the name of that apparition that brought me here?"

"My master and thine? That is the good knight and great lord Sir Kay the Seneschal, foster brother to our liege the king."

"Very good; go on, tell me everything."

He made a long story of it; but the part that had immediate interest for me was this. He said I was Sir Kay's prisoner, and that in the due course of custom I would be flung into a dungeon and left there on scant commons until my friends ransomed me—unless I chanced to rot, first. I saw that the last chance had the best show, but I didn't waste any bother about that; time was too precious. The page said, further, that dinner was about ended in the great hall by this time, and that as soon as the sociability and the heavy drinking should begin, Sir Kay would have me in and exhibit me before King Arthur and his illustrious knights seated at the Table Round, and would brag about his exploit in capturing me, and would probably exaggerate the facts a little, but it wouldn't be good form for me to correct him, and not over-safe, either; and when I was done being exhibited, then ho for the dungeon; but he, Clarence, would find a way to come and see me every now and then, and cheer me up, and help me get word to my friends.

Get word to my friends! I thanked him; I couldn't do less; and about this time a lackey came to say I was wanted; so Clarence led me in and took me off to one side and sat down by me.

Well, it was a curious kind of spectacle, and interesting. It was an immense place, and rather naked—yes, and full of loud contrasts. It was very, very lofty; so lofty that the banners depending from the arched beams and girders away up there floated in a sort of twilight; there was a stone-railed gallery at each end, high up, with musicians in the one, and women, clothed in stunning colors, in the other. The floor was of big stone flags laid in black and white squares, rather battered by age and use, and needing repair. As to ornament, there wasn't any, strictly speaking; though on the walls hung some huge tapestries which were probably taxed as works of art; battle pieces, they were, with horses shaped like those which children cut out of paper or create in ginger-bread; with men on them in scale armor whose scales are represented by round holes—so that the man's coat looks as if it had been done with a biscuit punch. There was a fireplace big enough to camp in; and its projecting sides and hood, of carved and pillared stonework, had the look of a cathedral door. Along the walls stood men-at-arms, in breast-plate and morion, with halberds for their only weapon—rigid as stat-ues; and that is what they looked like.

In the middle of this groined and vaulted public square was an oaken table which they called the Table Round. It was as large as a circus ring; and around it sat a great company of men dressed in such various and splendid colors that it hurt one's eyes to look at them. They wore their plumed hats, right along, except that whenever one addressed himself directly to the king, he lifted his hat a trifle just as he was begin-ning his remark.

Mainly they were drinking—from entire ox horns; but a few were still munching bread or gnawing beef bones. There was about an aver-age of two dogs to one man; and these sat in expectant attitudes till a spent bone was flung to them, and then they went for it by brigades and divisions, with a rush, and there ensued a fight which filled the prospect with a tumultuous chaos of plunging heads and bodies and flashing tails, and the storm of howlings and barkings deafened all speech for the time; but that was no matter, for the dogfight was always a bigger interest anyway; the men rose, sometimes, to observe it the bet-ter and bet on it, and the ladies and the musicians stretched themselves out over their balusters with the same object; and all broke into delighted ejaculations from time to time. In the end, the winning dog stretched himself out comfortably with his bone between his paws, and proceeded to growl over it, and gnaw it, and grease the floor with it, just as fifty others were already doing; and the rest of the court resumed their previous industries and entertainments.

As a rule the speech and behavior of these people were gracious and courtly; and I noticed that they were good and serious listeners when anybody was telling anything—I mean in a dogfightless interval. And plainly, too, they were a childlike and innocent lot; telling lies of the stateliest pattern with a most gentle and winning naïveté, and ready and willing to listen to anybody else's lie, and believe it, too. It was hard to associate them with anything cruel or dreadful; and yet they dealt in tales of blood and suffering with a guileless relish that made me almost forget to shudder.

I was not the only prisoner present. There were twenty or more. Poor devils, many of them were maimed, hacked, carved, in a frightful way; and their hair, their faces, their clothing, were caked with black and stiffened drenchings of blood. They were suffering sharp physical pain, of course; and weariness, and hunger and thirst, no doubt; and none had given them the comfort of a wash at least, or even the poor charity of a lotion for their wounds; yet you never heard them utter a moan or a groan, or saw them show any sign of restlessness, or any disposition to complain. The thought was forced upon me: "The rascals—*they* have served other people so in their day; it being their own turn, now, they were not expecting any better treatment than this; so their philosophical bearing is not an outcome of mental training, intellectual fortitude, reasoning; it is mere animal training; they are white Indians."

III. KNIGHTS OF THE TABLE ROUND

MAINLY THE Round Table talk was monologues—narrative accounts of the adventures in which these prisoners were captured and their friends and backers killed and stripped of their steeds and armor. As a general thing—as far as I could make out—these murderous adventures were not forays undertaken to avenge injuries, nor to settle old disputes or sudden fallings out; no, as a rule they were simple duels between strangers—duels between people who had never even been introduced to each other, and between whom existed no cause of offense whatever. Many a time I had seen a couple of boys, strangers, meet by chance, and say simultaneously, "I can lick you," and go at it on the spot; but I had always imagined until now, that that sort of thing belonged to children only, and was a sign and mark of childhood; but here were these big boobies sticking to it and taking pride in it clear up into full age and beyond. Yet there was something very engaging about these great simplehearted creatures, something attractive and lovable. There did not seem to be brains enough in the entire nursery, so to speak, to bait a fishhook with; but you didn't seem to mind that, after a little, because you soon saw that brains were not needed in a society like that, and, indeed would have marred it, hindered it, spoiled its symmetry—perhaps rendered its existence impossible.

There was a fine manliness observable in almost every face; and in some a certain loftiness and sweetness that rebuked your belittling criticisms and stilled them. A most noble benignity and purity reposed in the countenance of him they called Sir Galahad, and likewise in the king's also; and there was majesty and greatness in the giant frame and high bearing of Sir Launcelot of the Lake.

There was presently an incident which centered the general interest upon this Sir Launcelot. At a sign from a sort of master of ceremonies, six or eight of the prisoners rose and came forward in a body and knelt on the floor and lifted up their hands toward the ladies' gallery and begged the grace of a word with the queen. The most conspicuously

14

situated lady in that massed flower bed of feminine show and finery inclined her head by way of assent, and then the spokesman of the prisoners delivered himself and his fellows into her hands for free pardon, ransom, captivity or death, as she in her good pleasure might elect; and this, as he said, he was doing by command of Sir Kay the Seneschal, whose prisoners they were, he having vanquished them by his single might and prowess in sturdy conflict in the field.

Surprise and astonishment flashed from face to face all over the house; the queen's gratified smile faded out at the name of Sir Kay, and she looked disappointed; and the page whispered in my ear with an accent and manner expressive of extravagant derision —

"Sir *Kay*, forsooth! Oh, call me pet names, dearest, call me a marine! In twice a thousand years shall the unholy invention of man labor at odds to beget the fellow to this majestic lie!"

Every eye was fastened with severe inquiry upon Sir Kay. But he was equal to the occasion. He got up and played his hand like a major — and took every trick. He said he would state the case, exactly according to the facts; he would tell the simple straightforward tale, without comment of his own; "and then," said he, "if ye find glory and honor due, ye will give it unto him who is the mightiest man of his hands that ever bare shield or strake with sword in the ranks of Christian battle — even him that sitteth there!" and he pointed to Sir Launcelot. Ah, he fetched them; it was a rattling good stroke. Then he went on and told how Sir Launcelot, seeking adventures, some brief time gone by, killed seven giants at one sweep of his sword, and set a hundred and forty-two captive maidens free; and then went farther, still seeking adventures, and found him (Sir Kay) fighting a desperate fight against nine foreign knights, and straightway took the battle solely into his own hands, and conquered the nine; and that night Sir Launcelot rose quietly, and dressed him in Sir Kay's armor and took Sir Kay's horse and gat him away into distant lands, and vanquished sixteen knights in one pitched battle and thirty-four in another; and all these and the former nine he made to swear that about Whitsuntide they would ride to Arthur's court and yield them to Queen Guenever's hands as captives of Sir Kay the Seneschal, spoil of his knightly prowess; and now here were these half dozen, and the rest would be along as soon as they might be healed of their desperate wounds.

Well, it was touching to see the queen blush and smile, and look embarrassed and happy, and fling furtive glances at Sir Launcelot that would have got him shot in Arkansas, to a dead certainty.

Everybody praised the valor and magnanimity of Sir Launcelot; and as for me, I was perfectly amazed, that one man, all by himself, should have been able to beat down and capture such battalions of practiced fighters. I said as much to Clarence; but this mocking featherhead only said—

"An Sir Kay had had time to get another skin of sour wine into him, ye had seen the accompt doubled."

I looked at the boy in sorrow; and as I looked I saw the cloud of a deep despondency settle upon his countenance. I followed the direction of his eye, and saw that a very old and white-bearded man, clothed in a flowing black gown, had risen and was standing at the table upon unsteady legs, and feebly swaying his ancient head and surveying the company with his watery and wandering eye. The same suffering look that was in the page's face was observable in all the faces around—the look of dumb creatures who know that they must endure and make no moan.

"Marry, we shall have it again," sighed the boy; "that same old weary tale that he hath told a thousand times in the same words, and that he *will* tell till he dieth, every time he hath gotten his barrel full and feeleth his exaggeration-mill a-working. Would God I had died or I saw this day!"

"Who is it?"

"Merlin, the mighty liar and magician, perdition singe him for the weariness he worketh with his one tale! But that men fear him for that he hath the storms and the lightnings and all the devils that be in hell at his beck and call, they would have dug his entrails out these many years ago to get at that tale and squelch it. He telleth it always in the third person, making believe he is too modest to glorify himself—maledictions light upon him, misfortune be his dole! Good friend, prithee call me for evensong."

The boy nestled himself upon my shoulder and pretended to go to sleep. The old man began his tale; and presently the lad was asleep in reality; so also were the dogs, and the court, the lackeys, and the files of men-at-arms. The droning voice droned on; a soft snoring arose on all sides and supported it like a deep and subdued accompaniment of wind instruments. Some heads were bowed upon folded arms, some lay back with open mouths that issued unconscious music; the flies buzzed and bit, unmolested, the rats swarmed softly out from a hundred holes, and pattered about, and made themselves at home everywhere; and one of them sat up like a squirrel on the king's head and held a bit of cheese in its hands and nibbled it, and dribbled the crumbs in the king's face with naïve and impudent irreverence. It was a tranquil scene, and restful to the weary eye and the jaded spirit.

This was the old man's tale. He said:

"Right so the king and Merlin departed, and went until an hermit that was a good man and a great leech. So the hermit searched all his wounds and gave him good salves; so the king was there three days, and then were his wounds well amended that he might ride and go, and so departed. And as they rode, Arthur said, I have no sword. No force,* said Merlin, hereby is a sword that shall be yours and I may. So they rode till they came to a lake, the which was a fair water and broad, and in the midst of the lake Arthur was ware of an arm clothed in white samite, that held a fair sword in that hand. Lo, said Merlin, yonder is that sword that I spake of. With that they saw a damsel going upon the lake. What damsel is that? said Arthur. That is the Lady of the lake, said Merlin; and within that lake is a rock, and therein is as fair a place as any on earth, and richly beseen, and this damsel will come to you anon, and then speak ye fair to her that she will give you that sword. Anon withal came the damsel unto Arthur and saluted him, and he her again. Damsel, said Arthur, what sword is that, that yonder the arm holdeth above the water? I would it were mine, for I have no sword. Sir Arthur King, said the damsel, that sword is mine, and if ye will give me a gift when I ask it you, ye shall have it. By my faith, said Arthur, I will give you what gift ye will ask. Well, said the damsel, go ye into yonder barge and row yourself to the sword, and take it and the scabbard with you, and I will ask my gift when I see my time. So Sir Arthur and Merlin alight, and tied their horses to two trees, and so they went into the ship, and when they came to the sword that the hand held, Sir Arthur took it up by the handles, and took it with him. And the arm and the hand went under the water; and so they came into the land and rode forth. And then Sir Arthur saw a rich pavilion. What signifieth yonder pavilion? It is the knight's pavilion, said Merlin, that ye fought with last, Sir Pellinore, but he is out, he is not there; he hath ado with a knight of yours, that hight Egglame, and they have fought together, but at the last Egglame fled, and else he had been dead, and he hath chased him even to Carlion, and we shall meet with him anon in the highway. That is well said, said Arthur, now have I a sword, now will I wage battle with him, and be avenged on him. Sir, ye shall not so, said Merlin, for the knight is weary of fighting and chasing, so that ye shall have no worship to have ado with him; also, he will not lightly be matched of one knight living; and therefore it is my counsel, let him pass, for he shall do you good service in short time, and his sons, after his days. Also ye shall see that day in short space ye shall be right glad to give him your sister to wed. When I see him, I will do as ye advise me, said Arthur. Then Sir Arthur looked on the sword, and liked it passing well. Whether liketh you better, said Merlin, the sword or the scabbard? Me liketh better the sword, said Arthur. Ye are more unwise, said

---

*No matter.

Merlin, for the scabbard is worth ten of the sword, for while ye have the scabbard upon you ye shall never lose no blood, be ye never so sore wounded; therefore, keep well the scabbard always with you. So they rode unto Carlion, and by the way they met with Sir Pellinore; but Merlin had done such a craft that Pellinore saw not Arthur, and he passed by without any words. I marvel, said Arthur, that the knight would not speak. Sir, said Merlin, he saw you not; for and he had seen you ye had not lightly departed. So they came unto Carlion, whereof his knights were passing glad. And when they heard of his adventures they marveled that he would jeopard his person so alone. But all men of worship said it was merry to be under such a chieftain that would put his person in adventure as other poor knights did."

IV. SIR DINADAN THE HUMORIST

IT SEEMED to me that this quaint lie was most simply and beautifully told; but then I had heard it only once, and that makes a difference; it was pleasant to the others when it was fresh, no doubt.

Sir Dinadan the Humorist was the first to awake, and he soon roused the rest with a practical joke of a sufficiently poor quality. He tied some metal mugs to a dog's tail and turned him loose, and he tore around and around the place in a frenzy of fright, with all the other dogs bellowing after him and battering and crashing against everything that came in their way and making altogether a chaos of confusion and a most deafening din and turmoil; at which every man and woman of the multitude laughed till the tears flowed, and some fell out of their chairs and wallowed on the floor in ecstasy. It was just like so many children. Sir Dinadan was so proud of his exploit that he could not keep from telling over and over again, to weariness, how the immortal idea happened to occur to him; and as is the way with humorists of his breed, he was still laughing at it after everybody else had got through. He was so set up that he concluded to make a speech—of course a humorous speech. I think I never heard so many old played-out jokes strung together in my life. He was worse than the minstrels, worse than the clown in the circus. It seemed peculiarly sad to sit here, thirteen hundred years before I was born and listen again to poor, flat, worm-eaten jokes that had given me the dry gripes when I was a boy thirteen hundred years afterwards. It about convinced me that there isn't any such thing as a new joke possible. Everybody laughed at these antiquities—but then they always do; I had noticed that, centuries later. However, of course the scoffer didn't laugh—I mean the boy. No, he scoffed; there wasn't anything he wouldn't scoff at. He said the most of Sir Dinadan's jokes were rotten and the rest were petrified. I said "petrified" was good; as I believed, myself, that the only right way to classify the majestic ages of some of those jokes was by geologic periods. But that neat idea hit the boy in a blank place, for geology hadn't

been invented yet. However, I made a note of the remark, and calculated to educate the commonwealth up to it if I pulled through. It is no
use to throw a good thing away merely because the market isn't ripe yet.

Now Sir Kay arose and began to fire up on his history-mill, with me
for fuel. It was time for me to feel serious, and I did. Sir Kay told how
he had encountered me in a far land of barbarians, who all wore the
same ridiculous garb that I did—a garb that was a work of enchantment, and intended to make the wearer secure from hurt by human
hands. However, he had nullified the force of the enchantment by
prayer, and had killed my thirteen knights in a three-hours' battle, and
taken me prisoner, sparing my life in order that so strange a curiosity as
I was might be exhibited to the wonder and admiration of the king
and the court. He spoke of me all the time, in the blandest way, as "this
prodigious giant," and "this horrible sky-towering monster," and "this
tusked and taloned man-devouring ogre"; and everybody took in all
this bosh in the naïvest way, and never smiled or seemed to notice that
there was any discrepancy between these watered statistics and me. He
said that in trying to escape from him I sprang into the top of a tree two
hundred cubits high at a single bound, but he dislodged me with a
stone the size of a cow, which "all-to-brast" the most of my bones, and
then swore me to appear at Arthur's court for sentence. He ended by
condemning me to die at noon on the twenty-first; and was so little concerned about it that he stopped to yawn before he named the date.

I was in a dismal state by this time; indeed, I was hardly enough in
my right mind to keep the run of a dispute that sprung up as to how I
had better be killed, the possibility of the killing being doubted by
some, because of the enchantment in my clothes. And yet it was nothing but an ordinary suit of fifteen-dollar slopshops. Still, I was sane
enough to notice this detail, to wit: many of the terms used in the most
matter-of-fact way by this great assemblage of the first ladies and gentlemen in the land would have made a Comanche blush. Indelicacy is
too mild a term to convey the idea. However, I had read *Tom Jones* and
Roderick Random, and other books of that kind, and knew that the
highest and first ladies and gentlemen in England had remained
little or no cleaner in their talk, and in the morals and conduct which
such talk implies, clear up to a hundred years ago; in fact clear into
our own nineteenth century—in which century, broadly speaking, the
earliest samples of the real lady and real gentleman discoverable in
English history—or in European history, for that matter—may be said
to have made their appearance. Suppose Sir Walter, instead of putting
the conversation into the mouths of his characters, had allowed the
characters to speak for themselves? We should have had talk from
Rachel and Ivanhoe and the soft lady Rowena which would embarrass

a tramp in our day. However, to the unconsciously indelicate all things are delicate. King Arthur's people were not aware that they were indecent, and I had presence of mind enough not to mention it.

They were so troubled about my enchanted clothes that they were mightily relieved, at last, when old Merlin swept the difficulty away for them with a commonsense hint. He asked them why they were so dull—why didn't it occur to them to strip me. In half a minute I was as naked as a pair of tongs! And dear, dear, to think of it: I was the only embarrassed person there. Everybody discussed me; and did it as unconcernedly as if I had been a cabbage. Queen Guenever was as naïvely interested as the rest, and said she had never seen anybody with legs just like mine before. It was the only compliment I got—if it was a compliment.

Finally I was carried off in one direction, and my perilous clothes in another. I was shoved into a dark and narrow cell in a dungeon, with some scant remnants for dinner, some moldy straw for a bed, and no end of rats for company.

V. AN INSPIRATION

I WAS SO tired that even my fears were not able to keep me awake long.

When I next came to myself, I seemed to have been asleep a very long time. My first thought was, "Well, what an astonishing dream I've had! I reckon I've waked only just in time to keep from being hanged or drowned or burned, or something. . . . I'll nap again till the whistle blows, and then I'll go down to the arms factory and have it out with Hercules."

But just then I heard the harsh music of rusty chains and bolts, a light flashed in my eyes, and that butterfly, Clarence, stood before me! I gasped with surprise; my breath almost got away from me.

"What!" I said, "you here yet? Go along with the rest of the dream! Scatter!"

But he only laughed, in his lighthearted way, and fell to making fun of my sorry plight.

"All right," I said resignedly, "let the dream go on; I'm in no hurry."

"Prithee what dream?"

"What dream? Why, the dream that I am in Arthur's court—a person who never existed; and that I am talking to you, who are nothing but a work of the imagination."

"Oh, la, indeed! And is it a dream that you're to be burned tomorrow? Ho-ho—answer me that!"

The shock that went through me was distressing. I now began to reason that my situation was in the last degree serious, dream or no dream; for I knew by past experience of the lifelike intensity of dreams, that to be burned to death, even in a dream, would be very far from being a jest, and was a thing to be avoided, by any means, fair or foul, that I could contrive. So I said beseechingly:

"Ah, Clarence, good boy, only friend I've got—for you *are* my friend, aren't you—don't fail me; help me to devise some way of escaping from this place!"

"Now do but hear thyself! Escape? Why, man, the corridors are in guard and keep of men-at-arms."

22

"No doubt, no doubt. But how many, Clarence? Not many, I hope?"

"Full a score. One may not hope to escape." After a pause—hesitatingly: "and there be other reasons—and weightier."

"Other ones? What are they?"

"Well, they say—oh, but I daren't, indeed I daren't!"

"Why, poor lad, what is the matter? Why do you blench? Why do you tremble so?"

"Oh, in sooth, there is need! I do not want to tell you, but—"

"Come, come, be brave, be a man—speak out, there's a good lad!"

He hesitated, pulled one way by desire, the other way by fear; then he stole to the door and peeped out, listening; and finally crept close to me and put his mouth to my ear and told me his fearful news in a whisper, and with all the cowering apprehension of one who was venturing upon awful ground and speaking of things whose very mention might be freighted with death.

"Merlin, in his malice, has woven a spell about this dungeon, and there bides not the man in these kingdoms that would be desperate enough to essay to cross its lines with you! Now God pity me, I have told it! Ah, be kind to me, be merciful to a poor boy who means thee well; for an thou betray me I am lost!"

I laughed the only really refreshing laugh I had had for some time; and shouted—

"Merlin has wrought a spell! *Merlin*, forsooth! That cheap old humbug, that maundering old ass? Bosh, pure bosh, the silliest bosh in the world! Why, it does seem to me that of all the childish, idiotic, chuckleheaded, chicken-livered superstitions that ev—oh, damn Merlin!"

But Clarence had slumped to his knees before I had half finished, and he was like to go out of his mind with fright.

"Oh, beware! These are awful words! Any moment these walls may crumble upon us if you say such things. Oh call them back before it is too late!"

Now this strange exhibition gave me a good idea and set me to thinking. If everybody about here was so honestly and sincerely afraid of Merlin's pretended magic as Clarence was, certainly a superior man like me ought to be shrewd enough to contrive some way to take advantage of such a state of things. I went on thinking, and worked out a plan. Then I said:

"Get up. Pull yourself together; look me in the eye. Do you know why I laughed?"

"No—but for our blessed Lady's sake, do it no more."

"Well, I'll tell you why I laughed. Because I'm a magician myself."

"Thou!" The boy recoiled a step, and caught his breath, for the thing hit him rather sudden; but the aspect which he took on was very, very respectful. I took quick note of that; it indicated that a humbug didn't need to have a reputation in this asylum; people stood ready to take him at his word, without that. I resumed:

"I've known Merlin seven hundred years, and he—"

"Seven hun—"

"Don't interrupt me. He has died and come alive again thirteen times, and traveled under a new name every time: Smith, Jones, Robinson, Jackson, Peters, Haskins, Merlin—a new alias every time he turns up. I knew him in Egypt three hundred years ago; I knew him in India five hundred years ago—he is always blethering around in my way, everywhere I go; he makes me tired. He don't amount to shucks, as a magician; knows some of the old common tricks, but has never got beyond the rudiments, and never will. He is well enough for the provinces—one-night stands and that sort of thing, you know—but dear me, *he* oughtn't to set up for an expert—anyway not where there's a real artist. Now look here, Clarence, I am going to stand your friend, right along, and in return you must be mine. I want you to do me a favor. I want you to get word to the king that I am a magician myself— and the Supreme Grand High-yu-Muckamuck and head of the tribe, at that; and I want him to be made to understand that I am just quietly arranging a little calamity here that will make the fur fly in these realms if Sir Kay's project is carried out and any harm comes to me. Will you get that to the king for me?"

The poor boy was in such a state that he could hardly answer me. It was pitiful to see a creature so terrified, so unnerved, so demoralized. But he promised everything; and on my side he made me promise over and over again that I would remain his friend, and never turn against him or cast any enchantments upon him. Then he worked his way out, staying himself with his hand along the wall, like a sick person.

Presently this thought occurred to me: how heedless I have been! When the boy gets calm, he will wonder why a great magician like me should have begged a boy like him to help me get out of this place; he will put this and that together, and will see that I am a humbug.

I worried over that heedless blunder for an hour, and called myself a great many hard names, meantime. But finally it occurred to me all of a sudden that these animals didn't reason; that *they* never put this and that together; that all their talk showed that they didn't know a discrepancy when they saw it. I was at rest, then.

But as soon as one is at rest, in this world, off he goes on something else to worry about. It occurred to me that I had made another blunder: I had sent the boy off to alarm his betters with a threat—I intending to invent a calamity at my leisure; now the people who are the readiest and eagerest and willingest to swallow miracles are the very ones who are the hungriest to see you perform them; suppose I should be called on for a sample? Suppose I should be asked to name my calamity? Yes, I had made a blunder; I ought to have invented my calamity first. "What shall I do? what can I say, to gain a little time?" I was in trouble again; in the deepest kind of trouble: . . . "There's a footstep—they're coming! If I had only just a moment to think. . . . Good, I've got it. I'm all right."

You see, it was the eclipse. It came into my mind, in the nick of time, how Columbus, or Cortez, or one of those people, played an eclipse as a saving trump once, on some savages, and I saw my chance. I could play it myself, now; and it wouldn't be any plagiarism, either, because I should get it in nearly a thousand years ahead of those parties.

Clarence came in, subdued, distressed, and said:

"I hasted the message to our liege the king, and straightway he had me to his presence. He was frighted even to the marrow, and was minded to give order for your instant enlargement, and that you be clothed in fine raiment and lodged as befitted one so great; but then came Merlin and spoiled all; for he persuaded the king that you are mad, and know not whereof you speak; and said your threat is but foolishness and idle vaporing. They disputed long, but in the end, Merlin, scoffing, said, 'Wherefore hath he not *named* his brave calamity? Verily it is because he cannot.' This thrust did in a most sudden sort close the king's mouth, and he could offer naught to turn the argument; and so, reluctant, and full loth to do you the discourtesy, he yet prayeth you to consider his perplexed case, as noting how the matter stands, and name the calamity—if so be you have determined the nature of it and the time of its coming. Oh, prithee delay not; to delay at such a time were to double and treble the perils that already compass thee about. Oh, be thou wise—name the calamity!"

I allowed silence to accumulate while I got my impressiveness together, and then said:

"How long have I been shut up in this hole?"

"Ye were shut up when yesterday was well spent. It is nine of the morning now."

"No! Then I have slept well, sure enough. Nine in the morning now! And yet it is the very complexion of midnight, to a shade. This is the 20th, then?"

"The 20th—yes."

"And I am to be burned alive tomorrow." The boy shuddered.

"At what hour?"

"At high noon."

"Now then, I will tell you what to say." I paused, and stood over that cowering lad a whole minute in awful silence; then in a voice deep, measured, charged with doom, I began, and rose by dramatically graded stages to my colossal climax, which I delivered in as sublime and noble a way as ever I did such a thing in my life: "Go back and tell the king that at that hour I will smother the whole world in the dead blackness of midnight; I will blot out the sun, and he shall never shine again; the fruits of the earth shall rot for lack of light and warmth, and the peoples of the earth shall famish and die, to the last man!"

I had to carry the boy out myself, he sunk into such a collapse. I handed him over to the soldiers, and went back.

VI. THE ECLIPSE

IN THE stillness and the darkness, realization began to supplement knowledge. The mere knowledge of a fact is pale; but when you come to *realize* your fact, it takes on color. It is all the difference between hearing of a man being stabbed to the heart, and seeing it done. In the stillness and the darkness, the knowledge that I was in deadly danger took to itself deeper and deeper meaning all the time; a something which was realization crept inch by inch through my veins and turned me cold.

But it is a blessed provision of nature that at times like these, as soon as a man's mercury has got down to a certain point there comes a revulsion, and he rallies. Hope springs up, and cheerfulness along with it, and then he is in good shape to do something for himself, if anything can be done. When my rally came, it came with a bound. I said to myself that my eclipse would be sure to save me, and make me the greatest man in the kingdom besides; and straightway my mercury went up to the top of the tube, and my solicitudes all vanished. I was as happy a man as there was in the world. I was even impatient for tomorrow to come, I so wanted to gather in that great triumph and be the center of all the nation's wonder and reverence. Besides, in a business way it would be the making of me; I knew that.

Meantime there was one thing which had got pushed into the background of my mind. That was the half conviction that when the nature of my proposed calamity should be reported to those superstitious people, it would have such an effect that they would want to compromise. So, by and by when I heard footsteps coming, that thought was recalled to me, and I said to myself, "As sure as anything, it's the compromise. Well, if it is good, all right, I will accept; but if it isn't, I mean to stand my ground and play my hand for all it is worth."

The door opened, and some men-at-arms appeared. The leader said—

"The stake is ready. Come!"

The stake! The strength went out of me, and I almost fell down. It is hard to get one's breath at such a time, such lumps come into one's throat, and such gaspings, but as soon as I could speak, I said:

"But this is a mistake—the execution is tomorrow."

"Orders changed; been set forward a day. Haste thee!"

I was lost. There was no help for me. I was dazed, stupefied; I had no command over myself; I only wandered purposelessly about, like one out of his mind; so the soldiers took hold of me, and pulled me along with them, out of the cell and along the maze of underground corridors, and finally into the fierce glare of daylight and the upper world. As we stepped into the vast enclosed court of the castle I got a shock; for the first thing I saw was the stake, standing in the center, and near it the piled fagots and a monk. On all four sides of the court the seated multitudes rose rank above rank, forming sloping terraces that were rich with color. The king and the queen sat in their thrones, the most conspicuous figures there, of course.

To note all this, occupied but a second. The next second Clarence had slipped from some place of concealment and was pouring news into my ear, his eyes beaming with triumph and gladness. He said:

"'Tis through *me* the change was wrought! And main hard have I worked to do it, too. But when I revealed to them the calamity in store, and saw how mighty was the terror it did engender, then saw I also that this was the time to strike! Wherefore I diligently pretended, unto this and that and the other one, that your power against the sun could not reach its full until the morrow; and so if any would save the sun and the world, you must be slain today, whilst your enchantments are but in the weaving and lack potency. Odsbodikins, it was but a dull lie, a most indifferent invention, but you should have seen them seize it and swallow it, in the frenzy of their fright, as it were salvation sent from heaven; and all the while was I laughing in my sleeve the one moment, to see them so cheaply deceived, and glorifying God the next, that He was content to let the meanest of His creatures be His instrument to the saving of thy life. Ah, how happy has the matter sped! You will not need to do the sun a *real* hurt—ah, forget not that, on your soul forget it not! Only make a little darkness—only the littlest darkness, mind, and cease with that. It will be sufficient. They will see that I spoke falsely,—being ignorant, as they will fancy—and with the falling of the first shadow of that darkness you shall see them go mad with fear; and they will set you free and make you great! Go to thy triumph, now! But remember—ah, good friend, I implore thee remember my supplication, and do the blessed sun no hurt. For *my* sake, thy true friend."

I choked out some words through my grief and misery; as much as to say I would spare the sun; for which the lad's eyes paid me back with such deep and loving gratitude that I had not the heart to tell him his good-hearted foolishness had ruined me and sent me to my death.

As the soldiers assisted me across the court the stillness was so profound that if I had been blindfold I should have supposed I was in a solitude instead of walled in by four thousand people. There was not a movement perceptible in those masses of humanity; they were as rigid as stone images, and as pale; and dread sat upon every countenance. This hush continued while I was being chained to the stake; it still continued while the fagots were carefully and tediously piled about my ankles, my knees, my thighs, my body. Then there was a pause, and a deeper hush, if possible, and a man knelt down at my feet with a blazing torch; the multitude strained forward, gazing, and parting slightly from their seats without knowing it; the monk raised his hands above my head, and his eyes toward the blue sky, and began some words in Latin; in this attitude he droned on and on, a little while, and then stopped. I waited two or three moments: then looked up; he was standing there petrified. With a common impulse the multitude rose slowly up and stared into the sky. I followed their eyes; as sure as guns, there was my eclipse beginning! The life went boiling through my veins; I was a new man! The rim of black spread slowly into the sun's disk, my heart beat higher and higher, and still the assemblage and the priest stared into the sky, motionless. I knew that this gaze would be turned upon me, next. When it was, I was ready. I was in one of the most grand attitudes I ever struck, with my arm stretched up pointing to the sun. It was a noble effect. You could *see* the shudder sweep the mass like a wave. Two shouts rang out, one close upon the heels of the other:

"Apply the torch!"

"I forbid it!"

The one was from Merlin, the other from the king. Merlin started from his place—to apply the torch himself, I judged. I said:

"Stay where you are. If any man moves—even the king—before I give him leave, I will blast him with thunder, I will consume him with lightnings!"

The multitude sank meekly into their seats, as I was just expecting they would. Merlin hesitated a moment or two, and I was on pins and needles during that little while. Then he sat down, and I took a good breath; for I knew I was master of the situation now. The king said:

"Be merciful, fair sir, and essay no further in this perilous matter, lest disaster follow. It was reported to us that your powers could not attain unto their full strength until the morrow; but"—

"Your Majesty thinks the report may have been a lie? It *was* a lie."

That made an immense effect; up went appealing hands everywhere, and the king was assailed with a storm of supplications that I might be bought off at any price, and the calamity stayed. The king was eager to comply. He said:

"Name any terms, reverend sir, even to the halving of my kingdom; but banish this calamity, spare the sun!"

My fortune was made. I would have taken him up in a minute, but I couldn't stop an eclipse; the thing was out of the question. So I asked time to consider. The king said—

"How long—ah, how long, good sir? Be merciful; look, it groweth darker, moment by moment. Prithee how long?"

"Not long. Half an hour—maybe an hour."

There were a thousand pathetic protests, but I couldn't shorten up any, for I couldn't remember how long a total eclipse lasts. I was in a puzzled condition, anyway, and wanted to think. Something was wrong about that eclipse, and the fact was very unsettling. If this wasn't the one I was after, how was I to tell whether this was the sixth century, or nothing but a dream? Dear me, if I could only prove it was the latter! Here was a glad new hope. If the boy was right about the date, and this was surely the twentieth, it *wasn't* the sixth century. I reached for the monk's sleeve, in considerable excitement, and asked him what day of the month it was.

Hang him, he said it was the *twenty-first!* It made me turn cold to hear him. I begged him not to make any mistake about it; but he was sure; he knew it was the twenty-first. So, that featherheaded boy had botched things again! The time of the day was right for the eclipse; I had seen that for myself, in the beginning, by the dial that was nearby. Yes, I *was* in King Arthur's court, and I might as well make the most out of it I could.

The darkness was steadily growing, the people becoming more and more distressed. I now said:

"I have reflected, Sir King. For a lesson, I will let this darkness proceed, and spread night in the world; but whether I blot out the sun for good, or restore it, shall rest with you. These are the terms, to wit: You shall remain king over all your dominions, and receive all the glories and honors that belong to the kingship; but you shall appoint me your perpetual minister and executive, and give me for my services one per cent of such actual increase of revenue over and above its present amount as I may succeed in creating for the state. If I can't live on that, I shan't ask anybody to give me a lift. Is it satisfactory?"

There was a prodigious roar of applause, and out of the midst of it the king's voice rose, saying:

"Away with his bonds, and set him free! and do him homage, high and low, rich and poor, for he is become the king's right hand, is clothed with power and authority, and his seat is upon the highest step of the throne! Now sweep away this creeping night, and bring the light and cheer again, that all the world may bless thee."

But I said:

"That a common man should be shamed before the world, is nothing; but it were dishonor to the *king* if any that saw his minister naked should not also see him delivered from his shame. If I might ask that my clothes be brought again—"

"They are not meet," the king broke in. "Fetch raiment of another sort; clothe him like a prince!"

My idea worked. I wanted to keep things as they were till the eclipse was total, otherwise they would be trying again to get me to dismiss the darkness, and of course I couldn't do it. Sending for the clothes gained some delay, but not enough. So I had to make another excuse. I said it would be but natural if the king should change his mind and repent to some extent of what he had done under excitement; therefore I would let the darkness grow a while, and if at the end of a reasonable time the king had kept his mind the same, the darkness should be dismissed. Neither the king nor anybody else was satisfied with that arrangement, but I had to stick to my point.

It grew darker and darker and blacker and blacker, while I struggled with those awkward sixth-century clothes. It got to be pitch dark, at last, and the multitude groaned with horror to feel the cold uncanny night breezes fan through the place and see the stars come out and twinkle in the sky. At last the eclipse was total, and I was very glad of it, but everybody else was in misery; which was quite natural. I said:

"The king, by his silence, still stands to the terms." Then I lifted up my hands—stood just so a moment—then I said, with the most awful solemnity: "Let the enchantment dissolve and pass harmless away!"

There was no response, for a moment, in that deep darkness and that graveyard hush. But when the silver rim of the sun pushed itself out a moment or two later, the assemblage broke loose with a vast shout and came pouring down like a deluge to smother me with blessings and gratitude; and Clarence was not the last of the wash, be sure.

VII. MERLIN'S TOWER

INASMUCH AS I was now the second personage in the Kingdom, as far as political power and authority were concerned, much was made of me. My raiment was of silks and velvets and cloth of gold, and by consequence was very showy, also uncomfortable. But habit would soon reconcile me to my clothes; I was aware of that. I was given the choicest suite of apartments in the castle, after the king's. They were aglow with loud-colored silken hangings, but the stone floors had nothing but rushes on them for a carpet, and they were misfit rushes at that, being not all of one breed. As for conveniences, properly speaking, there weren't any. I mean *little* conveniences; it is the little conveniences that make the real comfort of life. The big oaken chairs, graced with rude carvings, were well enough, but that was the stopping place. There was no soap, no matches, no looking glass—except a metal one, about as powerful as a pail of water. And not a chromo. I had been used to chromos for years, and I saw now that without my suspecting it a passion for art had got worked into the fabric of my being, and was become a part of me. It made me homesick to look around over this proud and gaudy but heartless barrenness and remember that in our house in East Hartford, all unpretending as it was, you couldn't go into a room but you would find an insurance chromo, or at least a three-color God-Bless-Our-Home over the door; and in the parlor we had nine. But here, even in my grand room of state, there wasn't anything in the nature of a picture except a thing the size of a bed quilt, which was either woven or knitted (it had darned places in it), and nothing in it was the right color or the right shape; and as for proportions, even Raphael himself couldn't have botched them more formidably, after all his practice on those nightmares they call his "celebrated Hampton Court cartoons." Raphael was a bird. We had several of his chromos; one was his "Miraculous Draught of Fishes," where he puts in a miracle of his own—puts three men into a canoe which wouldn't have held a dog without upsetting. I always admired to study R.'s art, it was so fresh and unconventional.

32

There wasn't even a bell or a speaking tube in the castle. I had a great many servants, and those that were on duty lolled in the ante-room; and when I wanted one of them I had to go and call for him. There was no gas, there were no candles; a bronze dish half full of boardinghouse butter with a blazing rag floating in it was the thing that produced what was regarded as light. A lot of these hung along the walls and modified the dark, just toned it down enough to make it dismal. If you went out at night, your servants carried torches. There were no books, pens, paper, or ink, and no glass in the openings they believed to be windows. It is a little thing—glass is—until it is absent, then it becomes a big thing. But perhaps the worst of all was, that there wasn't any sugar, coffee, tea, or tobacco. I saw that I was just another Robinson Crusoe cast away on an uninhabited island, with no society but some more or less tame animals, and if I wanted to make life bearable I must do as he did—invent, contrive, create, reorganize things; set brain and hand to work, and keep them busy. Well, that was in my line.

One thing troubled me along at first—the immense interest which people took in me. Apparently the whole nation wanted a look at me. It soon transpired that the eclipse had scared the British world almost to death: that while it lasted the whole country, from one end to the other, was in a pitiable state of panic, and the churches, hermitages, and monkeries overflowed with praying and weeping poor creatures who thought the end of the world was come. Then had followed the news that the producer of this awful event was a stranger, a mighty magician at Arthur's court; that he could have blown out the sun like a candle, and was just going to do it when his mercy was purchased, and he then dissolved his enchantments, and was now recognized and honored as the man who had by his unaided might saved the globe from destruction and its peoples from extinction. Now if you consider that everybody believed that, and not only believed it but never even dreamed of doubting it, you will easily understand that there was not a person in all Britain that would not have walked fifty miles to get a sight of me. Of course I was all the talk—all other subjects were dropped; even the king became suddenly a person of minor interest and notoriety. Within twenty-four hours the delegations began to arrive, and from that time onward for a fortnight they kept coming. The village was crowded, and all the countryside. I had to go out a dozen times a day and show myself to these reverent and awestricken multitudes. It came to be a great burden, as to time and trouble, but of course it was at the same time compensatingly agreeable to be so celebrated and such a center of homage. It turned Brer Merlin green with envy and spite, which was a great satisfaction to me. But there was one thing I couldn't understand; nobody had asked for an autograph. I spoke to Clarence about it. By George, I had to explain to him what it was. Then he said nobody in the country could read or write but a few dozen priests. Land! think of that.

There was another thing that troubled me a little. Those multitudes presently began to agitate for another miracle. That was natural. To be able to carry back to their far homes the boast that they had seen the man who could command the sun, riding in the heavens, and be obeyed, would make them great in the eyes of their neighbors, and envied by them all; but to be able to also say they had seen him work a miracle themselves—why, people would come a distance to see *them*. The pressure got to be pretty strong. There was going to be an eclipse of the moon, and I knew the date and hour, but it was too far away. Two years. I would have given a good deal for license to hurry it up and use it now when there was a big market for it. It seemed a great pity to have it wasted so, and come lagging along at a time when a body wouldn't have any use for it as like as not. If it had been booked for only a month away, I could have sold it short; but as matters stood, I couldn't seem to cipher out any way to make it do me any good, so I gave up trying. Next, Clarence found that old Merlin was making himself busy on the sly among those people. He was spreading a report that I was a humbug, and that the reason I didn't accommodate the people with a miracle was because I couldn't. I saw that I must do something. I presently thought out a plan.

By my authority as executive I threw Merlin into prison—the same cell I had occupied myself. Then I gave public notice by herald and trumpet that I should be busy with affairs of state for a fortnight, but about the end of that time I would take a moment's leisure and blow up Merlin's stone tower by fires from heaven; in the meantime, whoso listened to evil reports about me, let him beware. Furthermore, I would perform but this one miracle at this time, and no more; if it failed to satisfy and any murmured, I would turn the murmurers into horses, and make them useful. Quiet ensued.

I took Clarence into my confidence, to a certain degree, and we went to work privately. I told him that this was a sort of miracle that required a trifle of preparation; and that it would be sudden death to ever talk about these preparations to anybody. That made his mouth safe enough. Clandestinely we made a few bushels of first-rate blasting powder, and I superintended my armorers while they constructed a lightning rod and some wires. This old stone tower was very massive— and rather ruinous, too, for it was Roman, and four hundred years old. Yes, and handsome, after a rude fashion, and clothed with ivy from base to summit, as with a shirt of scale mail. It stood on a lonely eminence, in good view from the castle, and about half a mile away.

Working by night, we stowed the powder in the tower—dug stones out, on the inside, and buried the powder in the walls themselves, which were fifteen feet thick at the base. We put in a peck at a time, in a dozen places. We could have blown up the Tower of London with these charges. When the thirteenth night was come we put up our lightning rod, bedded it in one of the batches of powder, and ran wires from it to the other batches. Everybody had shunned that locality from the day of my proclamation, but on the morning of the fourteenth I thought best to warn the people, through the heralds, to keep clear away—a quarter of a mile away. Then added, by command, that at some time during the twenty-four hours I would consummate the miracle, but would first give a brief notice; by flags on the castle towers, if in the daytime, by torch baskets in the same places if at night.

Thundershowers had been tolerably frequent, of late, and I was not much afraid of a failure; still, I shouldn't have cared for a delay of a day or two; I should have explained that I was busy with affairs of state, yet, and the people must wait.

Of course we had a blazing sunny day—almost the first one without a cloud for three weeks; things always happen so. I kept secluded, and watched the weather. Clarence dropped in from time to time and said the public excitement was growing and growing all the time, and the whole country filling up with human masses as far as one could see from the battlements. At last the wind sprang up and a cloud appeared—in the right quarter, too, and just at nightfall. For a little while I watched that distant cloud spread and blacken, then I judged it was time for me to appear. I ordered the torch baskets to be lit, and Merlin liberated and sent to me. A quarter of an hour later I ascended the parapet and there found the king and the court assembled and gazing off in the darkness toward Merlin's tower. Already the darkness was so heavy that one could not see far; these people, and the old turrets, being partly in deep shadow and partly in the red glow from the great torch baskets overhead, made a good deal of a picture.

Merlin arrived in a gloomy mood. I said:

"You wanted to burn me alive when I had not done you any harm, and latterly you have been trying to injure my professional reputation. Therefore I am going to call down fire and blow up your tower, but it is only fair to give you a chance; now if you think you can break my enchantments and ward off the fires, step to the bat, it's your innings."

"I can, fair sir, and I will. Doubt it not."

He drew an imaginary circle on the stones of the roof, and burnt a pinch of powder in it which sent up a small cloud of aromatic smoke, whereat everybody fell back, and began to cross themselves and get uncomfortable. Then he began to mutter and make passes in the air

with his hands. He worked himself up slowly and gradually into a sort
of frenzy, and got to thrashing around with his arms like the sails of a
windmill. By this time the storm had about reached us; the gusts of
wind were flaring the torches and making the shadows swash about, the
first heavy drops of rain were falling, the world abroad was black as
pitch, the lightning began to wink fitfully. Of course my rod would be
loading itself now. In fact, things were imminent. So I said:

"You have had time enough. I have given you every advantage,
and not interfered. It is plain your magic is weak. It is only fair that I
begin now."

I made about three passes in the air, and then there was an awful
crash and that old tower leaped into the sky in chunks, along with a vast
volcanic fountain of fire that turned night to noonday, and showed a
thousand acres of human beings groveling on the ground in a general
collapse of consternation. Well, it rained mortar and masonry the rest
of the week. This was the report; but probably the facts would have
modified it.

It was an effective miracle. The great bothersome temporary population vanished. There were a good many thousand tracks in the mud
the next morning, but they were all outward bound. If I had advertised
another miracle I couldn't have raised an audience with a sheriff.

Merlin's stock was flat. The king wanted to stop his wages; he even
wanted to banish him, but I interfered. I said he would be useful to
work the weather, and attend to small matters like that, and I would
give him a lift now and then when his poor little parlor magic soured
on him. There wasn't a rag of his tower left, but I had the government
rebuild it for him, and advised him to take boarders; but he was too
high-toned for that. And as for being grateful, he never even said thank-
you. He was a rather hard lot, take him how you might; but then you
couldn't fairly expect a man to be sweet that had been set back so.

VIII. THE BOSS

TO BE vested with enormous authority is a fine thing; but to have the onlooking world consent to it is a finer. The tower episode solidified my power, and made it impregnable. If any were perchance disposed to be jealous and critical before that, they experienced a change of heart, now. There was not anyone in the kingdom who would have considered it good judgment to meddle with my matters.

I was fast getting adjusted to my situation and circumstances. For a time, I used to wake up, mornings, and smile at my "dream," and listen for the Colt's factory whistle; but that sort of thing played itself out, gradually, and at last I was fully able to realize that I was actually living in the sixth century, and in Arthur's court, not a lunatic asylum. After that, I was just as much at home in that century as I could have been in any other; and as for preference, I wouldn't have traded it for the twentieth. Look at the opportunities here for a man of knowledge, brains, pluck, and enterprise to sail in and grow up with the country. The grandest field that ever was; and all my own; not a competitor; not a man who wasn't a baby to me in acquirements and capacities; whereas, what would I amount to in the twentieth century? I should be foreman of a factory, that is about all; and could drag a seine downstreet any day and catch a hundred better men than myself.

What a jump I had made! I couldn't keep from thinking about it, and contemplating it, just as one does who has struck oil. There was nothing back of me that could approach it, unless it might be Joseph's case; and Joseph's only approached it, it didn't equal it, quite. For it stands to reason that as Joseph's splendid financial ingenuities advantaged nobody but the king, the general public must have regarded him with a good deal of disfavor, whereas I had done my entire public a kindness in sparing the sun, and was popular by reason of it.

I was no shadow of a king; I was the substance; the king himself was the shadow. My power was colossal; and it was not a mere name, as such things have generally been, it was the genuine article. I stood here, at the very spring and source of the second great period of the world's history; and could see the trickling stream of that history gather, and deepen and broaden, and roll its mighty tides down the far centuries; and I could note the upspringing of adventurers like myself in the shelter of its long array of thrones: De Montforts, Gavestons, Mortimers, Villierses; the war-making, campaign-directing wantons of France, and Charles the Second's scepter-wielding drabs; but nowhere in the procession was my full-sized fellow visible. I was a Unique; and glad to know that fact could not be dislodged or challenged for thirteen centuries and a half, for sure.

Yes, in power I was equal to the king. At the same time there was another power that was a trifle stronger than both of us put together. That was the Church. I do not wish to disguise that fact. I couldn't, if I wanted to. But never mind about that, now; it will show up, in its proper place, later on. It didn't cause me any trouble in the beginning—at least any of consequence.

Well, it was a curious country, and full of interest. And the people! They were the quaintest and simplest and trustingest race; why, they were nothing but rabbits. It was pitiful for a person born in a wholesome free atmosphere to listen to their humble and hearty outpourings of loyalty toward their king and Church and nobility; as if they had any more occasion to love and honor king and Church and noble than a slave has to love and honor the lash, or a dog has to love and honor the stranger that kicks him! Why, dear me, *any* kind of royalty, howsoever modified, *any* kind of aristocracy, howsoever pruned, is rightly an insult; but if you are born and brought up under that sort of arrangement you probably never find it out for yourself, and don't believe it when somebody else tells you. It is enough to make a body ashamed of his race to think of the sort of froth that has always occupied its thrones without shadow of right or reason, and the seventh-rate people that have always figured as its aristocracies—a company of monarchs and nobles who, as a rule, would have achieved only poverty and obscurity if left, like their betters, to their own exertions.

The most of King Arthur's British nation were slaves, pure and simple, and bore that name, and wore the iron collar on their necks; and the rest were slaves in fact, but without the name; they imagined themselves men and freemen, and called themselves so. The truth was, the nation as a body was in the world for one object, and one only: to grovel before king and Church and noble; to slave for them, sweat blood for them, starve that they might be fed, work that they might play, drink misery to the dregs that they might be happy, go naked that they might wear silks and jewels, pay taxes that they might be spared from paying them, be familiar all their lives with the degrading language and postures of adulation that they might walk in pride and think themselves the gods of this world. And for all this, the thanks they got were cuffs and contempt; and so poor-spirited were they that they took even this sort of attention as an honor.

Inherited ideas are a curious thing, and interesting to observe and examine. I had mine, the king and his people had theirs. In both cases they flowed in ruts worn deep by time and habit, and the man who should have proposed to divert them by reason and argument would have had a long contract on his hands. For instance, those people had inherited the idea that all men without title and a long pedigree, whether they had great natural gifts and acquirements or hadn't, were creatures of no more consideration than so many animals, bugs, insects; whereas I had inherited the idea that human daws who can consent to masquerade in the peacock-shams of inherited dignities and unearned titles are of no good but to be laughed at. The way I was looked upon was odd, but it was natural. You know how the keeper and the public regard the elephant in the menagerie: well, that is the idea. They are full of admiration of his vast bulk and his prodigious strength; they speak with pride of the fact that he can do a hundred marvels which are far and away beyond their own powers; and they speak with the same pride of the fact that in his wrath he is able to drive a thousand men before him. But does that make him one of *them?* No; the raggedest tramp in the pit would smile at the idea. He couldn't comprehend it; couldn't take it in; couldn't in any remote way conceive of it. Well, to the king, the nobles, and all the nation, down to the very slaves and tramps, I was just that kind of an elephant, and nothing more. I was admired, also feared; but it was as an animal is admired and feared. The animal is not reverenced, neither was I; I was not even respected. I had no pedigree, no inherited title; so in the king's and nobles' eyes I was mere dirt; the people regarded me with wonder and awe, but there was no reverence mixed with it; through the force of inherited ideas they were not able to conceive of anything being entitled to that except pedigree and lordship. There you see the hand of that awful power, the Roman Catholic Church. In two or three little centuries it had converted a nation of men to a nation of worms. Before the day of the Church's supremacy in the world, men were men, and held their heads up, and had a man's pride and spirit and independence; and what of greatness and position a person got, he got mainly by achievement, not by birth. But then the Church came to the front, with an ax to grind; and she was wise, subtle, and knew more than one way to skin a cat—or a nation; she invented "divine right of kings," and propped it all around, brick by brick, with the Beatitudes—wrenching them from their good purpose to make them fortify an evil one; she preached (to the commoner) humility, obedience to superiors, the beauty of self-sacrifice; she preached (to the commoner) meekness under insult; preached (still to the commoner, always to the commoner) patience, meanness of spirit, nonresistance under oppression; and she introduced heritable ranks and aristocracies, and taught all the Christian populations of the earth to bow down to them and worship them. Even down to my birth century that poison was still in the blood of Christendom, and the best of English commoners was still content to see his inferiors impudently continuing to hold a number of positions, such as lordships and the throne, to which the grotesque laws of his country did not allow him to aspire; in fact he was not merely contented with this strange condition of things, he was even able to persuade himself that he was proud of it. It seems to show that there isn't anything you can't stand, if you are only born and bred to it. Of course that taint, that reverence for rank and title, had been in our American blood, too—I know that; but when I left America it had disappeared—at least to all intents and purposes. The remnant of it was restricted to the dudes and dudesses. When a disease has worked its way down to that level, it may fairly be said to be out of the system.

But to return to my anomalous position in King Arthur's kingdom. Here I was, a giant among pigmies, a man among children, a master intelligence among intellectual moles: by all rational measurement the one and only actually great man in that whole British world; and yet there and then, just as in the remote England of my birth time, the sheep-witted earl who could claim long descent from a king's leman, acquired at secondhand from the slums of London, was a better man than I was. Such a personage was fawned upon in Arthur's realm and reverently looked up to by everybody, even though his dispositions were as mean as his intelligence, and his morals as base as his lineage. There were times when *he* could sit down in the king's presence, but I couldn't. I could have got a title easily enough, and that would have raised me a large step in everybody's eyes; even in the king's, the giver of it. But I didn't ask for it; and I declined it when it was offered. I couldn't have enjoyed such a thing with my notions; and it wouldn't have been fair, anyway, because as far back as I could go, our tribe had always been short of the bar sinister. I couldn't have felt really and satisfactorily fine and proud and set up over any title except one that should come from the nation itself, the only legitimate source; and such an one I hoped to win; and in the course of years of honest and honorable endeavor, I did win it and did wear it with a high and clean pride. This title fell casually from the lips of a blacksmith, one day, in a village, was caught up as a happy thought and tossed from mouth to mouth with a laugh and an affirmative vote; in ten days it had swept the kingdom, and was become as familiar as the king's name. I was never known by any other designation afterward, whether in the nation's talk or in grave debate upon matters of state at the council board of the sovereign. This title, translated into modern speech, would be THE BOSS. Elected by the nation. That suited me. And it was a pretty high title. There were very few THE'S, and I was one of them. If you spoke of the duke, or the earl, or the bishop, how could anybody tell which one you meant? But if you spoke of The King or The Queen or The Boss, it was different.

Well, I liked the king, and *as* king I respected him—respected the office; at least respected it as much as I was capable of respecting any unearned supremacy; but as *men* I looked down upon him and his nobles—privately. And he and they liked me, and respected my office; but as an animal, without birth or sham title, they looked down upon me—and were not particularly private about it, either. I didn't charge for my opinion about them, and they didn't charge for their opinion about me: the account was square, the books balanced, everybody was satisfied.

IX. THE TOURNAMENT

THEY WERE always having grand tournaments there at Camelot; and very stirring and picturesque and ridiculous human bullfights they were, too, but just a little wearisome to the practical mind. However, I was generally on hand—for two reasons: a man must not hold himself aloof from the things which his friends and his community have at heart if he would be liked—especially as a statesmen; and both as business man and statesman I wanted to study the tournament and see if I couldn't invent an improvement on it. That reminds me to remark, in passing, that the very first official thing I did, in my administration— and it was on the very first day of it, too—was to start a patent office; for I knew that a country without a patent office and good patent laws was just a crab, and couldn't travel any way but sideways or backwards.

Things ran along, a tournament nearly every week; and now and then the boys used to want me to take a hand—I mean Sir Launcelot and the rest—but I said I would by and by; no hurry yet, and too much government machinery to oil up and set to rights and start a-going.

We had one tournament which was continued from day to day during more than a week, and as many as five hundred knights took part in it, from first to last. They were weeks gathering. They came on horseback from everywhere; from the very ends of the country, and even from beyond the sea; and many brought ladies and all brought squires, and troops of servants. It was a most gaudy and gorgeous crowd, as to costumery, and very characteristic of the country and the time, in the way of high animal spirits, innocent indecencies of language, and happy-hearted indifference to morals. It was fight or look on, all day and every day; and sing, gamble, dance, carouse, half the night every night. They had a most noble good time. You never saw such people. Those banks of beautiful ladies, shining in their barbaric splendors, would see a knight sprawl from his horse in the lists with a lance shaft the thickness of your ankle clean through him and the blood spouting, and instead of fainting they would clap their hands and crowd each other for a better view; only sometimes one would dive into her handkerchief, and look ostentatiously brokenhearted, and then you could lay two to one that there was a scandal there somewhere and she was afraid the public hadn't found it out.

The noise at night would have been annoying to me ordinarily, but I didn't mind it in the present circumstances, because it kept me from hearing the quacks detaching legs and arms from the day's cripples. They ruined an uncommon good old crosscut saw for me, and broke the sawbuck, too, but I let it pass. And as for my ax—well, I made up my mind that the next time I lent an ax to a surgeon I would pick my century.

I not only watched this tournament from day to day, but detailed an intelligent priest from my Department of Public Morals and Agriculture, and ordered him to report it; for it was my purpose by and by, when I should have gotten the people along far enough, to start a newspaper. The first thing you want in a new country, is a patent office; then work up your school system; and after that, out with your paper. A newspaper has its faults, and plenty of them, but no matter, it's hark from the tomb for a dead nation, and don't you forget it. You can't resurrect a dead nation without it; there isn't any way. So I wanted to sample things, and be finding out what sort of reporter material I might be able to rake together out of the sixth century when I should come to need it.

Well, the priest did very well, considering. He got in all the details, and that is a good thing in a local item: you see he had kept books for the undertaker department of his church when he was younger, and there, you know, the money's in the details; the more details, the more swag; bearers, mutes, candles, prayers—everything counts; and if the bereaved don't buy prayers enough you mark up your candles with a forked pencil, and your bill shows up all right. And he had a good knack at getting in the complimentary thing here and there about a knight that was likely to advertise—no, I mean a knight that had influence; and he also had a neat gift of exaggeration, for in his time he had kept door for a pious hermit who lived in a sty and worked miracles.

Of course this novice's report lacked whoop and crash and lurid description, and therefore wanted the true ring; but its antique wording was quaint and sweet and simple, and full of the fragrances and flavors of the time, and these little merits made up in a measure for its more important lacks. Here is an extract from it:

Then Sir Brian de les Isles and Grummore Grummorsum, knights of the castle, encountered with Sir Aglovale and Sir Tor, and Sir Tor smote down Sir Grummore Grummorsum to the earth. Then came in Sir Carados of the dolorous tower, and Sir Turquine, knights of the castle, and there encountered with them Sir Percivale de Galis and Sir Lamorak de Galis, that were two brethren, and there encountered Sir Percivale with Sir Carados, and either brake their spears unto their hands, and then Sir Turquine with Sir Lamorak, and either of them smote down other, horse and all, to the earth, and either parties rescued other and horsed them again. And Sir Arnold, and Sir Gauter, knights of the castle, encountered with Sir Brandiles and Sir Kay, and these four knights encountered mightily, and brake their spears to their hands. Then came Sir Pertolope from the castle, and there encountered with him Sir Lionel, and there Sir Pertolope the green knight smote down Sir Lionel, brother to Sir Launcelot. All this was marked by noble heralds, who bare him best, and their names. Then Sir Bleobaris brake his spear upon Sir Gareth, but of that stroke Sir Bleobaris fell to the earth. When Sir Galihodin saw that, he bad Sir Gareth keep him, and Sir Gareth smote him to the earth. Then Sir Galihud gat a spear to avenge his brother, and in the same wise Sir Gareth served him, and Sir Dinadan and his brother La Cote Male Taile, and Sir Sagramor le Desirous, and Sir Dodinas le Savage; all these he bare down with one spear. When King Agwisance of Ireland saw Sir Gareth fare so he marvelled what he might be, that one time seemed green, and another time, at his again coming, he seemed blue. And thus at every course that he rode to and fro he changed his color, so that there might neither king nor knight have ready cognizance of him. Then Sir Agwisance the King of Ireland encountered with Sir Gareth, and there Sir Gareth smote him from his horse, saddle and all. And then came King Carados of Scotland, and Sir Gareth smote him down horse and man. And in the same wise he served King Uriens of the land of Gore. And then there came in Sir Bagdemagus, and Sir Gareth smote him down horse and man to the earth. And Bagdemagus's son Meliganus brake a spear upon Sir Gareth mightily and knightly. And then Sir Galahault the noble prince cried on high, Knight with the many colors, well hast thou justed; now make thee ready that I may just with thee. Sir Gareth heard him, and he gat a great spear, and so they encountered together, and there the prince brake his spear; but Sir Gareth smote him upon the left side of the helm, that he reeled here and there, and he had fallen down had not his men recovered him. Truly said King Arthur, that knight with the many colors is a good knight. Wherefore the king called unto him Sir Launcelot, and prayed him to encounter with that knight. Sir, said Launcelot, I may as well find in my heart for to forbear him at this time, for he hath had travail enough this day, and when a good knight doth so well upon some day, it is no good knight's part to let him of his worship, and, namely, when he seeth a knight hath done so great labour: for peradventure, said Sir Launcelot, his quarrel is here this day, and peradventure he is best beloved with this lady of all that be here, for I see well he painteth himself and enforceth him to do great deeds, and therefore, said Sir Launcelot, as for me, this day he shall have the honour; though it lay in my power to put him from it, I would not.

There was an unpleasant little episode that day, which for reasons of state I struck out of my priest's report. You will have noticed that Garry was doing some great fighting in the engagement. When I say Garry I mean Sir Gareth. Garry was my private pet name for him; it suggests that I had a deep affection for him, and that was the case. But it was a private pet name only, and never spoken aloud to any one, much less to him; being a noble, he would not have endured a familiarity like that from me. Well, to proceed: I sat in the private box set apart for me as the king's minister. While Sir Dinadan was waiting for his turn to enter the lists, he came in there and sat down and began to talk; for he was always making up to me, because I was a stranger and he liked to have a fresh market for his jokes, the most of them having reached that stage of wear where the teller has to do the laughing himself while the other person looks sick. I had always responded to his efforts as well as I could, and felt a very deep and real kindness for him, too, for the reason that if by malice of fate he knew the one particular anecdote which I had heard oftenest and had most hated and most loathed all my life, he had at least spared it me. It was one which I had heard attributed to every humorous person who had ever stood on American soil, from Columbus down to Artemus Ward. It was about a humorous lecturer who flooded an ignorant audience with the killingest jokes for an hour and never got a laugh; and then when he was leaving, some gray simpletons wrung him gratefully by the hand and said it had been the funniest thing they had ever heard, and "it was all they could do to keep from laughin' right out in meetin'." That anecdote never saw the day that it was worth the telling; and yet I had sat under the telling of it hundreds and thousands and millions and billions of times, and cried and cursed all the way through. Then who can hope to know what my feelings were, to hear this armor-plated ass start on it again, in the murky twilight of tradition, before the dawn of history, while even Lactantius might be referred to as "the late Lactantius," and the Crusades wouldn't be born for five hundred years yet? Just as he finished, the call boy came; so, haw-hawing like a demon, he went rattling and clanking out like a crate of loose castings, and I knew nothing more. It was some minutes before I came to, and then I opened my eyes just in time to see Sir Gareth fetch him an awful welt, and I unconsciously out with the prayer, "I hope to gracious he's killed!" But by ill luck, before I had got half through with the words, Sir Gareth crashed into Sir Sagramor le Desirous and sent him thundering over his horse's crupper, and Sir Sagramor caught my remark and thought I meant it for *him*.

Well, whenever one of those people got a thing into his head, there was no getting it out again. I knew that, so I saved my breath, and offered no explanations. As soon as Sir Sagramor got well, he notified me that there was a little account to settle between us, and he named a day three or four years in the future; place of settlement, the lists where the offense had been given. I said I would be ready when he got back. You see, he was going for the Holy Grail. The boys all took a flier at the Holy Grail now and then. It was several years' cruise. They always put in the long absence snooping around, in the most conscientious way, though none of them had any idea where the Holy Grail really was, and I don't think any of them actually expected to find it, or would have known what to do with it if he *had* run across it. You see, it was just the Northwest Passage of that day, as you may say; that was all. Every year expeditions went out holy grailing, and next year relief expeditions went out to hunt for *them*. There was worlds of reputation in it, but no money. Why, they actually wanted *me* to put in! Well, I should smile.

X. BEGINNINGS OF CIVILIZATION

THE ROUND TABLE soon heard of the challenge, and of course it was a good deal discussed, for such things interested the boys. The king thought I ought now to set forth in quest of adventures, so that I might gain renown and be the more worthy to meet Sir Sagramor when the several years should have rolled away. I excused myself for the present; I said it would take me three or four years yet to get things well fixed up and going smoothly; then I should be ready; all the chances were that at the end of that time Sir Sagramor would still be out grailing, so no valuable time would be lost by the postponement; I should then have been in office six or seven years, and I believed my system and machinery would be so well developed that I could take a holiday without its working any harm.

I was pretty well satisfied with what I had already accomplished. In various quiet nooks and corners I had the beginnings of all sorts of industries under way—nuclei of future vast factories, the iron and steel missionaries of my future civilization. In these were gathered together the brightest young minds I could find, and I kept agents out raking the country for more, all the time. I was training a crowd of ignorant folk into experts—experts in every sort of handiwork and scientific calling. These nurseries of mine went smoothly and privately along undisturbed in their obscure country retreats, for nobody was allowed to come into their precincts without a special permit—for I was afraid of the Church.

I had started a teacher factory and a lot of Sunday schools the first thing; as a result, I now had an admirable system of graded schools in full blast in those places, and also a complete variety of Protestant congregations all in a prosperous and growing condition. Everybody could be any kind of a Christian he wanted to; there was perfect freedom in that matter. But I confined public religious teaching to the churches and the Sunday schools, permitting nothing of it in my other educational buildings. I could have given my own sect the preference and made everybody a Presbyterian without any trouble, but that would have been to affront a law of human nature: spiritual wants and instincts are as various in the human family as are physical appetites, complexions, and features, and a man is only at his best, morally, when he is equipped with the religious garment whose color and shape and size most nicely accommodate themselves to the spiritual complexion, angularities, and stature of the individual who wears it; and besides I was afraid of a united Church; it makes a mighty power, the mightiest conceivable, and then when it by and by gets into selfish hands, as it is always bound to do, it means death to human liberty, and paralysis to human thought.

All mines were royal property, and there were a good many of them. They had formerly been worked as savages always work mines—holes grubbed in the earth and the mineral brought up in sacks of hide by hand, at the rate of a ton a day; but I had begun to put the mining on a scientific basis as early as I could.

Yes, I had made pretty handsome progress when Sir Sagramor's challenge struck me.

Four years rolled by—and then! Well, you would never imagine it in the world. Unlimited power *is* the ideal thing when it is in safe hands. The despotism of heaven is the one absolutely perfect government. An earthly despotism would be the absolutely perfect earthly government, if the conditions were the same, namely, the despot the perfectest individual of the human race, and his lease of life perpetual. But as a perishable perfect man must die, and leave his despotism in the hands of an imperfect successor, an earthly despotism is not merely a bad form of government, it is the worst form that is possible.

My works showed what a despot could do with the resources of a kingdom at his command. Unsuspected by this dark land, I had the civilization of the nineteenth century booming under its very nose! It was fenced away from the public view, but there it was, a gigantic and unassailable fact—and to be heard from, yet, if I lived and had luck. There it was, as sure a fact, and as substantial a fact as any serene volcano, standing innocent with its smokeless summit in the blue sky and giving no sign of the rising hell in its bowels. My schools and churches were children four years before; they were grown-up, now; my shops of that day were vast factories, now; where I had a dozen trained men then, I had a thousand, now; where I had one brilliant expert then, I had fifty now. I stood with my hand on the cock, so to speak, ready to turn it on and flood the midnight world with light at any moment. But I was not going to do the thing in that sudden way. It was not my policy. The people could not have stood it; and moreover I should have had the Established Roman Catholic Church on my back in a minute.

No, I had been going cautiously all the while. I had had confidential agents trickling through the country some time, whose office was to undermine knighthood by imperceptible degrees, and to gnaw a little at this and that and the other superstition, and so prepare the way gradually for a better order of things. I was turning on my light one candlepower at a time, and meant to continue to do so.

I had scattered some branch schools secretly about the kingdom, and they were doing very well. I meant to work this racket more and more, as time wore on, if nothing occurred to frighten me. One of my deepest secrets was my West Point—my military academy. I kept that most jealously out of sight; and I did the same with my naval academy which I had established at a remote seaport. Both were prospering to my satisfaction.

Clarence was twenty-two now, and was my head executive, my right hand. He was a darling; he was equal to anything; there wasn't anything he couldn't turn his hand to. Of late I had been training him for journalism, for the time seemed about right for a start in the newspaper line; nothing big, but just a small weekly for experimental circulation in my civilization-nurseries. He took to it like a duck; there was an editor concealed in him, sure. Already he had doubled himself in one way; he talked sixth century and wrote nineteenth. His journalistic style was climbing, steadily; it was already up to the back settlement Alabama mark, and couldn't be told from the editorial output of that region either by matter or flavor.

We had another large departure on hand, too. This was a telegraph and a telephone; our first venture in this line. These wires were for private service only, as yet, and must be kept private until a riper day should come. We had a gang of men on the road, working mainly by night. They were stringing ground wires; we were afraid to put up poles, for they would attract too much inquiry. Ground wires were good enough, in both instances, for my wires were protected by an insulation of my own invention which was perfect. My men had orders to strike across country, avoiding roads, and establishing connection with any considerable towns whose lights betrayed their presence, and leaving experts in charge. Nobody could tell you how to find any place in the kingdom, for nobody ever went intentionally to any place, but only struck it by accident in his wanderings, and then generally left it without thinking to inquire what its name was. At one time and another we had sent out topographical expeditions to survey and map the kingdom, but the priests had always interfered and raised trouble. So we had given the thing up, for the present; it would be poor wisdom to antagonize the Church.

As for the general condition of the country, it was as it had been when I arrived in it, to all intents and purposes. I had made changes, but they were necessarily slight, and they were not noticeable. Thus far, I had not even meddled with taxation, outside of the taxes which provided the royal revenues. I had systematized those, and put the service on an effective and righteous basis. As a result, these revenues were already quadrupled, and yet the burden was so much more equably distributed than before, that all the kingdom felt a sense of relief, and the praises of my administration were hearty and general.

Personally, I struck an interruption, now, but I did not mind it, it could not have happened at a better time. Earlier it could have annoyed me, but now everything was in good hands and swimming right along. The king had reminded me several times, of late, that the postponement I had asked for, four years before, had about run out, now. It was a hint that I ought to be starting out to seek adventures and get up a reputation of a size to make me worthy of the honor of breaking a lance with Sir Sagramor, who was still out grailing, but was being hunted for by various relief expeditions, and might be found any year, now. So you see I was expecting this interruption; it did not take me by surprise.

XI. THE YANKEE IN SEARCH
OF ADVENTURES

THERE NEVER was such a country for wandering liars; and they were of both sexes. Hardly a month went by without one of these tramps arriving; and generally loaded with a tale about some princess or other wanting help to get her out of some faraway castle where she was held in captivity by a lawless scoundrel, usually a giant. Now you would think that the first thing the king would do after listening to such a novelette from an entire stranger, would be to ask for credentials—yes, and a pointer or two as to locality of castle, best route to it, and so on. But nobody ever thought of so simple and commonsense a thing as that. No, everybody swallowed these people's lies whole, and never asked a question of any sort or about anything. Well, one day when I was not around, one of these people came along—it was a she one, this time—and told a tale of the usual pattern. Her mistress was a captive in a vast and gloomy castle, along with forty-four other young and beautiful girls, pretty much all of them princesses; they had been languishing in that cruel captivity for twenty-six years; the masters of the castle were three stupendous brothers, each with four arms and one eye—the eye in the center of the forehead, and as big as a fruit. Sort of fruit not mentioned; their usual slovenliness in statistics.

Would you believe it? The king and the whole Round Table were in raptures over this preposterous opportunity for adventure. Every knight of the Table jumped for the chance, and begged for it; but to their vexation and chagrin the king conferred it upon me, who had not asked for it at all.

By an effort, I contained my joy when Clarence brought me the news. But he—he could not contain his. His mouth gushed delight and gratitude in a steady discharge—delight in my good fortune, gratitude to the king for this splendid mark of his favor for me. He could keep neither his legs nor his body still, but pirouetted about the place in an airy ecstasy of happiness.

On my side, I could have cursed the kindness that conferred upon me this benefaction, but I kept my vexation under the surface for policy's sake, and did what I could to let on to be glad. Indeed, I *said* I was glad. And in a way it was true; I was as glad as a person is when he is scalped.

Well, one must make the best of things, and not waste time with useless fretting, but get down to business and see what can be done. In all lies there is wheat among the chaff; I must get at the wheat in this case: so I sent for the girl and she came. She was a comely enough creature, and soft and modest, but if signs went for anything, she didn't know as much as a lady's watch. I said—

"My dear, have you been questioned as to particulars?"

She said she hadn't.

"Well, I didn't expect you had, but I thought I would ask to make sure; it's the way I've been raised. Now you mustn't take it unkindly if I remind you that as we don't know you, we must go a little slow. You may be all right, of course, and we'll hope that you are; but to take it for granted isn't business. *You* understand that. I'm obliged to ask you a few questions; just answer up fair and square, and don't be afraid. Where do you live, when you are home?"

"In the land of Moder, fair sir."

"Land of Moder. I don't remember hearing of it before. Parents living?"

"As to that, I know not if they be yet on live, sith it is many years that I have lain shut up in the castle."

"Your name, please?"

"I hight the Demoiselle Alisande la Carteloise, an it please you."

"Do you know anybody here who can identify you?"

"That were not likely, fair lord, I being come hither now for the first time."

"Have you brought any letters—any documents—any proofs that you are trustworthy and truthful?"

"Of a surety, no; and wherefore should I? Have I not a tongue, and cannot I say all that myself?"

"But *your* saying it, you know, and somebody else's saying it, is different."

"Different? How might that be? I fear me I do not understand."

"Don't *understand*? Land of—why, you see—you see—why, great Scott, can't you understand a little thing like that? Can't you understand the difference between your—*why* do you look so innocent and idiotic!"

"I? In truth I know not, but an it were the will of God."

"Yes, yes, I reckon that's about the size of it. Don't mind my seeming excited; I'm not. Let us change the subject. Now as to this castle, with forty-five princesses in it, and three ogres at the head of it, tell me—where is this harem?"

"Harem?"

"The *castle*, you understand; where is the castle?"

"Oh, as to that, it is great, and strong, and well beseen, and lieth in a far country. Yes, it is many leagues."

"*How* many?"

"Ah, fair sir, it were woundily hard to tell, they are so many, and do so lap the one upon the other, and being made all in the same image and tincted with the same color, one may not know the one league from its fellow, nor how to count them except they be taken apart, and ye wit well it were God's work to do that, being not within man's capacity; for ye will note—"

"Hold on, hold on, never mind about the distance; *whereabouts* does the castle lie? What's the direction from here?"

"Ah, please you sir, it hath no direction from here; by reason that the road lieth not straight, but turneth evermore; wherefore the direction of its place abideth not, but is sometime under the one sky and anon under another, whereso if ye be minded that it is in the east, and wend thitherward, ye shall observe that the way of the road doth yet again turn upon itself by the space of half a circle, and this marvel happing again and yet again and still again, it will grieve you that you had thought by vanities of the mind to thwart and bring to naught the will of Him that giveth not a castle a direction from a place except it pleaseth Him, and if it please Him not, will the rather that even all castles and all directions thereunto vanish out of the earth, leaving the places wherein they tarried desolate and vacant, so warning His creatures that where He will He will, and where He will not He—"

"Oh, that's all right, that's all right, give us a rest; never mind about the direction, *hang* the direction—I beg pardon, I beg a thousand pardons, I am not well today; pay no attention when I soliloquize, it is an old habit, an old, bad habit, and hard to get rid of when one's digestion is all disordered with eating food that was raised forever and ever before he was born; good land! a man can't keep his functions regular on spring chickens thirteen hundred years old. But come—never mind about that; let's—have you got such a thing as a map of that region about you? Now a good map—"

"Is it peradventure that manner of thing which of late the unbelievers have brought from over the great seas, which, being boiled in oil, and an onion and salt added thereto, doth—"

"What, a map? What are you talking about? Don't you know what a map is? There, there, never mind, don't explain, I hate explanations;

they fog a thing up so that you can't tell anything about it. Run along, dear; good-day; show her the way, Clarence."

Oh, well, it was reasonably plain, now, why these donkeys didn't prospect these liars for details. It may be that this girl had a fact in her somewhere, but I don't believe you could have sluiced it out with a hydraulic; nor got it with the earlier forms of blasting, even; it was a case for dynamite. Why, she was a perfect ass; and yet the king and his knights had listened to her as if she had been a leaf out of the gospel. It kind of sizes up the whole party. And think of the simple ways of this court: this wandering wench hadn't any more trouble to get access to the king in his palace than she would have had to get into the poorhouse in my day and country. In fact he was glad to see her, glad to hear her tale; with that adventure of hers to offer, she was as welcome as a corpse is to a coroner.

Just as I was ending up these reflections, Clarence came back. I remarked upon the barren result of my efforts with the girl; hadn't got hold of a single point that could help me to find the castle. The youth looked a little surprised, or puzzled, or something, and intimated that he had been wondering to himself what I had wanted to ask the girl all those questions for.

"Why, great guns," I said, "don't I want to find the castle? And how else would I go about it?"

"La, sweet your worship, one may lightly answer that, I ween. She will go with thee. They always do. She will ride with thee."

"Ride with me? Nonsense!"

"But of a truth she will. She will ride with thee. Thou shalt see."

"What? She browse around the hills and scour the woods with me— alone—and I as good as engaged to be married? Why, it's scandalous. Think how it would look."

My, the dear face that rose before me! The boy was eager to know all about this tender matter. I swore him to secrecy and then whispered her name—"Puss Flanagan." He looked disappointed, and said he didn't remember the countess. How natural it was for the little courtier to give her a rank. He asked me where she lived.

"In East Har—" I came to myself and stopped, a little confused; then I said, "Never mind, now; I'll tell you sometime."

And might he see her? Would I let him see her some day?

It was but a little thing to promise—thirteen hundred years or so— and he so eager; so I said Yes. But I sighed; I couldn't help it. And yet there was no sense in sighing, for she wasn't born yet. But that is the way we are made: we don't reason, where we feel; we just feel.

My expedition was all the talk that day and that night, and the boys were very good to me, and made much of me, and seemed to have forgotten their vexation and disappointment, and come to be as anxious for me to hive those ogres and set those ripe old virgins loose as if it were themselves that had the contract. Well, they *were* good children— but just children, that is all. And they gave me no end of points about how to scout for giants, and how to scoop them in; and they told me all sorts of charms against enchantments, and gave me salves and other rubbish to put on my wounds. But it never occurred to one of them to reflect that if I was such a wonderful necromancer as I was pretending to be, I ought not to need salves or instructions, or charms against enchantments, and least of all, arms and armor, on a foray of any kind—even against fire-spouting dragons, and devils hot from per-dition, let alone such poor adversaries as these I was after, these commonplace ogres of the back settlements.

I was to have an early breakfast, and start at dawn, for that was the usual way; but I had the demon's own time with my armor, and this delayed me a little. It is troublesome to get into, and there is so much detail. First you wrap a layer or two of blanket around your body, for a sort of cushion and to keep off the cold iron; then you put on your sleeves and shirt of chain mail—these are made of small steel links woven together, and they form a fabric so flexible that if you toss your shirt onto the floor, it slumps into a pile like a peck of wet fishnet; it is very heavy and is nearly the uncomfortablest material in the world for a nightshirt, yet plenty used it for that—tax collectors, and reformers, and one-horse kings with a defective title, and those sorts of people; then you put on your shoes—flatboats roofed over with interleaving bands of steel—and screw your clumsy spurs into the heels. Next you buckle your greaves on your legs, and your cuisses on your thighs; then come your backplate and your breastplate, and you begin to feel crowded; then you hitch onto the breastplate and the half-petticoat of broad overlapping bands of steel which hangs down in front but is scal-loped out behind so you can sit down, and isn't any real improvement on an inverted coal scuttle, either for looks or for wear, or to wipe your hands on; next you belt on your sword; then you put your stovepipe joints onto your arms, your iron gauntlets onto your hands, your iron rattrap onto your head, with a rag of steel web hitched onto it to hang over the back of your neck—and there you are, snug as a candle in a candle mold. This is no time to dance. Well, a man that is packed away like that, is a nut that isn't worth the cracking, there is so little of the meat, when you get down to it, by comparison with the shell.

The boys helped me, or I never could have got in. Just as we finished, Sir Bedivere happened in, and I saw that as like as not I hadn't chosen the most convenient outfit for a long trip. How stately he looked; and tall and broad and grand. He had on his head a conical steel casque that only came down to his ears, and for visor had only a narrow steel bar that extended down to his upper lip and protected his nose; and all the rest of him, from neck to heel, was flexible chain mail, trousers and all. But pretty much all of him was hidden under his outside garment, which of course was of chain mail, as I said, and hung straight from his shoulders to his ankles; and from his middle to the bottom, both before and behind, was divided, so that he could ride and let the skirts hang down on each side. He was going grailing, and it was just the outfit for it, too. I would have given a good deal for that ulster, but it was too late now to be fooling around. The sun was just up, the king and the court were all on hand to see me off and wish me luck; so it wouldn't be etiquette for me to tarry. You don't get on your horse yourself; no, if you tried it you would get disappointed. They carry you out, just as they carry a sunstruck man to the drug store, and put you on, and help get you to rights, and fix your feet in the stirrups; and all the while you do feel so strange and stuffy and like somebody else—like somebody that has been married on a sudden, or struck by lightning, or something like that, and hasn't quite fetched around, yet, and is sort of numb, and can't just get his bearings. Then they stood up the mast they called a spear, in its socket by my left foot, and I gripped it with my hand; lastly they hung my shield around my neck, and I was all complete and ready to up anchor and get to sea. Everybody was as good to me as they could be, and a maid of honor gave me the stirrup cup her own self. There was nothing more to do, now, but for that damsel to get up behind me on a pillion, which she did, and put an arm or so around me to hold on.

And so we started; and everybody gave us a good-bye and waved their handkerchiefs or helmets. And everybody we met, going down the hill and through the village was respectful to us, except some shabby little boys on the outskirts. They said—

"Oh, what a guy!" And hove clods at us.

In my experience boys are the same in all ages. They don't respect anything, they don't care for anything or anybody. They say "Go up, baldhead" to the prophet going his unoffending way in the gray of antiquity; they sass me in the holy gloom of the Middle Ages; and I had seen them act the same way in Buchanan's administration; I remember, because I was there and helped. The prophet had his bears and settled with his boys; and I wanted to get down and settle with mine, but it wouldn't answer, because I couldn't have got up again. I hate a country without a derrick.

XII. SLOW TORTURE

STRAIGHT OFF, we were in the country. It was most lovely and pleasant in those sylvan solitudes in the early cool morning in the first freshness of autumn. From hilltops we saw fair green valleys lying spread out below, with streams winding through them, and island groves of trees here and there, and huge lonely oaks scattered about and casting black blots of shade; and beyond the valleys we saw the ranges of hills, blue with haze, stretching away in billowy perspective to the horizon, with at wide intervals a dim fleck of white or gray on a wave summit, which we knew as a castle. We crossed broad natural lawns sparkling with dew, and we moved like spirits, the cushioned turf giving out no sound of footfall; we dreamed along through glades in a mist of green light that got its tint from the sundrenched roof of leaves overhead, and by our feet the clearest and coldest of runlets went frisking and gossiping over its reefs and making a sort of whispering music comfortable to hear; and at times we left the world behind and entered into the solemn great deeps and rich gloom of the forest, where furtive wild things whisked and scurried by and were gone before you could even get your eye on the place where the noise was; and where only the earliest birds were turning out and getting to business with a song here and a quarrel yonder and a mysterious far-off hammering and drumming for worms on a tree trunk away somewhere in the impenetrable remoteness of the woods. And by and by out we would swing again into the glare.

About the third or fourth or fifth time that we swung out into the glare—it was along there somewhere, a couple of hours or so after sunup—it wasn't as pleasant as it had been. It was beginning to get hot. This was quite noticeable. We had a very long pull, after that, without any shade. Now it is curious how progressively little frets grow and multiply after they once get a start. Things which I didn't mind at all, at first, I began to mind now—and more and more, too, all the time. The first ten or fifteen times I wanted my handkerchief I didn't seem to care;

I got along, and said never mind, it isn't any matter, and dropped it out of my mind. But now it was different; I wanted it all the time; it was nag, nag, nag, right along, and no rest; I couldn't get it out of my mind; and so at last I lost my temper and said hang a man that would make a suit of armor without any pockets in it. You see I had my handkerchief in my helmet; and some other things; but it was that kind of a helmet that you can't take off by yourself. That hadn't occurred to me when I put it there; and in fact I didn't know it. I supposed it would be particularly convenient there. And so now, the thought of its being there, so handy and close by, and yet not get-at-able, made it all the worse and the harder to bear. Yes, the thing that you can't get is the thing that you want, mainly; everyone has noticed that. Well, it took my mind off from everything else; took it clear off, and centered it in my helmet; and mile after mile, there it stayed, imagining the handkerchief, picturing the handkerchief; and it was bitter and aggravating to have the salt sweat keep trickling down into my eyes, and I couldn't get at it. It seems like a little thing, on paper, but it was not a little thing at all; it was the most real kind of misery. I would not say it if it was not so. I made up my mind that I would carry along a reticule next time, let it look how it might, and people say what they would. Of course these iron dudes of the Round Table would think it was scandalous, and maybe raise Sheol about it, but as for me, give me comfort first, and style afterwards. So we jogged along, and now and then we struck a stretch of dust, and it would tumble up in clouds and get into my nose and make me sneeze and cry; and of course I said things I oughtn't to have said, I don't deny that. I am not better than others. We couldn't seem to meet anybody in this lonesome Britain, not even an ogre; and in the mood I was in then, it was well for the ogre; that is, an ogre with a handkerchief. Most knights would have thought of nothing but getting his armor; but so I got his bandanna, he could keep his hardware, for all me.

Meantime it was getting hotter and hotter in there. You see, the sun was beating down and warming up the iron more and more all the time. Well, when you are hot, that way, every little thing irritates you. When I trotted, I rattled like a crate of dishes, and that annoyed me; and moreover I couldn't seem to stand that shield slatting and banging, now about my breast, now around my back; and if I dropped into a walk my joints creaked and screeched in that wearisome way that a wheelbarrow does, and as we didn't create any breeze at that gait, I was like to get fried in that stove; and besides, the quieter you went the heavier the iron settled down on you and the more and more tons you seemed to weigh every minute. And you had to be always changing hands, and passing your spear over to the other foot, it got so irksome for one hand to hold it long at a time.

Well, you know, when you perspire that way, in rivers, there comes a time when you—when you—well, when you itch. You are inside, your hands are outside; so there you are; nothing but iron between. It is not a light thing, let it sound as it may. First it is one place; then another; then some more; and it goes on spreading and spreading, and at last the territory is all occupied, and nobody can imagine what you feel like, nor how unpleasant it is. And when it had got to the worst, and it seemed to me that I could not stand anything more, a fly got in through the bars and settled on my nose, and the bars were stuck and wouldn't work, and I couldn't get the visor up; and I could only shake my head, which was baking hot by this time and the fly—well, you know how a fly acts when he has got a certainty—he only minded the shaking long enough to change from nose to lip, and lip to ear, and buzz and buzz all around in there, and keep on lighting and biting, in a way that a person already so distressed as I was, simply could not stand. So I gave in, and got Alisande to unship the helmet and relieve me of it. Then she emptied the conveniences out of it and fetched it full of water, and I drank and then stood up and she poured the rest down inside the armor. One cannot think how refreshing it was. She continued to fetch and pour until I was well soaked and thoroughly comfortable.

It was good to have a rest—and peace. But nothing is quite perfect in this life, at any time. I had made a pipe a while back, and also some pretty fair tobacco; not the real thing, but what some of the Indians use: the inside bark of the willow, dried. These comforts had been in the helmet, and now I had them again, but no matches.

Gradually, as the time wore along, one annoying fact was borne in upon my understanding—that we were weather-bound. An armed novice cannot mount his horse without help and plenty of it. Sandy was not enough; not enough for me, anyway. We had to wait until somebody should come along. Waiting, in silence, would have been agreeable enough, for I was full of matter for reflection, and wanted to give it a chance to work. I wanted to try and think out how it was that rational or even half-rational men could ever have learned to wear armor, considering its inconveniences; and how they had managed to keep up such a fashion for generations when it was plain that what I had suffered today they had had to suffer all the days of their lives. I wanted to think that out; and moreover I wanted to think out some way to reform this evil and persuade the people to let the foolish fashion die out; but thinking was out of the question in the circumstances. You couldn't think, where Sandy was. She was a quite biddable creature and good-hearted, but she had a flow of talk that was as steady as a mill, and made your head sore like the drays and wagons in a city. If she had

had a cork she would have been a comfort. But you can't cork that kind; they would die. Her clack was going all day, and you would think something would surely happen to her works, by and by; but no, they never got out of order; and she never had to slack up for words. She could grind, and pump, and churn and buzz by the week, and never stop to oil up or blow out. And yet the result was just nothing but wind. She never had any ideas, any more than a fog has. She was a perfect blatherskite; I mean for jaw, jaw, jaw, talk, talk, talk, jabber, jabber, jabber; but just as good as she could be. I hadn't minded her mill that morning, on account of having that hornet's nest of other troubles; but more than once in the afternoon I had to say—

"Take a rest, child; the way you are using up all the domestic air, the kingdom will have to go to importing it by tomorrow, and it's a low enough treasury without that."

XIII. FREEMEN!

YES, IT is strange how little a while at a time a person can be contented. Only a little while back, when I was riding and suffering, what a heaven this peace, this rest, this sweet serenity in this secluded shady nook by this purling stream would have seemed, where I could keep perfectly comfortable all the time by pouring a dipper of water into my armor now and then; yet already I was getting dissatisfied; partly because I could not light my pipe—for although I had long ago started a match factory, I had forgotten to bring matches with me—and partly because we had nothing to eat. Here was another illustration of the childlike improvidence of this age and people. A man in armor always trusted to chance for his food on a journey, and would have been scandalized at the idea of hanging a basket of sandwiches on his spear. There was probably not a knight of all the Round Table combination who would not rather have died than been caught carrying such a thing as that on his flagstaff. And yet there could not be anything more sensible. It had been my intention to smuggle a couple of sandwiches into my helmet, but I was interrupted in the act, and had to make an excuse and lay them aside, and a dog got them.

Night approached, and with it a storm. The darkness came on fast. We must camp, of course. I found a good shelter for the demoiselle under a rock, and went off and found another for myself. But I was obliged to remain in my armor, because I could not get it off by myself and yet could not allow Alisande to help, because it would have seemed so like undressing before folk. It would not have amounted to that in reality, because I had clothes on underneath; but the prejudices of one's breeding are not gotten rid of just at a jump, and I knew that when it came to stripping off that bobtailed iron petticoat I should be embarrassed.

With the storm came a change of weather; and the stronger the wind blew, and the wilder the rain lashed around, the colder and colder it got. Pretty soon, various kinds of bugs and ants and worms and things began to flock in out of the wet and crawl down inside my armor to get warm; and while some of them behaved well enough, and snuggled up among my clothes and got quiet, the majority were of a restless, uncomfortable sort, and never stayed still, but went on prowling and hunting for they did not know what; especially the ants, which went tickling along in wearisome procession from one end of me to the other by the hour, and are a kind of creatures which I never wish to sleep with again. It would be my advice to persons situated in this way, to not roll or thrash around, because this excites the interest of all the different sorts of animals and makes every last one of them want to turn out and see what is going on, and this makes things worse than they were before, and of course makes you objurgate harder, too, if you can. Still, if one did not roll and thrash around he would die; so perhaps it is as well to do one way as the other, there is no real choice. Even after I was frozen solid I could still distinguish that tickling, just as a corpse does when he is taking electric treatment. I said I would never wear armor after this trip.

All those trying hours whilst I was frozen and yet was in a living fire, as you may say, on account of that swarm of crawlers, that same unanswerable question kept circling and circling through my tired head: How do people stand this miserable armor? How have they managed to stand it all these generations? How can they sleep at night for dreading the tortures of next day?

When the morning came at last, I was in a bad enough plight: seedy, drowsy, fagged, from want of sleep; weary from thrashing around, famished from long fasting; pining for a bath, and to get rid of the animals; and crippled with rheumatism. And how had it fared with the nobly born, the titled aristocrat, the Demoiselle Alisande la Carteloise? Why, she was as fresh as a squirrel; she had slept like the dead; and as for a bath, probably neither she nor any other noble in the land had ever had one, and so she was not missing it. Measured by modern standards, they were merely modified savages, those people. This noble lady showed no impatience to get to breakfast—and that smacks of the savage, too. On their journeys those Britons were used to long fasts, and knew how to bear them; and also how to freight up against probable fasts before starting, after the style of the Indian and the anaconda. As like as not, Sandy was loaded for a three-day stretch.

We were off before sunrise, Sandy riding and I limping along behind. In half an hour we came upon a group of ragged poor creatures who had assembled to mend the thing which was regarded as a road. They were as humble as animals to me; and when I proposed to breakfast with them, they were so flattered, so overwhelmed by this extraordinary condescension of mine that at first they were not able to believe that I was in earnest. My lady put up her scornful lip and withdrew to one side; she said in their hearing that she would as soon think of eating with the other cattle—a remark which embarrassed these poor devils merely because it referred to them, and not because it insulted or offended them, for it didn't. And yet they were not slaves, not chattels. By a sarcasm of law and phrase they were freemen. Seven-tenths of the free population of the country were of just their class and degree: small "independent" farmers, artisans, etc.; which is to say, they were the nation, the actual Nation; they were about all of it that was useful, or worth saving, or really respectworthy; and to subtract them would have been to subtract the Nation and leave behind some dregs, some refuse, in the shape of a king, nobility and gentry, idle, unproductive, acquainted mainly with the arts of wasting and destroying, and of no sort of use or value in any rationally constructed world. And yet, by ingenious contrivance, this gilded minority, instead of being in the tail of the procession where it belonged, was marching head up and banners flying, at the other end of it; had elected itself to be the Nation, and these innumerable clams had permitted it so long that they had come at last to accept it as a truth; and not only that, but to believe it right and as it should be. The priests had told their fathers and themselves that this ironical state of things was ordained of God; and so, not reflecting upon how unlike God it would be to amuse himself with sarcasms, and especially such poor transparent ones as this, they had dropped the matter there and become respectfully quiet.

The talk of these meek people had a strange enough sound in a formerly American ear. They were freemen, but they could not leave the estates of their lord or their bishop without his permission; they could not prepare their own bread, but must have their corn ground and their bread baked at his mill and his bakery, and pay roundly for the same; they could not sell a piece of their own property without paying him a handsome percentage of the proceeds, nor buy a piece of somebody else's without remembering him in cash for the privilege; they had to harvest his grain for him gratis, and be ready to come at a moment's notice, leaving their own crop to destruction by the threatened storm; they had to let him plant fruit trees in their fields, and then keep their indignation to themselves when his heedless fruit gatherers trampled the grain around the trees; they had to smother their anger when his hunting parties galloped through their fields laying waste the result of their patient toil; they were not allowed to keep doves themselves, and when the swarms from my lord's dovecote settled on their crops they must not lose their temper and kill a bird, for awful would the penalty be; when the harvest was at last gathered, then came the procession of robbers to levy their blackmail upon it: first the Church carted off its fat tenth, then the king's commissioner took his twentieth, then my lord's people made a mighty inroad upon the remainder; after which, the skinned freeman had liberty to bestow the remnant in his barn, in case it was worth the trouble; there were taxes, and taxes, and taxes, and more taxes, and taxes again, and yet other taxes—upon this free and independent pauper, but none upon his lord the baron or the bishop, none upon the wasteful nobility or the all-devouring Church; if the baron would sleep unvexed, the freeman must sit up all night after his day's work and whip the ponds to keep the frogs quiet; if the freeman's daughter—but no, that last infamy of monarchical government is unprintable; and finally, if the freeman, grown desperate with his tortures, found his life unendurable under such conditions, and sacrificed it and fled to death for mercy and refuge, the gentle Church condemned him to eternal fire, the gentle law buried him at midnight at the crossroads with a stake through his back, and his master the baron or the bishop confiscated all his property and turned his widow and his orphans out of doors.

And here were these freemen assembled in the early morning to work on their lord the bishop's road three days each—gratis; every head of a family, and every son of a family, three days each, gratis, and a day or so added for their servants. Why, it was like reading about France and the French, before the ever-memorable and blessed Revolution, which swept a thousand years of such villainy away in one swift tidal wave of blood—one: a settlement of that hoary debt in the proportion of half a drop of blood for each hogshead of it that had been pressed by slow tortures out of that people in the weary stretch of ten centuries of wrong and shame and misery the like of which was not to be mated but in hell. There were two "Reigns of Terror," if we would but remember it and consider it; the one wrought murder in hot passion, the other in heartless cold blood; the one lasted mere months, the other had lasted a thousand years; the one inflicted death upon ten thousand persons, the other upon a hundred millions; but our shudders are all for the "horrors" of the minor Terror, the momentary Terror, so to speak; whereas, what is the horror of swift death by the ax, compared with lifelong death from hunger, cold, insult, cruelty, and heartbreak? What is swift death by lightning compared with death by slow fire at the stake? A city cemetery could contain the coffins filled by that brief Terror which we have all been so diligently taught to shiver at and mourn over; but all France could hardly contain the coffins filled by that older and real Terror—that unspeakably bitter and awful Terror which none of us has been taught to see in its vastness or pity as it deserves.

These poor ostensible freemen who were sharing their breakfast and their talk with me, were as full of humble reverence for their king and Church and nobility as their worst enemy could desire. There was something pitifully ludicrous about it. I asked them if they supposed a nation of people ever existed, who, with a free vote in every man's hand, would elect that a single family and its descendants should rein over it forever, whether gifted or boobies, to the exclusion of all other families—including the voter's; and would also elect that a certain hundred families should be raised to dizzy summits of rank, and clothed on with offensive transmissible glories and privileges to the exclusion of the rest of the nation's families—*including his own*.

They all looked unhit, and said they didn't know; that they had never thought about it before, and it hadn't ever occurred to them that a nation could be so situated that every man *could* have a say in the government. I said I had seen one—and that it would last until it had an Established Church. Again they were all unhit—at first. But presently one man looked up and asked me to state that proposition again; and state it slowly, so it could soak into his understanding. I did it; and after a little he had the idea, and he brought his fist down and said *he* didn't believe a nation where every man had a vote would voluntarily get down in the mud and dirt in any such way; and that to steal from a nation its will and preference must be a crime and the first of all crimes.

I said to myself:

"This one's a man. If I were backed by enough of his sort, I would make a strike for the welfare of this country, and try to prove myself its loyalest citizen by making a wholesome change in its system of government."

You see my kind of loyalty was loyalty to one's country, not to its institutions or its officeholders. The country is the real thing, the substantial thing, the eternal thing; it is the thing to watch over, and care for, and be loyal to; institutions are extraneous, they are its mere clothing, and clothing can wear out, become ragged, cease to be comfortable, cease to protect the body from winter, disease, and death. To be loyal to rags, to shout for rags, to worship rags, to die for rags—that is a loyalty of unreason, it is pure animal; it belongs to monarchy, was invented by monarchy; let monarchy keep it. I was from Connecticut, whose Constitution declares "that all political power is inherent in the people, and all free governments are founded on their authority and instituted for their benefit; and that they have *at all times* an undeniable and indefeasible right to *alter their form of government* in such a manner as they may think expedient."

Under that gospel, the citizen who thinks he sees that the commonwealth's political clothes are worn out, and yet holds his peace and does not agitate for a new suit, is disloyal; he is a traitor. That he may be the only one who thinks he sees this decay, does not excuse him; it is his duty to agitate anyway, and it is the duty of the others to vote him down if they do not see the matter as he does.

And now here I was, in a country where a right to say how the country should be governed was restricted to six persons in each thousand of its population. For the nine hundred and ninety-four to express dissatisfaction with the regnant system and propose to change it, would have made the whole six shudder as one man, it would have been so disloyal, so dishonorable, such putrid black treason. So to speak, I was become a stockholder in a corporation where nine hundred and ninety-four of the members furnished all the money and did all the work, and the other six elected themselves a permanent board of direction and took all the dividends. It seemed to me that what the nine hundred and ninety-four dupes needed was a new deal. The thing that would have best suited the circus side of my nature would have been to resign the Boss-ship and get up an insurrection and turn it into a revolution; but I knew that the Jack Cade or the Wat Tyler who tries such a thing without first educating his materials up to revolution grade is almost absolutely certain to get left. I had never been accustomed to getting left, even if I do say it myself. Wherefore, the "deal" which had been for some time working into shape in my mind was of a quite different pattern from the Cade-Tyler sort.

So I did not talk blood and insurrection to that man there who sat munching black bread with that abused and mistaught herd of human sheep, but took him aside and talked matter of another sort to him. After I had finished, I got him to lend me a little ink from his veins; and with this and a sliver I wrote on a piece of bark—

Put him in the Man Factory—

and gave it to him, and said—

"Take it to the palace at Camelot and give it into the hands of Amyas le Poulet, whom I call Clarence, and he will understand."

"He is a priest, then," said the man, and some of the enthusiasm went out of his face.

"How—a priest? Didn't I tell you that no chattel of the Church, no bondslave of pope or bishop can enter my Man Factory? Didn't I tell you that *you* couldn't enter unless your religion, whatever it might be, was your own free property?"

"Marry, it is so, and for that I was glad; wherefore it liked me not, and bred in me a cold doubt, to hear of this priest being there."

"But he isn't a priest, I tell you."

The man looked far from satisfied. He said:

"He is not a priest, and yet can read?"

"He is not a priest and yet can read—yes, and write, too, for that matter. I taught him myself." The man's face cleared. "And it is the first thing that you yourself will be taught in that Factory—"

"I? I would give blood out of my heart to know that art. Why, I will be your slave, your—"

"No you won't, you won't be anybody's slave. Take your family and go along. Your lord the bishop will confiscate your small property, but no matter, Clarence will fix you all right."

XIV. "DEFEND THEE, LORD!"

I PAID THREE pennies for my breakfast, and a most extravagant price it was, too, seeing that one could have breakfasted a dozen persons for that money; but I was feeling good by this time, and I had always been a kind of spendthrift anyway; and then these people had wanted to give me the food for nothing, scant as their provision was, and so it was a grateful pleasure to emphasize my appreciation and sincere thankfulness with a good big financial lift where the money would do so much more good than it would in my helmet, where, these pennies being made of iron and not stinted in weight, my half dollar's worth was a good deal of a burden to me. I spent money rather too freely in those days, it is true; but one reason for it was that I hadn't got the proportions of things entirely adjusted, even yet, after so long a sojourn in Britain—hadn't got along to where I was able to absolutely realize that a penny in Arthur's land and a couple of dollars in Connecticut were about one and the same thing: just twins, as you may say, in purchasing power. If my start from Camelot could have been delayed a very few days I could have paid these people in beautiful new coins from our own mint, and that would have pleased me; and them, too, not less. I had adopted the American values exclusively. In a week or two now, cents, nickels, dimes, quarters and half dollars, and also a trifle of gold, would be trickling in thin but steady streams all through the commercial veins of the kingdom, and I looked to see this new blood freshen up its life.

The farmers were bound to throw in something, to sort of offset my liberality, whether I would or no; so I let them give me a flint and steel; and as soon as they had comfortably bestowed Sandy and me on our horse, I lit my pipe. When the first blast of smoke shot out through the bars of my helmet, all those people broke for the woods, and Sandy went over backwards and struck the ground with a dull thud. They thought I was one of those fire-belching dragons they had heard so much about from knights and other professional liars. I had infinite trouble to persuade those people to venture back within explaining distance. Then I told them that this was only a bit of enchantment which would work harm to none but my enemies. And I promised, with my hand on my heart, that if all who felt no enmity toward me would come forward and pass before me they should see that only those who remained behind would be struck dead. The procession moved with a good deal of promptness. There were no casualties to report, for nobody had curiosity enough to remain behind to see what would happen.

I lost some time, now, for these big children, their fears gone, became so ravished with wonder over my awe-compelling fireworks that I had to stay there and smoke a couple of pipes out before they would let me go. Still the delay was not wholly unproductive, for it took all that time to get Sandy thoroughly wonted to the new thing, she being so close to it, you know. It plugged up her conversation-mill, too, for a considerable while, and that was a gain. But above all other benefits accruing, I had learned something. I was ready for any giant or any ogre that might come along, now.

We tarried with a holy hermit, that night, and my opportunity came about the middle of the next afternoon. We were crossing a vast meadow by way of shortcut, and I was musing absently, hearing nothing, seeing nothing, when Sandy suddenly interrupted a remark which she had begun that morning, with the cry—

"Defend thee, lord—peril of life is toward!"

And she slipped down from the horse and ran a little way and stood. I looked up and saw, far off in the shade of a tree, half a dozen armed knights and their squires; and straightway there was bustle among them and tightening of saddle girths for the mount. My pipe was ready and would have been lit, if I had not been lost in thinking about how to banish oppression from this land and restore to all its people their stolen rights and manhood without disobliging anybody. I lit up at once, and by the time I had got a good head of reserved steam on, here they came. All together, too; none of those chivalrous magnanimities which one reads so much about—one courtly rascal at a time, and the rest standing by to see fair play. No, they came in a body, they came with a whirr and a rush, they came like a volley from a battery; came with heads low down, plumes streaming out behind, lances advanced at a level. It was a handsome sight, a beautiful sight—for a man up a tree. I laid my lance in rest and waited, with my heart beating, till the iron wave was just ready to break over me, then spouted a column of white smoke through the bars of my helmet. You should have seen the wave go to pieces and scatter! This was a finer sight than the other one.

But these people stopped, two or three hundred yards away, and this troubled me. My satisfaction collapsed, and fear came; I judged I was a lost man. But Sandy was radiant; and was going to be eloquent, but I stopped her, and told her my magic had miscarried, somehow or other, and she must mount, with all dispatch, and we must ride for life. No, she wouldn't. She said that my enchantment had disabled those knights; they were not riding on, because they couldn't; wait, they would drop out of their saddles presently, and we would get their horses and harness. I could not deceive such trusting simplicity, so I said it was a mistake; that when my fireworks killed at all, they killed instantly; no, the men would not die, there was something wrong about my apparatus, I couldn't tell what; but we must hurry and get away, for those people would attack us again, in a minute. Sandy laughed, and said—

"Lackaday, sir, they be not of that breed! Sir Launcelot will give battle to dragons, and will abide by them, and will assail them again, and yet again, and still again, until he do conquer and destroy them; and so likewise will Sir Pellinore and Sir Aglovale and Sir Carados, and mayhap others, but there be none else that will venture it, let the idle say what the idle will. And, la, as to yonder base rufflers, think ye they have not their fill, but yet desire more?"

"Well, then, what are they waiting for? Why don't they leave? Nobody's hindering. Good land, I'm willing to let bygones be bygones, I'm sure."

"Leave, is it? Oh, give thyself easement as to that. They dream not of it, no, not they. They wait to yield them."

"Come—really, is that 'sooth'—as you people say? If they want to, why don't they?"

"It would like them much; but an ye wot how dragons are esteemed, ye would not hold them blamable. They fear to come."

"Well, then, suppose I go to them instead, and——"

"Ah, wit ye well they would not abide your coming. I will go."

And she did. She was a handy person to have along on a raid. I would have considered this a doubtful errand, myself. I presently saw the knights riding away, and Sandy coming back. That was a relief. I judged she had somehow failed to get the first innings—I mean in the conversation; otherwise the interview wouldn't have been so short. But it turned out that she had managed the business well; in fact admirably. She said that when she told those people I was The Boss, it hit them where they lived: "smote them sore with fear and dread" was her word; and then they were ready to put up with anything she might require. So she swore them to appear at Arthur's court within two days and yield them, with horse and harness, and be my knights henceforth, and subject to my command. How much better she managed that thing than I should have done it myself! She was a daisy.

XV. SANDY'S TALE

"AND SO I'm proprietor of some knights," said I, as we rode off. "Who would ever have supposed that I should live to list up assets of that sort. I shan't know what to do with them; unless I raffle them off. How many of them are there, Sandy?"

"Seven, please you, sir, and their squires."

"It is a good haul. Who are they? Where do they hang out?"

"Where do they hang out?"

"Yes, where do they live?"

"Ah, I understood thee not. That will I tell thee eftsoons." Then she said musingly, and softly, turning the words daintily over her tongue: "Hang they out—hang they out—where hang—where do they hang out; eh, right so; where do they hang out. Of a truth the phrase hath a fair and winsome grace, and is prettily worded withal. I will repeat it anon and anon in mine idlesse, whereby I may peradventure learn it. Where do they hang out. Even so! Already it falleth trippingly from my tongue, and forasmuch as—"

"Don't forget the cowboys, Sandy."

"Cowboys?"

"Yes; the knights, you know: You were going to tell me about them. A while back, you remember. Figuratively speaking, game's called."

"Game—"

"Yes, yes, yes! Go to the bat. I mean, get to work on your statistics, and don't burn so much kindling getting your fire started. Tell me about the knights."

"I will well, and lightly will begin. So they two departed and rode into a great forest. And—"

"Great Scott!"

You see, I recognized my mistake at once. I had set her works agoing; it was my own fault; she would be thirty days getting down to those facts. And she generally began without a preface and finished without a result. If you interrupted her she would either go right along without

71

noticing, or answer with a couple of words, and go back and say the sentence over again. So, interruptions only did harm; and yet I had to interrupt, and interrupt pretty frequently, too, in order to save my life; a person would die if he let her monotony drip on him right along all day.

"Great Scott!" I said in my distress. She went right back and began over again:

"So they two departed and rode into a great forest. And——"

"*Which* two?"

"Sir Gawaine and Sir Uwaine. And so they came to an abbey of monks, and there were well lodged. So on the morn they heard their masses in the abbey, and so they rode forth till they came to a great forest; then was Sir Gawaine ware in a valley by a turret, of twelve fair damsels, and two knights armed on great horses, and the damsels went to and fro by a tree. And then was Sir Gawaine ware how there hung a white shield on that tree, and ever as the damsels came by it they spit upon it, and some threw mire upon the shield—"

"Now, if I hadn't seen the like myself in this country, Sandy, I wouldn't believe it. But I've seen it, and I can just see those creatures now, parading before that shield and acting like that. The women here do certainly act like all possessed. Yes, and I mean your best, too, society's very choicest brands. The humblest hello-girl along ten thousand miles of wire could teach gentleness, patience, modesty, manners, to the highest duchess in Arthur's land."

"Hello-girl?"

"Yes, but don't you ask me to explain; it's a new kind of girl; they don't have them here; one often speaks sharply to them when they are not the least in fault, and he can't get over feeling sorry for it and ashamed of himself in thirteen hundred years, it's such shabby mean conduct and so unprovoked; the fact is, no gentleman ever does it— though I—well, I myself, if I've got to confess—"

"Peradventure she—"

"Never mind her; never mind her; I tell you I couldn't ever explain her so you would understand."

"Even so be it, sith ye are so minded. Then Sir Gawaine and Sir Uwaine went and saluted them, and asked them why they did that despite to the shield. Sirs, said the damsels, we shall tell you. There is a knight in this country that owneth this white shield, and he is a passing good man of his hands, but he hateth all ladies and gentlewomen, and therefore we do all this despite to the shield. I will say you, said Sir Gawaine, it beseemeth evil a good knight to despise all ladies and gentlewomen, and peradventure though he hate you he hath some cause, and peradventure he loveth in some other places ladies and gentlewomen, and to be loved again, and he such a man of prowess as ye speak of"—

"Man of prowess—yes, that is the man to please them, Sandy. Man of brains—that is a thing they never think of. Tom Sayers—John Heenan—John L. Sullivan—pity but you could be here. You would have your legs under the Round Table and a Sir in front of your names within the twenty-four hours; and you could bring about a new distribution of the married princesses and duchesses of the Court in another twenty-four. The fact is, it is just a sort of polished up court of Comanches, and there isn't a squaw in it who doesn't stand ready at the dropping of a hat to desert to the buck with the biggest string of scalps at his belt."

——"and he be such a man of prowess as ye speak of, said Sir Gawaine. Now what is his name? Sir, said they, his name is Marhaus the king's son of Ireland."

"Son of the king of Ireland, you mean; the other form doesn't mean anything. And look out and hold on tight, now, we must jump this gully. . . . There, we are all right now. This horse belongs in the circus; he is born before his time."

"I know him well, said Sir Uwaine, he is a passing good knight as any is on live."

"*On live*. If you've got a fault in the world, Sandy, it is that you are a shade too archaic. But it isn't any matter."

—"for I saw him once proved at a justs where many knights were gathered, and that time there might no man withstand him. Ah, said Sir Gawaine, damsels, methinketh ye are to blame, for it is to suppose he that hung that shield there will not be long therefrom, and then may those knights match him on horseback, and that is more your worship than thus; for I will abide no longer to see a knight's shield dishonored. And therewith Sir Uwaine and Sir Gawaine departed a little from them, and then were they ware where Sir Marhaus came riding on a great horse straight toward them. And when the twelve damsels saw Sir Marhaus they fled into the turret as they were wild, so that some of them fell by the way. Then the one of the knights of the tower dressed his shield, and said on high, Sir Marhaus defend thee. And so they ran together that the knight brake his spear on Marhaus, and Sir Marhaus smote him so hard that he brake his neck and the horse's back—"

"Well, that is just the trouble about this state of things, it ruins so many horses."

"That saw the other knight of the turret, and dressed him toward Marhaus, and they went so eagerly together, that the knight of the turret was soon smitten down, horse and man, stark dead—"

"*Another* horse gone; I tell you it is a custom that ought to be broken up. I don't see how people with any feeling can applaud and support it."

* * *

"So these two knights came together with great random"—

I saw that I had been asleep and missed a chapter, but I didn't say anything. I judged that the Irish knight was in trouble with the visitors by this time, and this turned out to be the case.

—"that Sir Uwaine smote Sir Marhaus that his spear brast in pieces on the shield, and Sir Marhaus smote him so sore that horse and man he bare to the earth, and hurt Sir Uwaine on the left side—"

"The truth is, Alisande, these archaics are a little *too* simple; the vocabulary is too limited, and so, by consequence, descriptions suffer in the matter of variety; they run too much to level Saharas of fact, and not enough to picturesque detail; this throws about them a certain air of the monotonous; in fact the fights are all alike: a couple of people come together with great random—random is a good word, and so is exegesis, for that matter, and so is holocaust, and defalcation, and usufruct and a hundred others, but land! a body ought to discriminate—they come together with great random, and a spear is brast, and one party brake his shield and the other one goes down, horse and man, over his horsetail and brake his neck, and then the next candidate comes randoming in, and brast *his* spear, and the other man brast his shield, and down *he* goes, horse and man, over his horsetail, and brake *his* neck, and then there's another elected, and another and another and still another, till the material is all used up; and when you come to figure up results, you can't tell one fight from another, nor who whipped; and as a *picture*, of living, raging, roaring battle, sho! why, it's pale and noiseless—just ghosts scuffling in a fog. Dear me, what would this barren vocabulary get out of the mightiest spectacle— the burning of Rome in Nero's time, for instance? Why, it would merely say, 'Town burned down; no insurance; boy brast a window, fireman brake his neck!' Why, *that* ain't a picture!"

It was a good deal of a lecture, I thought, but it didn't disturb Sandy, didn't turn a feather; her steam soared steadily up again, the minute I took off the lid:

"Then Sir Marhaus turned his horse and rode toward Gawaine with his spear. And when Sir Gawaine saw that, he dressed his shield, and they aventred their spears, and they came together with all the might of their horses, that either knight smote other so hard in the midst of their shields, but Sir Gawaine's spear brake"—

"I knew it would."

—"but Sir Marhaus's spear held; and therewith Sir Gawaine and his horse rushed down to the earth"—

"Just so—and brake his back."

—"and lightly Sir Gawaine rose upon his feet and pulled out his sword, and dressed him toward Sir Marhaus on foot, and therewith either came unto other eagerly, and smote together with their swords, that their shields flew in cantles, and they bruised their helms and their hauberks, and wounded either other. But Sir Gawaine, fro it passed nine of the clock, waxed by the space of three hours ever stronger and stronger, and thrice his might was increased. All this espied Sir Marhaus, and had great wonder how his might increased, and so they wounded other passing sore; and then when it was come noon"—

The pelting singsong of it carried me forward to scenes and sounds of my boyhood days:

"N-e-e-ew Haven! ten minutes for refreshments—knductr 'll strike the gong-bell two minutes before train leaves—passengers for the Shore-line please take seats in the rear k'yar, this k'yar don't go no furder—*ahh*-pls, *aw*-rnjz, b'*nan*ners, *s-a-n-d*'ches, p——*op*-corn!"

—"and waxed past noon and drew towards evensong. Sir Gawaine's strength feebled and waxed passing faint, that unnethes he might dure any longer, and Sir Marhaus was then bigger and bigger"—

"Which strained his armor, of course; and yet little would one of these people mind a small thing like that."

—"and so, Sir Knight, said Sir Marhaus, I have well felt that ye are a passing good knight, and a marvelous man of might as ever I felt any, while it lasteth, and our quarrels are not great, and therefore it were a pity to do you hurt, for I feel you are passing feeble. Ah, said Sir Gawaine, gentle knight, ye say the word that I should say. And therewith they took off their helms and either kissed other, and there they swore together either to love other as brethren"—

But I lost the thread there, and dozed off to slumber, thinking about what a pity it was that men with such superb strength—strength enabling them to stand up cased in cruelly burdensome iron and drenched with perspiration, and hack and batter and bang each other for six hours on a stretch—should not have been born at a time when they could put it to some useful purpose. Take a jackass, for instance: a jackass has that kind of strength, and puts it to a useful purpose, and is valuable to this world because he *is* a jackass; but a nobleman is not valuable because he is a jackass. It is a mixture that is always ineffectual, and should never have been attempted in the first place. And yet, once you start a mistake, the trouble is done and you never know what is going to come of it.

When I came to myself again and began to listen, I perceived that I had lost another chapter, and that Alisande had wandered a long way off with her people.

"And so they rode and came into a deep valley full of stones, and thereby they saw a fair stream of water; above thereby was the head of the stream, a fair fountain, and three damsels sitting thereby. In this country, said Sir Marhaus, came never knight since it was christened, but he found strange adventures"—

"This is not good form, Alisande. Sir Marhaus the king's son of Ireland talks like all the rest; you ought to give him a brogue, or at least a characteristic expletive; by this means one would recognize him as soon as he spoke, without his ever being named. It is a common literary device with the great authors. You should make him say, 'In this country, be jabers, came never knight since it was christened, but he found strange adventures, be jabers.' You see how much better that sounds."

—"came never knight but he found strange adventures, be jabers. Of a truth it doth indeed, fair lord, albeit 'tis passing hard to say, though peradventure that will not tarry but better speed with usage. And then they rode to the damsels, and either saluted other, and the eldest had a garland of gold about her head, and she was threescore winter of age or more"—

"The *damsel* was?"

"Even so, dear lord—and her hair was white under the garland"—

"Celluloid teeth, nine dollars a set, as like as not—the loose-fit kind, that go up and down like a portcullis when you eat, and fall out when you laugh."

"The second damsel was of thirty winter of age, with a circlet of gold about her head. The third damsel was but fifteen year of age"—

Billows of thought came rolling over my soul, and the voice faded out of my hearing!

Fifteen! Break—my heart! Oh, my lost darling! Just her age who was so gentle, and lovely, and all the world to me, and whom I shall never see again! How the thought of her carries me back over wide seas of memory to a vague dim time, a happy time, so many, many centuries hence, when I used to wake in the soft summer mornings, out of sweet dreams of her, and say "Hello, Central!" just to hear her dear voice come melting back to me with a "Hello, Hank!" that was music of the spheres to my enchanted ear. She got three dollars a week, but she was worth it.

I could not follow Alisande's further explanation of who our captured knights were, now—I mean in case she should ever get to explaining who they were. My interest was gone, my thoughts were far away, and sad. By fitful glimpses of the drifting tale, caught here and there and now and then, I merely noted in a vague way that each of these three knights took one of these three damsels up behind him on his horse, and one rode north, another east, the other south, to seek adventures, and meet again and lie, after year and day. Year and day—and without baggage. It was of a piece with the general simplicity of the country.

The sun was now setting. It was about three in the afternoon when Alisande had begun to tell me who the cowboys were; so she had made pretty good progress with it—for her. She would arrive some time or other, no doubt, but she was not a person who could be hurried.

We were approaching a castle which stood on high ground: a huge, strong, venerable structure, whose gray towers and battlements were charmingly draped with ivy, and whose whole majestic mass was drenched with splendors flung from the sinking sun. It was the largest castle we had seen, and so I thought it might be the one we were after, but Sandy said no. She did not know who owned it; she said she had passed it without calling, when she went down to Camelot.

XVI. MORGAN LE FAY

IF KNIGHTS-ERRANT were to be believed, not all castles were desirable places to seek hospitality in. As a matter of fact, knights-errant were *not* persons to be believed—that is, measured by modern standards of veracity; yet, measured by the standards of their own time, and scaled accordingly, you got the truth. It was very simple: you discounted a statement ninety-seven percent; the rest was fact. Now after making this allowance, the truth remained that if I could find out something about a castle before ringing the doorbell—I mean hailing the warders—it was the sensible thing to do. So I was pleased when I saw in the distance a horseman making the bottom turn of the road that wound down from this castle.

As we approached each other, I saw that he wore a plumed helmet, and seemed to be otherwise clothed in steel, but bore a curious addition also—a stiff square garment like a herald's tabard. However, I had to smile at my own forgetfulness when I got nearer and read this sign on his tabard:

"PERSIMMON'S SOAP—ALL THE PRIME-DONNE USE IT."

That was a little idea of my own, and had several wholesome purposes in view toward the civilizing and uplifting of this nation. In the first place, it was a furtive, underhand blow at this nonsense of knight errantry, though nobody suspected that but me. I had started a number of these people out—the bravest knights I could get—each sandwiched between bulletin boards bearing one device or another, and I judged that by and by when they got to be numerous enough they would begin to look ridiculous; and then, even the steel-clad ass that *hadn't* any board would himself begin to look ridiculous because he was out of the fashion.

Secondly, these missionaries would gradually, and without creating suspicion or exciting alarm, introduce a rudimentary cleanliness among the nobility, and from them it would work down to the people, if the priests could be kept quiet. This would undermine the Church. I mean would be a step toward that. Next, education—next, freedom— and then she would begin to crumble. It being my conviction that any Established Church is an established crime, an established slave pen, I had no scruples, but was willing to assail it in any way or with any weapon that promised to hurt it. Why, in my own former day—in remote centuries not yet stirring in the womb of time—there were old Englishmen who imagined that they had been born in a free country: a "free" country with the Corporation Act and the Test still in force in it—timbers propped against men's liberties and dishonored consciences to shore up an Established Anachronism with.

My missionaries were taught to spell out the gilt signs on their tabards—the showy gilding was a neat idea, I could have got the king to wear a bulletin board for the sake of that barbaric splendor—they were to spell out these signs and then explain to the lords and ladies what soap was; and if the lords and ladies were afraid of it, get them to try it on a dog. The missionary's next move was to get the family together and try it on himself; he was to stop at no experiment, however desperate, that could convince the nobility that soap was harmless; if any final doubt remained, he must catch a hermit—the woods were full of them; saints they called themselves, and saints they were believed to be. They were unspeakably holy, and worked miracles, and everybody stood in awe of them. If a hermit could survive a wash, and that failed to convince a duke, give him up, let him alone.

Whenever my missionaries overcame a knight errant on the road they washed him, and when he got well they swore him to go and get a bulletin board and disseminate soap and civilization the rest of his days. As a consequence the workers in the field were increasing by degrees, and the reform was steadily spreading. My soap factory felt the strain early. At first I had only two hands; but before I had left home I was already employing fifteen, and running night and day; and the atmospheric result was getting so pronounced that the king went sort of fainting and gasping around and said he did not believe he could stand it much longer, and Sir Launcelot got so that he did hardly anything but walk up and down the roof and swear, although I told him it was worse up there than anywhere else, but he said he wanted plenty of air; and he was always complaining that a palace was no place for a soap factory, anyway, and said if a man was to start one in his house he would be damned if he wouldn't strangle him. There were ladies present, too, but much these people ever cared for that; they would swear before children, if the wind was their way when the factory was going.

The missionary knight's name was La Cote Male Taile, and he said that this castle was the abode of Morgan le Fay, sister of King Arthur, and wife of King Uriens, monarch of a realm about as big as the District of Columbia—you could stand in the middle of it and throw bricks into the next kingdom. "Kings" and "Kingdoms" were as thick in Britain as they had been in little Palestine in Joshua's time, when people had to sleep with their knees pulled up because they couldn't stretch out without a passport.

La Cote was much depressed, for he had scored here the worst failure of his campaign. He had not worked off a cake; yet he had tried all the tricks of the trade, even to the washing of a hermit; but the hermit died. This was indeed a bad failure, for this animal would now be dubbed a martyr, and would take his place among the saints of the Roman calendar. Thus made he his moan, this poor Sir La Cote Male Taile, and sorrowed passing sore. And so my heart bled for him, and I was moved to comfort and stay him. Wherefore I said—

"Forbear to grieve, fair knight, for this is not a defeat. We have brains, you and I; and for such as have brains there are no defeats, but only victories. Observe how we will turn this seeming disaster into an advertisement; an advertisement for our soap; and the biggest one, to draw, that was ever thought of; an advertisement that will transform that Mount Washington defeat into a Matterhorn victory. We will put on your bulletin board, *'Patronized by the Elect.'* How does that strike you?"

"Verily, it is wonderly bethought!"

"Well, a body is bound to admit that for just a modest little one-line ad, it's a corker."

So the poor colporteur's griefs vanished away. He was a brave fellow, and had done mighty feats of arms in his time. His chief celebrity rested upon the events of an excursion like this one of mine, which he had once made with a damsel named Maledisant, who was as handy with her tongue as was Sandy, though in a different way, for her tongue churned forth only railings and insult, whereas Sandy's music was of a kindlier sort. I knew his story well, and so I knew how to interpret the compassion that was in his face when he bade me farewell. He supposed I was having a bitter hard time of it.

Sandy and I discussed his story, as we rode along, and she said that La Cote's bad luck had begun with the very beginning of that trip; for the king's fool had overthrown him on the first day, and in such cases it was customary for the girl to desert to the conqueror, but Maledisant didn't do it; and also persisted afterward in sticking to him, after all his defeats. But, said I, suppose the victor should decline to accept his spoil? She said that that wouldn't answer—he must. He couldn't decline; it wouldn't be regular. I made a note of that. If Sandy's music got to be too burdensome, sometime I would let a knight defeat me, on the chance that she would desert to him.

In due time we were challenged by the warders, from the castle walls, and after a parley admitted. I have nothing pleasant to tell about that visit. But it was not a disappointment, for I knew Mrs. le Fay by reputation, and was not expecting anything pleasant. She was held in awe by the whole realm, for she had made everybody believe she was a great sorceress. All her ways were wicked, all her instincts devilish. She was loaded to the eyelids with cold malice. All her history was black with crime; and among her crimes murder was common. I was most curious to see her; as curious as I could have been to see Satan. To my surprise she was beautiful; black thoughts had failed to make her expression repulsive, age had failed to wrinkle her satin skin or mar its bloomy freshness. She could have passed for old Uriens's granddaughter, she could have been mistaken for sister to her own son.

As soon as we were fairly within the castle gates we were ordered into her presence. King Uriens was there, a kind-faced old man with a subdued look; and also the son, Sir Uwaine le Blanchemains, in whom I was of course interested on account of the tradition that he had once done battle with thirty knights, and also on account of his trip with Sir Gawaine and Sir Marhaus, which Sandy had been aging me with. But Morgan was the main attraction, the conspicuous personality here; she was head chief of this household, that was plain. She caused us to be seated, and then she began, with all manner of pretty graces and graciousness, to ask me questions. Dear me, it was like a bird or a flute, or something, talking. I felt persuaded that this woman must have been misrepresented, lied about. She trilled along, and trilled along, and presently a handsome young page, clothed like a rainbow, and as easy and undulatory of movement as a wave, came with something on a golden salver, and kneeling to present it to her, overdid his graces and lost his balance, and so fell lightly against her knee. She slipped a dirk into him in as matter-of-course a way as another person would have harpooned a rat!

Poor child, he slumped to the floor, twisted his silken limbs in one great straining contortion of pain, and was dead. Out of the old king was wrung an involuntary "O-h!" of compassion. The look he got, made him cut it suddenly short and not put any more hyphens in it. Sir Uwaine, at a sign from his mother, went to the anteroom and called some servants, and meanwhile madame went rippling sweetly along with her talk.

I saw that she was a good housekeeper, for while she talked she kept a corner of her eye on the servants to see that they made no balks in handling the body and getting it out; when they came with fresh clean towels, she sent back for the other kind; and when they had finished wiping the floor and were going, she indicated a crimson fleck the size of a tear which their duller eyes had overlooked. It was plain to me that La Cote Male Taile had failed to see the mistress of the house. Often, how louder and clearer than any tongue, does dumb circumstantial evidence speak.

Morgan le Fay rippled along as musically as ever. Marvelous woman. And what a glance she had: when it fell in reproof upon those servants, they shrunk and quailed as timid people do when the lightning flashes out of a cloud. I could have got the habit myself. It was the same with that poor old Brer Uriens; he was always on the ragged edge of apprehension; she could not even turn towards him but he winced.

In the midst of the talk I let drop a complimentary word about King Arthur, forgetting for the moment how this woman hated her brother. That one little compliment was enough. She clouded up like a storm; she called for her guards, and said—

"Hale me these varlets to the dungeons!"

That struck cold on my ears, for her dungeons had a reputation. Nothing occurred to me to say—or do. But not so with Sandy. As the guard laid a hand upon me, she piped up with the tranquilest confidence, and said—

"God's wownds, dost thou covet destruction, thou maniac? It is The Boss!"

Now what a happy idea that was—and so simple; yet it would never have occurred to me. I was born modest; not all over, but in spots; and this was one of the spots.

The effect upon madame was electrical. It cleared her countenance and brought back her smiles and all her persuasive graces and blandishments; but nevertheless she was not able to entirely cover up with them the fact that she was in a ghastly fright. She said:

"La, but do list to thine handmaid! As if one gifted with powers like to mine might say the thing which I have said unto one who has vanquished Merlin, and not be jesting. By mine enchantments I foresaw your coming, and by them I knew you when you entered here. I did but play this little jest with hope to surprise you into some display of your art, as not doubting you would blast the guards with occult fires, consuming them to ashes on the spot, a marvel much beyond mine own ability, yet one which I have long been childishly curious to see."

The guards were less curious, and got out as soon as they got permission.

XVII. A ROYAL BANQUET

MADAME, SEEING me pacific and unresentful, no doubt judged that I was deceived by her excuse; for her fright dissolved away, and she was soon so importunate to have me give an exhibition and kill somebody, that the thing grew to be embarrassing. However, to my relief she was presently interrupted by the call to prayers. I will say this much for the nobility: that, tyrannical, murderous, rapacious and morally rotten as they were, they were deeply and enthusiastically religious. Nothing could divert them from the regular and faithful performance of the pieties enjoined by the Church. More than once I had seen a noble who had gotten his enemy at a disadvantage, stop to pray before cutting his throat; more than once I had seen a noble, after ambushing and dispatching his enemy, retire to the nearest wayside shrine and humbly give thanks, without even waiting to rob the body. There was to be nothing finer or sweeter in the life of even Benvenuto Cellini, that roughhewn saint, ten centuries later. All the nobles of Britain, with their families, attended divine service morning and night daily, in their private chapels, and even the worst of them had family worship five or six times a day besides. The credit of this belonged entirely to the Church. Although I was no friend to that Catholic Church, I was obliged to admit this. And often, in spite of me, I found myself saying, "What would this country be without the Church?"

After prayers we had dinner in a great banqueting hall which was lighted by hundreds of grease jets, and everything was as fine and lavish and rudely splendid as might become the royal degree of the hosts. At the head of the hall, on a dais, was the table of the king, queen, and their son, Prince Uwaine. Stretching down the hall from this, was the general table, on the floor. At this, above the salt, sat the visiting nobles and the grown members of their families, of both sexes—the resident Court, in effect—sixty-one persons; below the salt sat minor officers of the household, with their principal subordinates: altogether a hundred and eighteen persons sitting, and about as many liveried servants standing behind their chairs, or serving in one capacity or another. It was a very fine show. In a gallery a band with cymbals, horns, harps, and other horrors opened the proceedings with what seemed to be the crude first draft or original agony of the wail known to later centuries as "In the Sweet Bye and Bye." It was new, and ought to have been rehearsed a little more. For some reason or other the queen had the composer hanged, after dinner.

After this music, the priest who stood behind the royal table said a noble long grace in ostensible Latin. Then the battalion of waiters broke away from their posts, and darted, rushed, flew, fetched, and carried, and the mighty feeding began; no words anywhere, but absorbing attention to business. The rows of chops opened and shut in vast unison, and the sound of it was like to the muffled burr of subterranean machinery.

The havoc continued an hour and a half, and unimaginable was the destruction of substantials. Of the chief feature of the feast—the huge wild boar that lay stretched out so portly and imposing at the start—nothing was left but the semblance of a hoopskirt; and he was but the type and symbol of what had happened to all the other dishes.

With the pastries and so on, the heavy drinking began—and the talk. Gallon after gallon of wine and mead disappeared, and everybody got comfortable, then happy, then sparklingly joyous—both sexes—and by and by pretty noisy. Men told anecdotes that were terrific to hear, but nobody blushed; and when the nub was sprung, the assemblage let go with a horselaugh that shook the fortress. Ladies answered back with historiettes that would almost have made Queen Margaret of Navarre or even the great Elizabeth of England hide behind a handkerchief, but nobody hid here, but only laughed—howled, you may say. In pretty much all of these dreadful stories, ecclesiastics were the hardy heroes, but that didn't worry the chaplain any, he had his laugh with the rest; more than that, upon invitation he roared out a song which was of as daring a sort as any that was sung that night.

By midnight everybody was fagged out, and sore with laughing; and as a rule, drunk: some weepingly, some affectionately, some hilariously, some quarrelsomely, some dead and under the table. Of the ladies, the worst spectacle was a lovely young duchess, whose wedding eve this was; and indeed she was a spectacle, sure enough. Just as she was she could have sat in advance for the portrait of the young daughter of the Regent d'Orleans, at the famous dinner whence she was carried, foul-mouthed, intoxicated, and helpless, to her bed, in the lost and lamented days of the Ancient Regime.

Suddenly, even while the priest was lifting his hands, and all conscious heads were bowed in reverent expectation of the coming blessing, there appeared under the arch of the far-off door at the bottom of the hall, an old and bent and white-haired lady, leaning upon a crutchstick; and she lifted the stick and pointed it toward the queen and cried out—

"The wrath and curse of God fall upon you, woman without pity, who have slain mine innocent grandchild and made desolate this old heart that had nor chick nor friend nor stay nor comfort in all this world but him!"

Everybody crossed himself in a ghastly fright, for a curse was an awful thing to those people; but the queen rose up majestic, with the death light in her eye, and flung back this ruthless command:

"Lay hands on her! To the stake with her!"

The guards left their posts to obey. It was a shame; it was a cruel thing to see. What could be done? Sandy gave me a look; I knew she had another inspiration. I said—

"Do what you choose."

She was up and facing toward the queen in a moment. She indicated me, and said:

"Madame, *he* saith this may not be. Recall the commandment, or he will dissolve the castle and it shall vanish away like the instable fabric of a dream!"

Confound it, what a crazy contract to pledge a person to! What if the queen—

But my consternation subsided there, and my panic passed off; for the queen, all in a collapse, made no show of resistance but gave a countermanding sign and sunk into her seat. When she reached it she was sober. So were many of the others. The assemblage rose, whiffed ceremony to the winds, and rushed for the door like a mob, overturning chairs, smashing crockery, tugging, struggling, shouldering, crowding—anything to get out before I should change my mind and puff the castle into the measureless dim vacancies of space. Well, well, well, they *were* a superstitious lot. It is all a body can do to conceive of it.

The poor queen was so scared and humbled that she was even afraid to hang the composer without first consulting me. I was very sorry for her—indeed any one would have been, for she was really suffering; so I was willing to do anything that was reasonable, and had no desire to carry things to wanton extremities. I therefore considered the matter thoughtfully, and ended by having the musicians ordered into our presence to play that Sweet Bye and Bye again, which they did. Then I saw that she was right, and gave her permission to hang the whole band. This little relaxation of sternness had a good effect upon the queen. A statesman gains little by the arbitrary exercise of ironclad authority upon all occasions that offer, for this wounds the just pride of his subordinates, and thus tends to undermine his strength. A little concession, now and then, where it can do no harm, is the wiser policy.

Now that the queen was at her ease in her mind once more, and measurably happy, her wine naturally began to assert itself again, and it got a little the start of her. I mean it set her music going—her silver bell of a tongue. Dear me, she was a master talker. It would not become me to suggest that it was pretty late and that I was a tired man and very sleepy. I wished I had gone off to bed when I had the chance. Now I must stick it out; there was no other way. So she tinkled along and along, in the otherwise profound and ghostly hush of the sleeping castle, until by and by there came, as if from deep down under us, a faraway sound, as of a muffled shriek—with an expression of agony about it that made my flesh crawl. The queen stopped, and her eyes lighted with pleasure; she tilted her graceful head as a bird does when it listens. The sound bored its way up through the stillness again.

"What is it?" I said.

"It is truly a stubborn soul, and endureth long. It is many hours now."

"Endureth what?"

"The rack. Come—ye shall see a blithe sight. An he yield not his secret now, ye shall see him torn asunder."

What a silky smooth hellion she was; and so composed and serene, when the cords all down my legs were hurting in sympathy with that man's pain. Conducted by mailed guards bearing flaring torches, we tramped along echoing corridors, and down stone stairways dank and dripping, and smelling of mold and ages of imprisoned night—a chill, uncanny journey and a long one, and not made the shorter or the cheerier by the sorceress' talk, which was about this sufferer and his crime. He had been accused by an anonymous informer, of having killed a stag in the royal preserves. I said—

"Anonymous testimony isn't just the right thing, your Highness. It were fairer to confront the accused with the accuser."

"I had not thought of that, it being but of small consequence. But an I would, I could not, for that the accuser came masked by night, and told the forester, and straightway got him hence again, and so the forester knoweth him not."

"Then is this Unknown the only person who saw the stag killed?"

"Marry, *no* man *saw* the killing, but this Unknown saw this hardy wretch near to the spot where the stag lay, and came with right loyal zeal and betrayed him to the forester."

"So the Unknown was near the dead stag, too? Isn't it just possible that he did the killing himself? His loyal zeal—in a mask—looks just a shade suspicious. But what is your Highness' idea for racking the prisoner? Where is the profit?"

"He will not confess, else; and then were his soul lost. For his crime his life is forfeited by the law—and of a surety will I see that he payeth it—but it were peril to my own soul to let him die unconfessed and unabsolved. Nay, I were a fool to fling me into hell for *his* accommodation."

"But, your Highness, suppose he has nothing to confess?"

"As to that, we shall see, anon. An I rack him to death and he confess not, it will peradventure show that he had indeed naught to confess— ye will grant that this is sooth? Then shall I not be damned for an unconfessed man that had naught to confess—wherefore, I shall be safe."

It was the stubborn unreasoning of the time. It was useless to argue with her. Arguments have no chance against petrified training; they wear it as little as the waves wear a cliff. And her training was everybody's. The brightest intellect in the land would not have been able to see that her position was defective.

As we entered the rack cell I caught a picture that will not go from me; I wish it would. A native young giant of thirty or thereabouts, lay stretched upon the frame on his back, with his wrists and ankles tied to ropes which led over windlasses at either end. There was no color in him; his features were contorted and set, and sweat drops stood upon his forehead. A priest bent over him on each side; the executioner stood by; guards were on duty; smoking torches stood in sockets along the walls; in a corner crouched a poor young creature, her face drawn with anguish, a half-wild and hunted look in her eyes, and in her lap lay a little child asleep. Just as we stepped across the threshold the executioner gave his machine a slight turn, which wrung a cry from both the prisoner and the woman; but I shouted and the executioner released the strain without waiting to see who spoke. I could not let this horror go on; it would have killed me to see it. I asked the queen to let me clear the place and speak to the prisoner privately; and when she was going to object I spoke in a low voice and said I did not want to make a scene before her servants, but I must have my way; for I was King Arthur's representative, and was speaking in his name. She saw she had to yield. I asked her to endorse me to these people, and then leave me. It was not pleasant for her, but she took the pill; and even went further than I was meaning to require. I only wanted the backing of her own authority; but she said—

"Ye will do in all things as this lord shall command. It is The Boss."

It was certainly a good word to conjure with: you could see it by the squirming of these rats. The queen's guards fell into line, and she and they marched away, with their torchbearers, and woke the echoes of the cavernous tunnels with the measured beat of their retreating footfalls. I had the prisoner taken from the rack and placed upon his bed, and medicaments applied to his hurts, and wine given him to drink. The woman crept near and looked on, eagerly, lovingly, but timorously—

like one who fears a repulse; indeed, she tried furtively to touch the man's forehead, and jumped back, the picture of fright, when I turned unconsciously toward her. It was pitiful to see.

"Lord," I said, "stroke him, lass, if you want to. Do anything you're a mind to; don't mind me."

Why, her eyes were as grateful as an animal's, when you do it a kindness that it understands. The baby was out of her way and she had her cheek against the man's in a minute, and her hands fondling his hair, and her happy tears running down. The man revived, and caressed his wife with his eyes, which was all he could do. I judged I might clear the den, now, and I did; cleared it of all but the family and myself. Then I said—

"Now my friend, tell me your side of this matter; I know the other side."

The man moved his head in sign of refusal. But the woman looked pleased—as it seemed to me—pleased with my suggestion. I went on:

"You know of me?"

"Yes. All do, in Arthur's realms."

"If my reputation has come to you right and straight, you should not be afraid to speak."

The woman broke in, eagerly:

"Ah, fair my lord, do thou persuade him! Thou canst an thou wilt. Ah, he suffereth so; and it is for me—for *me!* And how can I bear it? I would I might see him die—a sweet, swift death; oh, my Hugo, I cannot bear this one!"

And she fell to sobbing and groveling about my feet, and still imploring. Imploring what? The man's death? I could not quite get the bearings of the thing. But Hugo interrupted her and said—

"Peace! Ye wit not what ye ask. Shall I starve whom I love, to win a gentle death? I wend thou knewest me better."

"Well," I said, "I can't quite make this out. It is a puzzle. Now—"

"Ah, dear my lord, an ye will but persuade him! Consider how these his tortures wound me! Oh, and he will not speak—whereas, the healing, the solace that lie in a blessed swift death—"

"What *are* you maundering about? He's going out from here a free man and whole—he's not going to die."

The man's white face lit up, and the woman flung herself at me in a most surprising explosion of joy, and cried out—

"He is saved—for it is the King's word by the mouth of the king's servant—Arthur, the king whose word is gold!"

"Well, then you do believe I can be trusted, after all. Why didn't you before?"

"Who doubted? Not I, indeed; and not she."

"Well, why wouldn't you tell me your story, then?"

"Ye had made no promise; else had it been otherwise."

"I see, I see. . . . And yet I believe I don't quite see, after all. You stood the torture and refused to confess; which shows plain enough to even the dullest understanding that you had nothing to confess—"

"*I*, my lord? How so? It was I that killed the deer!"

"You *did*? Oh, dear, this is the most mixed-up business that ever—"

"Dear Lord, I begged him on my knees to confess, but—"

"You *did!* It gets thicker and thicker. What did you want him to do that for?"

"Sith it would bring him a quick death and save him all this cruel pain."

"Well—yes, there is reason in that. But *he* didn't want the quick death."

"He? Why, of a surety he *did*."

"Well, then, why in the world *didn't* he confess?"

"Ah, sweet sir, and leave my wife and chick without bread and shelter?"

"Oh, heart of gold, now I see it! The bitter law takes the convicted man's estate and beggars his widow and his orphans. They could torture you to death, but without conviction or confession they could not rob your wife and baby. You stood by them like a man; and *you*— true wife and true woman that you are—you would have bought him release from torture at cost to yourself of slow starvation and death— well, it humbles a body to think what your sex can do when it comes to self-sacrifice. I'll book you both for my colony; you'll like it there; it's a Factory where I'm going to turn groping and grubbing automata into *men*."

XVIII. IN THE QUEEN'S DUNGEONS

WELL, I ARRANGED all that; and I had the man sent to his home. I had a great desire to rack the executioner; not because he was a good, painstaking and paingiving official,—for surely it was not to his discredit that he performed his functions well—but to pay him back for wantonly cuffing and otherwise distressing that young woman. The priests told me about this, and were generously hot to have him punished. Something of this disagreeable sort was turning up every now and then. I mean, episodes that showed that not all priests were frauds and self-seekers, but that many, even the great majority, of these that were down on the ground among the common people, were sincere and right-hearted, and devoted to the alleviation of human troubles and sufferings. Well, it was a thing which could not be helped, so I seldom fretted about it, and never many minutes at a time; it has never been my way to bother much about things which you can't cure. But I did not like it, for it was just the sort of thing to keep people reconciled to an Established Church. We *must* have a religion—it goes without saying—but my idea is, to have it cut up into forty free sects, so that they will police each other, as had been the case in the United States in my time. Concentration of power in a political machine is bad; and an Established Church is only a political machine; it was invented for that; it is nursed, cradled, preserved for that; it is an enemy to human liberty, and does no good which it could not better do in a split-up and scattered condition. That wasn't law; it wasn't gospel: it was only an opinion—my opinion, and I was only a man, one man: so it wasn't worth any more than the Pope's—or any less, for that matter.

Well, I couldn't rack the executioner, neither would I overlook the just complaint of the priests. The man must be punished some how or other, so I degraded him from his office and made him leader of the band—the new one that was to be started. He begged hard, and said he couldn't play—a plausible excuse, but too thin; there wasn't a musician in the country that could.

The queen was a good deal outraged, next morning, when she found she was going to have neither Hugo's life nor his property. But I told her she must bear this cross; that while by law and custom she certainly was entitled to both the man's life and his property, there were extenuating circumstances, and so in Arthur the king's name I had pardoned him. The deer was ravaging the man's fields, and he had killed it in sudden passion, and not for gain; and he had carried it into the royal forest in the hope that that might make detection of the misdoer impossible. Confound her, I couldn't make her see that sudden passion is an extenuating circumstance in the killing of venison—or of a person—so I gave it up and let her sulk it out. I *did* think I was going to make her see it by remarking that her own sudden passion in the case of the page modified that crime.

"Crime!" she exclaimed. "How thou talkest! Crime, forsooth! Man, I am going to *pay* for him!"

Oh, it was no use to waste sense on her. Training—training is everything; training is all there is *to* a person. We speak of nature; it is folly; there is no such thing as nature; what we call by that misleading name is merely heredity and training. We have no thoughts of our own, no opinions of our own; they are transmitted to us, trained into us. All that is original in us, and therefore fairly creditable or discreditable to us, can be covered up and hidden by the point of a cambric needle, all the rest being atoms contributed by, and inherited from, a procession of ancestors that stretches back a billion years to the Adam-clam or grasshopper or monkey from whom our race has been so tediously and ostentatiously and unprofitably developed. And as for me, all that I think about in this plodding sad pilgrimage, this pathetic drift between the eternities, is to look out and humbly live a pure and high and blameless life, and save that one microscopic atom in me that is truly *me*: the rest may land in Sheol and welcome for all I care.

No, confound her, her intellect was good, she had brains enough, but her training made her an ass—that is, from a many-centuries-later point of view. To kill the page was no crime—it was her right; and upon her right she stood, serenely and unconscious of offense. She was a result of generations of training in the unexamined and unassailed belief that the law which permitted her to kill a subject when she chose was a perfectly right and righteous one.

Well, we must give even Satan his due. She deserved a compliment for one thing; and I tried to pay it, but the words stuck in my throat. She had a right to kill the boy, but she was in no wise obliged to pay for him. That was law for some other people, but not for her. She knew quite well that she was doing a large and generous thing to pay for that lad, and that I ought in common fairness to come out with something handsome about it, but I couldn't—my mouth refused. I couldn't help seeing, in my fancy, that poor old grandam with the broken heart, and that fair young creature lying butchered, his little silken pomps and vanities laced with his golden blood. How could she *pay* for him? *Whom* could she pay? and so, well knowing that this woman, trained as she had been, deserved praise, even adulation, I was yet not able to utter it, trained as *I* had been. The best I could do was to fish up a compliment from outside, so to speak—and the pity of it was, that it was true:

"Madame, your people will adore you for this."

Quite true, but I meant to hang her for it some day, if I lived. Some of those laws were too bad, altogether too bad. A master might kill his slave for nothing: for mere spite, malice, or to pass the time—just as we have seen that the crowned head could do it with *his* slave, that is to say, anybody. A gentleman could kill a free commoner, and pay for him—cash or garden truck. A noble could kill a noble without expense, as far as the law was concerned, but reprisals in kind were to be expected. *Any*body could kill *some*body, except the commoner and the slave; these had no privileges. If they killed, it was murder, and the law wouldn't stand murder. It made short work of the experimenter— and of his family, too, if he murdered somebody who belonged up among the ornamental ranks. If a commoner gave a noble even so much as a Damiens-scratch which didn't kill or even hurt, he got Damiens's dose for it just the same; they pulled him to rags and tatters with horses, and all the world came to see the show, and crack jokes, and have a good time; and some of the performances of the best people present were as tough, and as properly unprintable, as any that have been printed by the pleasant Casanova in his chapter about the dismemberment of Louis XV's poor awkward enemy.

I had had enough of this grisly place by this time, and wanted to leave, but I couldn't, because I had something on my mind that my conscience kept prodding me about, and wouldn't let me forget. If I had the remaking of man, he wouldn't have any conscience. It is one of the most disagreeable things connected with a person; and although it certainly does a great deal of good, it cannot be said to pay, in the long run; it would be much better to have less good and more comfort. Still, this is only my opinion, and I am only one man; others, with less experience, may think differently. They have a right to their view. I only stand to this: I have noticed my conscience for many years, and I know it is more trouble and bother to me than anything else I started with. I suppose that in the beginning I prized it, because we prize anything that is ours; and yet how foolish it was to think so. If we look at it in another way, we see how absurd it is: if I had an anvil in me would I prize it? Of course not. And yet when you come to think, there is no real difference between a conscience and an anvil—I mean for comfort. I have noticed it a thousand times. And you could dissolve an anvil with acids, when you couldn't stand it any longer; but there isn't any way that you can work off a conscience—at least so it will stay worked off; not that I know of, anyway.

There was something I wanted to do before leaving, but it was a disagreeable matter, and I hated to go at it. Well, it bothered me all the morning. I could have mentioned it to the old king, but what would be the use—he was but an extinct volcano; he had been active in his time, but his fire was out, this good while, he was only a stately ash pile, now; gentle enough, and kindly enough for my purpose, without doubt, but not usable. He was nothing, this so-called king: the queen was the only power there. And she was a Vesuvius. As a favor, she might consent to warm a flock of sparrows for you, but then she might take that very opportunity to turn herself loose and bury a city. However, I reflected that as often as any other way, when you are expecting the worst, you get something that is not so bad, after all.

So I braced up and placed my matter before her royal Highness. I said I had been having a general jail delivery at Camelot and among neighboring castles, and with her permission I would like to examine her collection, her bric-a-brac—that is to say, her prisoners. She resisted; but I was expecting that. But she finally consented. I was expecting that, too, but not so soon. That about ended my discomfort. She called her guards and torches, and we went down into the dungeons. These were down under the castle's foundations, and mainly were small cells hollowed out of the living rock. Some of these cells had no light at all. In one of them was a woman, in foul rags, who sat on the ground, and would not answer a question, or speak a word, but only looked up at us once or twice, through a cobweb of tangled hair, as if to see what casual thing it might be that was disturbing with sound and light the meaningless dull dream that was become her life; after that, she sat bowed, with her dirt-caked fingers idly interlocked in her lap, and gave no further sign. This poor rack of bones was a woman of middle age, apparently; but only apparently; she had been there nine years, and was eighteen when she entered. She was a commoner, and had been sent here on her bridal night by Sir Breuse Sance Pité, a neighboring lord whose vassal her father was, and to which said lord she had refused what has since been called *le droit du Seigneur*; and moreover, had opposed violence to violence and spilt half a gill of his almost sacred blood. The young husband had interfered at that point, believing the bride's life in danger, and had flung the noble out into the midst of the humble and trembling wedding guests, in the parlor, and left him there astonished at this strange treatment, and implacably embittered against both bride and groom. The said lord being cramped for dungeon room had asked the queen to accommodate his two criminals, and here in her bastille they had been ever since; hither indeed, they had come before their crime was an hour old, and had never seen each other since. Here they were, kerneled like toads in the same rock; they had passed nine pitch dark years within fifty feet of each other, yet neither knew whether the other was alive or not. All the first years, their only question had been—asked with beseechings and tears that might have moved stones, "Is he alive?" "Is she alive?" But they had never got an answer; and at last that question was not asked any more—or any other.

I wanted to see the man, after hearing all this. He was thirty-four years old, and looked sixty. He sat upon a squared block of stone, with his head bent down, his forearms resting on his knees, his long hair hanging like a fringe before his face, and he was muttering to himself. He raised his chin and looked us slowly over, in a listless dull way, blinking with the distress of the torchlight, then dropped his head and fell to muttering again and took no further notice of us. There were some pathetically suggestive dumb witnesses present. On his wrists and ankles were cicatrices, old smooth scars, and fastened to the stone on which he sat was a chain with manacles and fetters attached; but this apparatus lay idle on the ground, and was thick with rust. Chains cease to be needed after the spirit has gone out of a prisoner.

I could not rouse the man; so I said we would take him to her, and see—to the bride who was the fairest thing in the earth to him, once—roses, pearls, and dew made flesh, for him; a wonderwork, the master-work of nature: with eyes like no other eyes, and voice like no other voice, and a freshness, and lithe young grace, and beauty that belonged properly to the creatures of dreams—as he thought—and to no other. The sight of her would set his stagnant blood leaping; the sight of her—

But it was a disappointment. They sat together on the ground and looked dimly wondering into each other's faces awhile, with a sort of weak animal curiosity; then forgot each other's presence, and dropped their eyes, and you saw that they were away again and wandering in some far land of dreams and shadows that we know nothing about.

I had them taken out and sent to their friends. The queen did not like it much. Not that she felt any personal interest in the matter, but she thought it disrespectful to Sir Breuse Sance Pité. However, I assured her that if he found he couldn't stand it I would fix him so that he could.

I set forty-seven prisoners loose out of those awful rat-holes, and left only one in captivity. He was a lord, and had killed another lord, a sort of kinsman of the queen. That other lord had ambushed him to assassinate him, but this fellow had got the best of him and cut his throat.

However, it was not for that that I left him jailed, but for maliciously destroying the only public well in one of his wretched villages. The queen was bound to hang him for killing her kinsman, but I would not allow it: it was no crime to kill an assassin. But I said I was willing to let her hang him for destroying the well; so she concluded to put up with that, as it was better than nothing.

Dear me, for what trifling offenses the most of those forty-seven men and women were shut up there! Indeed some were there for no distinct offense at all, but only to gratify somebody's spite; and not always the queen's by any means, but a friend's. The newest prisoner's crime was a mere remark, which he had made. He said he believed that men were about all alike, and one man as good as another, barring clothes. He said he believed that if you were to strip the nation naked and send a stranger through the crowd, he couldn't tell the king from a quack doctor, nor a duke from a hotel clerk. Apparently here was a man whose brains had not been reduced to an ineffectual mush by idiotic training. I set him loose and sent him to the Factory.

Some of the cells carved in the living rock were just behind the face of the precipice, and in each of these an arrow-slit had been pierced outward to the daylight, and so the captive had a thin ray from the blessed sun for his comfort. The case of one of these poor fellows was particularly hard. From his dusky swallow's hole high up in that vast wall of native rock he could peer out through the arrow-slit and see his own home off yonder in the valley; and for twenty-two years he had watched it, with heartache and longing, through that crack. He could see the lights shine there at night, and in the daytime he could see figures go in and come out—his wife and children, some of them, no doubt, though he could not make out, at that distance. In the course of years he noted festivities there, and tried to rejoice, and wondered if they were weddings or what they might be. And he noted funerals; and they wrung his heart. He could make out the coffin, but he could not determine its size, and so could not tell whether it was wife or child. He could see the procession form, with priests and mourners, and move solemnly away, bearing the secret with them. He had left behind him five children and a wife; and in nineteen years he had seen five funerals issue, and none of them humble enough in pomp to denote a servant. So he had lost five of his treasures; there must still be one remaining—one now infinitely, unspeakably precious—but *which* one? Wife, or child? That was the question that tortured him, by night and by day, asleep and awake. Well, to have an interest of some sort, and half a ray of light, when you are in a dungeon, is a great support to the body and preserver of the intellect. The man was in pretty good condition yet. By the time he had finished telling me his distressful tale, I was in the same state of mind that you would have been in yourself, if you have got average human curiosity: that is to say, I was as burning up as he was, to find out which member of the family it was that was left. So I took him over home myself; and an amazing kind of a surprise party it was, too—typhoons and cyclones of frantic joy, and whole Niagaras of happy tears; and by George we found the aforetime young matron graying toward the imminent verge of her half century, and the babies all men and women, and some of them married and experimenting familywise themselves—for not a soul of the tribe was dead! Conceive of the ingenious devilishness of that queen: she had a special hatred for the prisoner, and she had *invented* all those funerals herself, to scorch his heart with; and the sublimest stroke of genius of the whole thing was leaving the family invoice a funeral *short*, so as to let him wear his poor old soul out guessing.

But for me, he never would have got out. Morgan le Fay hated him with her whole heart, and she never would have softened toward him. And yet his crime was committed more in thoughtlessness than deliberate depravity. He had said she had red hair. Well, she had; but that was no way to speak of it. When red-headed people are above a certain social grade, their hair is auburn.

Consider it: among these forty-seven captives, there were five whose names, offenses and dates of incarceration were no longer known! One woman and four men—all bent, and wrinkled, and mind-extinguished patriarchs. They themselves had long ago forgotten these details; at any rate they had mere vague theories about them, nothing definite and nothing that they repeated twice in the same way. The succession of priests whose office it had been to pray daily with the captives and remind them that God had put them there, for some wise purpose or other, and teach them that patience, humbleness, and submission to oppression was what He loved to see in parties of a subordinate rank, had traditions about these poor old human ruins, but nothing more. These traditions went but little way, for they concerned the length of the incarceration only, and not the names or the offenses. And even by the help of tradition the only thing that could be proven was that none of the five had seen daylight for thirty-five years: how much longer this privation had lasted was not guessable. The king and the queen knew nothing about these poor creatures, except that they were heirlooms, assets inherited, along with the throne, from the former firm. Nothing of their history had been transmitted with their persons, and so the inheriting owners had considered them of no value, and had felt no interest in them. I said to the queen—

"Then why in the world didn't you set them free?"

The question was a puzzler. She didn't know *why* she hadn't; the thing had never come up in her mind. So here she was, forecasting the veritable history of future prisoners of the castle d'If, without knowing it. It seemed plain to me now, that with her training, those inherited prisoners were merely property—nothing more, nothing less. Well, when we inherit property, it does not occur to us to throw it away, even when we do not value it.

When I brought my procession of human bats up into the open world and the glare of the afternoon sun—previously blind-folding them, in charity for eyes so long untortured by light—they were a spectacle to look at. Skeletons, scarecrows, goblins, pathetic frights, every one: legitimatest possible children of Monarchy by the Grace of God and the Established Church. I muttered absently—

"I *wish* I could photograph them!"

You have seen that kind of people who will never let on that they don't know the meaning of a new big word. The more ignorant they are, the more pitifully certain they are to pretend you haven't shot over their heads. The queen was just one of that sort, and was always making the stupidest blunders by reason of it. She hesitated a moment; then her face brightened up with sudden comprehension, and she said she would do it for me.

I thought to myself: She? why what can she know about photography? But it was a poor time to be thinking. When I looked around, she was moving on the procession with an ax!

Well, she certainly was a curious one, was Morgan le Fay. I have seen a good many kinds of women in my time, but she laid over them all, for variety. And how sharply characteristic of her this episode was. She had no more idea than a horse of how to photograph a procession; but being in doubt, it was just like her to try to do it with an ax.

XIX. KNIGHT-ERRANTRY AS A TRADE

SANDY AND I were on the road again, next morning, bright and early. It was so good to open up one's lungs and take in whole luscious barrelfuls of the blessed God's untainted, dew-freshened, woodland-scented air once more, after suffocating body and mind for two days and nights in the moral and physical stenches of that intolerable old buzzard roost! I mean, for me: of course the place was all right and agreeable for Sandy, for she had been used to high life all her days.

Poor girl, her jaws had had a wearisome rest, now for a while, and I was expecting to get the consequences. I was right; but she had stood by me most helpfully in the castle, and had mightily supported and reinforced me with gigantic foolishnesses which were worth more for the occasion than wisdoms double their size; so I thought she had earned a right to work her mill for a while, if she wanted to, and I felt not a pang when she started it up:

"Now turn we unto Sir Marhaus that rode with the damsel of thirty winter of age southward"—

"Are you going to see if you can work up another half-stretch on the trail of the cowboys, Sandy?"

"Even so, fair my lord."

"Go ahead, then. I won't interrupt this time, if I can help it. Begin over again; start fair, and shake out all your reefs, and I will load my pipe and give good attention."

"Now turn we unto Sir Marhaus that rode with the damsel of thirty winter of age southward. And so they came into a deep forest, and by fortune they were nighted, and rode along in a deep way, and at the last they came into a courtelage where abode the duke of South Marches, and there they asked harbor. And on the morn the duke sent unto Sir Marhaus, and bad him make him ready. And so Sir Marhaus arose and armed him, and there was a mass sung afore him, and he brake his fast, and so mounted on horseback in the court of the castle, there they should do the battle. So there was the duke already on horseback, clean armed, and his six sons by him, and every each had a spear in his hand, and so they encountered, whereas the duke and his two sons brake their spears upon him, but Sir Marhaus held up his spear and touched none of them. Then came the four sons by couples, and two of them brake their spears, and so did the other two. And all this while Sir Marhaus touched him not. Then Sir Marhaus ran to the duke, and smote him with his spear that horse and man fell to the earth. And so he served his sons. And then Sir Marhaus alight down, and bad the duke yield him or else he would slay him. And then some of his sons recovered, and would have set upon Sir Marhaus. Then Sir Marhaus said to the duke, Cease thy sons, or else I will do the uttermost to you all. When the duke saw he might not escape the death, he cried to his sons, and charged them to yield them to Sir Marhaus. And they kneeled all down and put the pommels of their swords to the knight, and so he received them. And then they holp up their father, and so by their common assent promised unto Sir Marhaus never to be foes unto King Arthur, and thereupon at Whitsuntide after, to come he and his sons, and put them in the king's grace.*

"Even so standeth the history, fair Sir Boss. Now ye shall wit that that very duke and his six sons are they whom but few days past you also did overcome and send to Arthur's court!"

"Why, Sandy, you can't mean it."

"An I speak not sooth, let it be the worse for me."

"Well, well, well—now who would ever have thought it? One whole duke and six dukelets; why, Sandy, it was an elegant haul. Knight-errantry is a most chuckle-headed trade, and it is tedious hard work, too, but I begin to see that there *is* money in it, after all, if you have luck. Not that I would ever engage in it as a business; for I wouldn't. No sound and legitimate business can be established on a basis of speculation. A successful whirl in the knight-errantry line—now what is it when you blow away the nonsense and come down to the cold facts? It's just a corner in pork, that's all, and you can't make anything else out of it. You're rich—yes—suddenly rich—for about a day, maybe a week: then somebody corners the market on *you*, and down goes your bucket shop; ain't that so, Sandy?"

"Whethersoever it be that my mind miscarrieth, bewraying simple language in such sort that the words do seem to come endlong and overthwart—"

"There's no use in beating about the bush and trying to get around it that way, Sandy, it's *so*, just as I say. I *know* it's so. And, moreover, when you come right down to the bedrock, knight-errantry is *worse*

---

*The story is borrowed, language and all, from the *Morte d'Arthur*.—M.T.

than pork; for whatever happens, the pork's left, and so somebody's benefited, anyway; but when the market breaks, in a knight-errantry whirl, and every knight in the pool passes in his checks, what have you got for assets? Just a rubbish pile of battered corpses and a barrel or two of busted hardware. Can you call *those* assets? Give me pork, every time. Am I right?"

"Ah, peradventure my head being distraught by the manifold matters whereunto the confusions of these but late adventured haps and fortunings whereby not I alone nor you alone, but every each of us, meseemeth—"

"No, it's not your head, Sandy. Your head's all right, as far as it goes, but you don't know business; that's where the trouble is. It unfits you to argue about business, and you're wrong to be always trying. However, that aside, it was a good haul, anyway, and will breed a handsome crop of reputation in Arthur's court. And speaking of the cowboys, what a curious country this is for women and men that never get old. Now there's Morgan le Fay, as fresh and young as a Vassar pullet, to all appearances, and here is this old duke of the South Marches still slashing away with sword and lance at his time of life, after raising such a family as he has raised. As I understand it, Sir Gawaine killed seven of his sons, and still he had six left for Sir Marhaus and me to take into camp. And then there was that damsel of sixty winter of age still excursioning around in her frosty bloom—How old are you, Sandy?"

It was the first time I ever struck a still place in her. The mill had shut down for repairs, or something.

XX. THE OGRE'S CASTLE

BETWEEN SIX and nine we made ten miles, which was plenty for a horse carrying triple—man, woman, and armor; then we stopped for a long nooning, under some trees by a limpid brook.

Right so came by and by a knight riding; and as he drew near he made dolorous moan, and by the words of it I perceived that he was cursing and swearing; yet nevertheless was I glad of his coming, for that I saw he bore a bulletin board whereon in letters all of shining gold was writ—

"USE PETERSON'S PROPHYLACTIC TOOTHBRUSH
—ALL THE GO."

I was glad of his coming, for even by this token I knew him for knight of mine. It was Sir Madok de la Montaine, a burly great fellow whose chief distinction was that he had come within an ace of sending Sir Launcelot down over his horsetail once. He was never long in a stranger's presence without finding some pretext or other to let out that great fact. But there was other fact of nearly the same size, which he never pushed upon anybody unasked, and yet never withheld when asked: that was, that the reason he didn't quite succeed was, that he was interrupted and sent down over horsetail himself. This innocent vast lubber did not see any particular difference between the two facts. I liked him, for he was earnest in his work, and very valuable. And he was so fine to look at, with his broad mailed shoulders, and the grand leonine set of his plumed head, and his big shield with its quaint device of a gauntleted hand clutching a prophylactic toothbrush, with motto: "*Try Noyoudont.*" This was a toothbrush that I was introducing.

He was aweary, he said, and indeed he looked it; but he would not alight. He said he was after the stove-polish man; and with this he broke out cursing and swearing anew. The bulletin boarder referred to was Sir Ossaise of Surluse, a brave knight, and of considerable celebrity on

101

account of his having tried conclusions in a tournament, once, with no less a Mogul than Sir Gaheris himself—although not successfully. He was of a light and laughing disposition, and to him nothing in this world was serious. It was for this reason that I had chosen him to work up a stove-polish sentiment. There were no stoves yet, and so there could be nothing serious about stove polish. All that the agent needed to do was to deftly and by degrees prepare the public for the great change, and have them established in predilections toward neatness against the time when the stove should appear upon the stage.

Sir Madok was very bitter, and brake out anew with cursings. He said he had cursed his soul to rags; and yet he would not get down from his horse, neither would he take any rest, or listen to any comfort, until he should have found Sir Ossaise and settled this account. It appeared, by what I could piece together of the unprofane fragments of his statement, that he had chanced upon Sir Ossaise at dawn of the morning, and been told that if he would make a shortcut across the fields and swamps and broken hills and glades, he could head off a company of travelers who would be rare customers for prophylactics and toothwash. With characteristic zeal Sir Madok had plunged away at once upon this quest, and after three hours of awful crosslot riding had overhauled his game. And behold, it was the five patriarchs that had been released from the dungeons the evening before! Poor old creatures, it was all of twenty years since any one of them had known what it was to be equipped with any remaining snag or remnant of a tooth.

"Blank-blank-blank him," said Sir Madok, "an I do not stove polish him an I may find him, leave it to me; for never no knight that hight Ossaise or aught else may do me this disservice and bide on live, an I may find him, the which I have thereunto sworn a great oath this day."

And with these words, and others, he lightly took his spear and gat him thence. In the middle of the afternoon we came upon one of those very patriarchs ourselves, on the edge of a poor village. He was basking in the love of relatives and friends whom he had not seen for fifty years; and about him and caressing him were also descendants of his own body whom he had never seen at all till now; but to him these were all strangers, his memory was gone, his mind was stagnant. It seemed incredible that a man could outlast half a century shut up in a dark hole like a rat, but here were his old wife and some old comrades to testify to it. They could remember him as he was in the freshness and strength of his young manhood, when he kissed his child and delivered it to its mother's hands and went away into that long oblivion. The people at the castle could not tell within half a generation the length of time the man had been shut up there for his unrecorded and forgotten offense; but this old wife knew; and so did her old child, who stood there among her married sons and daughters trying to realize a father who had been to her a name, a thought, a formless image, a tradition, all her life, and now was suddenly concreted into actual flesh and blood and set before her face.

It was a curious situation; yet it is not on that account that I have made room for it here, but on account of a thing which seemed to me still more curious. To wit, that this dreadful matter brought from these downtrodden people no outburst of rage against their oppressors. They had been heritors and subjects of cruelty and outrage so long that nothing could have startled them but a kindness. Yes, here was a curious revelation indeed, of the depth to which this people had been sunk in slavery. Their entire being was reduced to a monotonous dead level of patience, resignation, dumb uncomplaining acceptance of whatever might befall them in this life. Their very imagination was dead. When you can say that of a man, he has struck bottom, I reckon; there is no lower deep for him.

I rather wished I had gone some other road. This was not the sort of experience for a statesman to encounter who was planning out a peaceful revolution in his mind. For it could not help bringing up the un-get-aroundable fact that, all gentle cant and philosophising to the contrary notwithstanding, no people in the world ever did achieve their freedom by goody-goody talk and moral suasion: it being immutable law that all revolutions that will succeed, must *begin* in blood, whatever may answer afterward. If history teaches anything, it teaches that. What this folk needed, then, was a Reign of Terror and a guillotine, and I was the wrong man for them.

Two days later, toward noon, Sandy began to show signs of excitement and feverish expectancy. She said we were approaching the ogre's castle. I was surprised into an uncomfortable shock. The object of our quest had gradually dropped out of my mind; this sudden resurrection of it made it seem quite a real and startling thing, for a moment, and roused up in me a smart interest. Sandy's excitement increased every moment; and so did mine, for that sort of thing is catching. My heart got to thumping. You can't reason with your heart; it has its own laws, and thumps about things which the intellect scorns. Presently, when Sandy slid from the horse, motioned me to stop, and went creeping stealthily, with her head bent nearly to her knees, toward a row of bushes that bordered a declivity, the thumpings grew stronger and quicker. And they kept it up while she was gaining her ambush and getting her glimpse over the declivity and also while I was creeping to her side on my knees. Her eyes were burning, now, as she pointed with her finger, and said in a panting whisper—

"The castle! The castle! Lo, where it looms!"

What a welcome disappointment I experienced! I said—

"Castle? It is nothing but a pigsty; a pigsty with a wattled fence around it."

She looked surprised and distressed. The animation faded out of her face, and during many moments she was lost in thought and silent. Then—

"It was not enchanted aforetime," she said in a musing fashion, as if to herself. "And how strange is this marvel, and how awful—that to the one perception it is enchanted and dight in a base and shameful aspect; yet to the perception of the other it is not enchanted, hath suffered no change, but stands firm and stately still, girt with its moat and waving its banners in the blue air from its towers. And God shield us, how it pricks the heart to see again these gracious captives, and the sorrow deepened in their sweet faces! We have tarried long, and are to blame."

I saw my cue. The castle was enchanted to *me*, not to her. It would be wasted time to try to argue her out of her delusion, it couldn't be done; I must just humor it. So I said—

"This is a common case—the enchanting of a thing to one eye and leaving it in its proper form to another. You have heard of it before, Sandy, though you haven't happened to experience it. But no harm is done. In fact it is lucky the way it is. If these ladies were hogs to everybody and to themselves, it would be necessary to break the enchantment, and that might be impossible if one failed to find out the particular process of the enchantment. And hazardous, too; for in attempting a disenchantment without the true key, you are liable to err, and turn your hogs into dogs, and the dogs into cats, the cats into rats, and so on, and end by reducing your materials to nothing, finally, or to an odorless gas which you can't follow—which of course amounts to the same thing. But here, by good luck, no one's eyes but mine are under the enchantment, and so it is of no consequence to dissolve it. These ladies remain ladies to you, and to themselves, and to everybody else; and at the same time they will suffer in no way from my delusion, for when I know that an ostensible hog is a lady, that is enough for me, I know how to treat her."

"Thanks, oh sweet my lord, thou talkest like an angel. And I know that thou wilt deliver them, for that thou art minded to great deeds and art as strong a knight of your hands and as brave to will and to do, as any that is on live."

"I will not leave a princess in the sty, Sandy. Are those three yonder that to my disordered eyes are starveling swineherds"—

"The ogres? Are *they* changed also? It is most wonderful. Now am I fearful; for how canst thou strike with sure aim when five of their nine cubits of stature are to thee invisible? Ah, go warily, fair sir; this is a mightier emprise than I wend."

"You be easy, Sandy. All I need to know is, how *much* of an ogre is invisible; then I know how to locate his vitals. Don't you be afraid, I will make short work of these bunco steerers. Stay where you are."

I left Sandy kneeling there, corpse-faced but plucky and hopeful, and rode down to the pigsty, and struck up a trade with the swineherds. I won their gratitude by buying out all the hogs at the lump sum of sixteen pennies, which was rather above latest quotations. I was just in time; for the Church, the lord of the manor, and the rest of the tax gatherers would have been along next day and swept off pretty much all the stock, leaving the swineherds very short of hogs and Sandy out of princesses. But now the tax people could be paid in cash, and there would be a stake left besides. One of the men had ten children; and he said that last year when a priest came and of his ten pigs took the fattest one for tithes, the wife burst out upon him, and offered him a child and said—

"Thou beast without bowels of mercy, why leave me my child, yet rob me of the wherewithal to feed it?"

How curious. The same thing had happened in the Wales of my day, under this same old Established Church, which was supposed by many to have changed its nature when it changed its disguise.

I sent the three men away, and then opened the sty gate and beckoned Sandy to come—which she did; and not leisurely, but with the rush of a prairie fire. And when I saw her fling herself upon those hogs, with tears of joy running down her cheeks, and strain them to her heart, and kiss them, and caress them, and call them reverently by grand princely names, I was ashamed of her, ashamed of the human race.

We had to drive those hogs home—ten miles; and no ladies were ever more fickle-minded or contrary. They would stay in no road, no path; they broke out through the brush on all sides, and flowed away in all directions, over rocks, and hills, and the roughest places they could find. And they must not be struck, or roughly accosted; Sandy could not bear to see them treated in ways unbecoming their rank. The troublesomest old sow of the lot had to be called my Lady, and your Highness, like the rest. It is annoying and difficult to scour around after hogs, in armor. There was one small countess, with an iron ring in her snout and hardly any hair on her back, that was the devil for perversity. She gave me a race of an hour, over all sorts of country, and then we were right where we had started from, having made not a rod of real progress. I seized her at last by the tail, and brought her along, squealing. When I overtook Sandy, she was horrified, and said it was in the last degree indelicate to drag a countess by her train.

We got the hogs home just at dark—most of them. The princess Nerovens de Morganore was missing, and two of her ladies in waiting:

namely, Miss Angela Bohun, and the Demoiselle Elaine Courtemains, the former of these two being a young black sow with a white star in her forehead, and the latter a brown one with thin legs and a slight limp in the forward shank on the starboard side—a couple of the tryingest blisters to drive, that I ever saw. Also among the missing were several mere baronesses—and I wanted them to stay missing; but no, all that sausage meat had to be found; so, servants were sent out with torches to scour the woods and hills to that end.

Of course the whole drove was housed in the house, and great guns—well, I never saw anything like it! Nor ever heard anything like it. And never smelt anything like it. It was like an insurrection in a gasometer.

XXI. THE PILGRIMS

WHEN I DID get to bed at last I was unspeakably tired; the stretching out, and the relaxing of the long-tense muscles, how luxurious, how delicious! but that was as far as I could get—sleep was out of the question, for the present. The ripping and tearing and squealing of the nobility up and down the halls and corridors was pandemonium come again and kept me broad awake. Being awake, my thoughts were busy, of course, and mainly they busied themselves with Sandy's curious delusion. Here she was, as sane a person as the kingdom could produce, and yet, from my point of view she was acting like a crazy woman! My land, the power of training! Of influence! Of education! It can bring a body up to believe anything. I had to put myself in Sandy's place to realize that she was not a lunatic. Yes, and put her in mine, to demonstrate how easy it is to seem a lunatic to a person who has not been taught as you have been taught. If I had told Sandy I had seen a wagon, uninfluenced by enchantment, spin along fifty miles an hour; had seen a man, unequipped with magic powers, get into a basket and soar out of sight among the clouds; and had listened, without any necromancer's help, to the conversation of a person who was several hundred miles away, Sandy would not merely have supposed me to be crazy, she would have thought she knew it. Everybody around her believed in enchantments; nobody had any doubts; to doubt that a castle could be turned into a sty, and its occupants into hogs, would have been the same as my doubting, among Connecticut people, the actuality of the telephone and its wonders—and in both cases would be absolute proof of a diseased mind, an unsettled reason. Yes, Sandy was sane; that must be admitted. If I also would be sane—to Sandy—I must keep my superstitions about unenchanted and unmiraculous locomotives, balloons, and telephones to myself. Also, I believed that the world was not flat, and hadn't pillars under it to support it, nor a canopy over it to turn off a universe of water that occupied all space above: but as I was the only person in the kingdom afflicted with such impious and criminal

107

opinions, I recognized that it would be good wisdom to keep quiet about this matter, too, if I did not wish to be suddenly shunned and forsaken by everybody as a madman.

The next morning Sandy assembled the swine in the dining room and gave them their breakfast, waiting upon them personally and manifesting in every way the deep reverence which the natives of her island, ancient and modern, have always felt for rank, let its outward casket and the mental and moral contents be what they may. I could have eaten with the hogs if I had had birth approaching my lofty official rank; but I hadn't, and so accepted the unavoidable slight and made no complaint. Sandy and I had our breakfast at the second table. The family were not at home. I said:

"How many are in the family, Sandy, and where do they keep themselves?"

"Family?"

"Yes."

"Which family, good my lord?"

"Why, this family; your own family."

"Sooth to say, I understand you not. I have no family."

"No family? Why, Sandy, isn't this your home?"

"Now how indeed might that be? I have no home."

"Well, then, whose house is this?"

"Ah, wit you well I would tell you an I knew myself."

"Come—you don't even know these people? Then who invited us here?"

"None invited us. We but came; that is all."

"Why, woman, this is a most extraordinary performance. The effrontery of it is beyond admiration. We blandly march into a man's house, and cram it full of the only really valuable nobility the sun has yet discovered in the earth, and then it turns out that we don't even know the man's name. How did you ever venture to take this extravagant liberty? I supposed, of course, it was your home. What will the man say?"

"What will he say? Forsooth what can he say but give thanks?"

"Thanks for what?"

Her face was filled with a puzzled surprise:

"Verily, thou troublest mine understanding with strange words. Do ye dream that one of his estate is like to have the honor twice in his life to entertain company such as we have brought to grace his house withal?"

"Well, no—when you come to that. No, it's an even bet that this is the first time he has had a treat like this."

"Then let him be thankful, and manifest the same by grateful speech and due humility; he were a dog, else, and the heir and ancestor of dogs."

To my mind, the situation was uncomfortable. It might become more so. It might be a good idea to muster the hogs and move on. So I said:

"The day is wasting, Sandy. It is time to get the nobility together and be moving."

"Wherefore, fair sir and Boss?"

"We want to take them to their home, don't we?"

"La, but list to him! They be of all the regions of the earth! Each must hie to her own home; wend you we might do all these journeys in one so brief life as He hath appointed that created life, and thereto death likewise with help of Adam, who by sin done through persuasion of his helpmeet, she being wrought upon and bewrayed by the beguilements of the great enemy of man, that serpent hight Satan, aforetime consecrated and set apart unto that evil work by overmastering spite and envy begotten in his heart through fell ambitions that did blight and mildew a nature erst so white and pure whenso it hove with the shining multitudes its brethren-born in glade and shade of that fair heaven wherein all such as native be to that rich estate and——"

"Great Scott!"

"My lord?"

"Well, you know we haven't got time for this sort of thing. Don't you see, we could distribute these people around the earth in less time than it is going to take you to explain that we can't. We mustn't talk now, we must act. You want to be careful; you mustn't let your mill get the start of you that way, at a time like this. To business, now—and sharp's the word. Who is to take the aristocracy home?"

"Even their friends. These will come for them from the far parts of the earth."

This was lightning from a clear sky, for unexpectedness; and the relief of it was like pardon to a prisoner. She would remain to deliver the goods, of course.

"Well, then, Sandy, as our enterprise is handsomely and successfully ended, I will go home and report; and if ever another one—"

"I also am ready; I will go with thee."

This was recalling the pardon.

"How? You will go with me? Why should you?"

"Will I be traitor to my knight, dost think? That were dishonor. I may not part from thee until in knightly encounter in the field some overmatching champion shall fairly win and fairly wear me. I were to blame an I thought that that might ever hap."

"Elected for the long term," I sighed to myself. "I may as well make the best of it." So then I spoke up and said:

"All right; let us make a start."

While she was gone to cry her farewells over the pork, I gave that whole peerage away to the servants. And I asked them to take a duster and dust around a little where the nobilities had mainly lodged and promenaded, but they considered that that would be hardly worthwhile, and would moreover be a rather grave departure from custom, and therefore likely to make talk. A departure from custom—that settled it; it was a nation capable of committing any crime but that. The servants said they would follow the fashion, a fashion grown sacred through immemorial observance: they would scatter fresh rushes in all the rooms and halls, and then the evidence of the aristocratic visitation would be no longer visible. It was a kind of satire on Nature; it was the scientific method, the geologic method; it deposited the history of the family in a stratified record; and the antiquary could dig through it and tell by the remains of each period what changes of diet the family had introduced successively for a hundred years.

The first thing we struck that day was a procession of pilgrims. It was not going our way, but we joined it nevertheless; for it was hourly being borne in upon me, now, that if I would govern this country wisely, I must be posted in the details of its life, and not at second hand but by personal observation and scrutiny.

This company of pilgrims resembled Chaucer's in this: that it had in it a sample of about all the upper occupations and professions the country could show, and a corresponding variety of costume. There were young men and old men, young women and old women, lively folk and grave folk. They rode upon mules and horses, and there was not a sidesaddle in the party; for this specialty was to remain unknown in England for nine hundred years yet.

It was a pleasant, friendly, sociable herd; pious, happy, merry, and full of unconscious coarsenesses and innocent indecencies. What they regarded as the merry tale went the continual round and caused no more embarrassment than it would have caused in the best English society twelve centuries later. Practical jokes worthy of the English wits of the first quarter of the far-off nineteenth century were sprung here and there and yonder along the line, and compelled the delightedest applause; and sometimes when a bright remark was made at one end of the procession and started on its travels toward the other, you could note its progress all the way by the sparkling spray of laughter it threw off from its bows as it plowed along; and also by the blushes of the mules in its wake.

Sandy knew the goal and purpose of this pilgrimage and she posted me. She said:

"They journey to the Valley of Holiness, for to be blessed of the godly hermits and drink of the miraculous waters and be cleansed from sin."

"Where is this watering place?"

"It lieth a two day journey hence, by the borders of the land that hight the Cuckoo Kingdom."

"Tell me about it. Is it a celebrated place?"

"Oh, of a truth, yes. There be none more so. Of old time there lived there an abbot and his monks. Belike were none in the world more holy than these; for they gave themselves to study of pious books, and spoke not the one to the other, or indeed to any, and ate decayed herbs and naught thereto, and slept hard, and prayed much, and washed never; also they wore the same garment until it fell from their bodies through age and decay. Right so came they to be known of all the world by reason of these holy austerities, and visited by rich and poor, and reverenced."

"Proceed."

"But always there was lack of water there. Whereas, upon a time, the holy abbot prayed, and for answer a great stream of clear water burst forth by miracle in a desert place. Now were the fickle monks tempted of the Fiend, and they wrought with their abbot unceasingly by beggings and beseechings that he would construct a bath; and when he was become aweary and might not resist more, he said have ye your will, then, and granted that they asked. Now mark thou what 'tis to forsake the ways of purity the which He loveth, and wanton with such as be worldly and an offense. These monks did enter into the bath and come thence washed as white as snow; and lo, in that moment His sign appeared, in miraculous rebuke! for His insulted waters ceased to flow, and utterly vanished away."

"They fared mildly, Sandy, considering how that kind of crime is regarded in this country."

"Belike; but it was their first sin; and they had been of perfect life for long, and differing in naught from the angels. Prayers, tears, torturings of the flesh, all was vain to beguile that water to flow again. Even processions; even burnt offerings; even votive candles to the Virgin, did fail every each of them; and all in the land did marvel."

"How odd to find that even this industry has its financial panics, and at times sees its assignats and greenbacks languish to zero, and everything come to a standstill. Go on, Sandy."

"And so upon a time, after year and day, the good abbot made humble surrender and destroyed the bath. And behold, His anger was in that moment appeased, and the waters gushed richly forth again, and even unto this day they have not ceased to flow in that generous measure."

"Then I take it nobody has washed since."

"He that would essay it could have his halter free; yea, and swiftly would he need it, too."

"The community has prospered since?"

"Even from that very day. The fame of the miracle went abroad into all lands. From every land came monks to join; they came even as the fishes come, in shoals; and the monastery added building to building, and yet others to these, and so spread wide its arms and took them in. And nuns came, also; and more again, and yet more; and built over against the monastery on the yon side of the vale, and added building to building, until mighty was that nunnery. And these were friendly unto those, and they joined their loving labors together, and together they built a fair great foundling asylum midway of the valley between."

"You spoke of some hermits, Sandy."

"These have gathered there from the ends of the earth. A hermit thriveth best where there be multitudes of pilgrims. Ye shall not find no hermit of no sort wanting. If any shall mention a hermit of a kind he thinketh new and not to be found but in some far strange land, let him but scratch among the holes and caves and swamps that line that Valley of Holiness, and whatsoever be his breed, it skills not, he shall find a sample of it there."

I closed up alongside of a burly fellow with a fat good-humored face, purposing to make myself agreeable and pick up some further crumbs of fact; but I had hardly more than scraped acquaintance with him when he began eagerly and awkwardly to lead up, in the immemorial way, to that same old anecdote—the one Sir Dinadan told me, what time I got into trouble with Sir Sagramor and was challenged of him on account of it. I excused myself and dropped to the rear of the procession, sad at heart, willing to go hence from this troubled life, this vale of tears, this brief day of broken rest, of cloud and storm, of weary struggle and monotonous defeat; and yet shrinking from the change, as remembering how long eternity is, and how many have wended thither who know that anecdote.

Early in the afternoon we overtook another procession of pilgrims; but in this one was no merriment, no jokes, no laughter, no playful ways, nor any happy giddiness, whether of youth or age. Yet both were here, both age and youth: gray old men and women, strong men and women of middle age, young husbands, young wives, little boys and girls, and three babies at the breast. Even the children were smileless; there was not a face among all these half a hundred people but was cast down and bore that set expression of hopelessness which is bred of long and hard trials and old acquaintance with despair. They were slaves. Chains led from their fettered feet and their manacled hands to a sole-leather belt about their waists; and all except the children were also linked together in a file, six feet apart, by a single chain which led from collar to collar all down the line. They were on foot, and had tramped three hundred miles in eighteen days, upon the cheapest odds and ends of food, and stingy rations of that. They had slept in these chains every night, bundled together like swine. They had upon their bodies some poor rags, but they could not be said to be clothed. Their irons had chafed the skin from their ankles and made sores which were ulcerated and wormy. Their naked feet were torn, and none walked without a limp. Originally there had been a hundred of these unfortunates, but about half had been sold on the trip. The trader in charge of them rode a horse and carried a whip with a short handle and a long heavy lash divided into several knotted tails at the end. With this whip he cut the shoulders of any that tottered from weariness and pain, and straightened them up. He did not speak; the whip conveyed his desire without that. None of these poor creatures looked up as we rode along by; they showed no consciousness of our presence. And they made no sound but one; that was the dull and awful clank of their chains from end to end of the long file, as forty-three burdened feet rose and fell in unison. The file moved in a cloud of its own making.

All these faces were gray with a coating of dust. One has seen the like of this coating upon furniture in unoccupied houses, and has written his idle thought in it with his finger. I was reminded of this when I noticed the faces of some of those women, young mothers carrying babes that were near to death and freedom, how a something in their hearts was written in the dust upon their faces, plain to see, and lord how plain to read! For it was the track of tears. One of these young mothers was but a girl, and it hurt me to the heart to read that writing, and reflect that it was come up out of the breast of such a child, a breast that ought not to know trouble yet, but only the gladness of the morning of life; and no doubt—

She reeled just then, giddy with fatigue, and down came the lash and flicked a flake of skin from her naked shoulder. It stung me as if I had been hit instead. The master halted the file and jumped from his horse. He stormed and swore at this girl, and said she had made annoyance enough with her laziness, and as this was the last chance he should have, he would settle the account now. She dropped on her knees and put up her hands and began to beg and cry and implore, in a passion of terror, but the master gave no attention. He snatched the child from her, and then made the men slaves who were chained before and behind her throw her on the ground and hold her there and expose her body; and then he laid on with his lash like a madman till her back was flayed, she shrieking and struggling the while, piteously. One of the men who was holding her turned away his face, and for this humanity he was reviled and flogged.

All our pilgrims looked on and commented—on the expert way in which the whip was handled. They were too much hardened by life-long everyday familiarity with slavery to notice that there was anything else in the exhibition that invited comment. This was what slavery could do, in the way of ossifying what one may call the superior lobe of human feeling; for these pilgrims were kindhearted people, and they would not have allowed that man to treat a horse like that.

I wanted to stop the whole thing and set the slaves free, but that would not do. I must not interfere too much and get myself a name for riding over the country's laws and the citizen's rights roughshod. If I lived and prospered I would be the death of slavery, that I was resolved upon; but I would try to fix it so that when I became its executioner it should be by command of the nation.

Just here was the wayside shop of a smith; and now arrived a landed proprietor who had bought this girl a few miles back, deliverable here where her irons could be taken off. They were removed; then there was a squabble between the gentleman and the dealer as to which should pay the blacksmith. The moment the girl was delivered from her irons, she flung herself, all tears and frantic sobbings, into the arms of the slave who had turned away his face when she was whipped. He strained her to his breast, and smothered her face and the child's with kisses, and washed them with the rain of his tears. I suspected. I inquired. Yes, I was right: it was husband and wife. They had to be torn apart by force; the girl had to be dragged away, and she struggled and fought and shrieked like one gone mad till a turn of the road hid her from sight; and even after that, we could still make out the fading plaint of those receding shrieks. And the husband and father, with his wife and child gone, never to be seen by him again in life—well, the look of him one might not bear at all, and so I turned away; but I knew I should never get his picture out of my mind again, and there it is to this day, to wring my heartstrings whenever I think of it.

We put up at the inn in a village just at nightfall, and when I rose next morning and looked abroad, I was ware where a knight came riding in the golden glory of the new day, and recognized him for knight of mine—Sir Ozana le Cure Hardy. He was in the gentlemen's furnishing line, and his missionarying speciality was plug hats. He was clothed all in steel, in the beautifulest armor of the time—up to where his helmet ought to have been; but he hadn't any helmet, he wore a shiny stovepipe hat, and was as ridiculous a spectacle as one might want to see. It was another of my surreptitious schemes for extinguishing knighthood by making it grotesque and absurd. Sir Ozana's saddle was hung about with leather hatboxes, and every time he overcame a wandering knight he swore him into my service and fitted him with a plug and made him wear it. I dressed and ran down to welcome Sir Ozana and get his news.

"How is trade?" I asked.

"Ye will note that I have but these four left; yet were they sixteen whenas I got me from Camelot."

"Why, you have certainly done nobly, Sir Ozana. Where have you been foraging of late?"

"I am but now come from the Valley of Holiness, please you sir."

"I am pointed for that place myself. Is there anything stirring in the monkery, more than common?"

"By the mass ye may not question it! . . . Give him good feed, boy, and stint it not, an thou valuest thy crown; so get ye lightly to the stable and do even as I bid. . . . Sir, it is parlous news I bring, and—be these pilgrims? Then ye may not do better, good folk, than gather and hear the tale I have to tell, sith it concerneth you, forasmuch as ye go to find that ye will not find, and seek that ye will seek in vain, my life being hostage for my word, and my word and message being these, namely: That a hap has happened whereof the like has not been seen no more but once this two hundred years, which was the first and last time that that said misfortune strake the holy valley in that form by command-ment of the Most High whereto by reasons just and causes thereunto contributing, wherein the matter—"

"The miraculous fount hath ceased to flow!" This shout burst from twenty pilgrim mouths at once.

"Ye say well, good people. I was verging to it, even when ye spake."

"Has somebody been washing again?"

"Nay, it is suspected, but none believe it. It is thought to be some other sin, but none wit what."

"How are they feeling about the calamity?"

"None may describe it in words. The fount is these nine days dry. The prayers that did begin then, and the lamentations in sackcloth and ashes, and the holy processions, none of these have ceased nor night nor day; and so the monks and the nuns and the foundlings be all exhausted, and do hang up prayers writ upon parchment, sith that no strength is left in man to lift up voice. And at last they sent for thee, Sir Boss, to try magic and enchantment; and if you could not come, then was the messenger to fetch Merlin, and he is there these three days, now, and saith he will fetch that water though he burst the globe and wreck its kingdoms to accomplish it; and right bravely doth he work his magic and call upon his hellions to hie them hither and help, but not a whiff of moisture hath he started yet, even so much as might qualify as mist upon a copper mirror an ye count not the barrel of sweat he sweatheth betwixt sun and sun over the dire labors of his task; and if ye——"

Breakfast was ready. As soon as it was over I showed to Sir Ozana these words which I had written on the inside of his hat: *"Chemical Department, Laboratory extension, Section G. Pxxp. Send two of first size, two of No. 3 and six of No. 4, together with the proper complementary details—and two of my trained assistants."* And I said:

"Now get you to Camelot as fast as you can fly, brave knight, and show the writing to Clarence, and tell him to have these required matters in the Valley of Holiness with all possible dispatch."

"I will well, Sir Boss," and he was off.

XXII. THE HOLY FOUNTAIN

THE PILGRIMS were human beings. Otherwise they would have acted differently. They had come a long and difficult journey, and now when the journey was nearly finished, and they learned that the main thing they had come for had ceased to exist, they didn't do as horses or cats or angleworms would probably have done—turn back and get at something profitable—no, anxious as they had before been to see the miraculous fountain, they were as much as forty times as anxious now to see the place where it had used to be. There is no accounting for human beings.

We made good time, and a couple of hours before sunset we stood upon the high confines of the Valley of Holiness and our eyes swept it from end to end and noted its features. That is, its large features. These were the three masses of buildings. They were distant and isolated temporalities shrunken to toy constructions in the lonely waste of what seemed a desert—and was. Such a scene is always mournful, it is so impressively still, and looks so steeped in death. But there was a sound here which interrupted the stillness only to add to its mournfulness; this was the faint far sound of tolling bells which floated fitfully to us on the passing breeze, and so faintly, so softly, that we hardly knew whether we heard it with our ears or with our spirits.

We reached the monastery before dark, and there the males were given lodging, but the women were sent over to the nunnery. The bells were close at hand, now, and their solemn booming smote upon the ear like a message of doom. A superstitious despair possessed the heart of every monk and published itself in his ghastly face. Everywhere, these black-robed, soft-sandled, tallow-visaged specters appeared, flitted about, and disappeared, noiseless as the creatures of a troubled dream, and as uncanny.

The old abbot's joy to see me was pathetic. Even to tears; but he did the shedding himself. He said:

"Delay not, son, but get to thy saving work. An we bring not the water back again, and soon, we are ruined, and the good work of two hundred years must end. And see thou do it with enchantments that be holy, for the Church will not endure that work in her cause be done by devil's magic."

"When I work, Father, be sure there will be no devil's work connected with it. I shall use no arts that come of the devil, and no elements not created by the hand of God. But is Merlin working strictly on pious lines?"

"Ah, he said he would, my son, he said he would, and took oath to make his promise good."

"Well, in that case, let him proceed."

"But surely you will not sit idle by, but help?"

"It will not answer to mix methods, Father; neither would it be professional courtesy. Two of a trade must not underbid each other. We might as well cut rates and be done with it; it would arrive at that in the end. Merlin has the contract; no other magician can touch it till he throws it up."

"But I will take it from him; it is a terrible emergency and the act is thereby justified. And if it were not so, who will give law to the Church? The Church giveth law to all; and what she wills to do, that she may do, hurt whom it may. I will take it from him; you shall begin upon the moment."

"It may not be, Father. No doubt, as you say, where power is supreme, one can do as one likes and suffer no injury; but we poor magicians are not so situated. Merlin is a very good magician in a small way, and has quite a neat provincial reputation. He is struggling along, doing the best he can, and it would not be etiquette for me to take his job until he himself abandons it."

The abbot's face lighted.

"Ah, that is simple. There are ways to persuade him to abandon it."

"No-no, Father, it skills not, as these people say. If he were persuaded against his will, he would load that well with a malicious enchantment which would balk me until I found out its secret. It might take a month. I could set up a little enchantment of mine which I call the telephone, and he could not find out its secret in a hundred years. Yes, you perceive, he might block me for a month. Would you like to risk a month in a dry time like this?"

"A month! The mere thought of it maketh me to shudder. Have it thy way, my son. But my heart is heavy with this disappointment. Leave me, and let me wear my spirit with weariness and waiting, even as I have done these ten long days, counterfeiting thus the thing that is called rest, the prone body making outward sign of repose where inwardly is none."

Of course it would have been best, all round, for Merlin to waive etiquette and quit and call it half a day, since he would never be able to start that water, for he was a true magician of the time: which is to say, the big miracles, the ones that gave him his reputation, always had the luck to be performed when nobody but Merlin was present; he couldn't start this well with all this crowd around to see; a crowd was as bad for a magician's miracle in that day as it was for a spiritualist's miracle in mine: there was sure to be some skeptic on hand to turn up the gas at the crucial moment and spoil everything. But I did not want Merlin to retire from the job until I was ready to take hold of it effectively myself; and I could not do that until I got my things from Camelot, and that would take two or three days.

My presence gave the monks hope, and cheered them up a good deal; insomuch that they ate a square meal that night for the first time in ten days. As soon as their stomachs had been properly reinforced with food, their spirits began to rise fast; when the mead began to go round they rose faster. By the time everybody was half-seas over, the holy community was in good shape to make a night of it; so we stayed by the board and put it through on that line. Matters got to be very jolly. Good old questionable stories were told that made the tears run down and cavernous mouths stand wide and the round bellies shake with laughter; and questionable songs were bellowed out in a mighty chorus that drowned the boom of the tolling bells.

At last I ventured a story myself; and vast was the success of it. Not right off, of course, for the native of those islands does not as a rule dissolve upon the early applications of a humorous thing; but the fifth time I told it, they began to crack, in places; the eighth time I told it, they began to crumble; at the twelfth repetition they fell apart in chunks; and at the fifteenth they disintegrated, and I got a broom and swept them up. This language is figurative. Those islanders—well, they are slow pay, at first, in the matter of return for your investment of effort, but in the end they make the pay of all other nations poor and small by contrast.

I was at the well next day betimes. Merlin was there, enchanting away like a beaver, but not raising the moisture. He was not in a pleasant humor; and every time I hinted that perhaps this contract was a shade too hefty for a novice he unlimbered his tongue and cursed like a bishop—French bishop of the Regency days, I mean.

Matters were about as I expected to find them. "The "fountain" was an ordinary well, it had been dug in the ordinary way, and stoned up in the ordinary way. There was no miracle about it. Even the lie that had created its reputation was not miraculous; I could have told it myself, with one hand tied behind me. The well was in a dark chamber which stood in the center of a cut-stone chapel, whose walls were hung with pious pictures of a workmanship that would have made a chromo feel good; pictures historically commemorative of curative miracles which had been achieved by the waters when nobody was looking. That is, nobody but angels: they are always on deck when there is a miracle to the fore—so as to get put in the picture, perhaps. Angels are as fond of that as a fire company; look at the old masters.

The well chamber was dimly lighted by lamps; the water was drawn with a windlass and chain, by monks, and poured into troughs which delivered it into stone reservoirs outside, in the chapel—when there was water to draw, I mean—and none but monks could enter the well chamber. I entered it, for I had temporary authority to do so, by courtesy of my professional brother and subordinate. But he hadn't entered it himself. He did everything by incantations; he never worked his intellect. If he had stepped in there and used his eyes, instead of his disordered mind, he could have cured the well by natural means, and then turned it into a miracle in the customary way; but no, he was an old numskull, a magician who believed in his own magic; and no magician can thrive who is handicapped with a superstition like that.

I had an idea that the well had sprung a leak; that some of the wall stones near the bottom had fallen and exposed fissures that allowed the water to escape. I measured the chain—ninety-eight feet. Then I called in a couple of monks, locked the door, took a candle, and made them lower me in the bucket. When the chain was all paid out, the candle confirmed my suspicion; a considerable section of the wall was gone, exposing a good big fissure.

I almost regretted that my theory about the well's trouble was correct, because I had another one that had a showy point or two about it for a miracle. I remembered that in America, many centuries later, when an oil well ceased to flow, they used to blast it out with a dynamite torpedo. If I should find this well dry, and no explanation of it, I could astonish these people most nobly by having a person of no especial value drop a dynamite bomb into it. It was my idea to appoint Merlin. However, it was plain that there was no occasion for the bomb. One cannot have everything the way he would like it. A man has no business to be depressed by a disappointment, anyway; he ought to make up his mind to get even. That is what I did. I said to myself, I am in no hurry, I can wait; that bomb will come good, yet. And it did, too.

When I was above ground again, I turned out the monks, and let down a fishline: the well was a hundred and fifty feet deep, and there was forty-one feet of water in it! I called in a monk and asked:

"How deep is the well?"

"That, sir, I wit not, having never been told."

"How does the water usually stand in it?"

"Near to the top, these two centuries, as the testimony goeth, brought down to us through our predecessors."

It was true—as to recent times at least—for there was witness to it, and better witness than a monk: only about twenty or thirty feet of the chain showed wear and use, the rest of it was unworn and rusty. What had happened when the well gave out that other time? Without doubt some practical person had come along and mended the leak, and then had come up and told the abbot he had discovered by divination that if the sinful bath were destroyed the well would flow again. The leak had befallen again, now, and these children would have prayed, and processioned, and tolled their bells for heavenly succor till they all dried up and blew away, and no innocent of them all would ever have thought to drop a fishline into the well or go down in it and find out what was really the matter. Old habit of mind is one of the toughest things to get away from in the world. It transmits itself like physical form and feature; and for a man, in those days, to have had an idea that his ancestors hadn't had, would have brought him under suspicion of being illegitimate. I said to the monk:

"It is a difficult miracle to restore water in a dry well, but we will try, if my brother Merlin fails. Brother Merlin is a very passable artist, but only in the parlor magic line, and he may not succeed; in fact is not likely to succeed. But that should be nothing to his discredit; the man that can do *this* kind of miracle knows enough to keep hotel."

"Hotel? I mind not to have heard——"

"Of hotel? It's what you call hostel. The man that can do this miracle can keep hostel. I can do this miracle; I shall do this miracle; yet I do not try to conceal from you that it is a miracle to tax the occult powers to the last strain."

"None knoweth that truth better than the brotherhood, indeed; for it is of record that aforetime it was parlous difficult and took a year. Natheless, God send you good success, and to that end will we pray."

As a matter of business it was a good idea to get the notion around that the thing was difficult. Many a small thing has been made large by the right kind of advertising. That monk was filled up with the difficulty of this enterprise; he would fill up the others. In two days the solicitude would be booming.

On my way home at noon, I met Sandy. She had been sampling the hermits. I said:

"I would like to do that, myself. This is Wednesday. Is there a matinée?"

"A which, please you, sir?"

"Matinée. Do they keep open, afternoons?"

"Who?"

"The hermits, of course."

"Keep open?"

"Yes, keep open. Isn't that plain enough? Do they knock off at noon."

"Knock off?"

"Knock off—yes, knock off. What is the matter with knock off? I never saw such a dunderhead; can't you understand anything at all? In plain terms, do they shut up shop, draw the game, bank the fires—"

"Shut up shop, draw—"

"There, never mind, let it go. You make me tired. You can't seem to understand the simplest thing."

"I would I might please thee, sir, and it is to me dole and sorrow that I fail, albeit sith I am but a simple damsel and taught of none, being from the cradle unbaptized in those deep waters of learning that do anoint with a sovereignty him that partaketh of that most noble sacrament, investing him with reverend state to the mental eye of the humble mortal who, by bar and lack of that great consecration seeth in his own unlearned estate but a symbol of that other sort of lack and loss which men do publish to the pitying eye with sackcloth trappings whereon the ashes of grief do lie bepowdered and bestrewn, and so, when such shall in the darkness of his mind encounter these golden phrases of high mystery, these shut-up-shops, and draw-the-game, and bank-the-fires, it is but by the grace of God that he burst not for envy of the mind that can beget, and tongue that can deliver so great and mellow-sounding miracles of speech, and if there do ensue confusion in that humbler mind, and failure to divine the meanings of these wonders, then if so be this miscomprehension is not vain but sooth and true, wit ye well it is the very substance of worshipful dear homage and may not lightly be misprized, nor had been, an ye had noted this complexion of my mood and mind and understood that that I would I could not, and that I could not I might not, nor yet nor might *nor* could, nor might-not nor could-not, might be by advantage turned to the desired *would,* and so I pray you mercy of my fault, and that ye will of your kindness and your charity forgive it, good my master and most dear lord."

I couldn't make it all out—that is, the details—but I got the general idea; and enough of it, too, to be ashamed. It was not fair to spring those nineteenth century technicalities upon the untutored infant of the sixth and then rail at her because she couldn't get their drift; and when she was making the honest best drive at it she could, too, and no fault of hers that she couldn't fetch the home plate; and so I apologized. Then we meandered pleasantly away toward the hermit holes in sociable converse together, and better friends than ever.

I was gradually coming to have a mysterious and shuddery reverence for this girl; for nowadays whenever she pulled out from the station and got her train fairly started on one of those horizonless transcontinental sentences of hers, it was borne in upon me that I was standing in the awful presence of the Mother of the German Language. I was so impressed with this, that sometimes when she began to empty one of these sentences on me I unconsciously took the very attitude of reverence, and stood uncovered; and if words had been water, I had been drowned, sure. She had exactly the German way: whatever was in her mind to be delivered, whether a mere remark, or a sermon, or a cyclopedia, or the history of a war, she would get it into a single sentence, or die. Whenever the literary German dives into a sentence, that is the last you are going to see of him till he emerges on the other side of his Atlantic with his verb in his mouth.

We drifted from hermit to hermit all the afternoon. It was a most strange menagerie. The chief emulation among them seemed to be, to see which could manage to be the uncleanest and most prosperous with vermin. Their manner and attitudes were the last expression of complacent self-righteousness. It was one anchorite's pride to lie naked in the mud and let the insects bite him and blister him unmolested; it was another's to lean against a rock, all day long, conspicuous to the admiration of the throng of pilgrims, and pray; it was another's to go naked, and crawl around on all fours; it was another's to drag about with him, year in and year out, eighty pounds of iron; it was another's to never lie down when he slept, but to stand among the thornbushes and snore when there were pilgrims around to look; a woman, who had the white hair of age, and no other apparel, was black from crown to heel with forty-seven years of holy abstinence from water. Groups of gazing pilgrims stood around all and every of these strange objects, lost in reverent wonder, and envious of the fleckless sanctity which these pious austerities had won for them from an exacting heaven.

By and by we went to see one of the supremely great ones. He was a mighty celebrity; his face had penetrated all Christendom; the noble and the renowned journeyed from the remotest lands on the globe to pay him reverence. His stand was in the center of the widest part of the valley; and it took all that space to hold his crowds.

His stand was a pillar sixty feet high, with a broad platform on the top of it. He was now doing what he had been doing every day for twenty years up there—bowing his body ceaselessly and rapidly almost to his feet. It was his way of praying. I timed him with a stopwatch, and he made twelve hundred and forty-four revolutions in twenty-four minutes and forty-six seconds. It seemed a pity to have all this power going to waste. It was one of the most useful motions in mechanics, the pedal movement; so I made a note in my memorandum book, purposing some day to apply a system of elastic cords to him and run a sewing machine with it. I afterwards carried out that scheme, and got five years' good service out of him; in which time he turned out upwards of eighteen thousand first-rate tow-linen shirts, which was ten a day. I worked him Sundays and all; he was going Sundays the same as week-days, and it was no use to waste the power. These shirts cost me nothing but just the mere trifle for the materials—I furnished those myself, it would not have been right to make him do that—and they sold like smoke to pilgrims at a dollar and a half apiece, which was the price of fifty cows or a blooded racehorse in Arthurdom. They were regarded as a perfect protection against sin, and advertised as such by my knights everywhere, with the paintpot and stencil plate; insomuch that there was not a cliff or a boulder or a dead wall in England but you could read on it at a mile distance:

"Buy the only genuine St. Stylite; patronized by the Nobility. Patent applied for."

There was more money in the business than one knew what to do with. As it extended, I brought out a line of goods suitable for kings, and a nobby thing for duchesses and that sort, with ruffles down the fore hatch and the running gear clewed up with a featherstitch to leeward and then hauled aft with a backstay and triced up with a half-turn in the standing rigging forward of the weather gaskets. Yes, it was a daisy.

But about that time I noticed that the motive power had taken to standing on one leg, and I found that there was something the matter with the other one; so I stocked the business and unloaded, taking Sir Bors de Ganis into camp financially along with certain of his friends: for the works stopped within a year, and the good saint got him to his rest. But he had earned it. I can say that for him.

When I saw him that first time—however, his personal condition will not quite bear description here. You can read it in the Lives of the Saints.*

---

*All the details concerning the hermits, in this chapter, are from Lecky—but greatly modified. This book not being a history but only a tale, the majority of the historian's frank details were too strong for reproduction in it.—EDITOR.

XXIII. RESTORATION OF THE FOUNTAIN

SATURDAY NOON I went to the well and looked on a while. Merlin was still burning smoke powders, and pawing the air, and muttering gibberish as hard as ever, but looking pretty downhearted, for of course he had not started even a perspiration in that well yet. Finally I said:

"How does the thing promise by this time, partner?"

"Behold, I am even now busied with trial of the powerfulest enchantment known to the princes of the occult arts in the lands of the East; an it fail me, naught can avail. Peace, until I finish."

He raised a smoke this time that darkened all the region, and must have made matters uncomfortable for the hermits, for the wind was their way, and it rolled down over their dens in a dense and billowy fog. He poured out volumes of speech to match, and contorted his body and sawed the air with his hands in a most extraordinary way. At the end of twenty minutes he dropped down panting, and about exhausted. Now arrived the abbot and several hundred monks and nuns, and behind them a multitude of pilgrims and a couple of acres of foundlings, all drawn by the prodigious smoke, and all in a grand state of excitement. The abbot inquired anxiously for results. Merlin said:

"If any labor of mortal might break the spell that binds these waters, this which I have but just essayed had done it. It has failed; whereby I do now know that that which I had feared is a truth established: the sign of this failure is, that the most potent spirit known to the magicians of the East, and whose name none may utter and live, has laid his spell upon this well. The mortal does not breathe, nor ever will, who can penetrate the secret of that spell, and without that secret none can break it. The water will flow no more forever, good Father. I have done what man could. Suffer me to go."

Of course this threw the abbot into a good deal of consternation. He turned to me with the signs of it in his face, and said:

"Ye have heard him. Is it true?"

"Part of it is."

"Not all, then, not all! What part is true?"

"That that spirit with the Russian name has put his spell upon the well."

"God's wownds, then we are ruined!"

"Possibly."

"But not certainly? Ye mean, not certainly?"

"That is it."

"Wherefore, ye also mean that when he saith none can break the spell—"

"Yes, when he says that, he says what isn't necessarily true. There are conditions under which an effort to break it may have some chance—that is, some small, some trifling chance—of success."

"The conditions—"

"Oh, they are nothing difficult. Only these: I want the well and the surroundings for the space of half a mile, entirely to myself from sun-set today until I remove the ban—and nobody allowed to cross the ground but by my authority."

"Are these all?"

"Yes."

"And you have no fear to try?"

"Oh, none. One may fail, of course; and one may also succeed. One can try, and I am ready to chance it. I have my conditions?"

"These and all others ye may name. I will issue commandment to that effect."

"Wait," said Merlin, with an evil smile. "Ye wit that he that would break this spell must know that spirit's name?"

"Yes, I know his name."

"And wit you also that to know it skills not of itself, but ye must like-wise pronounce it? Ha-ha! Knew ye that?"

"Yes, I knew that, too."

"You have that knowledge! Art a fool? Are ye minded to utter that name and die?"

"Utter it? Why certainly. I would utter it if it was Welsh."

"Ye are even a dead man, then; and I go to tell Arthur."

"That's all right. Take your gripsack and get along. The thing for *you* to do is to go home and work the weather, John W. Merlin."

It was a home shot, and it made him wince; for he was the worst weather-failure in the kingdom. Whenever he ordered up the danger signals along the coast there was a week's dead calm, sure, and every time he prophesied fair weather it rained brickbats. But I kept him in the weather bureau right along, to undermine his reputation. However, that shot raised his bile, and instead of starting home to report my death, he said he would remain and enjoy it.

My two experts arrived in the evening, and pretty well fagged, for they had traveled double tides. They had pack mules along, and had brought everything I needed—tools, pump, lead pipe, Greek fire, sheaves of big rockets, roman candles, colored-fire sprays, electric apparatus, and a lot of sundries—everything necessary for the stateliest kind of a miracle. They got their supper and a nap, and about midnight we sallied out through a solitude so wholly vacant and complete that it quite overpassed the required conditions. We took possession of the well and its surroundings. My boys were experts in all sorts of things, from the stoning up of a well to the constructing of a mathematical instrument. An hour before sunrise we had that leak mended in ship-shape fashion, and the water began to rise. Then we stowed our fire-works in the chapel, locked up the place, and went home to bed.

Before the noon mass was over, we were at the well again; for there was a deal to do, yet, and I was determined to spring the miracle before midnight, for business reasons: for whereas a miracle worked for the Church on a weekday is worth a good deal, it is worth six times as much if you get it in on a Sunday. In nine hours the water had risen to its customary level, that is to say, it was within twenty-three feet of the top. We put in a little iron pump, one of the first turned out by my works near the capital; we bored into a stone reservoir which stood against the outer wall of the well chamber and inserted a section of lead pipe that was long enough to reach to the door of the chapel and project beyond the threshold, where the gushing water would be visible to the two hundred and fifty acres of people I was intending should be present on the flat plain in front of this little holy hillock at the proper time.

We knocked the head out of an empty hogshead and hoisted this hogshead to the flat roof of the chapel, where we clamped it down fast, poured in gunpowder till it lay loosely an inch deep on the bottom, then we stood up rockets in the hogshead as thick as they could loosely stand, all the different breeds of rockets there are; and they made a portly and imposing sheaf, I can tell you. We grounded the wire of a pocket electrical battery in that powder, we placed a whole magazine of Greek fire on each corner of the roof—blue on one corner, green on another, red on another, and purple on the last, and grounded a wire in each.

About two hundred yards off, in the flat, we built a pen of scantlings, about four feet high, and laid planks on it, and so made a platform. We covered it with swell tapestries borrowed for the occasion, and topped it off with the abbot's own throne. When you are going to do a miracle for an ignorant race, you want to get in every detail that will count; you want to make all the properties impressive to the public eye; you want to make matters comfortable for your head guest; then you can turn yourself loose and play your effects for all they are worth. I know the value of these things, for I know human nature. You can't throw too much style into a miracle. It costs trouble, and work, and sometimes money; but it pays in the end. Well, we brought the wires to the ground at the chapel, and then brought them under the ground to the platform, and hid the batteries there. We put a rope fence a hundred feet square around the platform to keep off the common multitude, and that finished the work. My idea was, doors open at ten thirty, performance to begin at eleven twenty-five sharp. I wished I could charge admission, but of course that wouldn't answer. I instructed my boys to be in the chapel as early as ten, before anybody was around, and be ready to man the pumps at the proper time, and make the fur fly. Then we went home to supper.

The news of the disaster to the well had traveled far, by this time; and now for two or three days a steady avalanche of people had been pouring into the valley. The lower end of the valley was become one huge camp; we should have a good house, no question about that. Criers went the rounds early in the evening and announced the coming attempt, which put every pulse up to fever heat. They gave notice that the abbot and his official suite would move in state and occupy the platform at ten thirty, up to which time all the region which was under my ban must be clear; the bells would then cease from tolling, and this sign should be permission to the multitudes to close in and take their places.

I was at the platform and all ready to do the honors when the abbot's solemn procession hove in sight—which it did not do till it was nearly to the rope fence, because it was a starless black night and no torches permitted. With it came Merlin, and took a front seat on the platform; he was as good as his word, for once. One could not see the multitudes banked together beyond the ban, but they were there, just the same. The moment the bells stopped, those banked masses broke and poured over the line like a vast black wave, and for as much as a half hour it continued to flow, and then it solidified itself, and you could have walked upon a pavement of human heads to—well, miles.

We had a solemn stage wait, now, for about twenty minutes—a thing I had counted on for effect; it is always good to let your audience have a chance to work up its expectancy. At length, out of the silence a noble Latin chant—men's voices—broke and swelled up and rolled away into the night, a majestic tide of melody. I had put that up, too, and it was one of the best effects I ever invented. When it was finished I stood up on the platform and extended my hands abroad, for two minutes, with my face uplifted—that always produces a dead hush—and then slowly pronounced this ghastly word with a kind of awfulness which caused hundreds to tremble, and many women to faint:

"Constantinopolitanischerdudelsackspfeifenmachersgesellschaftt!"

Just as I was moaning out the closing hunks of that word, I touched off one of my electric connections, and all that murky world of people stood revealed in a hideous blue glare! It was immense—that effect! Lots of people shrieked, women curled up and quit in every direction, foundlings collapsed by platoons. The abbot and the monks crossed themselves nimbly and their lips fluttered with agitated prayers. Merlin held his grip, but he was astonished clear down to his corns; he had never seen anything to begin with that, before. Now was the time to pile in the effects. I lifted my hands and groaned out this word—as it were in agony—

"Nihilistendynamittheaterkaestchenssprengungsattentaetsversuchungen!"

—and turned on the red fire! You should have heard that Atlantic of people moan and howl when that crimson hell joined the blue! After sixty seconds I shouted—

"Transvaaltruppentropentrasporttrampeltthiertreibertrauungsthraenentragoedie!"

—and lit up the green fire! After waiting only forty seconds, this time, I spread my arms abroad and thundered out the devastating syllables of this word of words—

"Mekkamuselmannenmassenmenchenmoerdermohrenmuttermarmormonumentenmacher!"

—and whirled on the purple glare! There they were, all going at once, red, blue, green, purple! Four furious volcanoes pouring vast clouds of radiant smoke aloft, and spreading a blinding rainbowed noonday to the furthest confines of that valley. In the distance one could see that fellow on the pillar standing rigid against the background of sky, his seesaw stopped for the first time in twenty years. I knew the boys were at the pump, now, and ready. So I said to the abbot:

"The time is come, Father. I am about to pronounce the dread name and command the spell to dissolve. You want to brace up and take hold of something." Then I shouted to the people: "Behold, in another minute the spell will be broken, or no mortal can break it. If it break, all will know it, for you will see the sacred water gush from the chapel door!"

I stood a few moments, to let the hearers have a chance to spread my announcement to those who couldn't hear, and so convey it to the furthest ranks, then I made a grand exhibition of extra posturing and gesturing, and shouted:

"Lo, I command the fell spirit that possesses the holy fountain to now disgorge into the skies all the infernal fires that still remain in him, and straightway dissolve his spell and flee hence to the pit, there to lie bound a thousand years. By his own dread name I command it—BGWJJILLIGKKK!"

Then I touched off the hogshead of rockets, and a vast fountain of dazzling lances of fire vomited itself toward the zenith with a hissing rush, and burst in mid-sky into a storm of flashing jewels! One mighty groan of terror started up from the massed people—then suddenly broke into a wild hosannah of joy—for there, fair and plain in the uncanny glare, they saw the freed water leaping forth! The old abbot could not speak a word, for tears and the chokings in his throat; without utterance of any sort, he folded me in his arms and mashed me. It was more eloquent than speech. And harder to get over, too, in a country where there were really no doctors that were worth a damaged nickel.

You should have seen those acres of people throw themselves down in that water and kiss it; kiss it, and pet it, and fondle it, and talk to it as if it were alive, and welcome it back with the dear names they gave their darlings, just as if it had been a friend who was long gone away and lost, and was come home again. Yes, it was pretty to see, and made me think more of them than I had done before.

I sent Merlin home on a shutter. He had caved in and gone down like a landslide when I pronounced that fearful name, and had never come to since. He never had heard that name before—neither had I— but to him it was the right one; any jumble would have been the right one. He admitted, afterward, that that spirit's own mother could not have pronounced that name better than I did. He never could understand how I survived it, and I didn't tell him. It is only young magicians that give away a secret like that. Merlin spent three months working enchantments to try to find out the deep trick of how to pronounce that name and outlive it. But he didn't arrive.

When I started to the chapel, the populace uncovered and fell back reverently to make a wide way for me, as if I had been some kind of a superior being—and I was. I was aware of that. I took along a night shift of monks, and taught them the mystery of the pump, and set them to work, for it was plain that a good part of the people out there were going to sit up with the water all night, consequently it was but right that they should have all they wanted of it. To those monks that pump was a good deal of a miracle itself, and they were full of wonder over it; and of admiration, too, of the exceeding effectiveness of its performance.

It was a great night, an immense night. There was reputation in it. I could hardly get to sleep for glorying over it.

XXIV. A RIVAL MAGICIAN

MY INFLUENCE in the Valley of Holiness was something prodigious now. It seemed worthwhile to try to turn it to some valuable account. The thought came to me the next morning and was suggested by my seeing one of my knights who was in the soap line come riding in. According to history, the monks of this place two centuries before, had been worldly minded enough to want to wash. It might be that there was a leaven of this unrighteousness still remaining. So I sounded a Brother:

"Wouldn't you like a bath?"

He shuddered at the thought—the thought of the peril of it to the well—but he said with feeling—

"One needs not to ask that of a poor body who has not known that blessed refreshment sith that he was a boy. Would God I might wash me! But it may not be, fair sir, tempt me not; it is forbidden."

And then he sighed in such a sorrowful way that I was resolved he should have at least one layer of his real estate removed, if it sized up my whole influence and bankrupted the pile. So I went to the abbot and asked for a permit for this Brother. He blenched at the idea—I don't mean that you could see him blench, for of course you couldn't see it without you scraped him, and I didn't care enough about it to scrape him, but I knew the blench was there, just the same, and within a book cover's thickness of the surface, too—blenched, and trembled. He said:

"Ah, son, ask aught else thou wilt, and it is thine, and freely granted out of a grateful heart—but this, oh this! Would you drive away the blessed water again?"

"No, Father, I will not drive it away. I have mysterious knowledge which teaches me that there was an error that other time when it was thought the institution of the bath banished the fountain." A large interest began to show up in the old man's face. "My knowledge informs me that the bath was innocent of that misfortune, which was caused by quite another sort of sin."

"These are brave words—but—but right welcome, if they be true."

"They are true, indeed. Let me build the bath again, Father. Let me build it again, and the fountain shall flow forever."

"You promise this—you promise it? Say the word—say you promise it!"

"I do promise it."

"Then will I have the first bath myself! Go—get ye to your work. Tarry not, tarry not, but go."

I and my boys were at work, straight off. The ruins of the old bath were there yet, in the basement of the monastery, not a stone missing. They had been left just so, all these lifetimes, and avoided with a pious fear, as things accursed. In two days we had it all done and the water in—a spacious pool of clear pure water that a body could swim in. It was running water, too. It came in and went out through the ancient pipes. The old abbot kept his word and was the first to try it. He went down black and shaky, leaving the whole black community above troubled and worried and full of bodings; but he came back white and joyful, and the game was made! Another triumph scored.

It was a good campaign that we made in that Valley of Holiness, and I was very well satisfied, and ready to move on, now, but I struck a disappointment. I caught a heavy cold, and it started up an old lurking rheumatism of mine. Of course the rheumatism hunted up my weakest place and located itself there. This was the place where the abbot put his arms about me and mashed me, what time he was moved to testify his gratitude to me with an embrace.

When at last I got out, I was a shadow. But everybody was full of attentions and kindnesses, and these brought cheer back into my life and were the right medicine to help a convalescent swiftly up toward health and strength again; so I gained fast.

Sandy was worn out with nursing, so I made up my mind to turn out and go a cruise alone, leaving her at the nunnery to rest up. My idea was to disguise myself as a freeman of peasant degree and wander through the country a week or two on foot. This would give me a chance to eat and lodge with the lowliest and poorest class of free citizens on equal terms. There was no other way to inform myself perfectly of their everyday life and the operation of the laws upon it. If I went among them as a gentleman, there would be restraints and conventionalities which would shut me out from their private joys and troubles, and I should get no further than the outside shell.

One morning I was out on a long walk to get up muscle for my trip and had climbed the ridge which bordered the northern extremity of the valley, when I came upon an artificial opening in the face of a low precipice, and recognized it by its location as a hermitage which had often been pointed out to me from a distance, as the den of a hermit of high renown for dirt and austerity. I knew he had lately been offered a situation in the Great Sahara, where lions and sandflies made the hermit life peculiarly attractive and difficult, and had gone to Africa to take possession, so I thought I would look in and see how the atmosphere of this den agreed with its reputation.

My surprise was great: the place was newly swept and scoured. Then there was another surprise. Back in the gloom of the cavern I heard the clink of a little bell, and then this exclamation:

"*Hello, Central! Is this you, Camelot?*——Behold, thou mayst glad thy heart an thou hast faith to believe the wonderful when that it cometh in unexpected guise and maketh itself manifest in impossible places—here standeth in the flesh his mightiness The Boss, and with thine own ears shall ye hear him speak!"

Now what a radical reversal of things this was; what a jumbling together of extravagant incongruities; what a fantastic conjunction of opposites and irreconcilables—the home of the bogus miracle become the home of a real one, the den of a medieval hermit turned into a telephone office!

The telephone clerk stepped into the light, and I recognized one of my young fellows. I said:

"How long has this office been established here, Ulfius?"

"But since midnight, fair Sir Boss, an it please you. We saw many lights in the valley, and so judged it well to make a station, for that where so many lights be needs must they indicate a town of goodly size."

"Quite right. It isn't a town in the customary sense, but it's a good stand, anyway. Do you know where you are?"

"Of that I have had no time to make inquiry; for whenas my comradeship moved hence upon their labors, leaving me in charge, I got me to needed rest, purposing to inquire when I waked, and report the place's name to Camelot for record."

"Well, this is the Valley of Holiness."

It didn't take; I mean, he didn't start at the name, as I had supposed he would. He merely said—

"I will so report it."

"Why, the surrounding regions are filled with the noise of late wonders that have happened here! You don't hear of them?"

"Ah, ye will remember we move by night, and avoid speech with all. We learn naught but that we get by the telephone from Camelot."

"Why *they* know all about this thing. Haven't they told you anything about the great miracle of the restoration of a holy fountain?"

"Oh, *that*? Indeed yes. But the name of *this* valley doth woundily differ from the name of *that* one; indeed to differ wider were not pos—"

"What was that name, then?"

"The Valley of Hellishness."

"*That* explains it. Confound a telephone, anyway. It is the very demon for conveying similarities of sound that are miracles of divergence from similarity of sense. But no matter, you know the name of the place now. Call up Camelot."

He did it, and had Clarence sent for. It was good to hear my boy's voice again. It was like being home. After some affectionate interchanges and some account of my late illness, I said:

"What is new?"

"The king and queen and many of the court do start even in this hour, to go to your Valley to pay pious homage to the waters ye have restored, and cleanse themselves of sin, and see the place where the infernal spirit spouted true hell flames to the clouds—an ye listen sharply ye may hear me wink and hear me likewise smile a smile, sith 'twas I that made selection of those flames from out our stock and sent them by your order."

"Does the king know the way to this place?"

"The king? No, nor to any other in his realms, mayhap; but the lads that holp you with your miracle will be his guide and lead the way, and appoint the places for rests at noons and sleeps at night."

"This will bring them here—when?"

"Midafternoon, or later, the third day."

"Anything else in the way of news?"

"The king hath begun the raising of the standing army ye suggested to him; one regiment is complete and officered."

"The mischief! I wanted a main hand in that, myself. There is only one body of men in the kingdom that are fitted to officer a regular army."

"Yes—and now ye will marvel to know there's not so much as one West Pointer in that regiment."

"What are you talking about? Are you in earnest?"

"It is truly as I have said."

"Why, this makes me uneasy. Who were chosen, and what was the method? Competitive examination?"

"Indeed I know naught of the method. I but know this—these officers be all of noble family, and are born—what is it you call it— chuckleheads."

"There's something wrong, Clarence."

"Comfort yourself, then; for two candidates for a lieutenancy do travel hence with the king—young nobles both—and if you but wait where you are you will hear them questioned."

"That is news to the purpose. I will get one West Pointer in, anyway. Mount a man and send him to that school with a message; let him kill horses, if necessary, but he must be there before sunset tonight and say—"

"There is no need. I have laid a ground wire to the school. Prithee let me connect you with it."

It sounded good! In this atmosphere of telephones and lightning communication with distant regions, I was breathing the breath of life again after long suffocation. I realized, then, what a creepy, dull, inanimate horror this land had been to me all these years, and how I had been in such a stifled condition of mind as to have grown used to it almost beyond the power to notice it.

I gave my order to the superintendent of the Academy personally. I also asked him to bring me some paper and a fountain pen and a box or so of safety matches. I was getting tired of doing without these conveniences. I could have them, now, as I wasn't going to wear armor any more at present, and therefore could get at my pockets.

When I got back to the monastery, I found a thing of interest going on. The abbot and his monks were assembled in the great hall, observing with childish wonder and faith the performances of a new magician, a fresh arrival. His dress was the extreme of the fantastic; as showy and foolish as the sort of thing an Indian medicine man wears. He was mowing, and mumbling, and gesticulating, and drawing mystical figures in the air and on the floor—the regular thing, you know. He was a celebrity from Asia—so he said, and that was enough. That sort of evidence was as good as gold, and passed current everywhere.

How easy and cheap it was to be a great magician on this fellow's terms. His specialty was to tell you what any individual on the face of the globe was doing at the moment; and what he had done at any time in the past, and what he would do at any time in the future. He asked if any would like to know what the Emperor of the East was doing now? The sparkling eyes and the delighted rubbing of hands made eloquent answer—this reverend crowd *would* like to know what that monarch was at, just at this moment. The fraud went through some more mummery, and then made grave announcement:

"The high and mighty Emperor of the East doth at this moment put money in the palm of a holy begging friar—one, two, three pieces, and they be all of silver."

A buzz of admiring exclamations broke out, all around:

"It is marvelous!" "Wonderful!" "What study, what labor, to have acquired a so amazing power as this!"

Would they like to know what the Supreme Lord of Inde was doing? Yes. He told them what the Supreme Lord of Inde was doing. Then he told them what the Sultan of Egypt was at; also what the King of the Remote Seas was about. And so on and so on; and with each new marvel the astonishment at his accuracy rose higher and higher. They thought he must surely strike an uncertain place sometime; but no, he never had to hesitate, he always knew, and always with unerring precision. I saw that if this thing went on I should lose my supremacy, this fellow would capture my following, I should be left out in the cold. I must put a cog in his wheel, and do it right away, too. I said:

"If I might ask, I should very greatly like to know what a certain person is doing."

"Speak, and freely. I will tell you."

"It will be difficult—perhaps impossible."

"My art knoweth not that word. The more difficult it is, the more certainly will I reveal it to you."

You see, I was working up the interest. It was getting pretty high, too; you could see that by the craning necks all around, and the half suspended breathing. So now I climaxed it:

"If you make no mistake—if you tell me truly what I want to know— I will give you two hundred silver pennies."

"The fortune is mine! I will tell you what you would know."

"Then tell me what I am doing with my right hand."

"Ah-h!" There was a general gasp of surprise. It had not occurred to anybody in the crowd—that simple trick of inquiring about somebody who wasn't ten thousand miles away. The magician was hit hard; it was an emergency that had never happened in his experience before, and it corked him; he didn't know how to meet it. He looked stunned, confused; he couldn't say a word. "Come," I said, "what are you waiting for? Is it possible you can answer up, right off, and tell what anybody on the other side of the earth is doing, and yet can't tell what a person is doing who isn't three yards from you? Persons behind me know what I am doing with my right hand—they will endorse you if you tell correctly." He was still dumb. "Very well, I'll tell you why you don't speak up and tell; it is because you don't know. You a magician! Good friends, this tramp is a mere fraud and liar."

This distressed the monks and terrified them. They were not used to hearing these awful beings called names, and they did not know what might be the consequence. There was a dead silence, now; superstitious bodings were in every mind. The magician began to pull his wits together, and when he presently smiled an easy, nonchalant smile, it spread a mighty relief around; for it indicated that his mood was not destructive. He said:

"It hath struck me speechless, the frivolity of this person's speech. Let all know, if perchance there be any who know it not, that enchanters of my degree deign not to concern themselves with the doings of any but

Kings, Princes, Emperors, them that be born in the purple and them only. Had ye asked me what Arthur the great king is doing, it were another matter, and I had told ye; but the doings of a subject interest me not."

"Oh, I misunderstood you. I thought you said 'anybody,' and so I supposed 'anybody' included—well, anybody; that is, everybody."

"It doth—anybody that is of lofty birth; and the better if he be royal."

"That, it meseemeth, might well be," said the abbot, who saw his opportunity to smooth things and avert disaster, "for it were not likely that so wonderful a gift as this would be conferred for the revelation of the concerns of lesser beings than such as be born near to the summits of greatness. Our Arthur the king—"

"Would you know of him?" broke in the enchanter.

"Most gladly, yea, and gratefully."

Everybody was full of awe and interest again, right away, the incorrigible idiots. They watched the incantations absorbingly, and looked at me with a "There, now, what can you say to that?" air, when the announcement came:

"The king is weary with the chase, and lieth in his palace these two hours sleeping a dreamless sleep."

"God's benison upon him!" said the abbot, and crossed himself; "may that sleep be to the refreshment of his body and his soul."

"And so it might be, if he were sleeping," I said, "but the king is not sleeping, the king rides."

Here was trouble again—a conflict of authority. Nobody knew which of us to believe; I still had some reputation left. The magician's scorn was stirred, and he said:

"Lo, I have seen many wonderful soothsayers and prophets and magicians in my life days, but none before that could sit idle and see to the heart of things with never an incantation to help."

"You have lived in the woods and lost much by it. I use incantations myself, as this good brotherhood are aware—but only on occasions of moment."

When it comes to sarcasming, I reckon I know how to keep my end up. That jab made this fellow squirm. The abbot inquired after the queen and the court, and got this information:

"They be all on sleep, being overcome by fatigue, like as to the king." I said:

"That is merely another lie. Half of them are about their amusements, the queen and the other half are not sleeping, they ride. Now perhaps you can spread yourself a little, and tell us where the king and queen and all that are this moment riding with them are going?"

"They sleep now, as I said; but on the morrow they will ride, for they go a journey toward the sea."

"And where will they be the day after tomorrow at vespers?"

"Far to the north of Camelot, and half their journey will be done."

"That is another lie, by the space of a hundred and fifty miles. Their journey will not be merely half done, it will be all done, and they will be *here*, in this valley."

That was a noble shot! It set the abbot and the monks in a whirl of excitement, and it rocked the enchanter to his base. I followed the thing right up:

"If the king does not arrive, I will have myself ridden on a rail; if he does I will ride you on a rail instead."

Next day I went up to the telephone office and found that the king had passed through two towns that were on the line. I spotted his progress on the succeeding day in the same way. I kept these matters to myself. The third day's reports showed that if he kept up his gait he would arrive by four in the afternoon. There was still no sign anywhere of interest in his coming; there seemed to be no preparations making to receive him in state; a strange thing, truly. Only one thing could explain this: that other magician had been cutting under me, sure. This was true. I asked a friend of mine, a monk, about it, and he said, yes, the magician had tried some further enchantments and found out that the court had concluded to make no journey at all, but stay at home. Think of that! Observe how much a reputation was worth in such a country. These people had seen me do the very showiest bit of magic in history, and the only one within their memory that had a positive value, and yet here they were, ready to take up with an adventurer who could offer no evidence of his powers but his mere unproven word.

However, it was not good politics to let the king come without any fuss and feathers at all, so I went down and drummed up a procession of pilgrims and smoked out a batch of hermits and started them out at two o'clock to meet him. And that was the sort of state he arrived in. The abbot was helpless with rage and humiliation when I brought him out on a balcony and showed him the head of the state marching in and never a monk on hand to offer him welcome, and no stir of life or clang of joy bell to glad his spirit. He took one look and then flew to rouse out his forces. The next minute the bells were dinning furiously, and the various buildings were vomiting monks and nuns, who went swarming in a rush toward the coming procession; and with them went that magician—and he was on a rail, too, by the abbot's order; and his reputation was in the mud, and mine was in the sky again. Yes, a man can keep his trademark current in such a country, but he can't sit around and do it; he has got to be on deck and attending to business, right along.

XXV. A COMPETITIVE EXAMINATION

WHEN THE king traveled for change of air, or made a progress, or visited a distant noble whom he wished to bankrupt with the cost of his keep, part of the administration moved with him. It was a fashion of the time. The Commission charged with the examination of candidates for posts in the army came with the king to the Valley, whereas they could have transacted their business just as well at home. And although this expedition was strictly a holiday excursion for the king, he kept some of his business functions going, just the same. He touched for the evil, as usual; he held court in the gate at sunrise and tried cases, for he was himself Chief Justice of the King's Bench.

He shone very well in this latter office. He was a wise and humane judge, and he clearly did his honest best and fairest—according to his lights. That is a large reservation. His lights—I mean his rearing—often colored his decisions. Whenever there was a dispute between a noble or gentleman and a person of lower degree, the king's leanings and sympathies were for the former class always, whether he suspected it or not. It was impossible that this should be otherwise. The blunting effects of slavery upon the slaveholder's moral perceptions are known and conceded, the world over, and a privileged class, an aristocracy, is but a band of slaveholders under another name. This has a harsh sound and yet should not be offensive to any—even to the noble himself—unless the fact itself be an offense: for the statement simply formulates a fact. The repulsive feature of slavery is the *thing*, not its name. One needs but to hear an aristocrat speak of the classes that are below him to recognize—and in but indifferently modified measure—the very air and tone of the actual slaveholder; and behind these are the slaveholder's spirit, the slaveholder's blunted feeling. They are the result of the same cause in both cases: the possessor's old and inbred custom of regarding himself as a superior being. The king's judgment wrought frequent injustices, but it was merely the fault of his training, his natural and unalterable sympathies. He was as unfitted for a judgeship as

140

would be the average mother for the position of milk-distributor to starving children in famine time; her own children would fare a shade better than the rest.

One very curious case came before the king. A young girl, an orphan, who had a considerable estate, married a fine young fellow who had nothing. The girl's property was within a seignory held by the Church. The bishop of the diocese, an arrogant scion of the great nobility, claimed the girl's estate on the ground that she had married privately, and thus had cheated the Church out of one of its rights as lord of the seignory—the one heretofore referred to as *le droit du seigneur*. The penalty of refusal or avoidance was confiscation. The girl's defense was that the lordship of the seignory was vested in the bishop, and the particular right here involved was not transferable, but must be exercised by the lord himself or stand vacated; and that an older law of the Church itself strictly barred the bishop from exercising it. It was a very odd case, indeed.

It reminded me of something I had read in my youth about the ingenious way in which the aldermen of London raised the money that built the Mansion House. A person who had not taken the Sacrament according to the Anglican rite, could not stand as a candidate for sheriff of London. Thus Dissenters were ineligible; they could not run if asked, they could not serve if elected. The aldermen, who without any question were Yankees in disguise, hit upon this neat device: they passed a bylaw imposing a fine of £400 upon any one who should refuse to be a candidate for sheriff, and a fine of £600 upon any person who, after being elected sheriff, refused to serve. Then they went to work and elected a lot of Dissenters, one after another, and kept it up until they had collected £15,000 in fines; and there stands the stately Mansion House to this day, to keep the blushing citizen in mind of a long past and lamented day when a band of Yankees slipped into London and played games of the sort that has given their race a unique and shady reputation among all truly good and holy peoples that be in the earth.

The girl's case seemed strong to me; the bishop's case was just as strong. I did not see how the king was going to get out of this hole. But he got out. I append his decision:

"Truly I find small difficulty here, the matter being even a child's affair for simpleness. An the young bride had conveyed notice, as in duty bound, to her feudal lord and proper master and protector the bishop, she had suffered no loss, for the said bishop could have got a dispensation making him, for temporary conveniency, eligible to the exercise of his said right, and thus would she have kept all she had. Whereas, failing in her first duty, she hath by that failure failed in all;

for whoso, clinging to a rope, severeth it above his hands, must fall; it being no defense to claim that the rest of the rope is sound, neither any deliverance from his peril, as he shall find. Pardy, the woman's case is rotten at the source. It is the decree of the Court that she forfeit to the said lord bishop all her goods, even to the last farthing that she doth possess, and be thereto mulcted in the costs. Next!"

Here was a tragic end to a beautiful honeymoon not yet three months old. Poor young creatures! They had lived these three months lapped to the lips in worldly comforts. These clothes and trinkets they were wearing were as fine and dainty as the shrewdest stretch of the sumptuary laws allowed to people of their degree; and in these pretty clothes, she crying on his shoulder, and he trying to comfort her with hopeful words set to the music of despair, they went from the judgment seat out into the world homeless, bedless, breadless; why, the very beggars by the roadsides were not so poor as they.

Well, the king was out of the hole; and on terms satisfactory to the Church and the rest of the aristocracy, no doubt. Men write many fine and plausible arguments in support of monarchy, but the fact remains that where every man in a State has a vote, brutal laws are impossible. Arthur's people were of course poor material for a republic, because they had been debased so long by monarchy, and yet even they would have been intelligent enough to make short work of that law which the king had just been administering if it had been submitted to their full and free vote. There is a phrase which has grown so common in the world's mouth that it has come to seem to have sense and meaning— the sense and meaning implied when it is used—that is, the phrase which refers to this or that or the other nation as possibly being "capable of self-government"; and the implied sense of it is, that there has been a nation somewhere, sometime or other which *wasn't* capable of it— wasn't as able to govern itself as some self-appointed specialists were or would be to govern it. The master minds of all nations, in all ages, have sprung in affluent multitude from the mass of the nation, and from the mass of the nation only—not from its privileged classes; and so, no matter what the nation's intellectual grade was, whether high or low, the bulk of its ability was in the long ranks of its nameless and its poor, and so it never saw the day that it had not the material in abundance whereby to govern itself. Which is to assert an always self-proven fact: that even the best governed and most free and most enlightened monarchy is still behind the best condition attainable by its people; and that the same is true of kindred governments of lower grades, all the way down to the lowest.

King Arthur had hurried up the army business altogether beyond my calculations. I had not supposed he would move in the matter while I was away; and so I had not mapped out a scheme for determining the merits of officers; I had only remarked that it would be wise to submit every candidate to a sharp and searching examination; and privately I meant to put together a list of military qualifications that nobody could answer to but my West Pointers. That ought to have been attended to before I left; for the king was so taken with the idea of a standing army that he couldn't wait but must get about it at once, and get up as good a scheme of examination as he could invent out of his own head.

I was impatient to see what this was; and to show, too, how much more admirable was the one which I should display to the Examining Board. I intimated this, gently, to the king, and it fired his curiosity. When the Board was assembled, I followed him in, and behind us came the candidates. One of these candidates was a bright young West Pointer of mine, and with him were a couple of my West Point professors.

When I saw the Board, I did not know whether to cry or to laugh. The head of it was the officer known to later centuries as Norroy King-at-Arms! The two other members were chiefs of bureaus in his department; and all three were priests, of course; all officials who had to know how to read and write were priests.

My candidate was called first, out of courtesy to me, and the head of the Board opened on him with official solemnity:

"Name?"

"Mal-ease."

"Son of?"

"Webster."

"Webster—Webster. Hm—I—my memory faileth to recall the name. Condition?"

"Weaver."

"Weaver—God keep us!"

The king was staggered, from his summit to his foundations; one clerk fainted, and the others came near it. The chairman pulled himself together, and said indignantly:

"It is sufficient. Get you hence."

But I appealed to the king. I begged that my candidate might be examined. The king was willing, but the Board, who were all well-born folk, implored the king to spare them the indignity of examining the weaver's son. I knew they didn't know enough to examine him anyway, so I joined my prayers to theirs and the king turned the duty over to my professors. I had had a blackboard prepared, and it was put up now, and the circus began. It was beautiful to hear the lad lay out the science of war, and wallow in details of battle and siege, of supply, transportation, mining and countermining, grand tactics, big strategy and little strategy, signal service, infantry, cavalry, artillery, and all about siege guns, field guns, gatling guns, rifled guns, smooth bores, musket practice, revolver practice—and not a solitary word of it all could these catfish make head or tail of, you understand—and it was handsome to see him chalk off mathematical nightmares on the blackboard that would stump the angels themselves, and do it like nothing, too—all about eclipses, and comets, and solstices, and constellations, and mean time, and sidereal time, and dinner time, and bedtime, and every other imaginable thing above the clouds or under them that you could harry or bullyrag an enemy with and make him wish he hadn't come—and when the boy made his military salute and stood aside at last, I was proud enough to hug him, and all those other people were so dazed they looked partly petrified, partly drunk, and wholly caught out and snowed under. I judged that the cake was ours, and by a large majority.

Education is a great thing. This was the same youth who had come to West Point so ignorant that when I asked him, "If a general officer should have a horse shot under him on the field of battle, what ought he to do?" answered up naïvely and said:

"Get up and brush himself."

One of the young nobles was called up, now. I thought I would question him a little myself. I said:

"Can your lordship read?"

His face flushed indignantly, and he fired this at me:

"Takest me for a clerk? I trow I am not of a blood that"—

"Answer the question!"

He crowded his wrath down and made out to answer "No."

"Can you write?"

He wanted to resent this, too, but I said:

"You will confine yourself to the questions, and make no comments. You are not here to air your blood or your graces, and nothing of the sort will be permitted. Can you write?"

"No."

"Do you know the multiplication table?"

"I wit not what ye refer to."

"How much is nine times six?"

"It is a mystery that is hidden from me by reason that the emergency requiring the fathoming of it hath not in my life-days occurred, and so, not having no need to know this thing, I abide barren of the knowledge."

"If A trade a barrel of onions to B, worth twopence the bushel, in exchange for a sheep worth fourpence and a dog worth a penny, and C kill the dog before delivery, because bitten by the same, who mistook him for D, what sum is still due to A from B, and which party pays for the dog, C or D, and who gets the money? If A, is the penny sufficient, or may he claim consequential damages in the form of additional money to represent the possible profit which might have inured from the dog, and classifiable as earned increment, that is to say, usufruct?"

"Verily, in the all-wise and unknowable providence of God, who moveth in mysterious ways his wonders to perform, have I never heard the fellow to this question for confusion of the mind and congestion of the ducts of thought. Wherefore I beseech you let the dog and the onions and these people of the strange and godless names work out their several salvations from their piteous and wonderful difficulties without help of mine, for indeed their trouble is sufficient as it is, whereas an I tried to help I should but damage their cause the more and yet mayhap not live myself to see the desolation wrought."

"What do you know of the laws of attraction and gravitation?"

"If there be such, mayhap his grace the king did promulgate them whilst that I lay sick about the beginning of the year and thereby failed to hear his proclamation."

"What do you know of the science of optics?"

"I know of governors of places, and seneschals of castles, and sheriffs of counties, and many like small offices and titles of honor, but him you call the Science of Optics I have not heard of before; peradventure it is a new dignity."

"Yes, in this country."

Try to conceive of this mollusk gravely applying for an official position, of any kind under the sun! Why, he had all the earmarks of a typewriter copyist, if you leave out the disposition to contribute uninvited emendations of your grammar and punctuation. It was unaccountable that he didn't attempt a little help of that sort out of his majestic supply of incapacity for the job. But that didn't prove that he hadn't material in him for the disposition, it only proved that he wasn't a typewriter copyist yet. After nagging him a little more, I let the professors loose on him and they turned him inside out, on the line of scientific war, and found him empty, of course. He knew somewhat about the warfare of the time—bushwhacking around for ogres, and bullfights in the tournament ring, and such things—but otherwise he was empty and useless. Then we took the other young noble in hand, and he was the first one's twin, for ignorance and incapacity. I delivered them into the hands of the chairman of the board with the comfortable consciousness that their cake was dough. They were examined in the previous order of precedence.

"Name, so please you?"

"Pertipole, son of Sir Pertipole, Baron of Barley Mash."

"Grandfather?"

"Also Sir Pertipole, Baron of Barley Mash."

"Great-grandfather?"

"The same name and title."

"Great-great-grandfather?"

"We had none, worshipful sir, the line failing before it had reached so far back."

"It mattereth not. It is a good four generations, and fulfilleth the requirements of the rule."

"Fulfills what rule?" I asked.

"The rule requiring four generations of nobility or else the candidate is not eligible."

"A man not eligible for a lieutenancy in the army unless he can prove four generations of noble descent?"

"Even so; neither lieutenant nor any other officer may be commissioned without that qualification."

"Oh come, this is an astonishing thing. What good is such a qualification as that?"

"What good? It is a hardy question, fair sir and Boss, since it doth go far to impugn the wisdom of even our holy Mother Church herself."

"As how?"

"For that she hath established the self-same rule regarding saints. By her law none may be canonized until he hath lain dead four generations."

"I see, I see—it is the same thing. It is wonderful. In the one case a man lies dead-alive four generations—mummified in ignorance and sloth—and that qualifies him to command live people, and take their weal and woe into his impotent hands; and in the other case, a man lies bedded with death and worms four generations, and that qualifies him for office in the celestial camp. Does the king's grace approve of this strange law?"

The king said:

"Why, truly I see naught about it that is strange. All places of honor and of profit do belong, by natural right, to them that be of noble blood, and so these dignities in the army are their property and would be so without this or any rule. The rule is but to mark a limit. Its purpose is to keep out too recent blood, which would bring into contempt these offices, and men of lofty lineage would turn their backs and scorn to take them. I were to blame an I permitted this calamity. You can permit it an you are minded so to do, for you have the delegated authority, but that the king should do it were a most strange madness and not comprehensible to any."

"I yield. Proceed, sir Chief of the Herald's College."

The chairman resumed as follows:

"By what illustrious achievement for the honor of the Throne and State did the founder of your great line lift himself to the sacred dignity of the British nobility?"

"He built a brewery."

"Sire, the Board finds this candidate perfect in all the requirements and qualifications for military command, and doth hold his case open for decision after due examination of his competitor."

The competitor came forward and proved exactly four generations of nobility himself. So there was a tie in military qualifications that far.

He stood aside, a moment, and Sir Pertipole was questioned further:

"Of what condition was the wife of the founder of your line?"

"She came of the highest landed gentry, yet she was not noble; she was gracious and pure and charitable, of a blameless life and character, insomuch that in these regards was she peer of the best lady in the land."

"That will do. Stand down." He called up the competing lordling again, and asked: "What was the rank and condition of the great-grandmother who conferred British nobility upon your great house?"

"She was a king's leman and did climb to that splendid eminence by her own unholpen merit from the sewer where she was born."

"Ah, this indeed is true nobility, this is the right and perfect inter-mixture. The lieutenancy is yours, fair lord. Hold it not in contempt; it is the humble step which will lead to grandeurs more worthy of the splendor of an origin like to thine."

I was down in the bottomless pit of humiliation. I had promised myself an easy and zenith-scouring triumph, and this was the outcome!

I was almost ashamed to look my poor disappointed cadet in the face. I told him to go home and be patient, this wasn't the end.

I had a private audience with the king, and made a proposition. I said it was quite right to officer that regiment with nobilities, and he couldn't have done a wiser thing. It would also be a good idea to add five hundred officers to it; in fact, add as many officers as there were nobles and relatives of nobles in the country, even if there should finally be five times as many officers as privates in it, and thus make it the crack regiment, the envied regiment, the King's Own regiment, and entitled to fight on its own hook and in its own way, and go whither it would and come when it pleased, in time of war, and be utterly swell and independent. This would make that regiment the heart's desire of all the nobility, and they would all be satisfied and happy. Then we would make up the rest of the standing army out of commonplace materials, and officer it with nobodies, as was proper—nobodies selected on a basis of mere efficiency—and we would make this regiment toe the line, allow it no aristocratic freedom from restraint, and force it to do all the work and persistent hammering, to the end that whenever the King's Own was tired and wanted to go off for a change and rummage around amongst ogres and have a good time, it could go without uneasiness, knowing that matters were in safe hands behind it, and business going to be continued at the old stand, same as usual. The king was charmed with the idea.

When I noticed that, it gave me a valuable notion. I thought I saw my way out of an old and stubborn difficulty at last. You see, the royalties of the Pendragon stock were a long-lived race and very fruitful. Whenever a child was born to any of these—and it was pretty often—there was wild joy in the nation's mouth, and piteous sorrow in the nation's heart. The joy was questionable, but the grief was honest. Because the event meant another call for a Royal Grant. Long was the list of these royalties, and they were a heavy and steadily increasing burden upon the treasury and a menace to the crown. Yet Arthur could not believe this latter fact, and he would not listen to any of my various projects for substituting something in the place of the royal grants. If I could have persuaded him to now and then provide a support for one of these outlying scions from his own pocket, I could have made a grand to-do over it, and it would have had a good effect with the nation; but no, he wouldn't hear of such a thing. He had something like a religious passion for a royal grant; he seemed to look upon it as a sort of sacred swag, and one could not irritate him in any way so quickly and so surely as by an attack upon that venerable institution. If I ventured to cautiously hint that there was not another respectable family in England that would humble itself to hold out the hat—however, that is as far as I ever got; he always cut me short, there, and peremptorily, too.

But I believed I saw my chance at last. I would form this crack regiment out of officers alone—not a single private. Half of it should consist of nobles, who should fill all the places up to Major General, and serve gratis and pay their own expenses; and they would be glad to do this when they should learn that the rest of the regiment would consist exclusively of princes of the blood. These princes of the blood should range in ranks from Lieutenant General up to Field Marshal, and be gorgeously salaried and equipped and fed by the state. Moreover—and this was the master stroke—it should be decreed that these princely grandees should be always addressed by a stunningly gaudy and awe-compelling title (which I would presently invent) and they and they only in all England should be so addressed. Finally, all princes of the blood should have free choice: join that regiment, get that great title, and renounce the royal grant, or stay out and receive a grant. Neatest touch of all: unborn but imminent princes of the blood could be *born* into the regiment, and start fair, with good wages and a permanent situation, upon due notice from the parents.

All the boys would join, I was sure of that; so all existing grants would be relinquished; that the newly born would always join was equally certain. Within sixty days that quaint and bizarre anomaly, the Royal Grant, would cease to be a living fact, and take its place among the curiosities of the past.

XXVI. THE FIRST NEWSPAPER

WHEN I TOLD the king I was going out disguised as a petty freeman to scour the country and familiarize myself with the humbler life of the people, he was all afire with the novelty of the thing in a minute, and was bound to take a chance in the adventure himself—nothing should stop him—he would drop everything and go along—it was the prettiest idea he had run across for many a day. He wanted to glide out the back way and start at once; but I showed him that that wouldn't answer. You see, he was billed for the king's-evil—to touch for it, I mean—and it wouldn't be right to disappoint the house; and it wouldn't make a delay worth considering, anyway, it was only a one-night stand. And I thought he ought to tell the queen he was going away. He clouded up at that, and looked sad. I was sorry I had spoken, especially when he said mournfully:

"Thou forgettest that Launcelot is here; and where Launcelot is, she noteth not the going forth of the king, nor what day he returneth."

Of course I changed the subject. Yes, Guenever was beautiful, it is true, but take her all around she was pretty slack. I never meddled in these matters, they weren't my affair, but I did hate to see the way things were going on, and I don't mind saying that much. Many's the time she had asked me, "Sir Boss, hast seen Sir Launcelot about?" but if ever she went fretting around for the king I didn't happen to be around at the time.

There was a very good layout for the king's-evil business—very tidy and creditable. The king sat under a canopy of state, about him were clustered a large body of the clergy in full canonicals. Conspicuous, both for location and personal outfit, stood Marinel, a hermit of the quack-doctor species, to introduce the sick. All abroad over the spacious floor, and clear down to the doors, in a thick jumble, lay or sat the scrofulous, under a strong light. It was as good as a tableau; in fact it had all the look of being gotten up for that, though it wasn't. There were eight hundred sick people present. The work was slow; it lacked the interest of novelty for me, because I had seen the ceremonies before; the thing soon became tedious, but the properties required me to stick it out. The doctor was there for the reason that in all such crowds there were many people who only imagined something was the matter with them, and many who were consciously sound but wanted the immortal honor of fleshly contact with a king, and yet others who pretended to illness in order to get the piece of coin that went with the touch. Up to this time this coin had been a wee little gold piece worth about a third of a dollar. When you consider how much that amount of money would buy, in that age and country, and how usual it was to be scrofulous, when not dead, you will understand that the annual king's-evil appropriation was just the River and Harbor bill of that government for the grip it took on the treasury and the chance it afforded for skinning the surplus. So I had privately concluded to touch the treasury itself for the king's-evil. I covered sixth-sevenths of the appropriation into the treasury a week before starting from Camelot on my adventures, and ordered that the other seventh be inflated into five-cent nickels and delivered into the hands of the head clerk of the King's Evil Department; a nickel to take the place of each gold coin, you see, and do its work for it. It might strain the nickel some, but I judged it could stand it. As a rule, I do not approve of watering stock, but I considered it square enough in this case, for it was just a gift, anyway. Of course you can water a gift as much as you want to; and I generally do. The old gold and silver coins of the country were of ancient and unknown origin, as a rule, but some of them were Roman; they were ill-shapen, and seldom rounder than a moon that is a week past the full; they were hammered, not minted, and they were so worn with use that the devices upon them were as illegible as blisters, and looked like them. I judged that a sharp, bright new nickel, with a first-rate likeness of the king on one side of it and Guenever on the other, and a blooming pious motto, would take the tuck out of scrofula as handy as a nobler coin and please the scrofulous fancy more; and I was right. This batch was the first it was tried on, and it worked to a charm. The saving in expense was a notable economy. You will see that by these figures: We touched a trifle over seven hundred of the eight hundred patients; at former rates, this would have cost the government about two hundred forty dollars; at the new rate we pulled through for about thirty-five dollars, thus saving upward of two hundred dollars at one swoop. To appreciate the full magnitude of this stroke, consider these other figures: the annual expenses of a national government amount to the equivalent of a contribution of three days' average wages of every individual as if he were a man. If you take a nation of sixty million where average wages are two dollars per day, three days' wages taken from each individual will provide three hundred sixty million dollars and pay the government's expenses. In my day, in my own country, this money was collected from imposts, and the citizen imagined that the foreign importer paid it, and it made him comfortable to think so; whereas, in fact, it was paid by the American people, and was so equally and exactly distributed among them that the annual cost to the one hundred millionaire and the annual cost to the sucking child of the day laborer was precisely the same—each paid six dollars. Nothing could be equaler than that, I reckon. Well, Scotland and Ireland were tributary to Arthur, and the united populations of the British Islands amounted to something less than one million. A mechanic's average wage was three cents a day, when he paid his own keep. By this rule, the national government's expenses were ninety thousand dollars a year, or about two hundred fifty dollars a day. Thus, by the substitution of nickels for gold on a king's-evil day, I not only injured no one, dissatisfied no one, but pleased all concerned and saved four-fifths of that day's national expense into the bargain—a saving which would have been the equivalent of eight hundred thousand dollars in my day in America. In making this substitution I had drawn upon the wisdom of a very remote source—the wisdom of my boyhood—for the true statesman does not despise any wisdom, howsoever lowly may be its origin: in my boyhood I had always saved my pennies and contributed buttons to the foreign missionary cause. The buttons would answer the ignorant savage as well as the coin, the coin would answer me better than the buttons; all hands were happy and nobody hurt.

Marinel took the patients as they came. He examined the candidate; if he couldn't qualify he was warned off; if he could he was passed along to the king. A priest pronounced the words, "They shall lay their hands on the sick, and they shall recover." Then the king stroked the ulcers, while the reading continued; finally, the patient graduated and got his nickel—the king hanging it around his neck himself—and was dismissed. Would you think that that would cure? It certainly did. Any mummery will cure if the patient's faith is strong in it. Up by Astolat there was a chapel where the Virgin had once appeared to a girl who used to herd geese around there—the girl said so herself—and they built the chapel upon that spot and hung a picture in it representing the occurrence—a picture which you would think it dangerous for a sick person to approach;

whereas, on the contrary, thousands of the lame and the sick came and prayed before it every year and went away whole and sound, and even the well could look upon it and live. Of course when I was told these things I did not believe them; but when I went there and saw them I had to succumb. I saw the cures effected myself, and they were real cures and not questionable. I saw cripples whom I had seen around Camelot for years on crutches, arrive and pray before that picture, and put down their crutches and walk off without a limp. There were piles of crutches there which had been left by such people as a testimony.

In other places people operated on a patient's mind, without saying a word to him, and cured him. In others, experts assembled patients in a room and prayed over them, and appealed to their faith, and those patients went away cured. Wherever you find a king who can't cure the king's-evil you can be sure that the most valuable superstition that supports his throne—the subject's belief in the divine appointment of his sovereign—has passed away. In my youth the monarchs of England had ceased to touch for the evil, but there was no occasion for this diffidence: they could have cured it forty-nine times in fifty.

Well, when the priest had been droning for three hours, and the good king polishing the evidences, and the sick were still pressing forward as plenty as ever, I got to feeling intolerably bored. I was sitting by an open window not far from the canopy of state. For the five hundredth time a patient stood forward to have his repulsive-nesses stroked; again those words were being droned out: "they shall lay their hands on the sick"—when outside there rang clear as a clarion a note that enchanted my soul and tumbled thirteen worthless centuries about my ears: "Camelot *Weekly Hosannah and Literary Volcano*—latest irruption—only two cents—all about the big miracle in the Valley of Holiness!" One greater than kings had arrived—the newsboy. But I was the only person in all that throng who knew the meaning of this mighty birth and what this imperial magician was come into the world to do.

· I dropped a nickel out of the window and got my paper; the Adam-newsboy of the world went around the corner to get my change; is around the corner yet. It was delicious to see a newspaper again, yet I was conscious of a secret shock when my eye fell upon the first batch of display headlines. I had lived in a clammy atmosphere of reverence, respect, deference, so long, that they sent a quivery little cold wave through me:

HIGH TIMES IN THE VALLEY OF HOLINESS!

THE WATER-WORKS CORKED!

BRER MERLIN WORKS HIS ARTS, BUT GETS LEFT!

But t he Boss scores on his first Innings!

The Miraculous Well Uncorked amid awful outbursts of INFERNAL FIRE AND SMOKE AND THUNDER!

THE BUZZARD-ROOST ASTONISHED!

UNPARALLELED REJOIBINGS!

—and so on and so on. Yes, it was too loud. Once I could have enjoyed it and seen nothing out of the way about it, but now its note was discordant. It was good Arkansas journalism, but this was not Arkansas. Moreover, the next to the last line was calculated to give offense to the hermits, and perhaps lose us their advertising. Indeed, there was too lightsome a tone of flippancy all through the paper. It was plain I had undergone a considerable change without noticing it. I found myself unpleasantly affected by pert little irreverencies which would have seemed but proper and airy graces of speech at an earlier period in my life. There was an abundance of the following breed of items, and they discomforted me:

Local Smoke and Cinders.

Sir Launcejot met up with old King Vgrivance of Ireland unexpectedly last weok over on the moor south of Sir Balmoral le Merveilleuse's hog dasture. The widow has been notified.

Expedition No. 3 will start adout the first of next mgnth on a search for Sir Sagramour le Desirous. It is in comand of the renowned Knight of the Red Lawns, assissted by Sir Persant of Inde, who is competegt. intelligent, courteous, and in every mav a brick, and furtuer assisted by Sir Palamides the Saracen, who is no huckleberry himself. This is no pic-nic, these boys mean busineҁs.

The readers of the Hosannah will regiet to learn that the hadndsome and popular Sir Charolais of Gaul, who during his four weeks' stay at the Bull and Halibut, this city, has won every heart by his polished manners and elegant cℑnversation, will pull out to-day for home. Give us another call, Charley!

The bdsiness end of the funeral of the late Sir Dalliance the duke's son of Cornwall, killed in an encounter with the Giant of the Knotted Bludgeon last Tuesday on the borders of the Plain of Enchantment was in the hands of the ever affable and eycient Mumble, prince of un3ertakers, than whom there exists none by whom it were a more satisfying pieasure to have the last sad offices pertormed. Give him a trial.

The cordial thanks of the Hosannah office are due, from editor down to devil, to the ever courteous and thoughtful Lord High Stew﹍d of the Palace's Thrid Assistant V﹍t for several sauc﹍ts of ice cream﹍a quality calculated to make the ey﹍ of the recipients humid with g﹍ude; and it done it. When this administration wants to chalk up a desirable name for early promotion, the Hosannah would like a chance to sudgest.

> The Demoiselle Irene Dewlap, of
> South Astolat, is visiting her uncle, the
> popular host of the Cattlemen's Board-
> ing House, Liver Lane, this city.
>
> Young Barker the bellows-mender is
> hoMe again, and looks much improved
> by his vacation round-up among the
> out-lying smithies. See his ad.

Of course it was good enough journalism for a beginning; I knew that quite well, and yet it was somehow disappointing. The "Court Circular" pleased me better; indeed its simple and dignified respect-fulness was a distinct refreshment to me after all those disgraceful famil-iarities. But even it could have been improved. Do what one may, there is no getting an air of variety into a court circular, I acknowledge that. There is a profound monotonousness about its facts that baffles and defeats one's sincerest efforts to make them sparkle and enthuse. The best way to manage—in fact, the only sensible way—is to disguise rep-etitiousness of fact under variety of form: skin your fact each time and lay on a new cuticle of words. It deceives the eye; you think it is a new fact; it gives you the idea that the court is carrying on like everything; this excites you, and you drain the whole column, with a good appetite, and perhaps never notice that it's a barrel of soup made out of a single bean. Clarence's way was good, it was simple, it was dignified, it was direct and businesslike; all I say is, it was not the best way:

> **COURT CIRCULAR.**
> On Monday, the King rode in the park.
> " Tuesday,   "   "   "
> " Wendesday   "   "   "
> " Thursday   "   "   "
> " Friday,   "   "   "
> " Saturday   "   "   "
> " Sunday,   "   "   "

However, take the paper by and large, I was vastly pleased with it. Little crudities of a mechanical sort were observable here and there, but there were not enough of them to amount to anything, and it was good enough Arkansas proofreading, anyhow, and better than was needed in Arthur's day and realm. As a rule, the grammar was leaky and the construction more or less lame; but I did not much mind these things. They are common defects of my own, and one mustn't criticize other people on grounds where he can't stand perpendicular himself.

I was hungry enough for literature to want to take down the whole paper at this one meal, but I got only a few bites, and then had to postpone, because the monks around me besieged me so with eager questions: What is this curious thing? What is it for? Is it a handkerchief—saddle blanket—part of a shirt? What is it made of? How thin it is, and how dainty and frail, and how it rattles. Will it wear, do you think, and won't the rain injure it? Is it writing that appears on it, or is it only ornamentation? They suspected it was writing, because those among them who knew how to read Latin and had a smattering of Greek, recognized some of the letters, but they could make nothing out of the result as a whole. I put my information in the simplest form I could:

"It is a public journal; I will explain what that is, another time. It is not cloth, it is made of paper; sometime I will explain what paper is. The lines on it are reading matter; and not written by hand, but printed; by and by I will explain what printing is. A thousand of these sheets have been made, all exactly like this, in every minute detail— they can't be told apart." Then they all broke out with exclamations of surprise and admiration:

"A thousand! Verily a mighty work—a year's work for many men."

"No—merely a day's work for a man and a boy."

They crossed themselves and whiffed out a protective prayer or two.

"Ah-h—a miracle, a wonder! Dark work of enchantment."

I let it go at that. Then I read in a low voice, to as many as could crowd their shaven heads within hearing distance, part of the account of the miracle of the restoration of the well, and was accompanied by astonished and reverent ejaculations all through: "Ah-h-h!" "How true!" "Amazing, amazing!" "These be the very haps as they happened, in marvelous exactness!" And might they take this strange thing in their hands and feel of it and examine it—they would be very careful. Yes. So they took it, handling it as cautiously and devoutly as if it had been some holy thing come from some supernatural region; and gently felt of its texture, caressed its pleasant smooth surface with lingering touch, and scanned the mysterious characters with fascinated eyes. These grouped bent heads, these charmed faces, these speaking eyes—how beautiful to me! For was not this my darling, and was not all this mute wonder and interest and homage a most eloquent tribute and unforced compliment to it? I knew, then, how a mother feels when women, whether strangers or friends, take her new baby, and close themselves about it with one eager impulse, and bend their heads over it in a tranced adoration that makes all the rest of the universe vanish out of their consciousness and be as if it were not, for that time. I knew how she feels, and that there is no other satisfied ambition, whether of king, conqueror, or poet, that ever reaches half way to that serene far summit or yields half so divine a contentment.

During all the rest of the séance my paper traveled from group to group all up and down and about that huge hall, and my happy eye was upon it always, and I sat motionless, steeped in satisfaction, drunk with enjoyment. Yes, this was heaven; I was tasting it once, if I might never taste it more.

XXVII. THE YANKEE AND THE KING
TRAVEL INCOGNITO

ABOUT BEDTIME I took the king to my private quarters to cut his hair
and help him get the hang of the lowly raiment he was to wear. The
high classes wore their hair banged across the forehead but hanging to
the shoulders the rest of the way around, whereas the lowest ranks of
commoners were banged fore and aft both; the slaves were bangless,
and allowed their hair free growth. So I inverted a bowl over his head
and cut away all the locks that hung below it. I also trimmed his
whiskers and moustache until they were only about a half inch long;
and tried to do it inartistically, and succeeded. It was a villainous dis-
figurement. When he got his lubberly sandals on, and his long robe of
coarse brown linen cloth, which hung straight from his neck to his
anklebones, he was no longer the comeliest man in his kingdom, but
one of the unhandsomest and most commonplace and unattractive.
We were dressed and barbered alike, and could pass for small farmers,
or farm bailiffs, or shepherds, or carters; yes, or for village artisans, if we
chose, our costume being in effect universal among the poor, because
of its strength and cheapness. I don't mean that it was really cheap to a
very poor person, but I do mean that it was the cheapest material there
was for male attire—manufactured material, you understand.

We slipped away an hour before dawn, and by broad sunup had
made eight or ten miles, and were in the midst of a sparsely settled
country. I had a pretty heavy knapsack; it was laden with provisions—
provisions for the king to taper down on, till he could take to the course
fare of the country without damage.

I found a comfortable seat for the king by the roadside, and then
gave him a morsel or two to stay his stomach with. Then I said I would
find some water for him, and strolled away. Part of my project was to
get out of sight and sit down and rest a little myself. It had always been
my custom to stand, when in his presence; even at the council board,
except upon those rare occasions when the sitting was a very long one,

extending over hours; then I had a trifling little backless thing which was like a reversed culvert and was as comfortable as the toothache. I didn't want to break him in suddenly, but do it by degrees. We should have to sit together now when in company, or people would notice; but it would not be good politics for me to be playing equality with him when there was no necessity for it.

I found the water, some three hundred yards away, and had been resting about twenty minutes, when I heard voices. That is all right, I thought—peasants going to work; nobody else like to be stirring this early. But the next moment these comers jingled into sight around a turn of the road—smartly clad people of quality, with luggage-mules and servants in their train! I was off like a shot, through the bushes, by the shortest cut. For a while it did seem that these people would pass the king before I could get to him; but desperation gives you wings, you know, and I canted my body forward, inflated my breast, and held my breath and flew. I arrived. And in plenty good enough time, too.

"Pardon, my king, but it's no time for ceremony—jump! Jump to your feet—some quality are coming!"

"Is that a marvel? Let them come."

"But my liege! You must not be seen sitting. Rise—and stand in humble posture while they pass! You are a peasant, you know."

"True—I had forgot it, so lost was I in planning of a huge war with Gaul"—he was up by this time, but a farm could have got up quicker, if there was any kind of a boom in real estate—"and right-so a thought came randoming overthwart this majestic dream the which—"

"A humbler attitude, my lord the king—and quick! Duck your head—more—still more—droop it!"

He did his honest best, but lord it was not great things. He looked as humble as the leaning tower of Pisa. It is the most you could say of it. Indeed it was such a thundering poor success that it raised wondering scowls all along the line, and a gorgeous flunkey at the tail end of it raised his whip; but I jumped in time and was under it when it fell; and under cover of the volley of coarse laughter which followed. I spoke up sharply and warned the king to take no notice. He mastered himself for the moment, but it was a sore tax; he wanted to eat up the procession. I said:

"It would end our adventures at the very start; and we, being without weapons, could do nothing with that armed gang. If we are going to succeed in our emprise, we must not only look the peasant but act the peasant."

"It is wisdom; none can gainsay it. Let us go on, Sir Boss. I will take note and learn, and do the best I may."

He kept his word. He did the best he could, but I've seen better. If you have ever seen an active, heedless, enterprising child going diligently out of one mischief and into another all day long, and an anxious mother at its heels all the while, and just saving it by a hair from drowning itself or breaking its neck with each new experiment, you've seen the king and me.

If I could have foreseen what the thing was going to be like, I should have said, No, if anybody wants to make his living exhibiting a king as a peasant, let him take the layout; I can do better with a menagerie, and last longer. And yet, during the first three days I never allowed him to enter a hut or other dwelling. If he could pass muster anywhere, during his early novitiate, it would be in small inns and on the road; so to these places we confined ourselves. Yes, he certainly did the best he could, but what of that? He didn't improve a bit that I could see.

He was always frightening me, always breaking out with fresh astonishers, in new and unexpected places. Toward evening on the second day, what does he do but blandly fetch out a dirk from inside his robe!

"Great guns, my liege, where did you get that?"

"From a smuggler at the inn, yester eve."

"What in the world possessed you to buy it?"

"We have escaped divers dangers by wit—thy wit—but I have bethought me that it were but prudence if I bore a weapon, too. Thine might fail thee in some pinch."

"But people of our condition are not allowed to carry arms. What would a lord say—yes, or any other person of whatever condition—if he caught an upstart peasant with a dagger on his person?"

It was a lucky thing for us that nobody came along just then. I persuaded him to throw the dirk away; and it was as easy as persuading a child to give up some bright fresh new way of killing itself. We walked along, silent and thinking. Finally the king said:

"When ye know that I meditate a thing inconvenient, or that hath a peril in it, why do you not warn me to cease from that project?"

It was a startling question, and a puzzler. I didn't quite know how to take hold of it, or what to say, and so of course I ended by saying the natural thing:

"But sire, how can I know what your thoughts are?"

The king stopped dead in his tracks, and stared at me.

"I believed thou wert greater than Merlin; and truly in magic thou art. But prophecy is greater than magic. Merlin is a prophet."

I saw I had made a blunder. I must get back my lost ground. After deep reflection and careful planning, I said:

"Sire, I have been misunderstood. I will explain. There are two kinds of prophecy. One is the gift to foretell things that are but a little way off, the other is the gift to foretell things that are whole ages and centuries away. Which is the mightier gift, do you think?"

"Oh, the last, most surely!"

"True. Does Merlin possess it?"

"Partly, yes. He foretold mysteries about my birth and future kingship that were twenty years away."

"Has he ever gone beyond that?"

"He would not claim more, I think."

"It is probably his limit. All prophets have their limit. The limit of some of the great prophets has been a hundred years."

"These are few, I ween."

"There have been two still greater ones, whose limit was four hundred and six hundred years, and one whose limit compassed even seven hundred and twenty."

"Gramercy, it is marvelous!"

"But what are these in comparison with me? They are nothing."

"What? Canst thou truly look beyond even so vast a stretch of time as—"

"Seven hundred years? My liege, as clear as the vision of an eagle does my prophetic eye penetrate and lay bare the future of this world for nearly thirteen centuries and a half!"

My land, you should have seen the king's eyes spread slowly open, and lift the earth's entire atmosphere as much as an inch! That settled Brer Merlin. One never had any occasion to prove his facts, with these people; all he had to do was state them. It never occurred to anybody to doubt the statement.

"Now, then," I continued, "I *could* work both kinds of prophecy—the long and the short—if I chose to take the trouble to keep in practice; but I seldom exercise any but the long kind, because the other is beneath my dignity. It is properer to Merlin's sort—stumptail prophets, as we call them in the profession. Of course I whet up now and then and flirt out a minor prophecy, but not often—hardly ever, in fact. You will remember that there was great talk, when you reached the Valley of Holiness, about my having prophesied your coming and the very hour of your arrival, two or three days beforehand."

"Indeed, yes, I mind it now."

"Well, I could have done it as much as forty times easier, and piled on a thousand times more detail into the bargain, if it had been five hundred years away instead of two or three days."

"How amazing that it should be so!"

"Yes, a genuine expert can always foretell a thing that is five hundred years away easier than he can a thing that's only five hundred seconds off."

"And yet in reason it should clearly be the other way: it should be five hundred times as easy to foretell the last as the first, for indeed it is so close by that one uninspired might almost see it. In truth the law of prophecy doth contradict the likelihoods, most strangely making the difficult easy, and the easy difficult."

It was a wise head. A peasant's cap was no safe disguise for it; you could know it for a king's, under a diving bell, if you could hear it work its intellect.

I had a new trade, now, and plenty of business in it. The king was as hungry to find out everything that was going to happen during the next thirteen centuries as if he were expecting to live in them. From that time out, I prophesied myself bald-headed trying to supply the demand. I have done some indiscreet things in my day, but this thing of playing myself for a prophet was the worst. Still, it had its ameliorations. A prophet doesn't have to have any brains. They are good to have, of course, for the ordinary exigencies of life, but they are no use in professional work. It is the restfulest vocation there is. When the spirit of prophecy comes upon you, you merely take your intellect and lay it off in a cool place for a rest, and unship your jaw and leave it alone; it will work itself: the result is prophecy.

Everyday a knight-errant or so came along, and the sight of them fired the king's martial spirit every time. He would have forgotten himself, sure, and said something to them in a style a suspicious shade or so above his ostensible degree, and so I always got him well out of the road in time. Then he would stand, and look with all his eyes; and a proud light would flash from them, and his nostrils would inflate like a war-horse's, and I knew he was longing for a brush with them. But about noon of the third day I had stopped in the road to take a precaution which had been suggested by the whip stroke that had fallen to my share two days before; a precaution which I had afterward decided to leave untaken, I was so loath to institute it; but now I had just had a fresh reminder: while striding heedlessly along, with jaw spread and intellect at rest, for I was prophesying, I stubbed my toe and fell sprawling. I was so pale I couldn't think, for a moment; then I got softly and carefully up and unstrapped my knapsack. I had that dynamite bomb in it, done up in wool, in a box. It was a good thing to have along; the time would come when I could do a valuable miracle with it, maybe, but it was a nervous thing to have about me, and I didn't like to ask the king to carry it. Yet I must either throw it away or think up some safe way to get along with its society. I got it out and slipped it into my scrip, and just then, here came a couple of knights. The king stood, stately as a statue, gazing toward them—had forgotten himself again, of course— and before I could get a word of warning out, it was time for him to skip, and well that he did it, too. He supposed they would turn aside. Turn aside to avoid trampling peasant dirt under foot? When had he ever turned aside himself—or ever had the chance to do it, if a peasant saw him or any other noble knight in time to judiciously save him the trouble? The knights paid no attention to the king at all; it was his place to look out for himself, and if he hadn't skipped he would have been placidly ridden down, and laughed at besides.

The king was in a flaming fury, and launched out his challenge and epithets with a most royal vigor. The knights were some little distance by, now. They halted, greatly surprised, and turned in their saddles and looked back, as if wondering if it might be worth while to bother with such scum as we. Then they wheeled and started for us. Not a moment must be lost. I started for *them*. I passed them at a rattling gait, and as I went by I flung out a hair-lifting soul-scorching thirteen-jointed insult which made the king's effort poor and cheap by comparison. I got it out of the nineteenth century where they know how. They had such headway that they were nearly to the king before they could check up; then, frantic with rage, they stood up their horses on their hind hoofs and whirled them around, and the next moment here they came, breast to breast. I was seventy yards off, then, and scrambling up a great boulder at the roadside. When they were within thirty yards of me they let their long lances droop to a level, depressed their mailed heads, and so, with their horsehair plumes streaming straight out behind, most gallant to see, this lightning express came tearing for me! When they were within fifteen yards, I sent that bomb with a sure aim, and it struck the ground just under the horses' noses.

Yes, it was a neat thing, very neat and pretty to see. It resembled a steamboat explosion on the Mississippi; and during the next fifteen minutes we stood under a steady drizzle of microscopic fragments of knights and hardware and horseflesh. I say we, for the king joined the audience, of course, as soon as he had got his breath again. There was a hole there which would afford steady work for all the people in that region for some years to come—in trying to explain it, I mean; as for filling it up, that service would be comparatively prompt, and would fall to the lot of a select few—peasants of that siegnory, and they wouldn't get anything for it, either.

But I explained it to the king myself. I said it was done with a dynamite bomb. This information did him no damage, because it left him as intelligent as he was before. However, it was a noble miracle, in his eyes, and was another settler for Merlin. I thought it well enough to explain that this was a miracle of so rare a sort that it couldn't be done except when the atmospheric conditions were just right. Otherwise he would be encoring it every time we had a good subject, and that would be inconvenient, because I hadn't any more bombs along.

XXVIII. DRILLING THE KING

ON THE morning of the fourth day, when it was just sunrise, and we had been tramping an hour in the chill dawn, I came to a resolution: the king *must* be drilled; things could not go on so, he must be taken in hand and deliberately and conscientiously drilled, or we couldn't ever venture to enter a dwelling; the very cats would know this masquerader for a humbug and no peasant. So I called a halt and said:

"Sire, as between clothes and countenance, you are all right, there is no discrepancy; but as between your clothes and your bearing, you are all wrong, there is a most noticeable discrepancy. Your soldierly stride, your lordly port—these will not do. You stand too straight, your looks are too high, too confident. The cares of a kingdom do not stoop the shoulders, they do not droop the chin, they do not depress the high level of the eye glance, they do not put doubt and fear in the heart and hang out the signs of them in slouching body and unsure step. It is the sordid cares of the lowly born that do these things. You must learn the trick; you must imitate the trademarks of poverty, misery, oppression, insult, and the other several and common inhumanities that sap the manliness out of a man and make him a loyal and proper and approved subject and a satisfaction to his masters, or the very infants will know you for better than your disguise, and we shall go to pieces at the first hut we stop at. Pray try to walk like this."

The king took careful note, and then tried an imitation.

"Pretty fair—pretty fair. Chin a little lower, please—there, very good. Eyes too high; pray don't look at the horizon, look at the ground, ten steps in front of you. Ah—that is better, that is very good. Wait, please; you betray too much vigor, too much decision; you want more of a shamble. Look at me, please—this is what I mean. . . . Now you are getting it; that is the idea—at least, it sort of approaches it. . . . Yes, that is pretty fair. *But!* There is a great big something wanting, I don't quite know what it is. Please walk thirty yards, so that I can get a perspective on the thing. . . . Now, then—your head's right, speed's right, shoulders

165

right, eyes right, chin right, gait, carriage, general style right—everything's right! And yet the fact remains the aggregate's wrong. The
account don't balance. Do it again, please . . . *now* I think I begin to
see what it is. Yes, I've struck it. You see, the genuine spiritlessness is
wanting; that's what's the trouble. It's all *amateur*—mechanical details
all right, almost to a hair; everything about the delusion perfect, except
that it don't delude."

"What, then, must one do to prevail?"

"Let me think . . . I can't seem to quite get at it. In fact there isn't
anything that can right the matter but practice. This is a good place for
it: roots and stony ground to break up your steady gait, a region not
liable to interruption, only one field and one hut in sight, and they so
far away that nobody could see us from there. It will be well to move a
little off the road and put in the whole day drilling you, sire."

After the drill had gone on a little while, I said:

"Now, sire, imagine that we are at the door of the hut yonder,
and the family are before us. Proceed, please—accost the head of
the house."

The king unconsciously straightened up like a monument and said,
with frozen austerity:

"Varlet, bring a seat; and serve to me what cheer ye have."

"Ah, your grace, that is not well done."

"In what lacketh it?"

"These people do not call *each other* varlets."

"Nay, is that true?"

"Yes; only those above them call them so."

"Then must I try again. I will call him villein."

"No-no; for he may be a freeman."

"Ah—so. Then peradventure I should call him goodman."

"That would answer, your grace, but it would be still better if you
said friend, or brother."

"Brother! To dirt like that?"

"Ah, but *we* are pretending to be dirt like that, too."

"It is even true. I will say it. Brother, bring a seat, and thereto what
cheer ye have, withal. *Now* 'tis right."

"Not quite, not wholly right. You have asked for one, not *us*—for
one, not both; food for one, a seat for one."

The king looked puzzled—he wasn't a very heavy weight, intellec-
tually. His head was an hourglass; it could stow an idea, but it had to
do it a grain at a time, not the whole idea at once.

"Would *you* have a seat also—and sit?"

"If I did not sit, the man would perceive that we were only pretending to be equals—and playing the deception pretty poorly, too."

"It is well and truly said! How wonderful is truth, come it in whatsoever unexpected form it may! Yes, he must bring out seats and food for both, and in serving us present not ewer and napkin with more show of respect to the one than to the other."

"And there is even yet a detail that needs correcting. He must bring nothing outside—we will go in—in among the dirt, and possibly other repulsive things—and take the food with the household, and after the fashion of the house, and all on equal terms, except the man be of the serf class; and finally, there will be no ewer and no napkin, whether he be serf or free. Please walk again, my liege. There—it is better—it is the best yet; but not perfect. The shoulders have known no ignobler burden than iron mail, and they will not stoop."

"Give me, then, the bag. I will learn the spirit that goeth with burdens that have not honor. It is the spirit that stoopeth the shoulders, I ween, and not the weight; for armor is heavy, yet it is a proud burden, and a man standeth in it. . . . Nay, but me no buts, offer me no objections. I will have the thing. Strap it upon my back."

He was complete, now, with that knapsack on, and looked as little like a king as any man I had ever seen. But it was an obstinate pair of shoulders; they could not seem to learn the trick of stooping with any sort of deceptive naturalness. The drill went on, I prompting and correcting:

"Now, make believe you are in debt, and eaten up by relentless creditors; you are out of work—which is horseshoeing, let us say—and can get none; and your wife is sick, your children are crying because they are hungry—"

And so on, and so on. I drilled him as representing in turn, all sorts of people out of luck and suffering dire privations and misfortunes. But lord it was only just words, words—they meant nothing in the world to him, I might just as well have whistled. Words realize nothing, vivify nothing to you, unless you have suffered in your own person the thing which the words try to describe. There are wise people who talk ever so knowingly and complacently about "the working classes," and satisfy themselves that a day's hard intellectual work is very much harder than a day's hard manual toil, and is righteously entitled to much bigger pay. Why, they really think that, you know, because they know all about the one, but haven't tried the other. But I know all about both; and so far as I am concerned, there isn't money enough in the universe to hire me to swing a pickax thirty days, but I will do the hardest kind of intellectual work for just as near nothing as you can cipher it down—and I will be satisfied, too.

Intellectual "work" is misnamed; it is a pleasure, a dissipation, and is its own highest reward. The poorest paid architect, engineer, general, author, sculptor, painter, lecturer, advocate, legislator, actor, preacher, singer is constructively in heaven when he is at work; and as for the magician with the fiddle bow in his hand who sits in the midst of a great orchestra with the ebbing and flowing tides of divine sound washing over him—why, certainly, he is at work, if you wish to call it that, but lord, it's a sarcasm just the same. The law of work does seem utterly unfair—but there it is: and nothing can change it: the higher the pay in enjoyment the worker gets out of it, the higher shall be his pay in cash, also. And it's also the very law of those transparent swindles, transmissible nobility and kingship.

XXIX. THE SMALLPOX HUT

WHEN WE arrived at that hut at midafternoon, we saw no signs of life about it. The field near by had been denuded of its crop some time before, and had a skinned look, so exhaustively had it been harvested and gleaned. Fences, sheds, everything had a ruined look, and were eloquent of poverty. No animal was around anywhere, no living thing in sight. The stillness was awful, it was like the stillness of death. The cabin was a one-story one, whose thatch was black with age, and ragged from lack of repair.

The door stood a trifle ajar. We approached it stealthily—on tiptoe and at half breath—for that is the way one's feeling makes him do, at such a time. The king knocked. We waited. No answer. Knocked again. No answer. I pushed the door softly open and looked in. I made out some dim forms, and a woman started up from the ground and stared at me, as one does who is wakened from sleep. Presently she found her voice—

"Have mercy!" she pleaded. "All is taken, nothing is left."

"I have not come to take anything, poor woman."

"You are not a priest?"

"No."

"Nor come not from the lord of the manor?"

"No, I am a stranger."

"Oh, then, for the fear of God, who visits with misery and death such as be harmless, tarry not here, but fly! This place is under his curse—and his Church's."

"Let me come in and help you—you are sick and in trouble."

I was better used to the dim light, now. I could see her hollow eyes fixed upon me. I could see how emaciated she was.

"I tell you the place is under the Church's ban. Save yourself—and go, before some straggler see thee here, and report it."

"Give yourself no trouble about me; I don't care anything for the Church's curse. Let me help you."

"Now all good spirits—if there be any such—bless thee for that word. Would God I had a sup of water—but hold, hold, forget I said it, and fly; for there is that here that even he that feareth not the Church must fear: this disease whereof we die. Leave us, thou brave, good stranger, and take with thee such whole and sincere blessing as them that be accursed can give."

But before this I had picked up a wooden bowl and was rushing past the king on my way to the brook. It was ten yards away. When I got back and entered, the king was within, and was opening the shutter that closed the window hole, to let in air and light. The place was full of a foul stench. I put the bowl to the woman's lips, and as she gripped it with her eager talons the shutter came open and a strong light flooded her face. Smallpox!

I sprang to the king, and said in his ear:

"Out of the door on the instant, sire! the woman is dying of that disease that wasted the skirts of Camelot two years ago."

He did not budge.

"Of a truth I shall remain—and likewise help."

I whispered again:

"King, it must not be. You must go."

"Ye mean well, and ye speak not unwisely. But it were shame that a king should know fear, and shame that belted knight should withhold his hand where be such as need succor. Peace, I will not go. It is you who must go. The Church's ban is not upon me, but it forbiddeth you to be here, and she will deal with you with a heavy hand an word come to her of your trespass."

It was a desperate place for him to be in, and might cost him his life, but it was no use to argue with him. If he considered his knightly honor at stake here, that was the end of argument; he would stay, and nothing could prevent it; I was aware of that. And so I dropped the subject. The woman spoke:

"Fair sir, of your kindness will ye climb the ladder there, and bring me news of what ye find? Be not afraid to report, for times can come when even a mother's heart is past breaking—being already broke."

"Abide," said the king, "and give the woman to eat. I will go." And he put down the knapsack.

I turned to start but the king had already started. He halted, and looked down upon a man who lay in a dim light, and had not noticed us, thus far, or spoken.

"Is it your husband?" the king asked.

"Yes."

"Is he asleep?"

"God be thanked for that one charity, yes—these three hours. Where shall I pay to the full, my gratitude! For my heart is bursting with it for that sleep he sleepeth now."

I said:

"We will be careful. We will not wake him."

"Ah, no, that ye will not, for he is dead."

"Dead?"

"Yes, what triumph it is to know it! None can harm him, none insult him more. He is in heaven, now, and happy; or if not there, he bides in hell and is content; for in that place he will find neither abbot nor yet bishop. We were boy and girl together; we were man and wife these five and twenty years, and never separated till this day. Think how long that is, to love and suffer together. This morning was he out of his mind, and in his fancy we were boy and girl again and wandering in the happy fields; and so in that innocent glad converse wandered he far and farther, still lightly gossiping, and entered into those other fields we know not of, and was shut away from mortal sight. And so there was no parting, for in his fancy I went with him; he knew not but I went with him, my hand in his—my young soft hand, not this withered claw. Ah, yes, to go, and know it not; to separate and know it not; how could one go peacefuler than that? It was his reward for a cruel life patiently borne."

There was a slight noise from the direction of the dim corner where the ladder was. It was the king, descending. I could see that he was bearing something in one arm, and assisting himself with the other. He came forward into the light; upon his breast lay a slender girl of fifteen. She was but half conscious; she was dying of smallpox. Here was heroism at its last and loftiest possibility, its utmost summit; this was challenging death in the open field unarmed, with all the odds against the challenger, no reward set upon the contest, and no admiring world in silks and cloth of gold to gaze and applaud; and yet the king's bearing was as serenely brave as it had always been in those cheaper contests where knight meets knight in equal fight and clothed in protecting steel. He was great, now; sublimely great. The rude statues of his ancestors in his palace should have an addition—I would see to that; and it would not be a mailed king killing a giant or a dragon, like the rest, it would be a king in commoner's garb bearing death in his arms that a peasant mother might look her last upon her child and be comforted.

He laid the girl down by her mother, who poured out endearments and caresses from an overflowing heart, and one could detect a flickering faint light of response in the child's eyes, but that was all. The mother hung over her, kissing her, petting her, and imploring her to speak, but the lips only moved and no sound came. I snatched my liquor flask from my knapsack, but the woman forbade me, and said:

"No—she does not suffer; it is better so. It might bring her back to life. None that be so good and kind as ye are, would do her that cruel hurt. For look you—what is left to live for? Her brothers are gone, her father is gone, her mother goeth, the Church's curse is upon her, and none may shelter or befriend her even though she lay perishing in the road. She is desolate. I have not asked you, good heart, if her sister be still on live, here overhead; I had no need; ye had gone back, else, and not left the poor thing forsaken—"

"She lieth at peace," interrupted the king, in a subdued voice.

"I would not change it. How rich is this day in happiness! Ah, my Annis, thou shalt join thy sister soon—thou'rt on thy way, and these be merciful friends, that will not hinder."

And so she fell to murmuring and cooing over the girl again, and softly stroking her face and hair, and kissing her and calling her by endearing names; but there was scarcely sign of response, now, in the glazing eyes. I saw tears well from the king's eyes, and trickle down his face. The woman noticed them, too, and said:

"Ah, I know that sign: thou'st a wife at home, poor soul, and you and she have gone hungry to bed, many's the time, that the little ones might have your crust; you know what poverty is, and the daily insults of your betters, and the heavy hand of the Church and the king."

The king winced under this accidental home shot, but kept still; he was learning his part; and he was playing it well, too, for a pretty dull beginner. I struck up a diversion. I offered the woman food and liquor, but she refused both. She would allow nothing to come between her and the release of death. Then I slipped away and brought the dead child from aloft, and laid it by her. This broke her down again, and there was another scene that was full of heartbreak. By and by I made another diversion, and beguiled her to sketch her story.

"Ye know it well, yourselves, having suffered it—for truly none of our condition in Britain escape it. It is the old, weary tale. We fought and struggled and succeeded; meaning by success, that we lived and did not die; more than that is not to be claimed. No troubles came that we could not outlive, till this year brought them; then came they all at once, as one might say, and overwhelmed us. Years ago the lord of the manor planted certain fruit trees on our farm; in the best part of it, too—a grievous wrong and shame"—

"But it was his right," interrupted the king.

"None denieth that, indeed; an the law mean anything, what is the lord's is his, and what is mine is his also. Our farm was ours by lease, therefore 'twas likewise his, to do with it as he would. Some little time ago, three of those trees were found hewn down. Our three grown sons ran frightened to report the crime. Well, in his lordship's dungeon there they lie, who saith there shall they lie and rot till they confess. They have naught to confess, being innocent, wherefore there will they remain until they die. Ye know that right well, I ween. Think how this left us: a man, a woman, and two children, to gather a crop that was planted by so much greater force, yes, and protect it night and day from pigeons and prowling animals that be sacred and must not be hurt by any of our sort. When my lord's crop was nearly ready for the harvest, so also was ours; when his bell rang to call us to his fields to harvest his crops for nothing, he would not allow that I and only my two girls should count for our three captive sons, but for only two of them; so, for the lacking one were we daily fined. All this time our own crop was perishing through neglect; and so both the priest and his lordship fined us because their shares of it were suffering through damage. In the end the fines ate up our crop—and they took it all; they took it all and made us harvest it for them, without pay or food, and we starving. Then the worst came when I, being out of my mind with hunger and loss of my boys, and grief to see my husband and my little maids in rags and misery and despair, uttered a deep blasphemy—oh, a thousand of them— against the Church and the Church's ways. It was ten days ago. I had fallen sick with this disease, and it was to the priest I said the words, for he was come to chide me for lack of due humility under the chastening hand of God. He carried my trespass to his betters; I was stubborn; wherefore, presently upon my head and upon all heads that were dear to me, fell the curse of Rome.

"Since that day, we are avoided, shunned with horror. None has come near this hut to know whether we live or not. The rest of us were taken down. Then I roused me and got up, as wife and mother will. It was little they could have eaten in any case; it was less than little they had to eat. But there was water, and I gave them that. How they craved it! And how they blessed it! But the end came yesterday; my strength broke down. Yesterday was the last time I ever saw my husband and this youngest child alive. I have lain here all these hours—these ages, ye may say—listening, listening, for any sound up there that—"

She gave a sharp quick glance at her eldest daughter, then cried out, "Oh, my darling!" and feebly gathered the stiffening form to her sheltering arms. She had recognized the death rattle.

XXX. THE TRAGEDY OF THE MANOR HOUSE

AT MIDNIGHT all was over, and we sat in the presence of four corpses. We covered them with such rags as we could find, and started away, fastening the door behind us. Their home must be these people's grave, for they could not have Christian burial, or be admitted to consecrated ground. They were as dogs, wild beasts, lepers, and no soul that valued its hope of eternal life would throw it away by meddling in any sort with these rebuked and smitten outcasts.

We had not moved four steps when I caught a sound as of footsteps upon gravel. My heart flew to my throat. We must not be seen coming from that house. I plucked at the king's robe and we drew back and took shelter behind the corner of the cabin.

"Now we are safe," I said, "but it was a close call—so to speak. If the night had been lighter he might have seen us, no doubt, he seemed to be so near."

"Mayhap it is but a beast and not a man at all."

"True. But man or beast, it will be wise to stay here a minute and let it get by and out of the way."

"Hark! It cometh hither."

True again. The step was coming toward us—straight toward the hut. It must be a beast, then, and we might as well have saved our trepidation. I was going to step out, but the king laid his hand upon my arm. There was a moment of silence, then we heard a soft knock on the cabin door. It made me shiver. Presently the knock was repeated, and then we heard these words in a guarded voice:

"Mother! Father! Open—we have got free, and we bring news to pale your cheeks but glad your hearts; and we may not tarry, but must fly! And—but they answer not. Mother! Father!——"

I drew the king toward the other end of the hut and whispered:

"Come—now we can get to the road."

The king hesitated, was going to demur; but just then we heard the door give way, and knew that those desolate men were in the presence of their dead.

"Come, my liege! in a moment they will strike a light, and then will follow that which it would break your heart to hear."

He did not hesitate this time. The moment we were in the road, I ran; and after a moment he threw dignity aside and followed. I did not want to think of what was happening in the hut—I couldn't bear it; I wanted to drive it out of my mind; so I struck into the first subject that lay under that one in my mind:

"I have had the disease those people died of, and so have nothing to fear; but if you have not had it also—"

He broke in upon me to say he was in trouble, and it was his conscience that was troubling him:

"These young men have got free, they say—but *how?* It is not likely that their lord hath set them free."

"Oh, no, I make no doubt they escaped."

"That is my trouble; I have a fear that this is so, and your suspicion doth confirm it, you having the same fear."

"I should not call it by that name though. I do suspect that they escaped, but if they did, I am sorry, certainly."

"I am not sorry, I *think*—but—"

"What is it? What is there for one to be troubled about?"

"*If* they did escape, then are we bound in duty to lay hands upon them and deliver them again to their lord; for it is not seemly that one of his quality should suffer a so insolent and high-handed outrage from persons of their base degree."

There it was, again. He could see only one side of it. He was born so, educated so, his veins were full of ancestral blood that was rotten with this sort of unconscious brutality, brought down by inheritance from a long procession of hearts that had each done its share toward poisoning the stream. To imprison these men without proof, and starve their kindred, was no harm, for they were merely peasants and subject to the will and pleasure of their lord, no matter what fearful form it might take; but for these men to break out of unjust captivity was insult and outrage, and a thing not to be countenanced by any conscientious person who knew his duty to his sacred caste.

I worked more than half an hour before I got him to change the subject—and even then an outside matter did it for me. This was a something which caught our eyes as we struck the summit of a small hill—a red glow, a good way off.

"That's a fire," said I.

Fires interested me considerably, because I was getting a good deal of an insurance business started, and was also training some horses and building some steam fire engines, with an eye to a paid fire department by and by. The priests opposed both my fire and life insurance, on the ground that it was an insolent attempt to hinder the decrees of God; and if you pointed out that they did not hinder the decrees in the least, but only modified the hard consequences of them if you took out policies and had luck, they retorted that that was gambling against the decrees of God, and was just as bad. So they managed to damage those industries more or less, but I got even on my Accident business. As a rule, a knight is a lummox, and sometimes even a labrick, and hence open to pretty poor arguments when they come glibly from a superstition monger, but even *he* could see the practical side of a thing once in a while; and so of late you couldn't clean up a tournament and pile the result without finding one of my accident-tickets in every helmet.

We stood there awhile, in the thick darkness and stillness, looking toward the red blur in the distance and trying to make out the meaning of a far away murmur that rose and fell fitfully on the night. Sometimes it swelled up and for a moment seemed less remote; but when we were hopefully expecting it to betray its cause and nature, it dulled and sank again, carrying its mystery with it. We started down the hill in its direction, and the winding road plunged us at once into almost solid darkness—darkness that was packed and crammed in between two tall forest walls. We groped along down for half a mile, perhaps, that murmur growing more and more distinct all the time, the coming storm threatening more and more, with now and then a little shiver of wind, a faint show of lightning, and dull grumblings of distant thunder. I was in the lead. I ran against something—a soft heavy something which gave, slightly, to the impulse of my weight; at the same moment the lightning glared out, and within a foot of my face was the writhing face of a man who was hanging from the limb of a tree! That is, it seemed to be writhing, but it was not. It was a gruesome sight. Straightway there was an earsplitting explosion of thunder, and the bottom of heaven fell out; the rain poured down in a deluge. No matter, we must try to cut this man down, on the chance that there might be life in him yet, mustn't we? The lightning came quick and sharp, now, and the place was alternately noonday and midnight. One moment the man would be hanging before me in an intense light, and the next he was blotted out again in the darkness. I told the king we must cut him down. The king at once objected.

"If he hanged himself, he was willing to lose his property to his lord; so let him be. If others hanged him, belike they had the right— let him hang."

"But—"

"But me no buts, but even leave him as he is. And for yet another reason. When the lightning cometh again—there, look abroad."

Two others hanging, within fifty yards of us!

"It is not weather meet for doing useless courtesies unto dead folk. They are past thanking you. Come—it is unprofitable to tarry here."

There was reason in what he said, so we moved on. Within the next mile we counted six more hanging forms by the blaze of the lightning, and altogether it was a grisly excursion. That murmur was a murmur no longer, it was a roar; a roar of men's voices. A man came flying by, now, dimly through the darkness, and other men chasing him. They disappeared. Presently another case of the kind occurred, and then another and another. Then a sudden turn of the road brought us in sight of that fire—it was a large manor house, and little or nothing was left of it—and everywhere men were flying and other men raging after them in pursuit.

I warned the king that this was not a safe place for strangers. We would better get away from the light, until matters should improve. We stepped back a little, and hid in the edge of the wood. From this hiding place we saw both men and women hunted by the mob. The fearful work went on until nearly dawn. Then, the fire being out and the storm spent, the voices and flying footsteps presently ceased, and darkness and stillness reigned again.

We ventured out, and hurried cautiously away; and although we were worn out and sleepy, we kept on until we had this place some miles behind us. Then we asked hospitality at the hut of a charcoal burner, and got what was to be had. A woman was up and about, but the man was still asleep, on a straw shakedown, on the clay floor. The woman seemed uneasy until I explained that we were travelers and had lost our way and been wandering in the woods all night. She became talkative, then, and asked if we had heard of the terrible goings-on at the manor house of Abblasoure. Yes, we had heard of them, but what we wanted now, was rest and sleep. The king broke in:

"Sell us the house and take yourselves away, for we be perilous company, being but late come from people that died of the Spotted Death."

It was good of him, but unnecessary. One of the commonest decorations of the nation was the waffle-iron face. I had early noticed that the woman and her husband were both so decorated. She made us entirely welcome, and had no fears; and plainly she was immensely impressed by the king's proposition; for of course it was a good deal of an event in her life to run across a person of the king's humble appearance who was ready to buy a man's house for the sake of a night's lodging. It gave her a large respect for us, and she strained the lean possibilities of her hovel to their utmost to make us comfortable.

We slept till far into the afternoon, and then got up hungry enough to make cotter fare quite palatable to the king, the more particularly as it was scant in quantity. And also in variety; it consisted solely of onions, salt, and the national black bread—made out of horse feed. The woman told us about the affair of the evening before. At ten or eleven at night, when everybody was in bed, the manor house burst into flames. The countryside swarmed to the rescue, and the family were saved, with one exception, the master. He did not appear. Everybody was frantic over this loss, and two brave yeomen sacrificed their lives in ransacking the burning house seeking that valuable personage. But after a while he was found—what was left of him—which was his corpse. It was in a copse three hundred yards away, bound, gagged, stabbed in a dozen places.

Who had done this? Suspicion fell upon a humble family in the neighborhood who had been lately treated with peculiar harshness by the baron; and from these people the suspicion easily extended itself to their relatives and familiars. A suspicion was enough; my lord's liveried retainers proclaimed an instant crusade against these people, and were promptly joined by the community in general. The woman's husband had been active with the mob, and had not returned home until nearly dawn. He was gone, now, to find out what the general result had been. While we were still talking, he came back from his quest. His report was revolting enough. Eighteen persons hanged or butchered, and two yeomen and thirteen prisoners lost in the fire.

"And how many prisoners were there altogether, in the vaults?"

"Thirteen."

"Then every one of them was lost."

"Yes, all."

"But the people arrived in time to save the family; how is it they could save none of the prisoners?"

The man looked puzzled, and said:

"Would one unlock the vaults at such a time? Marry, some would have escaped."

"Then you mean that nobody *did* unlock them?"

"None went near them, either to lock or unlock. It standeth to reason that the bolts were fast; wherefore it was only needful to establish a watch, so that if any broke the bonds he might not escape, but be taken. None were taken."

"Natheless, three did escape," said the king, "and ye will do well to publish it and set justice upon their track, for these murthered the baron and fired the house."

I was just expecting he would come out with that. For a moment the man and his wife showed an eager interest in this news and an impatience to go out and spread it; then a sudden something else betrayed itself in their faces, and they began to ask questions. I answered the questions myself, and narrowly watched the effects produced. I was soon satisfied that the knowledge of who these three prisoners were, had somehow changed the atmosphere; that our hosts' continued eagerness to go and spread the news was now only pretended and not real. The king did not notice the change, and I was glad of that. I worked the conversation around toward other details of the night's proceedings, and noted that these people were relieved to have it take that direction.

The painful thing observable about all this business was, the alacrity with which this oppressed community had turned their cruel hands against their own class in the interest of the common oppressor. This man and woman seemed to feel that in a quarrel between a person of their own class and his lord, it was the natural and proper and rightful thing for that poor devil's whole caste to side with the master and fight his battle for him, without ever stopping to inquire into the rights or wrongs of the matter. This man had been out helping to hang his neighbors, and had done his work with zeal, and yet was aware that there was nothing against them but a mere suspicion, with nothing back of it describable as evidence, still neither he nor his wife seemed to see anything horrible about it.

This was depressing—to a man with the dream of a republic in his head. It reminded me of a time thirteen centuries away, when the "poor whites" of our South who were always despised and frequently insulted, by the slave-lords around them, and who owed their base condition simply to the presence of slavery in the midst, were yet pusillanimously ready to side with slave-lords in all political moves for the upholding and perpetuating of slavery, and did also finally shoulder their muskets and pour out their lives in an effort to prevent the destruction of that very institution which degraded them. And there was only one redeeming feature connected with that pitiful piece of history; and that was, that secretly the "poor white" did detest the slave-lord, and did feel his own shame. That feeling was not brought to the surface, but the fact that it was there and could have been brought out, under favoring circumstances, was something—in fact it was enough; for it showed that a man is at bottom a man, after all, even if it doesn't show on the outside.

Well, as it turned out, this charcoal burner was just the twin of the Southern "poor white" of the far future. The king presently showed impatience, and said:

"An ye prattle here all the day, justice will miscarry. Think ye the criminals will abide in their father's house? They are fleeing, they are not waiting. You should look to it that a party of horse be set upon their track."

The woman paled slightly, but quite perceptibly, and the man looked flustered and irresolute. I said:

"Come, friend, I will walk a little way with you, and explain which

direction I think they would try to take. If they were merely resisters of
the gabelle or some kindred absurdity I would try to protect them from
capture; but when men murder a person of high degree and likewise
burn his house, that is another matter."

The last remark was for the king—to quiet him. On the road the
man pulled his resolution together, and began the march with a steady
gait, but there was no eagerness in it. By and by I said:

"What relation were these men to you—cousins?"

He turned as white as his layer of charcoal would let him, and
stopped, trembling.

"Ah, my God, how knew you that?"

"I didn't know it; it was a chance guess."

"Poor lads, they are lost. And good lads they were, too."

"Were you actually going yonder to tell on them?"

He didn't quite know how to take that; but he said, hesitatingly:
"Ye-s."

"Then I think you are a damned scoundrel!"

It made him as glad as if I had called him an angel.

"Say the good words again, brother! For surely ye mean that ye
would not betray me an I failed of my duty."

"Duty? There is no duty in the matter, except the duty to keep still
and let those men get away. They've done a righteous deed."

He looked pleased; pleased, and touched with apprehension at the
same time. He looked up and down the road to see that no one was
coming, and then said in a cautious voice:

"From what land come you, brother, that you speak such perilous
words, and seem not to be afraid?"

"They are not perilous words when spoken to one of my own caste,
I take it. You would not tell anybody I said them?"

"I? I would be drawn asunder by wild horses first."

"Well, then, let me say my say. I have no fears of your repeating it. I
think devil's work has been done last night upon those innocent poor
people. That old baron got only what he deserved. If I had my way, all
his kind should have the same luck."

Fear and depression vanished from the man's manner, and grateful-
ness and a brave animation took their place:

"Even though you be a spy, and your words a trap for my undoing,
yet are they such refreshment that to hear them again and others like
to them, I would go to the gallows happy, as having had one good feast
at least in a starved life. And I will say my say, now, and ye may report
it if ye be so minded. I helped to hang my neighbors for that it were
peril to my own life to show lack of zeal in the master's cause; the others
helped for none other reason. All rejoice today that he is dead, but all

do go about seemingly sorrowing, and shedding the hypocrite's tear, for in that lies safety. I have said the words. I have said the words! the only ones that have ever tasted good in my mouth, and the reward of that taste is sufficient. Lead on, an ye will, be it even to the scaffold, for I am ready."

There it was, you see. A man *is* a man, at bottom. Whole ages of abuse and oppression cannot crush the manhood clear out of him. Whoever thinks it a mistake, is himself mistaken. Yes, there is plenty good enough material for a republic in the most degraded people that ever existed—even the Russians; plenty of manhood in them—even in the Germans—if one could but force it out of its timid and suspicious privacy, to overthrow and trample in the mud any throne that ever was set up and any nobility that ever supported it. We should see certain things yet, let us hope and believe. First, a modified monarchy, till Arthur's days were done, then the destruction of the throne, nobility abolished, every member of it bound out to some useful trade, universal suffrage instituted, and the whole government placed in the hands of the men and women of the nation there to remain. Yes, there was no occasion to give up my dream yet awhile.

XXXI. MARCO

WE STROLLED along in a sufficiently indolent fashion, now, and talked. We must dispose of about the amount of time it ought to take to go to the little hamlet of Abblasoure and put justice on the track of those murderers and get back home again. And meantime I had an auxiliary interest which had never paled yet, never lost its novelty for me, since I had been in Arthur's kingdom: the behavior—born of nice and exact subdivisions of caste—of chance passersby toward each other. Toward the shaven monk who trudged along with his cowl tilted back and the sweat washing down his fat jowls, the coal burner was deeply reverent; to the gentleman he was abject; with the small farmer and the free mechanic he was cordial and gossipy; and when a slave passed by with a countenance respectfully lowered, this chap's nose was in the air—he couldn't even see him. Well, there are times when one would like to hang the whole human race and finish the farce.

Presently we struck an incident. A small mob of half naked boys and girls came tearing out of the woods, scared and shrieking. The eldest among them were not more than twelve or fourteen years old. They implored help, but they were so beside themselves that we couldn't make out what the matter was. However, we plunged into the wood, they scurrying in the lead, and the trouble was quickly revealed: they had hanged a little fellow with a bark rope, and he was kicking and struggling, in the process of choking to death. We rescued him, and fetched him around. It was some more human nature; the admiring little folk imitating their elders; they were playing mob, and had achieved a success which promised to be a good deal more serious than they had bargained for.

It was not a dull excursion for me. I managed to put in the time very well. I made various acquaintanceships, and in my quality of stranger was able to ask as many questions as I wanted to. A thing which naturally interested me, as a statesman, was the matter of wages. I picked up what I could under that head during the afternoon. A man who hasn't had much experience, and doesn't think, is apt to measure a nation's prosperity or lack of prosperity by the mere size of the prevailing wages: if the wages be high, the nation is prosperous; if low, it isn't. Which is an error. It isn't what sum you get, it's how much you can buy with it that's the important thing; and it's that that tells whether your wages are high in fact or only high in name. I could remember how it was in the time of our great civil war in the nineteenth century. In the North a carpenter got three dollars a day, gold valuation; in the South he got fifty—payable in Confederate shinplasters worth a dollar a bushel. In the North a suit of overalls cost three dollars—a day's wages; in the South, it cost seventy-five—which was two days' wages. Other things were in proportion. Consequently, wages were twice as high in the North as they were in the South, because the one wage had that much more purchasing power than the other had.

Yes, I made various acquaintances in the hamlet, and a thing that gratified me a good deal was to find our new coins in circulation—lots of milrays, lots of mills, lots of cents, a good many nickels, and some silver; all this among the artisans and commonalty generally; yes, and even some gold—but that was at the bank, that is to say, the goldsmith's. I dropped in there while Marco the son of Marco was haggling with a shopkeeper over a quarter of a pound of salt, and asked for change for a twenty dollar gold piece. They furnished it—that is, after they had chewed the piece, and rung it on the counter, and tried acid on it, and asked me where I got it, and who I was, and where I was from, and where I was going to, and when I expected to get there, and perhaps a couple of hundred more questions; and when they got aground, I went right on and furnished them a lot of information voluntarily; told them I owned a dog, and his name was Watch, and my first wife was a Free Will Baptist, and her grandfather was a Prohibitionist, and I used to know a man who had two thumbs on each hand and a wart on the inside of his upper lip, and died in the hope of a glorious resurrection and so on and so on and so on till even that hungry village questioner began to look satisfied, and also a shade put out; but he had to respect a man of my financial strength, and so he didn't give me any lip, but I noticed he took it out of his underlings, which was a perfectly natural thing to do. Yes, they changed my twenty, but I judged it strained the bank a little, which was a thing to be expected, for it was the same as walking into a paltry village store in the nineteenth century and requiring the boss of it to change a two-thousand dollar bill for you all of a sudden. He could do it, maybe; but at the same time he would wonder how a small farmer happened to be carrying so much money around in his pocket; which was probably this goldsmith's thought, too; for he followed me to the door and stood there gazing after me with reverent admiration.

Our new money was not only handsomely circulating, but its language was already glibly in use; that is to say, people had dropped the names of the former moneys, and spoke of things as being worth so many dollars or cents or mills or milrays, now. It was very gratifying. We were progressing, that was sure.

I got to know several master mechanics, but about the most interesting fellow among them was the blacksmith, Dowley. He was a live man and a brisk talker, and had two journeymen and three apprentices, and was doing a raging business. In fact, he was getting rich, hand over fist, and was vastly respected. Marco was very proud of having such a man for a friend. He had taken me there ostensibly to let me see the big establishment which bought so much of his charcoal, but really to let me see what easy and almost familiar terms he was on with this great man. Dowley and I fraternized at once; I had had just such picked men, splendid fellows, under me in the Colt Arms Factory. I was bound to see more of him, so I invited him to come out to Marco's, Sunday, and dine with us. Marco was appalled, and held his breath; and when the grandee accepted, he was so grateful that he almost forgot to be astonished at the condescension.

Marco's joy was exuberant—but only for a moment; then he grew thoughtful, then sad; and when he heard me tell Dowley I should have Dickon the boss mason, and Smug the boss wheelwright out there, too, the coal dust on his face turned to chalk, and he lost his grip. But I knew what was the matter with him; he judged that his financial days were numbered. However, on our way to invite the others, I said:

"You must allow me to have these friends come, and you must also allow me to pay the costs."

His face cleared, and he said with spirit:

"But not all of it, not all of it. Ye cannot well bear a burden like to this alone."

I stopped him, and said:

"Now let's understand each other on the spot, old friend. I am only a farm bailiff, it is true; but I am not poor, nevertheless. I have been very fortunate this year—you would be astonished to know how I have thriven. I tell you the honest truth when I say I could squander away as many as a dozen feasts like this and never care *that* for the expense!" And I snapped my fingers. I could see myself rise a foot at a time in Marco's estimation, and when I fetched out those last words I was become a very tower, for style and altitude. "So you see, you must let me have my way. You can't contribute a cent to this orgy, that's *settled*."

"It's grand and good of you—"

"No, it isn't. You've opened your house to Jones and me in the most generous way; Jones was remarking upon it today, just before you came back from the village; for although he wouldn't be likely to say such a thing to you,—because Jones isn't a talker, and is diffident in society— he has a good heart and a grateful, and knows how to appreciate it when he is well treated; yes, you and your wife have been very hospitable toward us—"

"Ah, brother, 'tis nothing—*such* hospitality!"

"But it *is* something; the best a man has, freely given, is always something, and is as good as a prince can do, and ranks right along beside it—for even a prince can but do his best. And so we'll shop around and get up this layout, now, and don't you worry about the expense. I'm one of the worst spendthrifts that ever was born. Why, do you know, sometimes in a single week I spend—but never mind about that—you'd never believe it anyway."

And so we went gadding along, dropping in here and there, pricing things, and gossiping with the shopkeepers about the riot, and now and then running across pathetic reminders of it, in the persons of shunned and tearful and houseless remnants of families whose homes had been taken from them and their parents butchered or hanged. The raiment of Marco and his wife was of coarse tow linen and linsey-woolsey respectively, and resembled township maps, it being made up pretty exclusively of patches which had been added, township by township, in the course of five or six years, until hardly a handbreadth of the original garments was surviving and present. Now I wanted to fit these people out with new suits, on account of that swell company, and I didn't know just how to get at it with delicacy, until at last it struck me that as I had already been liberal in inventing wordy gratitude for the king, it would be just the thing to back it up with evidence of a substantial sort; so I said:

"And Marco, there's another thing which you must permit—out of kindness for Jones—because you wouldn't want to offend him. He was very anxious to testify his appreciation in some way, but he is so diffident he couldn't venture it himself, and so he begged me to buy some little things and give them to you and Dame Phyllis and let him pay for them without your ever knowing they came from him—you know how a delicate person feels about that sort of thing—and so I said I would, and we would keep mum. Well, his idea was, a new outfit of clothes for you both—"

"Oh, it is wastefulness! It may not be, brother, it may not be. Consider the vastness of the sum—"

"Hang the vastness of the sum! Try to keep quiet for a moment, and see how it would seem; a body can't get in a word edgeways, you talk so much. You ought to cure that, Marco; it isn't good form, you know, and it will grow on you if you don't check it. Yes, we'll step in here, now, and price this man's stuff—and don't forget to remember to not let on to Jones that you know he had anything to do with it. You can't think how curiously sensitive and proud he is. He's a farmer—pretty fairly well-to-do farmer—and I'm his bailiff; *but*—the imagination of that man! Why, sometimes when he forgets himself and gets to blowing off, you'd think he was one of the swells of the earth; and you might listen to him a hundred years and never take him for a farmer—especially if he talked agriculture. He *thinks* he's a Sheol of a farmer; thinks he's old Grayback from Wayback; but between you and me privately he don't know as much about farming as he does about running a kingdom—still, whatever he talks about, you want to drop your underjaw and listen, the same as if you had never heard such incredible wisdom in all your life before, and were afraid you might die before you got enough of it. That will please Jones."

It tickled Marco to the marrow to hear about such an odd character; but it also prepared him for accidents; and in my experience when you travel with a king who is letting on to be something else and can't remember it more than about half the time, you can't take too many precautions.

This was the best store we had come across yet; it had everything in it, in small quantities, from anvils and dry goods all the way down to fish and pinchbeck jewelry. I concluded I would bunch my whole invoice right here, and not go pricing around any more. So I got rid of Marco, by sending him off to invite the mason and the wheelwright, which left the field free for me. For I never care to do a thing in a quiet way; it's got to be theatrical or I don't take any interest in it. I showed up money enough, in a careless way, to corral the shopkeeper's respect, and then I wrote down a list of the things I wanted, and handed it to him to see if he could read it. He could, and was proud to show that he could. He said he had been educated by a priest, and could read and write both. He ran it through, and remarked with satisfaction that it was a pretty heavy bill. Well, and so it was, for a little concern like that. I was not only providing a swell dinner, but some odds and ends of extras. I ordered that the things be carted out and delivered at the dwelling of Marco the son of Marco by Saturday evening, and send me the bill at dinner time Sunday. He said I could depend upon his promptness and exactitude, it was the rule of the house. He also observed that he would throw in a couple of miller-guns for the Marcos, gratis—that everybody was using them now. He had a mighty opinion of that clever device. I said:

"And please fill them up to the middle mark, too; and add that to the bill."

He would, with pleasure. He filled them, and I took them with me. I couldn't venture to tell him that the miller-gun was a little invention of my own, and that I had officially ordered that every shopkeeper in the kingdom keep them on hand and sell them at government price— which was the merest trifle, and the shopkeeper got that, not the government. We furnished them for nothing.

The king had hardly missed us when we got back at nightfall. He had early dropped again into his dream of a grand invasion of Gaul with the whole strength of his kingdom at his back, and the afternoon had slipped away without his ever coming to himself again.

XXXII. DOWLEY'S HUMILIATION

WELL, WHEN that cargo arrived, toward sunset, Saturday afternoon, I had my hands full to keep the Marcos from fainting. They were sure Jones and I were ruined past help, and they blamed themselves as accessories to this bankruptcy. You see, in addition to the dinner materials, which called for a sufficiently round sum, I had bought a lot of extras for the future comfort of the family: for instance, a big lot of wheat, a delicacy as rare to the tables of their class as was ice cream to a hermit's; also a sizable deal dinner table; also two entire pounds of salt, which was another piece of extravagance in those people's eyes; also crockery, stools, the clothes, a small cask of beer, and so on. I instructed the Marcos to keep quiet about this sumptuousness, so as to give me a chance to surprise the guests and show off a little. Concerning the new clothes, the simple couple were like children; they were up and down, all right, to see if it wasn't nearly daylight, so that they could put them on, and they were into them at last as much as an hour before dawn was due. Then their pleasure—not to say delirium—was so fresh and novel and inspiring that the sight of it paid me well for the interruptions which my sleep had suffered. The king had slept just as usual—like the dead. The Marcos could not thank him for their clothes, that being forbidden; but they tried every way they could think of to make him see how grateful they were. Which all went for nothing; he didn't notice any change.

It turned out to be one of those rich and rare fall days which is just a June day toned down to a degree where it is heaven to be out of doors. Toward noon the guests arrived and we assembled under a great tree and were soon as sociable as old acquaintances. Even the king's reserve melted a little, though it was some little trouble to him to adjust himself to the name of Jones along at first. I had asked him to try to not forget that he was a farmer; but I had also considered it prudent to ask him to let the thing stand at that, and not elaborate it any. Because he was just the kind of person you could depend on to spoil a little thing like that if you didn't warn him, his tongue was so handy, and his spirit so willing, and his information so uncertain.

Dowley was in fine feather, and I early got him started, and then adroitly worked him around onto his own history for a text and himself for a hero, and then it was good to sit there and hear him hum. Self-made man, you know. They know how to talk. They do deserve more credit than any other breed of men, yes, that is true; and they are among the very first to find it out, too. He told how he had begun life an orphan lad without money and without friends able to help him; how he had lived as the slaves of the meanest master lived; how his day's work was from sixteen to eighteen hours long, and yielded him only enough black bread to keep him in a half-fed condition; how his faithful endeavors finally attracted the attention of a good blacksmith, who came near knocking him dead with kindness by suddenly offering, when he was totally unprepared, to take him as his bound apprentice for nine years and give him board and clothes and teach him the trade—or "mystery" as Dowley called it. That was his first great rise, his first gorgeous stroke of fortune; and you saw that he couldn't yet speak of it without a sort of eloquent wonder and delight that such a gilded promotion should have fallen to the lot of a common human being. He got no new clothing during his apprenticeship, but on his graduation day his master tricked him out in spang-new tow linens and made him feel unspeakably rich and fine.

"I remember me of that day!" the wheelwright sang out, with enthusiasm.

"And I likewise!" cried the mason. "I would not believe they were thine own; in faith I could not."

"Nor others!" shouted Dowley, with sparkling eyes. "I was like to lose my character, the neighbors wending I had mayhap been stealing. It was a great day, a great day; one forgetteth not days like that."

Yes, and his master was a fine man, and prosperous, and always had a great feast of meat twice in the year, and with it white bread, true wheaten bread; in fact, lived like a lord, so to speak. And in time Dowley succeeded to the business and married the daughter.

"And now consider what is come to pass," said he, impressively. "Two times in every month there is fresh meat upon my table." He made a pause here, to let that fact sink home, then added—"and eight times, salt meat."

"It is even true," said the wheelwright, with bated breath.

"I know it of mine own knowledge," said the mason, in the same reverent fashion.

"On my table appeareth white bread every Sunday in the year," added the master smith, with solemnity. "I leave it to your own consciences, friends, if this is not also true?"

"By my head, yes!" cried the mason.

"I can testify it—and I do," said the wheelwright.

"And as to furniture, ye shall say yourselves what mine equipment is." He waved his hand in fine gesture of granting frank and unhampered freedom of speech, and added: "Speak as ye are moved; speak as ye would speak an I were not here."

"Ye have five stools, and of the sweetest workmanship at that, albeit your family is but three," said the wheelwright with deep respect.

"And six wooden goblets, and six platters of wood and two of pewter to eat and drink from withal," said the mason, impressively. "And I say it as knowing God is my judge, and we tarry not here alway, but must answer at the last day for the things said in the body, be they false or be they sooth."

"Now ye know what manner of man I am, brother Jones," said the smith, with a fine and friendly condescension, "and doubtless ye would look to find me a man jealous of his due of respect and but sparing of outgo to strangers till their rating and quality be assured, but trouble yourself not, as concerning that; wit ye well ye shall find me a man that regardeth not these matters but is willing to receive any he as his fellow and equal that carrieth a right heart in his body, be his worldly estate howsoever modest. And in token of it, here is my hand; and I say with my own mouth we are equals—equals"—and he smiled around on the company with the satisfaction of a god who is doing the handsome and gracious thing and is quite well aware of it.

The king took the hand with a poorly disguised reluctance, and let go of it as willingly as a lady lets go of a fish; all of which had a good effect, for it was mistaken for an embarrassment natural to one who was being beamed upon by greatness.

The dame brought out the table, now, and set it under the tree. It caused a visible stir of surprise, it being brand new and a sumptuous article of deal. But the surprise rose higher still, when the dame, with a body oozing easy indifference at every pore, but eyes that gave it all away by absolutely flaming with vanity, slowly unfolded an actual simon-pure tablecloth and spread it. That was a notch above even the blacksmith's domestic grandeurs, and it hit him hard; you could see it. But Marco was in Paradise; you could see that, too. Then the dame brought two fine new stools—whew! That was a sensation; it was visible in the eyes of every guest. Then she brought two more—as calmly as she could. Sensation again—with awed murmurs. Again she brought two—walking on air, she was so proud. The guests were petrified, and the mason muttered:

"There is that about earthly pomps which doth ever move to reverence."

As the dame turned away, Marco couldn't help slapping on the climax while the thing was hot; so he said with what was meant for a languid composure but was a poor imitation of it:

"These suffice; leave the rest."

So there were more yet! It was a fine effect. I couldn't have played the hand better myself.

From this out, the madame piled up the surprises with a rush that fired the general astonishment up to a hundred and fifty in the shade, and at the same time paralyzed expression of it down to gasped "Oh's" and "Ah's" and mute upliftings of hands and eyes. She fetched crockery—new, and plenty of it; new wooden goblets and other table furniture; and beer, fish, chicken, a goose, eggs, roast beef, roast mutton, a ham, a small roast pig, and a wealth of genuine white wheaten bread. Take it by and large, that spread laid everything far and away in the shade that ever that crowd had seen before. And while they sat there just simply stupefied with wonder and awe, I sort of waved my hand as if by accident, and the storekeeper's son emerged from space and said he had come to collect.

"That's all right," I said, indifferently. "What is the amount? Give us the items."

Then he read off this bill, while those three amazed men listened, and serene waves of satisfaction rolled over my soul and alternate waves of terror and admiration surged over Marco's:

2 pounds salt	200
8 dozen pints of beer, in the wood	800
3 bushels wheat	2,700
2 pounds fish	100
3 hens	400
1 goose	400
3 dozen eggs	150
1 roast of beef	450
1 " "mutton	400
1 ham	800
1 suckling pig	500
2 crockery dinner sets	6,000
2 men's suits and underwear	2,800
1 stuff and 1 linsey-woolsey gown and underwear	1,600
8 wooden goblets	800
Various table furniture	10,000
1 deal table	3,000
8 stools	4,000
2 miller-guns, loaded	3,000

He ceased. There was a pale and awful silence. Not a limb stirred. Not a nostril betrayed the passage of breath.

"Is that all?" I asked, in a voice of the most perfect calmness.

"All, fair sir, save that certain matters of light moment are placed together under a head hight sundries. If it would like you, I will sepa—"

"It is of no consequence," I said, accompanying the words with a gesture of the most utter indifference; "give me the grand total, please."

The clerk leaned against the tree to stay himself, and said:

"Thirty-nine thousand one hundred and fifty milrays!"

The wheelwright fell off his stool, the others grabbed the table to save themselves, and there was a deep and general ejaculation of—

"God be with us in the day of disaster!"

The clerk hastened to say:

"My father chargeth me to say he cannot honorably require you to pay it all at this time, and therefore only prayeth you—"

I paid no more heed than if it were the idle breeze, but with an air of indifference amounting almost to weariness, got out my money and tossed four dollars onto the table. Ah, you should have seen them stare!

The clerk was astonished and charmed. He asked me to retain one of the dollars as security, until he could go to town and—I interrupted:

"What, and fetch back nine cents? Nonsense. Take the whole. Keep the change."

There was an amazed murmur to this effect:

"Verily this being is *made* of money! He throweth it away even as it were dirt."

The blacksmith was a crushed man.

The clerk took his money and reeled away drunk with fortune. I said to Marco and his wife:

"Good folk, here is a little trifle for you"—handing the miller-guns as if it were a matter of no consequence though each of them contained fifteen cents in solid cash; and while the poor creatures went to pieces with astonishment and gratitude, I turned to the others and said calmly as one would ask the time of day:

"Well, if we are all ready, I judge the dinner is. Come, fall to."

Ah, well, it was immense; yes, it was a daisy. I don't know that I ever put a situation together better, or got happier spectacular effects out of the materials available. The blacksmith—well, he was simply mashed. Land! I wouldn't have felt what that man was feeling, for anything in the world. Here he had been blowing and bragging about his grand meat-feast twice a year, and his fresh meat twice a month, and his salt meat twice a week, and his white bread every Sunday the year round— all for a family of three: the entire cost for the year not above 69.2.6 (sixty-nine cents, two mills, and six milrays), and all of a sudden here comes along a man who slashes out nearly four dollars on a single blowout; and not only that, but acts as if it made him tired to handle such small sums. Yes, Dowley was a good deal wilted, and shrunk up and collapsed; he had the aspect of a bladder balloon that's been stepped on by a cow.

XXXIII. SIXTH-CENTURY POLITICAL ECONOMY

HOWEVER, I made a dead set at him, and before the first third of the dinner was reached, I had him happy again. It was easy to do—in a country of ranks and castes. You see, in a country where they have ranks and castes, a man isn't ever a man, he is only part of a man, he can't ever get his full growth. You prove your superiority over him in station, or rank, or fortune and that's the end of it—he knuckles down. You can't insult him after that. No, I don't mean quite that; of course you *can* insult him, I only mean it's difficult; and so, unless you've got a lot of useless time on your hands it doesn't pay to try. I had the smith's reverence, now, because I was apparently immensely prosperous and rich; I could have had his adoration if I had had some little gimcrack title of nobility. And not only his, but any commoner's in the land, though he were the mightiest production of all the ages, in intellect, worth, and character, and I bankrupt in all three. This was to remain so, as long as England should exist in the earth. With the spirit of prophecy upon me, I could look into the future and see her erect statues and monuments to her unspeakable Georges and other royal and noble clotheshorses, and leave unhonored the creators of this world—after God—Gutenberg, Watt, Arkwright, Whitney, Morse, Stephenson, Bell.

The king got his cargo aboard, and then, the talk not turning upon battle, conquest, or ironclad duel, he dulled down to drowsiness and went off to take a nap. Mrs. Marco cleared the table, placed the beer keg handy, and went away to eat her dinner of leavings in humble privacy, and the rest of us soon drifted into matters near and dear to the hearts of our sort—business and wages, of course. At a first glance, things appeared to be exceeding prosperous in this little tributary kingdom—whose lord was King Bagdemagus—as compared with the state of things in my own region. They had the "protection" system in full force here, whereas we were working along down towards free trade, by easy stages, and were now about half way. Before long,

Dowley and I were doing all the talking, the others hungrily listening. Dowley warmed to his work, snuffed an advantage in the air, and began to put questions which he considered pretty awkward ones for me, and they did have something of that look:

"In your country, brother, what is the wage of a master bailiff, master hind, carterer, shepherd, swineherd?"

"Twenty-five milrays a day; that is to say, a quarter of a cent."

The smith's face beamed with joy. He said:

"With us they are allowed the double of it! And what may a mechanic get—carpenter, dauber, mason, painter, blacksmith, wheelwright, and the like?"

"On the average, fifty milrays; half a cent a day."

"Ho-ho! With us they are allowed a hundred! With us any good mechanic is allowed a cent a day! I count out the tailor, but not the others—they are all allowed a cent a day, and in driving times they get more—yes, up to a hundred and ten and even fifteen milrays a day. I've paid a hundred and fifteen myself, within the week. 'Rah for protection—to Sheol with free trade!"

And his face shone upon the company like a sunburst. But I didn't scare at all. I rigged up my pile driver, and allowed myself fifteen minutes to drive him into the earth—drive him *all* in—drive him in till not even the curve of his skull should show above ground. Here is the way I started in on him. I asked:

"What do you pay a pound for salt?"

"A hundred milrays."

"We pay forty. What do you pay for beef and mutton—when you buy it?" That was a neat hit; it made the color come.

"It varieth somewhat, but not much; one may say seventy-five milrays the pound."

"We pay thirty-three. What do you pay for eggs?"

"Fifty milrays the dozen."

"We pay twenty. What do you pay for beer?"

"It costeth us eight and one half milrays the pint."

"We get it for four; twenty-five bottles for a cent. What do you pay for wheat?"

"At the rate of nine hundred milrays the bushel."

"We pay four hundred. What do you pay for a man's tow-linen suit?"

"Thirteen cents."

"We pay six. What do you pay for a stuff gown for the wife of the laborer or the mechanic?"

"We pay eight cents and four mills."

"Well, observe the difference: you pay eight cents and four mills, we pay only four cents." I prepared, now to sock it to him. I said: "Look here, dear friend, *what's become of your high wages you were bragging so about, a few minutes ago?*" And I looked around on the company with placid satisfaction, for I had slipped up on him gradually and tied him hand and foot, you see, without his ever noticing that he was being tied at all. "What's become of those noble high wages of yours? I seem to have knocked the stuffing all out of them, it appears to me."

But if you will believe me, he merely looked surprised, that is all! He didn't grasp the situation at all, didn't know he had walked into a trap, didn't discover that he was *in* a trap. I could have shot him, for sheer vexation. With cloudy eye and a struggling intellect, he fetched this out:

"Marry, I seem not to understand. It is *proved* that our wages be double thine; how then may it be that thou'st knocked therefrom the stuffing—an I miscall not the wonderly word, this being the first time under grace and providence of God it hath been granted me to hear it."

Well, I was stunned; partly with this unlooked-for stupidity on his part, and partly because his fellows so manifestly sided with him and were of his mind—if you might call it mind. My position was simple enough, plain enough; how could it ever be simplified more? However, I must try:

"Why, look here, brother Dowley, don't you see? Your wages are merely higher than ours in *name*, not in *fact*."

"Hear him! They are the *double*—ye have confessed it yourself."

"Yes-yes, I don't deny that at all. But that's got nothing to do with it; the *amount* of the wages in mere coins, with meaningless names attached to them to know them by, has got nothing to do with it. The thing is, how much can you *buy* with your wages? That's the idea. While it is true that with you a good mechanic is allowed about three dollars and a half a year, and with us only about a dollar and seventy-five—"

"There—ye're confessing it again, ye're confessing it again!"

"Confound it, I've never denied it I tell you! What I say is this. With us *half* a dollar buys more than a *dollar* buys with you—and *therefore* it stands to reason and the commonest kind of common sense, that our wages are *higher* than yours."

He looked dazed, and said, despairingly:

"Verily, I cannot make it out. Ye've just *said* ours are the higher, and with the same breath ye take it back."

"Oh, great Scott, isn't it possible to get such a simple thing through your head? Now look here—let me illustrate. We pay four cents for a woman's stuff gown, you pay eight cents and four mills which is four mills more than *double*. What do you allow a laboring woman who works on a farm?"

"Two mills a day."

"Very good; we allow but half as much; we pay her only a tenth of a cent a day; and—"

"Again ye're conf—"

"Wait! Now, you see, the thing is very simple; this time you'll understand it. For instance, it takes your woman forty-two days to earn her gown, at two mills a day—seven weeks' work; but ours earns her in forty days—two days *short* of seven weeks' wages are gone; ours has a gown, and two days' wages left, to buy something else with. There—*now* you understand it!"

He looked—well, he merely looked dubious, it's the most I can say; so did the others. I waited—to let the thing work. Dowley spoke at last—and betrayed the fact that he actually hadn't gotten away from his rooted and grounded superstitions yet. He said, with a trifle of hesitancy:

"But—but—ye cannot fail to grant that two mills a day is better than one."

Shucks! Well, of course I hated to give it up. So I chanced another flyer:

"Let us suppose a case. Suppose one of your journeymen goes out and buys the following articles:

> "1 pound of salt;
> 1 dozen eggs;
> 1 dozen pints of beer;
> 1 bushel of wheat;
> 1 tow-linen suit;
> 5 pounds of beef;
> 5 pounds of mutton.

"The lot will cost him thirty-two cents. It takes him thirty-two working days to earn the money—five weeks and two days. Let him come to us and work thirty-two days at *half* the wages; he can buy all those things for a shade under fourteen and one half cents; they will cost him a shade under twenty-nine days' work, and he will have about half a week's wages over. Carry it through the year; he would save nearly a week's wages every two months, *your* man nothing; thus saving five or six weeks' wages in a year, your man not a cent. *Now* I reckon you understand that 'high wages' and 'low wages' are phrases that don't mean anything in the world until you find out which of them will *buy* the most!"

It was a crusher.

But alas, it didn't crush. No, I had to give it up. What those people valued was *high wages*; it didn't seem to be a matter of any consequence to them whether the high wages would buy anything or not. They stood for "protection," and swore by it, which was reasonable enough, because interested parties had gulled them into the notion that it was protection which had created their high wages. I proved to them that in a quarter of a century their wages had advanced but thirty per cent, while the cost of living had gone up one hundred; and that with us, in a shorter time, wages had advanced forty per cent, while the cost of living had gone steadily down. But it didn't do any good. Nothing could unseat their strange beliefs.

Well, I was smarting under a sense of defeat. Undeserved defeat, but what of that? That didn't soften the smart any. And to think of the circumstances! The first statesman of the age, the capablest man, the best-informed man in the entire world, the loftiest uncrowned head that had moved through the clouds of any political firmament for centuries, sitting here apparently defeated in argument by an ignorant country blacksmith! And I could see that those others were sorry for me—which made me blush till I could smell my whiskers scorching. Put yourself in my place; feel as mean as I did, as ashamed as I felt—wouldn't you have struck below the belt to get even? Yes, you would; it is simply human nature. Well, that is what I did. I am not trying to justify it; I'm only saying that I was mad, and *anybody* would have done it.

Well, when I make up my mind to hit a man, I don't plan out a love tap; no, that isn't my way; as long as I'm going to hit him at all, I'm going to hit him a lifter. And I don't jump at him all of a sudden, and risk making a blundering halfway business of it; no, I get away off yonder to one side, and work up on him gradually, so that he never suspects that I'm going to hit him at all; and by and by, all in a flash, he's flat of his back, and he can't tell for the life of him how it all happened. That is the way I went for brother Dowley. I started to talking lazy and comfortable, as if I was just talking to pass the time; and the oldest man in the world couldn't have taken the bearings of my starting place and guessed where I was going to fetch up:

"Boys, there's a good many curious things about law, and custom, and usage, and all that sort of thing, when you come to look at it; yes, and about the drift and progress of human opinion and movement, too. There are written laws—they perish; but there are also unwritten laws—*they* are eternal. Take the unwritten law of wages: it says they've got to advance, little by little, straight through the centuries. And notice how it works. We know what wages are now, here and there and yonder; we strike an average, and say that's the wages of today. We know what the wages were a hundred years ago, and what they were two hundred years ago; that's as far back as we can get, but it suffices to give us

the law of progress, the measure and rate of the periodical augmenta-
tion; and so, without a document to help us, we can come pretty close
to determining what the wages were three and four and five hundred
years ago. Good, so far. Do we stop there? No. We stop looking backward; we face around and apply the law to the future. My friends, I can
tell you what people's wages are going to be at any date in the future
you want to know, for hundreds and hundreds of years."

"What, goodman, what!"

"Yes. In seven hundred years wages will have risen to six times what
they are now, here in your region, and farm hands will be allowed three
cents a day, and mechanics six."

"I would I might die now and live then!" interrupted Smug the
mason, with a fine avaricious glow in his eye.

"And that isn't all; they'll get their board besides—such as it is: it
won't bloat them. Two hundred and fifty years later—pay attention,
now—a mechanic's wages will be—mind you, this is law, not guess-
work; a mechanic's wages will then be *twenty* cents a day!"

There was a general gasp of awed astonishment. Dickon the wheelwright murmured, with raised eyes and hands:

"More than three weeks' pay for one day's work."

"Riches—of a truth, yes, riches!" muttered Marco, his breath coming quick and short, with excitement.

"Wages will keep on rising, little by little, little by little, as steadily as
a tree grows, and at the end of three hundred and forty years more
there'll be at least *one* country where the mechanic's average wage will
be *two hundred* cents a day!"

It knocked them absolutely dumb! Not a man of them could get
his breath for upwards of two minutes. Then the coal burner said
prayerfully:

"Might I but live to see it!"

"It is the income of an earl!" said Smug.

"An earl, say ye?" said Dowley; "ye could say more than that and speak
no lie; there's no earl in the realm of Bagdemagus that hath an income
like to that. Income of an earl—mf! It's the income of an angel!"

"Now then, that is what is going to happen as regards wages. In that
remote day, that man will earn, with *one* week's work, that bill of goods
which it takes you upwards of *five* weeks to earn now. Some other pretty
surprising things are going to happen, too. Brother Dowley, who is it
that determines, every spring, what the particular wage of each kind of
mechanic, laborer, and servant shall be for that year?"

"Sometimes the courts, sometimes the town council; but most of all,
the magistrate. Ye may say, in general terms, it is the magistrate that
fixes the wages."

"Doesn't ask any of those poor devils to *help* him fix their wages for them, does he?"

"Hm! That *were* an idea! The master that's to pay him the money is the one that's rightly concerned in that matter, ye will notice."

"Yes—but I thought the other man might have some little trifle at stake in it, too; and even his wife and children, poor creatures. The masters are these: nobles, rich men, the prosperous generally. These few, who do no work, determine what pay the vast hive shall have who *do* work. You see? They're a 'combine'—a trade union, to coin a new phrase—who band themselves together to force their lowly brother to take what they choose to give. Thirteen hundred years hence—so says the unwritten law—the 'combine' will be the other way, and then how these fine people's posterity will fume and fret and grit their teeth over the insolent tyranny of trade unions! Yes indeed! the magistrate will tranquilly arrange the wages from now clear away down into the nineteenth century; and then all of a sudden the wage earner will consider that a couple of thousand years or so is enough for this one-sided sort of thing; and he will rise up and take a hand in fixing his wages himself. Ah, he will have a long and bitter account of wrong and humiliation to settle."

"Do ye believe—"

"That he actually will help to fix his own wages? Yes, indeed. And he will be strong and able, then."

"Brave times, brave times, of a truth!" sneered the prosperous smith.

"Oh—and there's another detail. In that day, a master may hire a man for only just one day, or one week, or one month at a time, if he wants to."

"What?"

"It's true. Moreover, a magistrate won't be able to force a man to work for a master a whole year on a stretch whether the man wants to or not."

"Will there be *no* law or sense in that day?"

"Both of them, Dowley. In that day a man will be his own property, not the property of magistrate and master. And he can leave town whenever he wants to, if the wages don't suit him—and they can't put him in the pillory for it!"

"Perdition catch such an age!" shouted Dowley, in strong indignation. "An age of dogs, an age barren of reverence for superiors and respect for authority! The pillory—"

"Oh, wait, brother; say no good word for that institution. I think the pillory ought to be abolished."

"A most strange idea. Why?"

"Well, I'll tell you why. Is a man ever put in the pillory for a capital crime?"

"No."

"Is it right to condemn a man to a slight punishment for a small offense and then kill him?"

There was no answer. I had scored my first point! For the first time, the smith wasn't up and ready. The company noticed it. Good effect.

"You don't answer, brother. You were about to glorify the pillory a while ago, and shed some pity on a future age that isn't going to use it. I think the pillory ought to be abolished. What usually happens when a poor fellow is put in the pillory for some little offense that didn't amount to anything in the world? The mob try to have some fun with him, don't they?"

"Yes."

"They begin by clodding him; and they laugh themselves to pieces to see him try to dodge one clod and get hit with another?"

"Yes."

"Then they throw dead cats at him, don't they?"

"Yes."

"Well, then, suppose he has a few personal enemies in that mob—and here and there a man or a woman with a secret grudge against him—and suppose especially, that he is unpopular in the community, for his pride, or his prosperity, or one thing or another—stones and bricks take the place of clods and cats presently, don't they?"

"There is no doubt of it."

"As a rule he is crippled for life, isn't he—jaws broken, teeth smashed out—or legs mutilated, gangrened, presently cut off—or an eye knocked out, maybe both eyes?"

"It is true, God knoweth it."

"And if he is unpopular he can depend on *dying*, right there in the stocks, can't he?"

"He surely can! One may not deny it."

"I take it none of *you* are unpopular—by reason of pride or insolence, or conspicuous prosperity, or any of those things that excite envy and malice among the base scum of the village? *You* wouldn't think it much of a risk to take a chance in the stocks?"

Dowley winced, visibly. I judged he was hit. But he didn't betray it by any spoken word. As for the others, they spoke out plainly, and with strong feeling. They said they had seen enough of the stocks to know what a man's chance in them was, and they would never consent to enter them if they could compromise on a quick death by hanging.

"Well, to change the subject—for I think I've established my point that the stocks ought to be abolished. I think some of our laws are pretty unfair. For instance, if I do a thing which ought to deliver me to the stocks, and you know I did it and yet keep still and don't report me, *you* will get the stocks if anybody informs on you."

"Ah, but that would serve you but right," said Dowley, "for you *must* inform. So saith the law."

The others coincided.

"Well, all right, let it go, since you vote me down. But there's one thing which certainly isn't fair. The magistrate fixes a mechanic's wage at one cent a day, for instance. The law says that if any master shall venture even under utmost press of business, to pay anything *over* that cent a day, even for a single day, he shall be both fined and pilloried for it; and whoever knows he did it and doesn't inform, they also shall be fined and pilloried. Now it seems to me unfair, Dowley, and a deadly peril to all of us, that because you thoughtlessly confessed, a while ago, that within a week you have paid a cent and fifteen mil—"

Oh, I tell *you* it was a smasher! You ought to have seen them go to pieces, the whole gang. I had just slipped up on poor smiling and complacent Dowley so nice and easy and softly, that he never suspected anything was going to happen till the blow came crashing down and knocked him all to rags.

A fine effect. In fact as fine as any I ever produced, with so little time to work it up in.

But I saw in a moment that I had overdone the thing a little. I was expecting to scare them, but I wasn't expecting to scare them to death. They were mighty near it, though. You see they had been a whole lifetime learning to appreciate the pillory; and to have that thing staring them in the face, and every one of them distinctly at the mercy of me, a stranger, if I chose to go and report—well, it was awful, and they couldn't seem to recover from the shock, they couldn't seem to pull themselves together. Pale, shaky, dumb, pitiful? Why, they weren't any better than so many dead men. It was very uncomfortable. Of course I thought they would appeal to me to keep mum, and then we would shake hands, and take a drink all round, and laugh it off, and there an end. But no; you see I was an unknown person, among a cruelly oppressed and suspicious people, a people always accustomed to having advantage taken of their helplessness, and never expecting just or kind treatment from any but their own families and very closest intimates. Appeal to *me* to be gentle, to be fair, to be generous? Of course they wanted to, but they couldn't dare.

XXXIV. THE YANKEE AND THE KING SOLD AS SLAVES

WELL, WHAT had I better do? Nothing in a hurry, sure. I must get up a diversion; anything to employ me while I could think, and while these poor fellows could have a chance to come to life again. There sat Marco, petrified in the act of trying to get the hang of his miller-gun — turned to stone, just in the attitude he was in when my pile driver fell, the toy still gripped in his unconscious fingers. So I took it from him and proposed to explain its mystery. Mystery! a simple little thing like that; and yet it was mystery enough, for that race and that age.

I never saw such an awkward people, with machinery; you see, they were totally unused to it. The miller-gun was a little double-barreled tube of toughened glass, with a neat little trick of a spring to it, which upon pressure would let a shot escape. But the shot wouldn't hurt anybody, it would only drop into your hand. In the gun were two sizes — wee mustard-seed shot, and another sort that were several times larger. They were money. The mustard-seed shot represented milrays, the larger ones mills. So the gun was a purse; and very handy too; you could pay out money in the dark with it, with accuracy; and you could carry it in your mouth; or in your vest pocket, if you had one. I made them of several sizes — one size so large that it would carry the equivalent of a dollar. Using shot for money was a good thing for the government; the metal cost nothing, and the money couldn't be counterfeited, for I was the only person in the kingdom who knew how to manage a shot tower. "Paying the shot" soon came to be a common phrase. Yes, and I knew it would still be passing men's lips, away down in the nineteenth century, yet none would suspect how and when it originated.

The king joined us, about this time, mightily refreshed by his nap, and feeling good. Anything could make me nervous now, I was so uneasy — for our lives were in danger; and so it worried me to detect a complacent something in the king's eye which seemed to indicate that he had been loading himself up for a performance of some kind or other; confound it, why must he go and choose such a time as this?

I was right. He began, straight off, in the most innocently artful, and transparent, and lubberly way, to lead up to the subject of agriculture. The cold sweat broke out all over me. I wanted to whisper in his ear, "Man, we are in awful danger! Every moment is worth a principality till we get back these men's confidence; *don't* waste any of this golden time." But of course I couldn't do it. Whisper to him? It would look as if we were conspiring. So I had to sit there and look calm and pleasant while the king stood over that dynamite mine and mooned along about his damned onions and things. At first the tumult of my own thoughts, summoned by the danger signal and swarming to the rescue from every quarter of my skull, kept up such a hurrah and confusion and fifing and drumming that I couldn't take in a word; but presently when my mob of gathering plans began to crystallize and fall into position and form line of battle, a sort of order and quiet ensued and I caught the boom of the king's batteries, as if out of remote distance:

— "were not the best way, methinks, albeit it is not to be denied that authorities differ as concerning this point, some contending that the onion is but an unwholesome berry when stricken early from the tree—"

The audience showed signs of life, and sought each other's eyes in a surprised and troubled way.

— "whileas others do yet maintain, with much show of reason, that this is not of necessity the case, instancing that plums and other like cereals do be always dug in the unripe state"—

The audience exhibited distinct distress; yes, and also fear.

— "yet are they clearly wholesome, the more especially when one doth assuage the asperities of their nature by admixture of the tranquilizing juice of the wayward cabbage"—

The wild light of terror began to glow in these men's eyes, and one of them muttered, "These be errors, every one—God hath surely smitten the mind of this farmer." I was in miserable apprehension; I sat upon thorns.

— "and further instancing the known truth that in the case of animals, the young, which may be called the green fruit of the creature, is the better, all confessing that when a goat is ripe, his fur doth heat and sore engame his flesh, the which defect, taken in connection with his several rancid habits, and fulsome appetites, and godless attitudes of mind, and bilious quality of morals"—

They rose and went for him! With a fierce shout, "The one would betray us, the other is mad! Kill them! Kill them!" they flung themselves upon us. What joy flamed up in the king's eye! He might be lame in agriculture, but this kind of thing was just in his line. He had been fasting long, he was hungry for a fight. He hit the blacksmith a crack under the jaw that lifted him clear off his feet and stretched him flat of his back. "St. George for Britain!" And he downed the wheelwright. The mason was big, but I laid him out like nothing. The three gathered themselves up and came again; went down again; came again; and kept on repeating this, with native British pluck, until they were battered to jelly, reeling with exhaustion, and so blind that they couldn't tell us from each other; and yet they kept right on, hammering away with what might was left in them. Hammering each other—for we stepped aside and looked on while they rolled, and struggled, and gouged, and pounded, and bit, with the strict and wordless attention to business of so many bulldogs. We looked on without apprehension, for they were fast getting past ability to go for help against us, and the arena was far enough from the public road to be safe from intrusion.

Well, while they were gradually playing out, it suddenly occurred to me to wonder what had become of Marco. I looked around; he was nowhere to be seen. Oh, but this was ominous! I pulled the king's sleeve, and we glided away and rushed for the hut. No Marco there, no Phyllis there! They had gone to the road for help, sure. I told the king to give his heels wings, and I would explain later. We made good time across the open ground, and as we darted into the shelter of the wood I glanced back and saw a mob of excited peasants swarm into view, with Marco and his wife at their head. They were making a world of noise, but that couldn't hurt anybody; the wood was dense, and as soon as we were well into its depths we would take to a tree and let them whistle. Ah, but then came another sound—dogs! Yes, that was quite another matter. It magnified our contract—we must find running water.

We tore along at a good gait, and soon left the sounds far behind and modified to a murmur. We struck a stream and darted into it. We waded swiftly down it, in the dim forest light, for as much as three hundred yards, and then came across an oak with a great bough sticking out over the water. We climbed up on this bough, and began to work our way along it to the body of the tree; now we began to hear those sounds more plainly; so the mob had struck our trail. For a while the sounds approached pretty fast. And then for another while they didn't. No doubt the dogs had found the place where we had entered the stream, and were now waltzing up and down the shores trying to pick up the trail again.

When we were snugly lodged in the tree and curtained with foliage, the king was satisfied, but I was doubtful. I believed we could crawl along a branch and get into the next tree, and I judged it worth while to try. We tried it, and made a success of it, though the king slipped, at the junction, and came near failing to connect. We got comfortable lodgment and satisfactory concealment among the foliage, and then we had nothing to do but listen to the hunt.

Presently we heard it coming—and coming on the jump, too; yes, and down both sides of the stream. Louder—louder—next minute it swelled swiftly up into a roar of shoutings, barkings, tramplings, and swept by like a cyclone.

"I was afraid that the overhanging branch would suggest something to them," said I, "but I don't mind the disappointment. Come, my liege, it were well that we make good use of our time. We've flanked them. Dark is coming on, presently. If we can cross the stream and get a good start, and borrow a couple of horses from somebody's pasture to use for a few hours, we shall be safe enough."

We started down, and got nearly to the lowest limb, when we seemed to hear the hunt returning. We stopped to listen.

"Yes," said I, "they're baffled, they've given it up, they're on their way home. We will climb back to our roost again, and let them go by."

So we climbed back. The king listened a moment and said:

"They still search—I wit the sign. We did best to abide."

He was right. He knew more about hunting than I did. The noise approached steadily, but not with a rush. The king said:

"They reason that we were advantaged by no parlous start of them, and being on foot are as yet no mighty way from where we took the water."

"Yes, sire, that is about it, I am afraid, though I was hoping better things."

The noise drew nearer and nearer, and soon the van was drifting under us, on both sides of the water. A voice called a halt from the other bank, and said:

"An they were so minded, they could get to yon tree by this branch that overhangs, and yet not touch ground. Ye will do well to send a man up it."

"Marry, that will we do!"

I was obliged to admire my cuteness in foreseeing this very thing and swapping trees to beat it. But don't you know, there are some things that can beat smartness and foresight? Awkwardness and stupidity can. The best swordsman in the world doesn't need to fear the second best swordsman in the world; no, the person for him to be afraid of is some ignorant antagonist who has never had a sword in his hand before; he doesn't do the thing he ought to do, and so the expert isn't prepared for him; he does the thing he ought not to do: and often it catches the expert out and ends him on the spot. Well, how could I, with all my gifts, make any valuable preparation against a nearsighted, cross-eyed, puddingheaded clown who would aim himself at the wrong tree and hit the right one? And that is what he did. He went for the wrong tree, which was of course the right one by mistake, and up he started.

Matters were serious, now. We remained still and awaited developments. The peasant toiled his difficult way up. The king raised himself up and stood; he made a leg ready, and when the comer's head arrived in reach of it there was a dull thud, and down went the man floundering to the ground. There was a wild outbreak of anger, below, and the mob swarmed in from all around, and there we were treed, and prisoners. Another man started up; the bridging bough was detected, and a volunteer started up the tree that furnished the bridge. The king ordered me to play Horatius and keep the bridge. For a while the enemy came thick and fast; but no matter, the head man of each procession always got a buffet that dislodged him as soon as he came in reach. The king's spirits rose, his joy was limitless. He said that if nothing occurred to mar the prospect we should have a beautiful night, for on this line of tactics we could hold the tree against the whole countryside.

However, the mob soon came to that conclusion themselves; wherefore they called off the assault and began to debate other plans. They had no weapons, but there were plenty of stones, and stones might answer. We had no objections. A stone might possibly penetrate to us once in a while, but it wasn't very likely; we were well protected by boughs and foliage, and were not visible from any good aiming point. If they would but waste half an hour in stone throwing, the dark would come to our help. We were feeling very well satisfied. We could smile; almost laugh.

But we didn't; which was just as well, for we should have been interrupted. Before the stones had been raging through the leaves and bouncing from the boughs fifteen minutes, we began to notice a smell. A couple of sniffs of it was enough of an explanation: it was smoke! Our game was up at last. We recognized that. When smoke invites you, you have to come. They raised their pile of dry brush and damp weeds higher and higher, and when they saw the thick cloud begin to roll up and smother the tree, they broke out in a storm of joy-clamors. I got enough breath to say:

"Proceed, my liege; after you is manners."

The king gasped:

"Follow me down, and then back thyself against one side of the trunk, and leave me the other. Then will we fight. Let each pile his dead according to his own fashion and taste."

Then he descended barking and coughing, and I followed. I struck the ground an instant after him; we sprang to our appointed places, and began to give and take with all our might. The powwow and racket was prodigious; it was a tempest of riot and confusion and thick-falling blows. Suddenly some horsemen tore into the midst of the crowd, and a voice shouted:

"Hold—or ye are dead men!"

How good it sounded! The owner of the voice bore all the marks of a gentleman: picturesque and costly raiment, the aspect of command, a hard countenance with complexion and features marred by dissipation. The mob fell humbly back, like so many spaniels. The gentleman inspected us critically, then said sharply to the peasants:

"What are ye doing to these people?"

"They be madmen, worshipful sir, that have come wandering we know not whence, and—"

"Ye know not whence? Do ye pretend ye know them not?"

"Most honored sir, we speak but the truth. They are strangers and unknown to any in this region; and they be the most violent and bloodthirsty madmen that ever—"

"Peace! Ye know not what ye say. They are not mad. Who are ye? And whence are ye? Explain."

"We are but peaceful strangers, sir," I said, "and traveling upon our own concerns. We are from a far country, and unacquainted here. We have purposed no harm; and yet but for your brave interference and protection these people would have killed us. As you have divined, sir, we are not mad; neither are we violent or bloodthirsty."

The gentleman turned to his retinue and said calmly:

"Lash me these animals to their kennels!"

The mob vanished in an instant; and after them plunged the horsemen, laying about them with their whips and pitilessly riding down such as were witless enough to keep the road instead of taking to the bush. The shrieks and supplications presently died away in the distance, and soon the horsemen began to straggle back. Meantime the gentleman had been questioning us more closely, but had dug no particulars out of us. We were lavish of recognition of the service he was doing us, but we revealed nothing more than that we were friendless strangers from a far country. When the escort were all returned, the gentleman said to one of his servants:

"Bring the led horses and mount these people."

"Yes, my lord."

We were placed toward the rear, among the servants. We traveled pretty fast, and finally drew rein some time after dark at a roadside inn some ten or twelve miles from the scene of our troubles. My lord went immediately to his room, after ordering his supper, and we saw no more of him. At dawn in the morning we breakfasted and made ready to start.

My lord's chief attendant sauntered forward at that moment with indolent grace, and said:

"Ye have said ye should continue upon this road, which is our direction likewise; wherefore my lord, the earl Grip, hath given commandment that ye retain the horses and ride, and that certain of us ride with ye a twenty mile to a fair town that hight Cambenet, whenso ye shall be out of peril."

We could do nothing less than express our thanks and accept the offer. We jogged along, six in the party, at a moderate and comfortable gait, and in conversation learned that my lord Grip was a very great personage in his own region, which lay a day's journey beyond Cambenet. We loitered to such a degree that it was near the middle of the forenoon when we entered the market square of the town. We dismounted, and left our thanks once more for my lord, and then approached a crowd assembled in the center of the square, to see what might be the object of interest. It was the remnant of that old peregrinating band of slaves! So they had been dragging their chains about, all this weary time. That poor husband was gone, and also many others; and some few purchases had been added to the gang. The king was not interested, and wanted to move along, but I was absorbed, and full of pity. I could not take my eyes away from these worn and wasted wrecks of humanity. There they sat, grouped upon the ground, silent, uncomplaining, with bowed heads, a pathetic sight. And by hideous contrast, a redundant orator was making a speech to another gathering not thirty steps away, in fulsome laudation of "our glorious British liberties!"

I was boiling. I had forgotten I was a plebeian, I was remembering I was a man. Cost what it might, I would mount that rostrum and—

Click! the king and I were handcuffed together! Our companions, those servants, had done it; my lord Grip stood looking on. The king burst out in a fury, and said:

"What meaneth this ill-mannered jest?"

My lord merely said to his head miscreant, coolly:

"Put up the slaves and sell them!"

Slaves! The word had a new sound—and how unspeakably awful! The king lifted his manacles and brought them down with a deadly force; but my lord was out of the way when they arrived. A dozen of the rascal's servants sprang forward, and in a moment we were helpless, with our hands bound behind us. We so loudly and so earnestly proclaimed ourselves freemen, that we got the interested attention of that liberty-mouthing orator and his patriotic crowd, and they gathered about us and assumed a very determined attitude. The orator said:

"If indeed ye are freemen, ye have nought to fear—the God-given liberties of Britain are about ye for your shield and shelter! (Applause.) Ye shall soon see. Bring forth your proofs."

"What proofs?"

"Proof that ye are freemen."

Ah—I remembered! I came to myself; I said nothing. But the king stormed out:

"Thou'rt insane, man. It were better, and more in reason, that this thief and scoundrel here prove that we are *not* freemen."

You see, he knew his own laws just as other people so often know the laws: by words, not by effects. They take a *meaning*, and get to be very vivid, when you come to apply them to yourself.

All hands shook their heads and looked disappointed; some turned away, no longer interested. The orator said—and this time in the tones of business, not of sentiment:

"An ye do not know your country's laws, it were time ye learned them. Ye are strangers to us; ye will not deny that. Ye may be freemen, we do not deny that; but also ye may be slaves. The law is clear: it doth not require the claimant to prove ye are slaves, it requireth you to prove ye are *not*."

I said:

"Dear sir, give us only time to send to Astolat; or give us only time to send to the Valley of Holiness—"

"Peace, good man, these are extraordinary requests, and you may not hope to have them granted. It would cost much time, and would unwarrantably inconvenience your master—"

"*Master*, idiot!" stormed the king. "I have no master, I myself am the m——"

"Silence, for God's sake!"

I got the words out in time to stop the king. We were in trouble enough already; it could not help us any to give these people the notion that we were lunatics.

There is no use in stringing out the details. The earl put us up and sold us at auction. This same infernal law had existed in our own South in my own time, more than thirteen hundred years later, and under it hundreds of freemen who could not prove that they were freemen had been sold into lifelong slavery without the circumstance making any particular impression upon me; but the minute law and the auction block came into my personal experience, a thing which had been merely improper before became suddenly hellish. Well, that's the way we are made.

Yes, we were sold at auction, like swine. In a big town and an active market we should have brought a good price; but this place was utterly stagnant and so we sold at a figure which makes me ashamed, every time I think of it. The King of England brought seven dollars, and his prime minister nine; whereas the king was easily worth twelve dollars and I as easily worth fifteen. But that is the way things always go; if you force a sale on a dull market, I don't care what the property is, you are going to make a poor business of it, and you can make up your mind to it. If the earl had had wit enough to—

However, there is no occasion for my working my sympathies up on his account. Let him go, for the present: I took his number, so to speak.

The slave dealer bought us both, and hitched us onto that long chain of his, and we constituted the rear of his procession. We took up our line of march and passed out of Cambenet at noon; and it seemed to me unaccountably strange and odd that the King of England and his chief minister, marching manacled and fettered and yoked, in a slave convoy, could move by all manner of idle men and women, and under windows where sat the sweet and the lovely, and yet never attract a curious eye, never provoke a single remark. Dear, dear, it only shows that there is nothing diviner about a king than there is about a tramp, after all. He is just a cheap and hollow artificiality when you don't know he is a king. But reveal his quality, and dear me it takes your very breath away to look at him. I reckon we are all fools. Born so, no doubt.

XXXV. A PITIFUL INCIDENT

IT'S A WORLD of surprises. The king brooded; this was natural. What would he brood about, should you say? Why, about the prodigious nature of his fall, of course—from the loftiest place in the world to the lowest; from the most illustrious station in the world to the obscurest; from the grandest vocation among men to the basest. No, I take my oath that the thing that graveled him most, to start with, was not this, but the price he had fetched! He couldn't seem to get over that seven dollars. Well, it stunned me so, when I first found it out, that I couldn't believe it; it didn't seem natural. But as soon as my mental sight cleared and I got a right focus on it, I saw I was mistaken: it *was* natural. For this reason: a king is a mere artificiality, and so a king's feelings, like the impulses of an automatic doll, are mere artificialities; but as a man, he is a reality, and his feelings, as a man, are real, not phantoms. It shames the average man to be valued below his own estimate of his worth; and the king certainly wasn't anything more than an average man, if he was up that high.

Confound him, he wearied me with arguments to show that in anything like a fair market he could have fetched twenty-five dollars, sure—a thing which was plainly nonsense, and full of the baldest conceit; I wasn't worth it myself. But it was tender ground for me to argue on. In fact I had to simply shirk argument and do the diplomatic instead. I had to throw conscience aside, and brazenly concede that he ought to have brought twenty-five dollars; whereas I was quite well aware that in all the ages, the world had never seen a king that was worth half the money, and during the next thirteen centuries wouldn't see one that was worth the fourth of it. Yes, he tired me. If he began to talk about the crops, or about the recent weather, or about the condition of politics, or about dogs, or cats, or morals, or theology—no matter what—I sighed, for I knew what was coming: he was going to get out of it a palliation of that tiresome seven-dollar sale. Wherever we halted, where there was a crowd, he would give me a look which said,

211

plainly: "if that thing could be tried over again, now, with this kind of folk, you would see a different result." Well, when he was first sold, it secretly tickled me to see him go for seven dollars; but before he was done with his sweating and worrying I wished he had fetched a hundred. The thing never got a chance to die, for every day, at one place or another, possible purchasers looked us over, and as often as any other way, their comment on the king was something like this:

"Here's a two-dollar-and-a-half chump with a thirty-dollar style. Pity but style was marketable."

At last this sort of remark produced an evil result. Our owner was a practical person and he perceived that this defect must be mended if he hoped to find a purchaser for the king. So he went to work to take the style out of his sacred majesty. I could have given the man some valuable advice, but I didn't; you mustn't volunteer advice to a slave driver unless you want to damage the cause you are arguing for. I had found it a sufficiently difficult job to reduce the king's style to a peasant's style, even when he was a willing and anxious pupil; now then, to undertake to reduce the king's style to a slave's style—and by force—go to! It was a stately contract. Never mind the details—it will save me trouble to let you imagine them. I will only remark that at the end of a week there was plenty of evidence that lash and club and fist had done their work well; the king's body was a sight to see—and to weep over; but his spirit—why, it wasn't even fazed. Even that dull clod of a slave driver was able to see that there can be such a thing as a slave who will remain a man till he dies; whose bones you can break, but whose manhood you can't. This man found that from his first effort down to his latest, he couldn't ever come within reach of the king but the king was ready to plunge for him, and did it. So he gave up, at last, and left the king in possession of his style unimpaired. The fact is, the king was a good deal more than a king, he was a man; and when a man is a man, you can't knock it out of him.

We had a rough time for a month, tramping to and fro in the earth, and suffering. And what Englishman was the most interested in the slavery question by that time? His grace the king! Yes; from being the most indifferent, he was become the most interested. He was become the bitterest hater of the institution I had ever heard talk. And so I ventured to ask once more a question which I had asked years before and had gotten such a sharp answer that I had not thought it prudent to meddle in the matter further. Would he abolish slavery?

His answer was as sharp as before, but it was music this time; I shouldn't ever wish to hear pleasanter, though the profanity was not good, being awkwardly put together, and with the crash word almost in the middle instead of at the end, where of course it ought to have been.

I was ready and willing to get free, now; I hadn't wanted to get free any sooner. No, I cannot quite say that. I had wanted to, but I had not been willing to take desperate chances, and had always dissuaded the king from them. But now—ah, it was a new atmosphere! Liberty would be worth any cost that might be put upon it now. I set about a plan, and was straightway charmed with it. It would require time, yes, and patience, too, a great deal of both. One could invent quicker ways, and fully as sure ones; but none that would be as picturesque as this; none that could be made so dramatic. And so I was not going to give this one up. It might delay us months, but no matter, I would carry it out or break something.

Now and then we had an adventure. One night we were overtaken by a snowstorm while still a mile from the village we were making for. Almost instantly we were shut up as in a fog, the driving snow was so thick. You couldn't see a thing, and we were soon lost. The slave driver lashed us desperately, for he saw ruin before him, but his lashings only made matters worse, for they drove us further from the road and from likelihood of succor. So we had to stop, at last, and slump down in the snow where we were. The storm continued until toward midnight, then ceased. By this time two of our feebler men and three of our women were dead, and others past moving and threatened with death. Our master was nearly beside himself. He stirred up the living and made us stand, jump, slap ourselves, to restore our circulation, and he helped as well as he could with his whip.

Now came a diversion. We heard shrieks and yells, and soon a woman came running, and crying; and seeing our group, she flung herself into our midst and begged for protection. A mob of people came tearing after her, some with torches, and they said she was a witch who had caused several cows to die by a strange disease, and practiced her arts by help of a devil in the form of a black cat. This poor woman had been stoned until she hardly looked human, she was so battered and bloody. The mob wanted to burn her.

Well, now, what do you suppose our master did? When we closed around this poor creature to shelter her, he saw his chance. He said, burn her here, or they shouldn't have her at all. Imagine that! They were willing. They fastened her to a post; they brought wood and piled it about her; they applied the torch while she shrieked and pleaded and strained her two young daughters to her breast; and our brute, with a heart solely for business, lashed us into position about the stake and warmed us into life and commercial value by the same fire which took away the innocent life of that poor harmless mother. That was the sort of master we had. I took *his* number. That snowstorm cost him nine of his flock; and he was more brutal to us than ever, after that, for many days together, he was so enraged over his loss.

We had adventures, all along. One day we ran into a procession. And such a procession! All the riffraff of the kingdom seemed to be comprehended in it; and all drunk at that. In the van was a cart with a coffin in it, and on the coffin sat a comely young girl of about eighteen suckling a baby, which she squeezed to her breast in a passion of love every little while, and every little while wiped from its face the tears which her eyes rained down upon it; and always the foolish little thing smiled up at her, happy and content, kneading her breast with its dimpled fat hand, which she patted and fondled right over her breaking heart.

Men and women, boys and girls, trotted along beside or after the cart, hooting, shouting profane and ribald remarks, singing snatches of foul song, skipping, dancing—a very holiday of hellions, a sickening sight. We had struck a suburb of London, outside the walls, and this was a sample of one sort of London society. Our master secured a good place for us near the gallows. A priest was in attendance, and he helped the girl climb up, and said comforting words to her, and made the undersheriff provide a stool for her. Then he stood there by her on the gallows, and for a moment looked down upon the mass of upturned faces at his feet, then out over the solid pavement of heads that stretched away on every side occupying the vacancies far and near, and then began to tell the story of the case. And there was pity in his voice—how seldom a sound that was in that ignorant and savage land! I remember every detail of what he said, except the words he said it in; and so I change it into my own words:

"Law is intended to mete out justice. Sometimes it fails. This cannot be helped. We can only grieve, and be resigned, and pray for the soul of him who falls unfairly by the arm of the law, and that his fellows may be few. A law sends this poor young thing to death—and it is right. But another law had placed her where she must commit her crime or starve, with her child—and before God that law is responsible for both her crime and her ignominious death!

"A little while ago this young thing, this child of eighteen years, was as happy a wife and mother as any in England; and her lips were blithe with song, which is the native speech of glad and innocent hearts. Her young husband was as happy as she; for he was doing his whole duty, he worked early and late at his handicraft, his bread was honest bread well and fairly earned, he was prospering, he was furnishing shelter and sustenance to his family, he was adding his mite to the wealth of the nation. By consent of a treacherous law, instant destruction fell upon this holy home and swept it away! That young husband was waylaid and impressed, and sent to sea. The wife knew nothing of it. She sought him everywhere, she moved the hardest hearts with the supplications of her tears, the broken eloquence of her despair. Weeks dragged by, she watching, waiting, hoping, her mind going slowly to wreck under the burden of her misery. Little by little all her small possessions went for food. When she could no longer pay her rent, they turned her out of doors. She begged, while she had strength; when she was starving, at last, and her milk failing, she stole a piece of linen cloth of the value of a fourth part of a cent, thinking to sell it and save her child. But she was seen by the owner of the cloth. She was put in jail and brought to trial. The man testified to the facts. A plea was made for her, and her sorrowful story was told in her behalf. She spoke, too, by permission, and said she did steal the cloth, but that her mind was so disordered of late, by trouble, that when she was overborne with hunger all acts, criminal or other, swam meaningless through her brain and she knew nothing rightly, except that she was so hungry! For a moment all were touched, and there was disposition to deal mercifully with her, seeing that she was so young and friendless, and her case so piteous, and the law that robbed her of her support to blame as being the first and only cause of her transgression; but the prosecuting officer replied that whereas these things were all true, and most pitiful as well, still there was much small theft in these days, and mistimed mercy here would be a danger to property—oh, my God, is there no property in ruined homes, and orphaned babes, and broken hearts that British law holds precious— and so he must require sentence.

"When the judge put on his black cap, the owner of the stolen linen rose trembling up, his lip quivering, his face as gray as ashes; and when the awful words came, he cried out, 'Oh, poor child, poor child, I did not know it was death!' and fell as a tree falls. When they lifted him up his reason was gone; before the sun was set, he had taken his own life. A kindly man; a man whose heart was right, at bottom; add his murder to this that is to be now done here; and charge them both where they belong—to the rulers and the bitter laws of Britain. The time is come, my child; let me pray over thee—not for thee, dear abused poor heart and innocent, but for them that be guilty of thy ruin and death, who need it more."

After his prayer they put the noose around the young girl's neck, and they had great trouble to adjust the knot under her ear, because she was devouring the baby all the time, wildly kissing it, and snatching it to her face and her breast, and drenching it with tears, and half moaning, half shrieking all the while, and the baby crowing, and laughing, and kicking its feet with delight over what it took for romp and play. Even the hangman couldn't stand it, but turned away. When all was ready the priest gently pulled and tugged and forced the child out of the mother's arms, and stepped quickly out of her reach; but she clasped her hands, and made a wild spring toward him, with a shriek; but the rope—and the undersheriff—held her short. Then she went on her knees and stretched out her hands and cried:

"One more kiss—Oh, my God, one more, one more—it is the dying that begs it!"

She got it; she almost smothered the little thing. And when they got it away again, she cried out:

"Oh, my child, my darling, it will die! It has no home, it has no father, no friend, no mother—"

"It has them all!" said that good priest. "All these will I be to it till I die."

You should have seen her face then! Gratitude? Lord, what do you want with words to express that? Words are only painted fire; a look is the fire itself. She gave that look, and carried it away to the treasury of heaven, where all things that are divine belong.

XXXVI. AN ENCOUNTER IN THE DARK

LONDON—to a slave—was a sufficiently interesting place. It was merely a great big village; and mainly mud and thatch. The streets were muddy, crooked, unpaved. The populace was an ever flocking and drifting swarm of rags and splendors, of nodding plumes and shining armor. The king had a palace there; he saw the outside of it. It made him sigh; yes, and swear a little, in a poor juvenile sixth-century way. We saw knights and grandees whom we knew, but they didn't know us in our rags and dirt and raw welts and bruises, and wouldn't have recognized us if we had hailed them, nor stopped to answer, either, it being unlawful to speak with slaves on a chain. Sandy passed within ten yards of me on a mule—hunting for me, I imagined. But the thing which clean broke my heart was something which happened in front of our old barrack in a square, while we were enduring the spectacle of a man being boiled to death in oil for counterfeiting pennies. It was the sight of a newsboy—and I couldn't get at him! Still, I had one comfort; here was proof that Clarence was still alive and banging away. I meant to be with him before long; the thought was full of cheer.

I had one little glimpse of another thing, one day, which gave me a great uplift. It was a wire stretching from housetop to housetop. Telegraph or telephone, sure. I did very much wish I had a little piece of it. It was just what I needed, in order to carry out my project of escape. My idea was, to get loose some night, along with the king, then gag and bind our master, change clothes with him, batter him into the aspect of a stranger, hitch him to the slave chain, assume possession of the property, march to Camelot, and—

But you get my idea; you see what a stunning dramatic surprise I would wind up with at the palace. It was all feasible, if I could only get hold of a slender piece of iron which I could shape into a lockpick. I could then undo the lumbering padlocks with which our chains were fastened, whenever I might choose. But I never had any luck; no such thing ever happened to fall in my way. However, my chance came at last. A gentleman who had come twice before to dicker for me, without result, or indeed any approach to a result, came again. I was far from expecting ever to belong to him, for the price asked for me from the time I was first enslaved was exorbitant, and always provoked either anger or derision, yet my master stuck stubbornly to it—twenty-two dollars. He wouldn't bate a cent. The king was greatly admired, because of his grand physique, but his kingly style was against him, and he wasn't salable; nobody wanted that kind of a slave. I considered myself safe from parting from him because of my extravagant price. No, I was not expecting to ever belong to this gentleman whom I have spoken of, but he had something which I expected would belong to me eventually, if he would but visit us often enough. It was a steel thing with a long pin to it, with which his long cloth outside garment was fastened together in front. There were three of them. He had disappointed me twice, because he did not come quite close enough to me to make my project entirely safe; but this time I succeeded; I captured the lower clasp of the three, and when he missed it he thought he had lost it on the way.

I had a chance to be glad about a minute, then straightway a chance to be sad again. For when the purchase was about to fail, as usual, the master suddenly spoke up and said what would be worded thus—in modern English:

"I'll tell you what I'll do. I'm tired supporting these two for no good. Give me twenty-two dollars for this one, and I'll throw the other one in."

The king couldn't get his breath, he was in such a fury. He began to choke and gag, and meantime the master and the gentleman moved away, discussing.

"An ye will keep the offer open—"

"'Tis open till the morrow at this hour."

"Then will I answer you at that time," said the gentleman and disappeared, the master following him.

I had a time of it to cool the king down, but I managed it. I whispered in his ear, to this effect:

"Your grace *will* go for nothing, but after another fashion. And so shall I. Tonight we shall both be free."

"Ah! How is that?"

"With this thing which I have stolen, I will unlock these locks and cast off these chains tonight. When he comes about nine-thirty to inspect us for the night, we will seize him, gag him, batter him, and early in the morning we will march out of this town, proprietors of this caravan of slaves."

That was as far as I went, but the king was charmed and satisfied. That evening we waited patiently for our fellow slaves to get to sleep and signify it by the usual sign, for you must not take many chances on those poor fellows if you can avoid it. It is best to keep your own secrets. No doubt they fidgeted only about as usual, but it didn't seem so to me. It seemed to me that they were going to be forever getting down to their regular snoring. As the time dragged on I got nervously afraid we shouldn't have enough of it left for our needs; so I made several premature attempts, and merely delayed things by it; for I couldn't seem to touch a padlock, there in the dark, without starting a rattle out of it which interrupted somebody's sleep and made him turn over and wake some more of the gang.

But finally I did get my last iron off, and was a free man once more. I took a good breath of relief, and reached for the king's irons. Too late! in comes the master, with a light in one hand and his heavy walking staff in the other. I snuggled close among the wallow of snorers, to conceal as nearly as possible that I was naked of irons; and I kept a sharp lookout and prepared to spring for my man the moment he should bend over me.

But he didn't approach me. He stopped, gazed absently toward our dusky mass a minute, evidently thinking about something else; then set down his light, moved musingly toward the door, and before a body could imagine what he was doing, he was out of the door and had closed it behind him.

"Quick!" said the king. "Fetch him back!"

Of course it was the thing to do, and I was up and out in a moment. But dear me, there were no lamps in those days, and it was a dark night. But I glimpsed a dim figure a few steps away. I darted for it, threw myself upon it, and then there was a state of things and lively! We fought and scuffled and struggled, and drew a crowd in no time. They took an immense interest in the fight and encouraged us all they could, and in fact couldn't have been pleasanter or more cordial if it had been their own fight. Then a tremendous row broke out behind us, and as much as half of our audience left us, with a rush, to invest some sympathy in that. Lanterns began to swing in all directions; it was the watch, gathering from far and near. Presently a halberd fell across my back, as a reminder, and I knew what it meant. I was in custody. So was my adversary. We were marched off toward prison, one on each side of the watchman. Here was disaster, here was a fine scheme gone to sudden destruction! I tried to imagine what would happen when the master should discover that it was I who had been fighting him; and what would happen if they jailed us together in the general apartment for brawlers and petty law breakers, as was the custom; and what might—

Just then my antagonist turned his face around in my direction, the freckled light from the watchman's tin lantern fell on it, and by George he was the wrong man!

XXXVII. AN AWFUL PREDICAMENT

SLEEP? IT was impossible. It would naturally have been impossible in that noisome cavern of a jail, with its mangy crowd of drunken, quarrelsome and song-singing rapscallions. But the thing that made sleep all the more a thing not to be dreamed of, was my racking impatience to get out of this place and find out the whole size of what might have happened yonder in the slave quarters in consequence of that intolerable miscarriage of mine.

It was a long night but the morning got around at last. I made a full and frank explanation to the court. I said I was a slave, the property of the great Earl Grip, who had arrived just after dark at the Tabard inn in the village on the other side of the water, and had stopped there overnight, by compulsion, he being taken deadly sick with a strange and sudden disorder. I had been ordered to cross to the city in all haste and bring the best physician; I was doing my best; naturally I was running with all my might; the night was dark, I ran against this common person here, who seized me by the throat and began to pummel me, although I told him my errand, and implored him, for the sake of the great earl my master's mortal peril—

The common person interrupted and said it was a lie; and was going to explain how I rushed upon him and attacked him without a word—

"Silence, sirrah!" from the court. "Take him hence and give him a few stripes whereby to teach him how to treat the servant of a nobleman after a different fashion another time. Go!"

Then the court begged my pardon, and hoped I would not fail to tell his lordship it was in no wise the court's fault that this high-handed thing had happened. I said I would make it all right, and so took my leave. Took it just in time, too; he was starting to ask me why I didn't fetch out these facts the moment I was arrested. I said I would if I had thought of it—which was true—but that I was so battered by that man that all my wit was knocked out of me—and so forth and so on, and got myself away, still mumbling.

I didn't wait for breakfast. No grass grew under my feet. I was soon at the slave quarters. Empty—everybody gone! That is, everybody except one body—the slave master's. It lay there all battered to pulp; and all about were the evidences of a terrific fight. There was a rude board coffin on a cart at the door, and workmen, assisted by the police, were thinning a road through the gaping crowd in order that they might bring it in.

I picked out a man humble enough in life to condescend to talk with one so shabby as I, and got his account of the matter.

"There were sixteen slaves here. They rose against their master in the night, and thou seest how it ended."

"Yes. How did it begin?"

"There was no witness but the slaves. They said the slave that was most valuable got free of his bonds and escaped in some strange way—by magic arts 'twas thought, by reason that he had no key, and the locks were neither broke nor in any wise injured. When the master discovered his loss, he was mad with despair, and threw himself upon his people with his heavy stick, who resisted and brake his back and in other and divers ways did give him hurts that brought him swiftly to his end."

"This is dreadful. It will go hard with the slaves, no doubt, upon the trial."

"Marry, the trial is over."

"Over!"

"Would they be a week, think you—and the matter so simple? They were not the half of a quarter of an hour at it."

"Why, I don't see how they could determine which were the guilty ones in so short a time."

"*Which* ones? Indeed they considered not particulars like to that. They condemned them in a body. Wit ye not the law—which men say the Romans left behind them here when they went—that if one slave killeth his master all the slaves of that man must die for it."

"True. I had forgotten. And when will these die?"

"Belike within a four and twenty hours; albeit some say they will wait a pair of days more, if peradventure they may find the missing one meantime."

The missing one! It made me feel uncomfortable.

"Is it likely they will find him?"

"Before the day is spent—yes. They seek him everywhere. They stand at the gates of the town, with certain of the slaves who will discover him to them if he cometh, and none can pass out but he will be first examined."

"Might one see the place where the rest are confined?"

"The outside of it—yes. The inside of it—but ye will not want to see that."

I took the address of that prison, for future reference, and then sauntered off. At the first secondhand clothing shop I came to, up a back
street, I got a rough rig suitable for a common seaman who might be
going on a cold voyage, and bound up my face with a liberal bandage,
saying I had a toothache. This concealed my worst bruises. It was a
transformation. I no longer resembled my former self. Then I struck
out for that wire, found it and followed it to its den. It was a little room
over a butcher's shop—which meant that business wasn't very brisk in
the telegraphic line. The young chap in charge was drowsing at his
table. I locked the door and put the vast key in my bosom. This
alarmed the young fellow, and he was going to make a noise; but I said:

"Save your wind; if you open your mouth you are dead, sure. Tackle
your instrument. Lively, now! Call Camelot."

"This doth amaze me! How should such as you know aught of such
matters as—"

"Call Camelot! I am a desperate man. Call Camelot, or get away
from the instrument and I will do it myself."

"What—you?"

"Yes—certainly. Stop gabbling. Call the palace." He made the call.

"Now then, call Clarence."

"Clarence *who?*"

"Never mind Clarence who. Say you want Clarence; you'll get an
answer."

He did so. We waited five nerve-straining minutes—ten minutes—
how long it did seem!—and then came a click that was as familiar to
me as a human voice; for Clarence had been my own pupil.

"Now, my lad, vacate! They wouldn't have known *my* touch, maybe,
and so your call was surest; but I'm all right, now."

He vacated the place and cocked his ear to listen—but it didn't win.
I used a cipher. I didn't waste any time in sociabilities with Clarence,
but squared away for business, straight off—thus:

"The king is here and in danger. We were captured and brought here
as slaves. We should not be able to prove our identity—and the fact is,
I am not in a position to try. Send a telegram for the palace here which
will carry conviction with it."

His answer came straight back:

"They don't know anything about the telegraph; they haven't had
any experience yet, the line to London is so new. Better not venture
that. They might hang you. Think up something else."

Might hang us! Little he knew how closely he was crowding the
facts. I couldn't think up anything for the moment. Then an idea struck
me, and I started it along:

"Send five hundred picked knights with Launcelot in the lead; and send them on the jump. Let them enter by the southwest gate, and look out for the man with a white cloth around his right arm."

The answer was prompt:

"They shall start in half an hour."

"All right, Clarence; now tell this lad here that I'm a friend of yours and a deadhead; and that he must be discreet and say nothing about this visit of mine."

The instrument began to talk to the youth and I hurried away. I fell to ciphering. In half an hour it would be nine o'clock. Knights and horses in heavy armor couldn't travel very fast. These would make the best time they could, and now that the ground was in good condition, and no snow or mud, they would probably make a seven-mile gait; they would have to change horses a couple of times; they would arrive about six, or a little after; it would still be plenty light enough; they would see the white cloth which I should tie around my right arm, and I would take command. We would surround that prison and have the king out in no time. It would be showy and picturesque enough, all things considered, though I would have preferred noonday, on account of the more theatrical aspect the thing would have.

Now then, in order to increase the strings to my bow, I thought I would look up some of those people whom I had formerly recognized, and make myself known. That would help us out of our scrape, without the knights. But I must proceed cautiously, for it was a risky business. I must get into sumptuous raiment, and it wouldn't do to run and jump into it. No, I must work up to it by degrees, buying suit after suit of clothes, in shops wide apart, and getting a little finer article with each change, until I should finally reach silk and velvet, and be ready for my project. So I started.

But the scheme fell through like scat! The first corner I turned, I came plump upon one of our slaves, snooping around with a watchman. I coughed, at the moment, and he gave me a sudden look that bit right into my marrow. I judged he thought he had heard that cough before. I turned immediately into a shop and worked along down the counter, pricing things and watching out of the corner of my eye. Those people had stopped, and were talking together and looking in at the door. I made up my mind to get out the back way, if there was a back way, and I asked the shopwoman if I could step out there and look for the escaped slave, who was believed to be in hiding back there somewhere, and said I was an officer in disguise, and my pard was yonder at the door with one of the murderers in charge, and would she be good enough to step there and tell him he needn't wait, but had better go at once to the further end of the back alley and be ready to head him off when I rousted him out.

She was blazing with eagerness to see one of those already celebrated murderers, and she started on the errand at once. I slipped out the back way, locked the door behind me, put the key in my pocket and started off, chuckling to myself and comfortable.

Well, I had gone and spoiled it again, made another mistake. A double one, in fact. There were plenty of ways to get rid of that officer by some simple and plausible device, but no, I must pick out a picturesque one; it is the crying defect of my character. And then, I had ordered my procedure upon what the officer, being human, would *naturally* do; whereas when you are least expecting it, a man will now and then go and do the very thing which it's *not* natural for him to do. The natural thing for the officer to do, in this case, was to follow straight on my heels; he would find a stout oaken door, securely locked, between him and me; before he could break it down, I should be far away and engaged in slipping into a succession of baffling disguises which would soon get me into a sort of raiment which was a surer protection from meddling law dogs in Britain than any amount of mere innocence and purity of character. But instead of doing the natural thing, the officer took me at my word, and followed my instructions. And so, as I came trotting out of that cul-de-sac, full of satisfaction with my own cleverness, he turned the corner and I walked right into his handcuffs. If I had known it was a cul-de-sac—however, there isn't any excusing a blunder like that, let it go. Charge it up to profit and loss.

Of course I was indignant, and swore I had just come ashore from a long voyage, and all that sort of thing—just to see, you know, if it would deceive that slave. But it didn't. He knew me. Then I reproached him for betraying me. He was more surprised than hurt. He stretched his eyes wide, and said:

"What, wouldst have me let thee, of all men, escape and not hang with us, when thou're the very *cause* of our hanging? Go to!"

"Go to" was their way of saying "I should smile!" or "I like that!" Queer talkers, those people.

Well, there was a sort of bastard justice in his view of the case, and so I dropped the matter. When you can't cure a disaster by argument, what is the use to argue? It isn't my way. So I only said:

"You're not going to be hanged. None of us are."

Both men laughed, and the slave said:

"Ye have not ranked as a fool—before. You might better keep your reputation, seeing the strain would not be for long."

"It will stand it, I reckon. Before tomorrow we shall be out of prison, and free to go where we will, besides."

The witty officer lifted at his left ear with his thumb, made a rasping noise in his throat, and said:

"Out of prison—yes—ye say true. And free likewise to go where ye will, so ye wander not out of his grace the Devil's sultry realm."

I kept my temper, and said, indifferently:

"Now I suppose you really think we are going to hang within a day or two."

"I thought it not many minutes ago, for so the thing was decided and proclaimed."

"Ah, then you've changed your mind, is that it?"

"Even that. I only *thought*, then; I *know*, now."

I felt sarcastical, so I said:

"Oh, sapient servant of the law, condescend to tell us, then, what you *know*."

"That ye will all be hanged *today*, at midafternoon! Oho! that shot hit home! Lean upon me."

The fact is I did need to lean upon somebody. My knights couldn't arrive in time. They would be as much as three hours too late. Nothing in the world could save the King of England; nor me, which was more important. More important, not merely to me, but to the nation—the only nation on earth standing ready to blossom into civilization. I was sick. I said no more, there wasn't anything to say. I knew what the man meant; that if the missing slave was found, the postponement would be revoked, the execution take place today. Well, the missing slave was found.

XXXVIII. SIR LAUNCELOT AND KNIGHTS
TO THE RESCUE

NEARING FOUR in the afternoon. The scene was just outside the walls of London. A cool, comfortable, superb day, with a brilliant sun; the kind of day to make one want to live, not die. The multitude was prodigious and far-reaching; and yet we fifteen poor devils hadn't a friend in it. There was something painful in that thought, look at it how you might. There we sat, on our tall scaffold, the butt of the hate and mockery of all those enemies. We were being made a holiday spectacle. They had built a sort of grandstand for the nobility and gentry, and these were there in full force, with their ladies. We recognized a good many of them.

The crowd got a brief and unexpected dash of diversion out of the king. The moment we were freed of our bonds he sprang up, in his fantastic rags, with face bruised out of all recognition, and proclaimed himself Arthur, King of Britain, and denounced the awful penalties of treason upon every soul there present if hair of his sacred head were touched. It startled and surprised him to hear them break into a vast roar of laughter. It wounded his dignity, and he locked himself up in silence, then, although the crowd begged him to go on, and tried to provoke him to it by catcalls, jeers, and shouts of:

"Let him speak! The king! The king! his humble subjects hunger and thirst for words of wisdom out of the mouth of their master his Serene and Sacred Raggedness!"

But it went for nothing. He put on all his majesty and sat under this rain of contempt and insult unmoved. He certainly was great in his way. Absently, I had taken off my white bandage and wound it about my right arm. When the crowd noticed this, they began upon me. They said:

"Doubtless this sailorman is his minister—observe his costly badge of office!"

I let them go on until they got tired, and then I said:

"Yes, I am his minister. The Boss; and tomorrow you will hear that from Camelot which—"

I got no further. They drowned me out with joyous derision. But presently there was silence; for the sheriffs of London, in their official robes, with their subordinates, began to make a stir which indicated that business was about to begin. In the hush which followed, our crime was recited, the death warrant read, then everybody uncovered while a priest uttered a prayer.

Then a slave was blindfolded, the hangman unslung his rope. There lay the smooth road below us, we upon one side of it, the banked multitude walling its other side—a good clear road, and kept free by the police—how good it would be to see my five hundred horsemen come tearing down it! But, no, it was out of the possibilities. I followed its receding thread out into the distance—not a horseman on it, or sign of one.

There was a jerk, and the slave hung dangling; dangling and hideously squirming, for his limbs were not tied.

A second rope was unslung, in a moment another slave was dangling.

In a minute a third slave was struggling in the air. It was dreadful. I turned away my head a moment, and when I turned back I missed the king! They were blindfolding him! I was paralyzed; I couldn't move, I was choking, my tongue was petrified. They finished blindfolding him, they led him under the rope. I couldn't shake off that clinging impotence. But when I saw them put the noose around his neck, then everything let go in me and I made a spring to the rescue—and as I made it I shot one more glance abroad—by George, here they came, atilting—five hundred mailed and belted knights on bicycles!

The grandest sight that ever was seen. Lord, how the plumes streamed, how the sun flamed and flashed from the endless procession of webby wheels!

I waved my right arm as Launcelot swept in—he recognized my rag—I tore away noose and bandage, and shouted:

"On your knees, every rascal of you, and salute the king! Who fails shall sup in hell tonight!"

I always use that high style when I'm climaxing an effect. Well, it was noble to see Launcelot and the boys swarm up onto that scaffold and heave sheriffs and such overboard. And it was fine to see that astonished multitude go down on their knees and beg their lives of the king they had just been deriding and insulting. And as he stood apart, there, receiving this homage in his rags, I thought to myself, well really there *is* something peculiarly grand about the gait and bearing of a king, after all.

I was immensely satisfied. Take the whole situation all around, it was one of the gaudiest effects I ever instigated.

And presently up comes Clarence, his own self! And winks, and says, very modernly:

"Good deal of a surprise, wasn't it? I knew you'd like it. I've had the boys practicing, this long time, privately; and just hungry for a chance to show off."

XXXIX. THE YANKEE'S FIGHT
WITH THE KNIGHTS

HOME AGAIN, at Camelot. A morning or two later I found the paper, damp from the press, by my plate at the breakfast table. I turned to the advertising columns, knowing I should find something of personal interest to me there. It was this:

DE PAR LE ROI.

Know that the great lord and illustrious kni8ht SIR SAGRAMOUR LE DESIROUS having condescended to meet the King's Minister, Hank Morgan, the which is surnamed The Boss, for satisfaction of offence anciently given, these will engage in the lists by Camelot about the fourth hour of the morning of the sixteenth day of this next succeeding month. The battle will be à l'outrance, sith the said offence was of a deadly sort, admitting of no composition.

DE PAR LE ROI

Clarence's editorial reference to this affair was to this effect:

	It will be observed, by a glance at our advertising columns, that the community is to be favored with a treat of unusual interest in the tournament line. The names of the artists are warrant of	
...ndrew. work maintained there since, soon listic have with cked interest		our disappointn. promptly and ...t two of their felo erlain, and others have already

upon the ea—n d ve been m d oy the ar s, ent out ch y by yterian B t, and c some y ng men of our unde the i guidance of tha for and in a known he great enterprise of making pure; esem movement had its origin a preven has ever been a sions in our on of pris other one ospel, by- e The he same co represent med thirty of needs and bear- which years ago! foreign was organizing, the missions, so that both had to withdraw and much to their grief.

good entertainment. The box-office will be open at noon of the 13th; admission 3 cents, reserved seats 5; proceeds to go to the hospital fund. The royal pair and all the Court will be present. With these exceptions, and the press and the clergy, the free list is strictly suspended. Parties are hereby warned against buying tickets of speculators; they will not be good at the door. Everybody knows and likes The Boss, everybody knows and likes Sir Sag.; come, let us give the lads a good send-off. ReMember, the proceeds go to a great and free charity, and one whose broad benevolence stretches out its helping hand, warm with the blood of a loving heart, to all that suffer, regardless of race, creed, condition or color—the only charity yet established in the earth which has no politico-religious stop-cock on its compassion, but says Here flows the stream, let *all* come and drink! turn out, all hands! fetch along your doughnuts and your gum-drops and have a good time. Pie for sale on the grounds, and rocks to crack it with; also circus-lemonade—three drops of lime juice to a barrel of water.

N. B. *This is the first tournament under the new law, which allows each combatant to use any weapon he may prefer.* You want to make a note of that.

spoken, yon furnished for their use, make and the kind letters of introduction why they are units ing friends to us ried, and leave the thot kind words ent which you, m, 'oy-hind; and it is a home matter of b it is our durp direct them to now under the g fields as an These young men are warm-hearted azirl regions be not to "build ond,' and the der instruction ons of our another man founhati's on ociety, which They go un-say that "inr ionaries to mon say sending rain.

Up to the day set, there was no talk in all Britain of anything but this combat. All other topics sank into insignificance and passed out of men's thoughts and interest. It was not because a tournament was a great matter; it was not because Sir Sagramor had found the Holy Grail, for he had not, but had failed; it was not because the second (official) personage in the kingdom was one of the duelists; no, all these features were commonplace. Yet there was abundant reason for the extraordinary interest which this coming fight was creating. It was born of the fact that all the nation knew that this was not to be a duel between mere men, so to speak, but a duel between two mighty magicians; a duel not of muscle but of mind, not of human skill but of superhuman art and craft; a final struggle for supremacy between the two master enchanters of the age. It was realized that the most prodigious achievements of the most renowned knights could not be worthy of comparison with a spectacle like this; they could be but child's play, contrasted with this mysterious and awful battle of the gods. Yes, all the world knew it was going to be in reality a duel between Merlin and me, a measuring of his magic powers against mine. It was known that Merlin had been busy whole days and nights together, imbuing Sir Sagramor's arms and armor with supernal powers of offense and defense, and that he had procured for him from the spirits of the air a fleecy veil which would render the wearer invisible to his antagonist while still visible to other men. Against Sir Sagramor, so weaponed and protected, a thousand knights could accomplish nothing; against him no known enchantments could prevail. These facts were sure; regarding them there was no doubt, no reason for doubt. There was but one question: might there be still other enchantments, *unknown* to Merlin, which could render Sir Sagramor's veil transparent to me, and make his enchanted mail vulnerable to my weapons? This was the one thing to be decided in the lists. Until then the world must remain in suspense.

So the world thought there was a vast matter at stake here, and the world was right, but it was not the one they had in their minds. No, a far vaster one was upon the cast of this die: *the life of knight-errantry*. I was a champion, it was true, but not the champion of the frivolous black arts, I was the champion of hard unsentimental common sense and reason. I was entering the lists to either destroy knight-errantry or be its victim.

Vast as the showgrounds were, there were no vacant spaces in them outside of the lists, at ten o'clock on the morning of the 16th. The mammoth grandstand was clothed in flags, streamers, and rich tapestries, and packed with several acres of small-fry tributary kings, their suites, and the British aristocracy; with our own royal gang in the chief place, and each and every individual a flashing prism of gaudy silks and velvets—well, I never saw anything to begin with it but a fight between an Upper Mississippi sunset and the aurora borealis. The huge camp of beflagged and gay-colored tents at one end of the lists, with a stiff-standing sentinel at every door and a shining shield hanging by him for challenge, was another fine sight. You see, every knight was there who had any ambition or any caste feeling; for my feeling toward their order was not much of a secret, and so here was their chance. If I won my fight with Sir Sagramor, others would have the right to call me out as long as I might be willing to respond.

Down at our end there were but two tents; one for me, and another for my servants. At the appointed hour the king made a sign, and the heralds, in their tabards, appeared and made proclamation, naming the combatants and stating the cause of quarrel. There was a pause, then a ringing bugle blast, which was the signal for us to come forth. All the multitude caught their breath, and an eager curiosity flashed into every face.

Out from his tent rode great Sir Sagramor, an imposing tower of iron, stately and rigid, his huge spear standing upright in its socket and grasped in his strong hand, his grand horse's face and breast cased in steel, his body clothed in rich trappings that almost dragged the ground—oh, a most noble picture. A great shout went up, of welcome and admiration.

And then out I came. But I didn't get any shout. There was a won- dering and eloquent silence, for a moment, then a great wave of laugh- ter began to sweep along that human sea, but a warning bugle blast cut its career short. I was in the simplest and comfortablest of gymnast costumes—flesh-colored tights from neck to heel, with blue silk puff- ings about my loins, and bareheaded. My horse was not above medium size, but he was alert, slender-limbed, muscled with watch springs, and just a greyhound to go. He was a beauty, glossy as silk, and naked as he was when he was born, except for bridle and ranger saddle.

The iron tower and the gorgeous bed quilt came cumbrously but gracefully pirouetting down the lists, and we tripped lightly up to meet them. We halted; the tower saluted, I responded; then we wheeled and rode side by side to the grandstand and faced our king and queen, to whom we made obeisance. The queen exclaimed:

"Alack, Sir Boss, wilt fight naked, and without lance or sword or—"

But the king checked her and made her understand, with a polite phrase or two, that this was none of her business. The bugles rang again; and we separated and rode to the ends of the lists, and took position. Now old Merlin stepped into view and cast a dainty web of gossamer threads over Sir Sagramor which turned him into Hamlet's ghost; the king made a sign, the bugles blew, Sir Sagramor laid his great lance in rest, and the next moment here he came thundering down the course with his veil flying out behind, and I went whistling through the air like an arrow to meet him—cocking my ear, the while, as if noting the invisible knight's position and progress by hearing, not sight. A chorus of encouraging shouts burst out for him, and one brave voice flung out a heartening word for me—said:

"Go it, slim Jim!"

It was an even bet that Clarence had procured that favor for me— and furnished the language, too. When that formidable lance point was within a yard and a half of my breast I twitched my horse aside without an effort and the big knight swept by, scoring a blank. I got plenty of applause that time. We turned, braced up, and down we came again. Another blank for the knight, a roar of applause for me. This same thing was repeated once more; and it fetched such a whirlwind of applause that Sir Sagramor lost his temper, and at once changed his tactics and set himself the task of chasing me down. Why, he hadn't any show in the world at that; it was a game of tag, with all the advantage on my side; I whirled out of his path with ease whenever I chose, and once I slapped him on the back as I went to the rear. Finally I took the chase into my own hands; and after that, turn or twist, or do what he would, he was never able to get behind me again; he found himself always in front, at the end of his maneuver. So he gave up that business and retired to his end of the lists. His temper was clear gone, now, and he forgot himself and flung an insult at me which disposed of mine. I slipped my lasso from the horn of my saddle, and grasped the coil in my right hand. This time you should have seen him come! It was a business trip, sure; by his gait there was blood in his eye. I was sitting my horse at ease, and swinging the great loop of my lasso in wide circles about my head; the moment he was under way, I started for him; when the space between us had narrowed to forty feet, I sent the snaky spirals of the rope a-cleaving through the air, then darted aside and faced about and brought my trained animal to a halt with all his feet braced under him for a surge. The next moment the rope sprang taut and yanked Sir Sagramor out of the saddle! Great Scott, but there was a sensation!

Unquestionably the popular thing in this world is novelty. These people had never seen anything of that cowboy business before, and it carried them clear off their feet with delight. From all around and everywhere, the shout went up—

"Encore! encore!"

I wondered where they got the word, but there was no time to cipher on philological matters, because the whole knight-errantry hive was just humming, now, and my prospect for trade couldn't have been better. The moment my lasso was released and Sir Sagramor had been assisted to his tent, I hauled in the slack, took my station and began to swing my loop around my head again. I was sure to have use for it as soon as they could elect a successor for Sir Sagramor, and that couldn't take long where there were so many hungry candidates. Indeed, they elected one straight off—Sir Hervis de Revel.

Bzz! Here he came, like a house afire; I dodged; he passed like a flash, with my horsehair coils settling around his neck; a second or so later, *fst!* his saddle was empty.

I got another encore; and another, and another, and still another. When I had snaked five men out, things began to look serious to the ironclads, and they stopped and consulted together. As a result, they decided that it was time to waive etiquette and send their greatest and best against me. To the astonishment of that little world, I lassoed Sir Lamorak de Galis, and after him Sir Galahad. So you see there was simply nothing to be done, now, but play their right bower—bring out the superbest of the superb, the mightiest of the mighty, the great Sir Launcelot himself!

A proud moment for me? I should think so. Yonder was Arthur, King of Britain; yonder was Guenever; yes, and whole tribes of little provincial kings and kinglets; and in the tented camp yonder, renowned knights from many lands; and likewise the selectest body known to chivalry, the Knights of the Table Round, the most illustrious in Christendom; and biggest fact of all, the very sun of their shining system was yonder couching his lance, the focal point of forty thousand adoring eyes; and all by myself, here was I laying for him. Across my mind flitted the dear image of a certain hello-girl of West Hartford, and I wished she could see me now. In that moment, down came the Invincible, with the rush of a whirlwind—the courtly world rose to its feet and bent forward—the fateful coils went circling through the air, and before you could wink I was towing Sir Launcelot across the field on his back, and kissing my hand to the storm of waving kerchiefs and the thundercrash of applause that greeted me!

Said I to myself, as I coiled my lariat and hung it on my saddle horn, and sat there drunk with glory, "The victory is perfect—no other will venture against me—knight-errantry is dead." Now imagine my astonishment—and everybody else's too—to hear the peculiar bugle call which announces that another competitor is about to enter the lists! There was a mystery here; I couldn't account for this thing. Next, I noticed Merlin gliding away from me; and then I noticed that my lasso was gone! The old sleight-of-hand expert had stolen it, sure, and slipped it under his robe.

The bugle blew again. I looked, and down came Sagramor riding again, with his dust brushed off and his veil nicely rearranged. I trotted up to meet him, and pretended to find him by the sound of his horse's hoofs. He said:

"Thou'rt quick of ear, but it will not save thee from this!" and he touched the hilt of his great sword. "An ye are not able to see it, because of the influence of the veil, know that it is no cumbrous lance, but a sword—and I ween ye will not be able to avoid it."

His visor was up; there was death in his smile. I should never be able to dodge his sword, that was plain. Somebody was going to die, this time. If he got the drop on me, I could name the corpse. We rode forward together, and saluted the royalties. This time the king was disturbed. He said:

"Where is thy strange weapon?"

"It is stolen, sire."

"Hast another at hand?"

"No, sire, I brought only the one."

Then Merlin mixed in:

"He brought but the one because there was but the one to bring. There exists none other but that one. It belongeth to the king of the Demons of the Sea. This man is a pretender, and ignorant; else he had known that that weapon can be used in but eight bouts only, and then it vanisheth away to its home under the sea."

"Then is he weaponless," said the king. "Sir Sagramor, ye will grant him leave to borrow."

"And I will lend!" said Sir Launcelot, limping up. "He is as brave a knight of his hands as any that be on live, and he shall have mine."

He put his hand on his sword to draw it, but Sir Sagramor said:

"Stay, it may not be. He shall fight with his own weapons; it was his privilege to choose them and bring them. If he has erred, on his head be it."

"Knight!" said the king. "Thou'rt overwrought with passion; it disorders thy mind. Wouldst kill a naked man?"

"An he do it, he shall answer it to me," said Sir Launcelot.

"I will answer it to any he that desireth!" retorted Sir Sagramor hotly.

Merlin broke in, rubbing his hands and smiling his lowdownest smile of malicious gratification:

"'Tis well said, right well said! And 'tis enough of parleying, let my lord the king deliver the battle signal."

The king had to yield. The bugle made proclamation, and we turned apart and rode to our stations. There we stood, a hundred yards apart, facing each other, rigid and motionless, like horsed statues. And so we remained, in a soundless hush, as much as a full minute, everybody gazing, nobody stirring. It seemed as if the king could not take heart to give the signal. But at last he lifted his hand, the clear note of the bugle followed, Sir Sagramor's long blade described a flashing curve in the air, and it was superb to see him come. I sat still. On he came. I did not move. People got so excited that they shouted to me:

"Fly, fly! Save thyself! This is murther!"

I never budged so much as an inch, till that thundering apparition had got within fifteen paces of me; then I snatched a dragoon revolver out of my holster, there was a flash and a roar, and the revolver was back in the holster before anybody could tell what had happened.

Here was a riderless horse plunging by, and yonder lay Sir Sagramor, stone dead.

The people that ran to him were stricken dumb to find that the life was actually gone out of the man and no reason for it visible, no hurt upon his body, nothing like a wound. There was a hole through the breast of his chain mail, but they attached no importance to a little thing like that; and as a bullet wound there produces but little blood, none came in sight because of the clothing and swaddlings under the armor. The body was dragged over to let the king and the swells look down upon it. They were stupefied with astonishment, naturally. I was requested to come and explain the miracle. But I remained in my tracks, like a statue, and said:

"If it is a command, I will come, but my lord the king knows that I am where the laws of combat require me to remain while any desire to come against me."

I waited. Nobody challenged. Then I said:

"If there are any who doubt that this field is well and fairly won, I do not wait for them to challenge me, I challenge them."

"It is a gallant offer," said the king, "and well beseems you. Whom will you name, first?"

"I name none, I challenge all! Here I stand, and dare the chivalry of England to come against me — not by individuals, but in mass!"

"What!" shouted a score of knights.

"You have heard the challenge. Take it, or I proclaim you recreant knights and vanquished, every one!"

It was a "bluff" you know. At such a time it is sound judgment to put on a bold face and play your hand for a hundred times what it is worth; forty-nine times out of fifty nobody dares to "call," and you rake in the chips. But just this once — well, things looked squally! In just no time, five hundred knights were scrambling into their saddles, and before you could wink a widely scattering drove were under way and clattering down upon me. I snatched both revolvers from the holsters and began to measure distance and calculate chances.

Bang! One saddle empty. Bang! another one. Bang—bang! and I bagged two. Well it was nip and tuck with us, and I knew it. If I spent the eleventh shot without convincing these people, the twelfth man would kill me, sure.

And so I never did feel so happy as I did when my ninth downed its man and I detected the wavering in the crowd which is premonitory of panic. An instant lost now, could knock out my last chance. But I didn't lose it. I raised both revolvers and pointed them — the halted host stood their ground just about one good square moment, then broke and fled.

The day was mine. Knight-errantry was a doomed institution. The march of civilization was begun. How did I feel? Ah, you never could imagine it.

And Brer Merlin? His stock was flat again. Somehow, every time the magic of folderol tried conclusions with the magic of science, the magic of folderol got left.

XL. THREE YEARS LATER

WHEN I BROKE the back of knight-errantry that time, I no longer felt obliged to work in secret. So, the very next day I exposed my hidden schools, my mines, and my vast system of clandestine factories and workshops to an astonished world. That is to say, I exposed the nineteenth century to the inspection of the sixth.

Well it is always a good plan to follow up an advantage promptly. The knights were temporarily down, but if I would keep them so I must just simply paralyze them—nothing short of that would answer. You see, I was "bluffing" that last time, in the field; it would be natural for them to work around to that conclusion, if I gave them a chance. So I must not give them time: and I didn't.

I renewed my challenge, engraved it on brass, posted it up where any priest could read it to them, and also kept it standing, in the advertising columns of the paper.

I not only renewed it, but added to its proportions. I said, name the day, and I would take fifty assistants and stand up *against the massed chivalry of the whole earth and destroy it.*

I was not bluffing this time. I meant what I said; I could do what I promised. There wasn't any way to misunderstand the language of that challenge. Even the dullest of the chivalry perceived that this was a plain case of "put up, or shut up." They were wise and did the latter. In all the next three years they gave me no trouble worth mentioning.

Consider the three years sped. Now look around on England. A happy and prosperous country, and strangely altered. Schools everywhere, and several colleges; a number of pretty good newspapers. Even authorship was taking a start; Sir Dinadan the Humorist was first in the field, with a volume of gray-headed jokes which I had been familiar with during thirteen centuries. If he had left out that old rancid one about the lecturer I wouldn't have said anything; but I couldn't stand that one. I suppressed the book and hanged the author.

Slavery was dead and gone; all men were equal before the law; taxation had been equalized. The telegraph, the telephone, the phonograph, the typewriter, the sewing machine, and all the thousand willing and handy servants of steam and electricity were working their way into favor. We had a steamboat or two on the Thames, we had steam warships, and the beginnings of a steam commercial marine; I was getting ready to send out an expedition to discover America.

We were building several lines of railway, and our line from Camelot to London was already finished and in operation. I was shrewd enough to make all offices connected with the passenger service places of high and distinguished honor. My idea was to attract the chivalry and nobility, and make them useful and keep them out of mischief. The plan worked very well, the competition for the places was hot. The conductor of the 4:33 express was a duke, there wasn't a passenger conductor on the line below the degree of earl. They were good men, every one, but they had two defects which I couldn't cure, and so had to wink at: they wouldn't lay aside their armor, and they would "knock down" fares—I mean rob the company.

There was hardly a knight in all the land who wasn't in some useful employment. They were going from end to end of the country in all manner of useful missionary capacities; their penchant for wandering, and their experience in it, made them altogether the most effective spreaders of civilization we had. They went clothed in steel and equipped with sword and lance and battle-ax, and if they couldn't persuade a person to try a sewing machine on the installment plan, or a melodeon, or a barbed wire fence, or a prohibition journal, or any of the other thousand and one things they canvassed for, they removed him and passed on.

I was very happy. Things were working steadily toward a secretly longed-for point. You see, I had two schemes in my head which were the vastest of all my projects. The one was, to overthrow the Catholic Church and set up the Protestant faith on its ruins—not as an Established Church, but a go-as-you-please one; and the other project was, to get a decree issued by and by, commanding that upon Arthur's death unlimited suffrage should be introduced, and given to men and women alike—at any rate to all men, wise or unwise, and to all mothers who at middle age should be found to know nearly as much as their sons at twenty-one. Arthur was good for thirty years yet, he being about my own age—that is to say, forty—and I believed that in that time I could easily have the active part of the population of that day ready and eager for an event which should be the first of its kind in the history of the world—a rounded and complete governmental revolution without bloodshed. The result to be a republic. Well, I may as well confess, though I do feel ashamed when I think of it: I was beginning to have a base hankering to be its first president myself. Yes, there was more or less human nature in me; I found that out.

Clarence was with me as concerned the revolution, but in a modified way. His idea was a republic, without privileged orders but with a hereditary royal family at the head of it instead of an elective chief magistrate. He believed that no nation that had ever known the joy of worshiping a royal family could ever be robbed of it and not fade away and die of melancholy. I urged that kings were dangerous. He said, then have cats. He was sure that a royal family of cats would answer every purpose. They would be as useful as any other royal family, they would know as much, they would have the same virtues and the same treacheries, the same disposition to get up shindies with other royal cats, they would be laughably vain and absurd and never know it, they would be wholly inexpensive; finally, they would have as sound a divine right as any other royal house, and "Tom VII, or Tom XI, or Tom XIV by the grace of God King," would sound as well as it would when applied to the ordinary royal tomcat with tights on. "And as a rule," said he, in his neat modern English, "the character of these cats would be considerably above the character of the average king, and this would be an immense moral advantage to the nation, for the reason that a nation always models its morals after its monarch's. The worship of royalty being founded in unreason, these graceful and harmless cats would easily become as sacred as any other royalties, and indeed more so, because it would presently be noticed that they hanged nobody, beheaded nobody, imprisoned nobody, inflicted no cruelties or injustices of any sort, and so must be worthy of a deeper love and reverence than the customary human king, and would certainly get it. The eyes of the whole harried world would soon be fixed upon this humane and gentle system, and royal butchers would presently begin to disappear; their subjects would fill the vacancies with catlings from our own royal house; we should become a factory; we should supply the thrones of the world; within forty years all Europe would be governed by cats, and we should furnish the cats. The reign of universal peace would begin then, to end no more forever. . . . *Me-e-e-yow-ow-ow-ow—fzt—wow!*"

Hang him, I supposed he was in earnest, and was beginning to be persuaded by him, until he exploded that cathowl and startled me almost out of my clothes. But he never could be in earnest. He didn't know what it was. He had pictured a distinct and perfectly rational and feasible improvement upon constitutional monarchy, but he was too featherheaded to know it, or care anything about it, either. I was going to give him a scolding, but Sandy came flying in at that moment, wild with terror, and so choked with sobs that for a minute she could not get her voice. I ran and took her in my arms, and lavished caresses upon her and said, beseechingly:

"Speak, darling, speak! What is it?"

Her head fell limp upon my bosom, and she gasped, almost inaudibly: "HELLO-CENTRAL!"

"Quick!" I shouted to Clarence; "telephone the king's homeopath to come!"

In two minutes I was kneeling by the child's crib, and Sandy was dispatching servants here, there, and everywhere, all over the palace. I took in the situation almost at a glance—membranous croup! I bent down and whispered:

"Wake up, sweetheart! Hello-Central!"

She opened her soft eyes languidly, and made out to say—

"Papa."

That was a comfort. She was far from dead, yet. I sent for preparations of sulphur, I rousted out the croup kettle myself; for I don't sit down and wait for doctors when Sandy or the child is sick. I knew how to nurse both of them, and had had experience. This little chap had lived in my arms a good part of its small life, and often I could soothe away its troubles and get it to laugh through the tear-dews on its eyelashes when even its mother couldn't.

Sir Launcelot, in his richest armor, came striding along the great hall, now, on his way to the stock board; he was president of the stock board, and occupied the Siege Perilous, which he had bought of Sir Galahad; for the stock board consisted of the Knights of the Round Table, and they used the Round Table for business purposes, now. Seats at it were worth—well, you would never believe the figure, so it is no use to state it. Sir Launcelot was a bear, and he had put up a corner in one of the new lines, and was just getting ready to squeeze the shorts today; but what of that? He was the same old Launcelot, and when he glanced in as he was passing the door and found out that his pet was sick, that was enough for him; bulls and bears might fight it out their own way for all him, he would come right in here and stand by little Hello-Central for all he was worth. And that was what he did. He shied his helmet into the corner, and in half a minute he had a new wick in the alcohol lamp and was firing up on the croup kettle. By this time Sandy had built a blanket canopy over the crib, and everything was ready.

Sir Launcelot got up steam, he and I loaded up the kettle with unslaked lime and carbolic acid, with a touch of lactic acid added thereto, then filled the thing up with water and inserted the steam spout under the canopy. Everything was shipshape, now, and we sat down on either side of the crib to stand our watch. Sandy was so grateful and so comforted that she charged a couple of churchwardens with willowbark and sumac tobacco for us, and told us to smoke as much as we pleased, it couldn't get under the canopy, and she was used to smoke, being the first lady in the land who had ever seen a cloud blown. Well, there couldn't be a more contented or comfortable sight than Sir Launcelot in his noble armor sitting in gracious serenity at the end of a yard of snowy churchwarden. He was a beautiful man, a lovely man, and was just intended to make a wife and children happy. But of course, Guenever—however, it's no use to cry over what's done and can't be helped.

Well, he stood watch and watch with me, right straight through, for three days and nights, till the child was out of danger; then he took her up in his great arms and kissed her, with his plumes falling about her golden head, then laid her softly in Sandy's lap again and took his stately way down the vast hall, between the ranks of admiring men-at-arms and menials, and so disappeared. And no instinct warned me that I should never look upon him again in this world! Lord, what a world of heartbreak it is.

The doctors said we must take the child away, if we would coax her back to health and strength again. And she must have sea air. So we took a man-of-war, and a suite of two hundred and sixty persons, and went cruising about, and after a fortnight of this we stepped ashore on the French coast, and the doctors thought it would be a good idea to make something of a stay there. The little king of that region offered us his hospitalities, and we were glad to accept. If he had had as many conveniences as he lacked, we should have been plenty comfortable enough; even as it was, we made out very well, in his queer old castle, by the help of comforts and luxuries from the ship.

At the end of a month I sent the vessel home for fresh supplies, and for news. We expected her back in three or four days. She would bring me, along with other news, the result of a certain experiment which I had been starting. It was a project of mine to replace the tournament with something which might furnish an escape for the extra steam of the chivalry, keep those bucks entertained and out of mischief, and at the same time preserve the best thing in them, which was their hardy spirit of emulation. I had had a choice band of them in private training for some time, and the date was now arriving for their first public effort.

This experiment was baseball. In order to give the thing vogue from the start, and place it out of the reach of criticism, I chose my nines by rank, not capacity. There wasn't a knight in either team who wasn't a sceptered sovereign. As for material of this sort, there was a glut of it, always, around Arthur. You couldn't throw a brick in any direction and not cripple a king. Of course I couldn't get these people to leave off their armor; they wouldn't do that when they bathed. They consented to differentiate the armor so that a body could tell one team from the

other, but that was the most they would do. So, one of the teams wore
chain-mail ulsters, and the other wore plate armor made of my new
Bessemer steel. Their practice in the field was the most fantastic thing
I ever saw. Being ballproof, they never skipped out of the way, but stood
still and took the result; when a Bessemer was at the bat and a ball hit
him, it would bound a hundred and fifty yards, sometimes. And when
a man was running, and threw himself on his stomach to slide to his
base, it was like an ironclad coming into port. At first I appointed men
of no rank to act as umpires, but I had to discontinue that. These
people were no easier to please than other nines. The umpire's first
decision was usually his last; they broke him in two with a bat, and his
friends toted him home on a shutter. When it was noticed that no
umpire ever survived a game, umpiring got to be unpopular. So I was
obliged to appoint somebody whose rank and lofty position under the
government would protect him.

Here are the names of the nines:

BESSEMERS.	ULSTERS.
KING ARTHUR.	EMPEROR LUCIUS.
KING LOT OF LOTHIAN.	KING LOGRIS.
KING OF NORTHGALIS.	KING MARHALT OF IRELAND.
KING MARSIL.	KING MORGANORE.
KING OF LITTLE BRITAIN.	KING MARK OF CORNWALL.
KING LABOR.	KING NENTRES OF GARLOT.
KING PELLAM OF LISTENGESE.	KING MELIODAS OF LIONES.
KING BAGDEMAGUS.	KING OF THE LAKE.
KING TOLLEME LA FEINTES.	THE SOWDAN OF SYRIA.

Umpire—CLARENCE.

The first public game would certainly draw fifty thousand people;
and for solid fun would be worth going around the world to see.
Everything would be favorable; it was balmy and beautiful spring
weather, now, and Nature was all tailored out in her new clothes.

XLI. THE INTERDICT

HOWEVER, MY attention was suddenly snatched from such matters; our child began to lose ground again, and we had to go to sitting up with her, her case became so serious. We couldn't bear to allow anybody to help, in this service, so we two stood watch and watch, day in and day out. Ah, Sandy, what a right heart she had, how simple, and genuine, and good she was! She was a flawless wife and mother; and yet I had married her for no particular reason, except that by the customs of chivalry she was my property until some knight should win her from me in the field. She had hunted Britain over for me; had straightway resumed her old place at my side in the placidest way and as of right. I was a New Englander, and in my opinion this sort of partnership would compromise her, sooner or later. She couldn't see how, but I cut argument short and we had a wedding.

Now I didn't know I was drawing a prize, yet that was what I did draw. Within the twelvemonth I became her worshiper; and ours was the dearest and perfectest comradeship that ever was. People talk about beautiful friendships between two persons of the same sex. What is the best of that sort, as compared with the friendship of man and wife, where the best impulses and highest ideals of both are the same? There is no place for comparison between the two friendships; the one is earthly, the other divine.

In my dreams, along at first, I still wandered thirteen centuries away, and my unsatisfied spirit went calling and harking all up and down the unreplying vacancies of a vanished world. Many a time Sandy heard that imploring cry come from my lips in my sleep. With a grand magnanimity she saddled that cry of mine upon our child, conceiving it to be the name of some lost darling of mine. It touched me to tears, and it also nearly knocked me off my feet, too, when she smiled up in my face for an earned reward, and played her quaint and pretty surprise upon me:

"The name of one who was dear to thee is here preserved, here made holy, and the music of it will abide always in our ears. Now thou'll kiss me, as knowing the name I have given the child."

243

But I didn't know it, all the same. I hadn't an idea in the world; but it would have been cruel to confess it and spoil her pretty game; so I never let on, but said:

"Yes, I know, sweetheart—how dear and good it is of you, too! But I want to hear these lips of yours, which are also mine, utter it first—then its music will be perfect."

Pleased to the marrow, she murmured—

"HELLO-CENTRAL!"

I didn't laugh—I am always thankful for that—but the strain ruptured every cartilage in me, and for weeks afterward I could hear my bones clack when I walked. She never found out her mistake. The first time she heard that form of salute used at the telephone she was surprised, and not pleased; but I told her I had given order for it: that henceforth and forever the telephone must always be invoked with that reverent formality, in perpetual honor and remembrance of my lost friend and her small namesake. This was not true. But it answered.

Well, during two weeks and a half we watched by the crib, and in our deep solicitude we were unconscious of any world outside of that sickroom. Then our reward came: the center of the universe turned the corner and began to mend. Grateful? It isn't the term. There *isn't* any term for it. You know that, yourself, if you've watched your child through the Valley of the Shadow and seen it come back to life and sweep night out of the earth with one all-illuminating smile that you could cover with your hand.

Why, we were back in this world in one instant! Then we looked the same startled thought into each other's eyes at the same moment: more than two weeks gone, and that ship not back yet!

In another minute I appeared in the presence of my train. They had been steeped in troubled bodings all this time—their faces showed it. I called an escort and we galloped five miles to a hilltop overlooking the sea. Where was my great commerce that so lately had made these glistering expanses populous and beautiful with its white-winged flocks? Vanished, every one! Not a sail, from verge to verge, not a smoke bank— just a dead and empty solitude, in place of all that brisk and breezy life.

I went swiftly back, saying not a word to anybody. I told Sandy this ghastly news. We could imagine no explanation that would begin to explain. Had there been an invasion? An earthquake? A pestilence? Had the nation been swept out of existence? But guessing was profitless. I must go—at once. I borrowed the king's navy—a "ship" no bigger than a steam launch—and was soon ready.

The parting—ah, yes, that was hard. As I was devouring the child with last kisses, it brisked up and jabbered out its vocabulary—the first time in more than two weeks, and it made fools of us for joy. The darling mispronunciations of childhood! Dear me, there's no music that can touch it; and how one grieves when it wastes away and dissolves into correctness, knowing it will never visit his bereaved ear again. Well, how good it was to be able to carry that gracious memory away with me!

I approached England the next morning, with the wide highway of salt water all to myself. There were ships in the harbor, at Dover, but they were naked as to sails, and there was no sign of life about them. It was Sunday; yet at Canterbury the streets were empty; strangest of all, there was not even a priest in sight, and no stroke a bell fell upon my ear. The mournfulness of death was everywhere. I couldn't understand it. At last, in the further edge of that town I saw a small funeral procession—just a family and a few friends following a coffin—no priest; a funeral without bell, book, or candle; there was a church there, close at hand, but they passed it by, weeping, and did not enter it; I glanced up at the belfry, and there hung the bell, shrouded in black, and its tongue tied back. Now I knew! Now I understood the stupendous calamity that had overtaken England. Invasion? Invasion is a triviality to it. It was the INTERDICT!

I asked no questions; I didn't need to ask any. The Church had struck; the thing for me to do was to get into a disguise, and go warily. One of my servants gave me a suit of his clothes, and when we were safe beyond the town I put them on, and from that time I traveled alone; I could not risk the embarrassment of company.

A miserable journey. A desolate silence everywhere. Even in London itself. Traffic had ceased; men did not talk or laugh, or go in groups, or even in couples; they moved aimlessly about, each man by himself, with his head down, and woe and terror at his heart. The Tower showed recent war scars. Verily, much had been happening.

Of course I meant to take the train for Camelot. Train! Why, the station was as vacant as a cavern. I moved on. The journey to Camelot was a repetition of what I had already seen. The Monday and the Tuesday differed in no way from the Sunday. I arrived, far in the night. From being the best electric-lighted town in the kingdom and the most like a recumbent sun of anything you ever saw, it was become simply a blot—a blot upon darkness—that is to say, it was darker and solider than the rest of the darkness, and so you could see it a little better; it made me feel as if maybe it was symbolical—a sort of sign that the Church was going to *keep* the upper hand, now, and snuff out all my beautiful civilization just like that. I found no life stirring in the somber streets. I groped my way with a heavy heart. The vast castle loomed black upon the hilltop, not a spark visible about it. The drawbridge was down, the great gate stood wide, I entered without challenge, my own heels making the only sound I heard—and it was sepulchral enough, in those huge vacant courts.

XLII. WAR!

I FOUND CLARENCE, alone in his quarters, drowned in melancholy; and in place of the electric light, he had reinstituted the ancient rag-lamp, and sat there in a grisly twilight with all curtains drawn tight. He sprang up and rushed for me eagerly, saying:

"Oh, it's worth a billion milrays to look upon a live person again!"

He knew me as easily as if I hadn't been disguised at all. Which frightened me; one may easily believe that.

"Quick, now, tell me the meaning of this fearful disaster," I said. "How did it come about?"

"Well, if there hadn't been any Queen Guenever, it wouldn't have come so early; but it would have come, anyway. It would have come on your own account, by and by; by luck, it happened to come on the queen's."

"*And* Sir Launcelot's?"

"Just so."

"Give me the details."

"I reckon you will grant that during some years there has been only one pair of eyes in these kingdoms that has not been looking steadily askance at the queen and Sir Launcelot—"

"Yes, King Arthur's."

—"and only one heart that was without suspicion—"

"Yes—the king's; a heart that isn't capable of thinking evil of a friend."

"Well, the king might have gone on, still happy and unsuspecting, to the end of his days, but for one of your modern improvements—the stock board. When you left, three miles of the London, Canterbury and Dover were ready for the rails, and also ready and ripe for manipulation in the stock market. It was wildcat, and everybody knew it. The stock was for sale at a giveaway. What does Sir Launcelot do, but—"

"Yes, I know; he quietly picked up nearly all of it, for a song; then he bought about twice as much more, deliverable upon call; and he was about to call when I left."

"Very well, he did call. The boys couldn't deliver. Oh, he had them—and he just settled his grip and squeezed them. They were laughing in their sleeves over their smartness in selling stock to him at fifteen and sixteen and along there, that wasn't worth ten. Well, when they had laughed long enough on that side of their mouths, they rested up that side by shifting the laugh to the other side. That was when they compromised with the Invincible at two hundred eighty-three!"

"Good land!"

"He skinned them alive, and they deserved it—anyway, the whole kingdom rejoiced. Well, among the flayed were Sir Agravaine and Sir Mordred, nephews to the king. End of the first act. Act second, scene first, an apartment in Carlisle castle, where the court had gone for a few days' hunting. Persons present, the whole tribe of the king's nephews. Mordred and Agravaine propose to call the guileless Arthur's attention to Guenever and Sir Launcelot. Sir Gawaine, Sir Gareth, and Sir Gaheris will have nothing to do with it. A dispute ensues, with loud talk; in the midst of it, enter the king. Mordred and Agravaine spring their devastating tale upon him. *Tableau.* A trap is laid for Launcelot, by the king's command, and Sir Launcelot walks into it. He made it sufficiently uncomfortable for the ambushed witnesses—to wit, Mordred, Agravaine, and twelve knights of lesser rank, for he killed every one of them but Mordred; but of course that couldn't straighten matters between Launcelot and the king, and didn't."

"Oh, dear, only one thing could result—I see that. War, and the knights of the realm divided into a king's party and a Sir Launcelot's party."

"Yes—that was the way of it. The king sent the queen to the stake, proposing to purify her with fire. Launcelot and his knights rescued her, and in doing it slew certain good old friends of yours and mine— in fact, some of the best we ever had, to wit: Sir Belias le Orgulous, Sir Segwarides, Sir Griflet le Fils de Dieu, Sir Brandiles, Sir Aglovale"—

"Oh, you tear out my heartstrings."

—"wait, I'm not done yet—Sir Tor, Sir Gauter, Sir Gillimer—"

"The very best man in my subordinate nine. What a handy right fielder he was!"

—"Sir Reynold's three brothers, Sir Damus, Sir Priamus, Sir Kay the Stranger—"

"My peerless shortstop! I've seen him catch a daisy cutter in his teeth. Come, I can't stand this!"

—"Sir Driant, Sir Lambegus, Sir Herminde, Sir Pertilope, Sir Perimones, and—whom do you think?"

"Rush! Go on."

"Sir Gaheris, and Sir Gareth—both!"

"Oh, incredible! Their love for Launcelot was indestructible."

"Well, it was an accident. They were simply onlookers; they were unarmed, and were merely there to witness the queen's punishment. Sir Launcelot smote down whoever came in the way of his blind fury, and he killed these without noticing who they were. Here is an instantaneous photograph one of our boys got of the battle; it's for sale on every newsstand. There—the figures nearest the queen are Sir Launcelot with his sword up, and Sir Gareth gasping his latest breath. You can catch the agony in the queen's face through the curling smoke. It's a rattling battle picture."

"Indeed it is. We must take good care of it; its historical value is incalculable. Go on."

"Well, the rest of the tale is just war, pure and simple. Launcelot retreated to his town and castle of Joyous Gard, and gathered there a great following of knights. The king, with a great host, went there, and there was desperate fighting during several days, and as a result, all the plain around was paved with corpses and cast iron. Then the Church patched up a peace between Arthur and Launcelot and the queen and everybody—everybody but Sir Gawaine. He was bitter about the slaying of his brothers, Gareth and Gaheris, and would not be appeased. He notified Launcelot to get him thence, and make swift preparation, and look to be soon attacked. So Launcelot sailed to his Duchy of Guienne, with his following, and Gawaine soon followed, with an army, and he beguiled Arthur to go with him. Arthur left the kingdom in Sir Mordred's hands until you should return—"

"Ah—a king's customary wisdom!"

"Yes. Sir Mordred set himself at once to work to make his kingship permanent. He was going to marry Guenever, as a first move; but she fled and shut herself up in the Tower of London. Mordred attacked; the Bishop of Canterbury dropped down on him with the Interdict. The king returned; Mordred fought him at Dover, at Canterbury, and again at Barham Down. Then there was talk of peace and a composition. Terms, Mordred to have Cornwall and Kent during Arthur's life, and the whole kingdom afterward."

"Well, upon my word! My dream of a republic to *be* a dream, and so remain."

"Yes. The two armies lay near Salisbury. Gawaine—Gawaine's head is at Dover Castle, he fell in the fight there—Gawaine appeared to Arthur in a dream, at least his ghost did, and warned him to refrain from conflict for a month, let the delay cost what it might. But battle was precipitated by an accident. Arthur had given order that if a sword was raised during the consultation over the proposed treaty with Mordred, sound the trumpet and fall on! for he had no confidence in

Mordred. Mordred had given a similar order to *his* people. Well, by
and by an adder bit a knight's heel; the knight forgot all about the order,
and made a slash at the adder with his sword. Inside of half a minute
those two prodigious hosts came together with a crash! They butchered
away all day. Then the king—however, we have started something fresh
since you left—our paper has."

"No? What is that?"

"War correspondence!"

"Why, that's good."

"Yes, the paper was booming right along, for the Interdict made no
impression, got no grip, while the war lasted. I had war correspondents
with both armies. I will finish that battle by reading you what one of the
boys says:

"Then the king looked about him, and then was he ware of all his host and of
all his good knights were left no more on live but two knights, that was Sir Lucan
de Butlere, and his brother Sir Bedivere: and they were full sore wounded. Jesu
mercy, said the king, where are all my noble knights becomen? Alas that ever I
should see this doleful day. For now, said Arthur, I am come to mine end. But
would to God that I wist where were that traitor Sir Mordred, that hath caused
all this mischief. Then was King Arthur ware where Sir Mordred leaned upon
his sword among a great heap of dead men. Now give me my spear, said Arthur
unto Sir Lucan, for yonder I have espied the traitor that all this woe hath
wrought. Sir, let him be, said Sir Lucan, for he is unhappy; and if ye pass this
unhappy day, ye shall be right well revenged upon him. Good lord, remember
ye of your night's dream, and what the spirit of Sir Gawaine told you this night,
yet God of his great goodness hath preserved you hitherto. Therefore, for God's
sake, my lord, leave off by this. For blessed be God ye have won the field: for here
we be three on live, and with Sir Mordred is none on live. And if ye leave off
now, this wicked day of destiny is past. Tide me death, betide me life, saith the
king, now I see him yonder alone, he shall never escape mine hands, for at a
better avail shall I never have him. God speed you well, said Sir Bedivere. Then
the king gat his spear in both his hands, and ran toward Sir Mordred, crying,
Traitor, now is thy death day come. And when Sir Mordred heard Sir Arthur, he
ran until him with his sword drawn in his hand. And then King Arthur smote Sir
Mordred under the shield, with a foin of his spear throughout the body more
than a fathom. And when Sir Mordred felt that he had his death's wound, he
thrust himself, with the might that he had, up to the butt of King Arthur's spear.
And right so he smote his father Arthur with his sword holden in both his hands,
on the side of the head, that the sword pierced the helmet and the brain-pan, and
therewithal Sir Mordred fell stark dead to the earth. And noble Arthur fell in a
swoon to the earth, and there he swooned ofttimes."

"That is a good piece of war correspondence, Clarence; you are a
first-rate newspaper man. Well—is the king all right? Did he get well?"

"Poor soul, no. He is dead."

I was utterly stunned; it had not seemed to me that any wound could be mortal to him.

"And the queen, Clarence?"

"She is a nun, in Almesbury."

"What changes! and in such a short while. It is inconceivable. What next, I wonder?"

"I can tell you what next."

"Well?"

"Stake our lives and stand by them!"

"What do you mean by that?"

"The Church is master, now. The Interdict included you with Mordred; it is not to be removed while you remain alive. The clans are gathering. The Church has gathered all the knights that are left alive, and as soon as you are discovered we shall have business on our hands."

"Stuff! With our deadly scientific war material; with our hosts of trained—"

"Save your breath—we haven't sixty faithful left!"

"What are you saying? Our schools, our colleges, our vast workshops, our—"

"When those knights come, those establishments will empty themselves and go over to the enemy. Did you think you had educated the superstition out of those people?"

"I certainly did think it."

"Well, then, you may unthink it. They stood every strain easily—until the Interdict. Since then, they merely put on a bold outside—at heart they are quaking. Make up your mind to it—when the armies come, the mask will fall."

"It's hard news. We are lost. They will turn our own science against us."

"No they won't."

"Why?"

"Because I and a handful of the faithful have blocked that game. I'll tell you what I've done, and what moved me to it. Smart as you are, the Church was smarter. It was the Church that sent you cruising—through her servants the doctors."

"Clarence!"

"It is the truth. I know it. Every officer of your ship was the Church's picked servant, and so was every man of the crew."

"Oh, come!"

"It is just as I tell you. I did not find out these things at once, but I found them out finally. Did you send me verbal information, by the commander of the ship, to the effect that upon his return to you, with supplies, you were going to leave Cadiz"—

"Cadiz! I haven't been at Cadiz at all!"

— "going to leave Cadiz and cruise in distant seas indefinitely, for the health of your family? Did you send me that word?"

"Of course not. I would have written, wouldn't I?"

"Naturally. I was troubled and suspicious. When the commander sailed again I managed to ship a spy with him. I have never heard of vessel or spy since. I gave myself two weeks to hear from you in. Then I resolved to send a ship to Cadiz. There was a reason why I didn't."

"What was that?"

"Our navy had suddenly and mysteriously disappeared! Also as suddenly and as mysteriously, the railway and telegraph and telephone service ceased, the men all deserted, poles were cut down, the Church laid a ban upon the electric light! I had to be up and doing—and straight off. Your life was safe—nobody in these kingdoms but Merlin would venture to touch such a magician as you without ten thousand men at his back—I had nothing to think of but how to put preparations in the best trim against your coming. I felt safe myself—nobody would be anxious to touch a pet of yours. So this is what I did. From our various works I selected all the men—boys I mean—whose faithfulness under whatsoever pressure I could swear to, and I called them together secretly and gave them their instructions. There are fifty-two of them; none younger than fourteen, and none above seventeen years old."

"Why did you select boys?"

"Because all the others were born in an atmosphere of superstition and reared in it. It is in their blood and bones. We imagined we had educated it out of them; they thought so, too; the Interdict woke them up like a thunderclap! It revealed them to themselves, and it revealed them to me, too. With boys it was different. Such as have been under our training from seven to ten years have had no acquaintance with the Church's terrors, and it was among these that I found my fifty-two. As a next move, I paid a private visit to that old cave of Merlin's—not the small one—the big one—"

"Yes, the one where we secretly established our first great electric plant when I was projecting a miracle."

"Just so. And as that miracle hadn't become necessary then, I thought it might be a good idea to utilize the plant now. I've provisioned the cave for a siege—"

"A good idea, a first rate idea."

"I think so. I placed four of my boys there, as a guard—inside, and out of sight. Nobody was to be hurt—while outside; but any attempt to enter—well, we said just let anybody try it! Then I went out into the hills and uncovered and cut the secret wires which connected your bedroom with the wires that go to the dynamite deposits under all our vast factories, mills, workshops, magazines, etc., and about midnight I and my boys turned out and connected that wire with the cave, and nobody but you and I suspects where the other end of it goes to. We laid it under ground, of course, and it was all finished in a couple of hours or so. We shan't have to leave our fortress, now, when we want to blow up our civilization."

"It was the right move—and the natural one; a military necessity, in the changed condition of things. Well, what changes *have* come! We expected to be besieged in the palace some time or other, but—however, go on."

"Next, we built a wire fence."

"Wire fence?"

"Yes. You dropped the hint of it yourself, two or three years ago."

"Oh, I remember—the time the Church tried her strength against us the first time, and presently thought it wise to wait for a hopefuler season. Well, how have you arranged the fence?"

"I start twelve immensely strong wires—naked, not insulated—from a big dynamo in the cave—dynamo with no brushes except a positive and a negative one—"

"Yes, that's right."

"The wires go out from the cave and fence-in a circle of level ground a hundred yards in diameter; they make twelve independent fences, ten feet apart—that is to say, twelve circles within circles—and their ends come into the cave again."

"Right; go on."

"The fences are fastened to heavy oaken posts only three feet apart, and these posts are sunk five feet in the ground."

"That is good and strong."

"Yes. The wires have no ground connection outside of the cave. They go out from the positive brush of the dynamo; there is a ground connection through the negative brush; the other ends of the wire return to the cave, and each is grounded independently."

"No-no, that won't do!"

"Why?"

"It's too expensive—uses up force for nothing. You don't want any ground connection except the one through the negative brush. The other end of every wire must be brought back into the cave and fastened independently, and *without* any ground connection. Now, then, observe the economy of it. A cavalry charge hurls itself against the fence; you are using no power, you are spending no money, for there is only one ground connection till those horses come against the wire; the moment they touch it they form a connection with the negative brush *through the ground,* and drop dead. Don't you see—you are using no energy until it is needed; your lightning is there, and ready, like the load in a gun; but it isn't costing you a cent till you touch it off. Oh, yes, the single ground connection—"

"Of course! I don't know how I overlooked that. It's not only cheaper, but it's more effectual than the other way, for if wires break or get tangled, no harm is done."

"No, especially if we have a telltale in the cave and disconnect the broken wire. Well, go on. The gatlings?"

"Yes—that's arranged. In the center of the inner circle, on a spacious platform six feet high, I've grouped a battery of thirteen gatling guns, and provided plenty of ammunition."

"That's it. They command every approach, and when the Church's knights arrive, there's going to be music. The brow of the precipice over the cave—"

"I've got a wire fence there, and a gatling. They won't drop any rocks down on us."

"Well, and the glass-cylinder dynamite torpedoes?"

"That's attended to. It's the prettiest garden that was ever planted. It's a belt forty feet wide, and goes around the outer fence—distance between it and the fence one hundred yards—kind of neutral ground, that space is. There isn't a single square yard of that whole belt but is equipped with a torpedo. We laid them on the surface of the ground, and sprinkled a layer of sand over them. It's an innocent looking garden, but you let a man start in to hoe it once, and you'll see."

"You tested the torpedoes?"

"Well, I was going to, but—"

"But what? Why, it's an immense oversight not to apply a—"

"Test? Yes, I know; but they're all right; I laid a few in the public road beyond our lines and they've been tested."

"Oh, that alters the case. Who did it?"

"A Church committee."

"How kind!"

"Yes. They came to command us to make submission. You see they didn't really come to test the torpedoes; that was merely an incident."

"Did the committee make a report?"

"Yes, they made one. You could have heard it a mile."

"Unanimous?"

"That was the nature of it. After that I put up some signs, for the protection of future committees, and we have had no intruders since."

"Clarence, you've done a world of work, and done it perfectly."

"We had plenty of time for it; there wasn't any occasion for hurry."

We sat silent awhile, thinking. Then my mind was made up, and I said:

"Yes, everything is ready; everything is shipshape, no detail is wanting. I know what to do, now."

"So do I: sit down and wait."

"No, *sir*! rise up and *strike*!"

"Do you mean it?"

"Yes, indeed! The *de*fensive isn't in my line, and the *of*fensive is. That is, when I hold a fair hand—two-thirds as good a hand as the enemy. Oh, yes, we'll rise up and strike; that's our game."

"A hundred to one, you are right. When does the performance begin?"

"*Now!* We'll proclaim the Republic."

"Well, that *will* precipitate things, sure enough!"

"It will make them buzz, *I* tell you! England will be a hornet's nest before noon tomorrow, if the Church's hand hasn't lost its cunning—and we know it hasn't. Now you write and I'll dictate—thus:

"PROCLAMATION.

> "BE IT KNOWN UNTO ALL. Whereas the king having died and left no heir, it becomes my duty to continue the executive authority vested in me, until a government shall have been created and set in motion. The monarchy has lapsed, it no longer exists. By consequence, all political power has reverted to its original source, the people of the nation. With the monarchy, its several adjuncts died also; wherefore there is no longer a nobility, no longer a privileged class, no longer an Established Church: all men are become exactly equal, they are upon one common level, and religion is free. A *Republic is hereby proclaimed,* as being the natural estate of a nation when other authority has ceased. It is the duty of the British people to meet together immediately, and by their votes elect representatives and deliver into their hands the government."

I signed it "The Boss," and dated it from Merlin's Cave. Clarence said:

"Why, that tells where we are, and invites them to call right away."

"That is the idea. We *strike*—by the Proclamation—then it's their innings. Now have the thing set up and printed and posted, right off; that is, give the order; then, if you've got a couple of bicycles handy at the foot of the hill, ho for Merlin's Cave!"

"I shall be ready in ten minutes. What a cyclone there is going to be tomorrow when this piece of paper gets to work! . . . It's a pleasant old palace, this is; I wonder if we shall ever again—but never mind about that."

XLIII. THE BATTLE OF THE SAND BELT

IN MERLIN'S Cave—Clarence and I and fifty-two fresh, bright, well-educated, clean-minded young British boys. At dawn I sent an order to the factories and to all our great works to stop operations and remove all life to a safe distance, as everything was going to be blown up by secret mines, *"and no telling at what moment—therefore, vacate at once."* These people knew me, and had confidence in my word. They would clear out without waiting to part their hair, and I could take my own time about dating the explosion. You couldn't hire one of them to go back during the century, if the explosion was still impending.

We had a week of waiting. It was not dull for me, because I was writing all the time. During the first three days, I finished turning my old diary into this narrative form; it only required a chapter or so to bring it down to date. The rest of the week I took up in writing letters to my wife. It was always my habit to write to Sandy everyday, whenever we were separate, and now I kept up the habit for love of it, and of her, though I couldn't do anything with the letters, of course, after I had written them. But it put in the time, you see, and was almost like talking; it was almost as if I was saying, "Sandy, if you and Hello-Central were here in the cave, instead of only your photographs, what good times we could have!" And then, you know, I could imagine the baby goo-gooing something out in reply, with its fist in its mouth and itself stretched across its mother's lap on its back, and she a-laughing and admiring and worshiping, and now and then tickling under the baby's chin to set it cackling, and then maybe throwing in a word of answer to me herself—and so on and so on—well, don't you know, I could sit there in the cave with my pen, and keep it up, that way, by the hour with them. Why, it was almost like having us all together again.

I had spies out, every night, of course, to get news. Every report made things look more and more impressive. The hosts were gathering, gathering; down all the roads and paths of England the knights were riding, and priests rode with them, to hearten these original Crusaders, this being the Church's war. All the nobilities, big and little, were on their way, and all the gentry. This was all as was expected. We should thin out this sort of folk to such a degree that the people would have nothing to do but just step to the front with their republic and——

Ah, what a donkey I was! Toward the end of the week I began to get this large and disenchanting fact through my head: that the mass of the nation had swung their caps and shouted for the republic for about one day, and there an end! The Church, the nobles, and the gentry then turned one grand, all-disapproving frown upon them and shriveled them into sheep! From that moment the sheep had begun to gather to the fold—that is to say, the camps—and offer their valueless lives and their valuable wool to the "righteous cause." Why, even the very men who had lately been slaves were in the "righteous cause," and glorifying it, praying for it, sentimentally slabbering over it, just like all the other commoners. Imagine such human muck as this; conceive of this folly!

Yes, it was now "Death to the Republic!" everywhere—not a dissenting voice. All England was marching against us! Truly this was more than I had bargained for.

I watched my fifty-two boys narrowly; watched their faces, their walk, their unconscious attitudes: for all these are a language—a language given us purposely that it may betray us in times of emergency, when we have secrets which we want to keep. I knew that that thought would keep saying itself over and over again in their minds and hearts, *All England is marching against us!* and ever more strenuously imploring attention with each repetition, ever more sharply realizing itself to their imaginations, until even in their sleep they would find no rest from it, but hear the vague and flitting creatures of their dreams say, *All England*—ALL ENGLAND—*is marching against you!* I knew all this would happen; I knew that ultimately the pressure would become so great that it would compel utterance; therefore, I must be ready with an answer at that time—an answer well chosen and tranquilizing.

·I was right. The time came. They *had* to speak. Poor lads, it was pitiful to see, they were so pale, so worn, so troubled. At first their spokesman could hardly find voice or words; but he presently got both. This is what he said—and he put it in the neat modern English taught him in my schools:

"We have tried to forget what we are—English boys! We have tried to put reason before sentiment, duty before love; our minds approve, but our hearts reproach us. While apparently it was only the nobility, only the gentry, only the twenty-five or thirty thousand knights left alive out of the late wars, we were of one mind, and undisturbed by any troubling doubt; each and every one of these fifty-two lads who stand here before you, said, 'They have chosen—it is their affair.' But think—the matter is altered—*all England is marching against us!* Oh, sir, consider! Reflect! These people are our people, they are bone of our bone, flesh of our flesh, we love them—do not ask us to destroy our nation!"

Well, it shows the value of looking ahead, and being ready for a thing when it happens. If I hadn't foreseen this thing and been fixed, that boy would have had me—I couldn't have said a word. But I *was* fixed. I said:

"My boys, your hearts are in the right place, you have thought the worthy thought, you have done the worthy thing. You are English boys, you will remain English boys, and you will keep that name unsmirched. Give yourselves no further concern, let your minds be at peace. Consider this: while all England *is* marching against us, who is in the van? Who, by the commonest rules of war, will march in the front? Answer me."

"The mounted host of mailed knights."

"True. They are 30,000 strong. Acres deep, they will march. Now, observe: none but *they* will ever strike the sand belt! Then there will be an episode! Immediately after, the civilian multitude in the rear will retire, to meet business engagements elsewhere. None but nobles and gentry are knights, and *none but these* will remain to dance to our music after that episode. It is absolutely true that we shall have to fight nobody but these thirty thousand knights. Now speak, and it shall be as you decide. Shall we avoid the battle, retire from the field?"

"NO!!"

The shout was unanimous and hearty.

"Are you—are you—well, afraid of these thirty thousand knights?"

That joke brought out a good laugh, the boys' troubles vanished away, and they went gaily to their posts. Ah, they were a darling fifty-two! As pretty as girls, too.

I was ready for the enemy, now. Let the approaching big day come along—it would find us on deck.

The big day arrived on time. At dawn the sentry on watch in the corral came into the cave and reported a moving black mass under the horizon, and a faint sound which he thought to be military music. Breakfast was just ready; we sat down and ate it.

This over, I made the boys a little speech, and then sent out a detail to man the battery, with Clarence in command of it.

The sun rose presently and sent its unobstructed splendors over the land, and we saw a prodigious host moving slowly toward us, with the steady drift and aligned front of a wave of the sea. Nearer and nearer it came, and more and more sublimely imposing became its aspect; yes, all England were there, apparently. Soon we could see the innumerable banners fluttering, and then the sun struck the sea of armor and set it all a-flash. Yes, it was a fine sight; I hadn't ever seen anything to beat it.

At last we could make out details. All the front ranks, no telling how many acres deep, were horsemen—plumed knights in armor. Suddenly we heard the blare of trumpets; the slow walk burst into a gallop, and then—well, it was wonderful to see! Down swept that vast horseshoe wave—it approached the sand belt—my breath stood still; nearer, nearer—the strip of green turf beyond the yellow belt grew narrow—narrower still—became a mere ribbon in front of the horses— then disappeared under their hoofs. Great Scott! Why, the whole front of that host shot into the sky with a thundercrash, and became a whirling tempest of rags and fragments; and along the ground lay a thick wall of smoke that hid what was left of the multitude from our sight.

Time for the second step in the plan of campaign! I touched a button, and shook the bones of England loose from her spine!

In that explosion all our noble civilization-factories went up in the air and disappeared from the earth. It was a pity, but it was necessary. We could not afford to let the enemy turn our own weapons against us.

Now ensued one of the dullest quarter hours I had ever endured. We waited in a silent solitude enclosed by our circles of wire, and by a circle of heavy smoke outside of these. We couldn't see over the wall of smoke, and we couldn't see through it. But at last it began to shred away lazily, and by the end of another quarter hour the land was clear and our curiosity was enabled to satisfy itself. No living creature was in sight! We now perceived that additions had been made to our defenses. The dynamite had dug a ditch more than a hundred feet wide, all around us, and cast up an embankment some twenty-five feet high on both borders of it. As to destruction of life, it was amazing. Moreover, it was beyond estimate. Of course we could not *count* the dead, because they did not exist as individuals, but merely as homogeneous protoplasm, with alloys of iron and buttons.

No life was in sight, but necessarily there must have been some wounded in the rear ranks, who were carried off the field under cover of the wall of smoke; there would be sickness among the others—there always is, after an episode like that. But there would be no reinforcements; this was the last stand of the chivalry of England; it was all that was left of the order, after the recent annihilating wars. So I felt quite safe in believing that the utmost force that could for the future be brought against us would be but small; that is, of knights. I therefore issued a congratulatory proclamation to my army in these words:

SOLDIERS, CHAMPIONS OF HUMAN LIBERTY AND EQUALITY:
Your General congratulates you! In the pride of his strength and the vanity of his renown, an arrogant enemy came against you.

You were ready. The conflict was brief; on your side, glorious. This mighty victory having been achieved utterly without loss, stands without example in history. So long as the planets shall continue to move in their orbits, the BATTLE OF THE SAND BELT will not perish out of the memories of men.

THE BOSS.

I read it well, and the applause I got was very gratifying to me. I then wound up with these remarks:

"The war with the English nation, as a nation, is at an end. The nation has retired from the field and the war. Before it can be persuaded to return, war will have ceased. This campaign is the only one that is going to be fought. It will be brief—the briefest in history. Also the most destructive to life, considered from the standpoint of proportion of casualties to numbers engaged. We are done with the nation; henceforth we deal only with the knights. English knights can be killed, but they cannot be conquered. We know what is before us. While one of these men remains alive, our task is not finished, the war is not ended. We will kill them all." [Loud and long continued applause.]

I picketed the great embankments thrown up around our lines by the dynamite explosion—merely a lookout of a couple of boys to announce the enemy when he should appear again.

Next, I sent an engineer and forty men to a point just beyond our lines on the south, to turn a mountain brook that was there, and bring it within our lines and under our command, arranging it in such a way that I could make instant use of it in an emergency. The forty men were divided into two shifts of twenty each, and were to relieve each other every two hours. In ten hours the work was accomplished.

It was nightfall, now, and I withdrew my pickets. The one who had had the northern outlook reported a camp in sight, but visible with the glass only. He also reported that a few knights had been feeling their way toward us, and had driven some cattle across our lines, but that the knights themselves had not come very near. That was what I had been expecting. They were feeling us, you see; they wanted to know if we were going to play that red terror on them again. They would grow bolder in the night, perhaps. I believed I knew what project they would attempt, because it was plainly the thing I would attempt myself if I were in their places and as ignorant as they were. I mentioned it to Clarence.

"I think you are right," said he; "it is the obvious thing for them to try."

"Well, then," I said, "if they do it they are doomed."

"Certainly."

"They won't have the slightest show in the world."

"Of course they won't."

"It's dreadful, Clarence. It seems an awful pity."

The thing disturbed me so, that I couldn't get any peace of mind for thinking of it and worrying over it. So, at last, to quiet my conscience, I framed this message to the knights:

> TO THE HONORABLE THE COMMANDER OF THE INSURGENT CHIVALRY OF ENGLAND: You fight in vain. We know your strength— if one may call it by that name. We know that at the utmost you cannot bring against us above five and twenty thousand knights. Therefore, you have no chance—none whatever. Reflect: we are well equipped, well fortified, we number fifty-four. Fifth-four what? Men? No, *minds*—the capablest in the world; a force against which mere animal might may no more hope to prevail than may the idle waves of the sea hope to prevail against the granite barriers of England. Be advised. We offer you your lives; for the sake of your families, do not reject the gift. We offer you this chance, and it is the last: throw down your arms; surrender unconditionally to the Republic, and all will be forgiven.
>
> (Signed)　　　　　　　THE BOSS.

I read it to Clarence, and said I proposed to send it by a flag of truce. He laughed the sarcastic laugh he was born with, and said:

"Somehow it seems impossible for you to ever fully realize what these nobilities are. Now let us save a little time and trouble. Consider me the commander of the knights yonder. Now then, you are the flag of truce; approach and deliver me your message, and I will give you your answer."

I humored the idea. I came forward under an imaginary guard of the enemy's soldiers, produced my paper, and read it through. For answer, Clarence struck the paper out of my hand, pursed up a scornful lip and said with lofty disdain—

"Dismember me this animal, and return him in a basket to the base-born knave who sent him; other answer have I none!"

How empty is theory in presence of fact! And this was just fact, and nothing else. It was the thing that would have happened, there was no getting around that. I tore up the paper and granted my mistimed sentimentalities a permanent rest.

Then, to business. I tested the electric signals from the gatling platform to the cave, and made sure that they were all right; I tested and retested those which commanded the fences—these were signals whereby I could break and renew the electric current in each fence independently of the others, at will. I placed the brook connection under the guard and authority of three of my best boys, who would alternate in two-hour watches all night and promptly obey my signal, if I should have occasion to give it—three revolver-shots in quick succession. Sentry duty was discarded for the night, and the corral left empty of life; I ordered that quiet be maintained in the cave, and the electric lights turned down to a glimmer.

As soon as it was good and dark, I shut off the current from all of the fences, and then groped my way out to the embankment bordering our side of the great dynamite ditch. I crept to the top of it and lay there on the slant of the muck to watch. But it was too dark to see anything. As for sounds, there were none. The stillness was deathlike. True, there were the usual nightsounds of the country—the whir of night birds, the buzzing of insects, the barking of distant dogs, the mellow lowing of far-off kine—but these didn't seem to break the stillness, they only intensified it, and added a gruesome melancholy to it into the bargain.

I presently gave up looking, the night shut down so black, but I kept my ears strained to catch the least suspicious sound, for I judged I had only to wait and I shouldn't be disappointed. However, I had to wait a long time. At last I caught what you may call indistinct glimpses of sound—dulled metallic sound. I pricked up my ears, then, and held my breath, for this was the sort of thing I had been waiting for. This sound thickened, and approached—from toward the north. Presently I heard it at my own level—the ridgetop of the opposite embankment, a hundred feet or more away. Then I seemed to see a row of black dots appear along that ridge—human heads? I couldn't tell; it mightn't be anything at all; you can't depend on your eyes when your imagination is out of focus. However, the question was soon settled. I heard that metallic noise descending into the great ditch. It augmented fast, it spread all along, and it unmistakably furnished me this fact: an armed host was taking up its quarters in the ditch. Yes, these people were arranging a little surprise party for us. We could expect entertainment about dawn, possibly earlier.

I groped my way back to the corral, now; I had seen enough. I went to the platform and signaled to turn the current onto the two inner fences. Then I went into the cave, and found everything satisfactory there—nobody awake but the working watch. I woke Clarence and told him the great ditch was filling up with men, and that I believed all the knights were coming for us in a body. It was my notion that as soon as dawn approached we could expect the ditch's ambuscaded thousands to swarm up over the embankment and make an assault, and be followed immediately by the rest of their army.

Clarence said:

"They will be wanting to send out a scout or two in the dark to make preliminary observations. Why not take the lightning off the outer fences, and give them a chance?"

"I've already done it, Clarence. Did you ever know me to be inhospitable?"

"No, you are a good heart. I want to go and—"

"Be a reception committee? I will go, too."

We crossed the corral and lay down together between the two inside fences. Even the dim light of the cave had disordered our eyesight somewhat, but the focus straightway began to regulate itself and soon it was adjusted for present circumstances. We had had to feel our way before, but we could make out to see the fence posts now. We started a whispered conversation, but suddenly Clarence broke off and said:

"What is that?"

"What is what?"

"That thing yonder?"

"What thing—where?"

"There beyond you a little piece—a dark something—a dull shape of some kind—against the second fence."

I gazed and he gazed. I said:

"Could it be a man, Clarence?"

"No, I think not. If you notice, it looks like a lit—why, it *is* a man— leaning on the fence!"

"I certainly believe it is; let's go and see."

We crept along on our hands and knees until we were pretty close, and then looked up. Yes, it was a man—a dim great figure in armor, standing erect, with both hands on the upper wire—and of course there was a smell of burning flesh. Poor fellow, dead as a doornail, and never knew what hurt him. He stood there like a statue—no motion about him, except that his plumes swished about a little in the night wind. We rose up and looked in through the bars of his visor, but couldn't make out whether we knew him or not—features too dim and shadowed.

We heard muffled sounds approaching, and we sank down to the ground where we were. We made out another knight vaguely; he was coming very stealthily, and feeling his way. He was near enough, now, for us to see him put out a hand, find an upper wire, then bend and step under it and over the lower one. Now he arrived at the first knight—and started slightly when he discovered him. He stood a moment—no doubt wondering why the other one didn't move on; then he said, in a low voice, "Why dreamest thou here, good Sir Mar—" then he laid his hand on the corpse's shoulder—and just uttered a little soft moan and sunk down dead. Killed by a dead man, you see—killed by a dead friend, in fact. There was something awful about it.

These early birds came scattering along after each other, about one every five minutes in our vicinity, during half an hour. They brought no armor of offense but their swords; as a rule they carried the sword ready in the hand and put it forward and found the wires with it. We would now and then see a blue spark when the knight that caused it was so far away as to be invisible to us; but we knew what had happened, all the same, poor fellow; he had touched a charged wire with his sword and been elected. We had brief intervals of grim stillness, interrupted with piteous regularity by the clash made by the falling of an ironclad; and this sort of thing was going on, right along, and was very creepy, there in the dark and lonesomeness.

We concluded to make a tour between the inner fences. We elected to walk upright, for convenience sake; we argued that if discerned, we should be taken for friends rather than enemies, and in any case we should be out of reach of swords, and these gentry did not seem to have any spears along. Well, it was a curious trip. Everywhere dead men were lying outside the second fence—not plainly visible, but still visible; and we counted fifteen of those pathetic statues—dead knights standing with their hands on the upper wire.

One thing seemed to be sufficiently demonstrated: our current was so tremendous that it killed before the victim could cry out. Pretty soon we detected a muffled and heavy sound, and next moment we guessed what it was. It was a surprise in force coming! I whispered Clarence to go and wake the army, and notify it to wait in silence in the cave for further orders. He was soon back, and we stood by the inner fence and watched the silent lightning do its awful work upon that swarming host. One could make out but little of detail; but he could note that a black mass was piling itself up beyond the second fence. That swelling bulk was dead men! Our camp was enclosed with a solid wall of the dead—a bulwark, a breastwork, of corpses, you may say. One terrible thing about this thing was the absence of human voices; there were no cheers, no war cries: being intent upon a surprise, these men moved as noiselessly as they could; and always when the front rank was near enough to their goal to make it proper for them to begin to get a shout ready, of course they struck the fatal line and went down without testifying.

I sent a current through the third fence, now; and almost immediately through the fourth and fifth, so quickly were the gaps filled up. I believed the time was come, now, for my climax; I believed that the whole army was in our trap. Anyway, it was high time to find out. So I touched a button and set fifty electric suns aflame on the top of our precipice.

Land, what a sight! We were enclosed in three walls of dead men! All the other fences were pretty nearly filled with the living, who were stealthily working their way forward through the wires. The sudden glare paralyzed this host, petrified them, you may say, with astonishment; there was just one instant for me to utilize their immobility in, and I didn't lose the chance. You see, in another instant they would have recovered their faculties, then they'd have burst into a cheer and made a rush, and my wires would have gone down before it; but that lost instant lost them their opportunity forever; while even that slight fragment of time was still unspent, I shot the current through all the fences and struck the whole host dead in their tracks! *There* was a groan you could *hear*! It voiced the death pang of eleven thousand men. It swelled out on the night with awful pathos.

A glance showed that the rest of the enemy—perhaps ten thousand strong—were between us and the encircling ditch, and pressing forward to the assault. Consequently we had them *all*! and had them past help. Time for the last act of the tragedy. I fired the three appointed revolver shots—which meant:

"Turn on the water!"

There was a sudden rush and roar, and in a minute the mountain brook was raging through the big ditch and creating a river a hundred feet wise and twenty-five deep.

"Stand to your guns, men! Open fire!"

The thirteen gatlings began to vomit death into the fated ten thousand. They halted, they stood their ground a moment against that withering deluge of fire, then they broke, faced about and swept toward the ditch like chaff before a gale. A full fourth part of their force never reached the top of the lofty embankment; the three-fourths reached it and plunged over—to death by drowning.

Within ten short minutes after we had opened fire, armed resistance was totally annihilated, the campaign was ended, we fifty-four were masters of England! Twenty-five thousand men lay dead around us.

But how treacherous is fortune! In a little while—say an hour—happened a thing, by my own fault, which—but I have no heart to write that. Let the record end here.

XLIV. A POSTSCRIPT BY CLARENCE

I, CLARENCE, MUST write it for him. He proposed that we two go out and see if any help could be afforded the wounded. I was strenuous against the project. I said that if there were many, we could do but little for them; and it would not be wise for us to trust ourselves among them, anyway. But he could seldom be turned from a purpose once formed; so we shut off the electric current from the fences, took an escort along, climbed over the enclosing ramparts of dead knights, and moved out upon the field. The first wounded man who appealed for help, was sitting with his back against a dead comrade. When the Boss bent over him and spoke to him, the man recognized him and stabbed him. That knight was Sir Meliagraunce, as I found out by tearing off his helmet. He will not ask for help any more.

We carried the Boss to the cave and gave his wound, which was not very serious, the best care we could. In this service we had the help of Merlin, though we did not know it. He was disguised as a woman and appeared to be a simple old peasant goodwife. In this disguise, with brown-stained face and smooth-shaven, he had appeared a few days after the Boss was hurt, and offered to cook for us, saying her people had gone off to join certain new camps which the enemy were forming, and that she was starving. The Boss had been getting along very well, and had amused himself with finishing up his record.

We were glad to have this woman, for we were shorthanded. We were in a trap, you see—a trap of our own making. If we stayed where we were, our dead would kill us; if we moved out of our defenses, we should no longer be invincible. We had conquered; in turn we were conquered. The Boss recognized this; we all recognized it. If we could go to one of those new camps and patch up some kind of terms with the enemy—yes, but the Boss could not go, and neither could I, for I was among the first that were made sick by the poisonous air bred by those dead thousands. Others were taken down, and still others. Tomorrow—

Tomorrow. It is here. And with it the end. About midnight I awoke, and saw that hag making curious passes in the air about the Boss's head and face, and wondered what it meant. Everybody but the dynamo-watch lay steeped in sleep; there was no sound. The woman ceased from her mysterious foolery, and started tiptoeing toward the door. I called out—

"Stop! What have you been doing!"

She halted, and said with an accent of malicious satisfaction:

"Ye were conquerors; ye are conquered! These others are perishing—you also. Ye shall all die in this place—every one—except *him*. He sleepeth, now—and shall sleep thirteen centuries. I am Merlin!"

Then such a delirium of silly laughter overtook him that he reeled about like a drunken man, and presently fetched up against one of our wires. His mouth is spread open yet; apparently he is still laughing. I suppose the face will retain that petrified laugh until the corpse turns to dust.

The Boss has never stirred—sleeps like a stone. If he does not wake today we shall understand what kind of sleep it is, and his body will then be borne to a place in one of the remote recesses of the cave where none will ever find it to desecrate it. As for the rest of us—well, it is agreed that if any one of us ever escapes alive from this place, he will write the fact here, and loyally hide this Manuscript with the Boss, our dear good chief, whose property it is, be he alive or dead.

END OF THE MANUSCRIPT

FINAL P.S. BY M.T.

THE DAWN was come when I laid the manuscript aside. The rain had
almost ceased, the world was gray and sad, the exhausted storm was
sighing and sobbing itself to rest. I went to the stranger's room, and listened at his door, which was slightly ajar. I could hear his voice, and so
I knocked. There was no answer, but I still heard the voice. I peeped
in. The man lay on his back, in bed, talking brokenly but with spirit,
and punctuating with his arms, which he thrashed about, restlessly, as
sick people do in delirium. I slipped in softly and bent over him. His
mutterings and ejaculations went on. I spoke—merely a word, to call
his attention. His glassy eyes and his ashy face were alight in an instant
with pleasure, gratitude, gladness, welcome:

"O, Sandy, you are come at last—how I have longed for you! Sit by
me—do not leave me—never leave me again, Sandy, never again.
Where is your hand—give it me, dear, let me hold it—there—now all
is well, all is peace, and I am happy again—*we* are happy again, isn't it
so, Sandy? You are so dim, so vague, you are but a mist, a cloud, but
you are *here*, and that is blessedness sufficient; and I have your hand;
don't take it away—it is for only a little while, I shall not require it
long. . . . Was that the child? . . . Hello-Central! . . . She doesn't answer.
Asleep, perhaps? Bring her when she wakes, and let me touch her
hands, her face, her hair, and tell her goodbye. . . . Sandy! . . . Yes, you
are there. I lost myself a moment, and I thought you were gone. . . .
Have I been sick long? It must be so; it seems months to me. And
such dreams! Such strange and awful dreams, Sandy! Dreams that
were as real as reality—delirium, of course, but *so* real! Why, I thought
the king was dead, I thought you were in Gaul and couldn't get home,
I thought there was a revolution; in the fantastic frenzy of these dreams,
I thought that Clarence and I and a handful of my cadets fought and
exterminated the whole chivalry of England! But even that was not
the strangest. I seemed to be a creature out of a remote unborn age,

centuries hence, and even *that* was as real as the rest! Yes, I seemed to have flown back out of that age into this of ours, and then forward to it again, and was set down, a stranger and forlorn in that strange England, with an abyss of thirteen centuries yawning between me and you! between me and my home and my friends! between me and all that is dear to me, all that could make life worth the living! It was awful—awfuler than you can ever imagine, Sandy. Ah, watch by me, Sandy—stay by me every moment—*don't* let me go out of my mind again; death is nothing, let it come, but not with those dreams, not with the torture of those hideous dreams—I cannot endure *that* again. . . . Sandy? . . ."

He lay muttering incoherently some little time; then for a time he lay silent, and apparently sinking away toward death. Presently his fingers began to pick busily at the coverlet, and by that sign I knew that his end was at hand. With the first suggestion of the death rattle in his throat he started up slightly, and seemed to listen; then he said:

"A bugle? . . . It is the king! The drawbridge, there! Man the battlements—turn out the—"

He was getting up his last "effect"; but he never finished it.

DOVER · THRIFT · EDITIONS

POETRY

GUNGA DIN AND OTHER FAVORITE POEMS, Rudyard Kipling. 80pp. 26471-8

SNAKE AND OTHER POEMS, D. H. Lawrence. 64pp. 40647-4

THE CONGO AND OTHER POEMS, Vachel Lindsay. 96pp. 27272-9

EVANGELINE AND OTHER POEMS, Henry Wadsworth Longfellow. 64pp. 28255-4

FAVORITE POEMS, Henry Wadsworth Longfellow. 96pp. 27273-7

"TO HIS COY MISTRESS" AND OTHER POEMS, Andrew Marvell. 64pp. 29544-3

SPOON RIVER ANTHOLOGY, Edgar Lee Masters. 144pp. 27275-3

SELECTED POEMS, Claude McKay. 80pp. 40876-0

RENASCENCE AND OTHER POEMS, Edna St. Vincent Millay. 64pp. (Available in U.S. only.) 26873-X

SELECTED POEMS, John Milton. 128pp. 27554-X

CIVIL WAR POETRY: An Anthology, Paul Negri (ed.). 128pp. 29883-3

ENGLISH VICTORIAN POETRY: AN ANTHOLOGY, Paul Negri (ed.). 256pp. 40425-0

GREAT SONNETS, Paul Negri (ed.). 96pp. 28052-7

THE RAVEN AND OTHER FAVORITE POEMS, Edgar Allan Poe. 64pp. 26685-0

ESSAY ON MAN AND OTHER POEMS, Alexander Pope. 128pp. 28053-5

EARLY POEMS, Ezra Pound. 80pp. (Available in U.S. only.) 28745-9

GREAT POEMS BY AMERICAN WOMEN: An Anthology, Susan L. Rattiner (ed.). 224pp. (Available in U.S. only.) 40164-2

LITTLE ORPHANT ANNIE AND OTHER POEMS, James Whitcomb Riley. 80pp. 28260-0

GOBLIN MARKET AND OTHER POEMS, Christina Rossetti. 64pp. 28055-1

CHICAGO POEMS, Carl Sandburg. 80pp. 28057-8

CORNHUSKERS, Carl Sandburg. 157pp. 41409-4

THE SHOOTING OF DAN MCGREW AND OTHER POEMS, Robert Service. 96pp. (Available in U.S. only.) 27556-6

COMPLETE SONNETS, William Shakespeare. 80pp. 26686-9

SELECTED POEMS, Percy Bysshe Shelley. 128pp. 27558-2

AFRICAN-AMERICAN POETRY: An Anthology, 1773–1930, Joan R. Sherman (ed.). 96pp. 29604-0

100 BEST-LOVED POEMS, Philip Smith (ed.). 96pp. 28553-7

NATIVE AMERICAN SONGS AND POEMS: An Anthology, Brian Swann (ed.). 64pp. 29450-1

SELECTED POEMS, Alfred Lord Tennyson. 112pp. 27282-6

AENEID, Vergil (Publius Vergilius Maro). 256pp. 28749-1

CHRISTMAS CAROLS: COMPLETE VERSES, Shane Weller (ed.). 64pp. 27397-0

GREAT LOVE POEMS, Shane Weller (ed.). 128pp. 27284-2

CIVIL WAR POETRY AND PROSE, Walt Whitman. 96pp. 28507-3

SELECTED POEMS, Walt Whitman. 128pp. 26878-0

THE BALLAD OF READING GAOL AND OTHER POEMS, Oscar Wilde. 64pp. 27072-6

EARLY POEMS, William Carlos Williams. 64pp. (Available in U.S. only.) 29294-0

FAVORITE POEMS, William Wordsworth. 80pp. 27073-4

WORLD WAR ONE BRITISH POETS: Brooke, Owen, Sassoon, Rosenberg, and Others, Candace Ward (ed.). (Available in U.S. only.) 29568-0

EARLY POEMS, William Butler Yeats. 128pp. 27808-5

"EASTER, 1916" AND OTHER POEMS, William Butler Yeats. 80pp. (Available in U.S. only.) 29771-3

DOVER · THRIFT · EDITIONS

FICTION

DOVER · THRIFT · EDITIONS

FICTION

SIX GREAT SHERLOCK HOLMES STORIES, Sir Arthur Conan Doyle. 112pp. 27055-6

SHORT STORIES, Theodore Dreiser. 112pp. 28215-5

SILAS MARNER, George Eliot. 160pp. 29246-0

THIS SIDE OF PARADISE, F. Scott Fitzgerald. 208pp. 28999-0

"THE DIAMOND AS BIG AS THE RITZ" AND OTHER STORIES, F. Scott Fitzgerald. 29991-0

MADAME BOVARY, Gustave Flaubert. 256pp. 29257-6

THE REVOLT OF "MOTHER" AND OTHER STORIES, Mary E. Wilkins Freeman. 128pp. 40428-5

A ROOM WITH A VIEW, E. M. Forster. 176pp. (Available in U.S. only.) 28467-0

WHERE ANGELS FEAR TO TREAD, E. M. Forster. 128pp. (Available in U.S. only.) 27791-7

THE IMMORALIST, André Gide. 112pp. (Available in U.S. only.) 29237-1

HERLAND, Charlotte Perkins Gilman. 128pp. 40429-3

"THE YELLOW WALLPAPER" AND OTHER STORIES, Charlotte Perkins Gilman. 80pp. 29857-4

THE OVERCOAT AND OTHER STORIES, Nikolai Gogol. 112pp. 27057-2

CHELKASH AND OTHER STORIES, Maxim Gorky. 64pp. 40652-0

GREAT GHOST STORIES, John Grafton (ed.). 112pp. 27270-2

DETECTION BY GASLIGHT, Douglas G. Greene (ed.). 272pp. 29928-7

THE MABINOGION, Lady Charlotte E. Guest. 192pp. 29541-9

"THE FIDDLER OF THE REELS" AND OTHER SHORT STORIES, Thomas Hardy. 80pp. 29960-0

THE LUCK OF ROARING CAMP AND OTHER STORIES, Bret Harte. 96pp. 27271-0

THE HOUSE OF THE SEVEN GABLES, Nathaniel Hawthorne. 272pp. 40882-5

THE SCARLET LETTER, Nathaniel Hawthorne. 192pp. 28048-9

YOUNG GOODMAN BROWN AND OTHER STORIES, Nathaniel Hawthorne. 128pp. 27060-2

THE GIFT OF THE MAGI AND OTHER SHORT STORIES, O. Henry. 96pp. 27061-0

THE NUTCRACKER AND THE GOLDEN POT, E. T. A. Hoffmann. 128pp. 27806-9

THE BEAST IN THE JUNGLE AND OTHER STORIES, Henry James. 128pp. 27552-3

DAISY MILLER, Henry James. 64pp. 28773-4

THE TURN OF THE SCREW, Henry James. 96pp. 26684-2

WASHINGTON SQUARE, Henry James. 176pp. 40431-5

THE COUNTRY OF THE POINTED FIRS, Sarah Orne Jewett. 96pp. 28196-5

THE AUTOBIOGRAPHY OF AN EX-COLORED MAN, James Weldon Johnson. 112pp. 28512-X

DUBLINERS, James Joyce. 160pp. 26870-5

A PORTRAIT OF THE ARTIST AS A YOUNG MAN, James Joyce. 192pp. 28050-0

THE METAMORPHOSIS AND OTHER STORIES, Franz Kafka. 96pp. 29030-1

THE MAN WHO WOULD BE KING AND OTHER STORIES, Rudyard Kipling. 128pp. 28051-9

YOU KNOW ME AL, Ring Lardner. 128pp. 28513-8

SELECTED SHORT STORIES, D. H. Lawrence. 128pp. 27794-1

GREEN TEA AND OTHER GHOST STORIES, J. Sheridan LeFanu. 96pp. 27795-X

THE CALL OF THE WILD, Jack London. 64pp. 26472-6

FIVE GREAT SHORT STORIES, Jack London. 96pp. 27063-7

THE SEA-WOLF, Jack London. iv+244pp. 41108-7

WHITE FANG, Jack London. 160pp. 26968-X

DEATH IN VENICE, Thomas Mann. 96pp. (Available in U.S. only.) 28714-9

IN A GERMAN PENSION: 13 Stories, Katherine Mansfield. 112pp. 28719-X

DOVER · THRIFT · EDITIONS

FICTION

THE NECKLACE AND OTHER SHORT STORIES, Guy de Maupassant. 128pp. 27064-5

BARTLEBY AND BENITO CERENO, Herman Melville. 112pp. 26473-4

THE OIL JAR AND OTHER STORIES, Luigi Pirandello. 96pp. 28459-X

THE GOLD-BUG AND OTHER TALES, Edgar Allan Poe. 128pp. 26875-6

TALES OF TERROR AND DETECTION, Edgar Allan Poe. 96pp. 28744-0

THE QUEEN OF SPADES AND OTHER STORIES, Alexander Pushkin. 128pp. 28054-3

THE STORY OF AN AFRICAN FARM, Olive Schreiner. 256pp. 40165-0

FRANKENSTEIN, Mary Shelley. 176pp. 28211-2

THREE LIVES, Gertrude Stein. 176pp. (Available in U.S. only.) 28059-4

THE STRANGE CASE OF DR. JEKYLL AND MR. HYDE, Robert Louis Stevenson. 64pp. 26688-5

TREASURE ISLAND, Robert Louis Stevenson. 160pp. 27559-0

GULLIVER'S TRAVELS, Jonathan Swift. 240pp. 29273-8

THE KREUTZER SONATA AND OTHER SHORT STORIES, Leo Tolstoy. 144pp. 27805-0

THE WARDEN, Anthony Trollope. 176pp. 40076-X

FIRST LOVE AND DIARY OF A SUPERFLUOUS MAN, Ivan Turgenev. 96pp. 28775-0

FATHERS AND SONS, Ivan Turgenev. 176pp. 40073-5

ADVENTURES OF HUCKLEBERRY FINN, Mark Twain. 224pp. 28061-6

THE ADVENTURES OF TOM SAWYER, Mark Twain. 192pp. 40077-8

THE MYSTERIOUS STRANGER AND OTHER STORIES, Mark Twain. 128pp. 27069-6

HUMOROUS STORIES AND SKETCHES, Mark Twain. 80pp. 29279-7

AROUND THE WORLD IN EIGHTY DAYS, Jules Verne. 160pp. 41111-7

CANDIDE, Voltaire (François-Marie Arouet). 112pp. 26689-3

GREAT SHORT STORIES BY AMERICAN WOMEN, Candace Ward (ed.). 192pp. 28776-9

"THE COUNTRY OF THE BLIND" AND OTHER SCIENCE-FICTION STORIES, H. G. Wells. 160pp. (Available in U.S. only.) 29569-9

THE ISLAND OF DR. MOREAU, H. G. Wells. 112pp. (Available in U.S. only.) 29027-1

THE INVISIBLE MAN, H. G. Wells. 112pp. (Available in U.S. only.) 27071-8

THE TIME MACHINE, H. G. Wells. 80pp. (Available in U.S. only.) 28472-7

THE WAR OF THE WORLDS, H. G. Wells. 160pp. (Available in U.S. only.) 29506-0

ETHAN FROME, Edith Wharton. 96pp. 26690-7

SHORT STORIES, Edith Wharton. 128pp. 28235-X

THE AGE OF INNOCENCE, Edith Wharton. 288pp. 29803-5

THE PICTURE OF DORIAN GRAY, Oscar Wilde. 192pp. 27807-7

JACOB'S ROOM, Virginia Woolf. 144pp. (Available in U.S. only.) 40109-X

MONDAY OR TUESDAY: Eight Stories, Virginia Woolf. 64pp. (Available in U.S. only.) 29453-6

NONFICTION

POETICS, Aristotle. 64pp. 29577-X

POLITICS, Aristotle. 368pp. 41424-8

NICOMACHEAN ETHICS, Aristotle. 256pp. 40096-4

MEDITATIONS, Marcus Aurelius. 128pp. 29823-X

THE LAND OF LITTLE RAIN, Mary Austin. 96pp. 29037-9

THE DEVIL'S DICTIONARY, Ambrose Bierce. 144pp. 27542-6

THE ANALECTS, Confucius. 128pp. 28484-0

CONFESSIONS OF AN ENGLISH OPIUM EATER, Thomas De Quincey. 80pp. 28742-4

NARRATIVE OF THE LIFE OF FREDERICK DOUGLASS, Frederick Douglass. 96pp. 28499-9

DOVER · THRIFT · EDITIONS

NONFICTION

THE SOULS OF BLACK FOLK, W. E. B. Du Bois. 176pp. 28041-1

SELF-RELIANCE AND OTHER ESSAYS, Ralph Waldo Emerson. 128pp. 27790-9

THE LIFE OF OLAUDAH EQUIANO, OR GUSTAVUS VASSA, THE AFRICAN, Olaudah Equiano. 192pp. 40661-X

THE AUTOBIOGRAPHY OF BENJAMIN FRANKLIN, Benjamin Franklin. 144pp. 29073-5

TOTEM AND TABOO, Sigmund Freud. 176pp. (Available in U.S. only.) 40434-X

LOVE: A Book of Quotations, Herb Galewitz (ed.). 64pp. 40004-2

PRAGMATISM, William James. 128pp. 28270-8

THE STORY OF MY LIFE, Helen Keller. 80pp. 29249-5

TAO TE CHING, Lao Tze. 112pp. 29792-6

GREAT SPEECHES, Abraham Lincoln. 112pp. 26872-1

THE PRINCE, Niccolò Machiavelli. 80pp. 27274-5

THE SUBJECTION OF WOMEN, John Stuart Mill. 112pp. 29601-6

SELECTED ESSAYS, Michel de Montaigne. 96pp. 29109-X

UTOPIA, Sir Thomas More. 96pp. 29583-4

BEYOND GOOD AND EVIL: Prelude to a Philosophy of the Future, Friedrich Nietzsche. 176pp. 29868-X

THE BIRTH OF TRAGEDY, Friedrich Nietzsche. 96pp. 28515-4

COMMON SENSE, Thomas Paine. 64pp. 29602-4

SYMPOSIUM AND PHAEDRUS, Plato. 96pp. 27798-4

THE TRIAL AND DEATH OF SOCRATES: Four Dialogues, Plato. 128pp. 27066-1

A MODEST PROPOSAL AND OTHER SATIRICAL WORKS, Jonathan Swift. 64pp. 28759-9

CIVIL DISOBEDIENCE AND OTHER ESSAYS, Henry David Thoreau. 96pp. 27563-9

SELECTIONS FROM THE JOURNALS (Edited by Walter Harding), Henry David Thoreau. 96pp. 28760-2

WALDEN; OR, LIFE IN THE WOODS, Henry David Thoreau. 224pp. 28495-6

NARRATIVE OF SOJOURNER TRUTH, Sojourner Truth. 80pp. 29899-X

THE THEORY OF THE LEISURE CLASS, Thorstein Veblen. 256pp. 28062-4

DE PROFUNDIS, Oscar Wilde. 64pp. 29308-4

OSCAR WILDE'S WIT AND WISDOM: A Book of Quotations, Oscar Wilde. 64pp. 40146-4

UP FROM SLAVERY, Booker T. Washington. 160pp. 28738-6

A VINDICATION OF THE RIGHTS OF WOMAN, Mary Wollstonecraft. 224pp. 29036-0

PLAYS

PROMETHEUS BOUND, Aeschylus. 64pp. 28762-9

THE ORESTEIA TRILOGY: Agamemnon, The Libation-Bearers and The Furies, Aeschylus. 160pp. 29242-8

LYSISTRATA, Aristophanes. 64pp. 28225-2

WHAT EVERY WOMAN KNOWS, James Barrie. 80pp. (Available in U.S. only.) 29578-8

THE CHERRY ORCHARD, Anton Chekhov. 64pp. 26682-6

THE SEA GULL, Anton Chekhov. 64pp. 40656-3

THE THREE SISTERS, Anton Chekhov. 64pp. 27544-2

UNCLE VANYA, Anton Chekhov. 64pp. 40159-6

THE WAY OF THE WORLD, William Congreve. 80pp. 27787-9

BACCHAE, Euripides. 64pp. 29580-X

MEDEA, Euripides. 64pp. 27548-5

THE MIKADO, William Schwenck Gilbert. 64pp. 27268-0

DOVER · THRIFT · EDITIONS

PLAYS